Poland

D1644776

The principal sights:

< Lift flap for map

Ivan Bentchev, Eugeniusz Duda,
Dorota Leszczyńska, Michaela Marek,
Reinhold Vetter

Poland

Edited by Sebastian Wormell

With an historical introduction by
Manfred Alexander

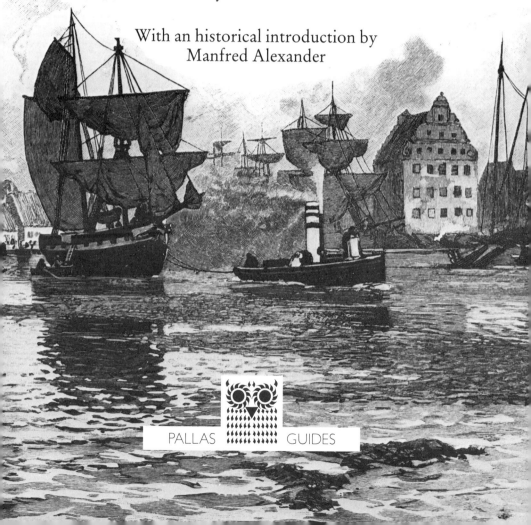

PALLAS GUIDES

Front cover: Wawel Cathedral, Kraków (Alexander Fyjis-Walker © Pallas Athene 1994)
Inside front cover: Farmer preparing for haymaking (Tim Sharman)

Back cover: Woman in traditional costume, Łowicz (Robert Harding Picture Library/Bildagentur Schuster/Deboicki)

Inside back cover: Map by Ted Hammond © Pallas Athene 1994, 2002

This book is part of the Pallas Guides series, published by Pallas Athene. If you would like further information about the series, please write to: Pallas Athene, 59 Linden Gardens, London W2 4HJ or visit our website on WWW.PALLASATHENE.CO.UK

Series editor: Alexander Fyjis-Walker
Assistant publisher: Ava Li
Series assistant: Tara Ely
Additional updatings provided by Chris Masters

German edition first published by DuMont Buchverlag GmbH & Co., Kbln 1989. English edition published by Pallas Athene, 59 Linden Gardens, London W2 4HJ © 1989 DuMont Buchverlag GmbH, Köln
All rights for all countries reserved by DuMont Buchverlag GmbH & Co., Limited Partnership, Cologne, Germany. The title of the German original is: Polen, by Ivan Bentchev, Dorota Lesezyoska, Michaela Marek, Reinhold Vetter

ISBN 1-873429-22-3

Printed through World Print, China

Contents

Editors' Foreword

Poland has been a potent myth for the English-speaking world for over two centuries. Polish democracy, Polish anarchy, romantic Polish nationalism – all these made a powerful if not always accurate impression in the eighteenth and nineteenth centuries. In our modern imagination, these have been replaced by the Miracle on the Vistula, Monte Cassino, Katyń, and the glorious march of Solidarity. Where for earlier generations Europe was saved from the Turk by Sobieski, and from the Red Army by Piłsudski, for our own she was also rescued from Communism by Lęch Wałęsa and Pope John Paul II.

Behind these mythical images, Poland itself lies almost unknown, a land full of unexpected treasures. Magnificent medieval architecture attests to the country's power in the middle ages, when Poland was one of the largest and most cosmopolitan states in Europe. The Renaissance saw patronage on a grand scale, of which perhaps the finest example is the completely preserved town of Zamość. And whatever the troubles of the later seventeenth and the eighteenth centuries, patrons continued to sponsor a vigorous intellectual life, which left monuments as diverse as great Baroque pilgrimage churches, princely palaces and art collections, and the first written constitution in Europe. However much the currents of the last two hundred years have obscured Polish achievements, Poland remains one of the cornerstones of the European experience.

Thankfully, the Polish spirit has proved itself magnificently since 1989 and the country is now fully at the heart of Europe, arguably more so than any other member of the former Eastern Bloc. The transformation since the first edition of this guide was published has been tremendous, and has come about with the sense of daring and the brio which have come to characterise Poles throughout history.

Editing this book has been a long but happy process, not least because of the generous help of English and Polish friends alike. Two Poles without whom this book would not have been possible are Natalia von Svolkien and Dr Christopher Ligota. All our thanks go also to Barbara Fyjis-Walker, Lidia Polubiec, Jurek Jarzębski, Elżbieta Lissowska, Tim Sharman, Andrew Poloczek, Jacek Lohmann, Tara Ely, Norman Reddaway, Emma Bassett, Ian Angus, Andrzej and Basiula Kuszell, Katarzyna Zur, Oleńka Radowicz, Grażyna Baker, Chris Masters, and Ava Li. Finally, special tribute should also be paid to two newer representatives of *Polonia in Anglia,* Emilia and Cecylia Wormell.

One word about editorial policy. Place names in Poland, as elsewhere in Eastern

Europe, have often changed over the years of turbulent history, and they are still occasionally contested. Purely for the benefit of readers referring to older books, the German names have been given in brackets where appropriate, and there is a concordance to help readers find their way through the index.

Sebastian Wormell and Alexander Fyjis-Walker
London, Spring 2002

History

Since prehistoric times many different peoples have been drawn to the area of Europe that is now Poland. The Slav population, including the Polanians who gave the country its name, migrated northwards and westwards from their ancestral homelands, mingled with the resident population, and adopted their culture. Conversion to Christianity brought Poland into the orbit of the West, and began a process of reciprocal cultural exchange with its neighbours, through which the Poles have created and enriched their own distinctive culture.

Poland has played a part in all the great cultural developments of the West: the Renaissance, Reformation and Counter-Reformation left their mark; Italian architecture and French literature were characteristic features of the life of the nobility, while German merchants and artists shaped the character of urban life. The water meadows were drained by Dutchmen, and English merchants were a frequent sight in the ports. Trade brought goods, people and ideas from western Europe far into the East – and vice versa.

All this gave rise to a fascinating civilization that was uniquely Polish and had a wide influence, reaching out eastwards beyond language and state boundaries. On its western side Poland tended to be on the receiving end (sometimes by force). At first Bohemia and the Germans gained political influence, then whole territories gradually became German-speaking, until the present century brought the culmination and reversal of this process.

Poland has historically been a land of transition between East and West. It has been a land where different Polish cultures have existed side by side: there was interaction between the nobility and bourgeoisie, while the peasantry pursued their own hard and dogged way of life. Architectural monuments bear witness to cultural variety. In Poznań, for instance, a city known to Germans as Posen, Prussian influence is evident, yet the Gothic cathedral contains a mid-19th-century Byzantine-style chapel with the tombs of the earliest Polish kings. The townscape of Lublin, on the other hand, is characterized by burghers' houses, wine cellars and churches with a distinctly Central European air. Historically Poland was a meeting-place of different religions and cultures, and the landscape still shows evidence of this: old Orthodox and Catholic churches, Calvinist chapels, synagogues and even mosques are found on Polish territory. The catastrophe of the Second World War, which brought with it the annihilation of the Jews and a part of the Polish population, and later caused the removal of the German population, has had the effect of creating an unhistorical homogeneity.

But although in language and religion Poland has never before been so uniform as since the Second World War, it still retains an awareness of the riches of the past.

The early period

Linguists have attempted to locate the ancestral homeland of the Slavs. By analysing the distribution of the Slavic words for 'white beech' and 'ivy' they have identified the eastern and western borders of the original Slavic settlement between the curve of the Carpathian range to the south and the Pripet marshes to the north. But their conclusions are no more secure than those based on archaeological finds, or the identification of peoples such as the Antes and Veneti mentioned in Greek and Latin sources.

The Slavic tribes come into clearer focus when the invasion of the Huns *c.*AD 375 forced them to join the migration of peoples, and like the Germanic peoples before them they now pressed forward in all directions. There is some controversy as to whether the Slav tribes came across the remnants of a settled population and joined with them, though this seems probable. The Slav migration reached its furthest northward extent in the area settled by the Balts and Finns. To the west they came in the course of the 6th and 7th centuries to the lower Elbe and from there took a circuitous route to the upper Main and further through the Bavarian Forest to the eastern Alps. In southern Europe the Slavs spread across the whole of the Balkans as far as the Peloponnese. The precursors of the later Slav states were built on the remains of earlier cultures, the ruins of Imperial Rome and on the margin of the Byzantine Empire. This geographical dispersal fostered the linguistic differences between the various Slavic groups, though these differences did not become as great as among the Germanic languages.

The earliest information concerning what later became Poland is given by a writer known as the 'Bavarian Geographer', who recorded the names of the tribes he knew around the middle of the 9th century. These included the Opolanians (Opolanie), Silesians (Ślężanie) and Vistulanians (Wiślanie) – names which often have geographical connotations. The Lachans recorded in the earliest Russian sources have been identified with Lech, the legendary father of the tribe.

This early Slavic settlement has been the subject of much heated controversy centred on whether the land the early Poles settled was unpopulated. A generation ago this question was still being argued between Poles and Germans along nationalistic lines. Archaeological finds provide undisputed evidence of the presence of people between the Carpathians and the Baltic in the Palaeolithic period. From the Neolithic period (i.e. from *c.*8000 BC onwards) there is evidence of continuous settlements, and in the Bronze Age (*c.*1600–700 BC) individual cultural groups can be distinguished. Uncertainty must remain as to what 'people' – or rather to what linguistic group – the unlettered 'Lusatian (or Lausitz) Culture' (late Bronze Age, *c.*1200–800 BC) belonged. This Lusatian Culture was supplanted at about the beginning of the present era by the Germanic peoples who settled the land from the Baltic coast and then pushed southwards or westwards in several waves. Swabians (Suebi), Goths and Gepids, Burgundians and Vandals passed through the region which

The Polish kings from Lech to Zygmunt III Waza, engraving by M. Merian ▷

later became Poland on their way to more southerly parts, where they founded their states or else fell into decline.

The Slavic occupation of the land was to prove more durable, a fact that has been used as an argument for the existence of an 'autochthonous' or aboriginal Slavic population. The unobtrusive migration of the Slavs has been described as 'seepage', but there is no evidence that this process was as peaceful as nationalist interpretations have sought to paint it in order to point a contrast with the warlike Germans. In any case at the beginning of written history, which coincided with the first political organization of a Polish state and conversion to Christianity, the Poles are found as the neighbours of other Slavs: the Czechs and the Moravians, the Pomeranians and the Lusatian Sorbs, the Rus' tribes in the east, and the non-Slavic Balts (Lithuanians and Pruzzi) to the northeast and north.

Nothing is known about the ordinary population of that time, but excavations of wooden and earth fortifications indicate that society was organized along aristocratic lines. From the great families a tribal organization developed, which was probably reinforced by shared religious cults. These included the worship of prominent hills in Poland's flat or undulating countryside, which were transformed in Christian times into pilgrimage shrines (Ślęża, Góra Św. Anny and others). It is notable that the Polish word for 'church' (*'kościół'*, from the Moravian *kostel*, Latin *castellum*) and 'priest' (*'ksiądz'*, from the Moravian *kněz*, German *kuning*, 'king') came to Poland from the neighbouring Great Moravian Empire, although it is not certain whether the 'Apostles of the Slavs', Cyril (also known as Constantine) and Methodios, were ever active in Poland itself.

The country was traversed by ancient trade routes, along which amber reached the Mediterranean; salt, furs and slaves were carried from east to west and from north to south. During his journey through the region in the mid-10th century, of which he wrote an account in Arabic, the Spanish Jew Ibrahim Ibn Ja'qūb was able to find fellow Jews, who were already familiar with the land and language and could give him information about the countries and their princes.

Poland under the Piasts (960–1370/86)

The first Polish ruler to appear in the documentary sources is Mieszko I (reigned *c.*960–99), who was an effective ruler of his princedom in the region of the Polanians between the Warta (Warthe) and Noteć (Netze). His predecessors are legendary figures, of whom the most important was Piast, a peasant who was supposed to have risen to become the founder of a dynasty. In 965 Mieszko I married a Bohemian princess, Dubrava, who brought the Christian faith with her. Mieszko had himself and his people baptized according to the Latin rite in 966, thus becoming part of the Christian West. The Bohemian influence on the religion and the country (the area around Kraków in the south was under the rule of the Bohemian prince Boleslav) was soon in competition with the influence of the Saxon Germans. From the time of Henry I (reigned 919–36) and Otto I (reigned 936–73) the Saxons were busy with the conquest and christianizing of the Slavs between the Elbe and Oder (Polish: Odra). By their acceptance of Christianity the Polish princely house placed itself on an equal footing with the Saxon nobility, and this soon found expression in marriage alliances, combined military campaigns and feudal disputes. Nevertheless, Mieszko I was able to attain a special position, was given the title *amicus imperatoris* and participated in the court diets of the German Emperors. He recognized the authority of the German King but seems to have taken a vassal's oath for only a part of his domains. He sought to strengthen his position by dynastic marriages, including that of his daughter, Świętosława, to the Danish king, Swein Forkbeard; Canute the Great, King of Denmark and England, was the fruit of this union.

Mieszko I was succeeded by his son (by Dubrava), Bolesław I Chrobry (the Brave, reigned 992–1025), whose four marriages are a vivid example of the way that 'family life' was closely bound up with foreign policy: two of his wives came from the Saxon nobility, one from Hungary and one was the daughter of the Slavic prince of Brandenburg (of the Hevellans). The burial of the Bohemian prince's son Vojtěch (Adalbert; Polish: Wojciech), who was murdered on the Baltic coast by the Pruzzi he was attempting to evangelize, gave Bolesław I the opportunity for the greatest ceremony of his reign: at the urging of the Pope, the young Emperor Otto III journeyed to Gniezno (Gnesen) in AD 1000 to pray at the grave of his friend whom he successfully persuaded the Pope to canonize. A chronicler from Lorraine, known as Gallus Anonimus, wrote later of the incredible wealth and unrivalled hospitality of the Polish prince, who was honoured by Otto III with the titles *dominus* and *amicus et socius*. The raising of Gniezno to archiepiscopal rank created a Polish ecclesiastical province with bishoprics at Kraków, Kołobrzeg (Kolberg) and Wrocław (Breslau). Although the leading figures in the church continued to be Czechs – the first archbishop was Radim (Gaudentius), half-brother of Wojciech – and Germans, the Polish church now developed independently from the church in the Empire.

After the death of the youthful Emperor Otto III in 1002, Bolesław I supported the candidature of the Margrave Ekkehard of Meissen, with whose family he was connected by marriage. But after Ekkehard's murder, he swung round to supporting Henry II of Bavaria (reigned 1002–24), though he maintained his claims to inherit Meissen. This territorial dispute grew into a lengthy struggle in which Henry II even had to call on the pagan Wendish tribes for help in fighting the army of the Christian Polish prince, much to the annoyance of the Saxon nobility and the clergy. These indecisive campaigns are often regarded as marking the start of a thousand-year border dispute between the Germans and Poles, but to contemporaries they were merely 'normal' inheritance disputes between kinsmen, played out at the highest level. In 1018 the Peace of Bautzen (Polish: Budziszyn) brought the end of the struggle between Emperor Henry and Bolesław I over the border regions (the margravate of Meissen), and allowed the Polish ruler to make good a large part of his territorial claims. For these regions of Lusatia and Upper Lusatia he swore an oath of fealty to Henry II. Bolesław I was still able to have himself made king at a coronation at Gniezno but died in the same year (1025).

His son, Mieszko II, who married the Lotharingian Rycheza in 1013, claimed his father's royal status, but soon came into conflict with the new German emperor, Conrad II (reigned 1024–39), whose military superiority forced him to renounce his royal title and imperial territories. Conflicts with a half-brother and revolts within the nobility also weakened his position, with the result that after his early death in 1034 the country fell into political confusion. The turbulence of the nobility and a pagan uprising threatened the country's internal unity, while it was assailed from without by almost all its neighbours. It was at this time that the Bohemian duke, Břetislav (Polish: Brzetysław) managed to destroy Kraków and Gniezno and steal the remains of St Wojciech, which he took back to Prague.

After going into exile Mieszko II's son Kazimierz (the Restorer) (reigned 1034 and 1039–58) was slowly able to regain his father's kingdom, from his base at Kraków. He reorganized the church, with the powerful support of his uncle, Archbishop Hermann of Cologne. By the time of his death Kazimierz I had earned his epithet 'Odnowiciel' ('the Restorer').

His son, Bolesław II Śmiały (the Bold, also called Szczodry, the Generous, reigned 1058–79) continued the work of reconstruction and gained independence from Bohemia, which was then weakened by quarrels between brothers in the ruling family. In the Empire Saxon revolts, the Investiture Contest and internecine strife brought about a collapse of central power during the reign of Emperor Henry IV (reigned 1056–1106), which made it possible for Bolesław to have himself crowned king – an event which took place immediately before Henry's submission to the Pope at Canossa. However, Bolesław could not prevent his own power from collapsing. In 1079 he had the Bishop of Kraków, Stanisław, brutally executed; according to legend he killed him with his own hands in a fit of rage at the Bishop's criticism of his personal behaviour. This murder, similar to Becket's a century later, turned the nobility even further against a king by whom they already felt threatened. Bolesław II was forced to flee and died at the turn of the year 1081–2 at an unknown place in Hungary or Carinthia.

Once again a strong central power was lacking and Poland sank into fratricidal strife with conflicts within the now strengthened nobility. The country also came under attack from outside. Not until the reign of Bolesław III Krzywousty (the Wry-mouthed, reigned 1102 and 1107–38) was there a measure of peace. By renouncing his claim to Silesia (1137) he brought to an end the hundred years of conflict with Bohemia, while on the other hand he was able to extend his territory in Pomerania. But the new law governing succession to the throne on the basis of seniority proved to be disastrous: as a way of preventing fraternal disputes an arrangement was introduced whereby the eldest son (Senior) was to have overall rule from Kraków over the clearly defined territories divided among all four sons. This resulted in various branches of Piasts splitting from one another and fighting between themselves. The only body that preserved the unity of the country was the church. The endless conflicts with the Emperor over the oath of fealty and payment of tribute were now conducted with the splinter provinces, especially Pomerania and Silesia.

Poland under Władysław I
Łokietek in 1320
-- borders of the King-
   dom of Poland
▓ fiefdom of the
   Bohemian Crown
░ independent
   duchies of
   the Piasts
▓ ruled since 1309 by
   the Teutonic Order

It was from Silesia that a new development came: Duke Henry I (Henryk Brodaty, the Bearded, reigned 1201–38) extended his dominions in Lower Silesia by adding other territories and laid the foundations for the expansion of the country. His wife, Hedwig (Polish: Jadwiga), a member of the family of the Counts of Andech and the Dukes of Meran, was later to become the patron saint of innumerable churches in Silesia (she was canonized in 1267); in her lifetime she encouraged the settlement of religious orders (Henryków/Heinrichau monastery 1225) and German immigrants. Towns 'under German laws' were founded, and German merchants and craftsmen were settled. German town laws spread slowly further eastwards even beyond the areas of German colonization. At the same time land that had remained uncultivated was colonized by farmers from the Empire, who brought with them new tools, agricultural methods, crops and specialized skills (mill construction and the draining of water meadows). This agricultural expansion led to an increase in the prosperity and taxable potential of the whole population, but it also led in some regions to the decline of the Polish language among the rural population.

Another special development took place in the land of the Pruzzi: at the request of Duke Konrad Mazowiecki (Conrad of Mazovia) the Teutonic Order of Knights (founded in 1197 at Acre) arrived there after the failure of their first attempt at colonization in Transylvania under the patronage of the Hungarian king. Their Grand Master Hermann

17

von Salza persuaded the Emperor Frederick II and the Pope to grant the (as yet uncon-quered) lands to the Order. The Teutonic Knights immediately began their advance, fighting the heathen and colonizing his lands, building castles and founding towns. The pacification of the Pruzzi was carried out by conversion, expulsion or extermination. The transfer of the seat of the Grand Master from Venice to Marienburg (Polish: Malbork, see page 376) marked the growing power of the Teutonic State. It was involved in the trade of the Hansa, and had an unusually effective internal organization, but its illegal conquest in 1308 of Gdańsk (Danzig) and East Pomerania (Pomorze Wschodnie, called Pomerellen in German) led to a long legal dispute with Poland.

In the face of forces inimical to Polish supremacy, which were evident both in the increasing strength of neighbouring states (Bohemia, Lithuania and the Teutonic State) and in the large German and Jewish element in the urban population, and which could be seen most clearly in the loss of control in Silesia, King Władysław I Łokietek (the Short, reigned 1320–33) attempted from his base in Sieradz to increase the royal power once again. With the support of the church and the nobility he was able, after the deaths of the two kings of Bohemia, Wacław I and Wacław II, to bring the land under his control again bit by bit, to break the resistance of the assertive towns, and to improve Poland's status in the outside world. One indication of this was his coronation as king in 1320 at Kraków, which from then on was to be coronation city (rather like Aachen in the Holy Roman Empire), even when the seat of government later moved to Warsaw.

Piasts

c.960–992	Mieszko I
992–1025	Bolesław I Chrobry (the Brave)
1025/1035–1034	Mieszko II
1031–1032	Bezprym
1034/1038–1058	Kazimierz I Odnowiciel (the Restorer)
1058–1079 (died 1081)	Bolesław II Śmiały/Szczodry (the Bold/Generous)
1079–1102	Władysław I Herman
1102/1107–1138	Bolesław III Krzywousty (the Wry-mouthed)

Period of the Regional Princes (Seniorate) 1138–c.1300

Bohemian Kings

1300–1305	Wacław I (in Bohemia Václav II)
1305–1306	Wacław II (in Bohemia Václav III)

Polish Kings

1305/1320–1333	Władysław I Łokietek (the Short)
1333–1370	Kazimierz III Wielki (the Great)

House of Anjou

1370–1382	Ludwik Węgierski (the Great)
1384–1399	Jadwiga (Hedwig) married to Władysław II Jagiełło

King Kazimierz III Wielki (reg. 1333–70), 17th-century engraving

Kazimierz III Wielki (the Great, reigned 1333–70) was able to build on his father's success and, after consolidating the country internally, resumed the pursuit of an active foreign policy. In the end Silesia went to Charles IV and the crown of Bohemia was lost, but new territories were added to the southeast. The tolerance of the ruler is shown by the fact that during the years of the Black Death (which did not affect Poland), when the Jews were being systematically persecuted and expelled throughout central Europe, Kazimierz offered them a new home and even granted them an autonomous administration, which was unique in Europe. This marked the beginning of the large Jewish presence which was such a feature of Poland until the Nazi Final Solution. During Kazimierz's reign the nobility in Poland developed into a politically unified estate with special rights, the basis for the later Republic of Nobles: the poorer members of the gentry ('szlachta', from the German 'Geschlecht', meaning 'family, race') permitted to hold administrative offices, while the great magnates were able to use their immense wealth to influence the succession to the throne, since Kazimierz III Wielki had no male heirs. His founding of the University of Kraków in 1364 was intended to enable young noblemen to be educated in their own land, thus saving them the journey to Padua or Bologna and keeping their youthful spirits in check.

Kazimierz III Wielki had tried to pave the way for a smooth succession by concluding a succession treaty with the Hungarian royal house of Anjou. On his death therefore Louis the Great (or Ludwik Węgierski, as he is known to Poles), the son of the late king's sister, hurried to Kraków and had himself crowned there. He reigned from 1370 to 1382, but his frequent absences encouraged the nobility to opposition. In return for the nobles' conceding the succession to one of his two daughters Louis granted them (almost complete) freedom from taxation and a say in the rule of the state, which was to remain intact. This Privilege of Košice (Polish: Koszyce) (1374) meant that the szlachta had attained a pre-eminent position, surpassing even the towns in influence. By the time Louis died, the country was already in turmoil and the self-confident nobility made use of the situation to set conditions for the succession of his young daughter Jadwiga (Hedwig). She was crowned at the age of eleven in Kraków in 1384, and reigned as 'rex' (king) until her death in 1399.

Poland under the Jagiellonians (1386–1572)

Jadwiga, a young girl in a strange country and with no family, became the nobility's pawn. Under these conditions a decision was made with far-reaching consequences: to marry the Piast heiress to Jogaila, Grand Duke of Lithuania, known to the Poles as Jagiełło, whose extensive territories in the east gave him the power to rival Poland. Lithuania was the last pagan state in Europe, and its warlike nobles based on the Baltic ruled a large empire that stretched to the Black Sea. Most of its population was Christian, and there were many links with the Orthodox Christians and with the Moslems to the east and southeast. Jadwiga has entered Polish myth as the innocent girl compelled by the barons to forego her personal happiness and enter into an arranged marriage with a man more than twenty years older, for the sake of the interests of the country, and of the szlachta. She devoted the rest of her life, until her early death in 1399 at the age of twenty-four, to good works, left all her money to the refounding of the University of Kraków, and was eventually canonized in 1997. Meanwhile Jagiełło was received into the Church in the Latin Rite on 15 February 1386. He received the baptismal name of Władysław and reigned as Władysław II (1386/99–1434). He married Jadwiga and was crowned on 4 March 1386 as *Tutor et Gubernator Regni Poloniae*. At a stroke Poland now had an experienced ruler, peace in the east with a wide scope for the spread of Polish culture and Polish influence, and a powerful partner in its struggle against the Teutonic Order, while on the other side the Lithuanian nobility was able to preserve its independence, gain access to the West and gradually attain the same rights as the Polish szlachta, though the personal union did not mean a constitutional unification of the two countries. This continued independence was ensured by the quarrelling in the Lithuanian ruling family: Witold (Lithuanian: Vytautas), who was made Grand Duke of Lithuania for life in 1401, was able to a large extent to disregard the claims of his cousin Jagiełło and pursue his own Eastern policy.

But a gradual process of unification did take place between Poland and Lithuania. The nobility met at Horodło in 1413 and agreed on co-operation between the representative bodies of the nobles of the two countries. Many Lithuanian noble families were accepted into Polish heraldic clans and were thus recognized as having equal rights. This reconciliation was preceded by a combined victory over the Teutonic Order at Grunwald (Tannenberg) in 1410. Poland, which for a century had been conducting a fruitless legal dispute over Eastern Pomerania and Gdańsk, joined forces with Lithuania, which had been involved in a continuous war over the territory of Samogitia (Żmudź), and together they defeated the Teutonic army, killing a large number of the leading members of the Order. Only Malbork (Marienburg) was retained by Heinrich von Plauen, who as the new Grand Master had to agree to the First Peace of Toruń (Thorn) (1411). In fact, this was relatively favourable to the Order, since it lost only a few of its lands and it held on to Gdańsk. However, the enormous sum it was compelled to pay ruined the Order's administration,

◁ *Genealogy of the Jagiellonians, 16th-century woodcut*

and the estates (the nobility and the towns) were able to assume an increasingly important part in the administration and the approval of taxes in the Teutonic State.

To the west the Hussite wars (following Hus' martyrdom at Constanz in 1415) gave the Jagiellonians the opportunity to interfere in the affairs of Bohemia. Although Władysław II refused the crown of Bohemia that was offered him by the Hussites in 1420, and Witold's nephew, Zygmunt Korybut, had a short and unsuccessful reign, the options for future claims were left open.

It was not until his fourth marriage, when he was in his seventies, that Władysław II Jagiełło fathered any sons; in 1424 and 1427 Władysław and Kazimierz were born, putting an end to the hopes of gaining the Polish crown that had been cherished by rival ruling houses, chief among them the Hohenzollern, led by Friedrich of Brandenburg, who had married Hedwig, the daughter of Queen Jadwiga. It also gave the Polish nobility, led by the Bishop of Kraków, Zbigniew Oleśnicki, the possibility of influencing the regents. In 1430 the nobility was granted the right to elect the king and the fundamental right of protection under the law ('*Neminem captivabimus nisi iure victim*' – 'We shall detain no-one unless he is convicted by law', roughly the equivalent of the English *Habeas corpus*). This marked a further stage in the laying of the foundations on which the Polish Republic of Nobles was to be built.

On the death of Władysław II at the age of eighty, his ten-year-old son Władysław III succeeded him (reigned 1434–44). Once again the nobility under Oleśnicki had the opportunity to strengthen their rights, especially since victories in the east had removed the danger from behind their back, allowing them to pursue an active policy towards Bohemia, Hungary and the German Empire. But the struggle for Hungary which followed the death of Sigismund of Luxemburg seemed on the verge of success, when it was cut short by the victory of the Turks at Varna (1444), in which the young Polish king was killed.

His successor was to be his seventeen-year-old brother Kazimierz, who had meanwhile established his own power base in Lithuania. After long negotiations in which the independence of Lithuania was confirmed and the Lithuanian nobility were given the same rights as the Polish, Kazimierz IV Jagiellończyk (the Jagiellonian, reigned 1447–92) was crowned at Kraków. His reign saw renewed struggles with the Teutonic State and the first serious confrontation with the rising power of Muscovite Russia. In the Teutonic State the estates (burghers and nobility) had grown in self-confidence, and now called on Poland for assistance against their oppressive overlords. In 1454 the Polish king incorporated the territory of the Teutonic Order into the Polish state and granted the rural nobility and the towns extensive rights. In the course of the protracted, indecisive wars with Poland, the Order was forced to pay its mercenaries by ceding Malbork to them (they in turn promptly sold it to the Polish king), and a second peace agreement was concluded at Toruń. This time the Polish king forced the Order to cede him eastern Pomerania and Gdańsk, Warmia, Ziemia Chełmińska (Kulmer Land) and other territories, thus gaining the whole of the lower course of the Vistula and unhindered access to the sea. What

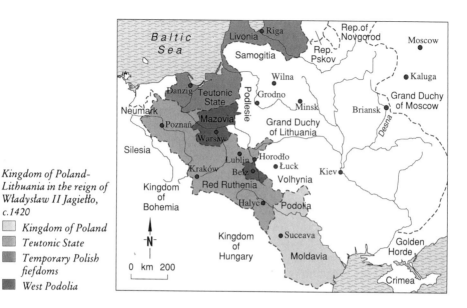

Kingdom of Poland-Lithuania in the reign of Władysław II Jagiełło, c.1420

Kingdom of Poland

Teutonic State

Temporary Polish fiefdoms

West Podolia

0 km 200

-N-

remained of the Teutonic State was declared a fief of the Polish king, and the Grand Master, with his new seat at Königsberg, was required to make a personal oath of allegiance and military service. But the Order's struggle with Poland was not yet ended.

The death of George of Poděbrady, the Bohemian nobleman who had risen with Hussite support to become king of Bohemia, enabled the Polish king to have his one-year-old son Władysław crowned in Bohemia in 1471, and on the death of his rival, King Matthias Corvinus of Hungary, Władysław also acquired the Crown of St Stephen in 1491. Four states, Poland, Lithuania, Bohemia and Hungary, were thus under the rule of the Jagiellonians, although they were not able to attain an internal unification of the lands they ruled, or to make their position secure. The powers ranged in opposition – the Polish nobility, Moscow, the Turks and the house of Habsburg – made any consolidation of the Jagiellonian position impossible.

In Poland-Lithuania Kazimierz's third son, Jan I Olbracht, came to the throne in 1492 (he died in 1501), and soon found himself involved in fighting the Crimean Tatars on the Black Sea coast. At Piotrków he granted the Polish nobility further rights in return for their military assistance. From now on only the nobility were to own land; the peasants were to be tied to the land owned by their feudal lord, and thus lose the right to seek another lord and land; and at Radom in 1505 the nobility were promised *Nihil novi*, that is, no political change without their consent at the local assemblies (dietines, or *sejmiki*). Kazimierz IV had made his fourth son, Aleksander Grand Duke of Lithuania (king from 1501 to 1506). Aleksander soon became embroiled in war with his father-in-law, Ivan III of Moscow. Numerous small concessions of land, which were confirmed in 1508 by an

23

'eternal treaty' in Moscow, were not enough to stop Ivan and his son Vassily III from pushing further westwards, and incorporating more territories with the acquisition of Smolensk (1514) and Pskov (1537).

Zygmunt I Stary (Sigismund the Old, reigned 1506–48) also had to endure indecisive wars in the southeast with Crimean Tatars, the rulers of Moldavia, and their overlord, the Turkish Sultan. Nevertheless Polish culture slowly spread into the steppes, where the Cossacks – fugitive East-Slavic serfs, who had adopted the life of the nomads of the steppes – acted as a buffer, though their loyalty could not be relied on.

Zygmunt I Stary's greatest success was, unexpectedly, in the Teutonic State. Since the Second Peace of Toruń the Order had been in continual decline, and the increasingly powerful estates wanted participation in the government of the land, which was in the hands of the ever-decreasing group of members of the Order. Further difficulties were created by the fact that the Order had had to allow quarrelsome mercenaries to settle in the country, and was no longer in a position to pay them any wage. All these groups regarded the liberties of the Polish nobility as a model for their own country. The last two Grand Masters of the Order, contrary to tradition, were drawn from the higher nobility of the Empire, and with the support of Emperor Maximilian I, they refused to take the personal oath of loyalty to the Polish king. Albrecht von Hohenzollern-Ansbach had been elected

Polish merchants in a 15th-century miniature from a Jagiellonian manuscript

Grand Master in 1511 at an early age, and attempted, by means of a combination of procrastination and guerrilla warfare, to claim full independence from his uncle Zygmunt I Stary. In the end Albrecht was able to take advantage of an unforeseen turn of events: the Reformation. Together with the fifty or so remaining members of the Order, he adopted the new teachings of Martin Luther, and at Luther's suggestion turned the Teutonic State into a secular duchy, hereditary to the Hohenzollerns, under the crown of Poland. The 'Prussian Act of Homage' took place ceremoniously on 10 April 1525 in Kraków. Thus peace came at last to the northern border. There were many sceptics, the most famous of whom was supposed to have been the court jester Stańczyk, who feigned sickness rather than celebrate the peace (vividly portrayed in a famous picture of the scene by the 19th-century painter Jan Matejko in the National Museum in Kraków), but none could have foreseen the future emergence of Poland's most dangerous enemy out of the connection that was now forged between East Prussia (as the Teutonic State was now called) and the Hohenzollern land of Brandenburg.

The Jagiellonians lost out in another inheritance agreement, this time with the Habsburgs. Before his death Władysław (Vladislav) of Bohemia had promised the Hungarian succession to the Habsburgs at Pressburg (Bratislava) in 1491. In 1507, and again in 1515, the Bohemian claims of King Zygmunt I Stary were thwarted by the marriage alliances of his rivals. Luck had already led the Habsburgs to their unexpected Luxemburg inheritance, and she smiled again when Władysław's son, the young King Louis, lost his life in the Battle of Mohács (1526). Thus the Bohemian Crown of St Wenceslas and the Hungarian Crown of St Stephen both finally passed to the house of Habsburg. The Jagiellonians were now reduced to their ancestral lands of Poland-Lithuania, where the wife of Zygmunt I Stary, Bona (queen from 1518, died 1557) of the Milanese condottieri family of Sforza, sought to strengthen the power of the king and his dynasty, occasionally by dubious means. In 1529 Zygmunt I Stary had his nine-year-old son Zygmunt August made Grand Duke in Lithuania, and in the same year the Polish Sejm, meeting at Piotrków, followed suit and elected him successor *vivente rege* (in the king's lifetime). This, however, struck at the *pupilla libertatis* (the right of the szlachta to hold their own free election of the king) and strengthened the resistance against the central power of the monarch. The royal house was criticized at the Sejm, and accused of lawbreaking, corruption and the accumulation of offices. There were three major issues at stake: preserving the union of Poland and Lithuania, safeguarding the rights of the nobility and protecting the Reformation. Not all these issues could be settled in the lifetime of Zygmunt II August (reigned 1548–72).

In the course of time the personal union between Poland and Lithuania gained the broad support of the nobility. The rights of the Polish szlachta and of Polish language and culture had greatly influenced the Lithuanian nobility and awakened the desire for a closer connection between the two states. This was countered only by the rich higher nobility, the magnates, who were endeavouring to gain greater independence. But they could not prevent an Act of Union being signed at the Sejm at Lublin in 1569 after stormy debates and with considerable participation by the rural nobility. The Grand Duchy of Lithuania

The Polish Parliament (Sejm) in the Jagiellonian period, contemporary woodcut

was thereafter joined to the Kingdom of Poland in an indissoluble union, but retained a certain independence in matters of its armed forces, administration, law and official appointments. The parallel is often made between Poland-Lithuania and England-Scotland. The Union of Lublin made Poland and Lithuania a single state consisting of two parts with an extraordinarily heterogeneous population as regards language and religion. However, the nobility's consciousness of the greatness of their empire and status became a means of binding the state together, and of ensuring that, except in the areas settled by Germans, the Polish language was widespread.

In this 'Golden Age' (*Złoty Wiek:* the reigns of the last two Jagiellonian kings 1506–72) an admirable – though temporary – solution was found to the problem of religious freedom. Despite the ban on importing reforming texts, the teachings of Luther quickly found their way into Poland – understandably, this occurred most easily in the German-speaking areas and among the German burghers of the Polish towns. The state's coercive measures had only a temporary success, since the reforming ideas of Calvin had already gained a foothold among the nobility, mainly because they seemed to give a religious

The 'Golden Age' (1506–1572)

Dynasty:	Rule of the Jagiellonians in Poland and Lithuania, and also, until 1526, in Bohemia and Hungary.
State:	1525 'Prussian Homage', the Teutonic Order is secularized and its territory comes under the Polish Crown; Union of Lublin 1569, union of Poland with Lithuania.
Nobility:	1505 *Nihil novi* at the Sejm at Radom: the nobility gains a political voice and a right of veto; 1573 rights codified in the *Articuli Henriciani*.
Religion:	During the Reformation Poland becomes a land of religious tolerance: besides Catholics, there are also Calvinists, Lutherans, Antitrinitarians (Socinians), Bohemian Brethren, Orthodox and Uniate Christians (from 1595), Armenians, Jews and Moslems.
Economy:	Thriving trade (via Gdańsk) of grain, timber, livestock, hemp, flax and potash.
Learning:	The centre of learning is the University of Kraków: famous scholars include the astronomer Nicolaus Copernicus (1473–1543), the humanists Filippo Buonaccorsi, 'Callimachus', (1437–96, the tutor of the sons of Kazimierz IV Jagiellończyk), Andrzej Frycz Modrzewski (1503–72), the writer of utopian works of political theory; among historians the most notable are Jan Długosz (1415–80), 'Annales seu cronice inclyti Regni Poloniae' up to 1480, Marcin Bielski (1495–1575), 'World Chronicle' in Polish appeared in 1597, Maciej Stryjkowski (1547–82), 'Chronicle of Poland, Lithuania, Sarmatia and all Russia', 1580.
Printing:	Between 1514 and 1524 the first books were printed in Polish, the first Bible in 1534; many works in Latin printed (*c.*1580 there were eight printing houses in Kraków).
Literature:	Flourishing of religious and secular literature in Polish: Mikołaj Rej (1505–69), verses and plays; Jan Kochanowski (1530–84) satirical and lyrical verse.
Art:	Giovanni Maria Padovano (died 1574), Bartolommeo Berrecci (*c.*1480–1573), Santi Gucci (*c.*1538–*c.*1600); Stanisław Samostrzelnik (died 1541), miniature painter.
Architecture:	Remodelling of Wawel 1505–36 by Italians Francesco Fiorentino (Franciszek Florentczyk) and Bartolommeo Berrecci; Collegium Maius, Kraków (finished 1519); the building of noblemen's seats, town palaces, town halls, market halls (Cloth Hall, Kraków), churches and monasteries.

foundation to the nobles' cherished notion of individual liberty. Anticlerical tendencies were combined with humanist trends, and strengthened the nobility's opposition to the excessive accumulation of power by the Catholic Church. Soon there were also refugees, Antitrinitarians and other radical groups, from Bohemia and elsewhere. King Zygmunt II August remained true to the old faith, but he took no very energetic steps to defend it. In several decisions of the Sejm a settlement was evolved which in 1555 guaranteed the nobility the right to freedom of belief, and in 1565 abolished ecclesiastical jurisdiction; in 1573, during the interregnum, complete religious freedom was attained. Poland was thus a 'land of tolerance', in which, besides the religious groups already mentioned, Orthodox Christians, Jews, Moslems and Armenians co-existed. But this was not to last; the Counter-Reformation was soon to arrive in Poland. It was to be particularly associated with Stanisław Hozjusz, the bishop appointed in 1551 to the 'exempt' (i.e. directly subordinate to the Vatican) diocese of Warmia. Most important was the Jesuit Order, which, under royal protection, was active in Poland from 1565 onwards, mainly in the field of education, and worked tirelessly for the re-Catholicization of the country.

The 'Golden Age' prepared the way for the specifically Polish institution of rule by the nobility, the guidelines for which were to be laid down at the end of the Jagiellonian period. Starting from the maxim that all the nobility (by law) was equal and spoke on behalf of the whole state, the szlachta succeeded in further diminishing the rights of the peasantry by introducing hereditary serfdom (1543) and restricting the trade of the towns, while securing duty-free imports and exports for themselves. The profits from Poland's basic commodity, grain, thus remained firmly in noble hands, while the towns were reduced in importance, because they were prevented from developing into the autonomous units they became in the Empire. Although a (largely German) patriciate dominated the 'great towns' of Kraków, Poznań, Warsaw and Gdańsk, culture emanated mainly from the nobility, the royal court and the residences of the magnates. Queen Bona Sforza symbolized and strengthened the Italian influence, which had already become apparent in humanist ideas and the Renaissance style. From the noblemen's seats this development spread to the towns, where Gothic now began to give way to Renaissance art and architecture.

The lives of two major figures exemplify the complexity of the period. One is the

---

Jagiellonians

1386–1434	Władysław II Jagiełło
1434–1444	Władysław III Warneńczyk (Varna)
1444/1447–1492	Kazimierz IV Jagiellończyk
1492–1501	Jan I Olbracht
1501–1506	Aleksander
1506–1548	Zygmunt I Stary (Sigismund the Old)
1548–1572	Zygmunt II August

astronomer Nicolaus Copernicus (Mikołaj Kopernik, 1473–1543), a canon of Frombork. It is not clear whether his mother tongue was German or Polish. He wrote his pioneering work *De revolutionibus orbium coelestium* in Latin, but only published it at the end of his life (in 1543 at Nuremberg), because his mathematical proofs contradicted the teachings of the church. The other is Veit Stoss (Wit Stwosz, *c.*1448–1533), the Nuremberg sculptor and painter, who lived in Kraków from 1477 to 1496, where – even before the 'Golden Age' had started – he created the Late Gothic high altar in St Mary's Church.

The Period of the Elective Monarchy in the Republic of Nobles (up to 1795)

In 1572 King Zygmunt II August died without leaving a male heir. The extinction of the Jagiellonian house in the male line made it possible for the first time for the right of the free election of the king to be exercised. This right had existed in theory since 1429 but had hitherto been overruled by dynastic claims. Now, however, lack of agreement about procedure, the private interests of the magnates, religious differences and foreign influence combined to make a swift decision impossible.

A convocation Sejm in Catholic Warsaw first appointed the Primate of the Catholic Church, Archbishop Jakub Uchański of Gniezno, as *Interrex*; the election of the king was to be made *viritim*, that is, every adult nobleman could participate in person at Wola near Warsaw. This *ad hoc* arrangement was later to become a fixed rule. Under external pressure, split by bribery and group interests, the nobility finally chose the brother of King Charles IX of France, Henri de Valois (in Polish Henryk Walezy) as the new King of Poland on 11 May 1573. The rights won so far by the nobility were laid down in the *Articuli Henriciani* and henceforth each new king had to swear to them; particular conditions for each reign were embodied in the *Pacta conventa*. But such a restriction was not familiar to Henri de Valois from his French background. Moreover, he showed little inclination to marry Anna, the sister of Zygmunt II, who was thirty years his senior, and rejected the imposition of further restrictions after his coronation in 1574. The death of his brother in May of the same year gave him a reason to escape from Kraków and make his way to France, where he ascended the throne as Henri III. He chose not to hold the French and Polish crowns jointly, and after a year had elapsed the Polish nobility, offended at his behaviour, deposed him and held another royal election.

This time the candidates included three Habsburgs, as well as Ivan IV (the Terrible) of Muscovy, and princes from Sweden, Bohemia and Italy – henceforth the race for the Polish crown was to become a party game for the European aristocracy. Already there was even discussion of partitioning the country. In this complicated situation two candidates were finally chosen: the Emperor Maximilian II, who was favoured by the *Interrex*, and the Prince of Transylvania, Stefan Batory, who succeeded simply because he was quicker off the mark in assembling his supporters and taking control of the coronation city of Kraków. He married Anna, the Jagiellonian heiress, and the couple were crowned on 1 May 1576.

This process of electing the king was to remain almost unaltered until the Polish state came to a temporary end in 1795. The king was merely the *primus inter pares*; not only was he elected by the nobility, he always had to confirm their rights, and if he broke his promises they could depose him. The fear was that the king might gain a *dominium absolutum*, so his powers were restricted to being the representative of the state, for which, however, he was richly compensated by income from state property. He could influence the making of laws and appointments to the most important offices of state, but final decisions lay with the magnates or with the Sejm as a whole.

King Stefan Batory, engraving by Jost Amman, 1576

The Polish Diet (*Sejm*) consisted of the Senate, to which the King, the Bishops and the holders of the highest offices of state belonged, and the Chamber of Deputies (*Izba poselska*), made up of the representatives of the whole nobility (*szlachta*). These deputies were elected at local diets (dietines or *sejmiki*) to represent the viewpoint of their sejmik on particular questions, which the king had presented before each session of the Sejm. The nobility also elected at local level the holders of lesser offices in the administration and judiciary, while the higher officials – Palatines (*Wojewodowie*) and Castellans (*Kasztelani*) – were appointed by the King or the Senate.

Nevertheless, a king as forceful and educated as Stefan Batory (reigned 1576–86) could still make his mark. His first aim was to establish the security of the country within and without, after the years of paralysis. A conflict with Gdańsk ended with the confirmation of the autonomy of the city in its internal affairs and its monopoly of the grain trade, though this had to be paid for with a hefty contribution to the state's coffers.

Stefan Batory conducted several successful military campaigns against Ivan IV, occupying Moscow in 1612, but was unable to win back the territories that had been lost. In matters of religion he was guided by tolerance. The Jews in the 'Generality of the Jewish Nation' were allowed their own national assembly of deputies drawn from the local self-governing communities (*Kahal*), and a fixed procedure was laid down in cases of conflict with other religious groups. Although his reign was short, Stefan Batory's reputation in Polish history remains high.

After his death there was once again a choice between several candidates. In the double election of 1587 the eventual victor was Zygmunt III Waza (reigned 1587–1632), the son of King John III (Vasa) of Sweden. In many respects Zygmunt was the antithesis of his predecessor on the Polish throne; mistrustful and fanatical in religion, he soon made many enemies among the powerful magnates, especially after 1592, when he also became king of Sweden and paid more attention to that country than to Poland. From his new residence in Warsaw (from 1596) he attempted to rule both states and reach a compromise in the Baltic lands between the competing interests of Sweden and Poland. In 1604 he lost the Swedish crown *de facto* (though not *de jure*) to the Calvinist usurper Charles IX, but he was able to prevent Poland becoming embroiled in the Thirty Years War, in which Gustavus Adolphus, the son of his opponent, played a decisive part. Zygmunt III Waza found success in the east, where, after the extinction of the Rurik dynasty Russia sank into the 'time of troubles' (*Smuta*). At first Zygmunt supported the 'False Dmitri' (Polish: Dymitr Samozwaniec), who was married to Maryna Mniszech, the daughter of a Polish magnate. (In fact there were two consecutive False Dmitris, both supported by the Poles: in 1607 a second impostor appeared, claiming to have miraculously survived after the first had been put to death by the Muscovites. Maryna claimed to recognize him as his predecessor – though she went through another wedding ceremony just in case.) In 1610 Zygmunt presented his own son Władysław in Moscow as his own candidate to the throne after a successful military campaign. Zygmunt's inept and domineering manner, forbidding Władysław, once he had been elected tsar, to adopt the Orthodox faith, led to a *volte-face*. The Russians drove out the Poles and in 1613 enthroned Mikhail Feodorovich Romanov as the new tsar. His family soon put an end to Poland's expansion eastwards and extended Russian territory at the expense of Poland-Lithuania.

The strongly Catholic attitude of the King also left a mark in the internal affairs of the country. First, in 1595 a Papal Bull created the Uniate Church, allowing the clergy – once they had recognized papal supremacy – to keep their Eastern Rite and continue to take wives; nevertheless the new dispensation was not generally accepted by Polish catholics of the Western Rite. Secondly, Zygmunt did all he could to foster the Counter-Reformation and discriminate against the Protestant nobility. This policy was helped by the good education given to the young noblemen in the Jesuit schools, and at the beginning of the 17th century was to bring a large part of the Protestant nobility back to the Catholic Church. On the other hand his attempts to strengthen the central power by means of reforms, such as fixed taxes and a standing army, met with opposition. These efforts gave rise to a revolt against the feared *dominium absolutum* in 1607. The King came through this victorious, but he was nevertheless forced to give up any intentions of introducing significant reforms. The old institution of the 'confederation' (*rokosz*), a sort of legitimate conspiracy against the king, now took on a constitutional character as a means of safeguarding the freedom of the nobility.

Despite the nobility's claim to hold a free election, the young Władysław IV Waza (reigned 1632–48) assumed the throne of his father virtually unopposed. After struggles with the Russians he renounced his claim to the title of tsar, which by now – like that to

A serf complains about his masters; pen and ink drawing, mid-17th century

the crown of Sweden – no longer bore any relation to reality. The war against the Turks, in which his father had been victorious at the Battle of Chocim (1621), petered out because of lack of funds. Inside the country the re-Catholicizing of the nobility made great strides, and at the same time the long tradition of religious tolerance gradually changed; increasingly the suppression of 'dissidents' was combined with attacks on non-Catholics.

The man elected as Władysław's successor was his stepbrother Jan, who had been a Jesuit priest and a cardinal. He now became Jan II Kazimierz Waza (reigned 1648–68) and married his stepbrother's widow. He was forced at once to become involved in the troubles in the Ukraine, where the Hetman (commander) of the Zaporozhian Cossacks, Bohdan Chmel'ny'cky (Polish: Chmielnicki) had started a rebellion against slowly encroaching Polish influence. Since the time of Stefan Batory a small number of Cossacks had been in the pay of the Polish king and had become part of the Polish nobility, while the rest continued to live by banditry. The king's lack of military skill, his conflicts with the aristocracy, and financial difficulties on the Polish side all helped the Cossacks, some of whom were in alliance with the Turks and Tatars, to inflict cruel persecution on the peasantry and Jews in the small towns in the Polish-Ukrainian region. The Treaty of Pereyaslavl in 1654 brought Moscow into the fray as an increasingly important rival to the Polish king, and marked the Tsar's first venture into the steppes north of the Black Sea. This was to lead in the reign of Catherine II to the Turks being driven from the empire of the tsars forever.

This war, in which the Cossacks placed themselves under the Moscow Tsar, became known as the 'Deluge' (*Potop*), and is described by Henryk Sienkiewicz in the novel of that name, which forms the second part of his great historical trilogy. In 1655 its scope widened with the entry of Sweden, under King Charles X Gustavus, who occupied the whole of Poland almost without a struggle. A turn in Polish fortunes was linked – more psychologically than in reality – with the raising of the siege of the monastery of Jasna Góra at Częstochowa, where the image of the Virgin was in future to symbolize the unity and liberty of the Catholic Poles against the Protestant Swedes, Orthodox Cossacks and Muslim Turks. On 1 April 1656 at Lwów (Lemberg, Ukrainian: Lviv) Jan II Kazimierz Waza proclaimed the Mother of God to be 'Queen of Poland', thus inaugurating the special veneration of the 'Black Madonna' ('Czarna Madonna') which is still such an important part of Polish life. Soon afterwards Poland had its first success in a guerrilla war of attrition against the Swedish troops. The Swedes then called on Brandenburg for help and in return transferred full sovereignty of East Prussia to Elector Friedrich Wilhelm of Brandenburg (the Great Elector) in 1656. In the end almost all of its neighbours were involved in the struggle in and around Poland. By the time the war came to an end in 1660 with the Peace of Oliwa, the country was devastated. Apart from losses to Brandenburg, which had gained new territory as well as influence in Royal Prussia, Poland survived intact. The fighting in the Ukraine developed into a struggle between Poland and Russia, which resulted in 1667 in a compromise at the Peace of Andruszów (Andrusovo): Smolensk remained in Russia, Lithuania retained its 1569 borders, and Moscow received the Ukraine east of the Dnieper including Kiev.

The cost of the 'Deluge' to Poland had been immense: not only had it lost some of its territory and its status as a great power in eastern Europe, but half the population had been killed, whole areas depopulated, the countryside and towns were devastated, and urban life and culture were in ruins. The losses among the Jews were particularly high: the Jewish population was reduced from around 450,000 to around 180,000. The damage caused by the destruction of Jewish community life and prosperity was never to be made good.

During the Swedish Wars groups of nobles had continued to pursue their own interests and therefore had no great wish for the return of the *status quo ante* once the wars were over. Certain catchphrases now became symbolic of the decline of the country's prosperity and political order, most notable the *Liberum Veto* and 'Polish anarchy'. The *Liberum Veto* had come about in 1652 by chance, when a deputy from a sejmik, who was normally there to represent the electoral wishes of the nobility of his area at the Sejm, used a veto against a decision before discussion had been concluded and then walked out of the Sejm, leaving the helpless members with no option but to suspend the sitting. This precedent for a 'veto' (Polish: 'nie pozwalam' – 'I do not allow it') became one of the pillars of the constitution. Henceforth magnates, groups of nobles and foreign powers, by 'buying' deputies were able to thwart any reform of the state or society they disliked. The highest ideal of justice – the freedom of the noble members – became an instrument for the destruction of the whole state. The much-quoted phrase 'Polish anarchy' derives from a misunderstanding: the complicated system of elections and consultations, and the require-ment that decisions be unanimous, appeared to contemporaries to be time-consuming, elaborate and unpredictable, and they expressed this attitude in the formula *'Polonia confusione regitur'* ('Poland is ruled by disorder'). After the 'Deluge' this 'disorder' was turned into 'chaos' by a decline in morality, state institutions, and above all in prosperity.

No greater contrast can be imagined than between Poland and its neighbour, the rising Prussian state, where, from the time of the Great Elector up to Frederick the Great, the internal administration was organized along rational lines: in Prussia the ideal citizens were not the nobles enjoying their 'Golden Freedom' but the officials, soldiers and loyal subjects of the Hohenzollerns.

To halt the decline of the state into anarchy, Jan II Kazimierz attempted to hold the election of the heir to the throne in his own lifetime (*vivente rege*) and to introduce decision-making by majority in the Sejm. When the republicans (the defenders of the privileges of the Republic of Nobles) revolted against this and with foreign help won a bloody victory at the Battle of Mątwy (1666), the embittered king abdicated. Poland threatened to fall into complete impotence and chaos, and degenerate into the plaything of the magnates.

The election that followed brought to the throne Michał Korybut Wiśniowiecki (reigned 1669–73), the son of a rich magnate who had served with distinction in the war, a 'Piast', as the native Polish candidates were called. In his short and unhappy reign the war against the Turks was revived. The Grand Hetman of the Crown (as the commander-in-chief was styled) gained a few victories, but he had to return on the death of Wiśniowiecki and was unable to take advantage of these successes. The election of Jan III Sobieski as the new king (reigned 1674–96) showed that an energetic and clever candidate could make the hard climb to the Polish throne, though he was also helped by the propitious moment and by the money of the French family of his wife Marysieńka (Marie-Casimire de la Grange d'Arquien, 1641–1716), who had come to Poland in the entourage of Jan Kazimierz's French queen. King Jan III used French money to bring the war to an end, thus ending the payment of tribute to the Sublime Porte. He earned European fame in 1683, when, in alliance with the Emperor, he saved the city of Vienna from capture by the Turkish army. After further fighting the attacking power of the Ottoman Empire was broken in 1699 with the Peace of Karlovitz, though the borders of the Ottoman Empire remained almost unaltered. The military successes of the Polish king masked the further decline of the state. The magnates pursued their private interests regardless, and Jan III Sobieski himself unscrupulously ensured material advantages for his family. The king was unable to provide a stable arrangement for his succession; even the far-ranging marriage alliances of his children gave no lasting gains, since the nobility's aversion to his queen was so strong that after Jan's death their children were expressly excluded from candidature for the throne.

Ten candidates presented themselves for election in 1697, gladly taking money from all sides. The French prince François Louis de Conti received the most votes, but his opponent the Elector Augustus of Saxony moved more quickly to be crowned at Kraków. His reign as King August II Mocny (the Strong – so called for his physical prowess rather than his abilities as a ruler, reigned 1697–1733) marked the beginning of the 'Saxon Period' in Poland. Under the Saxons life was easy-going, but their rule also symbolized the continuing decline and foreign interference in the paralysed state. Poland now became the plaything of its neighbours. The Great Northern War, which Augustus had sketched out in a slapdash way during a drinking spree with Tsar Peter the Great, made Poland an area

King Jan III Sobieski in the battle against the Turks, 17th-century engraving

for foreign troops to pass through. By the time it ended, Russia was able to interfere freely in Poland's affairs. The support of Peter the Great after the Battle of Poltava (1709) brought Augustus back to the throne, which he had lost to Stanisław Leszczyński in 1704. Struggles with the Turks and interference by the Hohenzollerns, who after the proclamation in 1701 of the Elector Friedrich I as 'King in Prussia' were involved in discussions about possible partition plans, completed the picture of a state condemned to impotence. In 1720 Russia and Prussia agreed to stop any political reforms in Poland.

Once again Poland had lost a quarter of its population through war, famine and plague. Still more dramatic was the internal collapse, marked by drunkenness, self-interest, impoverishment and growing religious fanaticism. Non-Catholics were forced out of office and deprived of their rights. This gave their co-religionists abroad a new opportunity to interfere in the internal affairs of the country under the pretext of helping the Protestant and Orthodox dissidents to regain their rights (Prusso-Russian Alliance of 1730).

August II Mocny left a lasting impression on Poland more through his life of baroque excess, the architecture he commissioned, and the vast number of children he fathered, than through his political activities. After his death Stanisław Leszczyński tried to revive his claim to the throne, but was forced to resign in favour of August III (reigned 1733–63), the candidate supported by Moscow, and was given the Duchy of Lorraine in compensation by his son-in-law, Louis XV of France. August III was a moderate in politics and had

35

'The Royal Cake', an allegory of the First Partition of Poland in 1773; left to right: Empress Catherine II of Russia, King Stanisław August Poniatowski, Joseph II of Austria and Frederick II of Prussia

little interest in Poland. Under his ministers government degenerated into favouritism. The countryside was ruled by the magnate families who governed their vast estates like little kings (królewięta) and watched each other suspiciously. The greater part of the szlachta was courted by the rich families, and some were used as their political agents. Nevertheless, the country gradually recovered, prosperity increased and was shown in the building of great country houses and towns owned by the magnates. Highly cultured noblemen busied themselves with proposals for reform, which sought to mend the weaknesses of state and society. But good beginnings, such as the school reforms of the Piarist Stanisław Konarski, always stopped when they came up against the interests of the neighbouring countries and the magnates. Russian troops behaved as if they were in their own country; Austria and Prussia infringed Polish neutrality, especially after the conquest of Silesia (Peace of Dresden 1745), and adversely affected Polish trade. During the Seven Years War (1756–63) Poland became a deployment area for the warring neighbours, and Frederick II of Prussia (the Great) unscrupulously squeezed a sizeable part of his war costs from Poland by flooding the country with counterfeit money and imposing illegal tolls on the Vistula. With the death of August III Poland itself seemed finished.

The death of the Empress Elizabeth in 1762 not only saved Frederick II but also offered Poland an unexpected chance. The powerful noble family of Czartoryski (known simply as 'the Family') was able to have its candidate, Stanisław August Poniatowski (reigned 1764–95), elected as king. He was not only a gifted and knowledgeable man with a passionate interest in the arts, but he had also been the lover of the new Russian Empress, Catherine II. With Russian backing he quickly established himself, but found little support inside or outside the country for his enlightened ideas. Although the economic and tax reforms were accepted, the strengthening of the army and in particular the restriction of the *Liberum Veto* were firmly rejected by the neighbouring states.

Under the pretext of safeguarding the rights of (Orthodox) dissidents, Russia forced an 'eternal treaty' in 1767, which guaranteed the borders of the Republic and – hypocritically – the 'cardinal rights' of the nobility (free election of kings, *Liberum Veto*, equal rights for dissidents). The once high ideals of the nobleman-citizen were thus used to perpetuate the impotence of the state. A 'silent' session of the Sejm in 1768 was forced to approve the treaty without being allowed any discussion of its contents. Russia had thus achieved effective supremacy in Poland: its troops passed freely through the country; the Russian ambassador in Warsaw ruled beside and intrigued against the king. Opposition forces, which the Russians wanted to drive out, but which were not particularly in favour of reform, gathered in the Confederation of Bar (1768). The civil war that ensued spread to include an uprising of the Ukrainian peasants (*Hajdamaks*), in which around 100,000 Poles and Jews were brutally slaughtered.

The rekindled Russo-Turkish War, in which the tsars were finally to gain the upper hand (Peace of Küçük Kaynarci 1774), led to more definite ideas about a partitioning of Poland. Before the first partition Austrian and Prussian troops already occupied areas of the Republic of Nobles that were dominated *de facto* by Russia. Nevertheless the 1772 partition treaties, which came about because of Prussian pressure, were a surprise. While it is true that Prussia received the smallest part of the booty, it was the most important part, since it provided a land connection from Brandenburg-Pomerania to East Prussia and so cut Poland off from the Baltic Sea. By the time the feudal dependence of the Prussian region on the Polish Crown was severed in 1773, it already seemed an anachronism of interest only to legal scholars. Austria, whose Empress, Maria Theresa, was supposed to have shed tears over the fate of Poland, made sure that it had the largest part in terms of

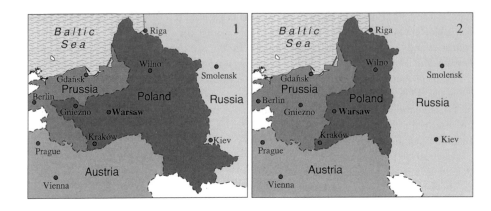

population, and realized its supposed historic claims to Galicia and Lodomeria (Halyč – Volodymyr). Russia annexed the eastern regions as far as the Dvina. The powerless Sejm was forced under military threat to accept the loss of 203,000 km^2 and 4.5 million people.

The shock of the partition awakened a new willingness for reform, which was expressed in the transformation of the government (organized into departments of state), the reform of the tax law, the army and the education system. All this culminated in the Polish enthusiasm for reform during the Four Years Sejm (1788–92) which created the Constitution of 3 May 1791. Poland had produced what was then the most modern constitution in Europe, a legal framework which could have converted the old estate-based Republic of Nobles into a modern constitutional democracy.

These reforms pleased neither the conservative forces in Poland nor the country's neighbours, who saw their interests threatened by the ending of 'Polish Anarchy'. Prussia, which had made a defensive treaty with Poland in 1790, left its ally in the lurch, while Empress Catherine, who was still preoccupied with Turkey, now condemned as a 'French plague' on the Vistula those very reforming ideas which she herself had once praised in her correspondence with Voltaire. The Confederation of Targowica in April 1792 brought together the conservative forces in Poland, whom Catherine 'selflessly' provided with 100,000 soldiers. Against these neither Polish belief in free will nor the patriotic zeal and military skill of Tadeusz Kościuszko, who had had his training in the American War of Independence, were of any avail. Early in 1793 a second partition of Poland was agreed, and a 'silent Sejm' had to accept it. After another desperate uprising under Kościuszko the Third Partition in 1795 forced the abdication of the king and the end of the Polish state.

It is true that the history of Europe had seen many partitions of countries, but the eradication of a whole state from the map was something quite remarkable. The more so since the arrogance of autocratic monarchs was already becoming an anachronism: in the United States of America since the Declaration of Independence, and in France since the Revolution of 1789 the idea of the sovereignty of the people had begun its victorious

First Partition 1772
Prussia takes West Prussia (except Danzig),
Russia takes Poland's eastern provinces, and
Austria annexes Galicia

Second Partition 1793
Prussia occupies Greater Poland (Wielkopolska)
and Danzig, Russia incorporates all the eastern
Polish region

Third Partition 1795
Prussia extends its territory to Warsaw, the
other regions of the Polish rump state are taken
by Russia and Austria

progress. The brutal partition of Poland aroused unanimous outrage among the enlightened public of Europe. The partitioning powers concealed their guilty consciences behind high-sounding propaganda and a policy of oppression, which was intended to disguise the differences that in fact existed between them. The Polish state – the land that had been part of the European family of nations since its conversion to Christianity, the great power of the late middle ages, the country where the free will of its (noble) citizens had counted for more than the rational perfection of the machinery of state – had indeed been eradicated from the map, but Poland lived on in the consciousness of its inhabitants. The 'Polish Question' was to remain a challenge for Europe until the state's re-emergence in the First World War.

Elected Kings (dates from election)

1573–1574	Henryk Walezy (Henri de Valois, deposed)
1576–1586	Stefan Batory
1587–1632	Zygmunt III Waza
1632–1648	Władysław IV Waza
1648–1668	Jan II Kazimierz Waza
1669–1673	Michał Korybut Wiśniowiecki
1674–1696	Jan III Sobieski
1697–1706	August II Mocny (the Strong)
1704–1709	Stanisław Leszczyński
1709–1733	August II Mocny (the Strong)
1733–1736	Stanisław Leszczyński
1733–1763	August III
1764–1795	Stanisław August Poniatowski

Poland under the rule of the Partitioning Powers (1795–1918)

With the Third Partition the history of the Polish state came to a temporary end, but not the history of the Polish nation. However, each of the partitioned areas developed in different directions, and the emigré movement – the *emigracja* – also played a crucial role. The differences profoundly marked the history of Poland's revived state during this century.

During the Napoleonic years the standard of hope for Poland was borne mainly by the emigrés, who believed that French help might be available for the re-establishment of Poland. One substantial move in this direction was the creation of a Polish Legion, which grew to number 10,000 men under the command of General Dąbrowski. It was, however, deployed by the French mainly in Italy; what was left of it died of swamp fever as a French colonial army on Haiti. A lasting reminder of this legion is the mazurka that later became the national anthem: 'Poland has not perished yet' with its refrain 'March, march, Dąbrowski! / From Italy to Poland', a song symbolizing both hope and hopelessness.

Napoleon similarly made use of the Polish Question for his own ends. After the victory over Prussia and his entry into Warsaw he was urged to create a new Polish state, but he did not want to play the Polish card too soon against Tsar Alexander, lest he restrict his room for manoeuvre. His cynical statement that the Poles should show that they were worthy of their state was another side of his relationship with the country from that shown in his love affair with Madame Walewska. What Napoleon needed above all was soldiers. Around 100,000 Poles marched with the Grande Armée in 1812 to Moscow, with the heroic Józef Poniatowski at their head. Those who survived the disastrous retreat were finally and successfully sacrificed at the Battle of the Nations near Leipzig in 1813.

Politically the creation of the Duchy of Warsaw in 1807 was a bad compromise, though it did bring with it the *Code Napoléon*, the French system of administration, and the involvement of non-nobles in politics. Napoleon had never made any specific promises to Poland, and his presence there remained merely an episode, but it brought the Poles closer to the fulfilment of their hopes than they were to be for a long time.

At the Congress of Vienna the representatives of all the great powers spoke about Poland, but only a few of them discussed it with Poland's representatives. Once again the map was changed and Prussia gave up most of the territory gained in the Third Partition. All the partitioning powers made vague promises to the Poles about how the unity of the nation would be safeguarded across the partition borders, but among themselves they were motivated primarily by their own interests. Poland's greatest hope was of all people Tsar Alexander, who was not only fêted as the 'Liberator of Europe' but had also acquired a lion's share of the booty: 82 per cent of the territory of the former Polish state. His promise to set up a 'Kingdom of Poland' in personal union with Russia was the most the Poles were able to achieve.

The regions that had passed to Russia in the First Partition in 1772 were never included

*The Polish gentry
(szlachta) in an early
19th-century illustration*

in these promises, since they were regarded as 'recovered territories' and later as 'Western Gouvernements'. In the three Central Gouvernements of Lithuania, Byelorussia and the Ukraine the social structure and the influence of the nobility remained largely intact, though the nobility often liked to impose the Russian form of serfdom on their peasantry. The landless Polish nobility, however, tended to lose their privileges and merge with the peasantry. While the Orthodox experienced a certain improvement of their condition, the position of the Jews – about 10 per cent of the population – became more difficult. The wars of the 'Deluge', Cossack attacks and pogroms had ruined once prosperous communities. People of Jewish faith sought to earn their living in two ways: either by working for themselves as tradesmen or craftsmen in enclosed districts (*shtetl*) or by acting as middlemen between the landlords and peasants, as stewards, tradesmen or tavern-keepers. In times of hardship both sides tended to blame and revenge themselves on the Jews. There was also tension between the pious and anti-intellectual *Hasidim* and those Jews who tended towards the Enlightenment (the *Haskalah*). The oppression of the tsarist police denied Jews all rights: they were concentrated in the cities, where surveillance was easier, they were prohibited from following certain occupations, and they were often forced to be constantly on the move.

Meanwhile the political opportunities for Poles at the uppermost part of the social pyramid seemed more favourable. Prince Adam Jerzy Czartoryski was taken as a hostage to Russia as a member of 'the Family'. There he had come into contact with the circle of Alexander, the heir to the throne, on whose accession he was made Russian foreign minister. Although he was able to achieve much for the Poles in the field of education, his political efforts to re-establish the Polish state remained unsuccessful. His ideas were incorporated into the constitution of the Kingdom of Poland, proclaimed on 20 July 1815, but this legal framework relied entirely on the goodwill of the Tsar, and Czartoryski did not become the Tsar's viceroy, as he had hoped. At first the political life in the Kingdom allowed for great expectations, even though the Tsar's brother Constantine held control over the administration and the army. But the gap between Tsar Alexander, who was moving further and further away from his youthful ideals, on one side and Polish society with its demands for participation in government and for the rule of law on the other, became ever deeper. His successor Tsar Nicholas (reigned 1825–55), deeply shaken by the Decembrist Revolt which opened his reign, was even less willing to entertain Polish special requests. A perceptible revival in the economy and the hope that Russia might give way formed the background for the November Uprising in 1830 in Warsaw which echoed the Paris July Revolution. Misreading the balance of power and with no advance planning, some young officers started a revolt and soon had general support. But by formally

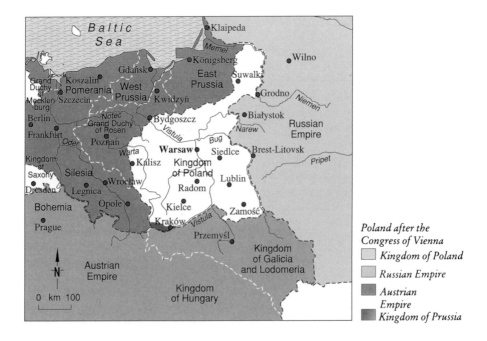

Poland after the Congress of Vienna

deposing the Romanov dynasty from the Polish throne they broke what were already slender channels of negotiation with Moscow and shifted the conflict to the military sphere. For all their courage, the Poles could not match Russian troops and the Uprising led to the abolition of Polish institutions and heavy penalties. Many estates were confiscated, the universities were closed, those accused and their sympathizers were severely punished or exiled. Although the provinces retained a Polish character Russian influence was asserted with far less restraint.

The flower of the Polish intellectuals emigrated, mostly to France. On their way westwards the refugees found innumerable sympathizers among the German middle classes, who saw the vanquished Poles as representing their own yearnings for political freedom. The many 'Polenlieder' of the period show that Poles and Germans had come closer together than ever before or since. From Paris Prince Adam Jerzy Czartoryski now organized resistance for the noble-conservative camp. Henceforth the Polish question was to play a part in all European conflicts, although nothing altered in the balance of power. The greatest Polish poet, Adam Mickiewicz died in Constantinople in 1855, seeking allies for the Polish cause. The democratic camp of the 'Great Emigration' under the leadership of the historian Joachim Lelewel attempted, by courting the non-noble classes, particularly the peasants, to create the sense of revolutionary nationhood which was a prerequisite for earning freedom. Fryderyk Chopin played an important rôle promoting Polish culture and nationhood in the salons of the European bourgeoisie.

In the Austrian territories of Galicia and Lodomeria, which had been in the south and southeast of the old Polish state, things were somewhat different. The population consisted of almost equal numbers of Catholic Poles, and Orthodox or Uniate Ukrainians (called Ruthenians by the Austrians). National and religious differences made any united resistance impossible. Moreover, in the few towns the Jews were also a strong presence, while the administration was in the hands of German-speaking Austrian officials. Galicia was economically a backward region, and high taxation, the preferential treatment given to the landowning nobility, and a lack of investment allowed the area in the course of the century to become one of the poorest in the Austrian Empire. On the other hand the Austrian administration allowed the Polish nobility to preserve more of their liberties than did the other two partitioning powers.

The city of Kraków was a special case. In 1815 Russia had been unwilling to allow its return to Austria, so the city had been made a republic, whose 88,000 inhabitants nevertheless remained under the control of the partitioning powers. As a university city with an oligarchical constitution devised by Adam Czartoryski and using a property-based franchise, Kraków was a place where Poles could act freely and it became a focus of national aspirations. After the November Uprising in 1830 the 'Protecting Powers' restricted the liberties of the city, and an attempted uprising planned by Polish emigrés resulted in 1846 in the ending of the autonomy of Kraków and the incorporation of the region into Austria. The population of the city welcomed the entry of Austrian troops into Kraków for protection against the revolt of the Ukrainian peasants. The linguistic and religious differences now intensified further as social tensions grew between Polish landlords and Ukrainian peasants.

In the Prussian partition, the authorities at first allowed their new provinces a large degree of self-government. The social structure was left unchanged, while various reforms in administration, economics and education created a climate of respect until 1830. But this relative harmony ended with the November Uprising, when the Viceroy, Prince Radziwiłł, was replaced by a new *Oberpräsident*, Eduard von Flottwell. The previously subtle attempts at Germanization now became more overt: the Polish nobility was to be suppressed, German immigration was encouraged and an attempt was made to drive a wedge between the aristocratic Polish intelligentsia and the Polish peasants, whom they regarded as their allies. German became the language of government, and Polish administration of schools was discontinued. The campaign against the Catholic Church, which demanded that children of mixed marriages be brought up in the Catholic faith, created a new solidarity among the Poles. Economically successful and politically assured spokesmen emerged among the urban population. The accession of Friedrich Wilhelm IV in 1840 brought a temporary pause in the anti-Polish thrust of the Prussian administration, and

The 1863 Uprising as seen in a Punch cartoon by John Tenniel

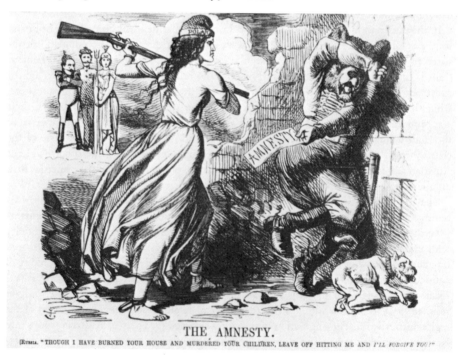

THE AMNESTY.

[Russia. "THOUGH I HAVE BURNED YOUR HOUSE AND MURDERED YOUR CHILDREN, LEAVE OFF HITTING ME AND *I'LL FORGIVE YOU!*"

instead a more liberal policy was followed in an attempt to make the Poles into 'good Prussians'. The attempted uprising in Kraków in 1846 and the unrest in 1848, in which the Poles had articulated their hopes for democracy and a national state, developed into military conflicts and thus alienated the German bourgeoisie from the Polish cause. The old linguistic and religious differences now turned into a nationalistic quarrel within the population; both sides now had a greater sense of conflict and began to vie with each other using the same political weapons (nationalist associations, economic unions, public relations campaigns). By 1870 it was clear that if it had been difficult to make the Poles 'loyal Prussians', under no circumstances – despite increased Germanization measures – could they be turned into 'good Germans'.

In 1848, the year of revolutions, there had been no unrest in Russian Congress Poland, and the reign of Nicholas I brought the Poles a period of 'moderate oppression'. Slow modernization of the economy made it possible for even the non-noble sections of the population to enjoy an improvement in their incomes. Aleksander Wielopolski became the representative of a cautious policy, which aimed at autonomy, while among the young intelligentsia there was increasing support for the nationalist 'Democrats' or 'Reds', who incited anti-Russian feeling. A series of incidents in 1861 brought about a large degree of solidarity among the Polish population. The tensions erupted in January 1863 in a badly planned uprising. In spite of the overwhelming military superiority of the Russians, the Poles were able to hold their own under changing leadership until April 1864. The Russians then imposed a terrible punishment on the country: the Polish nobility, intelligentsia and Catholic clergy suffered executions, expropriations, and were sentenced to hard labour and Siberian exile. The nobility, however, were not completely deprived of power, though they lost their status as the almost undisputed spokesmen of the nation. The bourgeoisie and intelligentsia gained in influence, and the peasantry now appeared as a new source of strength. A new generation under the slogan 'Organic Work' sought to improve the education and prosperity of the people in Congress Poland, and so achieve an internal sense of nationhood, before gaining independence as a state.

After the suppression of the January Uprising, the Poles were further from political autonomy than ever; it was only then in fact that the deliberate oppression began: the name of Poland disappeared completely, the country was governed by Russians according to Russian law, teaching had to be in Russian (from 1867, with the exception of religious instruction). As a result of these regulations there was an increase in the number of illiterates. The Catholic Church was not allowed to fill vacant sees. But all these draconian measures could not break the Polish people's will for self-determination. From the ranks of the bourgeois and noble intelligentsia attempts were made, through journalism and literature, to strengthen national resistance, to lay the foundations for a modern national society and to spread an awareness of history, which would embrace all Poles. The historical novels of Henryk Sienkiewicz and the paintings of Matejko were to make a great contribution to this process. A sharp rise in population was combined with growth in productivity in the economy, drawing the superfluous workforce from the countryside to the towns. The socialist movement, which developed among the industrial workers, split into two tendencies over the question of whether socialism was primarily an international or a Polish nationalist movement. This led in 1892 to the founding by Ludwik Waryński of the Polish Socialist Party (PPS), in which Józef Piłsudki was to gain some influence. The internationally minded socialists came mostly from the Jewish intelligentsia, who could expect no betterment of their situation from the increasing nationalist tensions. The most prominent example of this was Rosa Luxemburg (Róża Luksemburg), born in Zamość and founder member of the communist movement in Poland and Germany. The bourgeois camp gathered in political and business associations, which eventually came together to form the *Liga Narodowa* (National League), in which historical consciousness of Greater Poland combined with anti-semitism and anti-Germanism to form an ideology of national integration. Its most important representative was Roman Dmowski.

A small town in Galicia photographed in 1900

At the beginning of the 20th century the shape of Polish society in the Russian partition territories had become clear: the nobility had largely relinquished its leading role to – or rather had merged with – the bourgeosie represented politically by National Democracy (ND). Opposite them stood the great mass of the peasants, who were still waiting for full social recognition, and descendants of peasants, who had become industrial workers and were attracted to socialism. Some resolution of the conflicts of interest was possible under Russian rule only during the Russo-Japanese War of 1904, the 1905 Revolution and the First World War. The internationalist socialists, who were striving to work together with the Russian proletariat and overcome nationalistic sentiment, were squeezed out in the increasingly nationalistic climate on both sides, with the combination of anti-Russian and anti-Jewish feeling. The tsarist government temporarily moderated its Russification programme after the turn of the century (in 1905 Polish was permitted in schools), but the clashes with the state increased at the same time, borne along by the forces which were later to emerge in Piłsudski's Legions in the First World War.

All hopes for a democratization of the Tsarist empire, which would have helped the Poles achieve their new statehood in Slavic solidarity, had disappeared at the beginning of the First World War, although the Russian Commander-in-Chief, Grand Duke Nikolai Nikolaevich, had attempted to awaken such hopes in his manifesto of 14 August 1914. Congress Poland had little reason to be grateful to the Tsarist empire, under the name of 'Vistulaland' it had second-class status on the periphery of the empire. Despite a certain amount of economic success – for instance in the textile industry in Łódź – the country was still largely agricultural and geared to Russian needs. The transport connections were also suited to Russian requirements (for instance, the gauge of railway tracks). The population had with difficulty accustomed itself to obedience, but beneath this obedience lurked a fundamental mistrust of the authorities. There was no experience of democratic parliamentary processes; the intellectuals exhausted themselves in endless debates and had never learned to carry political responsibility. From the Polish province of the Russian Empire there was no ready-made or even visible path to independent statehood.

Austria had not exactly spoiled its Polish provinces after 1848 either. At the end of the neo-absolutist era of the interior minister, Alexander Bach, the Polish nobility was at least permitted to participate in the administration of the provinces, and in 1868 Galicia was even granted autonomous status. From 1870 the schools and universities (Lwów, 1869, and Kraków) used the Polish language, which also became the language of administration again. Galician Poles even reached the central administrative offices in Vienna, where at the beginning of the century they were *de facto* promoted to the status of a third major ethnic group (after the Germans and Hungarians) with an acknowledged political role.

These successes of the noble representatives also had a negative side. The increasing Polish influence served to mobilize ever more clearly Ukrainian nationalism, since the Ukrainians felt themselves to be doubly oppressed by foreign domination. What the

Ukrainian intellectuals could articulate, the Ukrainian peasants suffered in silence: the neglect of the economy, poverty and exploitation of villages. In many small towns the Jews formed the majority of the population and dominated trade. It was all too easy for them to become everyone's scapegoat in the delicate balance between Polish and Ukrainian nationalism, Catholic, Uniate and Orthodox Christianity, town and countryside. While enlightened Jews entered the intellectual professions (doctors, lawyers), latent anti-semitism simply followed the social shift.

The greater degree of intellectual freedom in this, the poorhouse of the Austrian Monarchy, allowed the peasants to organize themselves. They articulated their interests in the Polish Peasants' Party and its numerous splinter groups, which existed side by side with the bourgeois and socialist parties. Around the parties secret organizations grew up in the revolutionary year 1905, which conducted propaganda and military attacks on the Tsarist empire from their bases in Galicia. This school of the underground produced most of the leading politicians and soldiers in the new Republic of Poland. They had parliamentary and military experience, but were often helpless when it came to questions of economics.

Prussia – from 1871 the German Reich – affected its Polish population in a quite different way. Prussian-German administration and access to the German economic cycle brought the Polish section of the population undoubted advantages, but in the consciousness of the people these counted for little, when they had to fight long and hard for their language and religion. Contemporaries did not realize that Prussia was training its opponents to use the same weapons for their own ends. Nationalist and economic associations strengthened both the Poles' will to resist and their abilities to organize. Each conflict between the authorities and the Catholic Church during the Kulturkampf strengthened the connection in people's mind between Polishness and Catholicism: 'Polakatolik'. Bismarck's brutal Germanization policy aimed to marginalize the Polish nobility, the Catholic Church and the Polish language, but – by an irony of history – it had quite the opposite effect. Nowhere else did Polish society unite so strongly despite class barriers to form a national resistance and many associations were founded with the aim of correcting the short-comings and injustices of the Prussian administration (by encouraging agriculture, schools, land-ownership in Polish hands). The harder the coercive measures of the official policies of language and land, which were intended to 'Germanize' people and land by means of the Ostmarkenverein ('Society for the Eastern Borders'), known to the Poles as Hakata from the initials of its founders, the greater was Polish solidarity. The Poles fought with the same nationalist weapons as the Germans, and honoured their symbols of resistance, such as the peasant Michał Drzymała, who set up home in a caravan in 1904 because he was not allowed to build a farm on his land. Polish deputies in the Reichstag and a combative Polish press learned how to hold their own in the competition between the nationalities, and they did so successfully against the best administration of the time. Did the Poles of the Province of Posen therefore have cause to be grateful to the Germans for this hard school? A large part of the fateful German-Polish conflict was based on the experience of this nationalist struggle. The new Polish state was to inherit from the Prussian province a structured, modern and self-confident society, which, with its prosperity and national consciousness, was trained in the competitive struggle. It was effective but had also learned not to compromise.

The First World War brought another low point in the fortunes of the Polish people: Poles fought on both sides of the eastern front, which for a long time ran through Polish territory. Many vague promises were made by all three partitioning powers in order to obtain more soldiers for their own ends. The most far-reaching assurances came from the Central Powers, Germany and Austria-Hungary, in a joint declaration on 5 November 1916, when they proclaimed the re-establishment of a Polish state, but without precisely defining its frontiers. However, other events were already underway. With the support of the German occupying power, Piłsudski succeeded in building a military organization which formed the nucleus of a Polish army. Before the end of the war a timely quarrel with the German military over his refusal to swear an oath to the Kaiser led to Piłsudski's imprisonment in Magdeburg Castle on 22 July 1917, and so saved him from the accusation of being a collaborator. The military authorities had also permitted the Poles civilian institutions (the Regency Council, 27 October 1917). Although these only represented the upper strata of society, they prepared the way for the Poles to take over government.

The Polish emigrés represented an incalculable force during the war. Poland had long been a card of doubtful value in the policy of the Allies, despite the active propaganda of such emigrés as the pianist Paderewski, and it was not until the October Revolution that the West felt itself freed from the duty of being considerate to its Russian allies. As early as 22 January 1917 President Wilson had publicly emphasized the right of the Poles to have their own state, and in the course of 1917 the Polish National Committee in Paris was able to gain recognition by the Allies and, by creating an emigré army, to achieve the status of a belligerent power. President Wilson's Fourteen Points of 8 January 1918 stated as one of the Allies' war aims the raising to statehood of an 'area inhabited by indisputably Polish population', with the additional demand that it should have 'free, unrestricted access to the sea'.

The Second Polish Republic and the Second World War (1918–1945)

The progress of the First World War had revived the Polish question and brought it to international prominence. Here, finally, was the opportunity for the Polish people to create the state for which they had worked in vain through the whole course of the 19th century. Moreover, since all the partitioning powers had been defeated, the new Poland was able to emerge unhampered by its neighbours; the Poles were able in Namier's words 'to build Poland while Russia and Germany slept'.

The end of the First World War provided Poland with a combination of political circumstances which would have been unthinkable before: the partitioning powers had fought a war against each other and both sides had lost. This made it possible for Poland to make a new beginning as a state without being indebted to the German or the Russian side.

Several factions were involved in the foundation of the state, which took place in phases over October and November 1918. The German military authorities set up a Regency Council and attempted to gain authority by proclaiming an independent Poland on 7 October 1918. Their last ditch efforts were completely undermined by the spontaneous organization of soldiers and workers into soviets. In the Austrian partition the Provisional People's Government of Lublin (founded 6–7 November) was only one of many competing elements. At this moment Piłsudski was released from German detention; he arrived in Warsaw on 10 November, the only man capable of controlling Poland. The next day he became Commander-in-Chief of the Polish military forces, and on 22 November was appointed 'provisional head of state'. Abroad Roman Dmowski was at the head of the Polish National Council and the Exile Army. And lastly the Allies played a role that should not be underestimated, for it was their support alone that brought the question of Poland to the negotiating table and they had to give international recognition to the new borders of the country, subject though these were to fierce controversy and even derision.

The border question also played a central part in discussions within Poland. There were two opposing ideas: Piłsudski envisaged a sort of federation of the various ethnic groups which had belonged to the old Republic of Nobles before 1772; this would have involved a hostile stance towards Russia and a certain rapprochement with Germany (the 'Jagiellonian Principle'). His opponent Dmowski was prepared to be content to leave things in the east as they were, but planned to make massive acquisitions of land at Germany's expense in the west, taking over 'ancient Slavic land' up to the Oder, though this would have brought the lasting enmity of Germany (the 'Piast Principle'). In the end what came about was a combination of the two; Soviet Russia had now dropped out as a power in the east and in the Ukraine the unclear political situation seemed almost to invite Polish nationalists to take their chance. Consequently the borders of the new Polish Republic extended far beyond the areas with a mainly ethnic Polish population. Poland thus achieved its greatest possible extent, largely by military force. This brought on the country the enmity of almost all its neighbours. The borders with Germany were laid down in part by the Allies at the Peace Conference; in areas where the situation was unclear (Upper Silesia, southeast Prussia) plebiscites were to be held; Gdańsk became a Free State under the supervision of the League of Nations (15 November 1920). In January 1919 Poland fought a short war with Czechoslovakia over Cieszyn (Czech: Těšín, German: Teschen), and after lengthy disputes a partitioning of the region was achieved. Poland's military advance on Kiev, which was occupied on 7 May 1920, almost ended in defeat when the Red Army, under Tukhachevsky and Piłsudski's classmate Feliks Dzierżyński, counterattacked and advanced as far as Warsaw, where in August 1920 in a daring manoeuvre the Poles were able to encircle the Soviet forces and inflict a devastating defeat (the 'Miracle on the Vistula'). (For this victory Piłsudski, like Sobieski, has been claimed as a saviour of Christendom from the pagan hordes of the East.) The Treaty of Riga (18 March 1921) gave Poland almost the same borders as in 1772. On 9 October 1920 Piłsudski organized a surprise attack, led by General Żeligowski, against the new state of Lithuania which ceded to Poland the territories it claimed including Piłsudski's native city of Wilno (Lithuanian: Vilnius), but also brought lasting conflict with the new Lithuanian Republic. To the west, the outlook seemed particularly bleak regarding relations with the German Reich. The cession of territories was regarded in Germany as a grave loss, and there was particular resentment at the partitioning of Upper Silesia, which had gone ahead despite the fact that the Germans had won the plebiscites. After the Polish uprisings and the counter-measures taken by the German *Freikorps* the issue was imbued with such emotion that neither side accepted the eventual solution. Within the context of the old Prussian-Polish conflict this represented the most intractable problem between the new neighbours.

Within its new borders Poland had become a multi-ethnic state. In 1921 the population of approximately 27 million included about 70 per cent Poles, as well as 14 per cent

Marshal Józef Piłsudski,
photographed in 1918

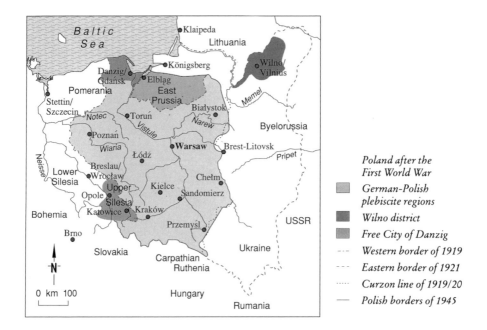

Poland after the
First World War

German-Polish
plebiscite regions

Wilno district

Free City of Danzig

- - - Western border of 1919

- - - Eastern border of 1921

...... Curzon line of 1919/20

——— Polish borders of 1945

Ukrainians (3.8 million), Byelorussians and Germans 3.9 per cent each (1 million), 7.8 per cent Jews (2.1 million) – though the census figures for the minorities are not invariably correct. The relations between the nationalities and the state were made worse by the nationalism of the Polish leaders, who wished to organize their state along lines which contradicted minority rights. Another problem was the legacy of partition, which meant that three distinct economic areas and infrastructures had to be assimilated into a single coherent entity.

In the face of these many internal and external problems the political parties of Poland were fatally fragmented. There were three main political camps, which were split into many individual groupings, always blurred at the edges, and which could only be held together by the personalities of the leaders: the bourgeois forces under Roman Dmowski (National Democracy); the parties on the left, particularly the PPS under Piłsudski, who had however left the party ('I rode in the tramcar called Socialism but I got off at the stop called Independence.'), and the peasant groups under Wincenty Witos. The relationships between the parties and the camps were complicated by irreconcilable differences between the leaders.

After the foundation of the state Piłsudski at first took dictatorial powers as head of state. The rapid changes of government reflected his attempts to achieve national unity. An institutional framework was created first by the Little Constitution of 20 February 1919, and finally by the Great Constitution of 17 March 1921. In accordance with the old tradition of Polish parliamentary thinking, the constitution stressed the controlling function of the people's representative assembly (*Sejm*), and so did not encourage the development of a strong executive. The fissiparous parties, the personal conflicts between the party leaders, quarrels between officials and officers in the various partition regions and the emigrés created a climate in which the internal controversies took priority over matters of common interest. Instead of the period of calm needed for internal consolidation, the country had to endure constantly changing governments. Poland was an agricultural country (72 per cent of the workforce worked on the land) and the land was extremely unevenly divided between the few rich big landowners and a large number of peasants, some of whom were very poor. Industry was not well developed: it was badly located and had little capital. The bourgeoisie of the towns included a high percentage of the ethnic minorities; in particular the large proportion of Jews in professional and intellectual occupations aroused the criticism of the nationalists. Strikes, a high level of unemployment, both official and hidden (particularly in agriculture), population growth and emigration (in the years before 1939 more than two million people emigrated) were features of a society which could only confirm the impression abroad of the 'instability of the Polish conditions'.

Piłsudski, whose prestige as a national hero could have made him a figure for national integration, resigned in exasperation from all political and military posts and withdrew to his estate. There he was courted by elements in the army and kept abreast of political developments, until finally in May 1926 he appeared outside Warsaw at the head of his troops. This demonstration of power turned into a bloody *coup d'état*, which Piłsudski justified as the 'cleaning up' (*Sanacja*) of internal affairs. This first move against the laws of democracy was followed by others, and as time went on it became increasingly clear that the new regime had turned into a real dictatorship, not just a moral one. Piłsudski took little personal control of the running of the country, leaving day-to-day politics to his close associates, particularly the officers of his Legions. He was soon on bad terms with the Sejm, whose controlling function he restricted, and in which he curbed the influence of the parties. The Sejm's only weapon was the budget, and as the parties were growing increasingly vehement in their opposition to him, Piłsudski created his own party, the 'Non-Party Bloc for Co-operation with the Government' (BBWR, 1927). However, the election of 1928 did not give Piłsudski a majority (he obtained only 122 of the 444 seats in the Sejm), so in 1930 he turned to openly dictatorial methods. He dissolved the Sejm and had about seventy of his political opponents imprisoned in the citadel at Brześć (Brest-Litovsk). Although the government now had a narrow majority, Piłsudski alienated the opposition politicians in the process. The emigration of many opposition figures led to his alienation of a large part of the Polish public as well. Piłsudski's increasing isolation was the background to the creation of the new constitution of 1935, which, behind the façade of the separation of powers, sought to concentrate real power in the hands of the president. But Piłsudski was unable to make use of this constitution that had been specially made for him; he died on 12 May 1935. Despite his attacks on the principles of democracy, Piłsudski is still much revered by Poles for the contribution he made to the foundation of the state and for his victory over the Soviet Army, as the fresh flowers always to be found on his tomb in Wawel Cathedral in Kraków demonstrate.

Piłsudski's tailor-made constitution did not fit any of his successors, and the Regime of the Colonels which came after him was increasingly at odds with Polish society. The regime was unable to produce any convincing successes either in its economic or social policies. Only the army represented an element of national pride, but for all its splendour there were serious structural weaknesses and a lack of modern weaponry.

Home policy was characterized by an even greater restriction of democratic rights. In the nationalistic climate the ethnic and religious minorities were subject to severe discrimination, to which the Ukrainians had already responded with violence in 1929. In the winter of 1936–7 the tensions even reached the brink of civil war. Anti-semitism, which had been nurtured by the right-wing parties, was confirmed in the last years of the colonels' regime by legal measures, which limited the number of Jewish students, provided special laws for the professions, and forbade ritual slaughter. Such measures, which hit Jewish communities and individuals hard, were intended to encourage Jews to emigrate.

The German community was to be caught in the crossfire of international politics. The Weimar Republic had called on the Germans to remain in the country and supported them in their political activities; but in the spring of 1939 Hitler began to exploit their political situation in a propaganda campaign which aimed to weaken and provoke the Polish state. The resulting escalation of violence on both sides created a climate of hatred, which was partly responsible for the atrocities of the Second World War.

In foreign policy the former close links with France, already damaged by the Locarno Treaty of 1925 in which France had guaranteed Germany's borders with France and Belgium but not with Poland, were further loosened by Poland's increasing self-confidence, especially after the nonaggression treaty with Hitler in 1934 had brought an easing of relations with Germany. After Piłsudski's death the foreign minister Colonel Beck even entertained the notion of making a bid to become a great power, formulated in terms of a 'Third Europe' between Germany and the Soviet Union. It was symptomatic of this overestimation of the real balance of power that Poland took advantage of the Munich Agreement (29 September 1938) to seize the Czech part of Cieszyn. Before Hitler's policy of aggression intensified in the spring of 1939 Poland had no real friends in Europe and was surrounded by hostile neighbours. Because of their own weakness the Western powers followed a policy of appeasement, which only gradually gave way to a hardening of their attitude towards Hitler. Poland's internal policies had not attracted much sympathy from the Western democracies either. Nevertheless, the guarantee that had been so signally denied to Czechoslovakia was offered to Poland by Britain and France in March 1939. Hitler could be under no illusion that an attack on Poland would trigger world war.

The pact Hitler made with the Soviet Union on 23 August 1939 created the configuration which Poland had always feared: both neighbours were agreed about their 'spheres of influence', which were in effect a new partition of the country. The actual *casus belli*, a

German troops tearing down a frontier barrier in September 1939

border incident faked by the Germans at Gliwice (Gleiwitz), was unimportant; the military plans for the 'Weiss' scenario had been prepared long before. German troops crossed the border on 1 September 1939. In the blitzkrieg that followed, the overwhelming superiority of the modern German Wehrmacht took the Poles by surprise, and despite bold resistance the Polish army was overcome. When on 17 September 1939 the Red Army advanced from the East to the line agreed in the Hitler-Stalin Pact, the Polish Government fled to Rumania, where they were interned. The independent Polish state had ceased to exist; its representation could only be assumed by those forces which had opposed Piłsudski from exile in London.

Neither the Germans nor the Soviets lost any time in instigating complete terror. What had broken out over Poland was not a 'normal' war. After the short sharp offensives of the Wehrmacht there followed the slow policy of Nazi strategies, intended to bring about the annihilation of large sections of the Polish population, the expulsion of the rural population from many regions and the enslavement of those that remained. This exceptional war against the civilian population was based on the Nazi ideas of the 'biological superiority' of the German 'race' over the Slavs, and especially over the Jews; it 'also had the aim of conquering 'Lebensraum' in the East, which Hitler wished to empty of the population living there and settle with 'germanische Wehrbauern' ('Germanic warrior peasants'). The Soviet occupation, though less ideologically driven, was if anything, more bloody. No country was to suffer more than Poland during the Second World War.

Formally a few regions in the West (Posen, Wartheland) were incorporated directly into the German Reich, while the rest was made a 'Generalgouvernement' under German administration, governed from the old royal castle of the Wawel in Kraków by Reichsminister Hans Frank. The Soviet Union held fraudulent plebiscites in its regions in October, and then annexed the territories to the Soviet Union.

However, this description of developments at formal government level says little about what was actually happening. In the autumn of 1939 the race war against the Poles had already begun, with expulsions from the Warthegau, which was now to be settled by repatriated Germans from the Soviet Union. Acts such as the arrest and deportation of the teaching staff of the University of Kraków (6 November 1939) represent only the tip of a multitude of individual actions, the murder, arrest and enslavement of Poles (disguised as 'labour deployment in the Reich'). The plans of the SS aimed at extinguishing the Polish people as a historic nation of Europe, the lower classes of which could find justification for their existence only in hard labour for the 'Aryan race'. The fate of the Jews was even worse: Hitler saw them as the 'adversaries of the Germanic race' and planned their extermination. By way of forced resettlement in ghettoes, deportation and death camps set up for the Jews from almost the whole of Europe, the way led to the crematoria of Brzezinka (Birkenau), Treblinka and others, where in all about six million people (two million of them Jews who were Polish citizens) were murdered. Other death camps, such as Majdanek, located within sight of the city of Lublin, were also used to annihilate opponents of the Nazis from all over Europe and to cow the local population.

The Polish people fought against this systematic annihilation in two ways. The first was through the Government-in-Exile in London under General Władysław Sikorski, which joined the war against the German Reich; Polish soldiers fought against the enemy of their country bravely and at a high cost, from the beginning (at Dunkirk) to the end (at Monte Cassino, for example). Polish airmen were responsible for 15% of enemy losses in the Battle of Britain, and the Polish contribution to breaking the Enigma code was immense. The other way to fight for Poland was through the Home Army (*Armia Krajowa*) which brought together military and civilian resistance. The situation of the Poles seemed to be eased by the German attack on the Soviet Union on 22 June 1941, since this meant that the ring around Poland was broken. However, continued Polish demands for the return of the eastern territories taken by the Soviet Union caused increasing damage to Polish-Soviet relations. Nor did the Soviet Union prove reliable in honouring its promises to release Poles deported to Siberia. The discovery at Katyń in the spring of 1943 of the bodies of 4321 Polish officers murdered by the Soviet forces, (as German propaganda correctly stated though it hypocritically exploited the fact), served as a pretext for Stalin to break off relations with the London Government-in-Exile. The long Soviet silence about the fate of over 27,000 officers and of sections of the civilian population after the Russian advance into Poland continued to embitter relations between the two peoples after the war, and it is only recently that Soviet responsibility for these atrocities has been admitted.

In the anti-Hitler coalition the Poles, for whose sake the Allies had entered the war, increasingly found themselves cast in the role of trouble-makers, whose best interests were decided over their heads at the Teheran and Yalta Conferences. But the Polish resistance was able to achieve some successes on its own. The most important of these was the preservation of Polish intellectual life; some of the intelligentsia were active in the military resistance or could continue the education of some of the nation's youth in secret schools and universities. Harrying operations against the occupiers were conducted by partisans from some of the impenetrable forests of Poland. The two uprisings in Warsaw have become bywords for tragedy with a central place in the consciousness of the Jewish and Polish peoples. The desperate uprising of the Ghetto in April 1943 was doomed from the start, but showed that the Jewish people could fight against their oppressors. The uprising of the Home Army towards the end of the summer of 1944 was better planned, since it was a last opportunity for Poles to seize the initiative. In the event, the Red Army waited impassively at the gates of Warsaw while the SS carried out Hitler's orders to raze the city to the ground. Stalin's army was able to occupy a wasteland.

As well as the centres of resistance already mentioned – the Government-in-Exile in London and the Home Army – mention must also be made of the communist resistance which, together with the Red Army, was to determine the destiny of Poland after its liberation from German occupation. After 1918 the communists in Poland, because of their pro-Russian and pro-Soviet orientation, had been marginalized: the party was finally dissolved by Comintern in 1938 and its leaders summoned to Moscow and mostly liquidated. The world war offered the communists the opportunity for a new beginning: in the country itself where they built up their own military units (*Armia Ludowa*, People's Army, formerly 'People's Guard') and party organization, and in exile in Moscow, where those Poles who had survived Stalin's purges were trained for new tasks. The communist forces, decimated by the German secret services, were reorganized in accordance with the wishes of Moscow. Władysław Gomułka, the leader of the resistance in Poland, and Bolesław Bierut, Stalin's spokesman and envoy, were the representatives of two opposing tendencies – a potential conflict which did not erupt until after the war. Stalin's diplomatic grip on the outcome in Poland became all the stronger during the war since the Red Army had had to bear the brunt of the struggle against the German Wehrmacht. It was Stalin who decided on the future borders of Poland at the conferences of the 'Big Three'. He insisted on shifting the country westwards by annexing territories from Germany, though the Eastern Territories that had been annexed by the Soviet Union in 1939 were never up for discussion. Stalin intended to exploit his agreed sphere of influence to the full. The march of the Red Army across the line that Stalin regarded as the eastern border of Poland marked the beginning of the 'reconstruction' of the country. Here again it must be pointed out that this was not a 'normal' reconstruction after wartime devastation, but a new construction of state and society organized by the communists. It entailed the dissolution, and, if necessary, suppression by military force of rival military and civilian forces in the non-communist resistance, the changing of the conditions of ownership by expropriation, the building of a system of administration on Soviet principles and its staffing by Soviet agents. The moving force was the 'Lublin Committee', which first emerged on 22 July 1944 at Chełm and three days later was holding office at Lublin.

The retreat of the defeated German Wehrmacht turned into a catastrophe for the civilian population. A scorched earth policy meant the senseless destruction of towns and industrial installations. The advancing Red Army, for its part, destroyed anything that stood in its path. Hundreds of thousands of Germans paid with their lives for the horrors of the Nazi campaign in Russia. Those who managed to flee often succumbed to the rigours of the winter trek to the west.

For the Polish population too things did not happen as the Government-in-Exile in the

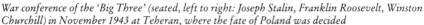

War conference of the 'Big Three' (seated, left to right: Joseph Stalin, Franklin Roosevelt, Winston Churchill) in November 1943 at Teheran, where the fate of Poland was decided

West and the Home Army had hoped. The Lublin Committee declared itself to be a provisional government on 1 January 1945, and in the same month moved to what was left of Warsaw. It was only with difficulty that the Western Allies were able to have a few of the members of the London Government-in-Exile (including Stanisław Mikołajczyk, the leader of the Peasant Party) accepted into the government which was now recognized by the Soviet Union. The promise of free elections rested only on the word of Stalin, and he was not willing to allow any external surveillance. To confirm Soviet power in Poland he drew up the Polish-Soviet Treaty for his puppet government to sign. Independent politicians resigned. The Home Army was disbanded, and its leaders were 'invited' by Stalin to Moscow, where they were tried and disappeared into camps. The Polish government that was represented at the Potsdam Conference (17 July to 2 August 1945) was essentially composed of Stalin's agents. The Polish state which resulted from this conference had new frontiers; only the southern border was the same as that of the Second Republic. The territories east of the Oder and Nysa (Neisse) – extending beyond the Oder at Szczecin (Stettin) – passed to Poland. The Poles called these the 'recovered territories'; the Germans referred to them as the 'districts under Polish administration', and the finality of this decision was long questioned (in some quarters it still is), but to Poland and its allies the decision was never in doubt. Those Germans who had not fled or been killed, were expelled, and the rest were resettled by force later. Of the population of about twelve million German-speakers who lived in these areas before the war, more than nine million – after the losses at the end of the war and in the resettlement operations – found new homes in the West. Their place was taken by Poles, most of whom were also victims of resettlement, this time from the territories that had been annexed by the Soviet Union. The wounds opened by these forced resettlements must take longer than the span of a single generation to heal; and the scars still mark the politics and personal lives of millions of Europeans.

Post-war Poland was a different country. Several times the machinery of war had rolled across it, bringing disaster. Most of the towns were destroyed, industrial plant had been plundered and devastated, the villages in the west were deserted. More than six million people (not quite half of whom were Polish Jews) had been killed by the Germans: one in five of the pre-war population. The new beginning under Soviet auspices had led to yet more victims. In particular both oppressors had aimed to eliminate the Polish intelligentsia: the Germans alone killed almost half the doctors and more than half the lawyers in Poland; many skilled workers were killed too. The new Poland was thus overwhelmingly working class and, for the first time in its history, overwhelmingly Catholic and Polish-speaking. Physically, this was a new Poland too, but the land gained to the west damaged relations with Germany for years to come, while on the other hand there was an inescapable close embrace with the traditional enemy to the east, which guaranteed the new frontiers but which also moulded the internal politics of the country. The toll of the Second World War in Poland was greater than in any other country, and to many it must have seemed as if Poland had lost the war twice.

Polish Republic (Second Republic)

1918–1922	Józef Piłsudski (Head of State)
1922	Gabriel Narutowicz (President, assassinated)
1922–1926	Stanisław Wojciechowski (President)
1926–1939	Ignacy Mościcki (President)

Exile

1939–1945	Władysław Raczkiewicz

Poland as a People's Republic

The main political force in the new Poland was the Communist Party, which used the name PPR (Polish Workers' Party) and was sustained by the Red Army and Soviet advisers. Other parties came from the resistance and from exile, including the Polish Peasant Party (PSL) with its leader Mikołajczyk, who brought the voice of the Western Allies into the government. But from the very beginning it was clear that the communists held the reins of power and that the most they would do was tolerate the presence of other political forces beside themselves. The communist power base in the country was strengthened – after initial problems – by a growth in membership which reached 950,000 in 1948. The communists occupied the key positions or had their representatives in the background if a ministry was held by a member of another party. This system, by which the Party had the power to keep a firm control behind what was formally multi-party rule in a 'Democratic Bloc', was what distinguished this transitional state from a 'people's democracy'. The Party deliberately built up power over the police, the security service, the army and the armed militia, and soon controlled Polish society and the country, though it was not until 1947 that the last vestiges of active resistance were removed.

Once the political forces of the Democratic Bloc had been brought into line, only the PSL under Mikołajczyk, now agriculture minister, was left as an independent party. It hoped to receive a clear vote of confidence from the population in a free election. To test the feeling in the country, the government under the Socialist Osóbka-Morawski announced a referendum to be held on 30 June 1946. Approval was sought on three issues: the abolition of the Senate, the programme of agricultural reform and nationalization, and the finality of the western border. On the last two points there was little dispute among the population, so the argument centred on the first question. Its actual significance became secondary, and instead it turned into a trial of strength with the Democratic Bloc. The results of the referendum were not announced until ten days afterwards and showed a 32 per cent No vote for the first question. The figure had been reduced by government manipulation, but Mikołajczyk's supporters were able to celebrate it as a victory. Internal political differences intensified still further.

In elections for the *Sejm* on 19 January 1947 the PSL was the only opposition party standing against the communist-led bloc. Foreign observers declared the conduct of this election to be irregular, and the result, which gave the Democratic Bloc 80 per cent of the vote, while the PSL received only 10 per cent, had clearly been 'touched up'. The new *Sejm* elected Bolesław Bierut as President of the Republic, and the First Secretary of the Socialist Party Józef Cyrankiewicz as Prime Minister. As a result of endeavours to criminalize any opposition to the government as treason and to punish it in show trials, the political spectrum narrowed still further, until with the flight of Mikołajczyk and some of his supporters in October 1947, the opposition was eliminated altogether. Power in Poland now lay completely in the hands of the communists, and the unity of the working class was demonstrated to the outside world by the merging of the PPR with the previously independent PPS (Polish Socialist Party) in December 1948 to form the PZPR (Polish United Workers' Party).

The internal transformation of the country had begun immediately after the liberation from German occupation: expropriations, nationalization of industrial and artisan businesses and land reform, which gave the peasants smallholdings with an average of 5 hectares, formed the basis of a new economic system in which the state reserved the organizing role for itself. Henceforth Poland was to have a planned economy on the Soviet model with an emphasis on heavy industry. Like the other countries under Soviet control, Poland was prevented by Stalin from participating in the Marshall Plan in 1947.

The bringing of the economy and society into line was followed by a power struggle within the Party. Various waves of purges had already swept over it, but from the autumn of 1948 onwards the 'Muscovites' under Bierut were able systematically to silence the 'Homeland Communists', with Gomułka at their head, by accusing them of 'Titoism' and nationalism. The 'Polish Road to Socialism' advocated by Gomułka and his stand against the collectivization of agriculture had brought on him the charge of being a 'radish': red on the outside, white on the inside – which are also the Polish national colours. However, the forced departure from power of Gomułka and many others was not followed by show trials and executions (as in Hungary or Czechoslovakia), only with imprisonment.

The power struggle within the Party was matched by a wider reshaping of all areas of life in accordance with the Soviet model – the 'Sovietization' of Poland. The Party, itself centrally organized, controlled the economy and society, guided art, scholarship and education and fought any impulse for independence from the Soviet masters. The 1952 constitution created a system in which the principle of the separation of powers was abolished. In October of the same year the 99.8 per cent vote for the list of the Party's National Front showed that the Soviet model was being copied in election procedure as well. But in one aspect the country was essentially different from the Soviet Union: since 1945 Poland had been almost 98 per cent Catholic, and the moral strength of the Church could not be swept away by nationalization. The government did, however, use a variety of means to diminish the competition represented by the Church: the clergy were forced to take an oath of loyalty to the state; and while the existence of certain institutions, such as the Catholic University of Lublin, was guaranteed, the Primate, Stefan Wyszyński, had to suffer a long period of imprisonment and temporary removal from office for his protests against restrictions and persecutions. Many priests and members of religious orders were also imprisoned.

Although this low point in the country's fortunes passed with the death of Stalin on 5 March 1953, the road to liberalization was at first very difficult. The forced collectivization of agriculture and the preferential treatment given to heavy industry proved to be the main contentious issues linked with the power struggle in the Party. It came into the open when Bierut died unexpectedly in Moscow, shortly after Khrushchev's anti-Stalin speech in February 1956. The cautious relaxation speeded up considerably after a strike in Poznań in June which was bloodily suppressed. Against the resistance of the Stalinists, Gomułka, who had only been fully rehabilitated in August, was able to assume the post of First Secretary of the PZPR in October 1956 and to get rid of the Stalinists. For the Soviet Union, which was also facing the dramatic intensification of unrest in Hungary, this seemed the lesser evil. Under cover of the Hungarian events Gomułka managed to manoeuvre skilfully between the various party groupings, feeding the hopes of the people for more freedom, expressed in the slogan 'Spring in October'. Forced collectivization was stopped and agricultural productivity was increased by providing credit and reducing the compulsory yields. This was accompanied by a reduction of state influence in other parts of the economy, as various branches of industry were allowed more initiative.

But the initial hopes were not fulfilled. True, Poland was able to retain a greater freedom of action in its internal policy than other socialist states, and in foreign policy – after the settlement with the GDR (Görlitz Agreement of 6 July 1950) – it was able through the Rapacki Plan to propose an atomic-weapon-free zone in central Europe, but the whole Party apparatus suffered in the 1960's from stagnation and Gomułka's estrangement from everyday reality. A power struggle between Gomułka and the interior minister, General Moczar, led to a renewed restriction of intellectual freedom and the rule of law from 1964, and from 1967 to a distasteful campaign against the 'Zionism' of those Jews who were left in the country. In the 'Prague Spring' of 1968 Poland sided with the anti-reform forces, and contributed troops to the Warsaw Pact invasion. It was in Warsaw too that Brezhnev enunciated his doctrine of intervention. In the last phase of his rule Gomułka surrounded himself with technocrats, from whose ranks his successor, Edward Gierek, was drawn. The end of the Gomułka era was connected with two dramatic events. One was the signing on 7 December 1970 in Warsaw of a treaty with the West German government of Willy Brandt. This not only marked a long overdue coming to terms with the past regarding the border question, it also opened opportunities for better co-operation in the future. The other was a long-smouldering internal political crisis, which erupted explosively after a price increase for consumer goods on 12 December of the same year. It was Gomułka's tragedy that his period in power, which had started with such high hopes, ended with a bloody suppression of the workers' strikes in Gdańsk. On 20 December 1970 Gomułka was removed from office and made an unperson.

The election of Gierek as First Secretary of the Party was likewise accompanied by high expectations, and to begin with this pragmatic politician from Katowice was able to fulfil them. Gierek replaced the old leadership of the Party, went to the factories to hear the workers' complaints, and introduced measures for economic improvement. The Polish people were promised a new generation of leaders and a 'new beginning'; they received more foreign credit and repaid the government's offers (such as more opportunities for foreign travel) with an increase in industrial productivity. But the far-reaching plans collapsed abruptly following the rise in world oil prices. The balance of payments deficit ballooned, and the country could only be kept going by massive credits. The economic difficulties led in the mid-1970's to a slow withdrawal of the previous liberalization measures. In June 1976 an increase in food prices caused strikes which were put down by force. Gierek had reached the point where the Party could keep the population quiet only by coercion.

Willy Brandt in Warsaw on 7 December 1970

This time, however, opposition movements were beginning to stir in Polish society. In protest against the actions of the police against the striking workers and to support needy families a 'Workers' Defence Committee' (KOR) was established, with the support of many intellectuals. Soon other associations sprang up, in which Poland's past and present problems were discussed and written about in uncensored publications. The failure of the government's economic policy was now under public scrutiny, particularly the country's high burden of debt; the signs of a moral decline of the Party did not go unnoticed. Another new factor for the regime was the increased influence of the Catholic Church. At first Gierek had generally co-operated with the Church, for instance permitting the building of new churches, but the charismatic figure of the old Primate, Cardinal Stefan Wyszyński, who was esteemed and feared as the admonisher and opponent of the government, received an unexpected boost from the election of the Bishop of Kraków, Cardinal Karol Wojtyła, as Pope John Paul II on 16 October 1978. Eight months later the Pope's triumphant tour of Poland reinforced the Church's authority as the legitimate and visible focus of national pride and moral aspirations.

The people's discontent at the gradual worsening of the food supply situation culminated in July 1980 in a vehement reaction to a rise in meat prices. The laying off of workers who had ideas about setting up an independent trade union was quickly followed by strikes in Gdańsk and other cities. What was new was the creation of an unofficial strike committee, whose leader, the Gdańsk electrician Lech Wałęsa, soon made more far-reaching demands for a nationwide independent trade union. Walk-outs and the united front presented by workers throughout the country, supported by intellectuals and priests, forced the Party to the negotiating table – since the 'Workers' Party' hoped to avoid using violence against the workers it was supposed to represent. The government accepted fundamental criticisms made by the workers, and the Gdańsk Agreement (31 August 1980) made substantial concessions. Although the leading role of the Party was officially confirmed, the emergence of a self-governing trade union 'Solidarity' ('Solidarność') – implicitly broke the monopoly of power. Five days after the Gdańsk agreement, Gierek paid the price as the Party removed him from office.

The new Party chief, Stanisław Kania, went even further in meeting the workers' demands. In October he 'registered' Solidarność; in other words, he permitted it to exist. But in the months that followed the Party came under pressure from two sides: to the neighbouring socialist countries it seemed that the Party's concessions had gone too far, while to the trade union they had not gone far enough. Solidarność too was increasingly troubled by internal problems, as individual groups made ever more far-reaching demands, which, had they been fulfilled, would have meant the break up of the post-war system. The union's only weapon, strike action, was over-used and brought the country to the brink of chaos. Soviet intervention seemed only a matter of time.

The events of 1981 have been hotly disputed. On 9 February the defence minister and commander-in-chief of the army, General Wojciech Jaruzelski was appointed prime minister. This was a first step towards a potential military coup, which could either be seen as a pre-emptive move to forestall Soviet invasion, or as a direct response to Moscow's commands. Meanwhile, the Party itself was proving all too susceptible to the new spirit of discussion. On 18 October Jaruzelski also took over from Kania as Party chief, acquiring a concentration of power unprecedented in the history of the new Poland. Food supply problems worsened, but at the same time there was an unaccustomed freedom of expression. Old pre-war ideas re-emerged as well as radical demands which discounted geopolitical realities. Solidarity tried to put its house in order at two conferences in the autumn of 1981, but Jaruzelski struck a surprise move on 13 December 1981, by declaring a 'State of War' ('Stan wojenny'). Under martial law thousands of Solidarity members and some of the old Party leadership were interned in camps.

By proclaiming the State of War and banning Solidarity General Jaruzelski had restored calm to the country – but this was a calm of paralysis and resignation, far removed from

1 WARSAW   Church of the Nuns of the Visitation ▷

2 WARSAW   Panorama of the old city centre; the Borch Palace in the foreground ▷

3 WARSAW Ostrogski Palace

4 WARSAW
Church of St Alexander

5 WARSAW Teatr Wielki (Great Theatre)

6   WARSAW   Ghetto Memorial

7   WARSAW   Old Town Square ▷

8/9   WARSAW   Wilanów Palace: the bathroom of Izabela Lubomirska and the Crimson Room

10 WARSAW Łazienki Park, the Theatre on the Island

11 WARSAW Łazienki Park, Ujazdów Castle

12 Arkadia Temple of Diana, north side

13 Pułtusk Church of St Matthew ▷

14 ZAKROCZYM Parish church

15 GOLUB-DOBRZYŃ Castle

16   RADZYŃ PODLASKI   Palace

17   OPINOGÓRA   Castle of Zygmunt Krasiński

19   LESZNO   Town Hall
18   POZNAŃ   Town Hall, interior
20   POZNAŃ   Town Hall

21   PAWŁOWICE
Column Room in the Mielżyński Palace ▷

the 'normalization' that was promised. Besides the pacification of society (to which the cautious attitude of the new Primate, Cardinal Glemp contributed), the most urgent issue was the reorganization of the economy. The country's debt stood at about 30 billion dollars and scope for reduction was limited, especially since the response of many countries to the declaration of martial law was to impose sanctions. Prices of everyday goods went through the roof, and ration cards were introduced for important foodstuffs such as meat. Since wage increases did not keep step with these inflationary price rises there was a clear decline in living standards, which led to the development of a black economy in hard currency and a rise in emigration (in some cases temporary, to earn foreign currency).

The potential for conflict between State and Church was realized with the murder of Jerzy Popiełuszko, a Warsaw priest, by officials of the security services on 19 October 1984. That the arrest and trial of these officials was sanctioned by Jaruzelski's government was intended to demonstrate that the country had returned to the rule of law. Popiełuszko's grave in Warsaw has since become an unofficial national shrine (see page 169).

More generally the Party was unable to overcome growing apathy and civil resistance.

Zbigniew Messner, a professor of economics, was appointed Prime Minister by Jaruzelski in 1985. Attempts at economic reform foundered however, and the Party's moral mandate was utterly rejected by a referendum on price rises and limited liberalization in 1987. Crippling strikes followed throughout the next year. Messner's replacement in 1988 was Mieczysław Rakowski, who had gained a reputation as a liberal when he was a journalist (in Bonn and elsewhere), but who had represented a consistent, though moderate party line in the various state and Party offices he had held. Meanwhile confusion and hope were being generated by Mikhail Gorbachev's policy of *glasnost* and *perestroika* in the Soviet Union, which was changing the direction of the Communist Party there.

In the autumn of 1988 lengthy round-table negotiations were held with Solidarity, which argued for a gradual transformation of the People's Republic into a democratic constitutional state. The main feature of the various stages in this transformation was the participation of the authorities of the old system in the progressive removal of their own powers. As a result of the negotiations a series of laws was passed by the Sejm on 7 April 1989: the Sejm was to have long terms so that it could limit the power of the anonymous Party apparatus, the office of State President was revived, rules for democratic elections were laid down, and there was a new law to unshackle trade unions and associations. In May censorship was abolished, and the freedoms of conscience and worship were safeguarded by law. The first free elections since the end of the Second World War were held under transitional rules, by which the Communists, together with allied parties and groups, were assured of 65 per cent of seats in the Sejm, while at the same time the election for the newly created Senate was to be entirely free. The results of the elections on 4 June 1989 showed unmistakably what the people thought of their old rulers: Solidarity won 99 per cent of the seats in the Senate, while in the lower house the Communists had difficulty finding representatives to fill the seats that had been allotted them, and even those

Lech Wałęsa, the leader of Solidarity, elected President of Poland in December 1990

Communists who had shown themselves to be reformers, such as Rakowski, failed to be elected.

Poland was thus a state in transition, a transition that was embodied by Wojciech Jaruzelski, whom the Sejm elected State President by a narrow majority on 19 June 1989. Communist candidates for the post of Prime Minister failed to gain a majority in the *Sejm*, and at Lech Wałęsa's suggestion on 24 August 1989 his Solidarity colleague Tadeusz Mazowiecki was elected as the first non-Communist Prime Minister since the war. Mazowiecki's cabinet, however, still reflected this period of transition; it contained, besides representatives of Solidarity, 'independents' such as the Foreign Minister Krzysztof Skubiszewski, and even Communists in the 'sensitive areas' of Interior Affairs and the Army.

A further stage in the creation of the new Poland was marked by the reforming amendment of 30 December 1989 by which the country's name once again became the 'Republic of Poland' and the crown was restored to the white eagle as a sign of sovereignty. The repeal of the article which maintained the 'leading role of the Party', and the change of wording to identify not 'the workers' but 'the people' as the source of authority in the state, marked another step away from the coercive state based on 'people's democracy'.

The most difficult problem was the change-over to a market economy. The Finance Minister, Leszek Balcerowicz, introduced austerity measures intended to halt hyperinflation and replace the old structures of the controlled economy with market forces. This shock therapy had achieved its aims by the beginning of 1991, when the lifting of controls on exchange rates stabilized the currency and filled the shops, though at the cost of a reduced standard of living for some sections of the population. Besides the unemployed, now numbering more than a million, pensioners in particular found themselves poorer, while others tried to take advantage of the new opportunities for making money through trade, temporary emigration or entrepreneurial activity.

Poland's transitional character was also reflected in the reshaping of the political landscape. In the 1980's politics had been dominated by the triad comprising the Party, the Church and Solidarity, but now the Communist Party had gone. It dissolved itself in January 1990, hoping for a new future as a party of social democracy. The Catholic

Church too had to redefine its role in a pluralist society. The new personalities in politics were recruited from the spectrum of groups represented in Solidarity, as well as from the old Democratic Party and the Peasants' Party. Solidarity had a particular burden to bear because of its double function as a party in government and a trade union in opposition. During 1990 this conflict became increasingly personalized in the controversy between the cautious Prime Minister Mazowiecki and Lech Wałęsa, who pressed for a speeding up of the process of change. After the Communist ministers were removed from office in July 1990, the resignation of President Jaruzelski made possible the first free presidential election in December 1990. Mazowiecki and Wałęsa, representing the two tendencies in Solidarity, stood against each other, but they were joined by a surprise candidate, a mysterious emigré Pole called Stanisław Tymiński, whose commercial, transatlantic glamour pushed him into second place in the first poll. Mazowiecki was thus eliminated from the second round on 16 December 1990, in which Lech Wałęsa won 75 per cent of the votes. This could not really be called a great electoral triumph, however, since 47 per cent of the electorate stayed away from the polls. On 22 December 1990 Lech Wałęsa was installed as the first freely elected President of the Republic of Poland, an event which signalled the end of the postwar period for Poland.

The astonishing events of 1989, with the liberalization and transformation of Hungary, the collapse of the GDR and the 'Velvet Revolution' in Czechoslovakia, and the end of Soviet supremacy, culminating in the dissolution of the Warsaw Pact on 1 April 1991, opened up for the states and peoples of Eastern and Central Europe the prospect of returning to the community of free nations. State borders, so bitterly argued over after 1918 and fortified with walls and barbed wire after 1945, were now open. The political map of Europe was changed in 1990 with the reunification of Germany, and it was particularly important for the Poles that, as a condition for Allied recognition of reunification, the Federal Republic of Germany formally recognized the border along the Oder-Neisse line. The treaty, the first in which Germany accepted the postwar frontier, was a vital prerequisite for a realistic and friendly relationship between neighbours.

Poland's return to normality as a free and sovereign state also brought with it the re-emergence of many features of the old political culture of the country – a complex party system and an emphasis on strong personalities rather than programmes and organisations.

A running quarrel broke out between President Wałęsa and the Sejm, which objected to Wałęsa's attempt to impose his candidate, Jan Krzysztof Bielecki, as prime minister. After a year of increasing tension, the Sejm succeeded in forcing the President to appoint its own candidate, Jan Olszewski, on 5 December 1991. Because uncertainty about parliamentary majorities prevented the formation of a stable government, the struggle between parliament and president, exacerbated by Wałęsa's authoritarian tendencies became a recurrent feature of the Polish political scene in the early years. Olszewski resigned after a few months and was succeeded in June 1992 by Hanna Suchocka, Poland's first woman prime minister.

Suchocka's government lost no time in introducing strict anti-abortion laws, which, together with continuing economic hardship, may have contributed to its sharp decline in popularity.

Rulers of Poland since 1944
People's Republic of Poland

Heads of State

Party Leaders

1943–48 Władysław Gomułka
(First Secretary Polish United
Workers' Party (PZPR);
Deputy Prime Minister 1947–51)

1944–47 Bolesław Bierut (President of the
National Homeland Council (KRN)
       1947–52 Bolesław Bierut (President of the Republic;
Party Chairman and First Secretary PZPR
from 1948)

1952–56 Bolesław Bierut (Party Chairman
and First Secretary PZPR; Prime
Minister 1954–56)

1952–64 Aleksander Zawadzki
(Chairman of Council of State)

1956–70 Władysław Gomułka
(First Secretary PZPR)

1964–68 Edward Ochab
(Chairman of Council of State)
1968–70 Marian Spychalski
(Chairman of Council of State)
1970–72 Józef Cyrankiewicz
(Chairman of Council of State)

1970–80 Edward Gierek
(First Secretary PZPR)

1972–85 Henryk Jabłoński
(Chairman of Council of State)

1980–81 Stanisław Kania
(First Secretary PZPR)
1981–85 Wojciech Jaruzelski
(First Secretary PZPR and
Prime Minister etc.)

1985–89 Wojciech Jaruzelski
(Chairman of Council of State 1985–89)

Republic of Poland

Presidents

1989–90 Wojciech Jaruzelski
1990–95 Lech Wałęsa

1995–   Aleksander Kwaśniewski
(re-elected in 2000)

Prime Ministers

1989–90 Tadeusz Mazowiecki
1991   Jan Bielecki
1991–92 Jan Olszewski
1992–93 Hanna Suchocka
1993–95 Waldemar Pawlak
1995–96 Józef Oleksy
1996–97 Włodzimierz Cimoszewicz
1997-2001 Jerzy Buzek
2001–   Leszek Miller

After the parliamentary elections of 1993 a new left-wing government was formed by Waldemar Pawlak, who soon became involved in bitter conflicts with President Wałęsa over constitutional reform and taxation. Pawlak eventually resigned, to be replaced by another leftist prime minister, Józef Oleksy (whose career was subsequently destroyed by spying allegations).

Soon after Pawlak's resignation, in 1995, Wałęsa himself lost a closely fought presidential contest to Aleksander Kwaśniewski, the leader of the ex-Communist Democratic Left Alliance (SLD), who was to go on to win a second term in 2000. However, between 1997 and 2001 Kwaśniewski had to work with a centre-right coalition government composed of the Solidarity Election Campaign (AWS) and the Freedom Union (UW), with Jerzy Buzek as Poland's longest-serving premier.

Poland's economy thrived unexpectedly in the mid-1990s. For most the decade the country experienced steady economic growth, making it the most successful of the former Eastern Bloc, until recession set in. Restructuring has caused some anguish, particularly in the area of heavy industry. The bankrupt Gdańsk shipyards, birthplace of Solidarity, threatened with closure, have been saved by the neighbouring Gdynia yards, which recently acquired them. The cotton mills of Łódź have closed, and the coalminers and steelworkers in the Upper Silesian industrial area around Katowice have had to face changes. Also problematic is Poland's agriculture, which still relies largely on peasant farmers. Although admirable from an ecological point of view, this inefficient system presents serious difficulties for the country's forthcoming integration into the European Union.

Meanwhile, the Roman Catholic Church, while retaining the allegiance of the great majority of the population, has lost much of the authority it wielded during the communist years. Its influence failed to prevent the election of former communist Kwaśniewski, or the adoption of a new liberal constitution in 1997. Nevertheless, a conservative-nationalistic Catholic wing continues to attract some popular support through such media outlets as Radio Marija.

Popular dissatisfaction with the AWS-UW government, especially among former manual workers and peasant farmers, for many of whom Poland's economic success had brought little benefit, culminated in the routing of Solidarity in the parliamentary elections of September 2001. The left-wing SLD was swept back to power, with its leader Leszek Miller at the head of a government coalition with the small Peasants' Party.

Despite the continuing complexities and infighting of Polish political life, it is undeniable that a strong democratic system has developed and is now securely established. It is regulated by a new constitution, promulgated in 1997, which vests legislative power in a bicameral national assembly. In 1999 Poland joined NATO and is expected to enter the European Union in the near future.

Manfred Alexander

Chronology of Poland's History

966	Baptism of the Polish prince Mieszko I
997	Martyrdom of St Wojciech by pagan tribes
1000	Creation of the Archbishopric of Gniezno as a Polish ecclesiastical province
1024	Bolesław I Chrobry becomes the first King of Poland
1079	Murder of St Stanisław
1138	Initiation of the Seniorate by Bolesław III Krzywousty
1226	Arrival of the Teutonic Knights
1241	The Mongols are repelled at Legnica by a Polish-German army
1264	Statute of Jewish liberties proclaimed at Kalisz
1308	The Teutonic Knights seize Gdańsk
1320	Władysław I Łokietek is crowned King, ending the period of fragmentation
1333–1370	Reign of Kazimierz III Wielki; Polish state consolidated
1335	Cession of Silesia to Bohemia
1374	Privilege of Košice: the nobility are granted political rights
1386	Union of Poland and Lithuania with marriage of Jadwiga to Grand Duke Jogaila (Władysław II Jagiełło)
1400	Refounding of Kraków University
1410	Battle of Grunwald (Tannenberg) spells end of Teutonic Knights
1454	Incorporation of Royal Prussia
1466	Second Peace of Toruń; Poland gains access to the Baltic and the country reaches its greatest extent, from the Baltic to the Black Sea
1493	First Diet (*Sejm*) at Piotrków: representatives of the local dietines (*Sejmiki*) are sent as deputies to the Sejm
1505	The constitution *Nihil novi* at the Sejm of Radom: the rights of the nobility in the Sejm are established, marking the beginning of the 'Noble Democracy'
1525	'The Prussian Homage': the secularized Teutonic State under Albrecht von Hohenzollern becomes a Polish fiefdom
1552	The Sejm establishes the right to freedom of conscience
1564	Arrival of the Jesuits marks start of Counter-Reformation
1569	Union of Lublin: Poland and Lithuania are to form an 'indivisible whole'
1573	*Articuli Henriciani* lay foundations of the Republic of Nobles after election of Henri de Valois as King
1595	Creation of the Greek-Catholic (Uniate) Church by the Union of Brześć
1606	Rokosz of Zebrzydowski against high-handedness of the King; decline of the Reformation in Poland
1611	Capture of Moscow
1621	East Prussia inherited by the Elector of Brandenburg
1617–1629	First Swedish War
1648–1657	Revolt of the Cossacks led by Bohdan Chmielnicki

1652	First *Liberum Veto* ('Breaking of the Sejm')
1655–60	Swedish Invasion – the 'Deluge'
1660	Peace of Oliwa ends Swedish-Polish struggle for the throne; Brandenburg keeps Ducal Prussia
1667	Armistice of Andrusovo; Moscow obtains Kiev and the Western Ukraine; Poland's status as a great power in Eastern Europe at an end
1683	Turkish siege of Vienna raised by Jan III Sobieski
1697	Friedrich Augustus of Saxony elected King; beginning of the Saxon Era
1700–1721	Great Northern War
1704–1709	Reign of Stanisław Leszczyński
1717	Silent Sejm – beginning of Russian protectorate
1724	Tumult of Toruń
1733–1735	War of the Polish Succession
1735–1763	Use of *Liberum Veto* prevents any decision in the Sejm
1764	Stanisław August Poniatowski elected (last) King of Poland
1768–1772	Confederation of Bar
1772	First Partition of Poland
1788–1792	Four Year Sejm: reform programme
1791	Constitution of 3 May
1792	Confederation of Targowice
1793	Second Partition of Poland
1794	Kościuszko Uprising: Battle of Racławice
1795	Third Partition of Poland; Stanisław August abdicates
1807–1813	Duchy of Warsaw, founded by Napoleon
1814–1815	Congress of Vienna creates Grand Duchy of Posen, Republic of Kraków, and Congress Kingdom of Poland with Tsar as King
1830	November Uprising followed by the Great Emigration
1832	Increased Russification and closure of Polish universities
1846	Insurrection in Kraków; end of Republic of Kraków
1848	Posnanian Uprising; end of Grand Duchy of Posen with increased Germanization
1863	January Uprising in Warsaw; severe reprisals and intensified Russification. Final abolition of serfdom
1867	Autonomy of Galicia established
1892	Polish Socialist Party (PPS) founded in Paris
1894	German nationalist Ostmarkenverein ('Hakata') founded
1897	National Democratic party founded by Roman Dmowski
1914–1918	First World War. Heavy fighting in Mazuria and Galicia
1915	German victory on Eastern Front
1916	Proclamation of Kingdom of Poland by Central Powers
1918	8 January: President Wilson's Fourteen Points
	3 June: Allies recognize principle of Polish independence
	7 October: The Council of Regency proclaims an independent Polish state

	11 November: Piłsudski assumes supreme command of the Polish army
	22 November: Piłsudski becomes 'provisional head of state'
1919	February: 'Little' Constitution
	August: First Polish Uprising in Upper Silesia
1920	10 January: Treaty of Versailles comes into force
	7 May: Polish army occupies Kiev
	16–25 August: Red Army beaten at the Battle of Warsaw: 'Miracle on the Vistula'
	9 October: Polish occupation of Wilno (Vilnius)
	15 November: Free City of Danzig constituted
1921	Partition of Upper Silesia by Council of Ambassadors after uprising
1922	Assassination of President Narutowicz after 7 days in office
1923	Piłsudski resigns official posts and withdraws to his estate
1925	Poland's eastern borders not guaranteed by Locarno Conference
1926	May: Piłsudski's coup d'état and installation of Sanacja government
1930	Arrest and imprisonment of opposition politicians
1932	Soviet-Polish non-aggression treaty
1934	German-Polish non-aggression treaty
1935	February: Opposition coalition (the 'Morges Front') formed in exile
	23 April: New constitution ('April' Constitution)
	12 May: Death of Piłsudski
1938	September: Occupation of Cieszyn region of Czechoslovakia
1939	31 March: Britain guarantees Poland's frontiers
	28 April: Hitler tears up non-aggression treaty
	23 August: Hitler-Stalin pact signed
	1 September: The German offensive begins the Second World War
	17 September: The Soviet Union invades Poland
	28 September: Poland partitioned
	30 September: President Raczkiewicz, interned in Romania, names General Władysław Sikorski as head of Government-in-Exile
1940	Government-in-Exile moves to London
1941	22 June: Operation Barbarossa begins
	Nazi genocide of Jews begins with death camps mainly on Polish territory
1942	January: the PPR (Polish Workers' Party) founded
	February: Underground army renamed Armia Krajowa (Home Army)
1943	13 April: First reports of the Soviet massacre of Polish officers at Katyń
	19 April–16 May: Uprising of the Warsaw Ghetto
	25 April: Stalin breaks with the Government-in-Exile
	4 July: Death of Sikorski in air accident at Gibraltar
	28 November–1 December: Teheran Conference
1944	July: Formation of the Lublin Committee under Soviet tutelage
	1 August–2 October: The Warsaw Uprising
	Poland occupied by Soviet forces

1945	4–11 February: Yalta Conference
	28 June: International recognition for Government of National Unity in Warsaw
	17 July – 2 August: Potsdam Conference
1946	30 June: Referendum as a test of strength for Communists
1947	19 January: Elections to the 'Constitution-making Sejm'
1948	September: Gomułka forced by Bierut to resign for 'rightist deviation'
	December: PPS and PPR joined as PZPR (United Polish Workers' Party);
	Poland becomes a one-party state
	25 December: Stefan Wyszyński installed as Primate
1950	Görlitz Agreement confirms border with GDR
1952	22 July: New constitution: Poland becomes a People's Democracy
1955	Warsaw Pact formed
1956	Strikes and unrest in Poznań; return of Gomułka
1966	Polish Millennium
1968	Unrest in Poland and invasion of Czechoslovakia by Warsaw Pact forces
	under command of Wojciech Jaruzelski
1970	Treaty of Normalization signed with West Germany under Brandt
	December: Strikes in Gdańsk; Gomułka replaced by Gierek
1976	June: Unrest following increase in meat prices
	27 September: 'Workers' Defence Committee' (KOR) founded
1978	Karol Wojtyła, Archbishop of Kraków, elected Pope; he visits Poland in 1979
1980	August: Strikes in Gdańsk and foundation of Solidarity
	September: Gierek replaced by Stanisław Kania
1981	February: General Wojciech Jaruzelski becomes Prime Minister
	25 May: Death of Cardinal Wyszyński, succeeded by Józef Glemp
	October: Jaruzelski becomes First Secretary of the Party
	13 December: Imposition of martial law (in force until July 1983)
1984	19 October: Murder of Father Jerzy Popiełuszko
1985	Mikhail Gorbachev becomes General Secretary of Soviet Communist Party
1987	Government loses referendum over question of prices and reform
1989	Round Table discussions between government and Solidarity lead to legalization
	of the organization and limited introduction of democratic freedoms
	4 June: First free elections: Mazowiecki is Prime Minister; Jaruzelski President
	30 December: Poland renamed 'Republic of Poland'
1990	Economic reforms introduced
	December: First direct elections for the Presidency won by Lech Wałęsa
1992	July: Hanna Suchocka first woman Prime Minister of Poland
1995	November: Wałęsa loses to Aleksander Kwaśniewski in presidential elections
1997	Jerzy Buzek becomes prime minister; the new constitution is adopted
1999	Poland joins NATO
2000	Kwaśniewski re-elected President for second term
2001	Former Communists win parliamentary elections: Leszek Miller Prime Minister

The Jews in Poland

Polonia: Poh-lan-ya (God rests here)
– Hebrew saying

The first sporadic contacts of Jews with the lands on the Oder and Vistula occurred in the early middle ages, during the formation of the Polish state. The account of Poland written around 965 by Ibrahim Ibn Ja'qūb, a Jewish traveller from Spain, mentions Jewish merchants among those who engaged in trade between Western Europe, Red Ruthenia and the Muslim East. Their route via Prague also took them to Kraków. From the end of the 11th century and for the next two hundred years Jews came to Poland from Czech and German towns to escape increasing persecution. At first these new immigrants settled mainly in Silesia. By the mid-15th century they could be found in at least 35 places there, as well as in major towns in other parts of the country, such as Kalisz, Płock, Sandomierz, Lublin, Kraków and Lwów. The economic and cultural development of Poland in the 14th century, which reached its high point in the reign of Kazimierz III Wielki (1333–70), offered new incentives for Jewish immigration, but the main reason for this immigration was still persecution, which continued unabated elsewhere. Many refugees came to Poland as a result of anti-Jewish attacks sparked off by the Black Death (Poland had largely escaped the plague). Another wave of immigrations was caused by the attacks on the Jews in Silesia following the preaching of the papal legate John of Capistrano against heretics. Already by the end of the 15th century 24,000 Jews had settled in Poland and Lithuania, but the influx reached its peak in the 16th century. Ashkenazi Jews forced to leave the Habsburg lands, Sephardi Jews banished from Spain and Portugal, and Sephardim who had chosen to leave Italy and the Ottoman Empire, were all arriving in Poland.

Towards the end of the century Jewish immigration had slowed down. At the same time the centre of Jewish life had ben shifting to the eastern regions of the Polish-Lithuanian Commonwealth. New Jewish communities grew up in the western and central parts of the country. This was a period with a high rate of population growth and the number of Jews increased rapidly. By the mid-17th century it had reached 500,000 (5 per cent of the total population), living in half the cities of Poland and Lithuania.

The social and legal status of Jews in medieval Poland was similar to that in neighbouring countries. The Kalisz Statute granted by Prince Bolesław Pobożny (the Pious) of Wielkopolska in 1264, the first set of privileges governing the status of Jews in Poland, described them as *servi camerae* ('bondsmen of the prince's treasury') and placed them under his direct jurisdiction. The prince guaranteed them economic and religious freedom, protection of life and property, and the right to follow their customs within their communities. In 1364 and 1367 Kazimierz III Wielki (according to legend, under the influence of his Jewish mistress, Esther) widened these privileges and extended them to the whole country. At the end of the 14th century equivalent privileges were granted to the Jews of the Grand Duchy of Lithuania by Prince Witold. These privileges were confirmed by subsequent rulers, until the Polish-Lithuanian Commonwealth was dissolved at the end of the 18th century. However, from 1539 Jews living in privately owned towns were subject to laws issued by the owners of the towns.

The Catholic clergy and the inhabitants of towns were often vocal in their opposition to the presence of Jews in Poland, and the religious and economic freedom accorded them. In extreme cases Jews were forced out of certain towns or prevented from settling in them. In the 16th century more than 20 royal towns were given the special privilege *de non tolerandis Judaeis* depriving Jews of the right of residence. In general, however, Jews in Poland enjoyed great freedom. They had autonomy within their communities, each of which was governed by a group of elders *(kahal)*. The greatest influence was exerted by the rabbis. In the first half of the 16th century these local communities began to form larger regional organizations *(ziemstwa)*. In 1581 a central body for the Jews of Poland and Lithuania called the Council of the Four Lands *(Vaad Arba Aratzot)* met for the first time in Lublin. It continued until its abolition in 1764, although from 1623 the representatives of Lithuanian Jews met separately. The Council was formed mainly to prepare Jewish tax returns for the Polish treasury, but it became involved in economic and legal questions, community organization, education, security and other matters of importance to Polish Jews.

Most Jews lived in towns. (In the eastern regions there were many small towns, *shtetl*, in which Jews formed the majority of the population.) They were mainly employed in local or international commerce. Money-lending, a practice forbidden to Christians by the Church, was an important occupation for Jews in the 14th century. One of the leading bankers was Lewko of Kraków, who lent money to the king and his courtiers, among others, administered the royal mint and leased the salt mines at Bochnia and Wieliczka. From the 16th century crafts began to grow in importance as a source of Jewish income. Another important area of Jewish activity was the leasing of inns, mills, distilleries and breweries. Gradually Jews began to lease whole business enterprises, and collect customs payments and tolls in large areas of the country. Outstanding among these was the chief collector of taxes from the Jews of Lithuania, Michał Ezofowicz, who was ennobled in 1525.

The cultural life of the Polish Jews flourished in the 16th century and the first half of the 17th. Scholarship and learning reached a high level and Talmudic scholars were highly acclaimed throughout the Jewish world. The greatest were Moses Isserles (1520–72) – a follower of his great 12th-century namesake, Moses Maimonides – and Lipman Heller (1579–1654) from Kraków, Salomon Luria (1510–73) from Lublin, and Jozue Falk (1550–

1614) from Lwów. At the numerous academies (*yeshivot*, singular: *yeshiva*) supported by rich communities, young men studied the Talmud. Jewish savants also made progress in science, particularly medicine. The number of religious and secular publications was greatly increased by the establishing of Hebrew printing houses, the first of which was founded in Kraków in 1534. This was also a great period for Jewish art and architecture, and many new synagogues were built. In Kraków alone five splendid brick and stone buildings were erected between 1550 and 1650. A new type of synagogue building appeared in southeastern Poland in the first half of the 17th century. It had a spacious interior divided into nine parts with the *bimah* placed between four massive pillars supporting a vaulted ceiling. The best surviving example is at Łańcut. Innumerable wooden synagogues were also built (usually in the local style) with polychrome wall decoration and liturgical objects of high quality, including candelabra, tapestries and silver decoration for the Torah scrolls. None of these has survived.

The mid-17th century brought a dramatic change in the fortunes of the Jews, whose life up to then had been generally tranquil and successful. Many thousands of Jews in the Ukraine were killed in the Cossack rebellion led by Bohdan Chmielnicki, as the rebels vented their fury against the hated Polish landlords and their Jewish agents. The country was then plunged into the chaos of the wars with Sweden, Russia and the Turks, which brought the Jews more misfortune as poverty, famine and pestilence decimated the population.

Against this background three important messianic movements began to spread among the Jews. The first of these was Sabbateism, called after Shabbetai Tzevi (1626–76) from Smyrna, who in 1648 and in 1666 proclaimed himself the Messiah. The second was Frankism founded by Jacob Frank (1726–91) from Podolia, who adopted some antinomian Sabbatean beliefs and rejected the authority of the Talmud. To escape the persecution of the Jewish authorities, he led his numerous followers to baptism in the Catholic Church, but soon found himself accused of heresy and imprisoned. On his release by the Russians he continued to lead the movement, finally settling in Germany, where he lived in baronial splendour surrounded by a gorgeously liveried retinue and supported by the offerings of his followers. After their conversion many Frankists were accepted into the nobility and given the names and coats of arms of noble families.

The only movement, however, to achieve widespread and deep religious significance was Hasidism (from the word *hasid* meaning pious). Its spiritual father was Israel ben Eliezer (1700–60), called the Baal Shem Tov ('Master of the Good Name'), who also came from Podolia. Hasidism offered Jews joy, simplicity and intense religious feelings through singing and dancing, instead of soulless, cold formalism. Having found fertile ground, this enthusiastic, anti-intellectual movement began to spread in the late 18th and early 19th centuries to Galicia, Byelorussia, Lithuania and the Congress Kingdom, and at first was criticized by the Jewish authorities. In the first half of the 19th century most of the Orthodox Polish Jews joined the movement, and so what had been a protest movement itself became accepted as a sort of institutionalized orthodoxy.

The small and often insignificant towns where the movement's leaders (*tzaddiks* – *tzaddik*, Polish: *cadyk*, means 'righteous man') had their residences *(dwory)*, such as Góra Kalwaria, Kock and Aleksandrów, became centres of Hasidism, attracting many pilgrims. *Tzaddiks* were considered to be miracle-workers and intermediaries between God and man. Their position as community leaders was originally charismatic, but soon became hereditary. This resulted in the creation of influential *tzaddik* dynasties and, more significantly, the gradual ossification of the movement. Hasidism disappeared from Eastern Europe in the Holocaust, and today the largest numbers of Hasidim live in the United States and Israel.

The Polish Enlightenment was not sympathetic to the otherness of the Jews; some otherwise tolerant reformers wrote virulently about them, and administrative privileges like the Council of the Four Lands were swept away. Debate about reforming Jewish life in Poland continued even during the Four Year Sejm (1788–92). After the final Partition the situation of the Jews depended on the policies of the occupying powers: Russia, Austria and Prussia. The autonomy which the Jews had enjoyed in the Polish Commonwealth had ended. Jews now had to be registered as citizens and given surnames. It was at this time many acquired such fanciful names as Rosenberg or Goldstein, assigned by civil servants, among them the writer E. T. A. Hoffmann. In the course of the 19th century the initial restrictions were gradually eased, leading eventually to full equality before the law in the second half of the century. In practice, however, this equality was not followed by any improvement to the conditions of life. Indeed, in Russia the reverse happened. Here the Jews were required from 1791 to live within the 'Pale of Settlement', which was defined in 1835 as encompassing the provinces (*gubernii*) in the Ukraine, Byelorussia and Lithuania (i.e. largely the territory taken from Poland in the Partitions). In 1882 the Tsarist authorities increased the restrictions on Jews living in the Pale and forced them to leave the villages. This was followed at the turn of the century by a series of pogroms in Jewish areas, encouraged by the state. These resulted in a massive wave of emigration of around 1.5 million people, most of whom made their way to America, though many stopped en route in cities in Polish provinces and Galicia, where the new arrivals, called 'Litvaks' (Lithuanians), were regarded warily by the established Jewish communities. The Tsarist terror caused an increase in Jewish political activity. In 1897 a socialist party, the Bund, was founded in Wilno. At the same time there was also Jewish emigration from the region under Austrian rule, though this was caused not by pogroms and persecution but by the proverbial poverty of Galicia.

In the 19th century the movement of Jewish Enlightenment *(Haskalah)*, began to increase in importance in Poland. It had originated in Germany in the 18th century in the circle of the great Jewish philosopher, Moses Mendelssohn (1729–86), the grandfather of the composer. Its activists thought that Jews should join the mainstream of society. The means of achieving this were, on the one hand, the reform of Judaism, and on the other, cultural assimilation. The movement was bitterly opposed by the Orthodox majority, but it was influential in obtaining emancipation for the Polish Jews. It also became the nucleus for the later nationalist idea, Zionism. The outstanding proponents of Haskalah in Poland included the philosopher Salomon Majmon (1754–1800) and the biologist and mathematician Mendel Lewin (1749–1826) from Satanów.

The more liberal attitude encouraged by Haskalah led to attempts to use the sacred language, Hebrew, for secular purposes. The pioneers in this revival included Józef Perl (1774–1839) of Tarnopol and Izaak Ber Levinsohn (1788–1860) of Krzemieniec, and by the end of the century Hebrew was emerging as a spoken language. The Hebrew Revival was linked with Zionism, as the Hebraists looked to Palestine as a place where they could speak their language without religious opposition.

In the second half of the 19th century the Jewish bourgeoisie and intelligentsia played a major role in various areas of Poland's economy and cultural life. In Warsaw, a number of culturally Polonized families attained great prominence, among them the Kronenbergs, Natansons, Toeplitzes and Wawelbergs. The rapid growth of Łódź, known as the 'Polish Manchester', was mainly the work of Jewish entrepreneurs, the best known being Israel Poznański (1833–1900). In art the Cracovian painter Maurycy Gottlieb (1856–79) achieved some success and now has a worldwide reputation.

At the same time a movement for the propagation of a separate Jewish culture based on the use of Yiddish also gained widespread popularity. Yiddish, the language of the Ashkenazi Jews, is based on German Rhineland dialects but strongly influenced by Hebrew and the Slavic languages, and written in Hebrew characters. It was now raised to a literary language, and poetry, plays and scientific works were written in it. The leading Yiddish writers were Juda Lejb Perec (1852–1915) from Zamość, and the humorist Szolem Alejchem (1859–1916) from Pereyaslavl, now in the Ukraine.

Many Jews took part in the struggle for an independent Poland, joining Piłsudski's Legions – as their forefathers had taken part in Kościuszko's Insurrection of 1794 and the Uprisings of 1830 and 1863. In the Second Republic (1918–39) with its many nationalities Jews formed the biggest national group after Poles and Ukrainians. Before 1939, 3.3 million Jews lived in Poland, 10 per cent of the population. Most Jews worked in commerce, manufacturing industries and in freelance professions. They were guaranteed minority rights by the state. In the 1920's new laws making Sunday a statutory rest day appeared to discriminate against Jews in nationalized industries. Other measures which antagonized the Jews were restrictions on ritual slaughter, and the *numerus clausus* limiting the number of Jewish students at universities. Increasing economic problems strengthened the influence of the more nationalist elements in Poland, and after 1935 and the death of Piłsudski, who had favoured the revival of Poland as a multi-national state, the anti-Jewish movement gained the official support of the state.

In inter-war Poland Jewish society was full of life. A well-developed network of elementary, secondary and vocational schools was supported by a variety of educational institutions with different religious and political orientations. There were Jewish libraries, reading rooms, literary and music clubs, scientific societies, theatres and sports clubs.

Newspapers in Yiddish, Hebrew and Polish were published. The religious communities were centres of spiritual life and engaged in wide-ranging charitable work, supporting hospitals, old people's homes and orphanages.

There was a colourful patchwork of Jewish political parties with representatives in the Sejm and on municipal councils. The largest groups in the Jewish population were represented by two parties, the Agudat Israel, which was Orthodox and supported Polish law, and the socialist Bund, as well as several smaller parties of various orientations which existed within Zionism (there was considerable emigration to Palestine from Poland in this period). Jews also belonged to Polish political parties, mainly the Polish Socialist Party (PPS) and the Communist Party (KPP).

Between the wars Poland was home to the largest Jewish community in Europe, with enormous cultural and intellectual vitality. Many outstanding figures in politics, science and the arts began their careers in Poland. They include the Israeli prime ministers David Ben Gurion, Menachem Begin and Yitzak Shamir, and the Yiddish writer Isaac Bashevis Singer (1904–91), who was awarded the Nobel Prize for Literature in 1978.

The Second World War brought unprecedented suffering to Jews in Poland. The Nazis began by segregating them into overcrowded and unhealthy ghettoes. Then in 1942, with the implementation of the 'Final Solution', systematic genocide began. The purpose-built death camps, where Jews were brought from the Polish ghettoes and from all over Europe to be killed, were all located in Poland. The Jews did not accept their fate as passive victims – the Warsaw Ghetto Uprising of 1943 was only the biggest of several acts of resistance. Conditions in Poland under the Nazi terror made it difficult for 'aryan' Poles to save Jews, though some risked their lives to do so.

Only a handful of Polish Jews survived the war. It is estimated that after 1945 around 50,000 were left. That number was later increased when some 150,000–200,000 Jews returned to Poland from the Soviet Union. Apart from the terrible loss of life, an enormous part of their cultural heritage and social structures had been destroyed.

In the summer of 1946, 42 Jews were killed in a pogrom at Kielce. This atrocity was one of the reasons why many Jewish survivors decided to leave Poland. There were two more waves of emigration: in 1956 and 1957, with the end of Stalinism and the advent of a more nationalist government, and between 1968 and 1970, when a new regime attempted to whip up 'anti-Zionist' feeling. It is estimated that there are 10,000 to 15,000 Jews living in Poland today, and most of them are elderly. This Jewish community is organized into sixteen regional Congregations of the Judaic Faith, which come under the central authority of the Religious Society of the Judaic Faith in Warsaw. The Jewish Social and Cultural Society (TSKŻ) had a similar structure, but has recently begun to lose its importance.

Despite the Holocaust, many silent witnesses of the Jewish presence in Poland have survived: synagogues, cemeteries and public buildings. In recent years there has been a revival of interest in Jewish heritage and much has been done in Poland to restore Jewish monuments, often as a result of voluntary initiatives. Even more importantly, there have been moves to increase the understanding of the thousand years of shared Polish and Jewish history. This is made easier by the normalization of relations between Poland and Israel, which had been broken in 1967 under pressure from the USSR, and the contacts that Polish Jews from all over the world can now make with Poles and Poland.

Eugeniusz Duda

Literature

Poland has one of the richest literary traditions in the Slavic world. It is well worth exploring for the non-Polish reader, but while it is relatively easy to find English editions of leading 20th-century writers (see page 644), translations of some of the earlier authors are more difficult to track down. English translations of Polish classics are published in Poland itself and should be looked out for.

As in other European languages, literature in Polish developed partly from pre-Christian oral traditions, and partly from Christian religious literature originally written in Latin.

The earliest evidence of writing in Poland is the 'Chronicle of Gallus Anonimus' (the Anonymous Gaul) dating from 1112–13. The 'Chronicles of Master Vincent' (Wincenty Kadłubek 1150–1233), written around 1200, are an outstanding example of medieval didactic and panegyrical rhetoric. The 'Chronicle of Greater Poland' from the late 13th century is a consciously literary writing of history; its author is thought to be either Janko of Czarnów, the Vice-Chancellor of Kazimierz III Wielki, or Baszno, a cleric at the court of the bishop of Posnań. A large-scale history of Poland, known as the 'Annales Poloniae', was written by Jan Długosz (1415–80) in the years 1455–80 (an English abridgement was published in 1997). Political writing is represented by Paweł Włodkowic (1370–1435), who argued Poland's case against the Teutonic Order at the Council of Constance, and by Jan Ostroróg (1436–1501), Poland's first political writer not to be a churchman, who defended royal policy against the claims of the Vatican, as well as against the endeavours of the Polish Church and the nobil-ity to gain more autonomy; his political tract 'Monumentum pro rei publicae ordinatione' ('On the Organization of the Commonwealth') is the first work of this kind in Poland.

The vernacular does not appear in writing until the early 14th century, with the 'Holy Cross Sermons' ('Kazania Świętokrzyskie'). The earliest Polish poem known is found in a manuscript of 1407. This is 'Bogurodzica' ('Mother of God'), a religious hymn probably sung before battle and dating from the early 13th century; the name derives from Old Church Slavonic and corresponds to the Greek 'Theotokos', an indication that the poem was based on Eastern, not Latin sources. At the request of Queen Jadwiga biblical texts and legal tracts were often translated into Polish. From the 14th and 15th centuries there are translations of the psalms, such as 'Queen Jadwiga's Psalter'. In 1455 Father Andrzej of Jaszowice prepared a complete translation of the Bible, which became known as the 'Bible of Queen Zofia' after King Władysław II Jagiełło's widow.

Religious writings in romance form include 'The Reflections on the Life of the Lord Jesus' as well as biographies of saints and sermons (the 'Kazania Świętokrzyskie' mentioned above and the 'Kazania Gnieźnieńskie' of the 15th century). Late medieval literature also took account of current secular problems, first in the form of occasional writing of a satirical character ('On Behaviour at Table') or on themes of social criticism ('Satire of the Lazy Peasants' or the 'Song of Tęczyński's Murder' – both these songs are directed against the lower orders and served to bolster the self-esteem of the nobility).

Mikołaj Rej, woodcut, 1562

The events of the Reformation were reflected in the Hussite 'Wycliffe Song' written by Jędrzej Gałka of Dobczyn, a professor at the University of Kraków. Another example of secular poetry is the 'Conversation of the Master with Death', written in dialogue form. Both pieces are characterized by imaginative language and vivid depictions of local customs; they have an important place in Polish literature.

The period of the Renaissance was also the Golden Age of Polish literature, which was now increasingly influenced by secular, humanist and classical tendencies. It developed in several genres including epigrams, odes, didactic drama, tragedy, satire and political poetry. The first generation of writers of the Polish Renaissance, who still wrote in Latin, included Jan Ostroróg, the poets Klemens Janicki and Jan Dantyszek, as well as Grzegorz of Sanok, Andrzej Kycki and Mikołaj Hussowski. Biernat of Lublin (*c*.1465–1529), who had Hussite sympathies, was the first to write exclusively in the vernacular, and he published the first printed book in Polish: 'The Paradise of the Soul' (1513), a sort of prayer book, which was later placed on the Index by the Roman Catholic Church. His major work, a verse translation of 'The Life of Aesop the Phrygian' was widely read.

The first of the great Renaissance writers was Mikołaj Rej (1505–69), the 'father of Polish literature'. Rej had close links with his social class, the nobility, and played an important part in public life, working not only as a man of letters but also as a political publicist and religious propagandist. In his verse dialogues 'Short Dispute between a Squire, a Bailiff and a Village Priest' (1543), his many epigrams and his prose text 'The Faithful Image of an Honest Man' (1558), he accurately captured the mentality and habits of the nobility.

Jan Kochanowski (1530–84), the 'poet of Czarnolas', was considered until the 19th century not only to be the greatest poet of the Polish Renaissance, but also the most important writer of this period in the whole Slavic world. A humanist, patriot and erudite antiquarian, his output was mostly lyrical: poems and laments. He also wrote 'The Dismissal of the Greek Envoys' (1578), an attempt to imitate classical tragedy in form and content, which is regarded as one of the great masterpieces of Polish humanism. Kochanowski's satires 'Harmony' and 'Satyr' touch on political as well as social problems. They could be called journalism in rhyme. His greatest lyrics are the 'Treny', threnodies written after the death of his young daughter (1580; English translation 1928).

Kochanowski's patron Jan Zamoyski established his Zamość Academy with the help of another poet, Szymon Szymonowic, whose 'Sielanki', a collection of bucolic idylls, balances classical learning with informed observation of Polish peasant life.

The 16th century also saw the development of writing on public affairs. Andrzej Frycz Modrzewski (1503–72) gained international importance with his work 'De republica emendanda' ('Concerning the Reform of the State'), which appeared in 1551, because the issues he dealt with (problems of the theory of the state, the role of the Church, education and the judicial system) were much discussed throughout Europe at that time. 1551 also saw the publication, by Marcin Bielski, of the first world history in Polish. Stanisław Orzechowski (1513–66) was active as a publicist, as was the Jesuit, preacher and champion of the Counter-Reformation, Piotr Skarga (1536–1612).

The Counter-Reformation brought a growing interest in the literature of Italy: Piotr Kochanowski (a nephew of Jan) translated Ariosto's 'Orlando Furioso' and Tasso's 'Gerusalemme Liberata'. Metaphysical yearning and world-weariness, introduced into lyrical poetry by Mikołaj Sęp-Szarziński (1550–81), are dominant themes in the Polish Baroque.

The 17th century was a period of military and religious conflict, which shook the Polish state to its foundations and destroyed its cultural achievements. Polish prose of the 17th century consists mainly of memoirs and political literature. It was written in what became known as the 'Macaronic Style', a mixture of Polish and Latin, and was characterized by the spirit of 'Sarmatism'. Sarmatism, which took its name from the Sarmatians, a non-Slavic warrior people from whom the szlachta (wrongly) claimed descent, was a view of life based on a patriotic-historical myth. Its specifically Polish and aristocratic ideology firmly rejected Western European, centralist absolutism. The epic achievements and attitudes of the nobility found their most complete expression in the colourful 'Memoirs' of the irrepressible Jan Chryzostom Pasek (1636–1701; English translation, 1976), in the historical poem 'The War of Chocim' by Wacław Potocki (1625–95), and in the 'Polish Psalmody', historical-

SATYR
Albo Dziki Mąż.
Iana Kochanowskiego,

Title page of Jan Kochanowski's 'Satyr', 16th century

philosophical psalms by Wespazjan Kochowski (1633–1700).

The Baroque style, in which form predominated over content, was best expressed in the lyric poetry, which is remarkable for its pomposity. Among the most outstanding representatives of the Baroque lyricists were Andrzej Morsztyn (1613–93), a master of the conceit, and Szymon Zimorowicz (1608–29), the author of the 'Roxolanki', a set of erotic pastorals.

The first half of the 18th century, known in Polish literary history as the 'Saxon Night', was a particularly bizarre phase in Baroque poetry that took the form of an obscurantist Sarmatism. Among a large number of mediocre poets one group of energetic intellectuals stands out. This group saw the necessity of reform in politics and education: Stanisław Konarski (1700–73) in his work 'Concerning an Efficient Method of Government' prepared the way for future literature on citizenship; Stanisław Leszczyński, the Polish King from 1704 to 1709 and again from 1733 to 1736, wrote a political tract entitled 'A Free Voice ensuring Freedom' (1749) after he had retired to exile at Lunéville; and Andrzej Załuski (1702–72) founded the famous library in Warsaw named after him.

These initiatives already heralded the Age of the Enlightenment. With the accession to the throne of Stanisław August Poniatowski, literary culture found a considerable defender and patron. The thirty years of the 'Stanisław Era' (1764–95) were characterized by a literature which had didactic aims and sought to make a contribution to social, political and economic reform. This was served not only by lively public writings, in which Stanisław Staszic (1755–1826) and Hugo Kołłątaj (1750–1812) stood out as champions of radical reform, it also led to the foundation of literary periodicals such as 'Monitor' (on the model of Addison's 'Spectator') and 'Pleasant and Useful Diversions'. In 1765 Wojciech Bogusławski founded the National Theatre in Warsaw, which did much to raise the capital's standing as a cultural centre.

In the literature of the Polish Enlightenment genres such as stories, dramas, fables and comic heroic poems were especially popular. Bishop Ignacy Krasicki (1735–1801), a 'prince of poets' and the chief representative of the Enlightenment, was a regular guest at King Stanisław's Thursday lunches, where artists, scientists and men of letters met. Krasicki is thought to be the author of the first Polish novel, 'The Adventures of Mikołaj Doświadczyński' (1776), a mixture in Miłosz's words, of an adventure story in the manner of Robinson Crusoe, a Voltairean satirical-philosophical tale, an *Erziehungsroman* in the manner of Rousseau, and an Utopian fantasy in the spirit of Jonathan Swift.

Another project connected with Stanisław Poniatowski was the compilation, using modern

Ignacy Krasicki (1735–1801)

research methods, of a massive history of Poland (1780–5) by his friend, the poet and bishop Adam Naruszewicz (1733–96). Six volumes of his 'History of the Polish Nation since the Conversion to Christianity' appeared, covering the period up to 1386 (the personal union of Poland and Lithuania). Stanisław Trembecki (1739–1812), the translator of Voltaire, in his work 'Sofjówka' presented a materialistic world view which he combined with masterly descriptions of nature. Other guests at the king's Thursday lunches were the scapegrace Kajetan Węgierski (1755–87), the satirist and translator of Pope, and Jan Jasiński (1761–94), a convinced republican and promoter of Jacobin virtues, who died in the defence of Warsaw during the 1794 Uprising.

The other cultural centre of Poland in the late 18th century was the town of Puławy (on the Vistula not far from Lublin), which was a Czartoryski property. The salon of Princess Izabela Czartoryska, the daughter of the poet Andrzej Morsztyn, was frequented by Franciszek Karpiński (1741–1825) and Dionizy Kniaźnin (1750–1807), both of them representatives of

Polish Sentimentalism, and whose poetry contains folkloric and idyllic pastoral elements.

Writers for the theatre included Franciszek Zabłocki (1754–1821), who aimed his comedies particularly at Sarmatism, and Julian Ursyn Niemcewicz (1757–1841), who was commissioned by the Reform Party, during the 1791 session of the Sejm, to write the comedy 'The Return of the Deputy'. The play's explosive political content instantly seized the imagination of Warsaw audiences and gave impetus to the movement for a new constitution.

The Third Partition of Poland in 1795, which erased Poland from the map, strengthened the writers' sense of patriotic duty. It also meant that Polish became the major factor in creating national consciousness and national unity. The Classicists sought a new genre after the French model to depict themes from their own history. Among these 'national tragedies' was 'Barbara

Adam Mickiewicz (1798–1855) by Walenty Wańkowicz

Radziwiłłówna' by Alojzy Feliński (1771–1820), first performed in 1817 and later translated into German and French. The leading figures in the transition from Classicism to Romanticism were Julian Ursyn Niemcewicz and Kazimierz Brodziński (1791–1835). In 1818 Brodziński published his wide-ranging treatise 'Concerning Classicism and Romanticism and the Spirit of Polish Poetry'. Patriotic verse flourished in the legions that fought on the side of Napoleon under General Jan Henryk Dąbrowski. The work of Cyprian Godebski (1765–1809) should be mentioned, especially his poem 'To the Polish Legions in Italy' (1805). From Italy came the new hopeful tones of the patriotic song (written by Józef Wybicki (1747–1822) in 1797), which later became the national anthem: 'Jeszcze Polska nie zginęła' ('Poland has not perished yet').

The idealized image of the rebellious Romantic and Byronic hero represented in works of Adam Mickiewicz (1798–1855), Juliusz Słowacki (1809–49), Antoni Malczewski (1793–1826), Seweryn Goszczyński (1801–76) and Józef Bohdan Zaleski (1802–86) made Romanticism the main literary movement after the suppression of the November Uprising of 1831. An important feature of Romanticism in Poland was a messianic theme, by which Poland was portrayed as the 'Christ among the Nations'. Its chief proponents were Mickiewicz, Słowacki and Zygmunt Krasiński (1812–59). In their plays (Mickiewicz: 'Forefathers' Eve', 1832; Słowacki: 'Kordian', 1834, 'Lilla Weneda', 1839; and Krasiński: 'The Undivine Comedy', 1833) they attempted to define and represent the conflicts of the Romantic hero in terms of moral philosophy. The national epic, 'Pan Tadeusz' (1834, English translations 1962, 1964) by Mickiewicz and the play 'Beniowski' (1841) by Słowacki are high points of world literature.

The strongly intellectualized poetry of Cyprian Kamil Norwid (1841–83) earns him a special place in the Polish pantheon. He wrote poems, plays and philosophical essays (including

Adam Mickiewicz reciting his poems at a literary salon, by G. Mjasoldov

'Vademecum', a collection of poems published in 1886), but it was not until after his death that Norwid received his just recognition. All these writers produced most of their work as emigrés in Paris or Rome, but there were also writers working in the country itself, such as Aleksander Fredro (1793–1876), a writer of comedies (English translations, 1969), whose best known works are 'Maiden's Vows' (1827), 'Revenge' (1833) and 'Pan Jowialski' (1832), and Józef Ignacy Kraszewski (1812–87), whose cycle of historical novels made a great contribution to the popularization of national history in the period of partition. In lyric poetry there were rebels – Wincenty Pol (1807–1872) and Ryszard Brewiński – as well as ruralists – Teofil Lenartowicz (1822–1893) and Władysław Syrokomla (1823–1863). The romanticism of the writer and patriotic agitator Apollo Korzeniowski (1820–69) was a formative influence on the work of his vagabond son Joseph Conrad.

The suppression of the January Uprising of 1863–4 was followed by an anti-Romantic, Positivist counter-movement, beginning around 1870. One of its leading figures was Aleksander Świętochowski (1849–1938). Positivism encouraged realism and gave literature a didactic, edifying function, which was intended to contribute to the solution of practical problems. This tendency was most evident in prose writings. The movement's outstanding achievement was the realistic novel, which had three great exponents: Bolesław Prus (1845–1912), Eliza Orzeszkowa (1841–1910) and the Nobel Prize winner, Henryk Sienkiewicz (1846–1916). The magnum opus of Bolesław Prus, 'The Doll' (1890, English translation 1972) deals in epic breadth with the social and spiritual life of 19th-century Poland. Eliza Orzeszkowa's novel, 'On the Banks of the Niemen' (1887) is her greatest book and movingly describes the fate of the eastern Polish nobility in the aftermath of the January Uprising. A deliberate rejection of the prophetic-messianic tendencies of Polish Romanticism gave rise to historical novels like Bolesław Prus's 'Pharaoh' (1897, English translation 1910), which deals with the dynamics of political power, and the novels of Henryk Sienkiewicz ('Trilogy': 'With Fire and the Sword', 'The Deluge' and 'Pan Wołodyjowski', 1884–8; 'The Knights of the Cross', 1900; and the world-famous 'Quo Vadis', 1896, all available in English). In these immensely popular works Sienkiewicz rejected the idea that history could function as an optimistic mirror for present-day Poland.

The crisis of Positivism at the end of the 1880's led to the emergence of Naturalism, whose principal exponents were Adolf Dygasiński (1839–1903), Antoni Sygietyński (1850–1923) and Gabriela Zapolska (1857–1921). Naturalism marked the beginning of a new period in Polish literature: the appearance of 'Młoda Polska' ('Young

Henryk Sienkiewicz (1846–1916)

Poland'). In the 1890's two factors dominated the consciousness of the new generation of writers and their move away from Positivism: the increase in social tension and a revival of militant patriotism. Nevertheless, 'art for art's sake' remained the formula in the numerous manifestoes produced by the writer and dramatist Stanisław Przybyszewski (1868–1927). The poetry of Kazimierz Przerwa-Tetmajer (1865–1940) dealt with philosophical and erotic themes using Impressionist and Symbolist techniques.

At the beginning of the 20th century, after a certain disappointment at the widespread rejection of this Aestheticism, the achievements of 'Young Poland' gained in intellectual depth. In this further development Jan Kasprowicz, Kazimierz Przerwa-Tetmajer, the classic representative of 'Young Poland' Leopold Staff (1878–1957), and the Expressionist Tadeusz Miciński (1878–1918) turned to themes of moral philosophy.

Among the prose writers of this period Stefan Żeromski (1864–1925) should be mentioned in first place. He was a dramatist, novelist and man of letters who enriched the prose of critical realism with elements of lyricism and of intellectual reflection. His novels 'Homeless People' (1900), 'Ashes' (1904, English translation 1928), 'The Faithful River' (1913) combined beauty of language with patriotic commitment.

The novelist and story-writer Władysław Reymont (1867–1925) became especially famous. His novel 'The Peasants' (1902–9, English translation 1942), a description of contemporary village life and mores, helped him to win the Nobel Prize in 1924.

The most important figure in the drama of 'Young Poland' was the painter, poet and director Stanisław Wyspiański (1869–1907). His works, which used ideological polemic to attack the Polish aristocratic tradition and the indolence of Polish intellectuals, have remained in the repertoire of the Polish National Theatre.

The year 1918, which saw Poland regain its independence with the establishment of the Second Republic, was of immense importance to

Polish literature. Stefan Żeromski, representing what had now become the older generation of writers, published his novel 'Early Spring' (1925) expressing his enthusiasm at national liberation. (Similar tendencies were shown in Wacław Berent's 'Living Stones', Andrzej Strug's 'The Yellow Cross' and Leopold Staff's 'Field Paths'.) Comparable in their enthusiasm, but more radical in their rejection of tradition, was the new generation of writers. Taking up Italian and French influences, the Polish Futurists prepared the way for the 'Kraków Avantgarde'. Their most outstanding representative was Julian Przyboś (1901–70) and their chief ideologue Tadeusz Peiper (1891–1969); they admired technology and machinery, were sworn enemies of anything spontaneous or natural and saw themselves as working with poetic form like railway 'pointsmen'.

In parallel to this there also developed a new cult of artistic simplicity and a revival of classical tradition, with the founding in 1920 of the 'Skamander' Group, which drew together such diverse individuals as Julian Tuwim (1894–1953), Antoni Słonimski (1895–1976), Jan Lechoń (1899–1956), Kazimierz Wierzyński (1894–1969) and Jarosław Iwaszkiewicz (1894–1980). And although they were independent in the conception of their work, Maria Pawlikowska-Jasnorzewska (1894–1945) and Kazimiera Iłłakowiczówna were close to the Skamandrites. Revolutionary protest against the socio-political situation in Poland in the 1920's was voiced above all by the poet Władysław Broniewski (1897–1962). In prose too – for instance in 'Therese Hennert's Affair' by Zofia Nałkowska (1884–1954) – sharp criticism was directed at the government elite and the mechanics of its internal power struggles.

Stanisław Ignacy Witkiewicz (1885–1939), Witold Gombrowicz (1904–69) and Bruno Schulz (1892–1942) together formed a triad of genius that between the wars produced some major works, which were later to influence European literature. The work of Witkiewicz, a child prodigy who wrote his first play ('Cock roaches') at the age of eight, is coloured by 'Catastrophism'. His view of an all-embracing threat to civilization was expressed in grotesque-tragic works, 'Farewell to Autumn' (1927), 'Insatiability' (1932, English translation 1977) and in his dramatic swansong, 'Cobblers'. Gombrowicz in his novel 'Ferdydurke' (1937, English translation 1961) unmasked with mordant irony stereotypes of manners and morals in Polish society. Gombrowicz's novels, including 'Pornografia' (1960, English translation 1966), and his journals have achieved a deservedly high international reputation. Bruno Schulz, in 'The Cinnamon Shops' (1934, English translation, 1963, as 'The Street of Crocodiles') and 'Sanatorium under the Sign of the Hourglass' (1937, English translation 1979) conjured up visions of provincial Jewish life, and made use of surrealist techniques. Catastrophist motifs were also taken up by the generation of writers emerging in the 1930's: Czesław Miłosz (born 1911), winner of the Nobel Prize for Literature, Konstanty Ildefons Gałczyński (1905–53) and Mieczysław Jastrun (1903–83) used a variety of lyrical forms in their treatment of moral and ideological themes. Pioneering psychological novels were written by Jerzy Andrzejewski (1909–83), Tadeusz Breza (1905–70) and Adolf Rudnicki (1912-90). Other writers who should be mentioned are, in the world of journalism, the writer and translator of French classics Tadeusz Boy-Żeleński (1874-1941), and in documentary literature, the reporter Melchior Wańkowicz (1892–1974) and Ksawery Pruszyński (1907–50).

1939 marked a decisive break in the literary life of Poland. The Nazi occupation did irreversable damage in the cultural field. Many intellectuals died violent deaths, and the whole intelligentsia was systematically persecuted. The revival of Polish literature after the end of the Second World War could not have been foreseen. Literary periodicals were quickly founded, including the Marxist-orientated 'Kuźnica' ('Smithy') and the 'Tygodnik Powszechny'

Stanisław Wyspiański (1869–1907), self-portrait with his wife

('General Weekly Newspaper'), around which Catholic writers such as Jerzy Zawiejski (1902–69), Hanna Malewska (1911-83) and Antoni Gołubiew (1907–80) formed a group.

The literature of the first years after the war (1945–9) was at first restricted to wartime subjects, with particular emphasis on the concentration camps and the persecution of the Jews. These themes were mostly clearly seen in the prose works of Zofia Nałkowska ('Medallions' 1949) and Tadeusz Borowski (1922–51, 'This Way for the Gas, Ladies and Gentlemen', 1946, English translation 1967), in the essays of Adolf Rudnicki ('The Dead Sea and the Living Sea' 1952, English translation 1957) and in the poetry of Tadeusz Różewicz (born 1921). 'The Germans', a play by Leon Kruczkowski (1900–62), gives a subtly differentiated picture of the occupiers.

The other main theme, the cause of the September defeat in 1939, was dealt with in the novels 'The Walls of Jericho' (1946) by Tadeusz Breza, 'Life's Bonds' (1948) by Zofia Nałkowska, 'September' by Jerzy Putrament (1910-86),

and 'Between the Wars' (1948–51) by Kazimierz Brandys (born 1916). In poetry, besides Tadeusz Różewicz, writers who had already made a name before the war again rose to importance: Broniewski, Tuwim, Słonimski, Wat, Gałczyński, Przyboś, Ważyk, Jastrun and Miłosz. They dealt not only with the war period, but also with contemporary problems. One of the most delicate was the fate of the 'Home Army' (Armia Krajowa) in Socialist Poland, and this was the subject of Jerzy Andrzejewski's novel 'Ashes and Diamonds' (1947, English translation 1962; see also page 137).

The Stalinist period was almost entirely barren. It was not until the 'Polish October' of 1956 that literature was permitted wider possibilities, as the Stalinist dogmas were rejected and existentialism came to influence literary activity. Two collections of poetry, 'The Life of the Market Square' by Paweł Hertz (born 1918) and 'Cruel Star' by Wiktor Woroszylski (1927-96), and three prose works, Jerzy Andrzejewski's 'Darkness Covers the Earth', Kazimiera Brandys's 'Mother of the Kings', and Tadeusz Konwicki's (born 1926) 'From the Encircling City' were of crucial importance. The modernist work of Zbigniew Bieńkowski (born 1913) centres not on historical events but the relationship between words and meaning. Zbigniew Herbert (1924-98), with Jarosław Iwaszkiewicz (1894–1980) the most important representative of the classical tradition, tried in his poems to bring order to a world full of contrasts and dissonances, but without subordinating himself to it. Both Miron Białoszewski (born 1922) and Tymoteusz Karpowicz (born 1921) endeavoured, each in his own way, to find a new, pure language which would enable the writer to describe everyday life. Among the most inspired poets of this generation was the Nobel Laureate Wisława Szymborska (born 1923), whose irony and sophistication are combined with a disarmingly unaffected style.

A special place in prose is occupied by the historical novel: Teodor Parnicki (1908-98); Hanna Malewska (1911-83); Jan Parandowski (1895-1978). Jaroslaw Iwaszkiewicz in his novel 'Glory and Vainglory' (1956–62) depicted the futile endeavours of people to find stable forms of culture and life in the years between 1913 and 1947. Jacek Bocheński (born 1926) wrote about the Roman Empire ('The Divine Julius', 1961), Paweł Jasienica (1909–70) published a whole series of books about Poland's history, Andrzej Kijowski (born 1928) wrote essays on the politics of Romanticism. The breakdown of rural life inspired Julian Kawalec (born 1916, 'Dancing Hawk', 1964), Tadeusz Nowak (1930-91, 'Be thou King, Be thou Executioner'), and Edward Redliński (born 1940, 'Konopielka', 1973).

The novels of Stanisław Lem (born 1921) are masterpieces of serious and intelligent science fiction and he is one of the most popular and internationally known contemporary writers. His stories go far beyond the fantasies of his most important predecessors, Jules Verne and H. G. Wells, and raise exciting questions of boundaries in mathematics, sociology, micro-

biology and nuclear physics. They do not so much contain technological predictions as reflect the structure and methods of present-day scientific thought. Stanisław Lem has also written theoretical treatises on cybernetics, futurology and literary theory. Many of his books have been translated into English, including 'The Investigation' (1959, English 1976), 'Return from the Stars' (1961, English 1980), 'Solaris' (1961, English 1971) and 'Perfect Vacuum' (1973, English 1978). A famous film version of 'Solaris' was made by the Russian director Andrei Tarkovsky.

The prose writers Marek Hłasko (1934–69), Marek Nowakowski (born 1935) and Andrzej Brycht appeared to incline to cynicism, almost to nihilism. Rejecting the communist picture of society, and searching instead for the human scale, they turned to the marginal groups in society, concerning themselves with the fate of the individual and depicting the brutishness of life in the new towns.

For Tadeusz Konwicki contemporary reality took on absurd and grotesque forms; inner life was characterized by the suppression of emotions in a hypocritical social system. This is

Stanisław Lem (born 1921)

described, for instance, in 'A Minor Apocalypse' (1979), 'The Chronicle of Love Events' (1974) and 'A Dreambook for our Time' (1963). After the Second World War Konwicki was first editor of the magazine 'Odrodzenie' ('Rebirth') and later became a member of the editorial board of 'Nowa Kultura' (1950–57); he also wrote works in films as a screenwriter and director, and has been awarded prizes at Venice and Mannheim.

Absurd drama was developed by Tadeusz Różewicz and Sławomir Mrożek. Różewicz works as a dramatist, poet and short story writer in Wrocław. Among his best known plays are 'The Laocoon Group' (1961), 'The Witnesses or Our Little Stabilization' (1962), 'The Ridiculous Old Man' (1964) and 'He Left the House' (1965). He is a moralist, who 'by dismantling the decorative façades of language seeks to recreate the truth and dignity of words'.

Sławomir Mrożek. (born 1930) is today one of the best-known contemporary Polish writers; by way of humorous pieces in newspapers and sketches on radio and television he eventually created his own form of absurd and macabre drama, which includes social and political satire open to many interpretations. He gained lasting recognition abroad especially for his plays 'Striptease' (1961, English translation 1972) and 'Tango (1964, English translation 1968). as well as 'On the High Seas' (1970) and 'Emigrés' (1974). Mrożek has lived in Paris and Mexico, and was stripped of his Polish citizenship after his public protest against the invasion of Czechoslovakia in 1968. However, performances of his plays were again permitted in Poland after 1973, and he has recently moved back to Kraków.

Stanisław Dygat (1914–78) was regarded as a disciple of Gombrowicz. He portrays people trying to escape from their milieux and conventions.

A strikingly original writer was Stanisław Jerzy Lec (1909–66). His career as a coiner of aphorisms began at the time of the Polish October (1955–6) and since then his 'Unkempt Thoughts' written between 1957 and 1959 passed into common parlance. Lec gave new life to the aphorism, making it once again a literary art form. He unmasks prejudices and hypocrisy with a precision and insight only rarely attained in profound analyses by other authors. ('Stupidity is the mother of crime. But the fathers are often geniuses.' 'I had a dream about reality. It was a relief to wake up.')

At the end of the 1960's and beginning of the 1970's a new generation of writers emerged, calling themselves the 'New Wave'. Authors such as Stanisław Barańczak, Ryszard Krynicki, Ewa Lipska, Julian Kornhauser and Adam Zagajewski expressed resistance to the use of literature for propaganda purposes; for them literature was and is a tool for experiencing real, often hidden, social tensions in their contemporary manifestations. Language for them assumes an important moral function. The most important journalist of the time, Ryszard Kapuściński (born 1932) has explored these moral dilemmas in arenas as different as Addis Ababa, Tehran and the football pitches of Latin America.

Dorota Leszczyńska

Theatre

What little survives of Polish theatre from before the 16th century is mainly liturgical drama, performed in church and consisting of dramatized dialogues, songs and hymns based on the Gospels. In the later middle ages these plays were often moved out of the church and performed on the church steps.

The real starting point for Polish drama is the spread of Renaissance humanism in the 16th century. Around 1500 ecclesiastical drama gave way to a revival of classical Latin dialogue, and half a century later this was replaced in turn by Polish.

Plays from antiquity – particularly comedies – were first performed at the courts of noblemen and at the university. Theatrical performances were taking place at the royal court as early as 1515, as is shown by the notes made by the treasurer of King Zygmunt I Stary.

Humanist drama, based on antiquity, was first introduced to Poland in the 'Spectaculum de Judicio Parisis' by Jacobus Locher Philomusis. Locher's play, first performed in 1522 in Kraków, must have enjoyed great popularity, for in 1546 it appeared in a Polish version. It stands on the borderline between the middle ages and the Renaissance and is still a long way from Jan Kochanowski's celebrated play 'The Dismissal of the Greek Envoys' (first performed in 1578 at the court of the Chancellor Jan Zamoyski at Jezdów). The structure of Kochanowski's writing was imitated by Piotr Ciekliński (1558–1604), who wrote a Polish version of Plautus's comedy 'Trinummus'.

The first comedy to be written in Polish was the folk-humanist play 'The Beggars' Tragedy', printed in 1552. It was the first of a genre of 'Komedia rybałtowska', so called after the Rybałci (impoverished village schoolmasters, writers, clerics and artists, who were forced by ill fortune to become travelling players; the name comes from the Latin *ribaldus*). The genre flourished until about the middle of the 17th century.

The medieval folk theatre tradition of the mystery plays, performed at church festivals, now became more secular, as their basic form was supplemented by comic re-enactments of local events.

Among the best known of the mummers' comedies of this time is Piotr Baryka's 'From Peasant to King', first performed in 1634 and later taken into the repertoire of the court theatre. The dialogue, which originated in the middle ages, took on new theatrical forms in the period of religious conflict, even before Mikołaj Rej (see page 98) published his important work, the 'Short Dispute between a Squire, a Bailiff and a Village Priest'. This Shrovetide comedy from the mid-16th century features a long disputation between a Catholic priest, a Protestant burgher and a student, though the eventual winner is the pretty housekeeper.

By the end of the 16th century the 'theatre of the schools', which had been inaugurated by the Jesuits, Piarists and Theatines, had increased in importance, and was soon to be found everywhere, in towns large and small. The plays were acted at schools for didactic purposes and on festive occasions, and their subject matter was taken from the Old and New Testaments, as well as the legends of the saints, history and mythology.

Open-air theatre in Warsaw, engraving, 1871

Later the Jesuits made use of the theatre of the schools in their struggle against the Reformation. They had their own seminaries for the training of dramatists, an office to co-ordinate programmes and their own censorship. The history of the Polish Jesuit theatre lasted for more than two hundred years. Its greatest period was the early 17th century; later it tended to degenerate into showy stage effects. The Protestants in northern Poland also used the theatre, especially under the influence of Jan Amos Komenský (Comenius).

In the years from 1637 to 1646 Polish theatre appeared for the first time as a centralized institution after King Władysław IV Waza had the *Sala del teatro* built at the castle in Warsaw in 1637. This theatre was equipped for productions of opera, ballet and comedies; the scenery, costumes and props were modelled on the lavish Baroque theatre of Italy.

The Age of the Enlightenment marked a new departure for Polish theatre, beginning in 1765. At the instigation of King Stanisław August Poniatowski the first public theatre, the 'National Theatre', was established as a permanent institution in Warsaw, with the actor and playwright Wojciech Bogusławski as its first director. The didactic conception of the theatre was reflected in its repertoire: the works preferred were comedies and *vaudevilles* with musical interludes.

The comedies in the Stanisław Era were based on French models, and on Molière in particular. The first dramatist to write for the National Theatre was a Jesuit, Franciszek Bohomolec (1720–84); his successor Franciszek Zabłocki (1754–1821), probably the most important Polish playwright of the Enlightenment, wrote a popular comedy, 'The Fop-Suitor', which was a satire on the *jeunesse dorée* of the capital. Zabłocki described contemporary Polish milieux and characters in his plays, and used very expressive, down-to-earth language.

The first socio-political comedy in Poland, 'The Return of the Deputy' by Julian Ursyn Niemcewicz (1757–1841), caused a storm of indignation in the Sejm because of its denunciation of the backwardness of some of the nobility.

During the Romantic period Polish theatrical life was characterized by two opposing tendencies, exemplified by two figures: Aleksander Fredro (1793–1878) – the Polish Molière – and Józef Korzeniowski (1797–1863) (not to be confused with his namesake, the English novelist Joseph Conrad). Fredro is indisputably one of the greatest of Polish comic dramatists; his models were Molière and Goldoni but the settings and characters in his plays were Polish.

Józef Korzeniowski tried to overcome the public's preference for plays in the French style. His dramas sprang from a detailed observation of social conditions and how they were altered by economic changes.

During the period of partition the theatre in Warsaw played an important role in preserving Polish culture and language in the Russian area.

In the second half of the 19th century Polish theatre went through what was called the 'Era of the Stars', which was linked with the names of such brilliant players as Helena Modrzejewska (1840–1909) and Alojzy Żółkowski the younger (1814–89). In cities such as Lwów, Wilno and Poznań the professional theatre also thrived, but it reached a pinnacle of achievement in Kraków under the direction of Stanisław Koźmian (1836–1922). The works of the great Romantics, Mickiewicz, Słowacki and Krasiński (see page 101) began to be staged; until then they had been regarded as plays for reading only.

In Kraków the influence of contemporary theatrical reform movements in the rest of Europe was particularly strong, and modernistic drama was performed. Koźmian had a distinguished successor in Tadeusz Pawlikowski. The most important figure in the theatrical world of the time was Stanisław Wyspiański (1869–1907), the painter, poet and dramatist, who was also an innovator in stage design. His plays, 'The Wedding', 'November Night', 'Liberation', 'The Curse', which used polemic with an ideological tinge to attack the tradition of the nobility and the indolence of Polish intellectuals, are still

frequently performed. The first was made into a successful film by Wajda.

The 'Polish Theatre' in Warsaw opened in 1913 with a production of Zygmunt Krasiński's 'Irydion' staged and directed in what was for the time a startlingly modern way. The theatre's founder, Arnold Szyfman, sought in the years that followed to create a theatre which would appeal to a broad public, but which could also give expression to avantgarde tendencies. Another outstanding figure in the theatre in Poland, Leon Schiller (1877–1954), also had many connections with the 'Teatr Polski'. A pupil of Edward Gordon Craig and familiar with the western European and the Russian theatre (Stanislavsky, Tairov, Meyerhold), Schiller tried to bring about a massive reform of the theatre in Poland, doing away with illusion and naturalistic staging. Schiller remained the leading figure in Polish theatre until well after the Second World War. One of his great achievements was to introduce a systematic course of study for directors; many of his pupils were later to occupy leading positions in the cultural life of the People's Republic.

New possibilities were opened up after Poland regained its independence in 1918; theatres were founded all over the country. The 'Reduta', under the direction of Juliusz Osterwa (1885–1947), was a lively travelling company, which gave the first performances of several plays by the most popular dramatists of the years between the wars, especially those of Jerzy Szaniawski (1886–1970). As an avantgarde theatre 'Reduta' turned the focus of attention on the actors and their performing skills, rejecting the picturesque approach to stage design that had been predominant.

While the theatrical work of a Szaniawski was rooted in the Polish tradition, Stanisław Ignacy Witkiewicz, known as Witkacy (1885–1939), achieved a breakthrough in his dramatic work by turning to Modernism. Witkacy's theory of 'pure form' utterly rejected the last remnants of traditional theatre and illusion; he regarded drama as a pure product of the imagination. From 1932 onwards Leon Schiller too was working in an avantgarde theatre, the 'Ateneum' in Warsaw.

Apart from Warsaw and Kraków, the other centres of Polish theatrical life in the inter-war period were Lwów, Wilno, Łódź and Poznań.

The Second World War and the German occupation resulted in a complete collapse of the official theatre in Poland, but illegal theatre groups sprang up and a secret theatre council (including Schiller) was formed.

Partly as a result, the rebuilding of theatrical life in Poland after 1945 was able to get underway with remarkable élan. There was an immediate and lively interest in the productions, even though to begin with the repertoire tended to remain at the level of light entertainment – and in the period of shortages and privation after the war this was just what the audiences wanted.

A few years after the end of the war the new Ministry of Art and Culture began to remodel Polish theatre along the lines of the new political and social order. This did not pass unchallenged: directors like Erwin Axer, a pupil of Leon Schiller, campaigned against what they called 'any sort of idealism in the name of a realistic approach and of a reality seen from the point of view of class dialectic' in the theatre.

Axer, who at that time had been for thirty years the manager and artistic director of the 'Contemporary Theatre' ('Teatr Współczesny') in Warsaw, was one of those in 1956 who promoted the movement for renewal in the Polish theatre after years of stagnation and isolation from the West. The movement played a pioneering role at the 'Nowy Teatr' in Łódź, for example. Axer had always been mainly interested in plays by 20th-century writers, both Polish and foreign, and introduced Polish audi-

Theatre director Tadeusz Kantor (1915–91)

ences to the works of dramatists such as Friedrich Dürrenmatt and Max Frisch.

Kazimierz Dejmek, the mentor of the 'Nowy Teatr' founded in Łódź in 1949, was the most consistent continuator of Leon Schiller's work. His productions had apolitical as well as a poetic character. Classic works of Polish drama have also been performed under his direction, going hack to plays such as the medieval mystery 'The Story of the Most Glorious Resurrection of Our Lord' by Mikołaj of Wilkowiecko.

The most successful modernist director is Adam Hanuszkiewicz. Konrad Swinarski, Jerzy Jarocki and Andrzej Wajda (born 1926) are also names with an international reputation in the theatre: each served for a time as artistic director of the 'Stary Teatr' in Kraków. Swinarski, who had trained with the Berliner Ensemble, sought to 'make a dramatic polyphony', while Jarocki's productions always seemed able to find a key to unlock the most interesting works of modern Polish writers. Best known abroad as a film director, Wajda's reputation as a theatre director is based on dynamic productions of 'The Devils' (Dostoievsky), 'November Night' (Wyspiański) and 'The Case of Danton' (after Stanisława Przybyszewska), several of which have been filmed.

Jerzy Grotowski, Józef Szajna and Tadeusz Kantor were the leading figures in the Polish theatrical avantgarde. Grotowski (1933-99) created the 'Poor Theatre', which does without traditional theatrical props and shifts the message of the text into the background, treating the relationship between the actors and the audience as the essential instrument of the performance. Grotowski's approach also influenced the politically charged, physical heatre of the '8th Day Group' in Poznań. Szajna, who came to theatre from painting and since 1971 has been the director of the 'Studio' theatre in Warsaw, deals with the conflict between the artist and society; his productions make use of scenic construction, the components of which are not only scenery, costumes and props, but also the actors' bodies and particular stage situations. Tadeusz Kantor (1915–91) was a tireless innovator and the founder of the 'Cricot' theatre in Kraków. His 'theatre of the dead' used imaginative stagings, sometimes with life-size puppets, to create eerie, often disturbing, effects. Such productions as 'The Dead Class' (1976) gained an international celebrity.

In the aftermath of these giants, there have recently been some very heated discussions – not without justification – about whether directors and stage designers are too prominent, and whether perhaps the actors themselves should not be given greater scope for developing their own interpretations on stage.

Nonetheless, the Polish theatre is still dominated a small group of leading directors, among them Krystian Lupa and Jerzy Grzegorzewski, whose innovative, free productions of classic plays have enlivened the rebuilt National Theatre in Warsaw.

23 GNIEZNO Cathedral of St Wojciech, tomb of Bishop Krzycki
◁ 22 KRUSZWICA Collegiate Church of Sts Peter and Paul
24 SZAMOTUŁY Parish church, Rokossowski tomb

25 GNIEZNO   Cathedral of St Wojciech

26 TUM POD ŁĘCZYCĄ   Collegiate Church

27 Bytów   Castle of the Teutonic Order

28 Szczecin   Ducal Castle

29   PYRZYCE   Bańska Gate

30   KAMIEŃ POMORSKI   Cathedral

31   STARGARD SZCZECIŃSKI   Town Hall

32   GDAŃSK   Panorama of the Old Town ▷

33　Gdańsk　Długi Targ (Long Market)

34　Gdańsk　Neptune Fountain ▷

35 GDAŃSK Żuraw (Crane Gate)

36 GDAŃSK St Mary's Church

37 GDAŃSK Wielka Zbrojownia (Great Arsenal)

38 FROMBORK Cathedral

39 WŁOCŁAWEK Cathedral

40 TORUŃ Town Hall

41   MALBORK   Castle of the Teutonic Order: High and Middle Castles

42   BIAŁYSTOK   Branicki Palace

43   SUWAŁKI   Landscape with lakes ▷

Music

The beginnings of Polish music can be traced back to pagan times. Many of these early wedding songs and folk songs with their accompanying customs, such as the 'Procession around the Grove with Song' were later adopted as part of the Christian repertory.

By the 11th century Gregorian chant was being sung in Poland. The earliest known Polish song is the 'Bogurodzica' ('Mother of God'), which was probably sung on the field before joining battle. It cannot be traced in manuscript before 1407, but it is very likely that the song was known long before. Among the earliest evidence of musical life in Poland are the liturgical books in the Chapter Library of Gniezno.

In the 15th century Polish music attained the level of that of the greatest cultural centres of Europe. Already from 1406 music lectures were compulsory at the *Facultas Artium* of the University of Kraków. The professors and students there included the singers Grzegorz of Sanok, later Archbishop of Lwów, and Jędrzej Gałka, who wrote the 'Wycliffe Song' of 1447. The greatest composer of the period was Mikołaj Radom, whose music shows links with Dufay and the Burgundian Court.

During the 'Golden Age' there were important musicians at the court of both Zygmunt I Stary and Zygmunt II August. Mikołaj Gomółka (1535–91) was a member of the court chapel in their reigns and wrote the famous 'Melodies for a Polish Psalter' (published in Kraków in 1580); Wacław of Szamotuły (1520–60) and Marcin Leopolita (died 1589) were both court composers. The two earliest organ tablatures, those of

Jan of Lublin (1540) and of the Holy Ghost Monastery at Kraków (1548) testify to familiarity with the international repertory.

The most important composer at the transition from Renaissance to Baroque was Mikołaj Zieliński (*fl. c.*1610), the creator of 'Offeratoria totius anni' and 'Communiones totius anni', published in 1611 in Venice. Zieliński, who was organist in the chapel of the Primate Wojciech Baranowski at Łowicz, was the first Pole to master the new concerto style, combining orchestra with choir against a *basso continuo*. As in other fields, Italian influence became very evident at the beginning of the 17th century; after 1596 most of the musicians King Zygmunt III Waza brought to the new royal court at Warsaw were Italians. It was there in 1628 that the first Italian opera was performed in Poland, and during the reign of Władysław IV Waza opera in Warsaw experienced a boom. At the courts of the magnates during the 17th and part of the 18th century, many musicians still came from Italy.

In this period the composers Adam Jarzębski (1590–1648) and Bartłomiej Pękiel (died 1670) were among the most prominent Polish musicians. In the 17th century musical life in churches and monasteries also developed; the period saw more extensive formation of church orchestras. As in the theatre, initiative lay chiefly with the Jesuits in the 18th century.

The Stanisław Era (after 1764) was characterized by the endeavour to develop more strongly the national element in Polish music, and so

◁ 44 Święta Lipka Pilgrimage church

Polish folk musicians, Kraków, wood engraving ▷
after W. Wodzinowski, 1889

W.WODZINOWSKI.
KRAKÓW 89.

enhance the status of folk music. On 11 July 1778, an opera by Maciej Kamieński (1734–1821), 'Fortune in Adversity', was performed for the first time in Warsaw. It is generally regarded as the first Polish opera, though in fact the work is more like vaudeville, a popular play with songs and choirs accompanied by an orchestra. The first performance, in 1794, of the comic opera 'The Supposed Miracle, or the Cracovians and the Highlanders' with a libretto by Wojciech Bogusławski (1757–1829) and music by Jan Stefani (1764–1829), was an important event in Polish musical and political history. In the second half of the 18th century classical music in Poland came to life. The polonaise, originally a Polish folk dance, enjoyed great popularity and now entered the chamber music repertoire. Michał Ogiński (1728–1800), a theoretician, wrote some twenty polonaises, paving the way for the later achievements of Fryderyk Chopin who himself also popularized the mazurka, a dance from Mazuria. At the threshold of the 19th century the instrumental music of Chopin's teacher Józef Elsner (1769–1834) formed a link between the Classical style and early Polish Romanticism.

The increase in patriotic songs was connected with the political situation at the time of the Partitions and the loss of independence. In 1797 Józef Wybicki composed what became the national anthem, 'Poland has not perished yet, while we live' ('Jeszcze Polska nie zginęła póki my żyjemy').

Mature Romanticism, whose most famous representative was Fryderyk Chopin (1810–49), developed from a generation of composers who combined the style of Viennese Classicism with features taken from the 'empfindsamer Stil' – 'sensibility'. Michał Ogiński and Franciszek Lessel (c.1780–1838) represented the sentimental trend, while in the work of Maria Szymanowska (1789–1831) virtuosity predominated. At this time musical life also developed at the schools, particularly thanks to Elsner and Karol Kurpiński (1785–1857). From 1803 E. T. A. Hoffmann was living in Warsaw and arranged for the first performances of Beethoven's symphonies in the capital. This was the atmosphere in which Chopin grew up.

Chopin's genius has made Polish music world-famous. His music fuses Polish melodies and musical traditions with the stylistic elements of Romanticism. From 1831 Chopin worked as a teacher and composer in Paris, where he was in close contact with some of the most celebrated artists and writers of the time. He revolutionized piano technique, introducing a style of playing which has remained influential to the present day. His work is characterized by Polish-Slavic dances and their rhythms (polonaise, mazurka, krakowiak) combined with elegantly supple melodic line. The more poetical element of his music was developed particularly in small-scale works (ballades, nocturnes, scherzos, préludes, études).

Although the earliest beginnings of Polish opera are linked with the name of Maciej Kamieński, its true creator was Stanisław Moniuszko (1819–72) whose opera 'Halka', first performed in Warsaw in 1858, marked the birth of a specifically national tradition of Polish opera. 'Halka' enjoyed a triumphant success in Poland, and also attracted some attention abroad. Moniuszko's successors in the field of opera were Władysław Żeleński (1837–1921), whose work continued into the 20th century, and Zygmunt Noskowski (1846–1909).

In the second half of the 19th century the development of Polish musical life did not keep pace with events in European music as a whole. New impulses did not enter music until the advent of the movement known as 'Young Poland'. It sought to connect once again with developments in the West, especially in the symphonic field. One of these 'Young Poles' was Karol Szymanowski (1883–1937), who made a lasting mark on Polish musical life before and after the First World War. Szymanowski freed himself from German and French models and gave Polish music a new and unmistakeable

Fryderyk Chopin (1810–49),
drawing by George Sand

1933); his 'St Luke Passion', first performed in 1966 in Münster Cathedral, is an outstanding piece. His 'Paradise Lost' (1978) with a libretto by Christopher Fry was given its première in Chicago. The influence of minimalism has also been felt in Poland, notably in the work of Henryk Górecki (born 1933), whose 'Symphony of Sorrowful Songs' (1976) uses old Polish prayers and folk songs, together with fragments written by prisoners of the Nazis.

The development of contemporary music in Poland is encouraged by the active interest of the concert-going public and by the regular international and all-Poland festivals. The best known is probably 'Warszawska Jesień', ('Warsaw Autumn') held annually in September.

Early music is also popular, as can be seen from the founding of ensembles such as the 'Capella Bydgosiensis pro Musica Antiqua' and 'Fistulatores et Tubicinatores Varsovienses'. Since the 19th century Poland has had a long tradition of famous performers: Henryk Wieniawski, Ignacy Paderewski and Arthur Rubinstein, Wanda Landowska (a major figure in the revival of the harpsichord) and many pupils of the great Leszetycki.

Polish musical life today centres around some prestigious orchestras (National Philharmonic Orchestra, Silesian Philharmonic Orchestra, Great Symphony Orchestra of Polish Radio and Television). Recent leading conductors have included Witold Rowicki, Henryk Czyż, Kazimierz Kord and Bohdan Wodiczko.

The International Fryderyk Chopin Competition held every five years in Warsaw, demands the highest level of virtuosity; its best-known finalist of recent years is Krystian Zimerman. The International Wieniawski Violin Competition in Poznań is also quinquennial. Among the most famous Polish violinists are Wanda Wiłkomirska and Tadeusz Wroński. Well-known singers have included Teresa Żylis-Gara, Bernard Ładysz and Władysław Ochman, and, among younger artists, the mezzosoprano Urszula Kriger.

character; his influence also pointed the way for the contemporary generation of Polish musicians.

In the Polish musical world today pride of place must go to Witold Lutosławski (1913-94), who introduced the experience of the European avantgarde into Polish music. His 'Funeral Music for Béla Bartók' for 64 stringed instruments found an original solution to the problem of twelve-tone music. His contemporary Sir Andrzej Panufnik (1914-91) escaped to exile in England in 1954, but remained deeply concerned with Polish issues, as his 'Katyń Epitaph' (1968) and bassoon concerto dedicated to the memory of Jerzy Popiełuszko show. His elegant and refined work is only now gaining the recognition it deserves.

The leading Cracovian composer of the avant-garde is Krzysztof Penderecki (born

Besides this, Poland also has made contributions to the world of jazz, notably the work of Krysztof Komeda (1931-69), who provided memorable music for several of Roman Polański's films. An international audience attends such annual festivals as the Jazz Jamboree in Warsaw.

In popular music an individual Polish trend has developed since the Anglo-American domination in the 1970's. As part of the atmosphere of liberalization in the summer of 1980, the first Polish rock festival was held at Jarocin. This has since become an annual event and a firmly established institution in Polish youth culture. Bands such as 'Maanam' and 'Izrael' represented the Polish 'New Wave' in the 1980's, while in the 1990's 'Kult' and the rapper 'Liroy' have displayed technical skill and creativity by no means inferior to those of their Western counterparts.

Dorota Leszczyńska

*Krysztof Penderecki
(born 1933), caricature
by Edmund Mańczak*

Film

Until the end of the Second World War film-making in Poland was not particularly significant. Its origins go back to 1908–10; the first Polish film is thought to be the comedy 'Antoś's First Visit to Warsaw' made in Warsaw in 1908, with Antoni Fertner in the title role, directed by Józef Meyer. Generally speaking, the earliest Polish films were influenced by French examples; preference was given to making film versions of great literary works, and famous stage actors set the tone.

Even after Poland's return to political independence in 1918 the situation of Polish film production did not change to any great extent, and material obstacles and lack of interest on the part of the state hampered the development of film-making. It was not until after 1926 that any real life came into the medium; Aleksander Hertz, who before the First World War was already the leading Polish producer with his 'Sfinks' company, strengthened his commitment to the film industry, producing films such as 'Iwonka' and 'The Lepers' by Wiktor Biegański. For the first time these were original Polish works, which enjoyed box-office success in their own country. At the same time three directors later to be instrumental in putting Poland in the forefront of film-making after the war were learning their craft: Leonard Buczkowski, Aleksander Ford and Eugeniusz Cękalski.

In the early 1930's film versions were made of the works of great Polish writers such as Stefan Żeromski, Henryk Sienkiewicz, Gabriela Zapolska and Eliza Orzeszkowa; later filmmakers also turned to contemporary literature. A few films from before the war deserve special mention: 'Wild Fields' (1932) by Józef Lejtes, a faithful depiction of life on the land; 'Condemned by Life' (1934) by Juliusz Gardan, a psychological film; and 'The Legion of the Street' (1932) by Aleksander Ford, about the life of newspaper boys in Warsaw.

Important for later developments were some of the avantgarde groups of film-makers, who concerned themselves with the intensive training of directors and cameramen and endeavoured to make documentary films which were sophisticated yet would appeal to a wide audience. In Warsaw the 'Start' group included Aleksander Ford, Wanda Jakubowska and Jerzy Toeplitz. Other important groups included 'Linia' in Kraków, 'Awangardia' in Lwów, and lastly, also in Warsaw, the 'Fellowship of Film-makers'.

Polish film criticism was also making its mark. Karol Irzykowski's book 'The Tenth Muse', published as early as 1924, was one of the first theoretical treatises on film-making.

During the German occupation in the Second World War Polish film-makers could only continue their work with great difficulty. Nevertheless a few directors were trained, and a few films were made, such as the 'Chronicle of the Warsaw Uprising 1944'. Most directors went abroad and worked mostly in countries in which Polish army units were based (France, Britain, the Soviet Union).

Aleksander Ford and other members of the former 'Start' group formed a film-making team in 1943 in the Soviet Union as part of the Kościuszko Division. It was called the 'Film Avantgarde of the Polish Army', and later, as the Soviet troops advanced, it established the 'Film

Base of the Polish Army' first at Lublin, and then at Łódź. This formed the basis in November 1945 for the first (nationalized) film company 'Film Polski'. Thus the cinema received state supervision and support before any other branch of the arts. The new organization was concerned with all aspects of film: the making and marketing of films, the training of the next generation of film-makers, the manufacture of materials needed for film-making, and the exchange of ideas with other countries. Because of the destruction of Warsaw, Łódź became the new centre of Polish film-making; it was there that the first studio was established and in 1948 the famous film school was founded.

In view of the horrific experiences of the Second World War it was natural that the first Polish postwar films should take the German occupation as their theme. 'Forbidden Songs' (1947, directed by Leonard Buczkowski), the first feature film to be made in Łódź, recreated the extraordinary atmosphere of occupied Warsaw; satirical songs, which, although forbidden by the occupying power, were sung everywhere, and soldiers' songs of the underground movement were used to reflect the fate of the capital. The film was not very ambitious from an artistic point of view, but it was an overwhelming success with audiences, despite official press criticism that it dealt 'too gently' with the Germans.

The extermination of the Jews on Polish territory was the main theme of 'The Border Road' (1948, directed by Aleksander Ford). Ford also dealt in this film with the co-existence of the Polish and Jewish populations in pre-war Poland and their relationship during the war, and the film is both a condemnation of Nazi crimes and a critique of nationalist and inhumane tendencies in Polish society before the war.

The third Polish postwar film, 'The Last Stage' (1949, directed by Wanda Jakubowska), took the audience into Auschwitz and showed the horrific suffering of those imprisoned there. At the centre of the film is the figure of humiliated and enslaved humanity. This was the first Polish film to achieve worldwide success.

The official criticism of these three films already showed tendencies that were to be fully articulated in 1949: from then on the slogan was to be 'Against formalism and cosmopolitanism, for social realism'. The universalist and humanistic character of the first postwar films was dismissed as ideological weakness; films should show not the struggle of the Polish people but the class struggle, they should deal not with the past but with the present, and in this way they should further the building of socialism. As a result of this political orientation of cinema by the Party and state, hardly any aesthetically interesting and independent critical films were made until 1956. However, two films by Jerzy Kawalerowicz, 'Cellulosis' and 'Under the Phrygian Star' (both made in 1954), and in particular two films by Aleksander Ford, 'Chopin's Youth' (1952) and 'The Barska Street Five' (1954), should be mentioned. 'Chopin's Youth' portrayed the artistic and political activity of Fryderyk Chopin in the years between 1826 and 1830, while 'The Barska Street Five' dealt with the question of how the nation's youth, uprooted by the war, could be reintegrated into society.

The political events of 1956 opened up new avenues in Polish film-making. Most important was liberation from the firm guidance and control exerted by the Party, and the introduction of 'self-regulation', that is, the formation of film-making groups working independently, who were to be responsible for the artistic side of the films. This reform led to a great wave of new Polish films, which enjoyed success both in Poland and in the West. It also became possible to deal with the mistakes and injustices of the Stalinist era. This non-conformism was in stark contrast to the films then being made in other socialist countries.

The revival was associated above all with a group of young directors, who had all learned their trade at the Łódź film school: Andrzej

Munk, Andrzej Wajda, Jerzy Kawalerowicz and Wojciech Has. 'The Man on the Rails' (1957, directed by Andrzej Munk) deals with the re-habilitation of an old, experienced train driver, who had lost his job in the Stalinist era because he had not approved of the 'socialist innovations' of the early 1950's. 'Kanał' (1957, directed by Andrzej Wajda) dealt with the Warsaw Uprising and it was not only a corrective to the recent version of Polish history, since it rehabilitated the Home Army, which had borne the brunt of the resistance struggle, but it also sought to criticize the deep-rooted Polish belief in heroism for its own sake. 'Eroica' (1958, directed by Andrzej Munk) about life in an officers' prisoner-of-war camp had a similar theme, but whereas Wajda gave his characters in 'Kanał' heroic traits, Munk showed his characters and their predicament in a more grotesque light.

It was not surprising that 'Eroica' in particular aroused much protest, and the cultural politi-cians took the opportunity to find faults in good films about contemporary issues. One of the few acceptable films was Andrzej Wajda's 'Ashes and Diamonds' (1958), after the novel by Jerzy Andrzejewski. The film shows a group of young soldiers of the Home Army fighting against the new communist state power; their struggle is shown as pointless since the historical process is against them. The reception of the film by the critics was generally positive, because it did not condemn the young resistance fighters, but pre-sented them as tragic figures.

Pessimism was one of the three most impor-tant themes (with the war and the occupation) of Polish film-making after 1956. 'The Noose' (1958, directed by Wojciech Has), for example, shows the struggle of an alcoholic against his addiction, his ultimate failure and inevitable suicide. 'The Eighth Day of the Week' (1958, directed by Aleksander Ford) is a story of two young people in love, who cannot cope with the adversities of everyday life. 'Samson' (1961, directed by Andrzej Wajda), a film about the sufferings of Jakub Gold, a Polish Jew, also

belongs to this pessimistic trend. Pessimism was the expression of the mood of many young directors and writers, and sprang from their diminishing confidence in the political future of their country.

Inevitably this tendency provoked criticism in official quarters, where more commitment to the building of socialism was demanded. As a result the war and occupation became less important as themes, while pure entertainment flourished. Some of these popular films were of high artistic worth, such as 'The Knife in the Water' (1962) by Roman Polański. A few directors took the liberty of using a popular genre as a basis for dealing with themes from the recent past: 'All Souls' (1961, directed by Tadeusz Konwicki) (see page 106). 'The Art of Being Loved' (1962, directed by Wojciech Has), 'The Passenger' (1963, directed first by Andrzej Munk, then after his death by Witold Lesiewicz). Or they went further back in history: 'Mother Joan of the Angels' (1961, directed by Jerzy Kawalerowicz) after a novella by Jarosław Iwaszkiewicz; 'The Knights of the Cross' (1960, directed by Aleksander Ford) after the novel by Henryk Sienkiewicz; 'The Saragossa Manuscript' (1964, directed by Wojciech Has) after the novel by Jan Potocki; 'Ashes' (1965, directed by Andrzej Wajda) after Stefan Żeromski.

At the beginning of the 1970's two trends dominated Polish film-making. Andrzej Wajda continued the more romantic, emotional tendency of the Polish school, with such films as 'Birch Wood' (1970), 'The Wedding' (1972), 'Promised Land' (1974/5), 'Shadow Line' (1976). Then in 1977 'Man of Marble' appeared, in which Wajda dealt with the contradictions in the life of a 'Hero of Socialist Labour' during the Stalinism of the 1950's. It was followed in 1981 by 'Man of Iron', Wajda's contribution to the social debates in Poland in the summer of 1980.

Krzysztof Zanussi's most important films are 'Illumination' (1973), 'Protective Colours' (1977) and 'Constans' (1980). They are about people who set themselves high moral standards and reject any dubious compromise. Zanussi's moral unease, the concern with the ethical problems of the individual in the midst of a consumer-orientated society was echoed in films made in the 1970's by young directors such as Krzysztof Kieślowski, Agnieszka Holland, Antoni Krauze and Feliks Falk.

The history of Polish documentary films follows a similar course, particularly after the Second World War. At first films of international quality were made; these included 'The Warsaw Suite' (1946) by Tadeusz Makarczyński, 'The Inquiry' (1946) by Jerzy Bossak, and 'Warsaw (1952) by Ludwik Perski. From 1956 onwards films from what was known as the 'Black Series', in which social shortcomings and mistakes were criticized, attacked the stagnation of the Stalin era. At the beginning of the 1960's a distinctive Polish school of documentary film emerged. Kazimierz Karabarz ('Musicians', 1960; 'The First Step', 1962; 'Before the Leaves Fall', 1964; 'Family of Man', 1962) and Jan Łomnicki ('A Ship is Born', 1961; and three films about the industrial town of Nowa Huta) made use of poetic images; narration and commentary were strictly limited; reality was neither prettified nor made to seem too negative. Problems posed were shown always to be capable of resolution. This balanced style was confronted in the 1970's by the 'Contesters': Tomasz Zygadło, Grzegorz Królikiewicz, Krzysztof Kieślowski, Marek Piwowaki. Their brand of realism confronted social and moral problems unflinchingly. After August 1980 the main subject of documentary film was the political and social upheaval of that momentous year, such as 'Workers 80' or 'The Peasants' (1981).

Polish cartoons developed at the end of the 1950's in the hands of animators such as Waldemar Borowczyk, Jan Lenica and Witold Giersz. The films are well worth seeing for their humour, combined with philosophical reflection and formal originality. Seventy per cent of them are children's films, and characters such as Bolek and Lolek, Filemon the tomcat and Colargol the bear are very popular.

The Polish film industry celebrated one of its greatest successes in Berlin in 1988, when the European Film Prize for 'Best Film' went to 'A Short Film About Killing' directed by Krzysztof Kieślowski, which formed part of his widely acclaimed series of films based around the Ten Commandments ('Dekalog'). This was followed in the early 1990's by his equally acclaimed 'Three Colours' trilogy. Amongst Polish films the annual Festival of Shorts held in Kraków is particularly important.

Nonetheless, in general the cinema has not greatly prospered in recent years. As in the communist period, many directors have worked abroad, including Jerzy Antczak, Agnieszka Holland and Kieślowski (who died in 1996). It is now, however, inadequate investment which keeps so many leading figures away. The most commercially successful Polish films have usually followed the model of American action movies, although there has also been a demand for lavish costume dramas with patriotic themes. Notable examples of these are Wajda's version of Mickiewicz's national epic, 'Pan Tadeusz' (1999), and Jerzy Hoffman's 'With Fire and Sword' (1999), derived from the novel by Henryk Sienkiewicz.

Dorota Leszczyńska

Art and Architecture

The history of Poland, with its changing frontiers and diverse populations, its alternating periods as a great European power and a victim of foreign domination, is reflected in its art and architecture. As well as Poles, the Polish king included among his subjects Germans, Jews, Ukrainians and others, who all contributed to the country's rich artistic heritage. Architects and artists from many countries came to work in Poland – above all from Italy, Germany and the Netherlands. It is important also to remember that Poland's present frontiers exclude areas in the former eastern territories, where Polish art and architecture flourished – in particular the cities of Wilno (now Vilnius in Lithuania) and Lwów (now Lviv in Ukraine). On the other hand, the postwar western and northern frontiers now include regions (in Pomerania, Prussia and Silesia) where German culture had been dominant and where historic ties with the old Polish state were less strong.

The earliest civilization which has left identifiable evidence in what is now Poland is the Lusatian Culture (*c*.1200–*c*.400 BC). The fortified Iron Age settlement at *Biskupin* dates from around the 6th century BC. Objects found there (pottery and bronze implements) and the reconstructions of timber buildings give a good idea of the achievements of this culture. The mysterious stones and carvings at the ancient cult centre on *Mount Ślęża* in Silesia are probably the work of Celts who were living here in the 5th century BC.

Many of the earliest remains associated with the emergent Polish state are to be found in Wielkopolska. At the fortified settlement (or *gród*) on *Ostrów Lednicki*, an island in Lake Lednica, the Polanian princes in the 10th and 11th centuries built a palatium and attached chapel, following the model of the palaces of the Carolingian and Ottonian emperors. Other early Piast residences have been excavated at *Wiślica*, *Płock, Przemyśl* and *Kraków*. Palace chapels were often built on circular plans; the foundation of one such rotunda can be seen on the *Wawel, Kraków*, and there are surviving examples of round churches at *Inowłódz, Cieszyn* and *Strzelno (St Procopius)*.

The conversion of Poland to Christianity in the 10th century was followed in the early 11th century by the creation of new bishoprics. The original cathedrals of *Poznań, Gniezno* and *Kraków* were three-aisled Romanesque basilicas which were later replaced by Gothic buildings (though the early 12th-century crypt of *St Leonard* survives at *Kraków*). The generally austere character of Romanesque architecture in Poland can be seen in the remaining collegiate and monastic churches: *Kruszwica* (1120–40) (plate 22), *Tum pod Łęczycą* (consecrated 1161) (plate 26), *Strzelno* (*c*.1180), *Opatów* (early 12th century) and *St Andrew, Kraków* (11th–12th centuries).

Romanesque sculpture can be found on portals at *Tum*, and on the unusual shafts of the columns in the church at *Strzelno* with their fine carvings of Virtues and Vices (*c*.1180) (illustration, page 287). In Silesia there is Romanesque carving on the portal of *St Mary Magdalene, Wrocław* (late 12th century) (plate 72) and *Trzebnica Abbey* (*c*.1230). Perhaps the most impressive examples of Romanesque figurative art in Poland are the scenes of the life and death of St

Wojciech (Adalbert) on the 12th-century bronze doors at Gniezno (illustration page 281) preserved from the earlier cathedral. (The slightly earlier bronze doors from Płock Cathedral, with panels cast in Magdeburg, are copies; the originals were taken to the cathedral of Novgorod in Russia in the 14th century.) A rare survival is the incised floor in the crypt at *Wiślica* (second half of 12th century) depicting a family at prayer (illustration, page 504).

Some good examples of smaller-scale Romanesque metalwork can be seen in Polish museums and treasuries: the late 12th-century *Trzemeszno chalice and paten* (now in Gniezno Cathedral Treasury) (illustration, page 286) have engraved and nielloed decoration, as does the hilt of the famous *Szczerbiec Sword* (illustration, page 482) in the *Wawel Museum, Kraków* (12th–13th centuries).

13th Century

The transition to Gothic began with the arrival in Poland of the Cistercian Order. As their monastic reform movement spread through Europe, the Cistercians carried with them their characteristic building techniques, including the rib vault and the pointed arch. The early Cistercian churches in Poland can be divided into two main groups: those founded from the Order's heartland in Burgundy with its masonry tradition, such as *Wąchock* (1218–39), *Sulejów* (consecrated 1232) (plate 58) and *Koprzywnica* (1218–38), and those with affiliations to German Cistercian houses, where more brick was used, such as *Mogiła* (mid-13th century) in *Małopolska*; *Henryków* and *Trzebnica* in Silesia; and *Kołbacz* (1210-30), *Oliwa* (13th century) and *Pelplin* (late 13th century) (colour plate 20) in Pomerania. The influence of this Silesian Cistercian architecture can be seen in the square-ended choir of *Wrocław Cathedral* (1244–72). In Pomerania Cistercian architecture influenced the early buildings of the Teutonic Order, such as the former cathedral at *Chełmża* (1254–63).

The new mendicant orders also developed the Gothic style for their spacious preaching churches. The *Dominican Church, Sandomierz* (second quarter 13th century), with its moulded brick decoration, is the best preserved early example. Parts of the early *Franciscan* and *Dominican Churches* in *Kraków* are still visible amidst later alterations.

Following the Tatar invasions in the mid-13th century, many towns were rebuilt on a regular plan. At *Wrocław* (c.1242) and *Kraków* (1257) the grid of streets arranged around a central market square can still be seen in the old town centres.

Early Gothic sculpture can be found on the north portal of *Trzebnica Abbey Church* (c.1270) (plate 73) and in the *Dominican Church, Poznań*.

14th Century

Brick Gothic architecture developed in Pomerania and the territories of the Teutonic Knights. The Teutonic castles came to dominate the Prussian landscape in the 13th and 14th centuries. Among the most impressive extant castles are *Gniew* (after 1283), *Golub Dobrzyń* (1302–6) (plate 15), *Lidzbark Warmiński* (1330–40) with its arcaded courtyard, and the cathedral-cum-castle complex of *Kwidzyn* (second half 14th century) with its magnificent latrine tower (the Teutonic Knights had learned the importance of hygiene in Palestine). Most impressive of all is *Malbork* (plate 41), from 1309 the headquarters of the Order, which was enlarged in stages throughout the 14th century and combines awe-inspiring fortifications with exquisitely delicate decoration (*Grand Master's Palace*, 1389–99).

In Warmia spacious box-like hall churches followed the pattern of *Frombork Cathedral* (1329–88) (plate 38). Two of the best preserved are *Dobre Miasto* (1357–91) (colour plate 26) and *Olsztyn* (begun 1370-80). The most striking Warmian church exterior is *St James, Orneta* with patterned brickwork and 15th-century gabled side-chapel.

The prosperity and self-confidence of the

burghers in the thriving northern cities of Gdańsk, Toruń and Elbląg were expressed in their grand churches, public buildings and residences. This is best seen today in *Toruń* with its tall brick hall churches (*St John, St James* and *St Mary*) and magnificent late 14th-century *Town Hall* (by a Master Andreas) (plate 40). In *Gdańsk,* the burghers built *St Catherine's Church* (second half 14th century), the *Great Mill* and the *Town Hall of the Main Town* (from 1379).

In western Pomerania the work of Hinrich Brunsberg (*c.*1360-1430) in the brick churches of *St James, Szczecin* (*c.*1400), *Chojna* (1389–1407), and *St Mary, Stargard Szczeciński* (*c.*1400) (illustration, page 327), shows the influence of the architecture of the Parler family in Prague, combined with external polychrome ceramic brickwork.

In Silesia too the main building material in the 14th century was brick used in combination with stone. The distinctive character of Silesian Gothic can best be seen in the tall, narrow churches of *Wrocław: Holy Cross* (1320–50), *St Elizabeth* (begun 1330) and *St Mary Magdalene* (1358–71). A particular feature of Silesian churches are the 'Piast' or 'jumping' vaults (see Glossary). These first occur in the *Holy Cross Church*, but are most striking in the hall church of *St Mary 'Na Piasku'* (1334–80) in *Wrocław*.

In the Kingdom of Poland the reign of Kazimierz III Wielki (1333–70) saw much building activity, especially in Małopolska. Much of the building was military – remains of castles can be seen at *Kruszwica* and *Ojców*, and the town of *Szydłów* has retained its fortifications from the period. Many churches were also founded. The rebuilding of *Wawel Cathedral, Kraków*, begun in 1320 under Władysław I Łokietek, was completed in 1364. In the king's newly founded town of *Kazimierz*, hard by Kraków, the tall brick and stone churches of *Corpus Christi* and *St Catherine* were built in the second half of the century. One distinctive feature of basilican churches built in Małopolska at this time was a system of

supports with internal buttresses set against piers in the side aisles (the 'Cracovian system' first seen in the nave of *Wawel Cathedral*). The royal 'expiatory' churches of *Wiślica* (plate 54), *Stopnica*, *Szydłów* and *Niepołomice* form an unusual group: stone churches with piers placed along the axis, creating a double-nave effect held together visually by the vaulting. In this period the ancient cathedrals of Wielkopolska were rebuilt: *Gniezno* (after 1342) with an ambulatory choir following French models, and *Poznań* (1346–57).

In Małopolska architectural sculpture reached a high level (in *Kraków* the portals of *St Catherine's* and the *Dominican Church* and chancel of *St Mary's*, late 14th century), and the tombs of Władysław I Łokietek and Kazimierz III Wielki in *Wawel Cathedral* mark the beginning of the splendid sequence of royal funerary sculpture in the cathedral. In Silesia the influence of the aristocratic elegance of the 'Beautiful' or 'International Gothic' style, which spread from the Parler workshop in Prague, can be seen in the portal sculptures of *Strzegom* parish church. The international Gothic in sculpture is also found in the 'Beautiful Madonnas' from around 1400 in *Toruń* (now lost) and *Gdańsk*. The *Krużlowa Madonna* (now in the National Museum, Kraków) and the *Pietà* in *St Mary Magdalene, Wrocław* also show Parler influence. In the territories of the Teutonic Knights a characteristic type of statue was produced showing the Virgin Mary in complex contrapposto holding a standing Christ Child and treading on a lion; these 'Lion Madonnas' are also found in Silesia.

15th Century

Following the accession of the Lithuanian Władysław II Jagiełło in 1386, work was commissioned at the royal court not only from western artists working in the International Gothic style (Crucifix of Queen Jadwiga and the king's tomb effigy in Wawel Cathedral), but also from Ruthenian painters working in the Byzantine tradition. The new link with the Lithuanian empire meant there was a stronger connection with the Orthodox communities of Rus. Examples of Byzantine-style murals can be seen at *Lublin Castle (Trinity Chapel); Wawel Cathedral (Holy Cross Chapel), Wiślica* and *Sandomierz*. The original *Black Madonna of Częstochowa* seems to have been a Ruthenian icon. However, panel painting produced in Poland in the early 15th century was strongly influenced by Bohemian models, and it was not until the middle of the century that a distinctively Polish school of painting developed in Kraków.

Northern brick Gothic reached its apogee in the second half of the 15th century with the great hall churches of *Gdańsk: Holy Trinity* (1422–c.1550) with its elaborate brick gables, and above all the massive hall church of *St Mary*, (1447–1506) (plate 36), with its tall bare walls and decorative gables on the outside, and intricate net and diamond vaults within. Net vaults, probably derived from English Gothic, with numerous ribs forming complex patterns, also appear at *Pelplin*. Diamond vaults, in which the ribs are done away with and the vault is divided into faceted cells resembling folded paper, make a spectacular appearance in the transept at *Pelplin* and the aisles of *St Catherine, Gdańsk*. Such diamond vaults are also found in Warmia and in *Kraków* (courtyard of the *Collegium Maius*).

In Małopolska and Silesia church architecture in the 15th century was conservative, and the great Kraków basilicas continued to be the inspiration for some provincial churches (*Bodzentyn* and *Skalbmierz*). The most impressive example of Late Gothic church architecture in the region is *Biecz*. The large brick and stone clergy houses at *Sandomierz* and *Wiślica* were built for the canon and historian Jan Długosz. Country houses such as *Dębno* (plate 55) reflect the cultivated life now enjoyed by the nobility. Secular architecture showed the flourishing state of the towns: in Silesia *Wrocław Town Hall* was impressively enlarged (1471–1505) (plate 69), and *Lwówek Town Hall* (1522–4) by Wendel Rosskopf (c.1480–1549) has curvilinear vaulting influenced by the work of Benedikt Ried in Prague. Sophisticated town defences were built to confront the Turkish threat (*Kraków Barbican*, 1498–9) (illustration, page 455).

Some timber churches – a distinctive feature of the Polish landscape – date from the Late Gothic period. The finest group (many with lavishly painted interiors) is in Małopolska and includes *Dębno Podhalańskie* (plate 53), *Lipnica Murowana, Grywałd* and *Haczów*. Wooden churches, both Roman Catholic and Uniate, continued to be built in the following centuries in southern Poland. Uniate churches with their distinctive pyramidal roofs include *Hrebenne* (plate 63) and *Powroźnik*.

Winged altarpieces with painted and carved panels were produced inlarge numbers from the 1440's. In Silesia a local school of panel painting developed around the middle of the century (*St Barbara Altarpiece*, 1447, and *St Elizabeth Altarpiece*, 1470–80, from *Wrocław*, both now in the *National Museum, Warsaw*), and in Kraków a local style also grew up (*Trinity Altarpiece, Wawel Cathedral*). However, foreign artists were in demand. Veit Stoss (c.1450–1533) – known in Poland as Wit Stwosz – came to Kraków from Nuremberg in 1477 and stayed until 1496. His principal works there are the huge wooden altarpiece in *St Mary's* (colour plate 7) and the marble tomb of King Kazimierz IV Jagiellończyk in *Wawel Cathedral*. He also designed the bronze *monument* to the humanist scholar Filippo Buonaccorsi in the *Dominican Church, Kraków*, cast by Peter Vischer (1460–1529) of Nuremberg. The enormous influence of the Stoss workshop is apparent in such local works as the *Książnice Wielkie Altarpiece*.

16th Century

The Italian Renaissance made an early appearance in Polish architecture thanks to Buonaccorsi's pupil, King Zygmunt I Stary (reigned 1506–48), who was married to an Italian princess and had spent some years at the humanist court of Buda. He commissioned Francesco Fiorentino (died 1516) to design a classical niche for the tomb of King Jan Olbracht (1502–5) in *Wawel Cathedral*, and to begin the rebuilding of *Wawel Castle* with a grand arcaded courtyard (plate 47). Fiorentino was succeeded by Master Benedykt (probably a German), who in turn was followed by another Florentine, Bartolommeo Berrecci (*c*.1480–1537). The *Wawel portals* with their extraordinary combination of Late Gothic and Renaissance motifs are probably due to Master Benedykt. Berrecci's greatest work is the domed *burial chapel* (illustration, page 476) for Zygmunt (1517–33) attached to *Wawel Cathedral*. The form and decoration of the chapel are Italian in spirit, although there are no specific Italian models, and the mythological sculpture reflects the humanist ideals of the court. For the chapel's altarpiece Zygmunt turned to artists from Nuremberg. Hans Dürer (1490–*c*.1538), the less talented brother of Albrecht, worked on the decoration of *Wawel Castle*, and another Franconian, Hans Süss of Kulmbach (*c*.1480–1522) produced paintings for the burghers' church, *St Mary's*. The most important Polish painter working in Kraków was Stanisław Samostrzelnik (1480/90–1541), a Cistercian monk who was temporarily released from his monastery to serve the Crown Chancellor Krzysztof Szydłowiecki. His work as a miniaturist can be seen in his illustrations for the *Liber geneseos*, the Szydłowiecki family history (now in the library at *Kórnik*) (illustration, page 291) and mural paintings by him decorate his monastery of *Mogiła*.

Zygmunt's castle and chapel were very influential. The Silesian princes remodelled their castles at *Legnica* (portal by Georg of Amberg, 1533) and *Brzeg* (portal by Jacopo (d.1575) and Francesco Pahr (d.1580), completed 1560). In Małopolska King Zygmunt August built an Italianate palace at *Niepołomice* (1550–71).

A number of curious tunnel-vaulted churches were built (or remodelled) by Giovanni Battista da Venezia around the middle of the century in Mazovia. The first of them, *Pułtusk* (plate 13),

also has the earliest of many imitations of the Zygmunt Chapel which were to be built in Poland over the next century.

The most outstanding example of municipal architecture of the period is *Poznań Town Hall* (1550–60) by Giovanni Battista Quadro (d.1590–91) of Lugano, with its arcaded façade and decorated vaulting (plate 18). Italian craftsmen were also responsible for the remodelling of the *Sukiennice, Kraków* (since restored), which has perhaps the finest example of the 'Polish parapet' (colour plate 6). This characteristic wall-cresting is found throughout south-eastern Poland; it can be seen on the 16th-century town halls of *Sandomierz* and *Tarnów*. Such parapets are also found on synagogues (*Old Synagogue, Kraków*, remodelled 1557–70). The development of Renaissance architecture into a form of 'artisan Mannerism' can be seen in the charming confusion of Italianate forms on *Chełmno Town Hall* (1567–70).

The 16th century is one of the greatest periods for tomb sculpture in Poland. Good collections of Renaissance and Mannerist tombs can be found in a number of churches, notably *Tarnów Cathedral* with its series of Tarnowski family monuments. The most magnificent series is formed by the royal monuments in *Wawel Cathedral*, which includes works by Giovanni Maria Padovano (d.1573), Jan Michałowicz of Urzędów (active 1570–83), Girolamo Canavesi (d.1582) and Santi Gucci (*c*.1530–*c*.1600), who remodelled the Zygmunt Chapel, adding the tombs of Zygmunt August and his wife. Stone carving from the workshops at Pińczów influenced by Gucci, can be found in many churches (*Mniszech Chapel, Radzyń Podlaski*, the *Firlej Chapel, Bejsce*; and the *Montelupi monuments, St Mary's, Kraków*).

Gucci was the architect of the *Mirów Palace, Książ Wielki* (1585–95) inspired by Florentine Mannerism, and his hand can also be seen in the design of the palace of *Baranów* (1591–1606) (plate 64). With the castle of *Krasiczyn* (1598–1633) (colour plate 9), this is one of the most spectacular of Polish Mannerist magnatial residences.

Probably the greatest surviving achievement of late 16th-century Polish Mannerism is Zamość, founded as an ideal town by the scholar-statesman, Hetman Jan Zamoyski, and laid out on a unified plan by the Venetian Bernardo Morando (c.1540–1600).

Early 17th Century

The arrival of the Waza dynasty and the Counter-Reformation brought the Baroque to Poland. The Jesuit church of *Sts Peter and Paul, Kraków* (1605–19) followed the plan of the Order's mother church, the Gesù in Rome. It was designed by the Jesuit Giuseppe Brizio, working with the King's architect Giovanni Battista Trevano (active 1599–1641) from Lombardy, who also probably had a part in extending the *Royal Castle* (1588–1611) at the new capital, *Warsaw*, and the residence at *Ujazdów* (1606-19) (plate 11) nearby. The finest surviving Early Baroque residence in the Waza style is the *Palace of the Bishops of Kraków* at *Kielce* (1637–44) (plate 56) built by Tommaso Poncino (d.1659), probably to Trevano's designs. The new capital was given an impressive Early Baroque monument in the *Sigismund Column* (colour plate 13) commemorating Zygmunt III Waza, erected in 1633–4 outside the Royal Castle by Agostino Locci the Elder (d. after 1650) and Constantino Tencalla (fl. 1630–45).

Catholic magnates financed the building of impressive churches and monasteries for religious orders. The Camaldulensian monastery of *Bielany* (1605–42) near Kraków was founded by Mikołaj Wolski with a grand façade by Wallenstein's architect Andrea Spezza (d.1658). The Jesuit architect Gian Maria Bernardoni (1541–1605) designed the church of the Bernardine monastery at *Kalwaria Zebrzydowska* (1603–9) founded by Mikołaj Zebrzydowski. Arranged around the monastery is an elaborate series of chapels laid out as a Way of the Cross for pilgrims to follow. This was the first of many 'Calvaries', a characteristic feature of Counter-Reformation devotion in Poland; one of the most delightful examples, dating from the middle of the century, can be found at *Wejherowo* near Gdańsk. Loreto Chapels were also founded, such as the one at *Gołąb* (1634–8). The use of black marble decoration was characteristic of Early Baroque interiors in the south, such as the *Myszkowski Chapel* (1602–14) in the *Dominican Church, Kraków* and the *Waza Chapel* (begun 1605) in *Wawel Cathedral*.

Baroque painting was introduced to Poland by the Venetian Tommaso Dolabella (c.1570–1650). He lived in Kraków from 1589 onwards and most of his work is in or around the old capital: the *Chapel of St Jacek* in the *Dominican Church* (1619–25) and *Bielany* monastery church (1633–43). The painter Franciszek Lekszycki (d.1668), a Bernardine friar, produced altarpieces strongly influenced by Flemish art (*Bernardine Church, Kraków* and *Kalwaria Zebrzydowska*). The most prominent stuccatore in the region was Giovanni Battista Falconi (fl. c.1625–60), whose magnificent plasterwork can be seen in several churches in *Kraków* and in the *Oświęcim funerary chapel* in the Franciscan Church at *Krosno* (1647–8).

Side by side with the beginnings of Baroque, the Mannerist tradition continued, exemplified by the castle and church at *Wiśnicz Nowy* (1615–30), remodelled for the Lubomirskis by Maciej Trapola (d.1637), and the extraordinarily grandiose symbolical castle of *Krzyżtopór* at *Ujazd* (1627–44) by Lorenzo Senes (Muretto) (d. after 1649). The distinctive local Mannerist style of *Lublin* with its unusual plasterwork continued well into the 17th century. Early examples are the *Bernardine Church* in *Lublin* (1602–7) and the nave vault of the *Zamość, Collegiate Church* (1618–30). One of the best exponents of the Lublin style was Jan Wolff, the architect of the new *Town Hall in Zamość* (1639–51), and the richly decorated *Firlej Chapel* (1630) in the *Dominican Church* in *Lublin*. Mannerist decoration of a more naïve variety can be seen on the façades of houses at *Kazimierz Dolny* with their jumble of architectural elements and figures in relief (*Przybyło Houses*, 1615, and *Celej House*, 1635). In Wielkopolska a sophisticated Mannerist architecture was practised by Cristoforo Bonadura (*c.*1582–1667/70), the architect of the *Bernardine Church* at *Sieraków* (1627–39) and later, with Giorgio Catenacci (active 1664–90), of a number of churches in *Poznań*.

Dutch Mannerism dominated the architecture of the great Protestant northern cities of Gdańsk and Toruń. In *Gdańsk* the city architect, Anthonis van Opbergen (1543–1611), designed the *Great Arsenal* (1602–9) 'one of the most perfect examples of this north European style' (Białostocki), and the interior of the *Town Hall* was decorated with perspective paintings by Jan Vredeman de Vries (1526–1606) and Isaak van den Blocke (d.1626). His brother Abraham van den Blocke (*c.*1572–1628) built the *Golden Gate* (1612–14), remodelled the *Arthur Court* and designed the *Bahr tomb* (1614–20) in *St Mary's*. His father Willem van den Blocke (d.1628) designed the *Ostrogski tomb*, *Tarnów Cathedral* (1605–20), an early example of the new type of funerary monument with kneeling figures.

The leading painter in Gdańsk was Daniel Schultz (*c.*1615–83), who was also active elsewhere in Poland; his impressive *portrait of Bishop Andrzej Trzebicki* (1664) can be seen in the *Franciscan monastery, Kraków*. In Kraków another German, Marcin Kober (active 2nd half 16th century) painted some striking portraits (*Stefan Batory*, in the *Missionaries' monastery*).

Later 17th Century

After the destruction caused by the Swedish Wars building work continued. Architecture in *Warsaw* was dominated by Tylman van Gameren (1632–1706), a native of Utrecht, who brought a Dutch classicism to the new Polish capital. This is clearest in his *Sakramentki Church* (1688–9) (illustration, page 168), one of three centrally planned churches he built in the city. Of his secular buildings there the most

splendid is the *Krasiński Palace* (1677–82) with its great pedimented and arcaded façade, the result of his collaboration with the sculptor Andreas Schlüter (*c.*1660–1714) from Gdańsk. The country house of the Primate Michał Radziejowski at *Nieborów* near Warsaw (1690–96) is another of Tylman's designs. His buildings can also be seen at *Gdańsk* (the *Royal Chapel*, 1678–81) and *Kraków*, where the *Church of St Anne* (1689–1704) has superb plasterwork by Baldassare Fontana (*c.*1658–1738). King Jan III Sobieski's villa at *Wilanów* (1679–92) (colour plate 16) was designed by Agostino Locci the Younger (*c.*1650–1729) with a complex iconographic program of lavish reliefs and statuary by Schlüter and Giuseppi Simone Belotti (d.1608). The illusionistic frescoes of Jerzy Eleuter Szymonowicz-Siemiginowski (*c.*1660–1711) reveal the influence of his training in Rome.

The 17th century was the great age of Sarmatian culture (see Glossary). Portraits of the szlachta in characteristic Sarmatian costume can be found in most museums. Even more peculiarly Polish are the portraits painted on polygonal plates to be attached to coffins; good collections of these can be seen in *Wilanów* and the *National Museum, Poznań*. The Dance of Death became a popular theme: perhaps the finest example is the plaster cycle in the *Oleśnicki Chapel* at *Tarłów*.

Church building continued apace. Italianizing tendencies can be seen in such buildings as the *Oratorian Church* at *Gostyń* (1677), inspired by Longhena's S. Maria della Salute in Venice, and in the Roman grandeur of the *Jesuit Church*, *Poznań* eventually finished by Giovanni Catenacci (1649–1711). Work on the great Paulite monastery on *Jasna Góra, Częstochowa* continued, with many artists involved, most notably the painter Karl Dankwart, who was responsible for the redecoration of the main church (1690–93) (plate 59). Splendid new silver shrines for Poland's patrons, St Wojciech at *Gniezno* and St Stanisław at *Kraków*, were made by the Gdańsk silversmith Peter van der Rennen (1609–69). In Catholic Warmia in the north the pilgrimage complex of *Święta Lipka* (1687–92) (plate 44) was rebuilt for the Jesuits by the architect Georg Ertly of Wilno (d.1696); it is notable for the superb ironwork by the Schwarz brothers.

Timber church architecture was still important, but now tended to imitate masonry construction (*Mnichów* and *Tomaszów Lubelski*) (colour plate 11). Few timber houses of any importance have survived, but it should be remembered that the overwhelming majority of buildings of all types and sizes continued to be made in wood up to the 19th century, including the seats of many of the nobility.

The art and architecture of Silesia, now under Habsburg rule, was heavily influenced by Austria and Bohemia. However, some of the most impressive buildings there were the 'Peace Churches' which the authorities grudgingly allowed the Lutherans to erect after 1648. The surviving examples at *Świdnica* and *Jawor* (1654–8), by Albrecht von Säbisch (1610–68) are *tours de force* of timber-framed construction. Another wave of Protestant churches followed at the beginning of the 18th century ('Grace Churches'), when the Swedish-influenced masonry church at *Jelenia Góra* (1709–18) was built by Martin Frantz (1681–1742). By then Catholic building on a grand scale was underway in Silesia: *Lubiąż Abbey* (rebuilt 1690–1720) (colour plate 1), the *Jesuit College in Wrocław* (now Wrocław University) with sculptural decoration by Franz Joseph Mangold (*fl.* 1725–53) and *Jesuit Church* (1689–98) with paintings by Johann Michael Rottmayr (1654–1730). The greatest Silesian painter of the 17th century, Michael Willmann (1630–1706), was a native of Protestant Königsberg. He converted to Catholicism and spent much of his life at Lubiąż Abbey; his work can be seen at *Henryków* and *Wrocław Town Hall* and his late masterpiece is the cycle of paintings in *Krzeszów* parish church (1692–5).

Early 18th Century

The advent of the Saxon kings in Poland brought architects and artists from the Dresden court to Warsaw. The greatest of these, Matthäus Daniel Pöppelmann (1662–1736), produced grand (unexecuted) designs for the royal palace. His son, Karl Friedrich Pöppelmann (d.1750) collaborated with Johann Sigismund Deibel (d.1752), introducing Saxon Rococo in a number of buildings in *Warsaw* including the *Zamoyski Palace*, and reshaping the Polish capital by creating the 'Saxon Axis'. Deibel's work can also be found at the palace of *Białystok* (1728–58) (plate 42) for the Branickis, and later at *Siedlce* (1766–72). Other great palaces of the aristocracy were extended on a magnificent scale in the mid-18th century, the grandest of all being *Radzyń Podlaski* remodelled by the court architect Jacopo Fontana (1710–73) (plate 16).

Outside the orbit of Saxon patronage, the outstanding figure is the architect Pompeo Ferrari (1660–1736), whose patron, Stanisław Leszczyński, was twice ousted from the Polish throne by the Saxon candidates. Much of Ferrari's work is in the Leszczyńskis' town of *Leszno*. He also designed the Borrominesque *Potocki Chapel* in *Gniezno Cathedral*, and the spectacular remodelling of the *Cistercian Church* at *Ląd*. In the Lublin region a number of interesting elliptical churches with complex spatial effects were designed by Paolo Antonio Fontana (*c.*1696–1765) at *Chełm*, *Lubartów* and *Włodawa*. The churches of Kasper Bażanka (*c.*1680–1726) also show the influence of Roman Baroque: *Imbramowice*, and the *Piarist* and *Missionary Churches*, *Kraków*, which contain work by the finest Baroque sculptor in Kraków, Antoni Frąckiewicz (*fl.* 1726–55). A Rococo sculptural treatment of the church façade can be seen in the *Trinity Church*, *Kraków* (1752–8) by Francesco Placidi (*c.*1710–82).

The most prominent Polish painter of the period was Szymon Czechowicz (1689–1775), who had been a pupil of Carlo Maratta in Rome and whose religious paintings can be found in churches throughout Poland.

In Silesia influences from Vienna and Prague continued to dominate. The Viennese court architect Johann Bernhard Fischer von Erlach (1656–1723) designed the *Electoral Chapel* (1715–24) in *Wrocław Cathedral*, and the great master of Bohemian Baroque, Kilian Ignaz Dientzenhofer (1689–1751) built one of his finest churches for the Benedictines at *Legnickie Pole* (1727–31), with a ceiling painting by the Bavarian Cosmas Damian Asam (1689–1739). The Dientzenhofer style was taken up by the local architect Anton Jentsch (*fl.* 1725–50) in the rebuilding of the *Cistercian Church* at *Krzeszów* (1728–35), where statuary was provided by the great Prague sculptors Ferdinand Maximilian Brokoff (1688–1731) and Matthias Braun (1684–1738).

Later 18th Century

The reign of Stanisław II August was a period of consciously enlightened royal patronage. The king began with ambitious schemes, such as the unexecuted project by Victor Louis (1731-1800) for rebuilding the Royal Castle in Warsaw, but political setbacks soon reduced their scope. Nevertheless the King gathered about him a group of architects and artists with the aim of regenerating Polish art. In architecture Palladian Classicism was the favoured style. The king's principal architect was Domenico Merlini (1730–97), whose individuality can be seen in the palace at *Jabłonna* (1774–5) and the *Myślewicki Palace, Warsaw* (1775–8), and whose Palladianism is seen at its purest in the *Królikarnia Palace, Warsaw* (1772–86). Merlini remodelled interiors in the *Royal Palace, Warsaw* and designed the *Palace on the Water* and other buildings in *Łazienki Park, Warsaw*. Johann Christian Kamsetzer (1753–95) from Dresden, whom Stanisław had sent to study architecture in Italy, worked with Merlini on these projects (plate 10). Marcello Bacciarelli (1759–1810), was brought from Rome to become the king's principal painter and create a school of history painting. As well as producing some striking portraits of the king, he also painted canvases and frescoes for the *Royal Castle* and *Łazienki* glorifying Stanisław's reign

and other great events in Polish history. Other major artists who contributed to these Warsaw projects were the painter Jan Bogumił Plersch (1732–1817) and the king's leading sculptor, André Jean LeBrun (1737–1811), a pupil of Pigalle. Another sculptor working at the royal court was the talented Italian Giacopo Monaldi (1730–1793). Bernardo Bellotto (1720–80), also called Canaletto, spent twelve years in Warsaw, where he painted his great *Election Sejm of Stanislaw II August* (in Poznań) and many vivid views of the city. These, together with the topographical paintings of Zygmunt Vogel (1764–1826) were of great use in the reconstruction of Warsaw after the Second World War.

Kamsetzer also worked on aristocratic residences such as the *Raczyński Palace, Warsaw* (1786), the interiors at *Rogalin* (c.1787) and the church at *Petrykozy* (1791). Other architects working in Warsaw at this time included Ephraim Schroeger (1727–83) from Toruń, the designer of the columned façades of the *Church of the Nuns of the Visitation* (1754–66) (plate 1) and the *Carmelite Church* (1761–83), and Szymon Bogumił Zug (1733–1807), whose plain circular *Lutheran Church* (1777–9) was the first work of uncompromising Neoclassicism in the capital. Zug played an important part in the development of the English landscape garden in Poland with his work for Helena Radziwiłł at *Arkadia* (plate 12) and *Natolin*, and for Anna Potocka at *Jabłonna* (illustration, page 235). Another aristocratic woman, Izabela Czartoryska, created the park at *Puławy*, with the English landscape gardener James Savage (c.1768–1816).

Jean-Pierre Norblin (1745–1830) came to Poland from France in 1774 and stayed there, working mainly for the Czartoryski family (ceiling of *Temple of Diana, Arkadia*, 1783). He also painted scenes of aristocratic rural life, which show the influence of Watteau. Franciszek Smuglewicz (1745–1807) was sent to Rome by the king, who hoped he would become Poland's great history painter. The 'Wilno School' he founded is characterized by a rather naïve classicism.

The dismemberment of the Polish state did not end artistic activity. Many court artists and architects left Warsaw and spread the Neoclassical style developed there to the provinces. Stanisław Zawadzki (1743–1806) designed the Palladian house at *Lubostroń* (1795–1800), and Jakub Kubicki (1758–1833) designed the similarly Palladian palace of *Białaczów* (1797–1800) (though he is better known for the *Belweder, Warsaw*, 1818–22). The most prominent architect at the turn of the century was Chrystian Piotr Aigner (1746–1841). His circular church designs (*Puławy*, 1800–03, and *St Alexander, Warsaw*, 1818–25) (plate 4), refer to the Pantheon in Rome, and the façade of *St Anne, Warsaw* (1786–8), designed in collaboration with the influential dilettante Stanisław Kostka Potocki (1757–1821), is indebted to Palladio and contrasts with the austerity of Aigner's much later remodelling of its bell tower (1820–1). Aigner's work can also be found at the palaces of *Wilanów*, *Łańcut* and *Igołomia* as well as the *Koniecpolski Palace* in *Warsaw*.

Early 19th Century

In Congress Poland (1815–30) Neoclassicism was the style of architecture favoured by the authorities. In Warsaw, besides Aigner and Kubicki, there were Italian newcomers such as Enrico Marconi (1792–1863) (remodelling of the *Pac Palace*, 1824–6) and above all the young Antonio Corazzi (1792–1877), the designer of austere, French-inspired Neoclassical buildings including the *Treasury* (1824–30) and the *Great Theatre* (1826–33) (plate 5), as well as numerous official buildings in provincial centres throughout the kingdom. Francesco Maria Lanci (1799–1875) was inspired by the English Picturesque in his Gothic Revival castle at *Zagórzany* (1834–9) and eclecticism characterizes his later work at *Wilanów*. Another historicist was Adam Idźkowski (1798–1879) (*Skierniewice Railway Station*, 1846).

The greatest architect working in Poland in the early 19th century was the Prussian Karl Friedrich Schinkel (1781–1841). Many of his public buildings in Prussian territory are neo-Gothic, influenced by his restoration work at Malbork: *Kołobrzeg Town Hall* and the *Grammar School, Gdańsk* (1837). He also worked for Polish patrons, designing the picturesque *Kórnik Castle*, the timber hunting lodge at *Antonin*, and the church at *Krzeszowice*. Perhaps his finest building in present-day Poland is the great neo-Gothic palace of *Kamieniec Ząbkowicki* (1838–63) in Silesia, now ruined.

Most prominent of the Austrian architects active in southwestern Poland was Peter von Nobile (1774–1854) who designed the *Potocki Chapel, Wawel Cathedral* (1832–40).

The cool classicism of the sculpture of the Dane Bertel Thorvaldsen (1768–1844) was much admired in early 19th-century Poland (*statues* of Józef Poniatowski and Copernicus in *Warsaw* and of Włodimierz Potocki, *Wawel Cathedral*). In *Poznań* the Polish nobles who built the *Golden Chapel* commissioned statues of the early Polish princes from the leading Berlin sculptor Christian Daniel Rauch (1777–1857).

In painting the Romantic-heroic manner came to the fore. Outstanding among Polish painters was Piotr Michałowski (1800–55), whose dashing brushstrokes record deeds of Polish arms and peasant scenes, and Henryk Rodakowski (1823–94).

Later 19th Century

Painting was dominated by the massive patriotic canvases of Jan Matejko (1836–93) of Kraków, whose depictions of scenes from Polish history did much to stir national feeling, in the same way that Henryk Sienkiewicz brought history to life in his novels. Some of his greatest paintings are in the *Sukiennice Museum* in *Kraków*, notably the incident-packed *Prussian Homage*. In contrast to the sometimes bombastic character of Matejko's historical vision, the work of Aleksander Gierymski (1850–1901), reflecting a more

Positivist approach, concentrated on the depiction of everyday scenes in Warsaw.

In architecture eclecticism predominated. In Warsaw the Marconi dynasty of architects played a leading role. Enrico built the classical *Hotel Europejski* and designed the Gothic remodelling of the *Mokotów Palace* (1860–65). His sons Leonard (1835–99) and Władysław Marconi (1848–1915) followed their father as architects at *Wilanów*. Towards the end of the century there were several architectural trends. Full-blown neo-Renaissance can be seen in the *Zachęta Building, Warsaw* (1898–1900) by Stefan Szyller (1857–1933), while the *Church of the Saviour, Warsaw* (1902) by Józef Pius Dziekoński (1844–1927) and others, has something of the Polish Renaissance style. In the *Zakopane* area Stanisław Witkiewicz (1851–1915) was turning to vernacular timber architecture for his villas and churches (*Willa Pod Jedlami*, 1897 (plate 52), and *Jaszczurówka Chapel* (colour plate 12)). The influence of the Vienna Secession could be felt in *Kraków* in such buildings as the *Old Theatre* (1903–6) by Tadeusz Stryjeński (1849–1943) and Franciszek Mączyński (1874–1947) with its sinuous decoration. The most complete surviving example of Cracovian Art Nouveau decoration is the *Jama Michalika café (c.*1905). The Warsztaty Krakowskie (Kraków Workshops) were founded on the model of the Wiener Werkstätte.

The most original architectural decoration of the period is by the Cracovian painter and writer Stanisław Wyspiański (1869–1907) (self-portrait page 105), a leading figure in the *Młoda Polska* (Young Poland) movement, which sought to regenerate the arts in Poland, and was based in Kraków. His murals and stained glass in the *Franciscan Church, Kraków* (1896–1902) are particularly impressive. There is a *museum* dedicated to Wyspiański in *Kraków* and his paintings and delicate pastels can be seen in the major galleries. Like Wyspiański, Józef Mehoffer (1869–1946) had worked as Matejko's assistant on the decoration of *St Mary's Kraków*. His

Art Nouveau canvases have a bizarre visionary quality (*Strange Garden*, 1903, *National Museum, Warsaw*). Jacek Malczewski (1854–1929) produced a peculiarly Polish blend of Romantic nationalism and dreamlike symbolism (*Melancholy*, 1894, *National Museum, Poznań*). Józef Pankiewicz (1866–1940) and Władysław Podkowiński (1866–95) brought the influence of French Impressionism to Poland.

Early 20th Century

Some of the most striking early 20th-century architecture was in *Wrocław* (then Breslau), where the *Jahrhunderthalle* (1913) by Max Berg (1870–1947) is remarkable for its bold use of concrete.

After the First World War Warsaw expanded rapidly. Public architecture in the newly independent Poland after the war adopted a stripped classical style which can be seen in the *Education Ministry* (1927–30) by Zdzisław Mączeński (1878–1961) and the *National Museum* (1927–34) by Tadeusz Tołwiński (1887–1951) in *Warsaw*, and the *National Museum* in *Kraków* (1936–9) by Bolesław Szmit (born 1908) and others. The ideas of the Modern Movement were taken up by Polish architects, most notably in the developments by the Warsaw Housing Cooperative at *Żoliborz* by Barbara Brukalska (1899–1980) and her husband Stanisław Brukalski (1894–1967).

A group of avant-garde artists, among them Zbigniew Pronaszko (1885–1958) and Tytus Czyżewski (1880–1945), came together in 1917 calling themselves the Polish Expressionists, though they were influenced less by German Expressionism than by Cubism. They soon renamed themselves the Polish Formists. The leading theorists and painters among the Formists were Leon Chwistek (1884–1944), whose work tended towards Futurism and Stanisław Ignacy Witkiewicz (Witkacy) (1885–1939), whose disturbing paintings, like his novels, have a grotesque and surreal quality (*Temptation of St Anthony*, 1916–21, *National Gallery, Kraków*).

149

Mieczysław Szczuka (1898–1927), a member of the avant-garde Blok group formed in Warsaw in 1924, was the leading artist of Constructivism. The pure abstraction of Malevich's Suprematism influenced art in Poland through the work of Władysław Strzemiński (1893–1952) and his wife Katarzyna Kobro (1898–1951). One of the most interesting of the Polish artists who settled in Paris in this period was Tadeusz Makowski (1882–1932), whose strange paintings explore the world of children and are influenced by folk art.

While Warsaw and Łódź were the centres of avant-garde art between the wars, Kraków was the main centre of Colourism, which developed in the 1930's; its purest exponent was perhaps Karol Larisch (1902–35). Wojciech Kossak (1856–1942) continued the tradition of painting patriotic battle scenes, but the most influential representational artists were the portraitist Tadeusz Pruszkowski (1888–1942), Bolesław Cybis (1895-1957) and Jan Zamoyski (1901–86).

Later 20th Century

After the destruction of Poland's architectural heritage in the Second World War the achievements of the restorers who reconstructed the ruined cities were remarkable. In central *Warsaw* the old houses and palaces were rebuilt on the foundations surviving beneath piles of rubble, using old inventories, descriptions and pictures. In *Gdańsk* more freedom was allowed to the architects who recreated the old merchants' houses. New housing and industry were a high priority. The most notorious new development was *Nowa Huta*, the industrial suburb of Kraków. Impressive buildings were erected in the newly built cities, notably the flying-saucer-shaped *Sports and Entertainment Hall, Katowice* (1965–71) (plate 82) by Maciej Gintowt and others.

The most prominent building from the preceding Stalinist period is the *Palace of Culture* (1952–5) in *Warsaw* by the Soviet architect Lev Rudniev (1885–1956) which includes allusions to the decoration of the Kraków Sukiennice in its otherwise Russian design. In the early 1950's there was an attempt to impose Socialist Realism as the official style in painting and sculpture, which resulted in works such as *Pass Me a Brick* by Aleksander Kobzdej (1920–72). But after 1956 stylistic pluralism was accepted. Polish graphic art achieved a great reputation through the poster designs of Henryk Tomaszewski (b.1914), Jan Lenica (b.1928) and many others.

Some of the most striking works since the war have been the monuments to the victims of the concentration camps and ghettoes, such as the *Majdanek Monument* (1969) (illustration, page 541) by Wiktor Tołkin (b.1922) and Janusz Dembek (b.1929) and the *Treblinka Monument* (1964) by Franciszek Duszeńko (b.1925) and Adam Haupt (b.1920) (illustration, page 247). More recent examples of monumental art are the *Monument to the Shipyard Workers* (1980) (illustration, page 366) in Gdańsk by Bogdan Pietruszka, erected at the demand of Solidarity, and the *Monument to the Heroes of the Warsaw Uprising* (1989) by Wincenty Kućma.

Since the fall of communism, there has been little architecture of merit, although central Warsaw has been transformed by some ostentatious office blocks and controversial public buildings, such as the *Supreme Court Building* (1991-99) by Marek Budziński. Meanwhile, some of the old regime's relics have been moved to the Museum of Socialist Realism at Kozłówka Palace, near Lubartów (see page 544).

Finally, no account of Polish art could be complete without mentioning the superb achievements of Polish folk art, where unbroken traditions reach back a thousand years or more. The 'vernacular' architecture in Zakopane shows how folk art is consciously used in a high art context, but the visitor will also see many genuine artefacts, notably the wayside shrines (*kapliczki*). There are many good folk museums and skansens (open-air museums of vernacular architecture), such as the one in the grounds of the Missionaries' Seminary, Łowicz (see page 231).

Sebastian Wormell

Warsaw (Warszawa)

Warsaw is situated in the middle of the Mazovian plain, at the heart of Poland. Although it only became the country's capital in about 1600, and so did not begin to play a major part in Polish history until a relatively late stage, it soon developed into one of the most important capitals in Europe. It remains the heart of Polish nationalism and the Polish state, symbolized by Warsaw's resurrection after the last war.

Remains of Neolithic settlements (c.10,000 BC) have been found on the site of the present city: on the eastern bank of the Vistula (Polish: Wisła) stood a fortification with an adjacent trading settlement (Stare Bródno). According to legend this was the home of Wars and his sister Sawa, from whose names the earliest form of the city's name, Warszewa or Warszowa, was supposed to be derived. In the 12th century villages and markets grew up on both sides of the Vistula. The development of these settlements was due mainly to the trade that flowed along the routes from Wielkopolska (Greater Poland) and Silesia (Polish: Śląsk) to Lithuania and Muscovy. A town was founded here at the beginning of the 14th century, and as early as 1408 the construction of the New Town (Nowe Miasto) began on the land adjoining the Old Town (Stare Miasto). In 1413 Duke Janusz I of Mazovia (Polish: Mazowsze), moved the capital of his duchy from Czersk to Warsaw, and built his residence and a wooden chapel on the site of the present Royal Castle. The streets around these buildings were laid out on a chequerboard plan with a rectangular market place, next to which a town hall was built in 1459 (no longer extant), and the whole complex was surrounded by an earth rampart.

When the last two Mazovian dukes, the brothers Stanisław and Janusz, died (by poison) in 1524 and 1526 they left no heirs, so Mazovia passed to the Polish crown. This acquisition was celebrated by the ceremonial entry of King Zygmunt I Stary into Warsaw Castle in August 1526. The union of Mazovia with the Polish crown strengthened its links with other regions of Poland; its central position in the Polish-Lithuanian state made it an economic and political centre whose influence extended throughout Poland.

From 1569 onwards Warsaw was the permanent meeting place of the combined Diets (Sejm) of Poland and Lithuania, and from 1573 the 'Electoral Field' at Wola, to the west of the city, became the site where the kings were chosen by a vast and colourful concourse of nobles. Between 1598 and 1611 King Zygmunt III Waza moved the royal residence from Kraków to Warsaw and remodelled the 13th-century ducal castle. From the middle of the

Warsaw, engraving by N. Perelle after a drawing by E. J. Dahlberg, 1650

16th century onwards there was a continual expansion and transformation of the Old and New Towns. The Gothic burghers' houses on Rynek Starego Miasta (Old Town Square) underwent Renaissance and Baroque remodelling, the nobility established their town residences in the city, and new palaces and churches sprang up, especially in the district to the south of the Old Town. On the right bank of the Vistula the separate town of Praga developed, linked to the left bank by the first permanent bridge in 1573.

Henceforth the destiny of Poland was almost always linked with that of Warsaw. In the middle of the 17th century the development of the town was interrupted by the Swedish invasion; later, in the 18th century, Warsaw became an important cultural and economic centre, and a centre of progressive political ideas. The great political treatises of the reformers Kołłątaj and Staszic were written here, and it was here that the Constitution of 3 May was adopted. With the incorporation of Praga the various districts of the city grew

together to form a single entity. On the rubble of the buildings destroyed by the Swedish invasions, new, often more beautiful buildings arose: houses, palaces and churches. A key date in the later development of the city is 1757, when a grand new thoroughfare was laid out to the south of the Old Town. Named ul. Marszałkowska after the great Crown Marshal Franciszek Bieleński, it ran through his own development, Bielino. (Like many of the magnates of the 16th and 17th centuries Bieleński built on his own wards (*jurydyki*), since they were exempt from municipal control.)

The Second Partition of Poland in 1793 brought another interruption in the city's development. It was followed in 1794 by the Kościuszko Uprising and the massacre by the Russians in Praga. Then came the Third Partition in 1795 after which the city came under Prussian rule for a few years. Warsaw resumed its role as a capital, first of the Duchy of Warsaw created by Napoleon in 1807, and then – after 1815 – of the Kingdom of Poland

Warsaw, the Jewish population being deported from the Ghetto before the outbreak of the Uprising of 1943

(Congress Poland), nominally independent but in fact under Russian domination. It became the centre of the national and social liberation struggle, with the November Rising of 1830–31, the January Rising of 1863, and the emergence of the first Polish workers' movement. It was in Warsaw in 1882 that Ludwik Waryński founded the first Polish socialist party 'Wielki Proletariat' ('Great Proletariat'). The 19th century also saw a great increase in the Jewish population; by 1919 about 40 per cent of Warsaw's inhabitants were Jews.

Once Poland regained its independence in 1918–19, the city developed at breathtaking speed. New administrative buildings, residential districts, schools, theatres and museums were built. The city's boundaries were extended. Stefan Starzyński, the City President from 1934, did much for Warsaw and played a leading part in its defence in September 1939.

The years of the German occupation were a period of bloody terror in Warsaw. By the end of the war the city had suffered massive loss of life (approximately 800,000 dead – half the population) and enormous damage to its fabric. Many monuments, works of art, libraries, archives and museums were destroyed or looted. But a large number of citizens responded to the mass executions of hostages, forced labour and deportations to concentration camps, by joining in the resistance movement. This encompassed all aspects of life: the 'Flying University', for example, outfaced Nazi determination to extinguish Polish culture, and was to be a vital element for the continuation of intellectual life in Poland after the war. From 1941 onwards the activities of the underground organizations intensified. The Jewish community, the largest in Europe, had been penned up in the ghetto since 1940, but took up arms in April/May 1943, after more than 300,000 had already been murdered at Treblinka, and fought a brave and unequal battle. Thirteen thousand Jews were killed in the Uprising and the remainder were transported to Treblinka. The first day of the Ghetto Uprising, 19 April, is commemorated by Jews as Holocaust Remembrance Day. In 1944 the Home Army (*Armia Krajowa* or AK), which had borne the brunt of the resistance against the German occupation, decided to strike in advance of the Allies' arrival, in order to establish a democratic, pluralistic state and avoid Soviet control. The Warsaw Uprising of the AK lasted from 1 August to 2 October 1944 and became a by-word for hopeless struggle against the Nazi machinery of annihilation. As the Red Army stood passively by, the uprising was brutally put down by German units under the command of SS General Erich von dem Bach-Zelewski. More people were killed than died at Hiroshima. The surviving inhabitants were then moved out, and on Hitler's orders the city was systematically razed to the ground. By the time liberation came, on 17 January 1945, 90 per cent of central Warsaw had been destroyed, and only 7 per cent of buildings were still habitable. Nevertheless Poles were determined that Warsaw should remain the capital. Reconstruction was enormously expensive, both of money and of communal effort; but it was achieved with remarkable speed, and Polish workmanship, as much as Polish tenacity, has gained worldwide admiration. It is hard to believe, walking through the Old Town or along Nowy Świat, that practically all the buildings are less than 50 years old.

Stare Miasto (Old Town)

The tour of the Old Town begins in Pl. Zamkowy (Castle Square; colour plate 13). This originally served as the forecourt to the Royal Castle and to the gate on the road leading south out of the city (now ul. Krakowskie Przedmieście). It was laid out on a regular plan in 1644 as a suitably grand setting for the Sigismund Column. The square was enlarged in 1818–21 by the architect Jakub Kubicki, when it attained its present dimensions, though the postwar road which cuts across its southern end has blurred the regularity of its triangular shape.

In the centre of the square stands the **Kolumna Zygmunta III (Sigismund Column)** (1), 22 metres high. Erected in 1633–4 by King Władysław IV Waza in memory of his father, who had established the Swedish Vasa dynasty on the Polish throne, it is one of Poland's earliest and most famous political monuments. The column was designed by the

architects Agostino Locci the Elder and Constantino Tencalla, and the bronze statue is by Clemente Molli. After suffering severe damage in January 1945, the column had to be replaced and the statue restored.

The east side of the square is now once again occupied by the Early Baroque façade of the **Zamek Królewski (Royal Castle)** (2). In 1939 most of the building was burned out after bombardment, though a large part of the furnishings was saved. In the autumn of 1944, in the aftermath of the Uprising, the castle was blown up. After much controversy reconstruction eventually began in 1971. The aim was to recreate the castle's external appearance in the 17th century, but at the same time care was taken to represent every phase of a complicated building history (particularly visible in the courtyard elevations).

This history began in the 13th century with a wooden fort built by the Dukes of Mazovia on the bank of the Vistula. Around the middle of the 14th century the Wieża Grodzka (Town Tower) on the southern edge of the site was added. At the beginning of the 15th century the Gothic Great Courtyard *(Curia Maior)* was created as the ducal residence, followed shortly afterwards by the Lesser Courtyard *(Curia Minor)* and subsidiary buildings. These formed the nucleus of the complex, in the area now occupied by the present northeast range; Gothic vaulting in the cellars and the remains of the *Curia Maior* have been preserved. King Zygmunt II August had the castle remodelled as a magnificent Renaissance palace, and added the northeast range. The architect was Giovanni Battista Quadro, who had made his name as the architect of Poznań town hall not long before. Shortly afterwards Zygmunt III Waza moved his court to Warsaw,

The erection of the Sigismund Column, drawing by the architect A. Locci

Transport of the granite block for the re-construction of the Sigismund Column destroyed in 1945; photograph, 1948

and made the castle the seat of the Polish kings, and the administrative centre of Poland. From 1598 to 1619 Zygmunt extended it to its present form, with five ranges and a gate tower in the centre of the main façade. Again the architects were Italian: Giacopo Rotondo and Giovanni Trevano. The present exteriors recreate the monumental severity of the Vasa style, which eschewed decoration and relied on balanced proportions for its effect.

During the Swedish invasion of 1655–6 the castle did not escape damage. For a time the kings resided elsewhere (Jan III Sobieski, for example, moved his residence to Wilanów, see pages 217 ff). August II Mocny (the Strong), the first King of Poland of the Saxon dynasty, moved back into the Royal Castle. Since it was by now rather old-fashioned and unsuited for the requirements of a Baroque court, the castle was modernized by his successor, August III. Between 1741 and 1747 the architects Gaetano Chiaveri and Antonio Solari gave the northeast range a Rococo remodelling, and created a sequence of splendid state rooms with a ballroom, gallery and chapel, and a façade with three bays projecting at each end and a five-bay ballroom projecting in the centre, overlooking the Vistula.

Stanisław August Poniatowski, who had a passionate interest in architecture, continued the transformation of the castle (1767–86). Nothing came of the grandiose designs created by the young French architect Victor Louis (later the architect of the Palais-Royal in Paris), whom Stanisław August invited to Warsaw soon after his accession. Instead, work began with a redecoration of the residential apartments in the south range, which had been gutted by fire in 1767. Inspired by the French example, the king gathered a circle of

157

*Royal Castle a Private Chapel b Canaletto Room c Old Audience Chamber d Royal Bed-
chamber e Dressing Room f Study g Ballroom h Green Salon i Yellow Salon j Knights' Hall
k Throne Room l Conference Cabinet m Marble Hall*

outstanding artists at his court: Jacopo Fontana, Domenico Merlini, Johann Christian
Kamsetzer, Marcello Bacciarelli, Jan Bogumił Plersch, André LeBrun, Giacopo Monaldi
and Bernardo Bellotto (known confusingly as Canaletto). In the final years of the Polish
monarchical republic they created magnificent Late Baroque and Neoclassical interiors, in
which architecture, mural painting and sculptural decoration fused into an harmonious
whole.

The 19th century saw several more alterations made to the structure and decoration of
the building, but the east range now presents the appearance it had in the time of Stanisław
August. Many of the fittings, furniture and paintings, particularly in Stanisław August's
apartments, are original, having survived the war and been incorporated in the rebuilding.

The King's *Private Chapel* (a) on the first floor of the Wieża Grodzka, the Town Tower
at the south end of the enfilade of rooms, was decorated in 1774–7 by Domenico Merlini.
It is a small, square room with a semicircular sanctuary, but it creates an effect of both
monumentality and lightness. The window niches reduce the impression of narrowness,

and in the sanctuary a coffered dome supported by free-standing columns conceals the boundaries of the space. The delicate colours typical of Neoclassicism add to the lightness of the effect. An urn here contains the heart of Tadeusz Kościuszko, the leader of the 1794 insurrection and hero of the American War of Independence.

The *Sala Canaletta* (Canaletto Room) (b) serves as an anteroom to the chapel, linking it to the adjoining royal apartments. Its walls are covered with city views and landscapes of Warsaw and its environs by the Venetian painter Bernardo Bellotto, the nephew of the more famous Canaletto (Giovanni Antonio Canal), whose name he appropriated and by which he is generally known in Poland. These paintings were extensively used in the reconstruction of the city. There is also a version of Bellotto's 'Election Sejm of Stanisław August'. The *Old Audience Chamber* (c) is a fine example of Polish Neoclassicism, known as the 'Stanisław August Style' after its principal patron. The architectural articulation of the walls and ceiling, by Merlini, is at once delicate and severe. It incorporates a programme of paintings by Marcello Bacciarelli in praise of Stanisław August. The large ceiling painting celebrates the flourishing of culture, sciences, agriculture and trade in Poland, while the overdoors have allegories of the ruler's virtues: Bravery, Wisdom, Fear of God, and Justice. The rich parquet floor is one of several in the castle to use a variety of different woods.

Directly adjoining the Audience Chamber is the *Royal Bedchamber* (d), which had a public function as the setting for the ceremonial levées. Its decoration is one of the first that Merlini created here (1772–4), and a comparison between it and the Audience Chamber shows how the architect developed. Here his treatment of the walls is still in the tradition of the Late Baroque. The paintings by Marcello Bacciarelli show Old Testament scenes: Esther falling at the feet of Ahasuerus; Rebecca and Eliezer; Hagar and the Angel; and Hagar with Ishmael.

The sequence of rooms in the King's private apartments concludes, in the usual way, with his *Dressing Room* (e) and *Study* (f) which is hung with paintings by Stanisław August's court artists.

From here we enter the Saxon Wing. Passing through the *Green Salon* (h) and *Yellow Salon* (i), we come to the most sumptuous of the castle's interiors, the *Marble Hall* (m). The decoration was originally created for Władyslaw IV by Giovanni Battista Ghisleni in 1640–43, with portraits of Władysław's royal ancestors. It was altered in 1771 by Jacopo Fontana, when the old portraits were replaced by a sequence of Polish kings from Bolesław Chobry to August III painted by Bacciarelli. The room was destroyed in 1831 on the orders of Tsar Nicholas I and was not reconstructed until the 1980's, when the grey marble cladding of the walls was recreated. Bacciarelli's full-length portrait of Stanisław August now has pride of place.

The adjoining room, overlooking the Vistula, is the *Knights' Hall* (j) decorated with large canvases by Bacciarelli recalling great events in Polish history, and portraits of great Poles in the form of busts and roundel paintings. The statue of Chronos supporting the spherical clock is by Giacomo Monaldi, while the figure of Fame is by André LeBrun. The Knights'

Hall originally served as the waiting room for the Throne Room (k). This has a small octagonal *Conference Cabinet* (l) decorated with gilded panels of grotesques painted by Jan Jerzy Plersch and hung with portraits of the European rulers who were Stanisław August's contemporaries. They include Frederick II of Prussia (by Friedrich Lohrmann), Catherine II of Russia (by Antoni Albertrandi) and the British King George III (by Thomas Gainsborough).

Beyond the Knights' Hall is the largest room in the State Apartments. The *Ballroom* (g) received its architectural form in the mid-18th century, during the reign of August III. It forms the centre-piece of the sequence of rooms created at that time and is expressed on the exterior by the middle pavilion on the Vistula façade. The internal decorations, however, are due to the energies of Stanisław August Poniatowski. On his accession to the throne he at once set about grand projects for his palace, for which Jan Bogumił Plersch and the king's young friend Victor Louis provided plans. But in the aftermath of the First Partition, and of a fire, remodelling was limited to redecoration, for which a competition was announced in 1777, in which Ephraim Schroeger and Domenico Merlini took part, as did J. B. Plersch. Merlini's was the winning design, and work began in the same year. Johann Christian Kamsetzer designed some details of the decoration, Johann Michael Graff executed the plasterwork. The conception followed the ideals of the High Baroque: the wall set back behind a surrounding order of detached double columns raised on plinths, supporting a prominent entabla-ture. The window openings which appear as arcades on the exterior of the projecting bay are expressed internally as blind niches; the corners are rounded. The painting in the ceiling is an alle-gory glorifying the King. again by Marcello Bacciarelli. Above the entrance is a portrait medallion of the King held by the geniuses of Peace and Justice. The two figures flanking the door (like the over-door they are by André LeBrun) are Apollo, the god of the arts, and Minerva, the goddess of the sciences; they represent the intellectual revival that Stanisław August worked hard to foster in Poland. It was in this room, at a reception in 1806, that Napoleon made his celebrated remarks on the beauty of Polish women.

In the north range, the *Prince's Apartments* now house a collection of paintings by Jan Matejko, including the famous 'Rejtan'. An exhibition in the medieval vaults has a moving dis-play of silver recovered from the ruins of the Castle and Old Town.

Thr *Galeria Lanckorońskich* displays part of the Lanckoroński family's impressive collec-tion of paintings, donated to the state by Professor Karolina Lanckorońska in 1994. It includes fifteen paintings once owned by Stanisław August, among them two Rembrandts. In the recently opened *Galeria Sztuki Zdobniczej (Gallery of Applied Art)* are good examples of 18th-century Polish glass, as well as bronzes, porcelain, silver and jewellery .

The Castle has been the setting for many important events in Poland's history. It was in the *Senate Hall* in the west range on 3 May 1791 that the new Constitution, the first such codified constitution in Europe, was adopted. In the period of Congress Poland the Sejm and the Senate met here. During the Second Republic (1918–39) the Castle was the seat of the President of the Republic. A reconstruction of the study of President Ignacy Mościnski (1926-1939) can be vis-ited. There is also an exhibition of the insignia of the Polish Government in Exile in London, which were ceremoniously returned to Poland in 1990.

Just below the Castle, and now uncomfortably close to the Trasa WZ (Aleje Solidarności), a busy throughway cut through the centre of Warsaw after the war, is the Pałac Lubomirskich (Lubomirski Palace), or **'Pałac Pod Blachą' ('Under the Tin Roof')** (3), now part of the Royal Castle. Originally a simple 17th-century house, it came into royal possession in 1776 and was remodelled by Domenico Merlini as a palace with three ranges linked to the Royal Castle by a long, narrow, library wing. Later it became the residence of Prince Józef Poniatowski; today it houses the magnificent Sahakian collection of Caucasian rugs.

Ul. Swiętojańska (St John Street) is one of the oldest thoroughfares in the city. It links the Castle with Rynek Starego Miasta (Old Town Square) and leads further north into Nowe Miasto (New Town), along the course of an old road linking Czersk and Zakroczym.

On the right of the street are two interesting churches. The first is the **Katedra św. Jana (St John's Cathedral)** (4), a cathedral since 1798, but originally a collegiate church. Its history goes back to the time of the foundation of the city itself. At the beginning of the 15th century Duke Janusz I of Mazovia had a stone church built to replace an earlier wooden one. This occupied more or less the area of the present choir. There followed several alterations and extensions, with the vaults being constructed by masons from Gdańsk. At the end of the 16th century Anna Jagiellonka built a passage connecting the church with her rooms in the Royal Castle; the church now had the double function of parish church and palace chapel. Later a tall bell-tower was added, but shortly afterwards the church was badly damaged by fire, and in 1602 it collapsed completely. Gradually, in the course of the 17th and 18th centuries, it was rebuilt, and then in 1836–40 the whole building and façade were totally remodelled in an English Gothic style by Adam Idźkowski. The cathedral was blown up in 1944. The rebuilding in 1947–56 recreated the exterior in its original, plain Gothic form, without the later accretions.

It is a three-aisled hall church with fine star vaults and a bright three-sided choir. The interior contains a few remnants of the old furnishings, mostly heavily restored or reconstructed. The Baroque choir stalls, a gift from Jan III Sobieski, were reconstructed, but the font of 1632, signed by its maker Petrus Noire Gallus, survived. The Late Gothic crucifix in the Chapel of Christ was made by a Nuremberg workshop. In the south aisle is the Renaissance tomb of the last Dukes of Mazovia, Stanisław and Janusz, and the monument (designed by Bertel Thorvaldsen) to Stanisław Malachowski (1736–1809), the Marshal (i.e. Speaker) of the Four Years' Sejm, who played a prominent part in the drafting of the 1791 Constitution. The westernmost chapel in the north aisle contains the tomb of Cardinal Stefan Wyszyński, Primate of Poland for much of the communist period.

The crypt contains the tombs of the Bishops of Warsaw, as well as those of the historical novelist Henryk Sienkiewicz and Gabriel Narutowicz, a distinguished scientist who was elected as the first President of the Republic in 1922, but was assassinated shortly after his inauguration. A number of plaques have been placed here commemorating the priests of the archdiocese of Warsaw murdered by the Nazis during the Second World War, and the scouts of the Wigry Battalion who died in the Warsaw Uprising.

Next door to the cathedral is the little **Kościół Jezuitów (Jesuit Church)** (5), its busy pilastered and pinnacled front contrasting with its more austere neighbour. An aisleless

Old Town Square, elevation of reconstructed houses on the Dekert Side

building with a row of chapels on its north side, a chancel lit by a remarkably tall dome, and the tallest tower in the Old Town, it was built between 1608 and 1620 and endowed by King Zygmunt III Waza and a number of high-ranking city officials. Planning had already begun in 1598, immediately after the arrival of the Jesuits in Poland.

From here it is only a few steps to Old Town Square, but it is worth making a detour through the narrow alleys.

Passing under the gateway in the bell-tower of St John's and along the little ul. Dziekania the visitor reaches ul. Kanonia. At its entrance is the arcaded passageway, built by Anna Jagiellonka, through which the dukes and kings could pass unseen from the castle into the church. Beyond it is a picturesque square lined with Baroque canons' houses (all rebuilt 1958–61). The only reminder of the cemetery that was here until 1780 is a Rococo statue of the Virgin set up in 1771. No. 8 was the home of Stanisław Staszic (1755–1826) who, inspired by the French *philosophes*, in particular Rousseau, drew up a radical programme for reform in his 'Warning to Poland' published in 1790; he was also a founder of the Society of the Friends of Learning in 1808. Next door, at No. 10, lived the historian and first president of the Society of the Friends of Learning, Bishop Jan Chrzciciel Albertrandi, and at No. 12 the poet and preacher Archbishop Jan Paweł Woronicz (1757–1829). In the centre of the square is a Warsaw bell dating from 1646.

The house on the corner of ul. Jezuicka (No. 2), dating from the mid-16th century, is worth a glance for its beautiful window niche and an oriel window added in the 17th century. The neighbouring house (No. 4) with a columned façade was where two remarkable brothers, the Bishops Ludwik and Andrzej Załuski, founded their 'Gymnasium Zaluscianum' in the early 18th century. From 1773 it housed the first ministry of education in Europe (the Commission for National Education).

To return to the cathedral the visitor turns into ul. Piwna (Beer Street), which contains the imposing building of the **Kościół św. Marcina (Church of St Martin)** (6) with its adjoining former Augustinian monastery. Founded in the 14th century by Duke Ziemiowit of Mazovia, the original Gothic complex was remodelled several times. In the post-war rebuilding it was returned to its final, Late Baroque form; a few pieces of Gothic masonry were uncovered. The furnishings are modern.

The buildings of ul. Piwna all go back to the 15th century. The street's delightful appearance was reconstructed as a whole between 1952 and 1954. Going north from St Martin's we reach, at the next corner, Zapiecek, a little square in which a well-known art gallery of the same name is to be found.

The western extension of Zapiecek forms ul. Piekarska (Baker Street), which runs into ul. Podwale ('Under the Ramparts') which used to be outside the old city walls.

On the walls stands the **Pomnik Kilińskiego (Jan Kiliński Monument)** (7) made by Stanisław Jackowski (1936, moved here in 1959) to commemorate the cobbler who led the revolt of Warsaw citizenry against Tsarist rule in 1794. Beside it is the *Museum of Handicrafts* with a collection of old clocks.

From Zapiecek the view extends to the **Rynek Starego Miasta (Old Town Square)** (colour plate 15, plate 7) which was laid out around 1400 as a rectangular space in the severely geometric grid plan of the Old Town, with two streets at right angles entering it at each corner. The Town Hall stood in the middle of the square until its demolition in 1817. Until the beginning of the 19th century the square had been the centre of political, administrative, economic and cultural life in the town and was the setting of several historic events. It was here in 1764 that the citizens received the newly elected King Stanisław August Poniatowski, and here in 1794 that the Black Procession led by the City President Jan Dekert set off to demand rights for the citizens. Each of the four sides of the square is named after a prominent figure in the reform movement of the late 18th century: the east side after Franciszek Barss, a champion of civil rights during the Four Years' *Sejm*; the side opposite is called after Hugo Kołłątaj, Rector of Kraków University and one of the ideologists behind the 3 May Constitution; the south side after Ignacy Zakrzewski, the President of the city at the time of the Kościuszko Uprising in 1794; and the north side after Jan Dekert. Following heavy damage in 1944 the market square was reconstructed in the years up to 1953, with many Polish artists involved in the recreation of the façade decoration.

We begin our tour of the square on the *Kołłątaj Side*. No. 21, remodelled, like many of the burghers' houses on the square, after a fire around 1700, has preserved a Gothic doorway and the cellar vaults of the original house. The 'Krokodyl' café and restaurant now occupy the building. The neighbouring house (No. 21a), which dates from the 17th century, was the home of Hugo Kołłątaj in 1812. The Fukier House (No. 27), named after a descendant of the Fuggers of Augsburg, to whom it belonged from 1810, contains a three-hundred-year-old wine cellar ('Winiarnia Fukierowska'). The façade, with an upper storey rising above a pitched roof, as was common with business premises in the 18th century, has fine Neoclassical decoration, and the interior has also been reconstructed in this style. The corner house 'Pod św. Anną' ('Under St Anne'; No. 31) is one of the few houses in the square to have preserved much of its Gothic form; alterations are limited to a few details: in 1635 the height of the building was raised, the shape of the windows and doorway changed and an oriel window was added to the side façade. The statue of St Anne with the Virgin and Child in the corner niche dates from the first half of the 16th century.

The interiors of the houses along the *Dekert Side* were linked together in the post-war reconstruction to house the **Muzeum Historyczne Miasta Warszawy (Historical Museum of the City of Warsaw)** (8). On display here are plans, views, models and portraits documenting the history of the city from its beginnings until the post-war period. The entrance is at No. 42, which underwent a Late Renaissance remodelling in the 17th century for the Royal Postmaster Montelupi, a member of the polonized Italian family who were put in charge of the Polish postal service in the mid-16th century. The neighbouring house (No. 40), which also belonged to Montelupi for a time, has fine (reconstructed) sgraffito on its façade. The ground floor of No. 38 has retained Late Gothic vaulting, and there is also a fine wrought iron Rococo grille installed in 1735. The house known from its distinctive sign as 'Pod Murzynkiem' ('the Little Moor', No. 36) has a sgraffiti-decorated façade which dates from the Late Renaissance period (early 17th century). The initials I G are those of its owner, the vintner Jakub Gianotti. The next house but one, No. 32, merits particular attention for its richly decorated Late Renaissance façade (first half of the 17th century), and has retained its slightly later Early Baroque doorway and an attic; its builder Wojciech Baryczka was the purveyor of oats to the royal stables.

At the corner to the Barss Side is the entrance to the picturesque **Kamienne Schodki (Stone Steps)** (9) leading down the slope to the Vistula; they were already in existence around 1600.

On the *Barss Side*, in a house with remains of Gothic masonry and a 17th-century doorway (No. 20), is the **Muzeum Literatury im. Adama Mickiewicza (Adam Mickiewicz Museum of Literature)** (10), named after the most famous Polish poet of Romanticism (see page 101). The corner house (No. 2), which belonged to Franciszek Barss from 1780 to 1795, had to be completely rebuilt after the war; today it houses the Galeria Sztuki Nowoczenej (Gallery of Modern Art).

From here it is worth making a sortie into ul. Celna, a street laid out *c*.1300, leading to the city fortifications and Brama Gnojna (Dung Gate), which was demolished in 1830. The viewing terrace on the high bank gives a fine panorama over the Vistula and Praga on the other side of the river. Ul. Brzozowa, a turning on the left, originally ran along the city walls. Its left-hand side is made up of the picturesque backs of the burghers' houses which face the square, while the opposite side used to be lined with warehouses. At the corner with ul. Celna (where the Customs House stood) are the remains of a Gothic house uncovered in the course of the rebuilding.

We now return to the Rynek, to look at the *Zakrzewski Side*. No. 5, which now has an elegant Neoclassical façade, was once occupied by Wojciech Oczko, Court Physician to Zygmunt I Stary, Stefan Batory and Zygmunt III Waza; today it contains the popular 'Bazyliszek' ('Basilisk') Restaurant. The house at the corner (No. 13) has a 14th-century core, but is named 'Pod Lwem' ('the Lion') after the 18th-century relief on its façade. It was recreated after the war in the Late Renaissance form it was given in its last remodelling, and the façade painting by the Polish artist Zofia Stryjeńska, dating from 1928-9, was also replaced. A modern sundial has been added to the façade on ul. Świętojańska.

Walking northwards along ul. Nowomiejska, past fine Late Renaissance and Baroque patrician houses, we reach the **Barbakan (Barbican)** (11), a massive circular building which formed part of the city defences erected in the middle of the 16th century by Giovanni Battista da Venezia, a military architect brought from Venice. Around 1800 the Barbican was absorbed into the surrounding houses and used for residential purposes. In 1937-8 the building, including the moat and drawbridge, was cleared of its accretions. In the 1950's it was reconstructed in its original form, and today it is used as a hall for temporary exhibitions.

The ramparts give a good view of the **Kościół Paulinów św. Ducha (Paulite Church of the Holy Ghost)** (12), built in 1707-17 by the Italian architects Giuseppe Piola and Giuseppe Simone Bellotti. Since 1711 it has been the starting point for an annual pilgrimage to Częstochowa. Its gabled front with twin towers is restrained and harmonious in its use of pilasters, which give external expression to its three-aisled interior. The Baroque furnishings have been reconstructed; the most notable feature is an altar painting of the Crucified Christ by the greatest master of the Silesian Baroque, Michael Willmann, brought here from Lubiąż after the war.

Nowe Miasto (New Town) and Cytadela (Citadel)

On the north side of the Holy Ghost Church is the beginning of ul. Długa (Long Street), which was originally the road westwards out of the city. Its name dates from the 15th century; in the middle ages it was used as a market. It was given its present, Neoclassical appearance during the reign of Stanisław August. Among the famous people who lived here at No. 3, was Maurycy Mochnacki (1804-34), spokesman of the Patriotic Society, a brilliant young literary critic, political journalist and an activist in the November Uprising of 1830, when he wrote: 'Our life is already poetry. From now on, our metre will be the clash of swords and our rhyme the roar of guns.' No. 4, opposite, is the birthplace of his fellow patriot Joachim Lelewel (1786-1861), the founder of Polish historiography, member of the national government in 1830 and President of the Patriotic Society.

A few steps further on stands the imposing bulk of the **Pałac Raczyńskich (Raczyński Palace)**, (13) No. 7. Its present form is the result of Johann Christian Kamsetzer's thorough remodelling in 1786. The exterior articulation is a fine example of severe Neoclassicism; the features seem to be drawn on to the façade: the lines of the cornice, the windows simply cut into the wall with no decoration, the double-stepped centrepiece with its pilaster order and temple front. It was here in 1794 that Kościuszko's Supreme National Council met; the French Marshals Murat, Davout and Lannes stayed here after the Napoleonic army took Warsaw in 1806. In 1944 the building was used as a hospital for those wounded in the Uprising, and today it houses the State Archives.

Extending in front of the point where ul. Długa joins ul. Miodowa is the complex of the **Klasztor Pijarów (Piarist Monastery)** (14), with the Kościół Najświętszej Marii Panny Królowej Korony Polskiej (Church of the Blessed Virgin Mary, Queen of the Crown of Poland). After the suppression of the order in 1835, it became a Russian Orthodox church, and then, after 1918, a garrison church. Founded by King Jan II Kazimierz Waza, the building was completed in 1660–81; the façade is by Giuseppe Fontana and dates from 1712. After several later remodellings the monastery was returned to its original form when it was rebuilt in 1946–60. The magnificent, monumental Baroque façade is in the form of a colossal pedimented aedicule with paired pilasters, with a round-arched niche inserted, surmounted by two bell towers which are slightly set back. The rhythmic articulation of the façades of the symmetrical adjoining buildings tie the ensemble together visually. The interior is lined on either side by a row of chapels, and is now furnished with religious art brought from Lower Silesia (wings of a Late Gothic triptych, Baroque altar paintings).

Diagonally opposite is the elegant façade of the **Pałac Krasińskich (Krasiński Palace)** (15), also called the Pałac Rzeczypospolitej (Palace of the Republic), impressively sited behind a grand forecourt. Built in 1677–82 for the Crown Referendary Jan Dobrogost Krasiński, the palace is one of the foremost examples of Baroque architecture in Poland. It was designed by Tylman van Gameren of Utrecht, who settled in Poland in 1666 and became the leading master of Polish Baroque. In 1765 it was acquired by the state as the seat of government. Later alterations (1766–73 by Jacopo Fontana and 1783, after a fire, by Domenico Merlini) did not alter the essential layout. After severe damage in the Second World War the palace was reconstructed between 1948 and 1961. It is now occupied by the National Library; a number of outstanding special collections are housed here: manuscripts, early printed books, maps, prints and music.

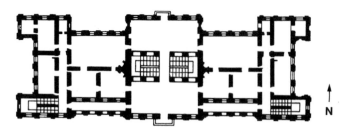

Plan of Krasiński Palace

N

The articulation of the long façade expresses the divisions of the ground-plan: behind the pedimented middle section is a grand staircase with the apartments extending to left and right. The pediment reliefs on the façade and the garden front celebrate the legendary origins of the Krasińskis from an ancient Roman patrician family. They are by Andreas Schlüter of Gdańsk, later to become famous for his work in Berlin. Behind the palace is the extensive *Ogród Krasińskich (Krasiński Park)* which was also designed by Tylman van Gameren. In 1766 it was remodelled and opened to the public.

Opposite the palace is the fine *Pomnik Bohaterów Powstania Warszawskiego (Monument to the Heroes of the Warsaw Uprising)* (1989) by Wincenty Kućma. Bronze figures representing the different sorts of people who took part in the Uprising emerge from the ground beneath concrete blocks, recalling the use of the city's sewers by the fighters. Unfortunately, the monument is now dwarfed by the postmodern *Pałac Sądu Najwyższego (Supreme Court Building)* (1991-99) by Marek Budzyński, fronted by by an array of peculiar green classical pillars.

Returning along ul. Długa, we reach the Nowe Miasto (New Town), which in fact is not much newer than the Old Town, as it was already in existence in the 14th century. At the corner of ul. Freta is the 17th-century Early Baroque *Kościół Dominikanów (Dominican Church)* (16), now a parish church. It was rebuilt in a modified form in 1947–59. The domed chapel of the Kotowski family, built by Tylman van Gameren and Giuseppe Simone Bellotti in 1691–4 on the north side, survived almost unscathed.

Of the Late Baroque and Neoclassical burghers' houses in ul. Freta the Kamienica Pod Samsonem (Samson House; No. 5) merits a closer look, because of the two reliefs on its Neoclassical façade showing *Samson fighting the Lion*, and *Delilah cutting Samson's Hair*, and because at the beginning of the 19th century it was briefly the home of E. T. A. Hoffmann. The author of 'The Nutcracker' lived here from 1804 to 1806, when he was an official in the Prussian administration. No. 16, rebuilt in 1770–80 by Szymon Bogumił Zug, is the **Muzeum Marii Skłodowskiej-Curie (Marie Skłodowska-Curie Museum)** (17); the great physicist, twice awarded the Nobel Prize (first in 1903 for the discovery of radioactivity and again in 1910 for isolating.polonium and radium), was born here on 7 November 1867.

Rynek Nowego Miasta (New Town Square) originally had a rectangular plan, like its Old Town counterpart. From the 15th century, the centre was occupied by the town hall, originally a timber building which was eventually replaced by a stone structure in 1680 after two fires. It was demolished in 1818. In the mid-18th century the surrounding buildings were completely renovated, and it was at that time that the square was given its present trapezoidal shape. Another thorough remodelling took place in about 1900, but the postwar rebuilding attempted to recreate an 18th-century appearance.

Dominating the square is the elegant centrally planned **Kościół Sakramentek (Church of the Sisters of the Blessed Sacrament)** (18), founded in 1688–9 by Maria Kazimiera Sobieska (Marie Casimière d'Arquien), the shrewish but beloved wife of King Jan III Sobieski, in thanks for his victory over the Turks. The pediment above the entrance contains the coats-of-arms of the royal couple. The building rises above a Greek-cross plan and is surmounted by a dome which develops with perfect logic out of the cruciform

167

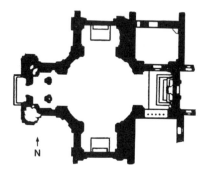

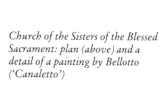

Church of the Sisters of the Blessed Sacrament: plan (above) and a detail of a painting by Bellotto ('Canaletto')

building by means of an octagonal drum. It is a productive translation by Tylman van Gameren of the achievements of the Roman Baroque, though the classical character of the building is very Dutch. Though the building itself was destroyed by bombing in 1944, the Late Baroque tomb of Sobieski's daughter Caroline de Bouillon (1746, by Lorenzo Mattielli) is original.

Continuing north from the church we reach ul. Kościelna, where the **Kościół Nawiedzenia Najświętszej Marii Panny (Church of the Visitation of the Virgin Mary)** (19) is a Late Gothic building (1411) with a 16th-century bell-tower. After many remodellings, it was not until 1906–15 that the church attained its present form, in which it was reconstructed after the war. Only the sanctuary retains its 'Baroque Gothic' appearance (1759–79).

Further along ul. Kościelna, past two 18th-century palaces, the Pałac Przeździeckich (Przeździecki Palace, No. 12) and the Pałac Brzezińskich (Brzeziński Palace, No. 10), (both remodelled in the 19th-century and reconstructed in 1951) the way continues to the Cytadela (Citadel).

At the corner of ul. Zakroczymska is the Franciscan monastery with the **Kościół św. Franciszka Serafickiego (Church of St Francis)** (20). This aisleless building lined with chapels dates mainly from the early 18th century (Giuseppe and Jacopo Fontana), and its present severe façade was completed in 1788 by Giuseppe Boretti. The obelisk-shaped superstructures above the projecting bays are an allusion to the church's function as a burial place for many well-born families.

Diagonally opposite is the Late Baroque **Pałac Sapiehów (Sapieha Palace)** (21) No. 6, built in the first half of the 18th century by the Dresden architect Johann Sigismund Deibel for the wojewoda of Troki, Jan Fryderyk Sapieha. The façade has fine Baroque decoration.

The **Cytadela (Citadel)** (22) on Żoliborz Hill, was built by the Tsarist authorities after the suppression of the November Uprising (1830–31). Many Polish patriots were incarcerated and executed here, including the leader of the 1863 January Uprising, Romuald Traugutt, and many members of the National Government he headed.

The complex was erected in 1832–4 by General Ivan Dehn, and was strengthened in 1857–75 by adding bastions, and surrounding it with a moat. Several Neoclassical gates have survived from the first phase of building. Inside the Citadel, at the north end between ul. Trojaka and ul. Czujna, is the Neoclassical **X. Pawilon (Block X)** (23) of 1822–7, which was later used as a prison; today it contains a museum commemorating the political prisoners.

From the Citadel al. Wojska Polskiego leads to the Żoliborz district created in the 1920's and 1930's. The name is Polonized French from 'jolis bords' – the pretty riverbanks. The **Osiedle Warszawskiej Spółdzielni Mieszkaniowej 'WSM' (Warsaw Housing Cooperative)** (24), which extends between Pl. T. Wilsona and Krasińskiego, Stołeczna and Słowackiego, is one of the high points of Functionalist housing-estate architecture in Europe. Two blocks further south, in ul. Niegolewskiego, stands the house (No. 8) of the architects Barbara and Stanisław Brukalski, who planned a large part of the 'WSM' estate. The house was built in 1927–8, and serves as a manifesto of Polish Functionalism.

Between ul. Hozjusza and ul. Alojzego Felińskiego, which leads back to Al. Wojska Polskiego, stands the **Kościół św. Stanisława Kostki (Church of St Stanisław Kostka)** (25) (1930–39, by Łukasz Wolski), where the tomb of Jerzy Popiełuszko, the priest murdered in 1984 by the state security services, has become a much-visited shrine.

Ul. Miodowa, ul. Senatorska; Teatr Wielki, Ogród Saski

The magnificence of the court of the Polish kings in the 17th and 18th centuries inspired many noble families to undertake their own ambitious building programmes. In their endeavour to match or even to surpass the king's latest architectural projects, these aristocratic patrons had their residences built by court architects, and entrusted the decoration to artists who enjoyed royal patronage. The most ambitious of these great palaces was that of the Krasiński family, but there was much competition along the three grand streets in the immediate vicinity of the Royal Castle: ul. Miodowa, ul. Senatorska, and, running southwards, ul. Krakowskie Przedmieście.

In 1944 all the buildings were badly damaged, and some of them were completely destroyed. What can be seen today is the result of thorough restoration. Often in the course of reconstruction buildings were rebuilt not as they were at the time they were destroyed but in an earlier state, omitting later modifications.

Ul. Miodowa, which begins at Pl. Krasińskich, was laid out in the 15th century to link the two old streets leading out of the city, ul. Długa and ul. Senatorska – hence its original name Poprzeczna (Transverse Street). Its northern side is lined with a row of large 18th-century palaces, all of them rebuilt after the war, and now occupied by various administrative and economic offices.

On the southern side of ul. Miodowa is the **Pałac Borchów (Borch Palace)** (26), Nos. 17–19, now the residence of the Primate of Poland. It is a U-shaped building dating from the early 18th century. In the course of postwar rebuilding the much remodelled palace was reconstructed in the form it attained after Neoclassical alterations by Domenico Merlini *c.*1780.

The adjoining complex of the **Pałac Paca (Pac Palace)** (27), No. 15, is the headquarters of the Ministry of Health. Like many of the palaces, it grew in several phases, and was remodelled and extended by each new owner. The original palace, which now forms the central block, was built in 1681–7 by Tylman van Gameren for Prince Dominik Mikołaj Radziwiłł. In 1757 Bishop Andrzej Stanisław Kostka Załuski, who was the owner of the palace for only a short time, had offices and stables added by Jacopo Fontana. Finally in 1824–8 Ludwik Pac commissioned the architect Enrico Marconi, an immigrant from Rome, to undertake a thorough remodelling, which gave the palace its present appearance: the main wing was given a new façade, side ranges and a gateway, thus creating a *cour d'honneur*.

The **Kościół Kapucynów (Capuchin Church)** (28), No. 13, at the corner of ul. Kapucyńska (founded by King Jan III Sobieski), was built by Tylman van Gameren and Agostino Locci, and completely rebuilt after the war. In the south aisle is the Kaplica Królewska (Royal Chapel), decorated in 1736 for King August III by his court architect Joachim Daniel Jauch as a burial place for the heart of his father, August II (the Strong), King of Poland 1697–1706 and 1709–33. In 1829 the chapel was modernized by Enrico Marconi for Tsar Nicholas I and a monument for the heart of King Jan III Sobieski was added.

At the end of ul. Miodowa stand two Late Baroque palaces, both completely rebuilt after the destruction of 1944: to the south the **Pałac Biskupów Krakowskich (Palace of the Bishops of Kraków)** (29), No. 5, on the corner of ul. Senatorska, and opposite it the **Pałac Branickich (Branicki Palace)** (30), No. 6, at the entrance to ul. Podwale. The Palace of the Bishops of Kraków dates from the first half of the 17th century; after a number of remodellings it was finally divided up into tenements in the 19th century. In the post-war rebuilding it was returned to its Late Baroque appearance: a blocky building projecting a far as the street, with a rusticated basement and a giant order of pilasters linking the two upper storeys. The Pałac Branickich is an example of another palace type, originally introduced from France: a two-storey, U-shaped complex with a courtyard entered through a gatehouse. Here too the patron used architects who were in royal service: from 1740 Johann Sigismund Deibel, and later Giuseppe Fontana.

At the Palace of the Bishops of Kraków we turn right along ul. Senatorska, which runs westwards out of the city and is another of Warsaw's oldest thoroughfares. The name (Senators' Street) derives from the fact that from the 16th century onwards the nobility and prelates had residences here near the Castle.

Borch Palace, watercolour by Z. Vogel, 1789

Opposite is the elegant **Pałac Prymasowski (Palace of the Primates of Poland)** (31), Nos. 13–15, now used as offices by the Ministry for Culture and Art; this has a villa-like layout with a low principal range set between two curving wings with pavilions at the ends, enclosing a grand *cour d'honneur*. Even this apparently unified and harmonious building is the result of a number of remodellings. The original residence, erected in 1593 for the Bishop of Płock (and Primate of Poland) Wojciech Baranowski, underwent a High Baroque transformation (probably by Tylman van Gameren) a hundred years later for the Primate Michał Radziejowski. In 1777–83 Ephraim Schroeger added the curved wings. Further lavish work continued until the end of the 18th century, under the direction of Szymon Bogumił Zug, finally giving the palace its present Neoclassical elegance. The finest interior is the magnificent ballroom by Schroeger and Zug (1777–83), with a gallery supported on Ionic columns.

A few steps further on ul. Senatorska opens into Pl. Teatralny (Theatre Square) dominated by the monumental complex of the **Teatr Wielki (Great Theatre)** (32) (plate 5).

The creation of a big enough site for the construction of the theatre (1825–33) in the centre of the city involved the demolition of one of the most remarkable examples of 17th-century town planning in Europe. This was Marywil (Marie-Ville), a commercial, residential and prestige development following the model of similar projects in Paris, such as the Place des Vosges. It was inspired and founded by Jan III Sobieski's French queen, Maria Kazimiera, after whom it was named. It was built to the designs of Tylman van

171

Gameren in 1692–5. As the name suggests it was a sort of 'town within a town', an extensive square, surrounded like a courtyard by five ranges of buildings containing shops on the ground floor and residential apartments above. One of the grand ranges was reserved for the royal court, and the square itself was the setting for court festivities.

The destruction of such an important architectural ensemble was only justified by the special importance attached to the building of the theatre. Throughout Europe the years around 1800 had seen a revival of interest in national traditions, a growth of research into national history and the nurturing of national culture. As an alternative to the court theatres, which were still based on the model of the French court and were accessible only to a small, well-born audience, new bourgeois national theatres were established where operas and plays by native authors were performed for a large audience who now wished to see their national aspirations reflected in a suitably impressive setting. Accordingly the Great Theatre was the expression and result of bourgeois nationalist efforts.

Antonio Corazzi, one of the leading architects of Neoclassicism in Poland, was entrusted with its design. The enormous complex includes not only an opera house with 2,500 seats, but also, in the wings adjoining the main block, meeting rooms for various official functions and ceremonies the National Theatre and a museum.

After suffering devastating damage in 1939 and 1944 the theatre was rebuilt between 1951 and 1965. Though there were some modifications, the historic character of a 'temple of national culture' was preserved. The Neoclassical façade – including the *porte cochère* which was added in 1890 – was reconstructed, but the interiors were given modern decoration.

The two monuments in front of the theatre (1965, by Jan Szczepkowski) honour two

important figures in Polish theatrical history: the playwright and actor Wojciech Bogu-sławski (1757–1829), regarded as the founder of Polish theatre, whose comic opera 'Cracovians and Mountaineers' played an important part in stirring insurrectionary feeling in 1794, and the composer and musician Stanisław Moniuszko (1819–72), whose 'Halka' (1858) is considered to be the first Polish national opera.

Opposite the theatre there now stands an uninspired reconstruction (1995–97) of the pre-war Town Hall. This necessitated the removal of the **Pomnik Bohaterów Warszawy (Monument to the Heroes of Warsaw)** to a new site not far away, on the embankment overlooking Al. Solidarności. The monument (also known as Nike, the Greek goddess of victory) was made in 1964 by Marian Konieczny, and commemorates the soldiers, resistance fighters and civilian victims of the war killed between 1939 and 1945. The figure seems almost vanquished, yet she still raises her head and sword to fight.

The **Pałac Blanka (Blank Palace)** (34) at ul. Senatorska, No. 14, was the residence in 1939 of the City President, Stefan Starzyński, and it was from here that he organized the defence of his city. The early Neoclassical palace, built in 1762–4 by Szymon Bogumił Zug, had been adapted between 1935 and 1938 for use as the seat of the city's administration. Today it is occupied by the workshops of the Office for Conservation of Historical Monuments.

Continuing along ul. Senatorska, beyond the corner of Pl. Teatralny, we pass **Kamienica Petyskusa (Petyskus House)** (35), No. 27, one of the earliest high-class

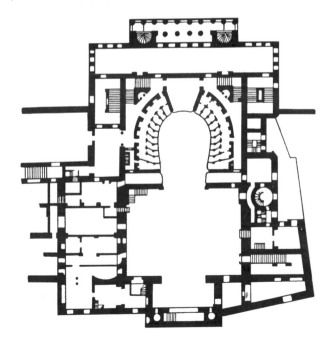

Plan of the Teatr Wielki ▷
(Great Theatre)

◁ *Teatr Wielki, engraving by*
F. Dietrich, 1833

tenement buildings in Warsaw. It was built in 1818–20 by Chrystian Piotr Aigner in the elegant style of a Neoclassical nobleman's palace.

The adjoining Franciscan Monastery with the **Kościół św. Antoniego Padewskiego (Church of St Antony of Padua)** (36), No. 31, is a fine example of Polish Baroque architecture (1671–81, architect unknown; destroyed 1944, rebuilt 1950–56). The church is aisleless, but over the years many Baroque and Neoclassical chapels were added. The altarpieces all date from the 18th century, as do the Stations of the Cross and many of the monuments.

A few steps further on is the Pałac Zamoyskich (Zamoyski Palace), more commonly known as the **Pałac Błękitny ('Azure Palace')** (37), Nos. 35–7, a building of interest both for its architecture and its history. It was built c.1700 by Teodor Potocki, Bishop of Warmia, but in 1726 the building was radically altered by King August II for his bastard daughter, Countess Anna Orzelska, Princess of Holstein. The king used his best architects, Joachim Daniel Jauch, Johann Sigismund Deibel and Karl Friedrich Pöppelmann. In 1730 the palace passed into the possession of the Czartoryski family, famous above all for their art collections. The Czartoryskis had the palace remodelled again in the current taste, in 1766–8 by Jacopo Fontana and in 1770–81 by Ephraim Schroeger. In 1812–19 (by which time the palace belonged to the Zamoyski family) Friedrich Albert Lassel added the wings and gave the building its final form (rebuilt in 1949–50 with slight alterations). The façade is an unusual, extremely austere variety of Neoclassicism. Apart from a cornice and simple window frames Lassel used no articulation of the wall surface, the entrance portico has severe cubic piers instead of the usual columns, and the centre of the façade is surmounted not by a pediment but by an attic-like projection. It was in this palace that Chopin gave one of his first recitals, at the age of six. In 1811 Stanisław Zamoyski opened his family's great library to the public, following the example of the Załuski brothers, who in 1748 had opened the first public library in Europe in the *Daniłowicz Palace* nearby. More than 500,000 of their books had, however, been carried off to St Petersburg by the Russians in 1795.

Diagonally opposite, set back behind a small garden, is the **Pałac Mniszchów (Mniszech Palace)** (38), Nos. 38–40, now the Belgian Embassy. The original Baroque building was given a Neoclassical remodelling by Adolf Schuch in 1829 when it became a merchants' club.

Next door (No. 42) is one of the finest examples of Art Nouveau architecture in Warsaw, the building of the **Bank Landaua (Landau Bank)** (39), built in 1904–6 by the architect Gustav Landau. It was the propaganda centre of the Communist Party.

Around the corner from the bank is **Pl. Bankowy** (40), which was laid out in its present form after the Second World War. Until recently the centre of the square contained the Pomnik Feliksa Dzierżyńskiego (Feliks Dzierżyński Monument) (1951, by Zbigniew Dunajewski). Dzierżyński, a member of the Polish szlachta from near Wilno, took an active part in the Bolshevik revolution and founded the Cheka, the notorious Soviet secret police. In 1920 he was instructed by Lenin to install a communist regime in Poland, a plan that was foiled by the Polish victory over the Red Army near Warsaw. This 'Miracle on the

View of the market at Rzeźnica Gate, drawing by J. P. Norblin

Vistula', engineered by Dzierżyński's class-mate Piłsudski, saved Western Europe from Communism.

At the other side of the corner to ul. Elektoralna is the former building of the **Stock Exchange and Bank of Poland** (41). It was built in a severe Neoclassical style by Antonio Corazzi between 1825 and 1828, and developed as the centre of financial administration. After its reconstruction in 1950–54 it housed the Museum of the History of the Polish Revolutionary Movement and it now contains a varied collection of Old Master paintings donated by Mr and Mrs Porczyński.

The twin buildings of the **Urząd Warszawy (Municipal Administration of Warsaw)** (42) on the east side of the square are also by Antonio Corazzi, and were built between 1823 and 1830, in an imposing Neoclassical style. Originally family palaces, they were converted into the offices of the Revenue and Treasury Commission. Today they are used by the municipal administration.

From here one can go a few steps further northwards along ul. Generała Władysława Andersa to the **Muzeum Archeologiczne (Archaeological Museum)** (43), entrance at ul. Długa 52. It contains a model of the settlement of Biskupin (6th century BC) (see page

284), the amber treasure of Basson (5th century) and archaeological finds from the Stone Age, Bronze Age and Iron Age. The building was erected in 1638–48 in the reign of Władysław IV Waza as an arsenal. It was later remodelled several times: in 1752–7 by Joachim Daniel Jauch and Johann Sigismund Deibel, in 1779–82 by Szymon Bogumił Zug. In 1935–8 the building was returned to its Early Baroque appearance, and the restoration plans used then were used again for the postwar rebuilding.

To the northeast is Muranów, laid out on the site of the Jewish ghetto created by the Germans during the Second World War. Warsaw's Jewish population had grown enormously at the end of the 19th century as Jews fled the pogroms and poverty of Russia. During the war almost 500,000 people were herded together in the ghetto, in horrifically cramped and squalid conditions, where they were weakened by famine and disease. In ten weeks in the summer of 1942 more than 300,000 Jews were deported to Treblinka, where they were murdered. The Ghetto Uprising (19 April to 3 May 1943) was a turning point in Jewish history; the anniversary of its start is observed in Israel as Holocaust Remembrance Day. In ul. Zamenhofa stands the **Pomnik Bohaterów Getta (Memorial to the Heroes of the Ghetto)** (44) created in 1948 by the sculptor Natan Rappaport and the architect Leon Marek Suzin using materials ordered by Hitler for a victory monument (plate 6). When the West German Chancellor Willy Brandt visited the monument in 1970, in an emotional gesture he knelt to honour the dead. From here a *Trakt Pamięci ('Path of Remembrance')* consisting of 19 black granite blocks leads to the site of the *Umschlagplatz* in ul. Sławki, where the deportations took place. The monument here (Hanna Schmalenberg and Władysław Klamerus, 1988) is a symbolic wall recalling the wall that surrounded the Ghetto.

Heading west, along ul. Mordechaja Anielewicza (named after the leader of the Ghetto Uprising), we reach the large, sadly unkempt *Cmentarz Żydowski (Jewish Cemetery)*, where the many impressive tombs include that of Ben Sonnenberg (1831, by David Friedländer), whose descendants include the philosopher Bergson. Adjacent is the city's main Catholic cemetery, the *Cmentarz Powązkowski*, which also has some fine tombs, and nearby are the Protestant cemeteries (Lutheran and Reformed), as well as a small Moslem cemetery with Tatar graves.

Visitors interested in Jewish culture should visit the *Jewish Historical Institute* and *Museum* at ul. Tłomackie 3–5 (near the site of Warsaw's main synagogue). There is also a *Jewish Theatre*, Pl. Grzybowski 12–16, and one working synagogue, *Synagoga Nożyków*, at ul. Twarda 6.

In ul. Dzielna stands the **Muzeum Więzienia 'Pawiak' (Museum of the Pawiak Prison)** (45) commemorating the Polish patriots and revolutionaries imprisoned here in the 19th century and the Second World War. During the Nazi occupation more than 100,000 Poles were held in this prison; 35,000 died in mass executions and 60,000 were taken to concentration camps.

From Pl. Bankowy we can head south along ul. Przechodnia to Pl. Żelaznej Bramy. This open space lay outside the city until the beginning of the 18th century and was used as a market place. Around 1725, in the reign of the Saxon King August II, it was incorporated

1 Lubiąż Cistercian Abbey on the Oder ▷

2 WROCŁAW Aula Leopoldina in the University

3 WROCŁAW Burghers' houses in the Plac Solny

4 LUBLIN Holy Cross Chapel
in the Dominican Church

5   Kraków   Hall of the Deputies in Wawel Castle

7   Kraków   St Mary's Church, altarpiece by Veit Stoss

6   Kraków   Market Square with the Cloth Hall and Town Hall Tower

9 KRASICZYN Renaissance castle

8 PRZEMYŚL Franciscan Church of St Mary Magdalene, west front

11   Mnichów   Timber Church of St Stephen

13　Warsaw　Plac Zamkowy with the Royal Castle and the Sigismund Column

14　Warsaw
　　Chopin Monument in Łazienki Park

15　Warsaw　Old Town Square

17   Baltic coast near Szczecin

◁ 16   Warsaw   Wilanów, garden front

18 Ląd Cistercian Abbey

19 Czerwińsk Augustinian Abbey

20 Pelplin Cistercian Church

22, 23　GDAŃSK　Burghers' houses and warehouses at the mouth of the Vistula

◁ 21　GDAŃSK　View of the Old Town　　　24　GDAŃSK　Długi Targ (Long Market) with the Town Hall

into the city. At its western end the Żelazna Brama (Iron Gate), after which the square is named, was built on the edge of the Ogród Saski (the Saxon Gardens). It is dominated on its eastern side by the **Pałac Lubomirskich (Lubomirski Palace)** (46). The nucleus of the palace dates from the period around 1700, but it was remodelled several times. More interesting than its exterior is the story of how it reached its present location. The palace originally stood further north, but in 1970 the authorities decided to use the building to improve the townscape. One side of it was to form the visual focus of the main axis of the Ogród Saski and hide the sports halls situated behind it. The building was therefore sawn off at its foundations and transported on special rails using hydraulic presses to its present site. This involved turning it through an angle of 78 degrees. The operation took six weeks and was mainly intended as a demonstration of what Polish engineering could do.

The way to ul. Krakowskie Przedmieście takes us across the Ogród Saski, which dates back to the 17th century. It was laid out by Tylman van Gameren in 1666–71, and originally belonged to a palace that was destroyed in the Second World War and not rebuilt. The Saxon Palace had been the residence of the Polish-Saxon kings, was de-molished in 1842 and replaced by two blocks linked by a colonnade; in 1869 it became the headquarters of the administration of the Warsaw Military District. The park was con-siderably extended by August III. In 1816–27 the English garden architect James Savage transformed it into a landscape garden of the sort that had been developed in England, with a straight avenue in the middle and apparently unorganized but well-balanced landscape ensembles. In the 19th century the garden became a popular place for Sunday entertainments, and its character gradually changed. A summer theatre, a confectioner's which became famous, and various kiosks were built. The park furnishings suffered badly in the wartime destruction and only the 25 allegorical statues, made in the 18th century by Franz Xaver Deibel have largely survived. At the western end of the garden, where the palace stood until 1944, only the fragment of an arcade remains. This is now the **Grób Nieznanego Żołnierza (Tomb of the Unknown Soldier)** (47). The changing of the guard here takes place every Sunday at 12 noon. It was here in June 1979 that Pope John Paul II celebrated the first public mass of his first official visit to Poland. The square was formerly Pl. Saski, and is now Pl. Piłsudskiego; the massive golden-domed Russian Orthodox Cathedral built here in 1894–1912 was demolished only a few years later as a symbol of hated Russian rule, shortly after Piłsudski came to power.

Following ul. Moliera and ul. Trębacka we head in the direction of ul. Krakowskie Przedmieście, but before going along this, the grandest street in Warsaw, we can cross it to make a short detour into ul. Bednarska, a turning diagonally opposite on the left, which has some delightful early 19th-century buildings. The Neoclassical and Gothic Revival houses were carefully restored in 1950. At the end of the street stands the **Dom Łaziebny (Bath**

house), (48) Nos. 2–4, an elegant, Neoclassical bathing establishment built in 1832 with an entrance portico whose Corinthian columns support a pediment with a relief of Neptune surrounded by his boisterous crew. Today the building is used as a primary school.

Ul. Krakowskie Przedmieście, Park Łazienkowski

The magnificent ul. Krakowskie Przedmieście ('Kraków Suburb Street') remains a favourite promenade for Varsovians. Together with ul. Nowy Świat and Al. Ujazdowskie, it forms the Trakt Królewski ('Royal Way') which runs for 4 km from the Royal Castle to the royal summer residences of Ujazdów and Łazienki, and then on to Wilanów. From the 17th century onwards this old road leading out of the city became one of the favourite areas for noble families connected with the court to build their residences.

Our walk begins at Pl. Zamkowy, where the kings set out in ceremonial procession from the Royal Castle to the cooler countryside. What they saw was more often than not an enormous building site, but one which bore evidence of prosperity and of the will to express this in grand architecture.

First we pass the **Kościół św. Anny (Church of St Anne)** (49). Until 1863 it belonged to the Bernardine order, and since 1929 it has been the parish church of the student community. It was founded in 1454 by Duke Bolesław IV of Mazovia and his wife Anna. The Gothic building was burned down in 1655 and was then rebuilt for Jan II Kazimierz as a Baroque church, though the interior still has remains of Gothic masonry. The Baroque decoration dates from the 17th and 18th centuries. The sacristy contains fine carved and inlaid doors and vestment cupboards made between 1729 and 1754 in the monastery's own workshops. The church was given its imposing and distinguished Palladian façade by the dilettante Stanisław Kostka Potocki and the architect Chrystian Piotr Aigner in 1786–8. In the four niches stand statues of the Evangelists by Giacopo Monaldi. The massive free-standing bell-tower to the left of the façade was erected in 1578 at the expense of Anna Jagiellonka; it was remodelled by Aigner in 1820–21 in a *Rundbogenstil* with blind arcading and rustication.

Adjoining the church on the right is the former **Odwach Wojskowy (Main Guard-house)** (50), No. 66. Originally part of the monastic buildings (also 1820–21, by Aigner) this is now the Central Library for Agriculture. For his façade, with its rusticated basement with arches and slender arcaded order in the upper storey, Aigner took as his model the Theatre of Marcellus in Rome.

The building next door (No. 64) with its plastically articulated neo-Renaissance façade is the **Resursa Obywatelska** (51), the Landowners' Club for well-to-do citizens built in 1860–61. The club appears in Bolesław Prus's great novel of 19th-century Warsaw, *The Doll*, as the meeting-place of the two main characters: Wokulski, the rising businessman, and Łęcki, the impoverished nobleman.

Next, extending as far as the corner of ul. Bednarska, are the buildings of the **Warszaw-**

skie Towarzystwo Dobroczynności (Warsaw Benevolent Society) (52), No. 62, which were created in 1840–7 by altering existing buildings. Giuseppe Simone Bellotti's statue of the 'Our Lady of Passau' was set up here in 1683.

At this point the street widens to form a square, which was created in 1860–62 by the demolition of a block of houses. In its centre stands the **Pomnik Adama Mickiewicza (Adam Mickiewicz Monument)** (53) erected in 1898; the writer is here a symbol of Poland's national literature, and the monument was paid for by public subscription. The sculptor was Cyprian Godebski. In 1942 it was taken down and removed to safety, and then in 1950 re-erected and solemnly unveiled for the second time.

At the southern end of the square are a number of buildings tightly grouped together, which merit a close look. On the left the bizarre façade of the **Kosciół Wniebowzięcia Najświętszej Marii Panny i św. Józefa (Church of the Assumption and St Joseph)** (54) projects into the square. Originally part of the monastery of the Discalced Carmelites, the church was built in the second half of the 17th century, probably by G. S. Bellotti. The façade, which was not completed until 1782, had been designed in 1761–2 by Ephraim Schroeger; it is one of the earliest attempts to introduce the latest Italian Neoclassicism to Warsaw. The luxuriant Baroque decoration of the interior dates from the 18th century, and the sculpture of the *Marriage of the Virgin* on the chancel screen is by Jan Jerzy Plersch.

The adjoining complex is the **Pałac Koniecpolskich (Koniecpolski Palace)** (55), Nos. 46–8, now the official residence of the President of the Republic. In the communist period this was the seat of the Council of Ministers. It was here in 1955 that the 'Treaty of Friendship, Co-operation and Mutual Assistance' (the 'Warsaw Pact') was signed, and in 1970 the treaty normalizing relations between Poland and the Federal Republic of Germany. The palace was built in the mid-17th century, altered several times and was given its present appearance by Chrystian Piotr Aigner in 1818–19. In its *cour d'honneur* an equestrian monument to Józef Poniatowski was erected here in 1965. Poniatowski, known as 'Pepi', the nephew of King Stanisław August, was a dandy lionized in the salons of Warsaw and Paris, but he distinguished himself as commander-in-chief of the Polish forces under Kościuszko and later under Napoleon; his romantic death at the Battle of Leipzig has come to stand for all that is noble in the Polish soul. The monument, a gift of Denmark, is a copy (1948-51) of the original statue by Bertel Thorvaldsen (1826–32) destroyed in the war. In the later 19th century the palace was the seat of the Russian Gouvernement; the courtyard then contained a statue of Ivan Paskievich, the Russian general who put down the 1830 Uprising with unexampled ferocity.

Opposite is the Palac Potockich (Potocki Palace) (56), No. 15, now the Ministry of Culture and Art, which also has three ranges around a *cour d'honneur*; it was formed in 1760–66 by altering an earlier building. The fine neo-Baroque wrought iron gates by Władysław Marconi were added in 1909.

Next, between ul. Ossolińskich and ul. Bagińskiego, comes the **Hotel Europejski** (57), the first modern hotel in Warsaw, built between 1855 and 1877 in the neo-Renaissance style by Enrico Marconi. It has undergone extensive alteration, as has the Hotel Bristol

Kazimierz Palace, 18th-century drawing

opposite (Nos. 42–4; 1899–1901 by Władysław Marconi), which is also worth a look, though its Secessionist decoration by Otto Wagner was destroyed when it was modernized in 1950.

The **Kościół Wizytek (Church of the Nuns of the Visitation)** (58) is one of Warsaw's most beautiful Baroque churches (plate 1). Queen Marie Louise Gonzaga summoned the nuns in 1654 from France and built the first (wooden) church for them. The present church was built in two phases in the 18th century: from 1728 to 1733 to the designs of Karol Bay and from 1754 to 1766 under the direction of Ephraim Schroeger. The sumptuous, plastic articulation of the columned façade is continued in the interior. The light-filled, aisleless space is a masterpiece of the Late Baroque, with its rhythmical arrangement of columns and oval domed side-chapels. Particularly notable is the high altar, designed by Ephraim Schroeger and executed by Jan Jerzy Plersch, with its obliquely arranged pairs of columns, and a group of sculptured figures breaking through the entablature like a mystic vision. The ebony tabernacle incorporated into the altar by Schroeger came from the earlier temporary church and was a gift of Queen Marie Louise.

The University of Warsaw (founded in 1816) occupies a whole complex of historic buildings. The **Pałac Tyszkiewiczów (Tyszkiewicz Palace)** (59), No. 32, from the end of the 18th century, stands on a corner and has two grand façades (Johann Christian Kamsetzer). The main front is identified by a balcony supported by four atlantes by André

Staszic Palace and the Copernicus Monument, 19th-century drawing

LeBrun (1787). The interior too is the work of the most celebrated artists, who were also engaged on the Royal Castle: Kamsetzer, Graff and later Enrico Marconi. It is now the University Library. The adjoining neo-Renaissance **Pałac Uruskich (Uruski Palace)** (60) dating from 1844–7 and the **Szpital św. Rocha (Hospital of St Roch)** (61), built *c.*1707 and extended *c.*1749 by Jacopo Fontana, are now parts of the University, as is the complex of the **Pałac Kazimierzowski (Kazimierz Palace)** (62), which with its park extends behind the street front. It was built in 1634 as the summer residence of Władysław IV Waza, though it takes its name from his brother, Jan II Kazimierz Waza, who had it remodelled in 1660. Between 1737 and 1739 there were further alterations by prominent artists such as Karl Friedrich Pöppelmann, Joachim Daniel Jauch and Johann Sigismund Deibel. A little later (1765–8) it was adapted by Domenico Merlini for use as a military academy, the Szkoła Rycerska, founded by Stanisław August. Tadeusz Kościuszko was one of the first students here. After destruction in the Second World War the palace was rebuilt with a Neoclassical façade to the street and a Late Baroque façade to the garden. The subsidiary buildings, which have been added piecemeal since 1815, were planned for the University; the Auditorium Maximum dates from 1930.

Opposite the University is the former **Pałac Czapskich (Czapski Palace)** (63), an 18th-century building, now the Akademia Sztuk Pięknych (Academy of Fine Arts). Fryderyk Chopin lived and worked here in the building on the left of the courtyard before leaving Warsaw in 1830. The statue in the courtyard is a 20th-century copy of the equestrian statue of Bartolomeo Colleoni by Andrea del Verrocchio in Venice (late 15th century).

The **Kościół św. Krzyża (Holy Cross Church)** (64) was founded by the Primate Stefan Radziejowski, and built between 1679 and 1696 by Giuseppe Simone Bellotti. The façade with its two towers was designed by Giuseppe Fontana (1725–37), and modified by Jacopo Fontana and Joachim Daniel Jauch (1756–60). Inside, on the first pier on the left, is a monument to Fryderyk Chopin with a portrait bust and an urn containing his heart. Indeed the church has a wealth of monuments to the famous: the writer Władysław Reymont (1867–1925), the historian, poet and literary critic Józef Ignacy Kraszewski (1812–78), the novelist Bolesław Prus (1845–1912), the poet Juliusz Słowacki (1809–49) and General Władysław Sikorski (1881–1943), the Prime Minister of the Polish Government in Exile in the Second World War and Commander-in-Chief of the Polish forces in the West. Several memorials commemorate the fact that the church was the scene of bitter fighting during the Uprising in August and September 1944.

The end of ul. Krakowskie Przedmieście is marked by Bertel Thorvaldsen's **Pomnik Mikołaja Kopernika (Nicolaus Copernicus Monument)** (65) erected in 1830 in front of the imposing Neoclassical façade of the **Pałac Staszica (Staszic Palace)** (66), which was built for the Warsaw Society of the Friends of Learning and is now the headquarters of the Academy of Sciences. It was built by Antonio Corazzi in 1820–23 with a stage-designer's feel for its position facing the ceremonial way. Its bizarre Russo-Byzantine remodelling of the 1890's was not adopted for the post-war rebuilding.

The rebuilt Nowy Świat ('New World'), which begins at this point, was until the beginning of the last century lined with unimpressive, timber buildings. The Neoclassical houses and palaces there today all date from the first half of the 19th century. It was here that great magnate families of the time, such as the Zamoyskis, Kossakowskis and Hołowczyces, built their summer residences, continuing the tradition of Krakowskie Przedmieście.

In ul. Tamka, which runs from here down to the Vistula, the **Pałac Gnińskich (Gniński Palace)** (67), No. 41, is worth a look. It was built towards the end of the 17th century by Tylman van Gameren as a pavilion of a large palace that was never completed, and was then remodelled several times in the 19th century, when it was the Warsaw School of Music. It is now the home of the Fryderyk Chopin Society. At the end of ul. Tamka, near the bank of the Vistula, is one of Warsaw's most famous symbols: the **Pomnik Syreny (Siren Statue)** (68), a mythical creature who is the city's emblem.

A few hundred metres further along ul. Nowy Świat brings us to the crossroads with Al. Jerozolimskie (Jerusalem Avenue), Rondo Charles de Gaulle, one of the main traffic junctions of modern Warsaw, with several important buildings. At the northwest corner is the headquarters of the International Book and Press Club; diagonally opposite it stands the former **Dom Partii (House of the Party)** (69), built between 1948 and 1951 and until recently the headquarters of the Central Committee of the Polish United Workers' Party.

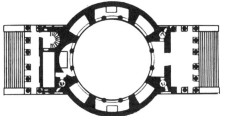

Church of St Alexander,
engraving by F. Dietrich,
1829; plan

It now houses the Stock Exchange.

Further south Nowy Świat opens into Pl. Trzech Krzyży (Square of the Three Crosses), which takes its name from the Calvary at the end of a Way of the Cross built by King August II in 1724–31 on the estate of Ujazdów. The middle of the square is occupied by the **Kościół św. Aleksandra (Parish Church of St Alexander)** (70), the outstanding example of mature Neoclassicism in Poland (plate 4). It was built between 1818 and 1825 by Chrystian Piotr Aigner, on a circular plan covered with a low dome, and it was this design that was reconstructed, rather than the neo-Renaissance remodelling of 1886–94 which stood here before the war. Placed with severe symmetry on the north and south sides are two pedimented porticoes with columns and steps. Inside, the wall surface is broken by chapels, rhythmically articulated with columns and pilasters.

Beyond Pl. Trzech Krzyży is al. Ujazdowskie, Warsaw's grandest and greenest avenue, lined with villas now mostly occupied by embassies and government departments. It was not unified architecturally until the second half of the 19th century. For a hundred and fifty years the parks and gardens here were a favourite meeting place for the well-to-do, rather like Rotten Row in London.

In a side street east of the avenue, ul. Wiejska, is the large complex of the **Sejm (Parliament)** (71) of the Polish Republic. Its nucleus dates from the middle of the 19th century. The semicircular plenary hall was added by Kazimierz Skórewicz as part of extensive alterations carried out between 1925 and 1928. In front of the former Yugoslav Embassy, formerly the Śleszyński Palace (Al. Ujazdowskie Nos. 23/25), a memorial tablet marks the place where the death sentence pronounced by a Polish underground court on SS Commander Franz Kutschera was carried out by members of the Home Army on 1 February 1944.

No. 25 al. Szucha, built in 1925–30 by Zdzisław Mączeński, was the Gestapo headquarters. The building now houses the Ministry of Education, while in the basement the former prison cells contain the **Muzeum Martyrologii Polskiej (Museum of Polish Martyrdom)** (72) commemorating the thousands who were tortured and murdered here.

The large thoroughfare running beneath Pl. na Rozdrożu is the Trasa Łazienkowska leading eastwards over the Vistula, built in 1971–4 and one of the biggest municipal building works undertaken in modern Warsaw.

It forms the northern boundary of the extensive **Park Łazienkowski (Łazienki Park)**, (plan page 209) the history of which goes back to the 16th century. In 1548 Queen Bona Sforza moved to the village of Ujazdów and converted a house there into a dower house for herself. In 1624-37 King Zygmunt III Waza built the *Zamek Ujazdowski (Ujazdów Castle)* (73) (a) (plate 11) on the estate, with four ranges around an inner courtyard, corner towers and loggia with a view overlooking the Vistula, in the tradition of the early, fortified villas of Italian princes. The estate became a deer-park for hunting. The architect is thought to have been Giovanni Battista Trevano. Additions were made in 1674-90 by Tylman van Gameren, and in 1766 King Stanisław August Poniatowski began work on a grandly conceived transformation of the whole complex. He planned a splendid royal residence, the equal of the Royal Castle, and used the team of first-class court artists he had assembled for his town residence: Domenico Merlini, Ephraim Schroeger, Jan Bogumił Plersch, Johann Christian Kamsetzer, André LeBrun, Marcello Bacciarelli and others. But in 1772 the ambitious project was interrupted when the political and financial crisis of the First Partition forced the King to restrict himself to a smaller project. The castle has been restored since 1973 and now houses the *Centrum Sztuki Wspołczesnej (Centre of Contemporary Art)*, which has an interesting programme of temporary exhibitions and an excellent restaurant.

To the south of the house, in the corner between Al. Ujazdowskie and ul. Agrykola is the University Botanical Garden founded in 1819. Also part of the university is the Neoclassical *Obserwatorium Astronomiczne (Observatory)* (b), built in 1820–24 by Chrystian Piotr Aigner.

Łazienki Park
a Zamek Ujazdowski (Ujazdów
   Castle)
b Obserwatorium Astronomiczne
   (Observatory)
c Stara Pomarańczarnia (Old
   Orangery)
d Wodozbiór (Reservoir)
e Biały Domek (White Lodge)
f Pomnik Fryderyka Chopina
   (Chopin Monument)
g Belweder (Belvedere Palace)
h Świątynia Diany (Temple of Diana)
i Świątynia Egipska (Egyptian
   Temple)
j Nowa Pomarańczarnia (New
   Orangery)
k Pałac na Wyspie (Palace on
   the Island)
l Teatr na Wyspie (Theatre on the
   Island)
m Wielka Oficyna (Great Offices)
n Pałac Myślewicki (Myślewicki Palace)
o Pomnik króla Jana III Sobieskiego
   (Sobieski Monument)

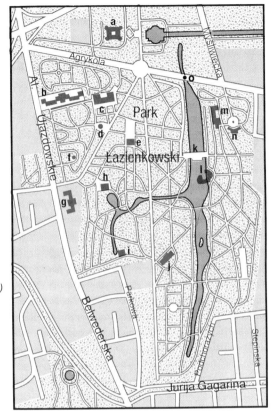

The neighbouring *Stara Pomarańczarnia (Old Orangery)* (c) is in the area of the park which survives from Stanisław August's time. Over the years the park developed in the hands of court architects to become one of the most beautiful English gardens in Poland: picturesque lakes were created, clumps of trees and lawns artfully arranged apparently at random. The principal creator of this charmingly composed landscape was Johann Christian Schuch, a landscape gardener from Dresden, who here made good use of the experience he had gained on travels through England, France and the Netherlands. Łazienki differs from its English models in having no artificial grottoes or merely picturesque ruins. The ideal of the landscape garden as the imitation of nature with its history is here modified by the influence of more formal French garden design.

The Old Orangery is one of a number of decorative buildings built for Stanisław August and scattered throughout the park. It was built in 1784–8 to the designs of Domenico Merlini. The lavish Baroque decoration of the theatre in its east wing is similar to that of the ballroom in the Royal Castle: Merlini worked here together with André LeBrun and

209

Giacopo Monaldi (sculpture) and Jan Bogumił Plersch (painted decoration). In the Orangery itself is a collection of sculpture of the 16th to the 20th centuries from the National Museum.

South of the Orangery the defensive-looking round structure is one of several *Wodozbiory (Reservoirs)* (d) (Merlini, 1823–7, remodelled by Chrystian Piotr Aigner). It is now a commercial art gallery. From here one can see the *Biały Domek (White Lodge)* (e) a rustic, but elegant timber building with decorative exterior plasterwork. It was built, probably in 1774–7, by Domenico Merlini with comfortable Rococo appointments, a dining room, bedchamber, boudoir and dressing room. Stanisław August lived here while the Łazienki Palace was being built, and in 1803 Louis XVIII of France spent some of his exile here. A sundial set up to the south of the Lodge in 1776 bears the Polish king's cypher: 'SA'.

Further to the southwest, we pass the *Pomnik Fryderyka Chopina (Fryderyk Chopin Monument)* (75) (f) (colour plate 14), an Art Nouveau sculpture by Wacław Szymanowski showing the composer seated beneath a willow tree. It was erected in 1904, destroyed by the Germans in 1940 and recreated in 1957-8. We then reach the *Belweder (Belvedere Palace)* (g). The land it is built on came into the possession of Stanisław August in 1767 and was incorporated into Łazienki Park. Its elegant Neoclassical appearance is the result of a remodelling by Jakub Kubicki c.1820 of a villa first built between 1730 and 1750 by Giuseppe Fontana. During Congress Poland this was the residence of the Grand Duke Constantine, nominally commander of the Polish army, but in fact the Tsar's viceroy. After independence in 1919 the palace became first the residence of the President of the Republic and then of Marshal Piłsudski. Since 1994 it has housed an exhibition of Piłsudski's life and work.

The little classical *Świątynia Diany (Temple of Diana)* (h), a timber building clad in stucco, situated a short distance away on the lake, was built at the same time, probably by Kubicki. At the southern end of the lake is a *Świątynia Egipska (Egyptian Temple)* (i) from the same period. Beyond the long, straight avenue, which divides the park in two, we arrive at the *Nowa Pomarańczarnia (New Orangery)* (j) (1860–61, by Adam Adolf Loewe), in which exotic plants are still grown. It is now a restaurant. The lakeside path leads back to the strikingly situated *Pałac na Wyspie (Palace on the Island)* (74) (k) on an artificial island in the middle of the lake.

Between 1683 and 1690 Tylman van Gameren had built a bath-house here ('łazienki' means 'baths') for the then owner, Stanisław Herakliusz Lubomirski. In the following century King Stanisław August gradually had the building altered and extended by Domenico Merlini: in 1775–6 the southern part had an extra storey added, in 1784 Merlini gave the building a new façade, and four years later the side wings were added, the north façade built and the belvedere placed on top. In 1792–3 the palace was given the two pavilions on the banks and the colonnades linking them to the main building. At the same time Stanisław's favourite artists were at work on the decoration of the interiors. In 1817 the palace was acquired by Tsar Alexander I and became the Imperial residence in Warsaw. Destroyed in 1944, Łazienki was painstakingly restored (though without its Russian Orthodox chapel) and is now a part of the National Museum displaying Baroque painting

The Palace on the Island in Łazieńki Park, watercolour by Z. Vogel, 1788

and sculpture (plan, page 212).

Despite its long and varied building history, the palace appears to be of a piece. Merlini united the various parts of the building by means of a uniform pilaster order and a balustrade surmounted by statues. The north front with its pedimented portico is rather severe, while the more plastic treatment of the south front, with its loggia and terrace in front, has the effect of a pleasure house. This carefully balanced two-faced quality of the building is underlined by the programme of the statuary: the pediment on the official front is decorated with figures of Fame and Peace, with the royal arms, accompanied by Minerva and Achilles. The statues at the corners represent the four continents, and those on the belvedere the four elements (all by André LeBrun). The south front, on the other hand, is decorated with figures representing the four seasons, while on the terrace there are Baroque love scenes from Ovid: a Satyr abducts a Nymph, and Hermaphroditus embraces the water nymph Salmacis. The two sculptures representing the rivers Vistula and Bug are by Ludwik Kaufman (1820).

Unlike the exterior, the interior still plainly reveals the history of the building's construction. The king retained the rooms decorated by Tylman van Gameren for the old bath pavilion. The *Bacchus Room* (I) on the left of the vestibule, which has decoration of blue and white painted tiles takes its name from a painting of Silenus with Bacchantes by Jacob Jordaens which hangs over the fireplace. The adjoining *Bathroom* (II) has also retained its old decoration by Tylman van Gameren. The wall reliefs show aquatic episodes from Ovid, such as Andromeda chained to a rock and threatened by a sea monster.

The *Ballroom* (III) is in one of the side wings added by Domenico Merlini. Its decoration is severely Neoclassical, and its pale colour brings out the details of the fine plasterwork. The decoration was designed by Johann Christian Kamsetzer; André LeBrun and Jan Bogumił Plersch executed the sculpture and grotesques. In the niches above the fireplaces are small-scale plaster copies of the most famous classical sculptures, the Farnese Hercules and the Apollo Belvedere, which the king brought back with him from a trip to Rome. Here the figures have a symbolic purpose as representatives of Virtue and the Arts, for, supporting the mantel shelf below are the cowering figures of those they vanquished: in Hercules's case Cerberus and a centaur, in Apollo's King Midas and the satyr Marsyas.

Passing through the small *Salon* (IV) in which portraits from the collection of the National Museum are exhibited, we reach the grandest room of the residence, the *Hall of Solomon* (V) which opens through a large arch into the central rotunda. It was the audience room, which explains why its gorgeous decoration takes the wisdom of Solomon as its theme. Marcello Bacciarelli painted several scenes from Solomon's life, which allude to the achievements of Stanisław August Poniatowski. The next room to the northeast has always been used as a *Picture Gallery* (VI), so its decoration is deliberately subdued.

The *Rotunda* (VII) was decorated by Domenico Merlini. The dome which reaches up into the upper storey, rests on a circle of columns, whose whiteness is delightfully set off

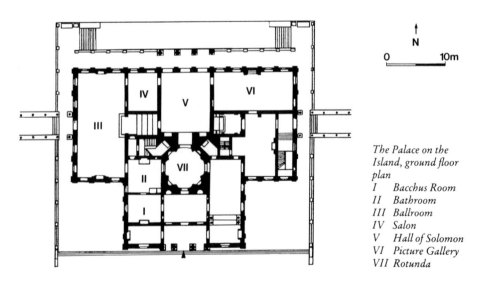

The Palace on the
Island, ground floor
plan
I   Bacchus Room
II   Bathroom
III Ballroom
IV   Salon
V   Hall of Solomon
VI   Picture Gallery
VII Rotunda

by yellow and green marbled walls. The room is inspired by the Roman Pantheon; the sculptural programme depicts a sort of glorious genealogy. In the four niches stand statues of the Polish kings Kazimierz III Wielki (by Giacopo Monaldi), Zygmunt I Stary and Stefan Batory (by André LeBrun) and Jan III Sobieski (by Franciszek Pink). Above the doors are busts of the Roman emperors Titus, Trajan and Marcus Aurelius. According to the inscription, freely adapted from Lucan, *Utile mundo editi exemplum*, these were intended to serve as an example to the world. Upstairs the king's private rooms have also been reconstructed since the war.

From the terrace in front of the south front it used to be possible to look across to the *Teatr na Wyspie (Theatre on the Island)* (1) (plate 10), but it is now almost completely hidden by trees. It is a classical amphitheatre built on an artificial island, with the audience on the bank separated from the stage by water. It was built as a picturesque ruin in 1790–91 by Johann Christian Kamsetzer. Performances are still held here.

In the northeast corner of the park, towards ul. Agrykola, stands the *Wielka Oficyna (Great Offices)* (m), which were used in the early 19th century as a cadet school. An attack by the cadets on the Belvedere Palace set off the November Uprising of 1830–31.

Nearby is the *Pałacyk Myślewicki (Myślewicki Palace)* (n), named after the village of Myślewice that used to be here. An early Neoclassical building erected in 1775–8 by Domenico Merlini, it has an unusual semicircular façade with a tall arched niche in the centre. It was used at first to accommodate important court officials, but later the king gave it to his nephew, Józef Poniatowski. Some rooms have kept their original decoration with paintings by Jan Bogumił Plersch.

On the bridge at the end of the lake is the *Pomnik króla Jana III Sobieskiego (Sobieski Monument)* (o).

If we make our way back through the park to the Belvedere Palace we find ourselves at what was the end of the original Royal Way. However, the road continues for another 10 km or so south to another royal palace at Wilanów (see page 217).

The City Centre: ul. Marszałkowska, Muzeum Narodowe, Mokotów

In the course of the rebuilding after the Second World War the centre of the city was shifted south from the Old Town. Few of the pre-war 19th-century buildings were reconstructed in ul. Marszałkowska and al. Jerozolimskie, the two large thorough-fares, both dating back to the 18th century, which intersect at right angles. Instead, this district, away from the 'museum-like' old centre, was rebuilt with modern structures. Ul. Marszałkowska was considerably widened and made the main traffic axis of the rebuilt city.

The landmark that has dominated modern Warsaw for the past 40 years is an – unloved – gift from the Soviet Union, the huge, pinnacled structure of the **Pałac Kultury i Nauki (Palace of Culture and Science)** (76) on Pl. Defilad. The building was completed in 1955

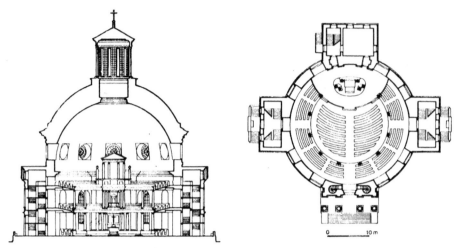

Lutheran Church, section and plan

after only three years and involved the clearing of a parade ground and the demolition of several apartment blocks which had survived the war. The architect, Lev V. Rudniev, a leading exponent of eclectic Stalinist monumentality, included some Polish elements in his design, notably the 'Polish parapets' surmounting the walls, a feature borrowed from the Sukiennice in Kraków. With a height of 234 metres and a total volume of 817,000 cubic metres it is the biggest building in the city. The institutions it shelters are many and varied: the Polish Academy of Sciences (PAN), the Polish section of the PEN Club, three theatres and three cinemas, the Museum of Technology and the Zoological Museum, exhibition halls, and three restaurants. The building has recently changed with the times – the Congress Hall is now a casino. There is a public viewing terrace on the thirtieth floor, which gives a view over the whole city. In front of the main façade to ul. Marszałkowska stand monuments to two important figures in Poland's cultural history: Mikołaj Kopernik (Nicolaus Copernicus) by Ludwik Nitsche, and Adam Mickiewicz by Stanisław Horno-Popławski. This large open space, Pl. Defilad, was used for communist parades and gymnastic displays; it is currently being redeveloped for commercial mixed use. The complex of buildings opposite, with the **Domy Towarowe 'Centrum' ('Centrum' Department Stores)** (77), was planned as an ensemble by Zbigniew Karpiński and built between 1960 and 1969. It includes residential, office and retail buildings.

Behind this complex, in ul. Jasna, stands the **Filharmonia (Philharmonic Hall)** (78), which replaces its predecessor, completely destroyed in 1944. It is the focus of Warsaw's lively musical life and the setting for the International Chopin Competition and the International Festival of Contemporary Music known as 'Warsaw Autumn'.

Continuing northwards along ul. Jasna for a few hundred metres we reach ul. Kredytowa, which was laid out in the 19th century and took its name from the Towarzystwo Kredytowe Ziemskie (Land Credit Society) whose headquarters (1854–8, Enrico Marconi and Józef Górecki) now contain the **Państwowe Muzeum Etnograficzne (State Ethnographical Museum)** (79) with wide-ranging collections of the folk art and culture of Poland, as well as of Africa, South America, Asia and Oceania.

Opposite stands the centrally-planned **Zbór Ewangelicko-Augsburgski (Lutheran Church)** (80), an uncompromising geometrical composition which is one of the most prominent examples of Neoclassicism in Warsaw (1777–81, Szymon Bogumił Zug; rebuilt 1950).

The building next door, the **Kamienica Heurichowska (Heurich House)** (81), is also of interest. It is one of the earliest (1907–10) Modernist buildings in the city, and was built by Jan Heurich the Younger for the Krasiński family. It is now the Ministry of Communications.

Opposite it is the famous **Zachęta Art Gallery** (82), built in 1898–1903 by Stefan Szyller in a grandiose neo-Baroque style for the Society for the Encouragement of the Fine Arts (Towarzystwo Zachęty Sztuk Pięknych). It holds regular exhibitions. The first President of Poland, Gabriel Narutowicz, was assassinated here in 1922.

From here we follow ul. Mazowiecka, Świętojańska and Nowy Świat to the **Muzeum Narodowe (National Museum)** (83), which, together with the Muzeum Wojska Polskiego (Museum of the Polish Armed Forces), occupies a large and important example of Functionalist architecture (1926–38, Tadeusz Tołwiński) in the eastern part of al. Jerozolimskie.

The National Museum developed from the Muzeum Sztuk Pięknych (Museum of Fine Arts), which was founded in 1862. The ground floor is used for the collection of prints from the School of Fine Arts, as well as a collection of casts once owned by King Stanisław August, together with about 200 paintings which had been bequeathed to the School of Fine Arts by Pietro Fiorentini, a merchant. Until the erection of the present building the Museum had no accommodation of its own. From 1898 it was provisionally placed in rented rooms in a house on Plac Teatralny. The collections grew not so much from purchases as from bequests from private owners. It was not until 1922 that the Museum, by now well stocked, was officially opened to the public. It had an outstanding collection of antiquities, an equally fine collection of European painting, applied arts, graphics and coins. During the war, and in particular during the Warsaw Uprising in 1944, the buildings and the collections suffered considerable damage. The reconstruction was accompanied by a significant expansion of the collection. Like all large museums in Poland it contains a number of works of art removed from churches, monasteries and various institutions during the war and not returned. Thus the most prominent exhibits in the collection of medieval art are the superb altarpieces from the castle chapel at Grudziądz, from St Elizabeth's Church, Wrocław, and from St Mary's Church, Gdańsk. The fine collection of European painting, which was considerably enriched by the incorporation of the Potocki collection in 1946, includes works by Pinturicchio, Lucas Cranach, Rembrandt, Jacob

Jordaens and Philippe de Champaigne. The development of Polish art is traced from the 16th century to the First World War; a large part of the collection comes from the Zachęta Society which was dissolved in 1945. Some of the great patriotic canvases of Jan Matejko (1838–93), notably the 'Battle of Grunwald', can be found here, as well as work by artists of the late 19th-century Young Poland movement, including the painter-playwright Stanisław Wyspiański (1869–1907). The museum's most unexpected exhibit is the remarkable series of wall paintings (8th to 12th centuries) from a church at Pharos in Nubia excavated by Polish archaeologists working in the Sudan in the 1970s.

From the National Museum we walk across ul. Nowy Świat and ul. Mokotowska to reach Pl. Konstytucji, the centre of the prominent **Marszałkowska Dzielnica Mieszkaniowa – 'MDM' (Marszałkowska Housing District)** (84), built in the Bierut era between 1949 and 1952 (architects: Stanisław Jankowski, Jan Knothe, Józef Sigalin and Zygmunt Stępiński).

Following ul. Marszałkowska southwards we come next to Pl. Zbawiciela with the **Kościół Zbawiciela (Church of the Saviour)** (85) built in 1901–11 by J. P. Dziekoński, L. Panczakiewicz and W. Żychiewicz. It displays an interesting mixture of elements from a variety of historical Polish styles, held in check by a tendency towards modern simplicity. Ul. Marszałkowska ends at Pl. Unii Lubelskiej with the Neoclassical **Rogatki Mokotowskie (Mokotów Toll Houses)** (86/87) dating from 1816–18 (Jakub Kubicki), which once marked the boundary of the city.

On ul. Puławska, which runs from here to Mokotów (once a village but now a district of Warsaw), just beyond Pl. Unii Lubelskej, the **'Supersam' Supermarket** (88), built in the 1960's, marks the beginning of an important part of the modern city. Further to the south is the former summer residence of the Lubomirski family, **Pałac Mokotowski (Mokotów Palace)**, Nos. 55–9 (89), a villa in a landscape garden, originally built in the late 18th century, but altered in 1822–5, and again in 1860–5 by Enrico Marconi in a neo-Gothic style. Its name is a polonization of 'Mon Côteau'.

Continuing even further south we finally reach the **Pałac Królikarnia (Królikarnia Palace)** – the name means 'rabbit warren' – No. 113 (90), now a branch of the National Museum housing works by the outstanding 20th-century sculptor Xawery Dunikowski. The name dates from the time of King August II, who used the estate as a hunting ground, filling it with game specially bred for the royal hunt. The palace was built between 1772 and 1786 by Domenico Merlini for the director of the Royal Theatre, Karol de Valery Thomatis. The two-storey square building, with its central domed rotunda and entrance portico, represents a type that has its origins in Andrea Palladio's Villa Rotonda near Vicenza. It is an outstanding example of the Palladian style, which strongly influenced the Neoclassicism of Stanisław August's Warsaw. The interior

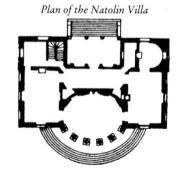

Plan of the Natolin Villa

was redecorated by Józef Huss after a fire in 1879; and, following complete destruction in the war, the palace was rebuilt in 1959–62.

Natolin and Wilanów

On the way to Wilanów (No. 193 bus from Al. Ujazdowskie or ul. Belwederska) we first pass through the satellite town of Ursynów-Natolin, created in the 1970's for a population of 160,000. But modern architecture is not the only feature of this district. In earlier centuries it had been developed by Jan III Sobieski and Stanisław August Poniatowski as part of a farsighted project to create a north-south axis through the city.

The historic centre of the district is the **Natolin** estate with its fine Neoclassical villa and a landscape garden. Originally part of the Wilanów estate, it passed to the Czartoryski family in the first half of the 18th century. In the 19th century it belonged to Aleksander Potocki, whose daughter, Natalia, gave the villa its name. The villa was built in 1780–82 for August Alexander Czartoryski by Szymon Bogumił Zug. Some of the elegant Neoclassical decoration of the interiors (by the Florentine Vincenzo Brenna) has survived all the later alterations, destruction and reconstruction. After alterations by Chrystian Piotr Aigner and Stanisław Kostka Potocki in 1808, some of the rooms were remodelled. One of these is the remarkable ballroom, which is conceived as an oval loggia open to the garden through six Ionic columns. The English garden was laid out between 1806 and 1815 by Anna Potocka; the entrance lodges are by Aigner (1823), but many of the smaller garden buildings – including a Doric temple, a classical aqueduct and a Moorish bridge – were built by Enrico Marconi in 1834–8.

The palace of **Wilanów**, part of the National Museum since 1945, is one of the most sumptuous châteaux in Poland (colour plate 16; plan page 223).

Until the 17th century it was an unpretentious country house. In 1650 work began on building a manor house, but this remained unfinished, and in 1677 it was acquired by Jan III Sobieski, who began its transformation into a royal residence. 'Wilanów' is a Polonization of 'Villa Nuova', and indeed the model for the palace was the Italian Baroque villa.

The *Palace* (a) itself is laid out on a horseshoe plan, with a main range flanked by two projecting wings, added in stages as and when funds permitted. The changes in style reflect this piecemeal planning. The complex which developed in this fashion is a characteristic example of a Baroque residence with a *cour d'honneur* on one side and a garden on the other.

The architect chosen by the king was his secretary, Agostino Locci, whose father (and namesake) had designed the Sigismund Column. The younger Locci was to become one of Poland's best-known Baroque architects.

The first section of the building was completed in 1679: using existing foundations, Locci built a modest, one-storey manor house with four corner pavilions. Work on the first extension to this house began soon afterwards (1681–7): it was raised by half a storey, and given gallery wings with towers at the ends. The manor house had thus already been transformed into a grand villa. At the same time the whole front was clad with a pilaster order, and a noble pedimented doorway with half-columns was inserted in the middle. The garden front was decorated with stucco ornaments.

From 1684 to 1696 Jan III Sobieski, always actively involved in the works at Wilanów, undertook another remodelling of the house. A further storey was added to the middle range and the pavilions were given attics at the front. The façade was also provided with a grandiose sculptural programme: on the attics were reliefs celebrating Sobieski's recent (1683) victory over the Turks at Kahlenberg near Vienna, and above them statues of the Muses with Pallas Athene, the goddess of learning (the latter is no longer extant). The statues were carved by Stefan Szwaner. The programme goes back to the classical motif of *arma et litterae* ('arms and letters'), which had become a topos in humanist encomia of princes: the ruler had to defend his land with arms against the outside, while ruling with learning and wisdom within it.

The decoration of the interiors of the palace also began in 1681. The programme was drawn up by Agostino Locci and Adam Kochański, the Royal Librarian, with the keen participation of the king himself. To execute the scheme he called upon a number of artists from home and abroad; the workshop they created was regarded as the nucleus for a future academy of art – on the model of the strictly organized patronage of Louis XIV.

The laying out of the park also dates from the beginning of work on the palace. It too was based on Italian models: a parterre on two levels with ornamental box hedges, a lake at the end and kitchen gardens at the sides for supplying the court. The domestic offices were built directly in front of the palace – a feature very much in the spirit of the classical ideal of the villa, which was supposed to be a self-sufficient organism. The constituent parts – the residence, park, domestic offices, farm – were to be treated largely as equals.

After Jan III Sobieski's death at Wilanów in 1696, not only did the residence remain unfinished, it also lost many of its valuable furnishings, which were divided between Queen Maria Kazimiera and her three sons. The heir to Wilanów, Prince Konstanty Sobieski, continued to work on the buildings for a little longer, but soon lost interest and allowed the palace to fall into disrepair.

However, Wilanów experienced a second heyday after 1720, when it passed into the hands of Elżbieta Sieniawska, the daughter of the great patron of the arts, Stanisław Herakliusz Lubomirski, and herself a well educated and ambitious connoisseur. Like Jan Sobieski, she gathered a circle of outstanding artists at Wilanów – including Johann Sigismund Deibel, Giovanni Spazzio, Giuseppe Fontana, Jan Jerzy Plersch and Giuseppe Rossi – and planned extensive rebuilding and alterations (notably the extension of the wings by Spazzio and Fontana), which were to continue for over a century. The next owners, August Aleksander Czartoryski and his daughter Izabela Lubomirska, continued to extend and modernize the complex of buildings, enlarging the park and bringing it into line with the new Rococo taste.

In 1799 Wilanów was inherited by Stanisław Kostka Potocki, and this marked the beginning of a new phase in the history of the palace. Potocki regarded it not just as a family seat but as a monument of a great epoch in Poland's past, and he planned to set it up as a memorial to King Jan III Sobieski. Potocki was the outstanding connoisseur and art theorist of his age and he brought together at Wilanów a variety of works dating from the period of Jan Sobieski. In 1802 Potocki also had a neo-Gothic gallery added to the north wing of the palace by Chrystian Piotr Aigner (remodelled in a neo-Renaissance style by Francesco Maria Lanci around 1850), to exhibit his collections of Polish and European portrait painting, classical sculpture, and Chinese and Japanese art. In 1805 the palace with its collections was opened to the public as a museum. The creation of the famous library was also his initiative. This treasure-house of rare manuscripts, illuminated incunables, engravings and maps was placed in what was formerly the palace's main hall, newly furnished for the purpose by Aigner.

The garden too underwent a thorough remodelling in this period. Potocki, who had a liking for the new English style of garden design, swept away the Baroque parterres with their statues and vases and laid out an extensive landscape garden. The offices and pavilions built by earlier owners were kept, but some were modified and they were supplemented by classical and chinoiserie buildings. As well as employing Chrystian Piotr Aigner and Szymon Bogumił Zug, Potocki prepared a number of designs and plans himself.

Under Stanisław Kostka Potocki's heirs, his son Aleksander, and later his grandson August, there were continual alterations to the fabric and decoration. From 1822 Enrico Marconi was working at Wilanów, followed around 1850 by Francesco Maria Lanci, and then by Marconi's sons, Władysław and Leonard.

The Second World War marked a decisive break in the history of Wilanów; the palace and gardens suffered serious damage; 90 per cent of the trees had been burned down. Immediately after the war work began on the restoration of the palace and the park, which have been returned, in part, to their Baroque forms.

Between 1954 and 1965 the palace underwent large-scale alterations to serve new functions. It was to continue to be a museum, but at the same time was to be used to accommodate guests on state visits. In the course of this work some of the 19th-century alterations were reversed and the appearance of the building as it had been in the 17th and 18th centuries was recreated. This required alterations to the exteriors; inside, hidden frescoes were found beneath layers of later plaster. The outbuildings too were put to new uses.

Wilanów today is once again primarily Jan III Sobieski's palace. The dominant theme is announced in the inscription on the façade: '*Quod vetus urbs coluit, nunc nova villa tenet*' – 'What the ancient city (Rome) honoured, the new villa (Wilanów) now possesses'. This message is reflected both in the architecture, with its allusions to Roman antiquity – such as the triumphal arch motif in the wings immediately next to the main range – and in the learned mythological-allegorical programme of the façade decoration.

The façade of the main range, distinguished by its Corinthian half-columns, is dominated by the golden sphere of the sun, whose rays are reflected by gilded shields bearing the Sobieski arms, held up by putti to the sun. A biblical quotation explains this motif: *'Refulsit sol / in clipeis'* – 'The sun is reflected in the shields'. The life-giving light of the sun, symbol of glory, radiates from King Jan III Sobieski onto the world. His glorious achievements are exemplified by the battle scenes on the reliefs and the Muses on the attic of the belvedere.

Allegorical praise is the function also of the two triumphal arches: the one on the right praises the King, that on the left the Queen, in front of their respective apartments.

The King's triumphal arch shows Alexander the Great dressed as Hercules, while the busts are those of classical emperors against whom the King measured his achievements; the statues in the niches below represent *Fortitudo* (Fortitude) and *Splendor Nominis* (Splendour of the Name, i.e. that of Jan III Sobieski). There is a triumphal procession in the lunette.

On the Queen's side the medallion above the doorway shows Dido, the Queen of Carthage, regarded as the embodiment of feminine beauty and intelligence. The figures in the niches are *Magnanimitas* (Magnanimity) and *Pudicitia* (Chastity).

The statues above the pavilions also form part of the programme: above the Queen's apartments stand Venus, Juno and Ceres, with Apollo, Jupiter and Mars opposite. On the façades of the ranges set at right angles to the main block the lunettes show mythological scenes taken from Ovid's Metamorphoses, with allegories of the virtues in the niches and busts of Roman emperors above (1723–9, by Gian Francesco Fumo and Pietro Innocente Comparetti).

The garden front balances this royal programme with fresco cycles of scenes from the Odyssey and the Aeneid. These too allude to heroic virtues, but also the nurturing of art, poetry and learning, which since antiquity had been regarded as the ideal of life in a villa, summed up in the motto *Otium cum dignitate* ('Leisure with dignity'). The pavilions have interesting sculptural decoration. On the south side is a sundial from the period around 1690 (Stephan Szwaner, Giuseppe Simone Bellotti): Saturn, the god of time, shown with wings and a scythe, spreads out the veil of the heavens, on which the hours and the zodiac are marked. The corresponding place on the north pavilion has a relief in honour of the Gdańsk astronomer Johannes Hevelius (or Hoewelke, 1611–87), who is supposed to have designed the sundial.

Despite many alterations, the interior of the palace has preserved its essential features. The symmetrical ground plan goes back to Agostino Locci's Italianate design: in the centre are two rooms one behind the other, flanked to left and right by the apartments of the King and Queen.

The columned great hall was a further monument to Sobieski, with an illusionistic frescoed ceiling showing him as Apollo driving away the powers of darkness and a monumental equestrian statue of himself as the vanquisher of the Turks. This was moved in the mid-18th century to the southern corner tower where it still remains; the fresco was replaced in the 19th century with ornamental plasterwork. The present wall decoration with Ionic half-columns and scagliola panels dates from a remodelling by Szymon Bogumił Zug at the end of the 18th century.

Beyond the hall is the 'Gabinet Holenderski' ('Dutch Cabinet'), so called because of a collection of Dutch paintings which Jan III Sobieski placed there. The ceiling fresco shows 'The Apotheosis of Prosperity, the Sciences and Arts under Saxon rule' and was painted c.1730, when Wilanów was occupied for a short time by August II. It is by the studio of the court painter Louis de Silvestre.

The bedrooms and their anterooms still have their painted decoration of Jan III Sobieski's time. The ceiling paintings show allegories of the four seasons (Jerzy Eleuter Szymonowicz-Siemiginowski), which once again are conceived as allusions to Jan III Sobieski and Maria Kazimiera: in the King's Bedroom is Summer (Apollo in the chariot of the Sun), in his anteroom Winter (Aeolus commanding the winds to rest – representing the peace-bringing ruler); in the Queen's Bedroom Spring (the season that awakens beauty and love) and in her anteroom Autumn (Vertumnus and Pomona, the god and goddess of fruitful nature).

View of Warsaw, early 17th-century engraving

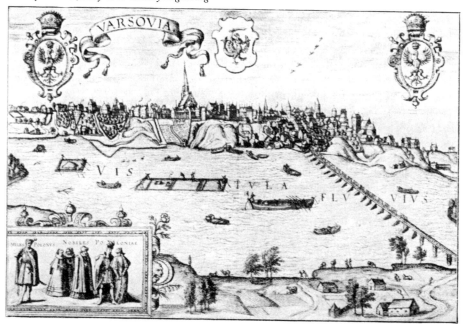

In the rich plasterwork of the friezes (by Giuseppe Simone Bellotti) are depicted scenes of bucolic life from Virgil's *Georgics*. The original decoration in the cabinets of the Queen's Apartments is also preserved. The 'Gabinet Zwierciadlany' ('Mirror Cabinet') has a circular ceiling painting by Claude Callot showing the Queen as Aurora. The putti and geniuses accompanying her are portraits of her sons Jakub, Aleksander and Konstantyn. Another cabinet has an illusionistic fresco imitating tapestries woven with scenes from the story of Apollo (Jerzy Eleuter Szymonowicz-Siemiginowski).

The decoration of the rest of the apartments dates from the period around 1730, including the third cabinet of the Queen with its depictions of the Loves of Jupiter (an appropriate subject for the amorous August II), and the King's 'Chinese Cabinet'.

Originally the rooms were expensively decorated with furniture from Italy, France and the Netherlands, and with paintings by famous artists, including Rembrandt, Van Dyck and Baciccia. The detailed inventory taken after Jan Sobieski's death in 1696 was a major source for reconstruction. The royal apartments today are a museum of Baroque interior decoration and portraiture.

In Jan III Sobieski's time the upper floor contained guest rooms, and the apartments of the princes and of the architect Agostino Locci. The painted decoration, less grandiose than that on the ground floor, is of more recent date. The interior is intended to suggest the decoration of a Polish manor house of the period around 1700.

The gallery wings linking the main block to the corner pavilions deserve close attention. They are decorated with frescoes by Michelangelo Palloni telling the story of Cupid and Psyche. At the end of the north gallery is Jacques Louis David's superb equestrian portrait of Stanisław Kostka Potocki.

In the south wing the apartments of Izabela Lubomirska have been recreated (plate 8). Originally decorated in the 1790's, they contain 18th-century French and Polish furniture and paintings by Italian, Flemish and Dutch artists. Also in the south wing is the great dining hall created in 1730 for August II by Johann Sigismund Deibel.

The north wing now once again has the decoration it received in the course of the 19th century at the time of the Potockis. The living rooms are in Empire style, as are the rooms and cabinets of the gallery, which were decorated to suit the various exhibits (an 'Etruscan Cabinet', for example, for the collection of classical ceramics).

Like the palace, the park in its present, restored form documents the history and development of the estate. It is entered through a *Gate* (b) with allegorical figures of war and peace from the time of Jan III Sobieski. The Baroque courtyard garden was replaced in the mid-19th century by an oval lawn. On the right are the Neoclassical *Wash-house* (c), *Kitchen* (d) and *Stables* (e) (1775–8, Szymon Bogumił Zug).

At the rear of the palace the Italian parterre garden has been reconstructed as it was created for Jan III Sobieski. On the *retaining wall* (f) which separates the two levels are allegorical statues of the Four Seasons and the Four Stages of Love dating from the first half of the 18th century.

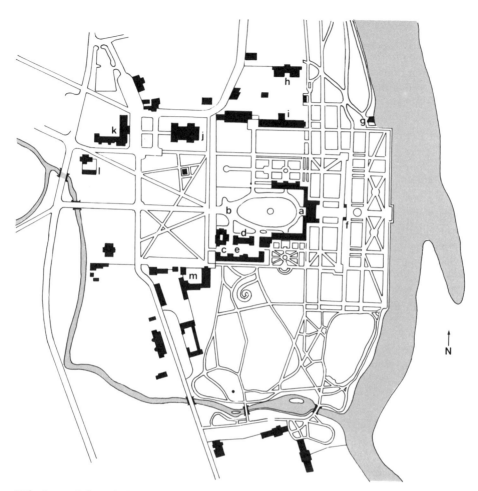

Wilanów a Palace b Gate c Wash-house d Kitchen e Stables f Retaining wall g Pumping station h Szpital św. Aleksandra (Hospital of St Alexander) i Oranżeria (Orangery) j Kościoł św. Anny (Church of St Anne) k Karczma (Inn) l Stara Karczma (Old Inn) m Muzeum Plakatu (Poster Museum)

South of the palace and the Baroque garden is an extensive English landscape garden laid out by Szymon Bogumił Zug for Izabela Lubomirska on the site of Jan III Sobieski's farm, with artificial hills and a fine collection of trees and shrubs.

Another English park extends north of the Baroque garden, along the banks of the lake of Wilanów. At the border between the two parks stands a brick Gothic *Pumping Station* (g) built in 1856 by Enrico Marconi for irrigating the gardens with water from the lake. Continuing further north we come to a Chinese Pavilion of 1806.

Returning to the palace we pass a complex of outbuildings, erected gradually from the 17th century onwards and intended for the inhabitants of the village of Wilanów and for travellers: first the *Szpital św. Aleksandra (Hospital of St Alexander)* (h), built in the 18th century and altered in 1845–7 by Enrico Marconi (it is now a storehouse); opposite is the *Oranżeria* (i) from the mid-18th century (remodelled 1806–21). Further west rises the domed *Kościół św. Anny (Parish Church of St Anne)* (j), of *c.*1770, altered in a neo-Renaissance style by Enrico Marconi between 1857 and 1870.

The *Karczma (Inn)* (k) opposite the church, now the Wilanów Restaurant, and the *Stara Karczma (Old Inn)* (l) were built in 1681 by Agostino Locci for Jan III Sobieski. Their present appearance is the result of neo-Renaissance alterations (*c.*1850, by Francesco Maria Lanci) and of renovation work in the 1960's.

Finally the outbuilding on the other side of the forecourt deserves attention. It is the former Riding School built in 1848–50 by Francesco Maria Lanci in a mixture of styles, which today, after conversion in 1968, contains the exceptionally interesting *Muzeum Plakatu (Poster Museum)* (m); the Poles have a worldwide reputation as poster designers. The way there takes us past the picturesque neo-Gothic mausoleum of Stanisław Kostka Potocki and his wife Aleksandra (1836, Enrico Marconi).

Dorota Leszczyńska and Michaela Marek

Mazowsze (Mazovia)

Sandy plains, broad forests and gently undulating moraine hills are the characteristic landscapes of Mazowsze (Mazovia), which includes the Nizina Mazowiecka (Mazovian Lowland) around Warsaw, the Nizina Podlaska (Podlasian Lowland) in the northeast and the Polesie Lubelskie (Lublin Woodland), part of the East European Plain.

Mazovia was once famous for its magnificent primeval forests (*puszcze* in Polish). There are still remnants of these in the Kampinoski National Park, Poland's largest nature reserve, which covers an area of 407 km² just to the west of Warsaw. Other remains of this primeval landscape, which has now become rare in Europe, are the Puszcza Biała (White Forest), between the rivers Narew and Bug, and the Puszcza Zielona (Green Forest) on the tributaries west of the Narew.

When the earliest settlements were formed in the area of the upper Vistula, Warta, Oder and on Lake Gopło, Mazovia as such did not yet exist. Not until the rule of Mieszko I did settlers from Kujawy establish themselves, mainly in the vicinity of already existing fortified towns on the wide, infertile, heathlands and primeval forests. They had to accept the authority of independent feudal lords who at first were successful in resisting the establishment of a central power in Poland.

Only ten years after the founding of the separate principality of Mazovia by the feudal ruler, Masław, in 1037, the region was conquered by the Polish prince Kazimierz I Odnowiciel, and then passed to a Piast lord with his residence at Płock. About a hundred years later, in 1138, Prince Bolesław III Krzywousty in his will ordered the founding of an autonomous principality, which also included part of Kujawy and the land of Sieradz as well as Mazovia, but in the ensuing period this was broken up into several separate principalities.

This was a period of intense colonization, which extended eastwards as far as Podlasie and southeast to Ruthenia. Border castles such as Drohiczyn and Bielsk were the objects of fierce struggles in the 12th and 13th centuries. To the north, the Mazovian colonization extended across the Ciechanów plateau to the land of the original pagan Prussians, or Pruzzi. The princes of Mazovia attempted to bring the latter under their rule as well, thereby

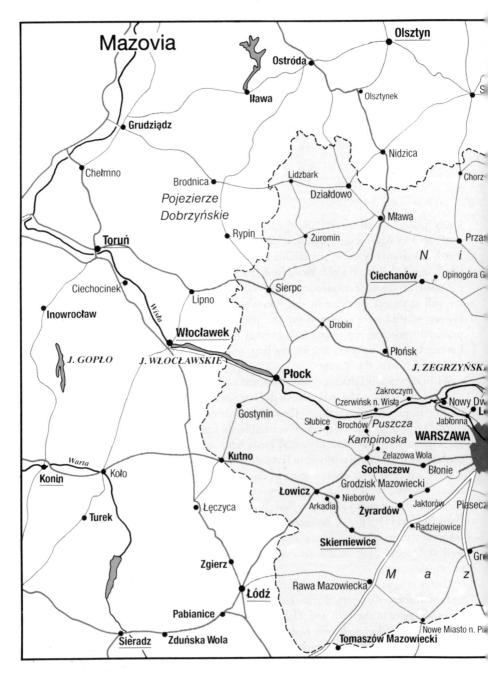

Mazovia

Olsztyn
Ostróda
Iława
Olsztynek
S
Grudziądz
Nidzica
Chełmno
Brodnica
Lidzbark
Chorz
Pojezierze
Działdowo
Dobrzyńskie
Mława
Rypin
Żuromin
Prza
Toruń
N   i
Ciechanów
Opinogóra G
Ciechocinek
Lipno
Sierpc
Inowrocław
Wisła
Drobin
Włocławek
J. GOPŁO   *J. WŁOCŁAWSKIE*
Płońsk
J. ZEGRZYŃSK
Płock
Zakroczym
Czerwińsk n. Wisłą
Nowy Dw
Gostynin
L
Słubice Brochów *Puszcza*
Jabłonna
Kampinoska
WARSZAWA
Warta
Kutno
Żelazowa Wola
Konin
Koło
Sochaczew
Błonie
Łowicz
Grodzisk Mazowiecki
Łęczyca
Nieborów
Jaktorów
Piasec
Turek
Arkadia
Żyrardów
Radziejowice
Skierniewice
Gr
Zgierz
M   a   z
Łódź
Rawa Mazowiecka
Pabianice
Nowe Miasto n. Pi
Sieradz Zduńska Wola
Tomaszów Mazowiecki

226

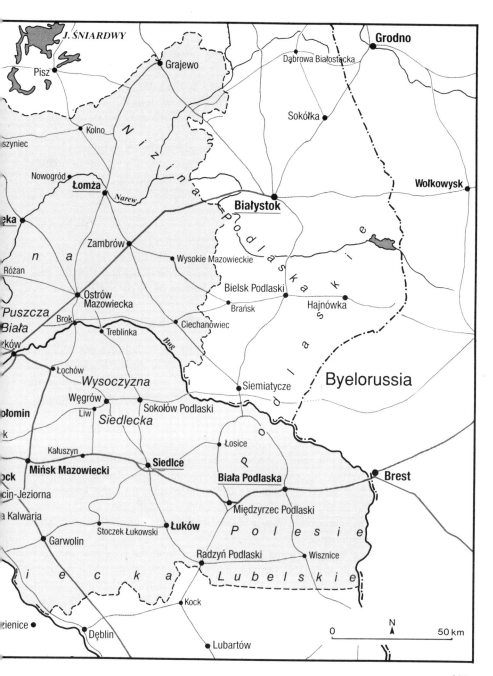

J. ŚNIARDWY

Pisz

Grajewo

Dąbrowa Białostocka

Grodno

Sokółka

Kolno

...szyniec

Nizina

Nowogród

Łomża

Narew

Białystok

Wołkowysk

...ęka

Zambrów

Podlaska

Wysokie Mazowieckie

...Różan

n a

Bielsk Podlaski

Hajnówka

Ostrów
Mazowiecka

Brańsk

Puszcza

Brok

Biała

Treblinka

Ciechanowiec

Bug

...ków

Łochów

Siemiatycze

Byelorussia

Wysoczyzna

Węgrów

...ołomin

Liw

Sokołów Podlaski

...k

Siedlecka

Łosice

Kałuszyn

Siedlce

Mińsk Mazowiecki

Biała Podlaska

Brest

...ock

...cin-Jeziorna

...a Kalwaria

Międzyrzec Podlaski

Łuków

Polesie

Garwolin

Stoczek Łukowski

Radzyń Podlaski

Wisznice

...i   e   c   k   a

Lubelskie

Kock

...ienice

Dęblin

Lubartów

N

0

50 km

227

provoking fierce retaliatory attacks. In 1226 Konrad Mazowiecki ('of Mazovia') sum-moned the Teutonic Knights to his aid from Hungary with the intention of converting them. The Knights succeeded in subduing the heathens, but themselves soon grew into a power that menaced both Mazovia and Lithuania.

In the 13th century and the first half of the 14th century Mazovia was in constant conflict with the Teutonic Order and with Lithuania. As a result of this unequal struggle Mazovia was so severely devastated that it was forced to become a vassal state of the Polish kingdom.

The personal union of Poland and Lithuania at the end of the 14th century created a favourable climate for Mazovia's development. Warsaw gained in importance as a trading centre and the newly acquired access to the Baltic along the Vistula (1466) opened up markets for agricultural produce from Mazovia, Lithuania and Ruthenia in Toruń and Gdańsk. The extinction of the dynasty of the princes of Mazovia brought about final unification with Poland in 1526, and with Podlasie, after the Union of Lublin, in 1569. In 1596 King Zygmunt III Waza transferred the capital from Kraków to Warsaw.

In the 16th and 17th centuries Mazovia was a densely populated territory filled with characteristic manors of the gentry (szlachta), while extensive latifundia of the mag-nates were created in the less populous regions in eastern Mazovia and Podlasie. The gentry were members of the large but impoverished knightly estate, and their political importance increased when they were given the right to participate in the election of the kings.

During the Age of Enlightenment Warsaw developed into a cultural and economic centre, where the struggle for the political and social rebirth of Poland began. After the Second Partition (1793) Prussia annexed the western region, and in the Third Partition the northern parts of the territory went to Prussia, while the rest was acquired by Austria.

Between 1807 and 1815 Mazovia, except for the northern part, which was annexed by Russia, formed part of the Duchy of Warsaw founded by Napoleon. After the Congress of Vienna, Russia, the great power to the north, was able to exercise its influence over the region: the district of Białystok remained directly under the control of the Tsarist Empire, while the rest of the territory became part of the Kingdom of Poland, with the Russian Tsar as King. The November Uprising (1830–31) once again cost the kingdom its sovereignty, and the January Uprising (1863–4), which saw fierce fighting in Mazovia and Podlasie, was unable to win it back. Russia reacted with severe punitive measures and a relentless policy of Russification.

The towns along the Warsaw-Vienna railway profited from the economic and social changes in the second half of the 19th century. Economic development, which continued after Poland regained its independence in 1918, was abruptly ended by the outbreak of the Second World War. Mazovia's closeness to East Prussia meant that it was quickly embroiled in the conflict. The horror of Nazi rule left its mark in this part of Poland. At Treblinka 800,000 people were killed, mainly Jews deported there from all over Poland.

Rural costumes in Mazovia, 19th-century lithograph

Kampinoski National Park – Żelazowa Wola – Brochów – Łowicz – Arkadia – Skierniewice – Radziejowice – Grodzisk Mazowiecki

The history of the area around Łowicz on the Bzura goes back to the 12th century. In 1136 the settlement that had developed around a castle belonging to the Dukes of Mazovia passed into the possession of the Bishops of Gniezno, who from the 15th century onwards were also Primates of Poland. Because of the status of the bishops and Łowicz's favourable situation at the intersection of the important trade routes between Toruń, Lwów, Poznań and Warsaw the region experienced a long, steady flowering.

The road from Warsaw to Łowicz skirts the **Kampinoski National Park**, still a wild and inaccessible area of forest and marshland, rich in wildlife (including wild boar). Its proximity to the capital made it an ideal refuge in times of trouble, particularly for the insurgents in 1863 and the partisans during the Second World War; the Nazis also used it for mass executions, some of whose victims are commemorated at the cemetery near the village of Palmiry (see page 241).

About 50 km from Warsaw is **Żelazowa Wola**, the birthplace of Fryderyk Chopin

(1810–49). The house of the Skarbek family, where his father (who was French) served as tutor, is no longer there, but the estate building where the family lived has survived and attracts music-lovers from all over the world. In 1931 the humble building was converted into a rather grander Chopin memorial house. In the Second World War the collection of authentic memorabilia was destroyed and has since been replaced with replicas. Early 19th-century furniture was collected for the rooms, and facsimiles of autograph scores and documents are displayed, with copies of family portraits. Piano recitals are held here on Sundays in the summer. Concerts also take place in the unusually charming park.

About 10 km to the north of Żelazowa Wola, in the village of **Brochów**, is a fortified *Church* characteristic of the Mazovian Renaissance. Originally Gothic, it was remodelled in the 1550's by the architect Giovanni Battista da Venezia, who had brought the severe monumentality of the North Italian High Renaissance from Venice to Mazovia (see also Pułtusk, page 241, and Brok, page 246). Despite rebuilding in 1665, destruction in the First World War and subsequent reconstruction the church has preserved its unique character. On the outside the compact brick building has three tall, round towers and a defensive passage, but the architecture within is bright and elegant. The nave has a barrel vault with flat ribbed coffering and simple arcades to the aisles; the blind arcading with engaged piers gives the aisles a crystalline plasticity. Fryderyk Chopin was baptized here and the parish records include an album listing the births, marriages and deaths in his family.

The town of **Łowicz** enjoyed its greatest prosperity as an important trading centre and the residence of the Primates of Poland. It has retained hardly any of its medieval architecture; its townscape was created between the 17th and 19th centuries, while the old castle of the Mazovian Piasts fell into ruin. Łowicz is famous for its Corpus Christi Day procession (usually in June), which is a good opportunity to see the colourful local costumes being worn.

The historic buildings are grouped around two market places, Rynek Kościuszki (Kościuszko Square) and Rynek Kilińskiego (Kiliński Square) two blocks further east.

In the middle of Rynek Kościuszki, at the centre of the town, stands the *Kościół Kolegiacki (Collegiate Church)*. This was originally a wooden building, which was rebuilt as a Gothic church in the 15th century and given a Baroque remodelling about two hundred years later (1652–68) by the Italian architects Tommaso and Andrea Poncino. The façade seems to be squeezed between the west towers, retained from a slightly earlier remodelling (1624) but given their spires by Ephraim Schroeger in the 18th century.

The church is the burial place of many of the Primates of Poland (and other prelates) and contains a large number of richly decorated chapels, tombs and altars. One of the most interesting is the chapel of Archbishop Jakub Uchański with his tomb, erected in 1580–83 by the leading Polish sculptor of the Late Renaissance, Jan Michałowicz, and remodelled in Neoclassical form by Ephraim Schroeger in 1782–3. The figure of the archbishop with wrinkled face, gnarled hands and gently falling drapery, shows the penetrating realism which had been introduced into Poland by Veit Stoss of Nuremberg a century before.

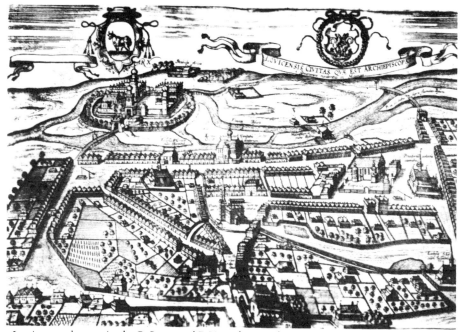

Łowicz, wood engraving by G. Braun and F. Hogenberg, 16th century

In the northwest corner of Rynek Kościuszki stand the 18th-century Baroque Vicars' Court and Canons' Houses. The Neoclassical *Town Hall*, built by Bonifacy Witkowski in 1825–8, is a characteristic example of the rather dry, mass-produced architecture of the administrative buildings erected in the first half of the 19th century in many towns of Congress Poland. Another example in Łowicz is the *Poczta Konna (Horse Post Office)* in ul. 3 Maja, built in 1829 and reconstructed in 1950 after the war.

The east side of Rynek Kościuszki is occupied by the former *Seminarium Misjonarzy (Missionaries' Seminary)*, built between 1689 and 1701 by Tylman van Gameren, the Utrecht architect who became the leading exponent of the Baroque in Poland. The building was reconstructed in its essentials after the Second World War, and it now houses a branch of the Warsaw National Museum with exhibits illustrating the history and folk traditions of the Łowicz district, which was famous for its brightly coloured costumes. In the adjoining grounds peasants' houses and agricultural implements can be seen. Baroque art from all over Poland is displayed in the former chapel of the seminary, one of Tylman van Gameren's most important works, with frescoes of the life of St Charles Borromeo by Michelangelo Palloni, court painter to Jan III Sobieski.

On the way to Rynek Kilińskiego along ul. Zduńska we pass the former *Kościół Pijarów*

(Piarist Church), a Baroque building of 1672–80 with a curved façade added in the mid-18th century and good Late Baroque ceiling paintings.

Ul. Zduńska, with its variety of burghers' houses dating from between the 16th and 19th centuries (the south side was completely rebuilt after war damage), opens into the triangular Rynek Kilińskiego, which is lined with picturesque houses of the Renaissance and Baroque periods.

Several former religious houses merit a short detour. One block to the north of the square, in ul. Podrzeczna, stands the *Klasztor Dominikanów (Dominican Monastery)*, originally a Baroque building dating from the second half of the 17th century. Like almost all monastic buildings it was altered several times to serve various purposes: in 1818, for example, it became a barracks. Today the building, which was restored in 1948–52, contains a technical college. A few steps further on, in ul. Zamkowa at the edge of the old town centre, stand the remains of the former *Zamek (Castle)*, which became the bishops' residence. Razed by the Swedes in the 17th century, it was rebuilt in the 18th century, destroyed again around 1800, and subsequently used as a quarry for new buildings in the town.

South of Rynek Kilińskiego, in ul. Stanisławskiego, we come first to the *Kościół św. Ducha (Holy Ghost Church)*, the oldest church in the town. It was begun in 1404, but its original character has been lost in the course of many alterations. Then comes the former *Klasztor Bernardynów (Bernardine Monastery)*, with its Gothic church (late 16th century) and Baroque monastic buildings (mid-18th century). This too was converted into barracks in the early 19th century and later into a school.

Returning in the direction of Rynek Kościuszki along ul. Sienkiewicza we pass the *Klasztor Bernardynek (Convent of Bernardine Nuns)*, a unified Baroque ensemble built by

Arkadia, plan of the Park

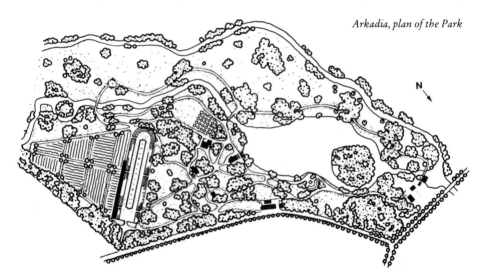

Tommaso Poncino *c*.1650. Turning right at the end of the street into ul. 1 Maja, a few minutes' walk brings us to the romantic *Villa* built in 1822–4 by the architect Karol Krauze for Stanisław Klicki, a general in Kościuszko's army. The remains of the landscape garden with its valuable collection of white poplars are preserved as a national monument. The buildings – palace and bastion – hark back to medieval castles with their banked base, turrets and battlements. The building material is iron ore, bare brick and rubble from the ruins of the bishops' castle.

On the road to Nieborów and Skierniewice, 6 km southeast of Łowicz, is **Arkadia**, a park created between 1778 and 1821 for Princess Helena Radziwiłł in the picturesque landscape style recently imported from England, though unlike most English parks it is not attached to a great house. Arkadia is one of the finest and best preserved examples of the landscape garden in Poland and is now part of the Warsaw National Museum. The architect was Szymon Bogumił Zug, the leading exponent of Polish Neoclassicism, who was much in demand as a garden designer. The artfully composed landscape he created, with a lake, streams, woods, groves, meadows and many winding paths, is dotted with pavilions, the artificial ruins of a classical amphitheatre and an aqueduct (1784), a pseudo-Gothic chapel and a Swiss chalet. There are also classical statues and fragments which the Princess herself collected for Arkadia on her extensive travels. Particularly delightful is Zug's little Neoclassical Temple of Diana (1783) on the shore of the lake (plate 12), with a ceiling painting by Jean-Pierre Norblin.

The *Palace* and *Park* at **Nieborów** 4 km away are also a characteristic product of the refined culture of the nobility in the 17th and 18th centuries in Poland. The ensemble has been painstakingly restored in all details of its decoration since the Second World War, and like Arkadia it is now a branch of the National Museum in Warsaw. The Baroque palace was built in 1690–96 by Tylman van Gameren for Cardinal Michał Radziejowski. The two-storey building with a high mansard roof, gabled centrepiece and tower-like pavilions flanking the façade stands at the end of a long driveway. Following the pattern of the gardens of French châteaux there is a parterre garden behind the palace with an axial avenue of lime trees. In the 1770's the palace passed into the possession of Prince Michał Hieronim Radziwiłł and Princess Helena, the creator of Arkadia. This was the heyday of Nieborów when the palace and gardens attained the form that made them famous. Szymon

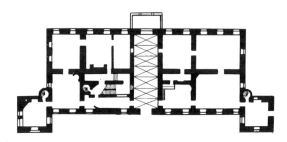

Nieborów, plan of the Palace

Bogumił Zug built several Neoclassical estate buildings including a brewery, stables and a carriage building, a guesthouse and an orangery, in which exotic plants are still grown today. To the west of the palace and its parterre garden Zug laid out an extensive English garden, as he had already done at Arkadia.

Nieborów is famous above all for the decoration of the palace (restored in its entirety), and for the extensive art collection assembled by Michał Hieronim Radziwiłł, which ranges from classical sculptures (including the famous Nieborów Niobe), through painting and porcelain of the Baroque and Neoclassical periods, to a library which contains valuable incunables from all the important publishing centres of Europe.

About 17 km southeast of Nieborów we come to **Skierniewice**, a small town whose Baroque-Neoclassical appearance dates from the 17th and 18th centuries when, like Łowicz, it belonged to the Archbishops of Gniezno. The station, built in 1846 by Adam Idźkowski in the *Rundbogenstil* at a junction on the Warsaw-Vienna line, has important historical associations. It was here in 1884 that Tsar Alexander III welcomed the Austrian Emperor Franz Joseph I and the German Emperor Wilhelm I to the conference which later became famous as the 'Meeting of the Three Emperors'. It was intended to find a solution to the disagreement between Russia and Austria-Hungary. The conference was held at the Palace of the Archbishops of Gniezno, which was then the seat of the Tsarist governor of Warsaw. The palace was built at the beginning of the 17th century and given a Baroque remodelling in the 1760's by Ephraim Schroeger. The park belonging to it now forms the centre of the town. On the edge of it stands another important work by Schroeger, the Neoclassical *Kościół Farny (Parish Church)* of 1780–81. Originally intended as the mausoleum of its founder, the Primate Antoni Ostrowski, it has a circular ground plan with a portico façade. In the long chancel the architect incorporated the remains of a Gothic tower. The interior, with blind arcading and a coffered ceiling, is inspired by the Roman Pantheon.

The road from Skierniewice to the village of **Radziejowice** about 30 km away runs through the Puszcza Jaktorowska, a primeval forest rich in game. When the Polish kings came hunting here, they stayed at the *Palace* of the Radziejowski family. It is worth making a short detour to visit this, since it is a typical example of the smaller aristocratic country seat popular all over Poland in the first half of the 19th century. As is often the case, it is a Neoclassical remodelling of an earlier palace dating from the late 17th century. The architect, Jakub Kubicki, was also responsible for converting the ruined fort into a little neo-Gothic castle and linking it to the palace by means of a gallery. Between the buildings and a pond that was also part of the estate lies a magnificent landscape garden, laid out by the architect Alexandre d'Alphonse de Saint-Omer in the course of the remodelling in 1817.

We can return to Warsaw by way of Jordanowice, a suburb of **Grodzisk Mazowiecki**, where there is another characteristic country manor (ul. Parkowa 1). The only indications that the plain, one-storey *Palace* of the second half of the 18th century is a nobleman's residence are the corner pilasters and a pedimented entrance. The interior contains some fine and carefully restored early Neoclassical decorative painting by Jan Bogumił Plersch, whose major works were created for the king in Warsaw.

Jabłonna – Nowy Dwór Mazowiecki – Zakroczym – Czerwińsk – Płock – Słubice

The way from Warsaw, the present capital of Mazovia, to Płock, its medieval capital, passes many interesting towns and villages which reflect various periods of the region's history.

About 20 km northwest of Warsaw, near the north bank of the Vistula, we reach the village of **Jabłonna**, where the Primate Michał Poniatowski, the brother of King Stanisław August, had his summer residence. The first architect he entrusted with the building of his *Palace* (1774–5) was Domenico Merlini; the corner pavilions were added by Szymon Bogumił Zug in 1783. The building, which now forms the principal range of the present palace, is arranged around a circular hall, which is visible from the outside rising above the other rooms. The façade is emphasized by a turret with a curious spire surmounted by a globe. The interior of the palace had lavish painted and plasterwork decoration created by the leading artists of the day.

After the death of Michał Poniatowski in 1794 during the Kościuszko Uprising, the estate was inherited by his nephew Prince Józef Poniatowski, who used it as a second residence after the Pałac Pod Blachą in Warsaw. Here he brought together his extensive collection of archives (now in Warsaw's Archiwum Główne Akt Dawnych – Principal Archive of Old Documents). In 1822 Jabłonna passed into the possession of the Potocki

Jabłonna, view of the Palace, drawing by F. Smuglewicz, c.1784

family, who owned it until the end of the Second World War. Anna Potocka, née Dunin-Wąsowiczowa, known as 'Anetka', was one of the highly cultivated, intellectual ladies in the early 19th century who devoted their fortunes and artistic expertise to the creation of exquisitely designed residences. In 1837 she commissioned the court architect Enrico Marconi to extend the palace. A new sequence of rooms was added to the main range and the façade was remodelled with an elegant decorative pilaster articulation. In the interior Domenico Merlini's Baroque-Neoclassical decoration was preserved only in the round hall: all the other rooms were redecorated.

In 1944 the palace was devastated by fire, and it was impossible to save any of the furnishings. What can be seen today is the result of painstaking reconstruction in the style of the years around 1800. The decoration has been recreated and the furniture brought together from elsewhere. The superb art collection did not return here after the war. The Potockis had moved it to safety in Warsaw shortly before the fire, and it was later sold and broken up.

Since 1953 the restored palace has been used by the Polska Akademia Nauk (Polish Academy of Sciences); it is not open to the public.

The residence always had extensive gardens, originally laid out with parterres. In 1783 Michał Poniatowski began to have it remodelled by Szymon Bogumił Zug. The romantic pavilions and Neoclassical guesthouse date from his time. The park was extended by Anna Potocka and transformed into an English landscape garden. The triumphal arch in honour of Prince Józef Poniatowski was also erected at her behest.

The road along the north bank of the Vistula comes after 16 km to the little town of **Nowy Dwór Mazowiecki**. On the western edge of the town on a hill above the strategically important confluence of the Narew and Vistula stands the *Twierdza Modlin (Modlin Fortress)*, an important example of 19th-century military architecture. It was planned in 1806–7 by General François de Chasseloup-Laubat for Napoleon. During the 19th century it was extended several times, surrounded with additional earthworks and bastions, and more residential and office quarters were built. Within a circumference of several kilometres about 20 forts sprang up. Among the many engineers, officers and architects involved in the planning of this, the most notable were the generals Ivan Dehn and Eduard von Todtleben, and the architect Jan Jakub Gay. The buildings are mostly Neoclassical and grandly conceived, whatever their function; some of them – the officers' mess, for example – are lavishly decorated. During the Second World War the fortress played an important strategic role, and in September 1939 it was fiercely defended, its garrison only abandoning the struggle once Warsaw had capitulated.

Only about 7 km further stands the little town of **Zakroczym** on the high bank of the Vistula. Its castle is mentioned as early as the 11th century, and it achieved its greatest importance in the 15th and 16th centuries, when it was the capital of the Ziemia Zakroczymska (Zakroczym Region) and the place where the princes of Mazovia met to debate legislation. In September 1831 this old tradition was renewed, when Zakroczym became the seat of government and of the Sejm of the insurrectionists. Of the old *Castle* on Góra Zamkowa (Castle Hill) only insignificant traces of the foundations remain, but there is a fine view from here over the Vistula to the Puszcza Kampinoska.

The *Kościół Podwyższenia św. Krzyża (Church of the Exaltation of the Holy Cross)* (plate 14) was built in the second half of the 16th century in an individualistic eclectic style combining Late Gothic and Renaissance features. It replaced an earlier, wooden building, which had burned down in 1511. The round windows in the side aisles date from alterations undertaken in the 17th century. The crushingly heavy proportions of the building are even more striking in the interior than outside. The church, as restored after severe damage in 1939, is simple and modest, but some pieces of the old decoration have survived, including monuments of the 16th and 17th centuries, and the painting on the high altar, which dates from around 1663 and is probably the work of Jeremiasz Melechowicz, then active as a court painter.

On the northern edge of the town is the *Klasztor Kapucynów (Capuchin Monastery)* with its *Kościół św. Wawrzyńca (Church of St Lawrence)*, an attractive group, which was restored in 1950 and 1980–81 after serious war damage. It was founded in the mid-18th century by the mayor, Józef Młocki.

The village of **Czerwińsk**, high above the Vistula, once enjoyed the status of a town. It developed from a small settlement and in the mid-11th century belonged to the Benedictine abbey of Mogilno. Around 1100 the village passed into the possession of the Bishops of Płock, who in 1148 invited Canons Regular from France and founded an abbey here. The *Opactwo (Abbey)* built at that time (colour plate 19) is one of the most important architectural monuments in Mazovia. The church, a three-aisled Romanesque basilica with a twin-towered west front, has regained its original medieval appearance after many later alterations thanks to its reconstruction after heavy damage during the Second World War. The beautiful Romanesque doorway merits special attention. The Late Gothic bell-tower was built in front of the church in 1497. In the course of the rebuilding, the arcades in the interior were found under Baroque cladding. They have been uncovered, as have three frescoes in the south part of the church. A fragment of Romanesque wall painting measuring about 10 m^2 and dating from the early 12th century is the largest and best preserved piece of painting of this period in Poland. The greater part of the church's furnishings dates from the Renaissance and Baroque periods.

The Late Gothic monastic buildings adjoining the church on the south sides were built in the 15th and 16th centuries (and rebuilt after 1950). One range was always intended to be a residence for the princes and kings passing through. Fine rib vaulting has survived in some of the rooms, particularly the refectory, which is now used as a chapel. Remains of Gothic wall paintings have also been uncovered here in places.

The heyday of the town, and also of the abbey, was in the 15th and 16th centuries, when wealthy merchants settled within its walls. In 1410 the army of Władysław Jagiełło crossed the Vistula here on the campaign against the Teutonic Order, using the first, pontoon, bridge to be built across the river. In the 15th century Czerwińsk was a place where the local Polish assemblies (dietines or *sejmiki*) met. During the Swedish wars in the 17th century the town was so badly damaged that it never recovered. In 1869 it lost its town status and today has a population of barely 700.

On another eminence above the Vistula lies the town of **Płock** which, as recent excavations have shown, was already in existence as a small settlement in the 9th century. From the 10th century until 1495 this was the seat of the Dukes of Mazovia. In 1075 Płock was raised to a bishopric, and in 1237 it became the first settlement in Mazovia to receive a town charter. From the mid-14th century onwards this important political centre also became significant economically, as it developed into one of the most important trading posts on the Vistula. Following the Swedish wars in the 17th century and a series of destructive fires, the town went into steady decline, and did not experience a revival of its economic and cultural fortunes until the 19th century, when it again became the centre of regional administration. The second half of the century saw the beginning of the establishment of industry here. Today Płock is a busy industrial town (mainly oil refining) with an active cultural life, as well as being full of reminders of its great past. It is still the seat of a mystical sect, the Mariavites, founded here at the end of the 19th century, but soon excommunicated owing to the excesses of these 'slaves of Mary'.

The history of Płock can be traced most clearly on the *Wzgórze Zamkowe (Castle Hill)* (also called Wzgórze Tumskie – Cathedral Hill), which slopes steeply down to the Vistula and is surmounted by a castle, a cathedral and an old Benedictine monastery. What can be seen today is the result of numerous alterations, extensions and modernizations over the centuries in the wake of wars and fires. When the ensemble was last restored in 1965–72, the various buildings were conserved as they were in the final stage of their development, but showing, where possible, the medieval masonry.

The earliest traces of the castle date back to the 10th century, when Duke Bolesław I Chrobry built a pre-Romanesque *palatium* on the site. Shortly afterwards Benedictines

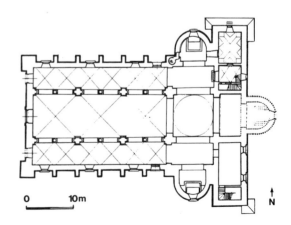

Płock, plan of the Cathedral

0   10m
N

established a community here. Already in this early period the complex was being altered and extended by each succeeding duke. The Romanesque *Cathedral* was built between 1136 and 1144 as a grand three-aisled basilica on a Latin-cross plan. (The magnificent bronze doors (1153–4), cast in Magdeburg, had already been moved to Norgovod in the 14th century; there are now excellent copies.) The Gothic towers were added in the first half of the 14th century. Of its many remodellings one of the most extensive was undertaken after a fire in the 1530's. The Italian architects Giovanni Cini and Bernardo Zanobi de Gianotis, followed by Giovanni Battista da Venezia, transformed the cathedral into a Renaissance building. In 1784 the court architect Domenico Merlini designed a Neoclassical façade. The restoration by Stefan Szyller (1901–3) sought to return the building to its medieval form; the present appearance of the cathedral is the result. In the course of the complete remodelling of the interior the decoration that had accumulated over the centuries was lost. The present painted decoration is by Władysław Drapiewski. The left-hand tower contains the *Kaplica Królewska (Royal Chapel)*; the remains of Dukes Władysław Herman and Bolesław Krzywousty were transferred to its crypt in 1825, and were placed in a single black marble sarcophagus with a white eagle on its lid. In the side aisles there is a large number of Renaissance and Baroque tombs and epitaphs.

The present appearance of the ruins of the *Castle*, which consists of four ranges round a courtyard, is due to its restoration in the 1960's. The medieval fortress was burned down in 1511. King Zygmunt I Stary had it rebuilt in the new Renaissance style, but incorporated masonry from the earlier building (some of this has now been exposed). At the end of the 18th century, when Płock was under Prussian rule, the now-dilapidated castle was partly demolished. All that remained was the southwest range with its two towers, which have become one of the town's trademarks: the *Wieża Szlachecka (Gentry Tower)* to the west

Płock, view of the Castle in the 17th century, drawing by A. Boot

239

was built in the 1350's (its upper storey was removed in 1796), and the *Wieża Zegarowa (Clock Tower)*, the core of which is Late Gothic, was built around 1492, later being used as the bell-tower of the cathedral, and was given its Baroque onion dome around 1730.

The castle now houses the *Muzeum Mazowieckie (Mazovian Museum)*, which besides material illustrating the history of the town also has a rich collection of art and applied arts, some of it displayed in reconstructed interiors of various periods. Pride of place is held by the fine Art Nouveau collection, which contains paintings by notable artists such as Józef Mehoffer, as well as furniture, glass, ceramics and metalwork.

Southwest of the castle site are the remains of the once magnificent *Opactwo Benedyktynów (Benedictine Abbey)*: a wall of the former Kościół św. Wojciecha (Church of St Adalbert) now forms part of the museum building. Church and monastery were destroyed and remodelled several times over the centuries. After secularization in the 19th century they were not rebuilt.

The complex of castle and cathedral has also included since 1903 the *Muzeum Diecezjalne (Diocesan Museum)* (on the corner of ul. Mostowa), which has an interesting collection of religious art. Opposite, at ul. Mostowa 1, the Late Gothic *Dom Pod Trąbami (Trumpet House)* has now been returned to its original appearance, after having undergone first a Baroque and then a Neoclassical remodelling.

On the way to the old town centre of Płock along the ul. Małachowskiego we pass the former *Kolegium Jezuickie (Jesuit College)* founded in 1608, with the *Kościół św. Michała (Church of St Michael)*. Since the end of the 18th century the buildings have been occupied by a school. Its present appearance dates from a Neoclassical remodelling in 1843 by Antonio Corazzi.

Ul. Małachowskiego opens into the *Stary Rynek (Old Market Place)*. Like other streets and squares in the old town, it contains a fine ensemble of Baroque and Neoclassical *burghers' houses* of the 18th and 19th centuries. The narrow north-west side is occupied by one of Poland's finest Neoclassical buildings, the elegant *Town Hall* by Jakub Kubicki of 1826–7.

To the left of the town hall, in the corner of the Old Market Place, stands the old *Kościół Farny (Parish Church)*. This was built in 1356 as a brick Gothic building and converted in the 16th century into a large hall church with an ambulatory and a succession of chapels around the choir. In the 18th century it was thoroughly remodelled. The building was shortened, and the chancel moved to the west end so that the façade could face the market place. The Early Baroque high altar, made by Giovanni Battista Ghisleni *c.*1632, comes from the old Benedictine abbey.

On the way back to Warsaw, following minor roads south of the Vistula, it is worth stopping at the village of **Słubice** about 28 km from Płock. A Neoclassical *Palace*, formerly the property of the Potocki family, stands in extensive Romantic parkland, which was laid out at the beginning of the 19th century. It is an elegant house built at the end of the 18th century by Hilary Szpilowski with a columned portico and projecting corner bays. Curved arcaded galleries link the main block with two cruciform pavilions. The magnificent furnishings of this very distinctive palace, and its important library, were taken by the Potockis to Wilanów (see page 217).

The *Kościół Farny (Parish Church)* was also designed by Hilary Szpilowski. It is remarkable above all for its façade, which was conceived by the architect in the form of a classical triumphal arch. Inside is a monument to Chancellor Andrzej Młodziejowski, made by the court sculptor Giacopo Monaldi.

From Słubice, via Iłów, Giżyce, Ruszki and Kamion, we reach the road which follows the south bank of the Vistula through picturesque countryside back to Warsaw.

A few kilometres beyond the village of Czosnów, on the right of the road in the forest called the Puszcza Kampinoska, is the *Cmentarz Palmiry*, a cemetery in which about 2,500 victims of the Nazi regime are buried. Between 1939 and 1941 prisoners from Warsaw were brought here to be murdered, among them many well-known politicians, scientists, writers and priests. Palmiry is the access point for the *Kampinoski National Park*, at 35,000 hectares the largest in Poland. Its pine forests, dunes and bogs are inhabited by boar, elk, roe deer, fox, badger, wolf, cranes, storks, herons, falcon and marsh owls.

Pułtusk – Ciechanów – Opinogóra – Przasnysz

On the western edge of the Puszcza Biała (White Forest), 60 km north of Warsaw, on the River Narew, lies the ancient town of **Pułtusk**, which was the property of the Bishops of Płock from the 11th century until 1796, and their permanent residence from the 14th century. The town developed as a flourishing centre of trade and of humanist culture. Despite devastating damage in the 17th-century wars and in 1944–5, the old heart of the town still shows evidence of its former greatness.

Pułtusk, view of the Castle, engraving of 1657

241

The centre of the medieval town, which stands on an island between two branches of the Narew, is the unusually long market place, lined with small, mostly Neoclassical houses dating from the early 19th century. In the middle of the square stands the Baroque *Town Hall*, built in 1728 and overshadowed by the Gothic tower of its predecessor, a military-looking structure, cubic below and octagonal above, which dates from the first half of the 16th century. It now contains the *Muzeum Regionalne (Regional Museum)* which documents the history of the town.

At the south end of the market place and surrounded by a park on the site of the old castle moat, stands the *Castle*, once the residence of the Bishops of Płock. When the wooden castle erected here in the 14th century was destroyed, a Renaissance castle was built on the same ground-plan. Work began in 1522 and lasted into the 17th century, with each new lord of the town introducing fresh extensions and alterations. Following its destruction by the Swedes, the complex underwent several remodellings, and after the Second World War it was rebuilt in the Neoclassical form it had been given at the beginning of the 19th century. In the interior no traces of earlier decoration have survived.

On the way back to the market place we pass the former Kaplica Zamkowa (Castle Chapel) now the *Kościół św. Marii Magdaleny (Church of St Mary Magdalene)*, a charming Renaissance building on a central plan (1538), which since its postwar reconstruction has been used as an exhibition hall.

The other end of the market place is occupied by the Collegiate Church, now the *Kościół św. Mateuscza (Church of St Matthew)* (plate 13), which despite appearances is one of the finest examples of Polish Renaissance architecture. The interior of this early 15th-century Gothic basilica was transformed in 1560 by Giovanni Battista da Venezia, using elements derived from the Venetian Renaissance, but he left the outside in its Gothic state; curiously enough, he retained this mixture of styles even in churches which he built from scratch (such as Brok, see page 246 and elsewhere in Mazovia).

The nave runs without a break to the polygonal apse, giving the interior an almost tunnel-like effect. On either side are arcades with the entrances to the side aisles and

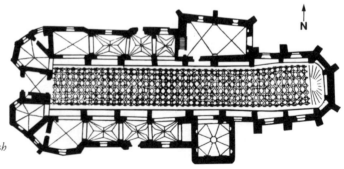

Pułtusk, plan of the parish Church of St Matthew

chapels below. The depth of the arcading is intended to suggest the spatial effect of an aisled church when seen in perspective, and thus to create the appearance of a monumental space. This concept is underlined also by the barrel vault and the niches at gallery level above the cornice, which are linked to the vault. The coffering is composed of flat plaster ribs of a sort known as 'Pułtusk vaulting', which was elsewhere developed into complicated patterns. Here, however, the architect restricted himself to a relatively simple network composed of circles linked by straight lines.

The furnishings of the church date from the Baroque period in the 17th and 18th centuries. The lavish altars were mostly donated by the bishops. Among the many monuments a Gothic tomb slab of the second half of the 15th century has survived on the north side of the chancel. The bishop who commissioned the remodelling, Andrzej Noskowski, had already used Giovanni Battista da Venezia to build his family chapel which is decorated with frescoes (1554); this was the first of many Polish funerary chapels inspired by the Sigismund Chapel in Wawel Cathedral (see page 476). The altarpiece is a 15th-century Gothic painting of the Deposition. On his tomb the bishop is shown in full pontifical vestments.

In ul. Gomulickiego, which runs along the western side of the island, is the *Kościół św. Józefa (Church of St Joseph)*, built in the 1560's for the Jesuit college. It was damaged and altered many times, but after the Second World War it was restored to its 18th century state.

Nearby, on the picturesque branch of the Narew, parts of the town walls of 1508–9 can still be seen, including a round battlemented bastion built of brick.

In the town of **Ciechanów**, 40 km northwest of Pułtusk, the ruin of a Gothic *Castle* of the Mazovian dukes has survived. It represents an unusually pure example of 15th-century castle building uninfluenced either by its predecessor or the well-known sophistication of the Teutonic castles.

The castle is situated at the eastern edge of the town, on the marshy banks of the River Lydynia, and was built in 1430 for Duke Janusz I. Accounts from the time of its construction identify the architect as Niklos, though his origins are unknown. From the ruins the original form of the complex can still be clearly made out; the massive walls surrounded a rectangular enclosure and created an impressive façade on the south side with two corner bastions between which the main gateway used to stand. Opposite, on the north wall, stood the original residential quarters of the castle.

In the 16th century the castle belonged to the Renaissance harpy Bona Sforza, widow of King Zygmunt I Stary. She transformed the residential building into a lavishly appointed residence (*c.*1550), but by 1580 this is already described as being in a state of neglect. In 1657 the castle was destroyed by the Swedes, and in the late 18th century it was being used as a quarry for building work in the town; as a result the last traces of the residential building disappeared.

About 8 km northeast of Ciechanów we reach the village of **Opinogóra**, which now lies off the main road, but in the middle ages was an important stage on the way from

Ciechanów to Przasnysz. In the 14th and 15th centuries the Dukes of Mazovia came here to hunt. From the 18th century onwards the village belonged to the noble family of Krasiński. Around 1825 Wincenty Krasiński, a general in Napoleon's army and later a senator and wojewoda in the Kingdom of Poland, where he was a loyal subject of the tsar, had a neo-Gothic *Castle* (plate 17) built for his son Zygmunt Krasiński, the great Romantic 'poet prophet' (see page 101). The castle is one of the most beautiful examples of the architecture of Romanticism in all Poland: an ornamental, one-storey building with a flat roof and a tall polygonal tower asymetrically placed at the southeast corner. The rich sculptured decoration on the windows and cornices is largely the result of restoration work in 1958–61. The building was badly damaged in the First World War, and by the end of the Second World War had become a ruin. After its rebuilding the castle was made into a Muzeum Romantyzmu (Museum of Romanticism); the rooms were furnished in the style of the period and there is a valuable collection of works of art which is continually being expanded. The Romantic *Park*, laid out at the beginning of the 19th century as an English landscape garden, is also maintained as part of the museum. In 1832 Amelia Załuska set up a stone bench here in memory of her unhappy youthful love affair with Zygmunt Krasiński, with the inscription 'Niech pamięć moja zawsze ci będzie miła' ('May the memory of me always be dear to you').

The Neoclassical *Kościół Farny (Parish Church)* in the village was founded by Wincenty Krasiński in 1825 as a burial place for his family. Inside are some important tombs and epitaphs, including the tomb of Maria Krasińska, Zygmunt's mother (1841, L. Pampaloni), and that of his sons Władysław and Zygmunt (1881, J. Franceschi). The poet is buried with the other members of his family in the crypt.

The town of **Przasnysz**, situated about 20 km northeast of Opinogóra on the River Węgierka, used to be an important commercial and administrative centre, especially in the 16th century. During this short-lived apogee, cut short by the Swedish Wars, Przasnysz

Ciechanów, view of the ruined Castle, 19th-century lithograph

was the scene of some vigorous and ambitious building activity. Wartime destruction and several great fires have considerably changed the appearance of the town since then, as has the prosperity which arrived in the later 19th century. However, there are still some interesting reminders of the town's late medieval heyday, especially the former *Kościół Bernardynów (Bernardine Church)* with its monastic buildings in ul. Marszałka J. Pilsudskiego.

In 1583 Paweł Kostka, the brother of the later canonized Stanisław Kostka, invited the Bernardine friars to the town and financed the building of their monastery. The church, a massive brick building with stepped gables decorated with blind tracery, was built between 1588 and 1595. The impression of sober strength is reinforced by the low saddle-roofed bell-tower on the north corner. The church's rich furnishings suffered heavy damage during the Second World War, when it was used as a storehouse. The old stained-glass windows and wall paintings were replaced with modern works during restoration in the 1950's. The net vault, however, came through the war unscathed. In the south chapel, set into a modern altar, is a fine Late Gothic Madonna of around 1500. In the narthex hangs an Early Baroque crucifix (*c*.1630).

The adjoining three ranges of monastery buildings were built shortly after the church was completed in the first half of the 17th century. Despite severe war damage, not all of which has been made good, it can still be seen how decisively the style of building changed within that short space of time: the pedimented articulation with its well-proportioned pilasters and cornice mouldings are typical of the Early Baroque.

Dating from the late 15th century, the *Kościół Farny (Parish Church)* in ul. 3. Maja, is a brick Gothic building, which has been altered many times. Its exterior is decorated with ornamental bricks of various colours. South of the sanctuary is a round stair-tower giving the church a fortress-like aspect. The bell-tower next to the church has remained unaltered since it was built (except for the upper storey) and is one of the finest examples of Mazovian Gothic. The decoration and layout of the interior date from the 18th and 19th centuries, and the layout has also been altered.

The generous proportions of the nearby market place go back to the middle ages. Since the 19th century the buildings have been gradually replaced, but the low, ornamented houses have still preserved the character of an old provincial market square. The *Town Hall* was rebuilt *c*.1800 in Neoclassical form. In the middle of the gardens, where the market used to be, a memorial was unveiled in 1962 commemorating the 535th anniversary of the granting of the town's charter in 1427. It is decorated with reliefs showing various important episodes in the history of the town.

Wyszków – Brok – Treblinka – Ostrołęka – Łomża – Nowogród

Wyszków, on the River Bug, is 54 km northeast of Warsaw. The town was already in existence as a trading centre in the 12th century, and was granted its charter in 1502. Yet until the end of the 18th century it only had a wooden parish church, which was constantly being burned down and rebuilt. In 1793 the Bishop of Płock, Krzysztof Hilary Szembek, who was also the proprietor of the town, commissioned the building of the present Neoclassical *Kościół Farny (Parish Church)*. This was probably based on an already existing design by Szymon Bogumił Zug. The façade with its flat pilaster articulation, the tall niche around the main doorway, and the tower that rises above the pediment are very austere and linear. Behind it is an unusually elegant church interior with three aisles separated by columns on tall pedestals. They do not support arches, as one might expect, but a horizontal lintel above which is a barrel vault. The motifs and proportions of the high altar are in keeping, and a unified perspective is created.

In Rybienko, a district of Wyszków to the west of the town centre on the south bank of the Bug is a park (once a landscape garden in the English style) containing a Neoclassical *Palace* built around 1780 by either Szymon Bogumił Zug or Johann Christian Kamsetzer.

It is a long building with two projecting bays at the sides and a columned portico in the middle. The interiors have preserved their fine classical decoration of the 1780's by Jan Bogumił Plersch.

Today it is used as a reformatory school, but in the 19th century, when the estate belonged to the Morzkowski family, it was a favourite meeting place for the bohemian world of Warsaw.

The small town of **Brok**, about 28 km from Wyszków, was an important commercial centre in the middle ages on the road along the River Bug. From the 13th century it was the property of the bishops of Płock, who had their summer residence there. The palace was rebuilt in the 17th century and is now a ruin.

The outstanding *Parish Church* was built in 1560 by Giovanni Battista da Venezia, the Italian architect who made an important contribution to the Mazovian Renaissance with his works at Pułtusk (see page 242), Brochów (see page 230) and elsewhere. This is a typical example of his churches, an aisleless building with a long chancel and external buttresses, which seems to continue the Gothic tradition. The construction of the gables is also influenced by local models, while the stylistic language – pilaster arcades arranged one above the other – already reflects a Renaissance sense of form. In the interior too the monumental forms of the Renaissance are employed: the nave and chancel have a barrel vault, which rests on plastically treated blind arcades and is decorated with a flat symmetrical plasterwork coffering (called 'Pułtusk vaulting' after its prototype, see page 242). One of the Baroque side-altars, with a representation of the Tree of Jesse, is worth noting.

At **Treblinka**, 14 km east of Brok, the Nazis first built a concentration camp (Treblinka I) in 1941. A year later they laid out the mass-extermination camp (Treblinka II), in which about 800,000 people were tortured and murdered, mostly Jews from Poland, but also from other occupied countries. In November 1943 the Nazis closed this camp down and bulldozed the site in an attempt to remove all trace of it.

They were not successful. 'I saw a sight which I shall never forget, a tremendous area of many kilometres, and all over this area there were scattered skulls, bones – tens of thousands; and piles of shoes – among them tens of thousands of little shoes,' wrote Dr Adolf Berman of what he saw in 1945. He picked up one of these shoes: 'I brought it as a very precious thing, because I knew that over a million of such little shoes, scattered all over the fields of death, could easily be found' (quoted by M. Gilbert, 'The Holocaust'.)

In 1964 a monument was erected on the site consisting of thousands of rough-hewn granite blocks – as symbolic gravestones. Sandstone blocks mark the way to the site of Treblinka I, 2 km away, where there is another memorial.

The main road leading northeast of Warsaw passes through Radzymin, the birthplace of Isaac Bashevis Singer, the great Yiddish writer. Here in August 1920 the Red Army broke through defences in the rush to Warsaw. The future Pius XI, then a Papal Nuncio, had watched the 'advancing hordes of Antichrist' and solemnly cursed them here. Within five days, the Soviets were encircled and their defeat was complete.

At an intersection of the old trade roads by land and by water from Mazovia to the land of the Pruzzi and to Lithuania lies **Ostrołęka**, which developed in the middle ages as a market settlement around a castle. In the 15th and 16th centuries the town was an important centre of manufacture and trade. In 1831 it witnessed a bloody battle in which the Russians finally managed to inflict a crushing blow to the insurrectionary forces under the bold General Bem.

Treblinka, monument on the site of the extermination camp

In Pl. gen. J. Bema, formerly the market square, a *memorial* erected in 1973 commemorates the military deeds of the great General Józef Bem and there is a *mausoleum* to the insurrectionists who died.

The fortified *Klasztor Bernardynów (Bernardine Monastery)*, site of the battle in 1831, with its *Kościół św. Antoniego Padewskiego (Church of St Antony of Padua)* in ul. Bogusławskiego, was built in 1666–96. Despite many alterations since the 18th century the complex has preserved its original character. In front of the church is a large rectangular courtyard dating from the first half of the 18th century, surrounded by arcades with a Way of the Cross. The church itself is a grandly conceived, cruciform, aisleless building with fine Baroque and Rococo decoration. The painted decoration, commissioned by a local patrician, was executed in 1762–4 by Walenty Żebrowski; it depicts numerous scenes from the life of St Antony of Padua. The majestic Rococo altar, erected in 1764 by Jan Dubanowski and Mikołaj Tomaszewski, is flanked on either side of the triumphal arch by a side altar with figures of Bernardine saints. The church contains many works of local painting and sculpture, including a Late Gothic crucifix dating from the early 16th century and a figure of the resurrected Christ from the same period.

The River Narew was once the only means of crossing the impenetrable primeval forests of Podlasie from Mazovia to the region of the Pruzzi. The town of **Łomża** started life around AD 1000 at the foot of a castle safeguarding a ford across the Narew, and in the 16th century developed into one of the biggest towns in Mazovia. The town's celebrated *Cathedral*, formerly the parish church (in ul. Dworna) was built during this prosperous period.

During the Second World War, when 75 per cent of the fabric of Łomża was destroyed, the church suffered severe damage. But since its rebuilding in 1953–6, it has once again taken its place as one of the most important works of architecture in Mazovia. It is a Late Gothic hall-church with a tall nave and slightly lower aisles. After damage in the 17th century the church was given a new Early Baroque pediment by Giuseppe Simone Bellotti in 1691–2. The interior has interesting star and diamond vaulting of the period around 1550. A number of important tombs and monuments survived the war unscathed. Particularly worthy of attention is the double tomb of the starosta (sheriff) Andrzej Dunin-Modliszewski and his wife Elżbieta, made around the end of the 16th century, perhaps by the Kraków-based Italian sculptor Santi Gucci. It has two reliefs showing the recumbent figures of the couple, and its structure follows Italian Renaissance models.

The cathedral is separated by a block of houses from the Old Market Square to the north. Here the only surviving old buildings are the Neoclassical *Town Hall*, built in 1826, and a burgher's house (No. 13) dating from a little later. The other buildings are mostly postwar.

Beyond the market square we reach the delightful ensemble of the *Kościół Kapucynów (Capuchin Church)* with its monastery, a Baroque complex dating from the 18th century, which has survived with its decoration largely unaltered.

In the western part of the old town centre, on the corner of ul. Dworna and ul. H. Sienkiewicza, stands the interesting building of the *Kościół Wniebowzięcia N.P. Marii (Church of the Assumption)*, which was built in 1877 as a Lutheran church. The anonymous architect was inspired by Byzantine churches. Until the Second World War the interior was decorated with mosaics and frescoes; only the remains of stained-glass windows have survived.

One block to the southwest, on the corner of ul. Kopernika and al. Legionów is the old *Cmentarz (Cemetery)* of the town with interesting Neoclassical tombs and mausolea.

16 km northwest from Łomża, in the *Puszcza Kurpiowska* on the south bank of the Narew, is the town of **Nowogród** with its interesting *Skansen (Open-Air Museum)* laid out in 1927 by the ethnologist Adam Chętnik with examples of regional vernacular architecture: peasant houses with all their furnishings, workshops with tools, as well as scenes of daily life.

Liw – Węgrów – Siedlce – Biała Podlaska – Radzyń Podlaski

The road from Warsaw into the Podlasie region passes first through Wesoła and Sulejówek into the eastern borders of Nizina Mazowiecka (the Mazovian Lowlands). After about

Nowogród, view of the open-air museum

75 km we reach the small town of **Liw**, which was an important centre of trade and regional administration in the middle ages (charter granted 1420). In the 14th century work began on the building of a *Castle* on the site of earlier defences to safeguard the ferry traffic across the River Liwiec. It was not completed until 1429 by the architect Niklos, who was already busy building the castle at Ciechanów (see page 244). In the 17th century the castle was destroyed in the Swedish Deluge, and the town suffered such heavy damage that it never recovered. Powerful competition from the neighbouring town of Węgrów also contributed to its decline. In 1869 Liw finally lost its municipal status.

Despite centuries of dilapidation large parts of the castle have survived, and it is easy to make out its original appearance. Projecting from the northeast side of the rectangular block with massive sloping walls is a thick-set polygonal tower, which was the bastion safeguarding the entrance to the castle precincts. Inside the complex a three-storey residential building was erected on the left-hand side, and known as the 'Dom Duży' ('Big House'). A little later the 'Dom Mniejszy' ('Smaller House') was built opposite; it was replaced in 1792 by the Baroque building of the Starostwo (sheriff's office). In 1956–61 the ruins were restored and the Starostwo, which had been destroyed in the mid-19th century was rebuilt. Its rooms are now used for the *Muzeum Zbrojowni na Zamku w Liwie (Armoury Museum at Liw Castle)*, with an interesting collection of European and Oriental weaponry, armour and battle paintings.

The little town of **Węgrów**, 5 km northeast of Liw, developed in the middle ages as a trading centre at the intersection of important routes between Warsaw, Lithuania and the land of the Pruzzi. Duke Bolesław IV granted it a town charter in 1441. In the 16th century Węgrów became one of the principal centres of the Reformation in Mazovia. However, the Krasiński family, the proprietors of the town between 1664 and 1762, sponsored a Counter-Reformation policy at great expense, giving Węgrów two important monuments of Baroque architecture: the parish church and the Franciscan monastery, both by Tylman van Gameren.

The façade and gateway of the *Kościół Farny (Parish Church)* occupy the east side of the *Market Square*, where a 16th-century Late Gothic hall-church originally stood. After a fire in 1703 Jan Dobrogost Krasiński, the wojewoda of Płock, and crown referendary, commissioned Tylman van Gameren to remodel the building, and his designs were executed over the following years by Carlo Ceroni and Johann Reisner. In 1707–8 the interior was given painted decoration by Michelangelo Palloni.

From the Gothic building Tylman retained the surrounding wall and the two little towers flanking the façade. Within the walls he transformed the church into a grand basilica: there is hardly any distinction between the chancel and the nave, which opens through broad arcades into the side-aisles. The principal space is entirely lined with pilasters, whose entablature supports the vault. On the east wall of the chancel Michelangelo Palloni painted an Assumption of the Virgin as if seen through a loggia. The altar

Liw, the remains of the Castle

paintings in the aisles and chancel chapels are also treated as illusionistic views of the world outside. The sacristy contains a notable collection of portraits of prelates.

The church stands in the centre of a graveyard, around which a wall was built in the 18th century with a gateway to the market square flanked by two low corner towers.

Next door to the church at No. 26, on the corner of ul. Staszica, stands the *Dom Gdański (Gdańsk House)* an 18th-century building which was once an inn.

Further east, in ul. Kościuszki, stand the former *Kościół i Klasztor Reformatów (Church and Monastery of the Reformed Franciscans)*, founded by Jan Kazimierz Krasiński in 1668. The original temporary timber buildings were replaced in 1693–1706 by the present complex. Here too Tylman van Gameren was the architect, and Carlo Ceroni and Johann Reisner carried out his plans. Michelangelo Palloni worked on the decoration of the interior up to the building's consecration in 1711. The façade with its tall centre bay and lower sides expresses the arrangement of the interior space. The short nave with ambitious vaulting is flanked on each side by domed chapels. A dome rises above the crossing. As in the parish church, a pilaster order runs all round the interior, and there is a high vault with a projecting cornice which links the various spaces. Palloni's dome fresco depicts the Adoration of the Holy Trinity, with scenes of the Creation of the World, the Expulsion from Paradise, Moses Receiving the Tablets of the Law, and the Baptism of Christ in the Jordan. In the side chapels Palloni painted scenes from the lives of various saints. The monumental high altar with a crucifix (by Andreas Schlüter) above the tabernacle, with the sorrowing Virgin and St John the Evangelist, and God the Father appearing in host of angels, was also designed by Tylman van Gameren. Above the door of the north chapel is the eclectic monument to Jan Dobrogost Krasiński, the patron of the rebuilding of the monastery and the parish church (and of the Krasiński Palace in Warsaw, see page 167), an allegory of Death and Posthumous Fame by Andreas Mackensen the Younger (1703).

90 km to the east of Warsaw, on the edge of the Siedlce Highlands, lies the provincial capital, **Siedlce**, a Baroque town, which developed in the 18th century into a place of some importance under the patronage of the aristocratic Czartoryski family. Its layout dates from this period and like other magnatial towns has no central market square.

The town's heyday began with the building of the Pałac Czartoryskich (Czartoryski Palace), now called the *Pałac Ogińskich (Ogiński Palace)* at the end of ul. Kościuszki in the early 18th century. It attained its final form in 1776–82, when Aleksandra Czartoryska (who married an Ogiński) commissioned Stanisław Zawadzki to extend it. The elegant Neoclassical palace is built on a rectangular plan. Its façade has a plain pilaster articulation; over the entrance in the middle is a pedimented portico on slender columns. The lower wings attached to the main block contain domestic offices. The palace was rebuilt in 1950 and since then has been the seat of the Urząd Miejski (Municipal Administration); the rich interior decoration has not survived.

The *Park Miejski (Town Park)*, which surrounds the residence, also goes back to an idea of Aleksandra Ogińska's. In 1768, before the alterations were made to the palace, the Princess began the transformation of the estate into a Romantic landscape garden on the English model. In so doing she started decades of rivalry between the Polish noblewomen, who vied with each other to create beautiful and imaginative gardens. The garden was remodelled again in anticipation of a visit by King Stanisław August Poniatowski in 1783: the existing lakes and watercourses were linked by additional canals, picturesque artificial islands were created, enchanted grottoes built, and the landscape was strewn with classical temples, miniature oriental shrines and rustic cottages. After Aleksandra Ogińska's death the park gradually fell into decay, the pavilions were demolished, canals and lakes filled in and the course of the paths altered.

Ul. Kościuszki leads past the guesthouse and stables of the palace to the town centre. The Neoclassical *Post Office* on the corner of ul. J. Piłsudskiego was built by Antonio Corazzi in 1827–8.

The *Kaplica Ogińskich* in the old cemetery a little further east on ul. Michała Żymierskiego is a charming Neoclassical domed building with three porticoes, designed in 1791 by the painter Zygmunt Vogel. Aleksandra Ogińska is buried in the crypt beneath.

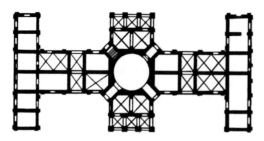

Siedlce, plan of the Town Hall

The *Kościół św. Stanisława (Church of St Stanislas)* on the corner of ul. Kościuszki was founded by Kazimierz Czartoryski, an earlier lord of the town. It is a Late Baroque building which was given a Neoclassical façade (1793, Stanisław Zawadzki) and a magnificent new high altar by Aleksandra Ogińska. The portico at the entrance of the church alludes to the architecture of the palace and hence to the church's benefactress. Of the surviving furnishings the great Baroque paintings by Szymon Czechowicz merit particular attention. Czechowicz's work is to be found in many churches in Podlasie. The high altar incorporates a 17th-century votive image of the Virgin and Child, with applied garments of silver and gilt copper set with precious stones.

The middle of the town is marked by the *Ratusz (Town Hall)* built in 1766–72 and impressively sited opposite the church on the other side of ul. Floriańska. This ensemble is another product of the initiative and patronage of Aleksandra Ogińska. The architect was Johann Sigismund Deibel, who at that time was also working at the royal court in Warsaw. The main function of the town hall was the organization of local commerce, and the expression of civic pride; there was no independent administration as such, since the town was in private hands. Consequently a small single-storey building with wings was all that was needed, though for reasons of prestige a projecting centrepiece with an entrance loggia, pilasters and a massive, richly decorated tower were also built, giving the town hall some of the splendour of an aristocratic residence.

During the Second World War the town hall was badly damaged, and since its rebuilding in 1945–52 it has housed the *Muzeum Okręgowe (District Museum)* with an interesting collection of material illustrating the history and culture of Podlasie, as well as the works of the contemporary Siedlce painter Małgorzata Łada-Maciągowa.

The old town centre of **Biała Podlaska** situated only 36 km from the Byelorussian border, was a creation of the aristocratic Radziwiłł family, which was of Lithuanian origin and became one of the mightiest in the Polish Commonwealth. The history of the town only began in the late 15th century and appeared to have come to an early end a mere 150 years later with the Swedish Wars. However, thanks to the patronage of the Radziwiłłs, it recovered in the 18th century. It suffered again in the Second World War; in 1940 the first of several large concentration camps was set up here, the last being created as late as spring 1944. In the woods around Biała Podlaska countless prisoners were shot.

The historic centre of the town consists of a few streets between Pl. Wolności and the Park Radziwiłłowski.

The *Park* surrounds the remains of the once magnificent *Palace* of the Radziwiłłs, built from 1622 onwards over a long period by the Italian architect Paolo Negroni, who was active mainly in Lublin. It was originally a castle laid out on a pentagonal plan with bastions, ramparts and moats; in its courtyard a splendid palace was built, complete with domestic offices and a chapel. On the south side, extending to the banks of the River Krzna, is an enclosed game reserve, where red deer, roe deer, bison and even bears used to roam. While it was still under construction the residence was destroyed by the Swedes; further destruction occurred in the course of the 18th century, affecting the whole town. The remaining parts of the castle were restored in 1976–8 and it now houses a cultural centre.

The castle precincts are entered from ul. Warszawska, past a gatehouse, whose restoration was only approximately faithful to the original. Guarding the entrance is the *Wieża Bramna (Gate Tower)*, a good vantage point for a view over the whole town. Beyond the gate is the L-shaped building of the former offices, built at the end of the 17th century and later raised in height, which enclosed the courtyard on two sides. They have preserved in parts their original pilastered façade. Directly opposite stood the palace, only the foundations of which remain. At their southeast corner rises another Baroque tower, which marked the end of the façade of the palace. The black eagle in the sgraffito decoration is the heraldic emblem of the Radziwiłłs. Beyond this tower stands the former palace chapel, which dates from the second half of the 17th century, though its Late Renaissance decoration has all been lost. Next to the palace complex the remains of the fortifications can be seen, though these give only a faint impression of their original imposing effect.

The way to Pl. Wolności passes the *Kościół Farny św. Anny (Parish Church of St Anne)* in ul. Warswawska, built around 1600 on the site of an earlier timber church. Its plain Renaissance exterior conceals the richly decorated family chapel of the Radziwiłłs. In the first half of the 17th century Karol Stanisław Radziwiłł commissioned the paintings and plaster reliefs which depict memorable events in the history of the family.

A little further east the street crosses the former market place, now called Pl. Wolności. It is lined with 19th-century houses, most of the building material for which came from the ruins of the fortified palace. Wooden market booths once stood in the centre of the square, but there was no town hall because the town was under private rule.

The monument on the northern side of the square commemorates the victims of public executions held here by the Nazis in the autumn of 1943.

On the corner of the ul. J. Piłsudskiego (entrance at ul. Pocztowa 4) is the *Muzeum Okręgowe (District Museum)* which documents the history of the town and has a fascinating collection of local folk art.

The continuation of ul. J. Piłsudskiego, ul. Reformacka, leads to the *Kościół św. Antoniego (Church of St Antony)* with its *Klasztor Reformatów (Monastery of the Reformed Franciscans)*. The Baroque monastic complex, a Radziwiłł foundation, was built in the 1670's. Despite a troubled history, including use by the Germans as a storehouse between 1938 and 1944, the church has suffered no serious damage. The ceiling fresco uses elements from the founder's family coat of arms. The conventual buildings are now used by a school.

The town of **Radzyń Podlaski** is recorded from the 15th century onwards as belonging to a succession of various noble families. It achieved fame in 1686, when the then proprietor, Stanisław Antoni Szczuka, commissioned Agostino Locci, the architect of

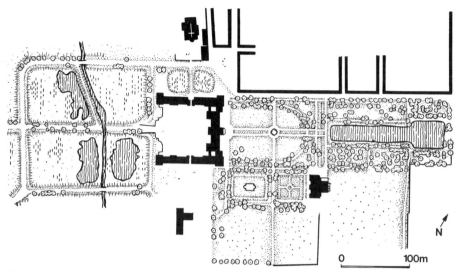

Radzyń Podlaski, plan of the palace and park

Wilanów (see page 217 ff.), to convert his small manor house into a palace. Shortly afterwards this was inherited by the Potocki family. Here as elsewhere the Potockis were busy builders and discerning patrons. Between 1750 and 1759 Jacopo Fontana, the court architect in Warsaw, transformed Locci's little palace into the grand Baroque complex it is today. The *Palace* soon became famous as *Wersal Podlaski* ('Podlasian Versailles'). The main building with three bays projecting slightly at each end and a taller projecting centrepiece, dominates the broad *cour d'honneur*, flanked on either side by a long wing. The open side of the courtyard is shut off by a curving wall. The principal axis – from the main gate to the palace façade – is intersected by a transverse axis indicated by two towered gateways in the centre of the wings, through which a road runs across the court to the parish church. This unusual arrangement, creating a new type of palace building, was Fontana's solution to the problem of linking the palace with the town, which was not situated opposite the main grand façade, but to one side.

Fontana was also responsible for the decoration of the interiors. His designs were executed for his patron, Eustachy Potocki, by such prominent artists as the court painter Jan Bogumił Plersch and the sculptor Johann Redler. However, of the luxurious Rococo decoration only the sculptures on the façades have survived; all the interior ornamentation has been lost.

Already in the 19th century – after the palace had passed into new ownership – the buildings were visibly falling into decay. In 1920 it was transferred to the state and until 1939 was used as a seat of local government. In 1944 it was gutted by fire. In the rebuilding, completed in 1973, no attempt was made to recreate the interiors, and the division of the rooms no longer corresponds to the original designs. The building is now once again used as a regional administrative headquarters.

Behind the palace are the *gardens* created for Eustachy Potocki in 1767 by the garden architect Knackfuss on a French Baroque model with geometrically structured parterres, espaliers, and hedges in ornamental lines interrupted by canals. The *orangery*, built by Jacopo Fontana during his remodelling of the palace, is one of the most beautiful examples of Rococo architecture in Poland. After its destruction in 1944 it was rebuilt in the same year while hostilities were still in progress, the first architectural monument in the whole of Poland to be reconstructed after war damage.

Góra Kalwaria – Czersk – Rezerwat Modrzewina – Mała Wieś

About 34 km south of Warsaw the old trade road to Czersk passes through the small town of **Góra Kalwaria** on the banks of the Vistula. A village is mentioned here in the 13th century, but it was in 1666 that its real development began, when it was acquired by Stefan Wierzbowski, Bishop of Poznań. He developed it as a pilgrimage centre and built a long Way of the Cross, modelled on Mount Calvary in Jerusalem. The layout of the town, in the shape of a Latin cross with its head at the point where a stream called the Cedron (after the brook in the Garden of Gethsemane) runs into the Vistula, has survived to the present day, though since the 19th century it has been increasingly surrounded by expanding residential developments. Along the town's two main axes, ul. Kalwaryjska and ul. Dominikańska with ul. Pijarska, the bishop created a large number of chapels and shrines, most of which were destroyed in the Second World War.

The Baroque *Kaplica Piłata (Pilate Chapel)* in ul. Dominikańska still survives from the bishop's original ensemble; it contains a cycle of paintings of the Passion. The *Kościół Bernardynów (Bernardine Church)*, now the parish church, was built at the same time. The present Late Baroque church was built by Jacopo Fontana in the 1750's, and still preserves almost all its original decoration and furnishings. In the former monastery garden, which extends to the bank of the river, the small *Kaplica św. Antoniego (Chapel of St Antony)* is still standing. Many (local) miracles are connected with the wooden figure of the saint which can be seen there.

In the 19th century, when the pilgrimage centre began to develop into a town, the Neoclassical *Town Hall* was built in the market square in 1829–34 by Bonifacy Witkow-ski. The same architect was responsible for the market hall next door, which was rebuilt after the war as a representative example of the type.

Christians were not the only pilgrims at Góra Kalwaria, or Gur as it was known to the Hasidic followers of the Alter family of tzaddiks. Döblin joined one of the daily trains taking pilgrims from Warsaw to see 'the greatest rebbe of them all'. The 'almost frightening bustling black throng' is met by specially chosen men and boys: 'How proudly these men, youths, boys stride along in clean black caftans, in high shiny black caps; they look romantic, rapturous, medieval. Their faces have an extraordinary look, an earnest stillness.' The Tzaddik's house still stands at ul. Pijarska 2, and there is a synagogue, now used as a furniture warehouse.

The picturesque town of **Czersk**, which can be approached by a delightful 3 km walk from Góra Kalwaria along the bank of the Vistula, was, until the rise of Warsaw, one of the most important towns in Mazovia.

Archaeological excavations have revealed that a settlement was already in existence in the 10th or 11th century on the highest point in the countryside. From the 13th century Czersk was the capital of a duchy, but it was not until the second half of the 14th century, when the settlement was granted municipal status, that work started on building the castle, whose impressive ruins bear witness to Czersk's eventful history. Because of its location on one of the oldest and most important trade routes the town soon grew in commercial and political importance, and in the 16th century it was also famous for its cloth production. In the following century, however, this period of prosperity came to an abrupt end with the devastation of the Swedish Deluge. Afterwards the development of Warsaw prevented any real revival of Czersk's fortunes. By the 19th century Czersk had become an insignificant village, and in 1869 its municipal status was revoked.

The rise and decline of the town is reflected in the history of the *Castle*. Its surrounding walls, which form an irregular quadrilateral, show that it was built on the site of the early medieval settlement. The three bastions are part of the original fortifications. The two round defensive towers did not at first rise above the coping; their original battlements have been filled in but can still clearly be made out. The towers were probably raised to their present height in the 16th century, when the northeast bastion was remodelled as a rectangular gate tower. The southeastern tower was used as a prison, and wooden stairs led up to the high entrance above the windowless ground floor. The west tower probably contained the arsenal. Within the surrounding walls traces of buildings have survived. Along the north side were the residential quarters, some of the foundations of which have been excavated. In the centre of the precincts stood a chapel, of which only the outlines of the foundations can now be seen. To the southwest, where the surrounding walls are missing, there is a view far across the Równina Warszawska (Warsaw Plain).

Near Grójec, 28 km southwest of Czersk, is the **Reserwat Modrzewina**, a nature reserve consisting of 41 hectares of larch forest with trees 160 to 240 years old. It is particularly attractive in autumn, and can be explored along signposted footpaths.

Close by is **Mała Wieś** ('Little Hamlet') with the *Palace* of the Walicki family. This is an elegant Neoclassical building with a pedimented portico at the entrance, built in 1783–6 by the important architect Hilary Szpilowski for the wojewoda Bazyli Walicki. The severe dignity of the façade is emphasized by the large size of the forecourt, which is flanked by offices like a *cour d'honneur*. What makes the Walicki Palace different from most comparable residences is that it has preserved its valuable (though restored) interior decoration. The plasterwork, sculptures and paintings are by Friedrich Albert Lessel and Robert

Stankiewicz. As was common in the late 18th century, great importance was attached to stylistic variety in the decoration of the different rooms. Particularly striking is the Sala Warszawska (Warsaw Room), one wall of which is filled with a virtuoso perspective painting of a loggia with a panorama of the capital.

The French parterre gardens are contemporary with the building of the palace but the landscape park was laid out in 1825.

Dorota Leszczyńska and Michaela Marek

Wielkopolska (Greater Poland)

In western and central Poland – the region between the German border and Poland's second largest city, Łódź – the letters Wlkp. appear after many of the names of towns and villages, such as Gorzów Wlkp., or Środa Wlkp. to the southeast of Poznań. Wlkp. stands for 'Wielkopolska' ('Greater Poland'), one of the historic core regions of Poland, and indeed the first centre from which the Polish state was organized. It contains the settlements which the Poles regard as their most ancient capitals: Poznań, Gniezno, and Kruszwica on Lake Goplo. The country is open and fertile, with many woods and lakes.

Since Poland's new voivodships were created in 1998, Wielkopolska has once again become a political entity. However, the following section includes places not only in the present voivodship of Wielkopolska, but also in areas beyond its borders, in what are now the neighbouring voivodships of Łódź and Lubsko.

Politically the history of Wielkopolska, in good times and in bad, was determined by its proximity to Germany. German interest in the region had developed since the 10th century, when the Poles and Germans, often at the same time and sometimes in collaboration, began subjugating and converting the pagan West Slavic peoples between the Elbe and the lower Vistula, and between the Saale and the Oder. In the region east of the Oder German and Polish influences constantly alternated and overlapped, so that both Germans and Poles would later be able to claim their 'historical rights' to the land. The region described here includes parts of former eastern German territories of Silesia, Brandenburg and Posen-West Prussia, which were within the German Reich in the 19th and early 20th centuries. Memories of the bitter disputes over land in the 19th century, when the Germans sought to acquire the property of Polish farmers, have recently been revived by Poles who fear that the country's entry to the European Union will enable Germans to buy Polish land again.

Archaeologists and historians assume that during the early Bronze Age large parts of what was to become Wielkopolska were inhabited by an Illyrian people, part of the Lusatian Cul-

259

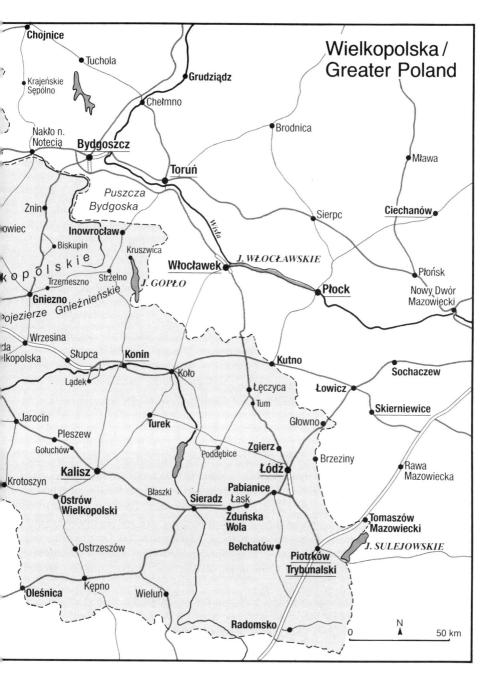

Chojnice

Tuchola

Krajeńskie
Sępólno

Grudziądz

Wielkopolska /
Greater Poland

Chełmno

Brodnica

Mława

Nakło n.
Notecią **Bydgoszcz**

Toruń

*Puszcza
Bydgoska*

Sierpc

Ciechanów

Żnin

owiec

Inowrocław

Biskupin

Kruszwica

Wisła

J. WŁOCŁAWSKIE

Płońsk

opolskie

Trzemeszno

Strzelno

Włocławek

J. GOPŁO

Płock

Nowy Dwór
Mazowiecki

Gniezno

ojezierze

Gnieźnieńskie

Wrzesina

da
lkopolska

Słupca

Konin

Koło

Kutno

Sochaczew

Lądek

Łęczyca

Łowicz

Tum

Skierniewice

Jarocin

Pleszew

Turek

Główno

Goluchów

Poddębice

Zgierz

Brzeziny

Rawa
Mazowiecka

Kalisz

Krotoszyn

Błaszki

Łódź

Pabianice

**Ostrów
Wielkopolski**

Sieradz

Łask

**Zduńska
Wola**

**Tomaszów
Mazowiecki**

Ostrzeszów

Bełchatów

**Piotrków
Trybunalski**

J. SULEJOWSKIE

Oleśnica

Kępno

Wieluń

Radomsko

0

N

50 km

ture, who were ousted by or merged with the southeastward migration of Nordic-Germanic tribes. At the beginning of the Christian era this Germanic acquisition of land came to an end. Then from AD 400 onwards, under pressure from the Hun invasion and Germanic migrations, Slavic tribes came from the east and trickled into what at that time were almost uninhabited lands, settling there right up to the line formed by the rivers Elbe and Saale.

In the ancestral region of the Polanians (Latin: *Poloni*; Polish: *Polanie*) on the middle Warta (Warthe) and the upper Noteć (Netze) it is possible to trace the beginnings of a formation of a state as far back as the 9th century. The emergence of Prince Mieszko I (*c.*960–92) as the ruler of an established state is reported in a variety of sources: the Chronicle of the Saxon monk Widukind of Corvey, the travel narrative of the Jewish merchant Ibrahim Ibn Ja'qūb, contemporary annals, and the Chronicle of Bishop Thietmar of Merseburg. In 966 Mieszko I adopted Christianity of the Latin Church for himself and his people, and in 968 a missionary bishopric was founded at Poznań. On his death Mieszko left behind him a large state, which extended eastwards from the Oder to far beyond the Vistula, and from the Sudeten Mountains to the Baltic Sea. The creation of the first Polish archbishopric at Gniezno in 1000 made possible the establishment of a separate Polish church organization, and above all emphasized Poland's independence from the German Empire. There was now much missionary activity in Poland, and the number of parishes was increased. The first monasteries were founded: Międzyrzecz and Tum pod Łęczycą (both *c.*1000), Lubin, Mogilno and Trzemeszno (second half of 11th century), all in Wielkopolska. With the agreement of Pope John XIX, Mieszko's son, Bolesław I Chrobry, was crowned King of Poland at Gniezno on Christmas Day 1024.

In his reign the system of castellan government was already complete: the whole country was covered with a network of castles, from which the castellans exercised their administrative, judicial and fiscal duties. In the shadow of these castles settlements (*podgrodzie*, 'under the castle') grew up to provide for them, and these gradually took on the status of towns (Gniezno, Poznań, Kruszwica).

From the middle ages until the 18th century the sovereignty of the Polish state was to determine the political history of Wielkopolska. In the 11th century Polish missionary activity and feudal overlordship extended for a short time as far as the March of Lusatia (bishopric of Lubusz) and remained the determining factor in Silesia for several centuries. It was during the subjugation and Christianization of the pagan Pomeranians east of the mouth of the Oder, particularly in the 12th century, that Poles and Germans began to work together. At the same time, in some parts of Wielkopolska the German migration eastwards (Drang nach Osten) was extending considerably further than the territories of the German Empire. The medieval German population that survived into the modern period did so mainly in the city communes.

After the Polish kings had renounced their claim to Silesia by treaties in the 14th century, and definitively excluded the territory from the Kingdom of Poland, the long border between Wielkopolska and Silesia remained almost unchanged until the Second Partition (1793). However, the frontier in the north, between the mouths of the Oder and

Vistula, was the subject of bitter disputes over rival Polish and German claims. In the 12th century Pomerania had become a German fiefdom; and until the 19th century the border of the German Empire ran 200 km east of the mouth of the Oder, i.e. from Łeba southwards. East Pomerania (Pommerellen) with Gdańsk (Danzig) at its centre remained politically under Polish and Church influence until the end of the 13th century; from 1309 until 1454 this region was under the rule of the Teutonic Order, before passing, together with the region around Chełmno (Kulmer Land), the diocese of Warmia (Ermeland) and part of West Prussia, to Poland again for the next 300 years.

As a result of the troubles and the fragmentation of Poland into a number of separate princedoms (1138–1320), the political centre of the Piast territory gradually shifted to Małopolska (Lesser Poland), with Kraków as its capital. It was from there that the renewal of the kingdom started at the beginning of the 14th century. In 1320 Kraków replaced Gniezno as the coronation city of the Polish kings.

The three partitions of Poland at the end of the 18th century changed the political face of Wielkopolska utterly. The First Partition, the result of an agreement made between Prussia, Russia and Austria on 2 August 1772 at St Petersburg, gave Prussia the Netze District, i.e. the territory on either side of the River Noteć (Netze), including the towns of Bydgoszcz (Bromberg) and Inowrocław (Hohensalza), which had always been part of Wielkopolska. On 23 January 1793 a partition treaty between Prussia and Russia led to the annexation by Prussia of the whole of Wielkopolska and part of Mazovia. The Third Partition, agreed in the treaty of the 24 October 1795, completely wiped the 800-year-old Polish state from the map of Europe, with Prussia receiving Warsaw and Białystok.

During the Napoleonic interlude between 1807 and 1815 the region formed part of the Duchy of Warsaw under Friedrich August of Saxony. At the Congress of Vienna Prussia regained only the Poznań region. Prussia's Polish policy entailed the enforced Germanization of West Prussia, but in the Grand Duchy of Posen the Polish nationality was at first tolerated. When the Prussian constitution was revised in 1850, however, the Grand Duchy was officially made a Prussian province, and in the forty or so years between the founding of the German Reich in 1870 and the First World War the government intensified state measures (laws governing school supervision in 1872, and the language used in business in 1877) in an attempt to crush the Polish sense of identity. This untrammelled Germanization only led to intensified nationalist agitation on both the Polish and the German sides in the years leading up to war, and many Germans emigrated.

The end of the First World War brought the resurrection of Poland. In the Treaty of Versailles on 28 June 1919 Poland was given the Province of Posen and the West Prussian Vistula corridor, which gave the new state access to the sea. In 1921–2 about two thirds of the 1.1 million Germans still living in these regions migrated to the Reich or were driven out by economic or administrative pressure. But nowhere on its western side had Poland after the First World War expanded beyond its historic borders of 1772. Indeed the area later known as 'Grenzmark Posen-Westpreussen' ('Border March of Posen-West Prussia'), which had been part of the Polish state before 1772, remained in Germany.

The Second World War and the (fourth) partition of Poland which had been agreed between Hitler and Stalin in a secret clause added to the German-Soviet non-aggression pact, brought Wielkopolska once more under a German yoke. By a decree of 8 October 1939 Hitler incorporated Poznań, West Prussia, Gdańsk and Upper Silesia, together with an area almost as large which had never belonged to Prussia, into the Reich. The new frontier ran from Upper Silesia to East Prussia, passing east of Kutno and Łódź and close to Warsaw. The obliteration of Poland was followed by the savage oppression of its people.

The shifting of Poland westwards as a result of the conferences of Teheran, Yalta and Potsdam meant that the whole of Wielkopolska was re-incorporated into the Polish state. Millions of Germans now had to pay for Hitler's crimes by being expelled from the territories east of the Oder and Noteć.

The 19th century, after the three partitions, was for Poland not only a period of lost sovereignty and the struggle to retain a national identity, in the three partitioned areas, but also a time of great changes in social conditions in the countryside, with industrialization and the development of new centres of population. Each of the three partitioning powers created a different set of conditions, which influenced economic, social and cultural development of the region. In the inter-war years and since the Second World War attempts were made to iron out the disparities, but they can still be felt today.

In eastern and south-eastern Poland jokes are still made about the 'Prussian virtues' (discipline and a talent for organization) of people from Poznań and its environs. Yet the accessibility of the German economic centres of Berlin and the Ruhr District had positive effects on those parts of Wielkopolska that were in Prussian hands, as a glance at the Polish railway network will show. The elementary school system set up by the Prussian authorities was considerably better than the state education provided in the rest of Poland. In agriculture a variety of types of farm developed early on, ranging from smallholdings to large estates.

Nor is it by chance that today the proportion of nationalized agriculture is greater in the west of Poland than in the central, eastern and southeastern provinces. Wielkopolska did not come near the level of fragmentation in agriculture found in Małopolska (between Kraków and Lublin) where private ownership is the norm. The industry of Wielkopolska is concentrated in three districts: the two traditional centres, Poznań and Łódź, which have expanded since the Second World War, and the region around Konin, a new postwar development. Both Konin and Łódź, however, stand today on the brink of ecological catastrophe.

Geographically Wielkopolska can be divided into three regions: the Ziemia Lubuska in the west, the great depression of the Nizina Wielkopolska, and the plateaux of Wyżyna Łódzka in the east and Wyżyna Wieluńska in the southeast. Between the three most important rivers, the Oder, Warta and Noteć, the Pojezierze Wielkopolskie (Greater Polish Lakeland) extends from Zielona Góra in the southwest to Inowrocław in the northeast, near the historically important town of Kruszwica. Particularly delightful are the Puszcza Rzepińska and the Puszcza Notecka forests, south and east respectively of Gorzów Wlkp.

*Biskupin, reconstructed
Lusatian Culture Fort*

The earliest architecture to be found in Wielkopolska is one of the wooden forts made between 550 and 400 BC by people of the Lusatian Culture, which has been reconstructed at Biskupin, north of Gniezno; clay and bronze vessels have also been found at Biskupin, decorated with cult motifs.

Because of its importance in the early development of the Polish state, Wielkopolska has a wealth of Romanesque art: in architecture Poznań Cathedral, the collegiate churches of Kruszwica and Tum pod Łęczycą, the abbey church of Strzelno; in sculpture the doors in Gniezno Cathedral; and in the applied arts the chalices from Trzemeszno.

Gothic architecture is represented by basilican churches such as Gniezno Cathedral (remodelled in 1342) and by hall churches like the collegiate church of St Mary in Poznań. Architectural sculpture also reached a high level in this period, as is shown by the tympanum of the Dominican Church in Poznań (c.1300).

The beginning of the Renaissance in Poland coincided with the apogee of the towns; in Wielkopolska this was particularly true of Poznań, although its famous town hall (c.1550) in fact belongs to the Late Renaissance. In any case it is true that during the Renaissance and Baroque periods the centres of artistic development were now mainly to be found in Małopolska (principally at Kraków), Mazovia (Warsaw) and in Silesia.

With Neoclassicism, however, the situation was different; Wielkopolska, like Mazovia, was one of its great centres. The revolutionary style was at first confined to palaces, as can be seen at Sierniki (north of Poznań) and Lewków (southwest of Kalisz), but the development of new industrial centres and the increasing importance of the towns and municipal administration set architects new tasks connected with industrial development, town planning and the creation of public buildings. Much of their work can still be seen in towns such as Łódź, Kalisz and Poznań.

Gorzów Wlkp. – Chojna – Cedynia – Kostrzyn – Myślibórz – Strzelce Krajeńskie – Drezdenko – Ośno Lubuskie – Sulęcin – Lagów – Międzyrzecz – Gościkowo – Świebodzin – Chlastawa – Kalsk – Sulechów – Krosno Odrzańskie – Żary – Żagań – Zielona Góra

Because of its convenient situation on the Warta not far from the confluence with the Noteć, **Gorzów Wlkp. (Landsberg an der Warthe)** developed early as an important trading centre. Originally a fishing village, it received its town charter (under the name of Landisberch nova) in 1257. The first setbacks in its commercial development occurred with the destruction wrought by the Thirty Years War (1618–48) and the Great Northern War (1700–21). In 1857 Gorzów was linked to the railway network, and it grew rapidly until 1900 to become the largest town in the territory then known as the Neumark. The principal industries of the town are chemicals, engineering, food, timber, textiles and paper. The East German writer Christa Wolf was born here in 1929. The main landmarks, apart from the remains of the 14th-century town walls, are the arches of the *railway bridge* and the *Kościół Mariacki (St Mary's Church)* (now a cathedral), which can be seen for miles. This massive church, begun *c.*1300, was later converted into a three-aisled Gothic hall church; its exterior appearance has remained unaltered since the late 15th century.

Chojna (Königsberg), in the north of the former Neumark, was already an important trading town in medieval times. The turreted *Świecka Brama (Schwedt Gate)* and the *Barnkowska Brama (Bernikow Gate)* have survived from its old fortifications. Work has now started on the rebuilding of the *Kościół Mariacki (St Mary's Church)* burned out in 1945. The ruins of this High Gothic hall church, begun in 1389 and mostly the work of Hinrich Brunsberg (the builder of the Gothic Town Hall and church of St John at Szczecin), together with its massive tower (still standing), give a vivid impression of the church's original splendour.

Beyond Chojna, the little town of **Cedynia** was the site in 972 of Mieszko I's defeat of a German army led by the Emperor Otto. It was also from Cedynia that the final thrust on Berlin by the Red Army began on 16 April 1945. Berlin can be seen from the top of the hill, where there is a concrete monument.

All that remains of the Prussian castle at **Kostrzyn (Küstrin)** near the German border, are a few external walls; from 1536 to 1815 the town was the capital of the Neumark. It was in the fortress at Kostrzyn that the future Frederick II of Prussia was imprisoned in 1730 by his stern father for planning to escape to France. His friend and accomplice von Katte was beheaded outside the young Crown Prince's window

In the middle ages capital status was claimed by **Myślibórz (Soldin)**. The *Kosciól śś. Piotra i Pawła (Church of Sts Peter and Paul)* was at that time the church of a provost, and the powerful building (altered to a three-aisled hall church c.1300) with its square west tower still dominates the market place. Myślibórz, situated by the shore of a lake, the Jezioro Myśliborskie (Soldiner See), is now primarily a health resort.

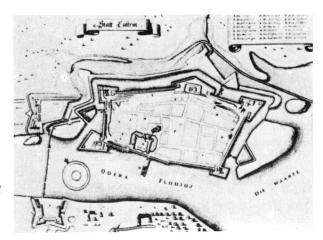

Kostrzyn, plan of the town and the Prussian fortifications in the 17th century, engraving by M. Merian

The *Kościół Mariacki (St Mary's Church)* in **Strzelce Krajeńskie (Friedeberg)** was reconsecrated in 1973. It is a three-aisled hall church of the 15th century. There are also remains of the town walls with the *Drezdenko Gate*. **Drezdenko (Driesen)** is first mentioned in 1092, when it was a castle with fortifications on the banks of the Noteć. The town still lies under the shadow of a late 19th-century red-brick administrative building typical of Kaiser Wilhelm II's Reich. To the east of Gorzów Wlkp., between the Warta to the south and the Noteć to the north lies the *Puszcza Notecka*, a large forest region, much used for riding. The usual starting point for visiting the forest is *Sieraków*, where there is a national stud farm.

The neo-Gothic alterations to the *Town Hall* of **Ośno Lubuskie (Drossen)** in the mid-19th century show the influence of the great Prussian architect Karl Friedrich Schinkel. The town's rise in the last century was due mainly to a brown coal mine in the nearby forest. Near the town hall stands the *Kościół św. Jakuba (Church of St James)*, first consecrated in 1298, a three-aisled brick building, thoroughly restored in the 19th century, and again repaired after damage in the Second World War. The *Kościół św. Mikołaja (Church of St Nicholas)* in **Sulęcin (Zielenzig)** was also restored after being completely gutted by fire in 1945; it is an aisleless brick building on a granite base and dates from the 14th/15th centuries.

The *Castle* of **Łagów (Lagow)** stands on a strip of land between two lakes. It is first mentioned in 1258 and in the 14th century was acquired by the Order of Knights Hospitaller and extended to form a powerful defensive stronghold. From the keep (35 metres high) there is a view across the lakes and beech woods of the countryside that used to be known as Sternberger Schweiz (Sternberg Switzerland – Sternberg being the German name for the nearby town of Torzym). An annual film week is held at Łagów (Lubuskie Lato Filmowe), and it is also a popular weekend resort.

Międzyrzecz (Meseritz) (meaning 'between the rivers') is a town with a long ecclesiastical tradition; the first Benedictine monastery in Poland was established here around 1000, though nothing more is heard about it in later periods. The *Kościół Farny św. Jana Chrzciciela (Parish Church of St John the Baptist)*, a three-aisled brick building with a star vault, is in a good state of preservation. The town hall (rebuilt in 1827 after a fire) and the Lutheran Church (before 1834, perhaps by Schinkel), both facing the market square, are examples of local Neoclassicism, as is the synagogue (now a warehouse). The remains of the castellan's castle (foundations, surrounding walls, a gateway), carefully restored after the Second World War date back to the very origins of Polish statehood in Wielkopolska. Międzyrzecz was the seat of the great preacher Dab Baer (the Maggid of Międzyrzecz), an early apostle of Hasidism who preserved many of the sayings of the Baal Shem Tov.

The former *Opactwo Cystersów (Cistercian Abbey)* 'in the Paradise of the Blessed Virgin Mary and Saint Martin' at **Gościkowo (Paradies)** – the abbey is also known in Polish as Paradyż – was founded by the Polish count Bonisius in 1234. The first monks came from Lehnin Abbey near Brandenburg. The plan of the brick-built abbey church still follows the structural system of large Romanesque churches based on the module of the square crossing, but in its detailing it follows the rules of Early Gothic, and it was given a thorough Baroque remodelling in the 18th century. Following the Second World War extensive restoration work was necessary. The high altar deserves especial mention: it was completed in 1740 and the two paintings by Felix Anton Scheffler show the Assumption of the Virgin, and St Martin.

The town of **Świebodzin (Schwiebus)**, situated at the intersection of two major trans-European roads, has one of the most important churches in what used to be part of the Mark Brandenburg: the *Kościół św. Michała (Church of St Michael)*. The 19th-century neo-Gothic west front is striking, with two extremely slender towers, which were built *c.*1860 after the church had been towerless since a fire in 1637. The church itself was begun in the 13th century as an Early Gothic building, and extended two hundred years later by the addition of a row of chapels on the south side and an aisle on the north side. Świebodzin is first mentioned as a town in 1251; the Renaissance *Town Hall* dates from around 1547, and has been much altered since.

One of the most remarkable features of the region around the towns of Świebodzin and Sulechów is the number of timber churches. The most beautiful of these is in **Chlastawa (Klastawe)**, built in 1647 by Protestants from Bohemia; its construction is half-timber with clay infill, wooden cladding and a shingle roof. Another timber church is at **Kalsk (Kalzig)**; it was built in 1521 on a base of granite masonry blocks, which may even date back to the foundation of the village around 1376.

The most famous landmarks in the town of **Sulechów (Züllichau)** are the Late Gothic *Kościół Farny NMP (Parish Church of St Mary)* and the *Town Hall*. Just off the market square, and slightly set back between two houses, St Mary's is a three-aisled brick-built hall church, with alterations after 1557; it was planned with two towers, but only the north tower was built. A plaque on the town hall commemorates Fryderyk Chopin's stay in the town. Of the old town defences the *Brama Krośnieńska (Krosno Gate)* (1704) is extant.

The *Kościół Farny NMP (Church of St Mary)* in **Krosno Odrzańskie (Crossen)** on the Oder not far from the confluence with the Bóbr (Bober) is one of the few significant Baroque churches in the region of the former Mark Brandenburg. It is a Gothic building remodelled for Protestant worship around 1708–29, with particularly impressive interior decoration, especially the ceiling. After destruction in the Second World War the old 13th-century Piast castle of Duke Henryk Brodaty (Henry the Bearded, Duke of Silesia and husband of St Jadwiga) was rebuilt. Krosno, which was primarily a merchant settlement, probably received its town charter around 1203.

In **Żary (Sorau)** the Baroque houses facing the market place (restored since 1960) are a reminder of the town's former prosperity. Żary had long been a centre of clothmaking and became an industrial centre for the production of linen. All that remains of the 14th/15th-century town fortifications are three towers, the 'Three Faithful Ones'. The *Kościół Farny NMP (Church of St Mary)*, a spacious hall church with a stepped west front, built mainly in the early 15th century, with the Baroque Promnitz Chapel (1670-72) on its north side. C. P. Telemann was Kapellmeister from 1704 to 1708 at the *Promnitz Palace* (1705–26, by Giulio Simonetti and Georg Spanninger), partly in ruins since 1944, one of three palaces in the town.

Although **Żagań (Sagan)** is only a few kilometres away, it is already in Silesia. Its architectural history is linked with the name of Albrecht von Wallenstein, the great general in the Thirty Years War, who was given the Princedom of Sagan by the Emperor Ferdinand II in 1628. An inveterate builder, Wallenstein began work on a new Renaissance *Palace* incorporating older buildings in 1631, only three years before his assassination. However, it was not until 1695 that the building was completed, by Antonio della Porta for Prince Lobkowitz, in the Baroque form which it has preserved to this day. The park has a Neoclassical orangery and other adornments. Important buildings in the town itself are the huge *Kościół Nawiedzenia NMP (Church of the Annunciation)*, the former Augustinian church with its magnificent stepped gable façade and delicate arcaded courtyard, a large 14th-century hall church dating from the 14th century, and the *Kościół śś. Piotra i Pawła* (Church of Sts Peter and Paul), also Gothic.

The Silesian town of **Zielona Góra (Grünberg)**, the centre of the voivodship administration, has a population of 110,000 and is now one of the most important industrial centres in western Poland. Historically the town's economy was based on clothmaking (the first guild of clothmakers was founded in 1438) and wine production. There is evidence of wine-making as far back as 1314, and today Zielona Góra is the only wine-producing town in Poland. The centre of the old town is a rectangular market square, with the *Town Hall* in

Silver cosmetic implements from Drezdenko, 11th century

the middle. The present town hall dates from 1590, with the tower rebuilt in 1670. The Late Gothic *Kościół Farny św. Jadwigi (Parish Church of St Jadwiga)* (1372–94) was last rebuilt, after a number of fires, in 1679. The former Lutheran church 'Zum Garten Christi' ('the Garden of Christ' – now the Roman Catholic *Kościół Matki Boskiej Częstochowskiej, Church of Our Lady of Częstochowa) is a half-timbered cruciform building of 1746–7* with a Neoclassical façade, which was given a tower in 1821. The *Wieża Głodowa* (Hunger Tower) and parts of the town walls have survived from the old town fortifications.

Poznań

'Posen, the capital of the Grand Duchy, has a gloomy, cheerless appearance. Its single attraction is the large number of Catholic churches. However, not one of these is beautiful. I went on a pilgrimage all morning in a vain search for beautiful old pictures. I did not find the old paintings beautiful, and those that have some beauty are not old. The Poles have the fatal habit of renovating their churches.' Despite Heinrich Heine's description in his 'Letter from Poland' (1823), **Poznań** (Posen) is worth exploring. It is one of the most ancient cities in Poland, was an important centre of the medieval Polish state, and is now the economic and cultural heart of Wielkopolska.

Poznań today is a bustling commercial centre, famous in Poland for its businesslike, Prussian demeanour. The first international fair was held in the city in 1925, and it has since grown into one of the biggest industrial exhibitions in the world. Poznań, the fifth largest city in Poland, with a population of 540,000, is chiefly important as a centre of industry and trade, but it has also played a decisive part in the development of Poland's culture and learning.

The founding of the city is closely connected with the beginnings of the Polish state. The first castle was built on Ostrów Tumski (Cathedral Island) in the River Warta in the 9th century. In 968 Mieszko I chose the town as the seat of the first Polish bishopric and the centre of the Piast state. Shortly afterwards a settlement of craftsmen and traders developed on the neighbouring island of Śródka to the east; the ducal castle was enlarged into the most powerful fortress in the country.

In the 13th century a new settlement grew up on the west bank of the Warta. This followed the chequerboard plan typical of a medieval new town, with a central market square. The granting of a town charter in 1253 underlined the pre-eminence of Poznań in Wielkopolska over Gniezno; at the same time Kraków was made the capital of all Poland.

In the following centuries Poznań became an increasingly important central European trading centre; merchants came from Germany, Italy, England and Greece to do business, and a large Jewish quarter developed. After the founding of the Lubrański Academy by Bishop Jan Lubrański (1456–1520), a great patron of learning, in 1518, Poznań quickly became a centre of culture and learning. Printing presses were established and there was a flowering of the applied arts.

View of Poznań, engraving after E. Raczyński, 1843

The Swedish Wars in the 17th century, together with the resentment felt by the higher nobility towards the burghers of the city, led to set-backs in its development. Religious conflicts also played a part in this, and it was not until the Polish Enlightenment during the reign of the last king, Stanisław August Poniatowski (1764–95) that Poznań felt any new impetus.

The Second Partition in 1793 brought the city under Prussian rule. Between 1807 and 1815 Poznań was a department of Napoleon's Duchy of Warsaw. After the Congress of Vienna it became the capital of the Prussian-dominated Grand Duchy of Posen, and from 1830 it was also the seat of provincial officials sent from Berlin.

The building of a massive citadel on the northern side of the city made Poznań into one of the strongest fortresses in Prussia. The large garrison meant an increase in the number of Prussian military and administrative personnel who settled with their families in the city. Many Jews also arrived, especially from Berlin, to make a new life for themselves in Poznań.

The middle of the 19th century saw the beginning of rapid industrial development. Both Poles and Germans had a part in this, though economic life in the town came increasingly under German domination. At the same time the Polish population came under the pressure of state-imposed Germanization, which gave rise to violent and bitter organized opposition. Political interest groups intensified their activities; one effective means of resistance was a boycott of all German shops.

In December 1918, the presence of Paderewski (who was passing through on his way to Warsaw) was enough to inspire rebellion. Shortly after Poznań became part of the new Polish state. The university was founded in 1919. The German population rapidly declined, and soon formed a mere five per cent of the city's total population. In the period

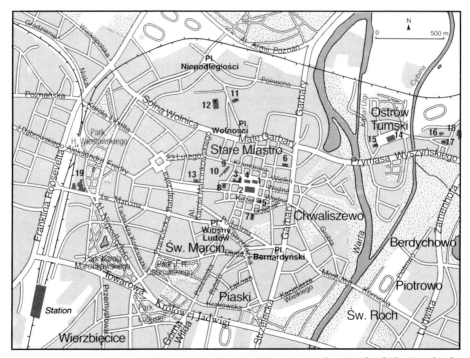

Poznań 1 Ratusz (Town Hall) 2 Odwach (Guardhouse) 3 Pałac Działyńskich (Działyński Palace) 4 Waga Miejska (Town Weigh-House) 5 Pałac Górków (Górka Palace) 6 Kościół Dominikanów (Dominican Church) 7 Kościół Farny (Parish Church) 8 Kościół Franciszkanów (Franciscan Church) 9 Zamek Przemysława (Przemysław Castle) 10 Mury Mieskie (City Walls) 11 Kościół św. Wojciecha (Church of St Adalbert) 12 Kościół Karmelitów Bosych (Church of the Discalced Carmelites) 13 Biblioteka Raczyńskich (Raczyński Library) 14 Katedra śś. Piotra i Pawła (Cathedral of Sts Peter and Paul) 15 Kościół Mariacki (Church of St Mary) 16 Dawny Klasztor Filipinów (former Oratorian Monastery) 17 Kościół św. Małgorzaty (Church of St Margaret) 18 Klasztor Reformatów (Monastery of the Reformed Franciscans) 19 Uniwersytet Adama Mickiewicza (Adam Mickiewicz University)

between the wars Poznań played an important role as an economic and educational centre in western Poland; the population grew to 280,000 and the city expanded greatly in size. The wartime years of German occupation were particularly terrible: many of the inhabitants were deported and Nazi terror was unremitting. Poznań was forcibly made the capital of the newly created Warthegau district.

The fabric of the city was not seriously damaged, however, until the Soviet counter-offensive at the beginning of 1945, when 75 per cent of the town centre was destroyed. As in Poland's other architecturally important towns, many of Poznań's historic monuments have been reconstructed.

The *Stare Miasto (Old Town)*, at the heart of the city centre, has retained its medieval plan with a grid street system and the spacious *Stary Rynek (Old Market Square)*, where all the administrative and commercial institutions of the city used to be concentrated.

The square is dominated by the **Ratusz (Town Hall)** (1), a gem of the Polish Renaissance and by far the most beautiful secular building in Poznań (plate 20). Its rooms now contain the *Muzeum Historyczne Miasta Poznania (Historical Museum of Poznań)*. The original Gothic town hall, built around 1300, was remodelled and extended in 1555–60 by Giovanni Battista Quadro, an architect from Ticino, to become one of the most splendid Renaissance town halls not only in Poland but in the whole of Central Europe.

Its rebuilding after partial destruction in the Second World War was completed in 1954. The main feature of the exterior is the façade with three storeys of arcades and an attic above, formed from a tall flat wall decorated with coloured portraits of Polish kings, with decorative cresting and three little towers. This attic also acts as a visual link with the tall main tower, which has a Neoclassical spire dating from the restoration in 1781–3.

The oldest parts of the town hall are the 13th-century cellars, consisting of four square rooms with Early Gothic cross-rib vaults. Room I now contains a model of the city showing the first cathedral of the 10th century; Room II has a display of Romanesque stonework; in Room III there is an authentic pillory (a copy of which now stands outside the town hall); and Room IV has a 13th-century stone sculpture of the Blessed Salomea.

The museum continues on the ground floor with the history of the city in the Renaissance, an exhibition about the various craft guilds of the time includes guild chests, where documents were kept, and the work of craftsmen.

The *Great Hall* (plate 18) on the first floor is one of the most beautiful Renaissance interiors in Poland; fortunately it was not destroyed in the Second World War. The splendid decoration of the hall, which extends behind the loggias across the whole width of the building, gives an idea of the way of life, ambition and pride of the 16th-century burghers. The coffered vault is supported on two piers, which divide the space into two parts. In one part the coffers in the vault are filled with the arms of Poland and Lithuania, the Habsburgs and the Sforzas, and the virtues of courage, steadfastness and patriotism symbolized by Samson, Hercules and other heroic figures. In the other part of the hall the coffers contain personifications of the sun and moon and various planets, with exotic and fantastic animals.

The barrel vault of the *Royal Hall*, also on the first floor, was reconstructed in 1910–13. Every new master admitted into the painters' guild was required to paint the portrait of the ruling monarch for the town. The ceremony of admission to the guild took place in this hall. At present the portraits of Zygmunt III Waza, Władysław IV Waza, Jan II Kazimierz Waza, August II Mocny and Stanisław Leszczyński are on display.

The *Courtroom* with its flattened domical vault has also preserved its Renaissance form. On the walls are Latin exhortations to the judges who used to preside here. The decorations on the vaulting are taken from Pompeiian patterns and were made by Szymon Bak in the mid-19th century. The rooms on the second floor were also rebuilt after destruction in

1945; the beams and coffered ceilings were made after patterns in houses in the market square that had survived the war. The largest room on the second floor is used for temporary exhibitions.

Directly in front of the town hall stands the *Fontanna Prozerpiny* (*Proserpine Fountain*), a Rococo structure of 1766. To the side is a terrace of shopkeepers' houses. These date back to the 15th century and have 16th-century arcades (reconstructed), where herrings, salt, cooking utensils, candles and other goods were sold. The arms on No. 17 are those of the shopkeepers' guild (a herring appears in them). The market square has many other interesting buildings. The Neoclassical **Odwach (Guardhouse)** (2) was built in 1788 by Johann Christian Kamsetzer for Kazimierz Raczyński, a member of a leading aristocratic family in Wielkopolska. The Late Baroque **Pałac Działyńskich (Działyński Palace)** (3) at No. 78, built in 1773–6, is now the seat of the Academy of Sciences and the Polish Western Institute. The great sculptured attic on the façade, with classical friezes surmounted by trophies, was added by Antoni Hoene in 1786–7.

The **Waga Miejska (Town Weigh-House)** (4) is an accurate copy of a Renaissance building by Giovanni Battista Quadro, which was demolished in 1890. The reconstructed 16th-century **Pałac Górków (Górka Palace)** (5) now houses the *Muzeum Archeologiczne (Archaeological Museum)*. The other burghers' houses surrounding the square were returned to their original Renaissance, Baroque or Neoclassical appearance in the course of postwar restoration. Among the interesting interiors is the *Apteka pod Białym Orłem (White Eagle Pharmacy)* at No. 14. The *Muzeum Instrumentów Muzycznich (Museum of Musical Instruments)* at No. 45 is the most important of its kind in Poland.

North of the market square, in ul. Dominikańska, stands the former **Kościół Dominikanów (Dominican Church)** (6). The Early Gothic west doorway survives from the original building of 1244–53. On the left of the nave is the Late Gothic *Rosary Chapel* (*c.*1500) with a magnificent vault (reconstructed). The St Jacek chapel on the upper storey (1622) leads into the cloister garden. At the beginning of the 18th century the church was given a Baroque remodelling by Giovanni Catenacci. The **Kościół Farny (Parish Church)** (7) is situated south of the market square, in ul. Gołębia. It forms part of the buildings of the former Kolegium Jezuicke (Jesuit College), and was built for the Jesuits

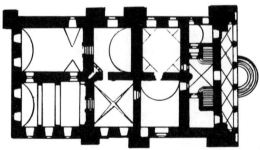

Poznań, plan of the Town Hall

from 1651 under the direction of a series of Italian architects: Tommaso Poncino, Giovanni Catenacci and Pompeo Ferrari, who completed the façade in 1732. The rich interior has painted decoration by Karl Dankwart, plasterwork by Giovanni Battista Bianco and a high altar with a painting by Szymon Czechowicz. The Jesuit College is now used by the Poznań City Council. At the back of the building is a park laid out around 1900, now named after Fryderyk Chopin.

At the foot of a small hill to the west of the Stary Rynek stands the **Kościół Francisz-kanów (Franciscan Church)** (8), a three-aisled Baroque building erected between 1665 and 1728 by Jan Koński, also with lavish interior decoration (paintings by Adam Swach); it was restored in 1964–5.

On the hill itself the *Muzeum Rzemiosł Artystycznych (Museum of Applied Arts)* is a building of no great architectural interest, but it incorporates remains of the **Zamek Przemysława (Przemysław Castle)** (9), which used to stand on the site. The castle built at the end of the 13th century by the Piast duke Przemysław I was destroyed during the Swedish Wars, partly rebuilt after 1783 and finally demolished in 1795; only a few bits of masonry remain. Not far away are parts of the medieval **Mury Miejskie (City Walls)** (10).

To the north of the Old Town is the **Kościół św. Wojciecha (Church of St Adalbert)** (11), a small 15th-century build-ing, which still has its (reconstructed) wooden bell-tower. The Gothic altar trip-tych (1500), with a carving of the Assump-tion of the Virgin, is probably the work of pupils of Veit Stoss. During restoration in

Poznań, view of al. Wilhelma, drawing, 1833

the early 1950's the church was given modern stained glass. Józef Wybicki (1747–1822), the author of the Polish national anthem 'Jeszcze Polska nie zginęła' ('Poland has not perished yet'), is buried in the crypt. Opposite St Adalbert's is the Baroque **Kościół Karmelitów Bosych (Church of the Discalced Carmelites)** (12), built by Cristoforo Bonadura and Giorgio Catenacci in the mid-17th century.

To the southeast of the Old Town, in ul. Garbary, is one of the city's grandest Baroque churches, the *Kościół Bernardynów (Bernardine Church)*, also by Bonadura and Catenacci (1658–71), while an interesting contrast to all this Italian Baroque is provided by the *Kościół Wszystkich Świętych (Church of All Saints)* in ul. Grobla, formerly the Lutheran church of the Holy Cross. It is a sober Neoclassical rectangular building enclosing a circular preaching hall, built in 1777 by Antoni Hoene. The Carmelite church, the *Kościół Bożego Ciała (Church of Corpus Christi)* in ul. Strzelecka, south of the Old Town, is the best of the city's surviving medieval churches, a tall Late Gothic brick building (1465–70), with Lady Chapel (1726) and high altar (*c.*1731) by Pompeo Ferrari.

While the Old Town with the Stary Rynek and town hall forms the historic centre of Poznań, the focus of city life today is Pl. Wolności (Freedom Square). Its north side is dominated by the imposing Neoclassical building of the **Biblioteka Raczyńskich (Raczyński Library)** (13) (1829), with a façade with 12 pairs of Corinthian columns clearly inspired by the east front of the Louvre. The library was founded by Count Edward Raczyński (see page 290) as a means of preserving Polish culture in what was then a Prussian-ruled city. (Another patriotic Edward Raczyński was the long-serving ambassador to the Court of St James, and later President of the Government in Exile in London.)

On the east side of the square is the *Muzeum Narodowe (National Museum)* with one of Poland's finest art collections. Its nucleus was the Raczyński collection containing works by some of the greatest Italian and Spanish masters. Bellotto's magnificent *Election Sejm of Stanisław August Poniatowski*, a detailed and vivid depiction of the last of the royal elections, should not be missed.

Ul. Wielka crosses the Most Chrobrego (literally: 'Bridge of the Brave' – after King Bolesław Chrobry) to the oldest part of Poznań: Ostrów Tumski (Cathedral Island) between the rivers Warta and Cybina, where the **Katedra śś. Piotra i Pawła (Cathedral of Sts Peter and Paul)** (14) stands. The pre-Romanesque stone-built basilica erected here by Mieszko I after 968, following his conversion to Christianity, was destroyed in 1038 but rebuilt in 1075. On the same site King Kazimierz III Wielki ordered the building of a new Gothic cathedral, a three-aisled basilica flanked by rows of chapels with a polygonal choir and ambulatory. This building later underwent Baroque and Neoclassical alterations, but after destruction in the Second World War the cathedral was rebuilt in its Gothic form, apart from the Baroque caps on the two west towers and the chapels.

The crypt has remains of the pre-Romanesque and Romanesque buildings, and parts of some royal tombs (probably of Mieszko I and Bolesław I Chrobry) as well as a 10th-

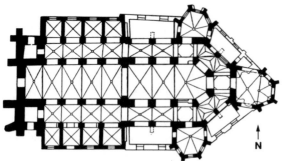

Poznań, plan of the Cathedral of Sts Peter and Paul

Poznań, view of the cathedral and Church of St Mary (left), wash drawing by J. von Minutoli, 1833

century font. The Late Gothic high altar and choir stalls date from the 16th century. There are eleven chapels surrounding the main body of the church; the most spectacular of these is the *Złota Kaplica (Golden Chapel)*, built in 1835–41 to the designs of Francesco Maria Lanci in a Byzantine style for the remains of Mieszko I and Bolesław I Chrobry, who share the sarcophagus there. The chapel also has bronze statues of the two princes by the Berlin sculptor Christian Daniel Rauch, the funerary sculptor of the Hohenzollerns and collaborator of Schinkel. Two Renaissance tombs are highlights of Polish sculpture: the tomb of Benedykt Idzbieński, Bishop of Poznań, is by the Polish sculptor Jan Michałowicz and was completed in 1560, while that of Barbara and Andrzej Górka was made by the Italian Girolamo Canavesi, who lived in Poland and had his workshop in Kraków.

Not far from the cathedral is the attractive ensemble of the little Late Gothic **Kościół Mariacki (Church of St Mary)** (15) built in 1431–44 and given modern stained glass and wall paintings in the early 1950's, and the former *Psalterium* and *Lubrański Academy*, a Renaissance building erected in 1518–20 and several times remodelled, now contains the Museum and Archives of the Archdiocese of Poznań.

Beyond the River Cybina is Śródka, the oldest suburb of Poznań, which also has several religious buildings reflecting its long history. The former **Klasztor Filipinów (Oratorian Monastery)** (16) is Late Baroque with neo-Romanesque additions (rebuilt after 1945), while the adjoining **Kościół św. Małgorzaty (Church of St Margaret)** (17) is a Late Gothic building with a fine star vault, and some Romanesque fragments. The former **Klasztor Reformatów (Monastery of the Reformed Franciscans)** (18) is another 17th-century Baroque work by Cristoforo Bonadura and Giorgio Catenacci. A little further

277

east is the *Kościół św. Jana Jerozolimskiego (Church of St John of Jerusalem)*, built by the Knights Hospitaller in the second half of the 13th century.

West of Pl. Wolności, ul. św. Marcina passes the *Pałac Kultury (Palace of Culture)* built as an imperial palace in 1905 by Franz Schwechten for Kaiser Wilhelm II on his visits to the city, and modified in 1940-44 by Franz Böhmer and Georg Petrich as a residence for Hitler. Its imposing Germanic Romanesque style is a conscious revival of the glories of the medieval German Empire. The **Uniwersytet Adama Mickiewicza (Adam Mickiewicz University)** (19) nearby, was built as a German academy in 1910 in the style of the Baltic Renaissance.

Ostrów Lednicki – Gniezno – Biskupin – Trzemeszno – Strzelno – Kruszwica

Northeast of Poznań, on Ostrów Lednicki, the largest island in Jezioro Lednica (Lake Lednica), is an archaeological *Skansen (Open-Air Museum)* with the remains of a ring-shaped fortification and some ruins. It seems likely that the nucleus of the Polanian state, from which the Polish state was founded in the 10th century, was to be found in this region. At any rate, a castle of the Polanian dukes stood here; it was destroyed in 1038 by Břetislav of Bohemia and not rebuilt; the castle chapel remained in use as a parish church until the 15th century.

Archaeological excavations have revealed that there was a settlement here as early as the 6th century. The first small castle, surrounded by an earthwork reinforced with wood, was built at the end of the 9th century and beginning of the 10th; next to it an outer ward was added for artisan workshops. The church, built on a Greek cross plan, probably in the 10th century, has an extension built of granite in the 11th century. At that time the road from Poznań to Gniezno crossed the lake and island over a wooden bridge 600 metres long. Timber piles were discovered in 1959.

Bishop Wojciech (Adalbert) of Prague, who had been driven from his Bohemian bishopric, was sent eastwards from Gdańsk to convert the pagan Pruzzi, who shortly afterwards murdered him. Bolesław I Chrobry bought back the martyr's body from the Pruzzi and had it brought to **Gniezno**, where after a quick canonization a vigorous Wojciech cult began to develop. Emperor Otto III, who had been a friend of the saint, felt compelled to make a pilgrimage to his grave in March 1000.

This imperial visit was to have great consequences for the young Polish state. Otto not only raised Bolesław to the status of a king, he also named him 'brother and associate in the Empire'. At the same time Pope Silvester II established the first Polish archbishopric at Gniezno under Wojciech's brother Radim, together with the bishoprics of Kraków, Kołobrzeg and Wrocław, enabling Poland to run its own church organization, which suited Bolesław's plan of achieving Polish autonomy. With the agreement of Pope John XIX, Bolesław was crowned King of Poland at Gniezno in 1024, in an act that symbolized Poland's independence from the Empire and was an expression of the state's internal consolidation and its cultural and ecclesiastical attachment to the Christian West.

It is hardly surprising, therefore, that the tomb of St Wojciech should be the origin and

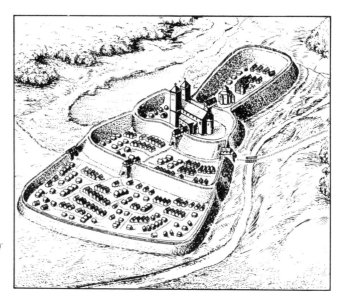

Gniezno, reconstruction of the town's appearance at the beginning of the 11th century

symbol of Polish sovereignty. The city's importance as the cradle of the Polish state is reflected today in the fact that the Primate of Poland is still the Archbishop of Gniezno. As a result of a great fire in 1819, which completely destroyed almost all the historic centre of the town, the development of Gniezno over the centuries can now only be traced on Wzgórze Lecha (Lech Hill), where Lech, the legendary leader of the Polanians, is supposed to have decided to settle on the site where he had seen a white eagle nesting. The hill was once the spiritual and intellectual centre of the town – indeed of all Poland – since it is where the *Katedra Wniebowzięcia N.P. Marii (Cathedral of the Assumption)* (plate 25) stands. Mieszko I had the first church built in 970–77 on the site of a pagan shrine. The remains of St Wojciech were brought here in 999, the year of his canonization.

In 1342 Jarosław Bogoria Skotnicki was appointed archbishop. A highly cultivated man with extraordinary abilities as a statesman, he was Rector of Bologna University and co-founder of the Jagiellonian University. In Kraków he was involved in the rebuilding of Wawel Cathedral, centre of the Piast kingdom based in Małopolska; on his translation to Gniezno he immediately began a similar rebuilding of his cathedral church to make it a worthy focal point of the historical Polish state based in Wielkopolska. Gniezno was to follow the model of the great French cathedrals. Skotnicki planned a three-aisled building with an ambulatory round the choir surrounded by a ring of chapels. The choir was completed in 1390, while work continued on the nave far into the 15th century. In 1760 the interior of the church, which had been remodelled several times, was burned out. For its rebuilding the architect Ephraim Schroeger was summoned from Warsaw and in the course of thirty years (1761–90) transformed part of the cathedral into a Neoclassical building. Severe damage in the Second World War made a comprehensive restoration necessary (1945–61), and the restorers seized the opportunity to return part of the church to its original form. From the result it is possible to read the building's history: the tall nave is flanked by low aisles with a choir ambulatory and ring of chapels, which have been left in their late 18th-century state. The statues above the buttresses representing saints venerated in Poland are the work of Marcin Różek (1932–6). The monumental two-towered west front also shows two stages of construction: the gabled centre in Dutch Late Gothic was built in the first half of the 17th century by an architect from Gdańsk, while the elegant towers with their slender buttresses and Baroque caps are part of Ephraim Schroeger's alterations (1779).

After walking around the outside of the church, we enter through the south doorway, where the most famous work of art in the cathedral – perhaps in the whole of Poland – is to be found: the early medieval *Drzwi Gnieźnieńskie (Gniezno Doors)*. These great monuments of Romanesque art were made in the 11th or 12th century at Magdeburg. According to legend they were commissioned by Bolesław III Krzywousty. The two doors, which are not quite symmetrical, are cast in solid bronze. Their eighteen rectangular panels contain scenes from the life of St Wojciech which are to be read from the bottom left to bottom right. The borders are filled with fantastic plant and animal motifs and little scenes of rural life, hunting and various fights. The saint's story is vividly told: on the left are scenes of his childhood and early life, while on the right we see his mission to the Pruzzi and martyrdom, the purchase of his body by Bolesław Chrobry and his solemn burial at Gniezno. What is most striking are the variety of gestures and expressions of the figures, and the vivid changes in mood from one scene to the next.

The nave and aisles are now in the form in which they were built in the early 15th century. The nave, separated from the choir only by the high choir arch, is a long space, emphasized by tall, narrow arcades and windows. The roughness and severity of the bare masonry are relieved only by unusual decorative mouldings with human and animal carvings on the archivolts, vaulting ribs and string course (reconstructed from fragments). This austere impression does not reflect the cathedral's original appearance: it has to be imagined richly decorated and furnished, and with at least ornamental paintwork (as can be deduced from some fragments of surviving painting that have been uncovered).

The present decoration of the choir is sparing but rich. On the (modern) *mensa* of the high altar stands the silver *Reliquary* of St Wojciech, made in 1662 in Gdańsk by the goldsmith Peter van der Rennen who later made the very similar Stanisław shrine in Kraków. It is in the form of a sarcophagus supported by six eagles, and on its lid lies the figure of the saint with his episcopal insignia. The lavishly decorated Early Baroque shape of the sarcophagus is ornamented with ten scenes from the saint's life. (The visitor may be puzzled about the contents of the reliquary, remembering that Duke Břetislav I of Bohemia had carried the relics of the saint back to Prague when he captured Gniezno in

The Gniezno Doors,
11th/12th century

1038. Fortunately, however, St Wojciech's head was miraculously rediscovered at Gniezno in 1123 – though this discovery was disputed by the Czechs.)

The whole of Catholic Poland was outraged when in March 1986 burglars broke into the Cathedral and stole the silver figure from the shrine. Fortunately they did not tamper with the saint's sarcophagus. The thieves were caught, but a copy had to be made of the figure, which was severely damaged.

The Gothic font of embossed copper, with its tall pointed lid, dates from the years after 1414. The Gothic rood (c.1430) now stands again on the beam spanning the choir arch.

Where the main west door used to be is now the richly furnished and painted Baroque *Stary Kapitularz (Old Chapter House)*, which is used for displaying a valuable collection of Gothic sculpture, including a carved triptych with a Coronation of the Virgin and figures of female saints, dating from c.1400.

On the west wall of the nave, on either side of the entrance to the chapter house, are two tombs which are among the cathedral's greatest treasures. The red marble tomb slab on the left was made in 1495 by Veit Stoss for Archbishop Zbigniew Oleśnicki. The realism of the figure, with his fleshy features and skewed pallium, is striking and forms a strange contrast to the traditional form of the tomb slab. The bronze panel of Archbishop Jakub of Sienno (died 1480), made only a few years earlier in a Flemish workshop, with a schematically drawn figure almost lost in the rich tracery of the church, seems archaic in comparison.

The western bays of the aisles have porches giving access to the outside through doorways which are interesting survivals of the original decoration of the church. The south door shows Christ the Judge accompanied by the Virgin and St John as intercessors, and angels bearing the instruments of the Passion. The artificial stone relief dates from the second half of the 14th century.

The north door, also decorated with artificial stone sculptures and dating from around 1400, shows the Crucifixion.

From here a side-door leads to the *Chapter Library*, which was originally accessible from the interior of the church. It was founded in the 11th century, together with a school attached to the cathedral chapter, and was the nucleus of a great tradition of spiritual and humanistic culture at Gniezno. Its rich collection includes a number of valuable medieval illuminated manuscripts.

A contrast to the sober appearance of the reconstructed Gothic of the nave is provided by the luxuriant Baroque and Neoclassical entrances to the chapels along the north aisle, with their wrought iron grilles. The long history of the cathedral is nowhere more strikingly apparent than here.

Before exploring the chapels, however, it is worth taking a look at the *tomb slab of St Wojciech* under the second arch to the nave. It was made towards the end of the 15th century by Hans Brandt of Gdańsk and was originally positioned under a baldachin in the nave, until it was replaced in the 17th century by the silver reliquary. Carved from red marble, it shows the figure of the saint represented as if standing. The sandstone base is decorated with two scenes from the saint's life and an inscription recording when it was made.

The richest of the chapels is the *Kaplica Potockiego (Potocki Chapel)*, the first on the north side. Founded by Archbishop Teodor Potocki, it was built by the Italian architect Pompeo Ferrari (1727–30). The architecture and decoration form a harmonious whole. The elliptical dome rising above pilasters and a subtly curved cornice creates the effect of a canopy and makes clear Ferrari's debt to Borromini. Potocki's tomb shows the archbishop kneeling in prayer facing the altar.

The neighbouring *Kaplica Bożego Ciała (Corpus Christi Chapel)* has been remodelled several times since it was first built around 1460; it contains a fine early Neoclassical altar by Ephraim Schroeger (*c*.1783).

The unimpressive-looking fragment of an early 11th-century Romanesque tomb slab, which can be seen in the north aisle here, is the earliest piece of writing on a work of art in Poland.

In the choir ambulatory are several fragments of the original Gothic arches with their sculptured decoration, as well as some fine tombs and monuments of the 16th century, including the tomb slab of the famous Chancellor and Archbishop Jan Łaski (a patron of humanist scholars and artists, and a defender of Poland against papal interference), which was made, together with three other monuments, by the Florentine sculptor Giovanni da Firenze in 1516 in the elegant style of the Italian Renaissance.

The *Kaplica Kołudzkich (Kołudzki Chapel)*, to the south of the east end of the choir, used to contain the Gniezno Doors, which have now been returned to the portal in the south aisle (see above).

In front of the last chapel in the ambulatory are two particularly fine Renaissance tombs. That of Archbishop Andrzej Krzycki (died 1537) has its original red marble tomb slab set into a later Neoclassical niche (plate 23). The recumbent figure is disturbingly lively: lying across his pillow the archbishop seems to gaze at the viewer through half-closed eyes while he clutches at his vestments. The figure is the work of the Italian architect and sculptor Bartolomeo Berrecci, who had been summoned to Kraków from Hungary and who brought with him to Poland the style of the High Renaissance. The neighbouring tomb of Archbishop Mikołaj Dziergowski (died 1554) is by Girolamo Canavesi, another Italian artist working in Kraków. What is particularly impressive about this tomb is its grand architectural construction. Flanking the figure of the archbishop are his patron (St Nicholas) and St Wojciech. In the tomb's superstructure the Virgin appears in a roundel supported by putti.

The *Skarbiec (Treasury)* contains a wealth of liturgical objects and votive offerings, one of the most valuable collections of precious metalwork in the whole of Poland. Its contents include two 12th-century chalices from Trzemeszno Abbey both elaborately decorated with Biblical scenes.

On the north flank of the cathedral is the *Kolegiata św. Jerzego (Collegiate Church of St George)*, which from the beginning has served as a parish church attached to the cathedral. It was originally an aisleless Romanesque church, but has undergone many alterations over the centuries. In 1782 Bernhard Langweber, an architect from Poznań, gave it the Baroque appearance it has today.

Behind the collegiate church is an impressive row of Late Baroque and Neoclassical *Canons' Houses* of the 18th and 19th centuries.

To the northeast of the cathedral complex, in ul. św. Jana (No. 9), is the *Muzeum Archeologiczne (Archaeological Museum)*, which has an interesting collection illustrating the early history of Ziemia Gnieźnieńska, the area around Gniezno. There are also some fragments of the sculptural decoration from the Romanesque predecessor of the present cathedral.

The *Kościół św. Jana Chrzciciela (Church of St John the Baptist)* at the end of ul. św. Jana is worth a visit. Formerly the monastery church of the Canons Regular of the Holy Sepulchre, it is an aisleless Gothic building of the 14th century, with a low polygonal choir and a massive square tower at the west front; it survived the war unscathed. Inside, the cross-rib vaults have rich sculptural decoration: the corbels and bosses have a variety of masks, animals and little scenes. The well-preserved Gothic painting in the chancel (third quarter of the 14th century) is of especial interest. The panels of the vaulting contain fourteen heads of Old Testament kings and prophets, while the walls have two rows of scenes from the lives of Christ, the Virgin and John the Baptist, as well as figures of saints.

Some 32 km north of Gniezno, in the midst of the Ziemia Pałucka with its many lakes, the *Skansen (Open-Air Museum)* of **Biskupin** provides an opportunity to find out about the earliest cultures of what is now Poland. In 1933 several fortified settlements were discovered here, the oldest of them dating back to the Stone Age. The settlement on the peninsula in Jezioro Biskupińskie (Lake Biskupin) dates from between 700 and 400 BC, the early Iron Age – the period of Lusatian Culture. It is the only one of the settlements to have been thoroughly excavated, and on the basis of the archaeological finds parts of the complex were reconstructed and opened to the public as an archaeological park in 1934. The complex fills an oval covering the whole of the peninsula, protected by a ring of breakwaters and a defensive rampart of earth and timber. On its southwest flank the entrance gate has been reconstructed (illustration, page 265). From here a causeway 120 metres long led to the mainland. The street system consisted of a ring road following the surrounding rampart and eleven parallel streets running across the settlement. An open area was left for assemblies. The housing, a section of which has been reconstructed along one of the streets, seems to reflect the social system of the inhabitants. There were originally 106 houses, all the same size and with the same layout. In each house lived a family of eleven or twelve, and something of their way of life is shown by the reconstructed furnishings. The tools excavated here show that the people here practised agriculture as well as animal husbandry and hunting. The cult objects indicate the ritual worship of natural forces and ancestors. Archaeological investigations at other sites, such as Gniezno, Poznań and Wrocław, have shown that this basic pattern for laying out a settlement, and the method of constructing houses and ramparts, remained in use until the time of the early Piasts.

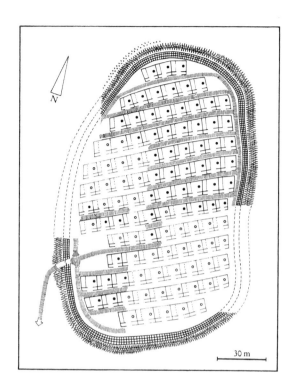

Biskupin, plan of the early Iron Age island settlement with a reconstruction of the arrangement of houses and hearths along boarded gangways

The town of **Trzemeszno**, 16 km east of Gniezno, is one of the oldest settlements in Wielkopolska. It grew up around a Benedictine monastery, which according to legend was founded by St Wojciech himself. The body of the murdered saint rested here before his canonization and translation to Gniezno.

The original monastic buildings were destroyed in the 11th century and today are known only from excavations. At the beginning of the 12th century the monastery was refounded by Duke Bolesław III Krzywousty as a house of Augustinian canons, who retained it, together with the town, until the monastery was secularized in 1793.

In 1130–46, as part of the rebuilding of the monastery, the canons erected a new three-aisled *basilica* with a transept and a west front with two towers. In 1760–91 this was drastically remodelled to become the present monumental Late Baroque church, a centrally planned, octagonal building with a large dome and a short nave on the west side, with side chapels. The west front still has two towers, and its pointed window and the vaulting in the porch were retained from the Gothic remodelling of the earlier church. At the east end, facing the town, the choir projects from the main building and presents a grand façade flanked by two towers and articulated by a giant pilaster order. The middle part of this façade, which is curved like an apse, is given emphasis by a richly decorated lower storey.

The interior decoration and furnishings were burned in 1945, and were only partially reconstructed in the years after the war. The *Confessio* of St Wojciech (Adalbert) below the dome, where relics of the saint were venerated, was lost, and consequently the church's place in the tradition of centrally planned mausolea and martyria is no longer immediately apparent.

Much of the rich sculptural decoration from the late 18th century has been reconstructed. The reliefs in the choir show the four Fathers of the Church, while the four Evangelists appear in the crossing, and the programme is completed by four Prophets above the nave arcades. The paintings in the dome and vaults show scenes illustrating the story of man's salvation, originally painted in the 1780's by Franciszek Smuglewicz, one of

the leading painters of the period of Stanisław August Poniatowski. After their destruction in 1945 they were completely remade except for the surviving original fragment in the south transept. The oval medallions in the dome show parallel sacrificial scenes from the Old and New Testaments: the Sacrifice of Isaac, the Sacrifice of Melchizedek, the Presentation of Christ in the Temple, and the Crucifixion. Further sacrifices appear in the trapezoidal panels: Moses on Mount Sinai, and Solomon, David and Abel. The paintings in the nave vaults show episodes from the life of St Wojciech.

The high altar was reconstructed in 1959 with a painting of the Assumption of the Virgin, which is a free copy of the original altarpiece by Franciszek Smuglewicz.

Opposite the church, in Pl. Kosmowskiego, stands the charming Late Baroque building of the *Kolegium*, a school founded by Abbot Michał Kosmowski in 1773 following the model of the Collegium Nobilium in Warsaw. The main building originally contained not only the school-

Trzemeszno, chalice given to the monastery by Kazimierz III Wielki in 1351 (now in Wawel Museum, Kraków)

rooms but also accommodation for boarders and apartments for the teachers; on the ground floor there is a chapel, and the wings are reserved for offices. The grand gateway, in the form of a triumphal arch, is decorated with a portrait roundel of King Stanisław August Poniatowski, who, the inscription says, is here honoured as a patron of learning.

Strzelno, a Cuiavian town 26 km north of Trzemeszno, was a picturesque place with medieval and Baroque buildings until its almost complete destruction in a great fire in 1761. The town began life in the early middle ages as a market settlement at the intersection of important trade routes, but the only evidence of this today is the irregular, angular street plan. In the 12th century the settlement was the property of the canons regular of Trzemeszno; but by 1193 it had passed to the Premonstratensian nuns, who shaped the history of the town until secularization in the 18th century.

The Premonstratensian nunnery on the *Wzgórze Klasztorne (Convent Hill)* to the east of the town, is the only historic building to have survived. The existence of the abbey is mentioned in the early 12th century, but the present buildings date from between 1175 and 1192. The original Romanesque complex underwent a number of alterations in the 15th, 17th and first half of the 18th centuries.

The nuns' church, now the parish church, the *Kościół św. Trójcy (Church of the Holy Trinity)* has retained its Romanesque form of the period around 1180. It is a three-aisled basilica with a long transept; the two-towered façade was given its Late Baroque cladding in 1743, with a pilaster order rising above a high base and topped by a cornice, above which the towers rise from the wall and flank the curved and richly decorated pediment.

In the interior the whole history of the church is revealed. Towards the end of the 15th century a fine star vault was built to replace the earlier flat wooden ceiling. In the mid-17th century the interior underwent a Baroque remodelling and the Romanesque columns

disappeared beneath a layer of plaster, which transformed them into massive piers. The wall surfaces were covered with Rococo ornament, and the furnishings of the church were also replaced; the Gothic vault was, however, allowed to remain.

During the restoration of the church after the Second World War, four Romanesque columns (*c.*1170) were rediscovered under the Baroque plasterwork. Their remarkable, richly carved relief decoration makes them some of the most important examples of Romanesque sculpture in Europe: the shafts of the two eastern columns are each decorated with three registers of ornamental arcading containing female personifications of the Virtues and Vices, which form a didactic moral programme.

A few other fragments of the Romanesque decoration of the church have survived in the Gothic-vaulted Kaplica św. Barbary (Chapel of St Barbara) south of the chancel, where they were later built into the wall. They include an arched relief panel with the Virgin and Prophets in roundels – originally a votive offering – and several fragments with individual figures, which probably come from tombs.

Strzelno, elevation of one of the four Romanesque columns in the Church of the Holy Trinity

The reliefs over the side doors to the church are also of interest. The south door, although it was remodelled in the 15th century, retains its 13th-century tympanum, showing St Anne holding the infant Virgin with the donor, Piotr Wszeborowic, kneeling on the right and presenting a model of the church. Opposite him is his wife, Anna. An inscription along the edge of the relief bears witness to the couple's devotion to St Anne. The trefoil-shaped tympanum on the north door (c.1216 or 1230) shows Christ in Majesty, with the praying figures of the Apostles Peter and Paul, two angels and the symbols of the Evangelists.

Originally the church must also have been richly painted, but only a few scanty fragments of decorative paintwork have survived. The furnishings, most of which date from the second quarter of the 18th century, suffered during restoration in the late 19th century, but the decorative ensemble still displays its luxuriant Baroque character.

Next to the abbey church is the smaller *Kościół św. Prokopa (Church of St Procopius)*, a rotunda built of ashlar masonry around 1160. It belongs to the widespread type of palace or castle chapel on a circular ground-plan with a chancel attached and a gallery, which here is housed in the tower and opens into the interior through a double arch. Unusual features include the two small apses on the north side, which probably contained side altars.

The primitive appearance of the bare masonry is the result of a reconstruction undertaken in 1946–52. In the 19th century the church was converted into a storehouse, which involved inserting false ceilings, making new windows and doors, and demolishing the two apses. In 1945 the building and the tympanum dating from 1180 suffered further damage from an explosion; not all the architectural features have been accurately reconstructed.

Taking a minor road northeast from Strzelno for about 17 km, we reach the little town of **Kruszwica** at the northern tip of Jezioro Gopło (Lake Gopło). It originally consisted of low wooden and half-timbered houses, dominated by the medieval castle and collegiate church. However, this townscape disappeared as early as the 17th century, when the castle and town were destroyed in the Swedish Wars. Since the late 19th century the old houses of the town have been replaced by modern buildings, with the exception of a few remnants, and the old street-plan of the town has also been altered. Today the only reminders of medieval Kruszwica are the collegiate church and the ruins of the castle.

The *Kolegiata N.P. Marii (Parish Church of St Mary)* (formerly dedicated to Sts Peter and Paul) (plate 22) was probably founded in the period between 1120 and 1140 in the time of Duke Bolesław III Krzywousty, probably as the seat of the Bishop of Kujawy, which was transferred to Włocławek in 1148. It is picturesquely sited on a hill by the shore of the lake and, since its thorough restoration in the 1950's, it now appears in its original form as a three-aisled Romanesque basilica with a Latin-cross plan. The chancel and transept have five apses in all. The choir apse was originally flanked by two secondary apses on the east side of the transept, but during construction the chancel was extended with two flanking

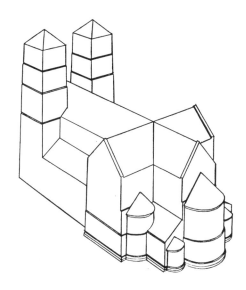

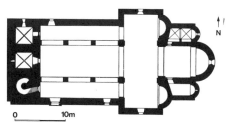

chapels, also with apsidal ends. This complex of interlocking geometrical forms – almost like a crystalline growth – goes back to the architectural tradition of the Benedictine abbey of Cluny in Burgundy, so it is not surprising to learn that Kruszwica was the first monastery in Poland settled by Cluniac monks.

From the west front of the church it can be seen that the original intention was to build a façade with two towers, but these were never executed. It was not until the 16th century, when some Late Gothic alterations were made to the church, that the present massive tower was built. Remarkably its articulation alludes to the Romanesque forms of the existing building.

Over the centuries the church was often altered and redecorated. In the mid-19th century (1856–9) it underwent a purist restoration, which revealed the exterior in its original form, but left the Baroque remodelling and furnishing of the interior. These were only removed in the most recent 'conservation' work, when all architectural alterations of later periods were swept away. However, there was no attempt to recreate the Romanesque decoration. Originally the masonry and the wooden ceiling would have been plastered, and probably also painted. The church's present appearance has a strangely attractive severity which has turned the church into a showpiece of pure Romanesque architecture.

The *Castle* of Kruszwica was built in the 14th century by King Kazimierz III Wielki on the site of an earlier fortified settlement. It originally covered a rectangular area protected by high, battlemented walls, but only the octagonal tower survived destruction in the 17th century. There are many folk legends attached to the picturesque ruin. Its name, *Mysia Wieża (Mice Tower)*, derives from the story, first told by the chronicler Gallus Anonimus, that the wicked Prince Popiel, rejected by his people, was devoured by mice in the castle; his successor was the peasant Piast, the founder of the Polish royal dynasty. In 1956 stairs were built in the tower to exploit the vantage point. From the top there is an impressive view over the town and lake.

Kórnik – Rogalin – Środa – Rakoniewice – Szamotuły

About 20 km south of Poznań, on the road to Jarocin, is the neo-Gothic **Pałac Kórnik** (**Kórnik Palace**) famous for its library and arboretum. It was originally built as a Renaissance palace for the Górka family, but its present English Picturesque Gothic appearance is the result of a 19th-century remodelling to designs by Karl Friedrich Schinkel for the Działyński family. But not all is Gothic inside: the most remarkable interior is a Moorish salon on the first floor. The castle is surrounded by a moat and stands near Lake Kórnik. The park has the finest dendrological collection in Poland with more than 10,000 exotic and native trees and shrubs.

The riches of the library and museum are the result of the efforts of the Działyński family, who acquired the estate in the 17th century, and of their successors, the Zamoyskis. In 1935 the last owner, Władysław Zamoyski bequeathed the whole property to the Polish state. The library contains many valuable books of the 16th and 17th centuries, manuscripts and printed books, including manuscripts by Napoleon and the Polish national bard, Adam Mickiewicz. But perhaps the most interesting items in the collection are the eleven portrait miniatures painted by Stanisław Samostrzelnik for the family album of the Szydłowiecki family, the 'Liber genoseos illustris familiae Schidloviciae'. They are a mark of Samostrzelnik's admiration for his patron and protector, the Crown Chancellor Krzysztof Szydłowiecki, and were painted in the early 1530's for Piotr Tomicki, Bishop of Kraków, a leading figure in Polish humanism, who was a great admirer of Samostrzelnik's work in the abbey at Mogiła (see page 489). The library also has the central panel of a triptych (1529) from the parish church at Mądre near Środa, 13 km south of Kórnik, combining two scenes from the life of the Virgin: the Annunciation in the foreground, and the Visitation in the background. The triptych is a good example of painting in Wielkopolska during the first half of the 16th century.

South of Poznań, on the edge of the Wielkopolski National Park, stands the **Pałac Rogalin** (**Rogalin Palace**), the Late Baroque country house of the Raczyński family, built around 1780 under the direction of Merlini, Kamsetzer and Graff. Rogalin has a wonderful park with one of the largest collections of oaks in Europe. Many are a thousand years old, and some have a circumference measuring as much as nine metres. Edward Raczyński, a great patron of the arts and sciences, laid the foundations of a magnificent collection, and it was added to by his successors. The collections were plundered by the Nazis, but the house still has fine Flemish tapestries, furniture and wall clocks. An adjoining art gallery, a

Portrait of Anne Szydłowiecka,
Kórnik Palace, page from
the 'Liber geneseos',
c.1530

branch of the Poznań National Gallery, contains history paintings by Jan Matejko and works by 19th-century French and German artists (Lenbach, Böcklin, Delaroche, Monet).

In the Kolegiata (Collegiate Church) at **Środa**, the Trinity Chapel, founded by Hieronim Gostomski, the wojewoda of Poznań, and built in 1598–1602, has wonderful plaster-work decoration. The ceiling is decorated with trapeze-shaped panels, all covered with lavish ornament (roundels, cartouches and garlands).

Rakoniewice, halfway between Poznań and Zielona Góra, has a beautiful and very unusual church entirely of half-timbered construction. It was built as a Lutheran place of worship in 1763 and the tower was added in 1781. It is now a museum.

Szamotuly, 35 km northwest of Poznań, was the home of the composer and musician Wacław Szamotulski, one of the leading figures of Poland's Golden Age in the 16th century. The *Kościół Farny (Parish Church)* contains the sandstone Renaissance tomb of the Royal Treasurer Jakub Rokossowski (died 1580) (plate 24). It is attributed to the sculptor Girolamo Canavesi, because of its similarity to the Górka tomb at Poznań (see page 277).

Leszno – Rydzyna – Wschowa – Kościan – Gostyń – Pawłowice

The history of the town of **Leszno** and the whole of the surrounding region has long been linked with the Leszczyński family. For more than three centuries Leszno (town charter 1547) was under the patronage of the Leszczyńskis. Stanisław Leszczyński, the last of the line, was twice King of Poland (1704–9 and 1733–6), but was ousted by his Saxon rivals, August II and August III and the town itself was punitively torched by the Russians in 1707. In the Renaissance the Leszczyńskis had made Leszno an important intellectual and cultural centre, where various nationalities – Poles, Czechs, Jews and Germans – lived together in peace. Clothmaking was then the main business in the town. Between 1628 and 1656 the celebrated Czech educationalist Jan Amos Komenský (Comenius) worked here at the invitation of the Protestant Leszczyńskis, having been forced with many of his followers to flee from his native Bohemia because of his Protestant faith. Comenius created a school here of European importance, which remained influential into the 19th century despite the misfortunes of various wars. There were strong connections with England, where there was much sympathy with the ideals of the Bohemian Brethren; it was English subscriptions which paid for the rebuilding of the school after raids by the Polish army. Leszno later declined in importance, but in the 19th century it became a centre of the Polish national movement against Prussian-German occupation. Since 1975 the town, which now has a population of 50,000, has been the administrative centre of a mainly agricultural voivodship; its main industry is small-scale food production.

Architecturally the most important buildings are the Late Gothic *Kościół św. Jana (Church of St John)*, which once belonged to the Bohemian Brethren, the *Kościół św. Krzyża (Church of the Holy Cross)* begun in 1707 as a Lutheran Church by Stanisław Leszczyński's architect, Pompeo Ferrari, and the Baroque *Kościół św. Mikołaja (Church of St Nicholas)*, built at the end of the 17th century by Giovanni and Giorgio Catenacci and completed by Pompeo Ferrari, which contains the Leszczyński family tombs; the Baroque *Town Hall*, a plain rectangular building with engaged columns at the corners and a tall spire, is also by Ferrari (1707–9).

The main feature of interest at **Rydzyna**, a small Late Baroque town a few kilometres southeast of Leszno, is the *Palace*, with its fine gardens. Built in 1696–1704 by Pompeo Ferrari for the Leszczyński family, it was altered in the 1740's for the Sułkowskis by Karl Martin Frantz, also responsible for the charming parish church. The palace was later redecorated by Ignaz Graff, who also built the Lutheran church. The *Town Hall* and some *burghers' houses* in the town centre have retained their Baroque form.

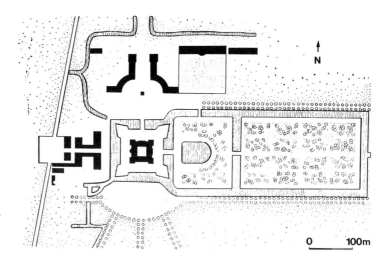

Rydzyna, plan of the Palace and Park

0   100m

Wschowa, 18 km west of Leszno, used to be a mint town. At the beginning of his reign Władysław II Jagiello (ruled 138–1434) established a new crown mint here (besides the already existing mint at Kraków) to produce a variety of coins. The history of coinage in the Jagiellonian period (1386-1572) demonstrates the changes brought about by the switch from the medieval groschen system, dominated by a silver currency, to the modern gold system, based on stabilized values of gold and silver. The denarii minted at Wschowa usually bear the arms of the Jagiellons: a cross with two transverse arms. The *Kościół Farny św. Stanisława (Parish Church of St Stanislaus)* was rebuilt by Pompeo Ferrari with an elliptical dome (1720–26), but it retains its 14th-century chancel with mid-16th century vaulting, and a late 16th-century tower. There is also a former *Bernardine Monastery* with a 17th-century church by Cristoforo Bonadura, and a number of attractive houses.

In the *Kościół Farny (Parish Church)* of **Kościan**, on the road from Leszno to Poznań, is the tomb of Maciej (died 1541) and Jadwiga Opaliński (died 1559), erected around 1590 and made by one of the Kraków workshops in the decorative Mannerist style. The two figures on the sarcophagus have a fullness and plasticity which distinguish them from most of the rather flatly carved works from the famous Santi Gucci workshop. The town is famous for its bagpipe music.

On the Holy Mountain of **Gostyń**, 30 km east of Leszno, stands the Baroque *Klasztor Filipinów (Oratorian Monastery)*, now an old people's home. The octagonal church, the only part of the complex still used for religious purposes, was begun by Giorgio Catenacci and completed by Pompeo Ferrari. It is modelled on the church of Sta Maria della Salute in

293

Venice and has a charming Virgin and Child of 1540. The nearby *Palace* of **Pawłowice** (1779–83, by Karl Gotthard Langhans) shows the influence of Robert Adam. The remodelling of the interior by Jan Krystian Kamsetzer in 1789 created a spectacular columned salon (plate 21).

Kalisz – Antonin – Gołuchów – Ląd

Kalisz, now a town with a population of 100,000, claims to be the oldest settlement in Poland. Ptolemy in the mid-2nd century AD mentions *Calisia*, probably referring to a Sarmatian settlement on this site. At the end of the 9th century and beginning of the 10th the first castle was built here together with a few houses. In 1253 Kalisz was granted its town charter, and in the 14th century it developed into a centre of weaving, favoured by its position on the trading route from the Baltic via Toruń to Wrocław and the south. The wars in the 17th century left deep scars on Kalisz. However, after the Congress of Vienna in 1815, the town experienced an economic boom mainly due to the development of spinning mills. Considerably more architectural evidence of the town's history would have survived, if large parts of the town centre had not been destroyed by German artillery in August 1914, and if the Jewish ghetto had not been blown up by the Nazis. Nevertheless Kalisz still largely preserves its street plan, within the semicircular town centre on the north bank of the River Prosna. Neoclassical architecture dominates the streets and alleyways around the market square.

In ul. Grodzka stands the *Kościół św. Mikołaja (Church of St Nicholas)*, founded in 1255, with a chancel dating from 1275. After a fire in 1706 the church was given a Baroque redecoration; the high altar and many sculptures, pictures and monuments date from this time. The church was partly re-Gothicized in the 19th century. Unfortunately another fire in 1973 destroyed a Baroque altar painting of the Descent from the Cross by the studio of Peter Paul Rubens.

Dominating the Pl. św. Józefa are the buildings of the former *Klasztor Jezuitów (Jesuit Monastery)* (1581) with its Early Baroque church (1595, Giovanni Maria Bernardoni and Albin Fontana), containing a Late Gothic tomb slab (1575), a Baroque high altar (early 18th century) and some monuments. To the left of the church is the old Jesuit College, and the former *Archbishop's Palace*, built in 1583–4 and given a Neoclassical remodelling in 1824–5. Also on Pl. św. Józefa is the *Kolegiata (Collegiate Church)*, which has a Gothic chancel of 1353. The most precious of its furnishings is the Kalisz Polyptych,'a Late Gothic painting (*c.*1500). Behind the church a portion remains of the medieval town walls, dating from the mid-14th century.

In ul. Narutowicza, running parallel to ul. Prosna, stands the *Klasztor Franciszkanów (Franciscan Monastery)* founded around the middle of the 13th century. The original Early Gothic church was altered in the mid-14th century and again between 1599 and 1632 by Albin Fontana, when vaulting with its Late Renaissance plasterwork and the Early Baroque gable were added. The furnishings are Baroque and Rococo.

Gołuchów, view of the Castle; drawing, 1893

The municipal park at Kalisz is larger than the whole town centre. On the edge of the park, near the River Prosna, stands the Neoclassical *Theatre* founded in 1830 and now named after Wojciech Bogusławski, one of the pioneers of Polish drama.

At **Antonin**, about 40 km southwest of Kalisz, on the road between Ostrów Wlkp. and Ostrzeszów, is one of the most remarkable buildings designed by the great Prussian architect Karl Friedrich Schinkel: an octagonal hunting lodge built entirely of larchwood. Inside, a single space surrounded by galleries occupies the whole four storeys of the building, with a massive iron stove and chimney in the centre. It was built for a member of the Radziwiłł family in 1822–4. Chopin stayed there a few years later, and recitals of his music are held on Sundays in the summer.

About 20 km northwest of Kalisz, in the direction of Poznań, stands the *Castle* of **Gołuchów**, set in the middle of a fine landscape park. It is now a branch of the Poznań National Museum displaying a collection of Greek vases, as well as paintings by Italian, Spanish, Portuguese and Flemish masters, applied art, furniture, carpets, arms and armour, and a fascinating collection of Polish portraits, most of them from the 17th century. The castle was built for the Leszczyński family *c*.1560, and at the beginning of the 17th century was extended as a magnificent magnatial residence on the initiative of Wacław Leszczyński, the wojewoda of Kalisz and later Chancellor. Three ranges with corner bastions surround a courtyard. The 17th-century arcades on the upper storey of the south range have survived, but all the other parts of the building date from 1872–85, when the châtelaine, Izabela Działyńska, the daughter of Prince Adam Czartoryski, commissioned a French architect, Maurice Ouradon, to remodel the castle in the French Renaissance style, incorporating genuine old architectural features from the 15th to the 17th centuries, which had been brought from France and Italy. The collections were looted by the Germans in 1939, but some items have been recovered and returned.

Further north, on the bank of the River Warta, stands the town of **Ląd**. A castle stood here as early as the 8th century, guarding the river crossing. After a fire in the 13th century it passed to the Cistercians, who kept it until 1819. The *Cistercian Monastery* had been founded around 1175, but the original Romanesque church was replaced by a splendid Baroque church in the 17th and 18th centuries (colour plate 18). The orientation of the building was reversed, and on the foundations of the old nave a new chancel was created (1651–90, Tommaso Poncino, Giorgio Catenacci and others). This was followed in 1728–35 by a new nave, which is one of Pompeo Ferrari's best works, an octagonal space spanned by a great dome. This spectacular interior has superb plasterwork with paintings by Adam Schwach and Georg Wilhelm Neunhertz, as well as sculptures. Schwach was also responsible for the paintings in the Abbot's Hall (1722). The 14th-century cloister and impressive chapter house survive from the medieval monastery, and there are remains of mid-14th-century mural paintings.

At the village of **Licheń**, 6 km north-west of Konin, stands one of Poland's most extraordinary recent buildings. The popular Marian pilgrimage shrine here has been transformed by the construction a vast domed concrete basilica begun in 1994. This is the largest church in the country (and seventh largest in Europe), paid for entirely by donations from the faithful. Its curious neo-classical style may not please purists. The architect is Barbara Bielecka.

Sieradz – Grąbień – Łask – Poddębice

Sieradz on the River Warta is one of the most ancient towns in Poland. A settlement is thought to have been in existence here in the 6th century. King Bolesław I Chrobry built a castle around 1025, and from the mid-13th century Sieradz was the capital of a duchy. From 1339 there was also a voivodship of Sieradz, and by the 14th century the town was a meeting place for synods of bishops and assemblies of nobles. Today Sieradz has a population of 35,000. The surrounding region is mainly agricultural but does include a few industries (cement, electrical engineering), and not far away is the big industrial conglomeration of Łódź. The *Kościół Farny (Parish Church)* near the market place dates from the second half of the 14th century and has a Late Gothic painting of the Holy Trinity. The interior furnishings are mostly Baroque. Also worth visiting are the former Dominican monastery and the castle ruins.

The timber *Church* of **Grąbień**, near Wieluń in the south of the voivodship, contains an important Renaissance ceiling painting. Created between 1520 and 1530, it depicts two musicians in realistic costume but in the midst of luxuriant foliage ornament, performing in honour of the Virgin, Apostles and Saints.

At **Łask**, halfway between Sieradz and Łódź, the Baroque Church has a chapel with an alabaster relief of the Madonna attributed to the workshop of Andrea della Robbia, the gift of Pope Clement XVII.

The *Pałac Grudzińskich (Grudziński Palace)* at **Poddębice**, at the northern end of the voivodship, was built in 1610–17. A thorough restoration in the early 1950's gave it back its Late Renaissance form, and it is now used as a school.

46 Kraków   Wawel, Royal Castle
◁ 45 Kraków   Ul. Floriańska and St Florian Gate   48   Kraków   Wawel Cathedral
47 Kraków   Wawel, arcaded courtyard of the Royal Castle

50 PIENINY MOUNTAINS   The Trzy Korony ('Three Crowns') and rafters on the Dunajec
◁ 49   KRAKÓW   Market place with St Mary's, the Adam Mickiewicz Monument and the Cloth Hall
51   ZAKOPANE   View of the town

52 ZAKOPANE Willa Pod Jedlami (The Firs)

53 DĘBNO PODHALAŃSKIE St Michael's

54 WIŚLICA
Church of
the Nativi•

55 DĘBNO [
Dębiński
Castle

56 KIELCE Palace of the Bishops of Kraków

57 WĄCHOCK Cistercian abbey

58   Sᴜʟᴇᴊᴏ́ᴡ-Pᴏᴅᴋʟᴀꜱᴢᴛᴏʀᴢᴇ   Main door of Cistercian abbey church

60   JĘDRZEJÓW   Cistercian church
59   CZĘSTOCHOWA   Paulite church

61   RADOM   Landscape near the town ▷

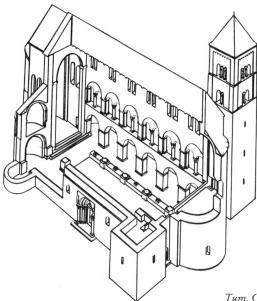

Tum, Collegiate Church of St Mary and St Alexius

Tum – Pabianice – Łódź

Tum, a village not far from the town of Łęczyca, has one of Wielkopolska's fine Romanesque churches. The *Kościół N.P. Marii i św. Aleksego (Collegiate Church of St Mary and St Alexius* (plate 26), consecrated in 1161, has been returned to its original form after partial destruction in the Second World War. The plan and overall shape of the building are derived from earlier, indigenous models. It consists of a basilica with arcades on rectangular piers separating the nave from the aisles, with galleries above them. The nave joins a rectangular chancel with an apse which has a small, lower apse at its east end. The church also has a west choir with another apse, and the building is flanked at the west end by two square towers, which project from the body of the church. Two squat round towers are attached at the north and south of the transept. Except for the upper parts of the west towers, the exterior walls are plain masonry with no articulation. On the north side of the church is a fine Romanesque doorway with shafts in the stepped jambs, and round-arched archivolts above a moulded cornice. The tympanum contains a seated Virgin and Child flanked by angels, one bearing a lily, the other a cross – the symbols of the beginning and end of Christ's earthly life.

Pabianice, southwest of Łódź, is another of Poland's ancient towns. Founded in 1297 by King Władysław I Łokietek, it later developed into an important weaving town and then in the 19th century into a centre of the textile and paper industry. The town has a fortified *Mansion*, typical of such buildings in Poland in the 16th century. It was built in

◁ 62 KRASICZYN Renaissance castle

1566–71 under the direction of the architect Wawrzyniec Lorek for the Kraków Chapter, and intended for the use of those entrusted with the inspection of church property in the area. The house has a rectangular ground-plan with two towers, and its façades are articulated with tall blind arcading, emphasizing its fortified character.

The year 1899 saw the publication of Władysław Reymont's novel 'Ziemia Obiecana' ('The Promised Land'), which is set in Łódź and describes the city as a paradigm of the dynamic capitalism of the 19th century. Reymont's book is perhaps best known from Andrzej Wajda's compelling film version made in 1974. In 1899 Łódź had already been established as a town for 476 years, having received its charter from King Władysław II Jagiełło in 1423. However, it had begun its rise to become 'the Polish Manchester' only 79 years earlier, on 18 September 1820, when a special decree of the Prefect of Mazovia designated the tiny hamlet as one of a group of new factory towns.

Liberal reformers such as Stanisław Staszic had taken the initiative of developing the textile industry in this part of Poland, and Łódź was to be its centre. A stream of highly qualified skilled workers, mainly Germans, most of whom were weavers, made their way to Łódź, as well as many unskilled workers, who came mainly from the Polish country round about. Many Jews from Galicia, Lithuania and Byelorussia also came to the burgeoning town. Between 1820 and 1870 the population increased forty-four-fold. German entrepreneurs, attracted by considerable concessions, took the leading part in the industrial development of the city. Small workshops, cotton spinning mills, dyeing works

Łódź, factory with workers' housing, 19th-century lithograph

and tanneries became the symbols of the new industrial era. They were soon followed by huge factories using the latest technology, much of it imported, together with engineers, from England. Manufacturing families such as the Poznańskis, Geyers and Scheiblers were able to make vast fortunes. Resentment at bad working and living conditions led to Łódź becoming an important centre of the Polish workers' movement before 1900. In 1892 and 1905 there were workers' uprisings here, and after 1918, in the new Polish state, Łódź was still the scene of massive strikes and demonstrations.

During the Second World War the city was renamed Litzmannstadt (after a retired general who had been an early brownshirt) and one of the first Jewish ghettoes was created. At the same time Łódź was one of the towns where the Polish underground resistance was successful against the German occupiers.

After 1945 Łódź retained its character as the main centre of the textile industry, as well as becoming an important centre of scientific and educational work. It has seven institutions of higher education, including the famous School of Film, Theatre and Television, which has produced such directors as Andrzej Wajda, Krzysztof Zanussi, Roman Polański and Krzysztof Kieślowski.

Almost 900,000 people now live in Łódź. However, the population is declining as the once numerous factories close down under the pressure of the free market.

Architecturally Łódź is a strange kaleidoscope of Neoclassicism, Historicism and Art Nouveau. Little has changed since the great days of the industrial revolution.

The main axis of the city centre is formed by ul. Piotrkowska, which runs from Pl. Wolności to Pl. Niepodległości. On the round Pl. Wolności stand the Neoclassical *Ratusz (Town Hall)* built in 1827 (now used as the archives of the voivodship), and the *Archaeological and Ethnographical Museum*. A little to the north from there, in ul. Ogrodowa, is the impressive building of the *Muzeum Historii Miasta (Museum of the History of Łódź)*. This was built in 1888 as one of the palaces of the Poznański manufacturing family; beside it is the huge brick complex of the family's spinning mill dating from the late 19th century when the great industrial firms were established in the city. Also in ul. Ogrodowa is Łódź's oldest building, a larchwood church erected in 1768.

Following ul. Zgierska we reach the northern district of Radogoszcz. On the corner of ul. Sowińskiego, on the site of the former prison is the *Radogoszcz Mausoleum* commemorating 2,000 Polish prisoners burnt alive by the Nazis before they evacuated the city in 1945. Near the railway station is the *Russian Orthodox Cathedral,* a rare survival of the many such churches built by the Tsars and usually demolished after the First World War as symbols of hated Russian rule. The *Jewish Cemetery*, located northeast of the city centre, was founded towards the end of the last century and is one of the most impressive and romantically evocative in Poland. Its southeast entrance can be reached along ul. Bracka. About 200,000 of the city's Jewish inhabitants are buried here; the mausolea of the powerful Silberstein and Poznański families are worth seeking out. Before the First World War there were around 300,000 Jews living in Łódź, a third of the total population, and their contribution to the commercial and cultural life of the city was immense (Arthur

Rubinstein was born here in 1887). Today the Jewish population numbers only 600.

In ul. Gdańska, which runs parallel to ul. Piotrkowska, stands another of the Poznański family properties, a neo-Renaissance *Palace* erected in 1904, and now used by the State Music College. Not far away, on the corner of ul. Więckowskiego, the *Muzeum Sztuki (Museum of Art)* is well worth a visit. The building, formerly the principal palace of the Poznańskis, and strikingly reminiscent of Venetian Renaissance palaces, has been used since 1925 to display art of the 19th and 20th centuries. This is one of the best places to find out about modern Polish art, as well as works by foreign artists, including Emil Nolde and Fernand Léger.

If we go southwards along ul. Piotrkowska we pass more buildings which recall the way of life of the Łódź bourgeoisie before and after 1900: a neo-Baroque residence (No. 90), a neo-Gothic apartment block (No. 99), a former office building (No. 100a), the eclectic palace of the Heinzel family of manufacturers (No. 104), and the residence built in 1910 for the industrialist Kindermann in a neo-Renaissance style (No. 151).

At the bottom end of ul. Piotrkowska, in Pl. Katedralny, stands the 19th-century *Cathedral*, a neo-Gothic building of yellow brick. Nearby, next to Reymont Park, is the impressive *Muzeum Włókiennictwa (Museum of Textile History)*, which tells the history of the development of spinning and weaving with examples of machines, tools and materials. The museum is housed in the 'White Factory', which was built in 1835–7 for the industrialist Ludwik Geyer.

To the east of ul. Piotrkowska, in ul. Jana Kilińskiego and ul. Targowa, are more factory buildings recalling Łódź's industrial past. Even the oldest mills were still in use until recently. Nearby, at the southern end of ul Przędzalniana, is the *Księży Młyn* with the *Palace* of the Herbst family, which has been opened to the public. Its beautifully restored interiors evoke the lifestyle of the 19th-century capitalists who created the city. The close proximity of the mill to the mill-owner's palace is characteristic of Łódź. The famous School of Film, Theatre and Television is not far away, in Pl. Zwycięstwa.

Even without making a tour of the slums around Rynek Bałucki, the visitor's impression of Łódź is of a city struggling with the contradictions and social problems of industrial change. The life of workers in the factories of Łódź has always been hard, and on several occasions in the summer of 1981 the workers' wives – more committed than their menfolk – took to the streets in their tens of thousands to demonstrate for better living conditions. The present economic upheavals will inevitably mean continued hardship in the new century.

Reinhold Vetter

Pomorze Zachodnie (Western Pomerania)

The region of Pomorze Zachodnie (Western Pomerania), formerly part of the Prussian province of Pommern (Pomerania), extends from the Baltic coast to the Pojezierze Drawskie (Drawa Lake District) in the south, and from the delta of the River Oder to a line south of Lake Łebsko in the east. It now contains three voivodships, Szczecin, Koszalin and Słupsk. The Oder delta, with the islands of Uznam and Wolin, was an important trading centre in early times, and attracted the various peoples settled around the Baltic, such as the Danes and Swedes, who were to play an important part in the history of the region.

The earliest traces of human settlement date from the beginning of the Mesolithic period (from 10,000 BC). At the beginning of the Bronze Age (end of the 3rd millennium BC) Pomorze ('po morzu' means 'by the sea') came under the influence of the Lusatian Culture. During the La Tène Period (500–100 BC) Pomerania was famous for its iron products. From archaeological finds of amber it has been possible to trace an amber trading route running from the Zatoka Gdańska (Bay of Gdańsk) to Rome. From the first century BC the Scandinavian Goths and the Gepids settled along the Pomeranian coastland.

The first to settle here at the beginning of the great migration of peoples in the 7th and 8th centuries were the Slavic tribes. They were followed by the Pomeranians and Kashubians. The 9th and 10th centuries saw rivalry between two important trading centres on the Baltic: Kołobrzeg and the island of Wolin, which already had a population of between 5,000 and 10,000.

Pomerania originally consisted of three distinct administrative organizations. Rügen and what is now Vorpommern (in Germany) formed one duchy, while the heart of the territory, with Szczecin as its centre, was ruled by the Gryf ('griffin') dynasty as the Duchy of Slavia, and the eastern regions (Pomerelia, called Pommerellen by the Germans) were ruled by the Samborids.

Under the Gryf dynasty the Pomeranian territories were united and gradually Christianized. However Poland, as the outpost of the Christian West, soon sought to gain control of the densely populated coastal areas. In 967, one year after Poland had been Christianized, Prince Mieszko I created himself Duke of Pomerania, and after his death his son Bolesław Chrobry made himself master of all Pomerania.

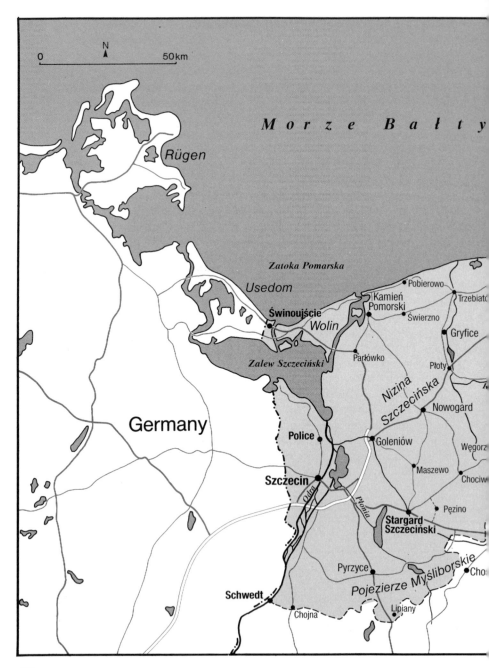

Morze Bałty

Rügen

Zatoka Pomarska

Usedom

Świnoujście

Wolin

Zalew Szczeciński

Pobierowo

Kamień Pomorski

Świerzno

Trzebiató

Gryfice

Parłówko

Płoty

Nizina Szczecińska

Nowogard

Germany

Police

Goleniów

Węgorz

Maszewo

Chociw

Szczecin

Odra

Pęzino

Stargard Szczeciński

Płonia

Pyrzyce

Pojezierze Myśliborskie

Cho

Schwedt

Chojna

Lipiany

0   50km

N

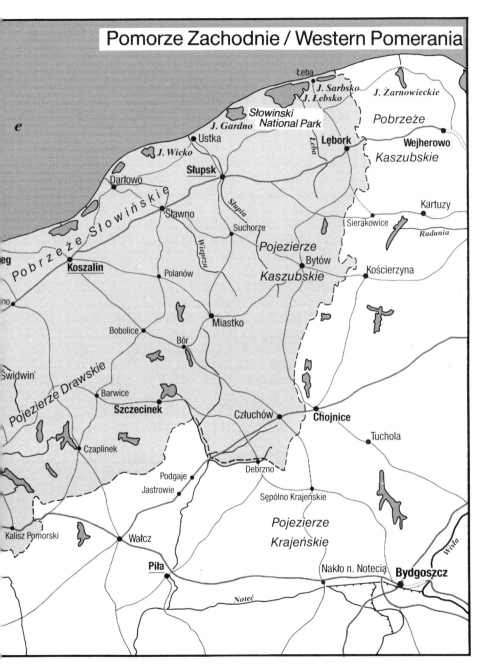

Pomorze Zachodnie / Western Pomerania

Łeba

J. Sarbsko

J. Lebsko

J. Żarnowieckie

Słowinski National Park

Pobrzeże

J. Gardno

Ustka

Lębork

Wejherowo

Kaszubskie

J. Wicko

Słupsk

Darłowo

J. Wicko

Sławno

Stupia

Kartuzy

Suchorze

Sierakowice

Radunia

Pobrzeże Słowińskie

Pojezierze

Bytów

Koścerzyna

Koszalin

Wieprza

Polanów

Kaszubskie

Miastko

Bobolice

Bór

Świdwin

Barwice

Pojezierze Drawskie

Szczecinek

Człuchów

Chojnice

Tuchola

Czaplinek

Podgaje

Debrzno

Jastrowie

Sępólno Krajeńskie

Kalisz Pomorski

Pojezierze

Wałcz

Krajeńskie

Wisła

Piła

Nakło n. Notecią

Bydgoszcz

Noteć

e

eg

no

Bolesław Chrobry, Poland's first king, founded the bishopric of Kołobrzeg in 1000. In the 12th century Bishop Otto of Bamberg, at the request of Bolesław III Krzywousty, made further, more successful attempts to convert the Pomeranian pagans to Christianity. Thus Pomerania came into the sphere of influence of its German neighbours to the west, and after Bolesław Krzywousty's death in 1138 the influence of Poland declined in Pomerania. In 1140 the bishopric of Wolin was founded, and in 1176 it moved its see to Kamień Pomorski (Cammin). Administratively, this meant that Pomerania was organized as a single ecclesiastical unit, though it was still split into a number of duchies. The dukes of Pomerania founded towns and monasteries and so encouraged a wave of immigrants. The towns adopted the municipal laws of Magdeburg or Lübeck, and gained their autonomy in the 13th century. The foreign merchants and craftsmen who settled in these towns dominated the Slavic population first by economic force, and later by force of numbers.

At the end of the 13th century the towns of Pomerania profited from their membership of the Hanseatic League, led by Lübeck, and there was a flourishing trade in agricultural products from Greater Poland, which, with linen and wool from Silesia, were exchanged for Flemish cloth, herrings and salt.

From the mid-13th century Brandenburg controlled the territory of Lubusz (Lebus), and its continued eastward expansion now threatened Pomerania. The ties with Poland were weakened. However, the Pomeranian ducal dynasty, which had split into two lines in 1295, was still concerned with maintaining a balance between the neighbouring powers, and some sort of strong dependence on the Kingdom of Poland lasted until the Reformation, when, in 1521, Pomerania recognized the feudal overlordship of the German Emperor. The influence of Brandenburg increased still further in 1618, when Poland finally declared itself willing to transfer the Prussian fiefdom to the Brandenburg line of the Hohenzollerns.

After the death of the last Gryf Duke, Bogusław XIV, in 1637, the Swedes annexed the whole of the coastal region during the Thirty Years War. The Peace of Westphalia in 1648 resulted in a partition of Pomerania between Prussia and Brandenburg. The new Kingdom of Prussia, formed in 1701, was able, by the Treaty of Stockholm in 1720 to extend its rule as far as Szczecin and the surrounding territories. The Prussian state system of creating provincial cities gave Pomerania a degree of autonomy again. The region remained part of Prussia and then of the German Empire until the collapse of the Third Reich, when another partition of historic Pomerania took place. The western section (Vorpommern) became part of the German Democratic Republic with the border running through the island of Uznam (Usedom), while to the east Pomorze Zachodne (Western Pomerania, known in German as Hinterpommern) extending as far as Pomerelia and the Bay of Gdańsk, now once again forms an integral part of Poland.

Szczecin

The port city of **Szczecin** (Stettin) is situated about 65 km inland from the Baltic Sea (colour plate 17), on the high western coastland of the Zalew Szczeciński (Stettiner Haff), at the mouth of the River Oder. Its history goes back to the 8th century and is closely bound up with the development of Pomerania.

In the 12th century the Polish Duke, Bolesław III Krzywousty, conquered the busy trading centre and brought in Bishop Otto from Bamberg to convert the inhabitants to Christianity. Between 1237 and 1243 Duke Barnim I of Pomerania granted the town a charter giving it self-government according to the laws of Magdeburg. In 1275 it became a member of the Hanseatic League, and remained the capital of the Dukes of Pomerania (the 'Dukes of the Griffin' – the griffin is still the emblem of the city) until 1630. The Reformation arrived in the city in 1535. From 1720 until 1945 Stettin was a Prussian city. At the end of the Second World War the German population was forced to leave, and since 1945 Szczecin has been Polish. It has recovered from wartime devastation to become Poland's seventh largest city, and the cultural, scientific and above all commercial centre of the region.

Our tour of the historic town centre begins at Pl. Zwycięstwa, with the **Brama Portowa (Port Gate)** (1) – formerly the Berliner Tor – at its eastern end. In the middle ages this was the entrance to the town from the west; the area beyond the limits of the old town was not developed until little more than a hundred years ago. The Baroque gate was built in 1725 by Gerhard Cornelius von Wallrawe, a Westphalian architect, and its rich relief decoration was made by the Berlin court sculptor Bartholomé Damast in 1740.

Continuing westwards from here we come to the **Katedra św. Jakuba (Jakobikirche,**

Szczecin at the end of the 19th century, engraving by H. Scherenberg

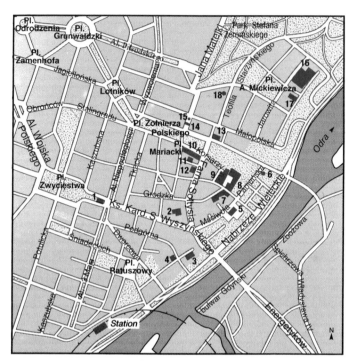

Szczecin
1 Brama Portowa (Port Gate)
2 Katedra św. Jakuba (Cathedral of St James)
3 Kościół św. Jana (Church of St John)
4 Part of the medieval fortifications
5 Ratusz (Town Hall)
6 Baszta Siedmiu Płaszczy (Tower of the Seven Coats)
7 Kamienica Loitza (Loitz House)
8 Zamek Książąt Pomorskich (Castle of the Dukes of Pomerania)
9 Pomnik Bogusława X (Monument to Duke Bogusław X and his wife Anna Jagiellonka)

10 Kamienice Profesorskie (Professors' Houses) 11 School 12 Site of Palace 13 Kościół śś. Piotra i Pawła (Church of Sts Peter and Paul) 14 Brama Hołdu Pruskiego (Gate of the Prussian Homage) 15 Statue of Flora 16 Prezydium Rady Wojewódzkiej (Presidium of the Voivodship Council) 17 Muzeum Narodowe (National Museum) 18 Pomnik Adama Mickiewicza (Adam Mickiewicz Monument)

Cathedral of St. James) (2), the largest church in Szczecin. It was founded around 1180 in the time of Bogusław I, but no trace of this original building has survived. The present Gothic hall church dates from the 14th century. The choir with its ambulatory and ring of chapels was built in 1375–87, the nave followed in about 1400, and the tower, which before the Second World War had a spire 119 metres high, was completed in 1504. Severe war damage was made good in the 1970's. The church is the work of masons from the circle of Hinrich Brunsberg, the creator of what has been called the 'malerisch' ('painterly', 'picturesque' or 'beautiful') style of architecture in Pomerania and Brandenburg.

Inside, the chapel of Our Lady of Częstochowa is worth a closer look; it has a fine cross-rib vault supported on two columns and a copy of the famous miraculous image of the Virgin. Little has remained of the old furnishings of the church. The high altar incorporates a 15th-century triptych, and in the Sacrament Chapel there is another winged altarpiece made in 1370. The windows have been given modern stained glass, and the organ too has been rebuilt in a modern style (1981). The composer Carl Loewe, famous for his Romantic ballads, was organist here between 1820 and 1866.

Next to the church, in a temporary belfry, hangs the giant St James's Bell, cast in 1681 by the Szczecin bell-founder Wawrzyniec Kokeritz. It weighs 5.7 tonnes.

Ul. Rybacka ('Fisherman's Street') brings us to the southern part of the old town. At the eastern end of ul. Podgórna rises the **Kościół św. Jana (Church of St John)** (3), which until 1856 belonged to the Franciscan Order. The friars had come to Szczecin in 1240 and built the church in the course of the 14th century, though the chancel probably dates from the 13th. It is a three-aisled hall church with a gabled façade crowned with pinnacles; the interior was thoroughly restored in the years after the war and now has modern decoration and furnishings.

In front of the church is the site of the Brama św. Ducha (Holy Ghost Gate), which once formed the entrance to the town from the south. It is recalled in the name of a street, ul. Pod Bramą ('under the gate'). Parts of the **medieval town fortifications** (4) dating from the 13th/14th centuries have survived at the corner of Pod Bramą and ul. Podgórna. In 1957 a plaque was placed here to commemorate the Hetman Stefan Czarniecki who defeated the Swedish army at this spot three hundred years earlier.

We now cross ul. Kardynała S. Wyszyńskiego and follow ul. Mściwoja to the Stary Rynek (Old Market Square), where the **Ratusz (Town Hall)** (5) stands. Fragments of vaulting of the original building have survived in the cellars, now an elegant wine bar 'U Wyszaka'. (Wyszak was a merchant and pirate said to have lived in Szczecin in the 12th century.) In the first half of the 15th century Hinrich Brunsberg erected a new, Gothic, building, which underwent a Baroque remodelling in 1677, under Swedish rule. After the Second World War, when the town hall was largely destroyed, the decision was made to re-build it in its earlier, 15th-century form. Since 1975 it has housed the *Muzeum Szczecińskie (Szczecin Museum)*, a branch of the National Museum.

Further north, in ul. Panieńska, stands the **Baszta Siedmiu Płaszczy (Tower of the Seven Coats)** (6), a section of the Gothic town walls. It guarded the city's north gate, which stood just nearby. The origin of the tower's curious name is sadly lost in the mist of tradition.

At the corner of ul. Kuśnierska is the **Kamienica Loitza (Loitz House)** (7), the most prominent example of a Szczecin burgher's house. Built in 1547 at the transition from Late Gothic to Early Renaissance, it was reconstructed after the war for use as the State School of Art. The Loitz family were prominent merchants, the owners of a large trading fleet, and bankers to the Jagiellonians. The end of the dynasty with the death of the enormously indebted Zygmunt II August, in 1572, brought about the collapse of the family bank.

In the immediate vicinity of the Kamienica Loitza are the old municipal weigh-house (on the corner of ul. Kuśnierska and ul. Grodzka) and several 15th-century warehouses.

Opposite these is the **Zamek Książąt Pomorskich (Castle of the Dukes of Pomerania)** (8). This is the nucleus from which the town of Szczecin developed. As early as the 10th century there was a fort protecting the harbour and a settlement which extended as far as the bank of the Oder. In the early 12th century, at the instigation of Duke Bolesław Krzywousty and Bishop Otto of Bamberg, the first Christian church was built here, replacing a pagan sanctuary.

The present castle grew continually from the mid-14th century onwards; it was repeatedly being extended, damaged and rebuilt. The unified appearance of the building (plate 28) is the result of work in the 1570's, when the castle – by now more of a palace – was given a Renaissance modernization by the Italian architect Guglielmo di Zaccaria for Duke Jan Fryderyk. Between 1616 and 1619 a fifth range – the museum wing (Philippsbau) – was added along ul. Rycerska. Over the following centuries, under Swedish and then Prussian rule, the castle suffered destruction and alterations, as well as war damage. Since post-war rebuilding, which has only recently been completed, the castle has been used as the cultural centre of the voivodship, with exhibition halls, workshops and a smart café and wine bar.

At the entrance to the castle precincts, at the northwest corner (ul. Korsarzy and ul. Rycerska) stands a bell-tower, whose platform affords a fine view over the city and port. On its south side is a copy of the famous statue of St Otto, the apostle of the Pomeranians.

Szczecin, Castle of the Dukes of Pomerania, engraving by M. Merian, 17th century

The original, one of the earliest examples of Pomeranian sculpture, is kept in the museum. This is located in the west wing of the castle, which was built as a museum by the Dukes Filip I and Franciszek I in the 17th century. A passageway through the middle range leads to the central courtyard, which is surrounded on two sides by loggias. In the basement of the east range is a Late Renaissance (17th-century) crypt, to which the sarcophagi of the dukes have been transferred from the crypt beneath the old chapel. The north range, built in the mid-14th century, is the oldest part of the complex, and contains the Bogusław Hall (named after Duke Bogusław X). This used to be the castle chapel, but has now been converted into a concert hall and is used for organ recitals, while the crypt below has been turned into a theatre. There is an attractive (restored) castle clock on the tower above the hall.

Before we leave the castle precincts, notice opposite the bell-tower the **Pomnik Bogus-ława X (Monument to Duke Bogusław X and his wife Anna Jagiellonka)** (9) created in 1974 by Leonia Chmielnik and Anna Paszkiewicz.

We now follow ul. Korsarzy as far as Pl. Żołnierza Polskiego. On the east side of this square (once known as Königsplatz) stand the **Kamienice Profesorskie (Professors' Houses)** (10) (houses Nos. 6–11), a terrace of single-storey residential houses with tall roofs and mansards. As early as the 14th century the houses on this site were lived in by the teachers at the school – the first in Szczecin – attached to the nearby Parish Church of St Mary. The houses were grouped around a whole block, bordered to the south by the Pl. Mariacki. The professors' houses faced inwards until around 1740, when they were turned outwards to the street. In 1831–4 they underwent another, Neoclassical, remodelling.

The **School** (11), founded in 1263 by Duke Barnim I, stood on the south side of the block, on Pl. Mariacki. The church in the centre of the square burned down in 1789 and was rebuilt in the Neoclassical style in 1832. It is now deconsecrated and forms part of the school buildings. During restoration work in the 1960's various remains of the original Gothic buildings came to light.

The **Palace** (12) that used to stand on the corner of ul. Farna, was the birthplace in 1729 of Princess Sophie Friederike Auguste von Anhalt-Zerbst, who later became Empress Catherine the Great of Russia. (Her father was serving with the Prussian army in the garrison here at the time.) Catherine's successor, Paul, also married a Szczecin-born princess, Sophia Dorothea von Württemberg.

We now return along ul. Farna back to Pl. Żołnierza Polskiego, on the opposite side of which stands the **Kościół ś.ś. Piotra i Pawła (Church of Sts Peter and Paul)** (13). The earliest church on this site was built in 1124, the year of Szczecin's conversion to Christianity. The present late 14th-century aisleless brick building has had many extensions and remodellings over the following centuries (especially in the 17th century), but it still preserves its Gothic appearance. In fact the façade was re-Gothicized in 1901–2 with a richly articulated stepped gable and a fine double doorway surmounted by a rose window. The exterior has decoration composed of glazed bricks, characteristic of the brick Gothic architecture of this region. On the north side of the church a porch was built in 1694, reusing the Romanesque piers from the Carthusian monastery at Grabów. The interior of the church has retained a fine 17th-century wooden ceiling. The slender, octagonal limestone piers at the sides of the nave are an indication that the building once had aisles.

A little further westwards, in Pl. Hołdu Pruskiego, stands the Baroque **Brama Hołdu Pruskiego (Gate of the Prussian Homage)** (14), formerly called the Anklamer Tor or Königstor. Like the Port Gate, this was built in 1725–8 by Gerhard Cornelius von Wallrawe. The rich sculptural decoration was again executed by Bartholomé Damast, while the wrought iron grilles date from the late 19th century. Beyond the gate stands a Baroque **Statue of Flora** (15).

The most beautiful part of Szczecin is the official quarter laid out in the early 20th century along the *Wały Chrobrego*, the earthworks now named after Bolesław Chrobry, but formerly known to the German inhabitants as Hakenterrasse. This is reached along ul. Małopolska and ul. Jarowita. The fortress that stood here in the 18th century was demolished in the late 19th century, and the area was given over to grand public buildings, prominent among them the **Prezydium Rady Wojewódzkiej (Presidium of the Voivodship Council)** (16) built in 1906–12. The central block on the boulevard is occupied by the **Muzeum Narodowe (National Museum)** (17), built in 1908–13 to the designs of the city architect Meyer and paid for by Stettin businessmen. The façade is decorated with roundels containing images of monuments of the great periods of art, including the Egyptian pyramids, a Gothic cathedral, and St Peter's in Rome. The collection has archaeological finds from Pomerania, material illustrating the history of fishing and folklore, as well as militaria.

In front of the museum the boulevard broadens into a square high above the banks of the Oder, surrounded by pavilions and approached up a flight of steps. In its centre stands a statue by Ludwig Manzel of Hercules fighting with the centaur. The wall along the front of the platform has a large fountain set into it and is decorated with the coats of arms of the coastal cities.

Behind the museum is Pl. Adama Mickiewicza, which has a picturesque garden. Here the **Pomnik Adama Mickiewicza (Adam Mickiewicz Monument)** (18) by Sławomir Lewiński, was erected in 1960, on the site of the equestrian statue of the Emperor Friedrich I, which stood here before the war. The greatest Polish poet of Romanticism thus set the seal of new-found Polishness on the post-war city. Further to the west is an extensive *Park* now named after *Stefan Żeromski*, with a marvellous stock of ancient trees both native and exotic.

Kołbacz – Pyrzyce – Stargard Szczeciński – Pęzino

This tour takes us into the south-eastern part of the Nizina Szczecińska (Szczecin Plain).

About 11 km south of Szczecin we reach the village of **Kołbacz (Kolbatz)** on the bank of the Płonia, with one of the most important religious buildings of the region, the *Church*

Stargard Szczeciński, St Mary's, from an old postcard

of the Cistercian Monastery founded in 1173 by Duke Warcisław II. The first monks came from the abbey of Esrom in Denmark. They began the construction of the abbey buildings around 1210. The Late Romanesque basilican church was completed around 1230. Like many Cistercian abbeys Kołbacz grew rich through its efficient farming, and so was able to undertake a modernization of the church a century later. The nave was given a Gothic remodelling and the choir rebuilt in the first half of the 13th century. The west front has elements of both the Romanesque and Gothic styles, with a round-arch frieze made of shaped bricks and a tracery rosette in the gable.

After the dissolution of the monastery in the 16th century the monastic buildings were transformed into a ducal residence, but only the Dom Opacki (Abbot's House) dating from the 13th century with a later half-timbered addition, the Dom Konwersów (Lay-Brothers' House) and a barn have survived, and they can still be seen near the church.

Kołbacz stands at the northern edge of the Ziemia Pyrzycka, a fertile region with practically no forests that the Cistercian agriculturalists exploited very successfully in the middle ages. The main town, **Pyrzyce (Pyritz)**, about 25 km further south, is mentioned in documentary sources as early as the 9th century, and until the Second World War it had an impressive ensemble of historic architecture. In February 1945 80 per cent of the fabric was destroyed. However, a large part of the town's medieval fortifications has survived, with two town gates, the *Brama Szczecińska (Stettin Gate)* to the north and the *Brama Bańska (Banie Gate)* (plate 29) to the south, as well as several towers. The town walls, built in the 14th century, had to be strengthened in the 16th century because of the constant threat from neighbouring Brandenburg. The *Kościół Farny (Parish Church)* in the town centre, a brick Gothic building with a choir ambulatory (14th/15th centuries), was rebuilt in 1969.

On a hill to the east of the town stand the ruins of a *castle* built between the 10th and 13th centuries.

Stargard Szczeciński (Stargard), 30 km northeast of here, also suffered terrible damage in the war, although some important architectural monuments were saved from complete destruction and have since been painstakingly restored. From the time of its foundation – or at least from the granting of its charter in 1253 – Stargard was one of the richest towns in Pomerania, thanks to its pre-eminence in the grain trade of Ziemia Pyrzycka. At times it even rivalled Szczecin.

In the market place stands the *Kościół N.P. Marii (Church of St Mary)* one of the greatest Gothic churches in the region: 'St Mary is the one church between the Oder and the banks of the Vistula that challenges the great basilicas of the Hanse, of Lübeck, Wismar, Stralsund' (Brian Knox). It was begun in the late 13th century as a brick hall church, but was extended around 1400 by the architect Hinrich Brunsberg into a large basilica with an ambulatory choir and a ring of chapels. Brunsberg's alterations began with the imposing façade with its two massive towers which take up almost the whole width of the façade, except for a small gable between them, and are covered with decorative blind arcading. The west door has extraordinary zigzag mouldings in its archivolts. Inside, the church has the classic structure of a Gothic basilica with a tall nave divided into arcade, triforium (almost unique among Baltic churches) and clearstorey levels. The star vaults were added in the 17th century. The church is lined with richly furnished family chapels. They include the Kaplica N.P. Marii (Lady Chapel) built around 1400 on the north side of the choir, with beautiful glazed brick decoration on its exterior.

Besides the church, the *Ratusz (Town Hall)* (plate 31) has been rebuilt, after being almost completely destroyed in the war. Originally a Gothic building, its Renaissance appearance was the result of a thorough remodelling in 1638. The lavish traceried decoration in the stepped gable of the entrance front dates from a re-Gothicization in 1868–76.

Next to the town hall stands the *Odwach (Guardhouse)* of 1720, which was rebuilt in the 1960's with an altered interior arrangement, to serve as the *Muzeum Regionalne (Regional Museum)*.

Behind the choir of St Mary's, at ul. Kazimierza Wielkiego No. 13, a Gothic burgher's house (15th century, altered in the mid-16th century) with a fine, richly articulated brick façade, has survived. Its interior too has been altered and is now used as a music school.

At the end of this interesting street, close to the bank of the River Ina, stands the *Arsenał (Arsenal)*, which was originally Gothic but underwent several later alterations. It was destroyed in the Second World War except for its outer wall, but was rebuilt in 1974–7 in its medieval form as the seat of the *Archiwum Miejskie (Municipal Archives)*.

From here we can begin a walk round the late 15th-century town fortifications, which are almost completely preserved. At the southwest corner of the walls, at the corner of ul. Bolesława Krzywoustego, stands the *Baszta Lodowa (Ice Tower)*, which dates from the mid-15th century and derives its name from the fact that ice was stored in its cellars in the 18th century. It has the usual shape of such towers in this area, with a rectangular base and a cylindrical superstructure. Next to the Ice Tower is the earliest of the surviving town gates, the *Brama Pyrzycka (Pyrzyce Gate)*, built at the end of the 13th century and altered in 1439, a mighty brick structure with a pointed arch passageway and a roofed defensive passage. The roof is surmounted by gables with blind arcading.

Nearby, at ul. Mieszka I. No. 43, is one of the few 16th-century *burghers' houses* not to have been completely destroyed in the war, although 80 per cent of its walls had to be reconstructed when it was restored to serve as the public library. The only decoration on the façade is the stepped gable and the simple, pointed blind arcading. The *Baszta Morze Czerwone (Red Sea Tower)*, whose name goes back to the bloody fighting in the Thirty Years War, is of the same type as the Ice Tower and has fine decoration composed of glazed bricks arranged in diamond shapes. The *Kościół św. Jana (Church of St John)* in Pl. Wolności, at the corner of ul. Chrobrego, is a Late Gothic hall church with a choir ambulatory and a ring of chapels, the result of a remodelling and enlargement of an earlier (13th-century) chapel of the Knights Hospitaller in 1408–64. The model for the choir is that of the parish church of St Mary. In the early 19th century, when Stargard was occupied by the Napoleonic army, the church was used as a military hospital and later as a storehouse. A thorough restoration towards the end of the century, which included raising to 99 metres the height of the tower that looms above the façade, gave the church its present external appearance. The church came through the Second World War relatively unscathed. The mural paintings and glazing of the windows date from the 1950's and 1960's.

Continuing along the town walls (ul. Wały Chrobrego), we reach two more impressive town gates in the north-eastern section of the fortifications. The first is the early 15th-century *Brama Młyńska (Mill Gate)*, which spans a branch of the River Ina. As the river was used as a waterway, this gate was not only used for defence but also as a customs post. Then, on the east side of the town centre, we come to the *Brama Wałowa (Rampart Gate)*, which was originally safeguarded by a round bastion projecting from the line of the wall. The blind arcade decoration in the gable dates from alterations in the 16th century.

About 14 km east of Stargard Szczeciński, on the plain southeast of the village of **Pęzino (Pansin)**, stands a *castle* built in the 13th and 14th centuries as a fortified monastery of the Knights Templar. From 1482 it was in the possession of the Knights Hospitaller, and between 1483 and 1493 it was the seat of a commandery of the order. The castle had been built of brick in the shape of an irregular rectangle with a square corner tower to the southeast, which was destroyed in 1674 and has remained as a picturesque ruin. On the

Międzyzdroje, photographed in 1930

south side of the castle is a gateway which still contains the remains of the equipment used to operate the drawbridge. In the first half of the 16th century the castle was extended by the addition of new residential quarters along the west wall, near the tower, with three storeys and Late Renaissance gables, as well as an oriel window. The roof structure is still extant. The neo-Gothic addition dates from the 19th century. After a fire in 1935 both buildings were given a single roof. The whole complex is set in a beautiful 19th-century park.

Wolin – Międzyzdroje – Kamień Pomorski – Świerzno – Pobierowo – Trzebiatów

The island of **Wolin** was inhabited from earliest times; finds that testify to its long trading history include beads from Egypt and coins from Persia. Much of it is now a national park, so its beech and pine forests and its unusual geological formations (steep banks and overhanging cliffs) are protected. Bison were reintroduced in 1976, and there are eagles. The little seaside town of **Międzyzdroje** is the starting point for excursions into the park.

    Kamień Pomorski (Cammin), a small town at the mouth of the River Dziwonna (Nemitz) in the Zalew Kamieński (Bay of Kamień), was an important political centre in the early middle ages. In the 11th and 12th centuries the Dukes of Pomerania resided here. In 1175 the town was raised to a status of a bishop's see in place of Wolin. Because of its position on a major trading waterway it soon became prosperous, and the period up to the 16th century saw the erection of a number of important buildings, most of which have survived, despite severe damage in the Second World War. In the 17th century damage was caused by two major sieges, the first by the Swedes (1630), and the second by the Prussian army (1679), and this, combined with the silting up of the river estuary, gradually brought · commercial life in the town to a standstill.

On a hill in the northeast part of the town stands the *Katedra św. Jana (Cathedral of St John)* (plate 30), one of Poland's most interesting medieval buildings. In 1175 work began on a Romanesque basilica on a Latin cross plan; as construction progressed the style gradually developed from Romanesque to Early Gothic. A Late Gothic remodelling followed in the 15th century. The church's present form, as restored in the 1960's, shows features from all the main phases of its history. Particularly fine is the rich decorative cresting on the exterior of the south transept, with openwork, traceried, triangular gables between pinnacles. In 1544 the church passed into the possession of the Protestant community, and all the old furnishings of the church were removed, except the high altar (*c.*1500) and the font. In the course of the 17th century the church was refurnished; the famous Baroque organ was donated in 1669 by Duke Ernest Bogusław von Croy.

The capitular buildings adjoin the cathedral on the north side. The Gothic cloister (14th/15th centuries) is the only surviving cloister of its kind in Pomerania. The former treasury on the upper floor of the east range is now a museum.

Not far from the cathedral stands the *Pałac Biskupi (Bishop's Palace)*, created in the 16th century by remodelling two Gothic houses, and now used as a library. One of its narrow ends sports an elegant gable, and a carved staircase, decorated with soldiers' heads, has survived inside.

The *Town Hall* in the market place was reconstructed in 1972, but was originally built in two easily distinguishable phases in the 15th and 16th centuries. The east front with its open porch, once used as a public law court, is surmounted by a Gothic stepped gable with slender pointed blind arcading. The gables at the narrow west end were remodelled in the late 17th century with ornate, traceried decoration. At the north corner of the market place an 18th-century half-timbered house is still standing.

Fragments of the town walls, dating from the 13th and 14th centuries, can be seen along the ul. Kościelna on the western edge of the old town centre. One of the original three town gates is also still extant, the *Brama Wolińska (Wolin Gate)*, built in 1308 and altered in the late 14th century. From the top of its massive tower there is a good view over the town.

13 km east of Kamień Pomorski, at **Świerzno (Schwirsen)**, is the *manor house* of the Flemming family, set in a park which was formally laid out in the French manner. Construction began in 1718 and was completed in 1730; in the 19th century the house was extended with two projecting sections. The design is symmetrical with three wings

constructed of oak half-timbering on rubble foundations, and roofed with a double layer of flat tiles. The entrance from the courtyard into the park to the north is flanked by two dovecotes with pointed roofs.

The seaside resort of **Pobierowo (Poberow)** is one of the most beautiful on the Baltic coast. It was founded in 1906 and its centre is composed of charming, small-scale buildings.

A few kilometres inland, on the bank of the River Rega, is the ancient town of **Trzebiatów (Treptow)**. It was already in existence in the 9th century as a small Slavic settlement, and after receiving its charter in 1277 soon developed into a flourishing centre of trade. As a member of the Hanseatic League the town had its own port, Regoujście, at the mouth of the Rega. The 15th century saw an escalation of rivalry with the neighbouring town of Kołobrzeg, which ended with the destruction of this harbour – though this did not stop the development of the town. Trzebiatów did not escape damage in the Second World War, but its historical appearance has been largely preserved.

The market square still has Gothic houses, some remodelled in the Baroque period. One of these, on the corner of ul. Zajazdowa, is decorated with a picture of an elephant balancing a ball on its trunk. This piece of sgraffito work was probably made around 1639, the year when an elephant was first put on show in Pomerania to general amazement. One worried clergyman exclaimed: 'May God grant that this extraordinary beast bring no evil to our homeland.' The *Town Hall* in the centre of the market place was enlarged in 1701 in the Baroque manner, but remains of the original Gothic building can still be seen on the west front.

The *Kościół N.P. Marii (Church of St Mary)*, a hall church built in the 14th century with a choir ambulatory, fine star vaults (15th century) and Gothic mural paintings on the choir arch, has two unusual bells: 'Gabriel' dating from the 14th century, one of the oldest bells in Poland, and 'Maria', cast in 1515, at 7.2 tonnes the third heaviest in Poland.

In Pl. Zjednoczenia, set in a curve in the river at the northeast corner of the old town centre, stands the *Castle*. It has recently been restored to its Baroque appearance (17th and 18th centuries) and reveals little of its long history, which goes back to an early medieval Slavic *castrum*.

Southwards along the river bank large parts of the 13th- and 14th-century town walls have survived, including the *Baszta Kaszana (Gruel Tower)*. This slender, round watchtower derives its name from a legend. One night, when a raiding party from the town of Gryfice (Greifenberg) was about to attack Trzebiatów, a soldier on watch here tripped over with a plate of gruel; alerted by the clatter of the plate, the townsfolk were able to fend off the attack.

Kołobrzeg – Świdwin – Koszalin

The largest town on the Pomeranian coast is **Kołobrzeg (Kolberg)** about 30 km northeast of Trzebiatów. Not only is it a well-known seaside resort, it is also famous for its traditional fortified architecture. Ninety per cent of the town was destroyed in 1945, but the most important architectural monuments have since been rebuilt.

The town existed as a small trading settlement 3 km to the south as early as the 10th century, when it was made the seat of one of the earliest Polish bishoprics. It was laid out on its present site when the town charter was granted in 1255, and soon became rich through its salt works and herring fisheries. Kołobrzeg joined the Hanseatic League at the beginning of the 14th century. From the Thirty Years War onwards the town was subject to repeated attacks. It was laid waste by the Swedes, and later captured by the Margravate of Brandenburg. In 1807, during the Napoleonic wars, it was besieged but successfully defended by General Gneisenau and the brewer Nettelbeck. In the mid-19th century work began on extending the harbour and setting up the facilities needed for a health resort.

The *Town Hall* in the market place is a neo-Gothic building with three ranges round a courtyard and battlemented turrets. It was built in 1829–30 to replace a Late Gothic town hall destroyed in the Napoleonic Wars. The design by Karl Friedrich Schinkel was executed under the direction of Ernst Friedrich Zwirner, the architect in charge of the completion of Cologne Cathedral. On its eastern side is a granite column once used as a pillory. The mask in its capital is said to be a portrait of the patrician Jakob Adebar, who was beheaded for leading an uprising of the guilds in 1526. Next to the town hall is a 17th-century warehouse.

Southwest of here, in ul. Katedralna, the interesting Gothic *Kolegiata N.P. Marii (Collegiate Church of St Mary)* has recently been resurrected from its wartime ruins. Originally a three-aisled hall-nave was attached to a 13th-century choir, but it was widened to five aisles in the second half of the 14th century. The ensemble was designed as a 'Stufenhalle' (the side-aisles progressively lower than the nave) so that all five aisles shelter under one wide-spreading roof. The impressive west front (15th century) is a single massive block; the towers that were intended to rise above it were never completed. Inside the church are some survivals from the medieval furnishings, saved from wartime devastation, as well as fragments of Gothic wall paintings and some Late Gothic altars, but the most important item is the bronze font dated 1355 and signed by Johann Alart. It rests on four recumbent lions, and its outer surface is decorated with gilded reliefs of scenes from the Life of Christ, arranged in two registers. The canons' stalls (*c.*1340) are carved with fantastic beasts, and the intricate pendant chandelier (1523) encloses a statue of the Virgin and Child.

One block east of the collegiate church, at ul. E. Gierczaka No. 15, is the *Dom Schlieffenów (Schlieffen House)*, a Gothic patrician house of the 15th century, remodelled in 1540 and altered after the war to serve as a museum of the history of the town. On the way to the sea-front promenade, it is worth making a slight detour to see the *Złota Uliczka (Golden Alley)*, a reconstructed picturesque group of medieval craftsmen's houses. Here stands the only surviving remnant of the once famous town fortifications, the *Baszta Prochowa (Powder Tower)* built in the 15th century, a brick Gothic structure with blind arcading, a saddleback roof and two richly decorated gables.

Koszalin, photograph taken in 1929

Going westward along the sea-front, we reach the *Spa Park*, which still contains the *Lighthouse* in the precincts of the former fortress ('Fort Münde', 1770–74). On the shore a *Pomnik Zaślubin Polski z Morzem (Monument to the Marriage of Poland with the Sea)* has been erected. This commemorates a spontaneous ceremony held on 18 March 1945 by a group of Polish soldiers, in which they swore that the land here would remain Polish. One of the female officers threw her ring into the sea in a suitably symbolic gesture. (Poland's Union with the Sea was first celebrated 25 years earlier, in 1920, when Poland was awarded a stretch of the Baltic coast by the Versailles Treaty.)

On the way to Koszalin the town of **Świdwin (Schivelbein)** has a *Castle* rebuilt in 1400 and later by the Teutonic Order. This is the birthplace of Rudolf Virchow (1821–1902), a great pathologist and anthropologist, who went to school at nearby Köslin and wrote a treatise about the monastery there.

The cultural and economic centre of the middle Baltic coast is the voivodship capital **Koszalin (Köslin)**, 44 km east of Kołobrzeg. A village called Cossalitz, later Cossalin, was already in existence here in the first half of the 12th century. In 1277 the Bishop of Kamień, to whose territory it belonged, granted the town a charter with the laws of Lübeck. Koszalin then developed into a flourishing commercial town. By the 14th century it had its own port on Jezioro Jamno (Jamunder See), and between 1574 and 1622 it was the see of a prince-bishop. It came under the rule of Brandenburg in 1648, and after the great fire of 1718, King Friedrich Wilhelm I rebuilt the town principally to house Prussian officials.

Post-war reconstruction was careful to preserve traces of the various phases of the town's development.

The *Town Hall* in the market place was built after the war. Its tower contains a carillon, as had been usual in the middle ages.

The Gothic *Kościół N.P. Marii (Church of St Mary)*, in the southwest corner of the square, became the cathedral of the refounded diocese of Kołobrzeg in 1972. Built at the beginning of the 14th century, it is a three-aisled basilica with a massive square west tower; the side-aisles have a series of steep transverse saddleback roofs. The church was thoroughly restored in the 19th century, when all later additions were stripped away, and the furnishings, which until then had remained intact, were removed. All that was left was the Gothic font and some life-sized figures from the former high altar (1512).

In ul. Kazimierza Wielkiego, on the north-western edge of the old town centre, a stretch of the brick and stone town walls, built in the 14th century, can still be found. Following the walls westwards we soon come to ul. Grodzka, the site on the bank of the little River Dzierzęcinka, where the castle of the prince-bishops stood in the 16th century. The former *Kaplica Zamkowa (Castle Chapel)* is a 17th-century Baroque building, but some Early Gothic masonry of the 13th century is visible on its east side. It is now used by Orthodox immigrants from the Eastern Territories.

A little further along ul. Grodzka stands the *Domek Kata (Executioner's House)*, a Gothic house remodelled in the 16th century, where the town executioner is said to have lived. Since restoration it has been used as a theatre.

Near Pl. Gwiaździsty, to the south of the town centre, on the site of the former cemetery outside the old town walls, stands the old cemetery chapel, the *Kaplica św. Gertrudy (Chapel of St Gertrude)*, a small centrally planned octagonal building of 1383, with a pyramidal roof and a fine star vault.

Darłowo – Słupsk – Bytów – Łeba

The town of **Darłowo (Rügenwalde)** on the Wieprza (Wipper), with its modern bathing resort suburb *Darłówko (Rügenwaldermünde)*, extends as far as the coast. It avoided destruction in the Second World War and still preserves its historic character.

There was a settlement here in the early middle ages. It received its town charter in 1270, and its rapid development into a prosperous commercial centre was based mainly on its busy trading links with Scandinavia. In 1412 it became a member of the Hanseatic League. The Thirty Years War resulted in an economic decline in the 17th century, which was hastened by several great fires and plagues. Not until the 18th century did the town recover, and this second period of prosperity, like the first, has left its mark on the townscape.

The market place, now called Pl. Tadeusza Kościuszki, still has its 18th-century *arcaded houses*, as does the street now called ul. Powstańców Warszawskich, where the leading patricians used to have their residences. The *Town Hall* in the market place was built in 1725, and so also belongs to this new phase of building in the town. The *Fontanna Rybaka (Fisherman Fountain)* was erected in 1919. Opposite the Town Hall stands the *Kościół Farny N.P. Marii (Parish Church of St Mary)*, a three-aisled basilica dating from the second half of the 14th century, remodelled around 1500, with a massive tower, 60 metres tall, which doubles as the church's west front. The church was burned out several times (1589, 1624, 1722) and was restored in the late 19th century. Its interior has some fine star vaults, and the fan vaulting in the sacristy merits particular attention. In a sarcophagus made in 1882 lie the remains of Duke Erik of Pomerania, who reigned as King Erik VII of Denmark, Sweden and Norway until his deposition in 1439. For the next ten years he lived as a pirate on the island of Gotland, before retiring to Darłowo, where he died in 1459. Two other sarcophagi, of the Baroque period, contain the remains of two duchesses: Elżbieta, the wife of Bogusław XIV, the last Duke of Pomerania, and Jadwiga, the wife of his brother Ulryk.

The *Brama Kamienna (Stone Gate)*, built in the 14th century and altered in 1737, stands to the north of here, and is visible from the market place. It is all that is left of the town fortifications, and represents a type of Gothic town gate very common in this region: cubic in shape, tall, with a simple passageway cut through its base and the upper part articulated with slender, decorative blind arcading.

The cemetery on the other side of the town walls, beyond the Stone Gate, was already in existence in the middle ages. The Late Gothic *Kaplica św. Gertrudy (Chapel of St Gertrude)* is said to have been founded by Duke Erik. Like its counterpart at Koszalin, it is a centrally planned building with a polygonal ground plan: the hexagonal centre is surrounded by a twelve-sided vaulted ambulatory, and the star vault supported by a central pier is echoed in the dodecagonal roof.

The *Castle*, once the residence of the Dukes of Pomerania and the seat of ex-King Erik in his old age (1449–59), stands on the southern edge of the town, between two branches of the Wieprza. It was erected in the second half of the 14th century and was first remodelled by Erik. Originally it was a four-sided building with a courtyard and strong fortifications. The state rooms were in the east range, with the chapel on the ground floor. After the castle was plundered in 1629 the last ducal resident, Elżbieta (the wife of Bogusław XIV), commissioned the extension of the chapel, which was reconsecrated in its new Early Baroque form in 1639. Its most precious furnishing was a silver altar, some fragments of which can be seen in the Muzeum Pomorza Środkowego (Museum of Central Pomerania) at Słupsk.

In the 19th century the castle was partly demolished, and the remaining buildings were used as storehouses and a prison. They now contain the *Muzeum Regionalne (Regional Museum)* with collections illustrating local geology and natural history, the archaeology, ethnography and history of Darłowo and the surrounding area, and works of art.

Słupsk (Stolp), which became the capital of the voivodship in 1975, lies inland, about 60 km east of Darłowo, on the banks of the River Słupia (Stolpe). It has had a long and

Słupsk, Mill Gate, photograph taken c.1900

turbulent history. A settlement is recorded here as early as the 9th century; it later became an important stopping place between Szczecin and Gdańsk and in 1310 was granted a town charter. Throughout the 14th century the town often changed hands until finally in the 15th century Słupsk became part of the Duchy of West Pomerania. It had meanwhile joined the Hanseatic League, and gained considerable prosperity, thanks to the great skills of its craftsmen, particularly in amber-work. A great fire in 1476 left a large part of the town in ashes, and marked a considerable setback in its fortunes, but Słupsk made a steady recovery. Słupsk came under Prussian rule in 1653.

The centre of the Stare Miasto (Old Town) is a square created in 1886 as part of large-scale replanning of the town. The Romantic neo-Gothic *Town Hall* was built here in 1901. The square extends beyond the original limits of the Old Town, marked by the *Nowa Brama (New Gate)* through which the medieval visitor would have entered Słupsk on the Koszalin road. This sturdy Late Gothic brick building was erected around 1500 with decorative blind arcading above the undecorated lower storey. The Baroque helm was added to the pyramid roof around 1650.

Ul. Łukaszewicza leads to the *Kościół N.P. Marii (Church of St Mary)*, the parish church of the Old Town. It dates from the second half of the 14th century but had to be remodelled after the catastrophic fire of 1476. It is a three-aisled basilica, with an exterior enlivened by decorative gables above the side-aisles and an ornamental frieze with tracery motifs. Until 1945 the mighty tower at the west front was surmounted by a tall Baroque spire. The interior still has many funerary monuments, as well as a Late Gothic Crucifixion and a fine Baroque pulpit.

North of the church is the market square with some Baroque and Neoclassical *burghers' houses* of the 18th and 19th centuries. Ul. Grodzka runs from here to the bank of the Słupia, where some remnants of the town walls (early 15th century) can still be seen. Following the walls southeastwards we reach the only surviving defensive tower, the *Baszta Czarownic (Witches' Tower)*, which in the 17th century was made into a prison for women suspected of witchcraft. Between 1600 and 1650 eighteen death sentences were carried out here.

At the end of the fortifications, in the southeast corner of the Old Town is the picturesque *Zamek Książęcy (Ducal Castle)* with the *Kościół św. Jacka (Church of St Hyacinth)*, formerly a Dominican friary church, and the *Młyn Zamkowy (Castle Mill)* (one of the principal sources of income for the dukes) attached to the back of the Gothic *Brama Młyńska (Mill Gate)*.

Construction of the castle lasted a long time, beginning in 1507. Its unusually thick walls, protected by a moat, suggest that it was intended as an inner fortress within the framework of the town fortifications. In the 1580's, when the building was still unfinished, Duke Jan Fryderyk called in the architect Guiglielmo di Zaccaria and had the building remodelled as a Renaissance residence. It remained in this form until the 18th century. In 1731 King Friedrich Wilhelm I had all the furnishings taken off to Berlin, and the castle was converted first into a barracks and then into a storehouse. Between 1959 and 1965 the castle was reconstructed in its severe, elegant Renaissance form to house the *Muzeum Pomorza Środkowego (Museum of Central Pomerania)*. The varied collections include a number of precious works of art from the region, among them parts of the silver altar of Darłowo (see page 336), Renaissance and Baroque tapestries, icons, coins, weapons, and pieces of King Jan III Sobieski's triumphal car from his battle against the Turks outside Vienna.

The museum's ethnographical collection is displayed in the castle mill. This was built to serve as a granary too and is probably older than the castle itself. When the latter was remodelled in 1580–87, the mill too was modernized. It remained in operation in the 20th century, though in 1925 the mill-wheel was replaced by a turbine. It has been part of the museum since 1968.

Until the Reformation the Gothic *Church of St Jacek* belonged to the Dominican order, which had been invited here by Duke Mściwój in 1274. This plain building, long and narrow, with a richly articulated, pierced gable above the choir façade and a tall tower at the west end, was erected in the 15th century to replace an earlier church. In 1524 the furnishings were removed in the course of the Reformation, and the building itself suffered damage, which was not made good until the early 17th century, when the building was

Bytów, town seal, probably 14th century

restored by the Duchess Erdmund, widow of Jan Fryderyk, as the castle church. The Late Renaissance high altar and the pulpit, the two most impressive items among the present furnishings, date from this period. Later a fine Baroque organ was added and two splendid tombs: the richly sculptured monument of Duchess Anna, and the white and black marble tomb of Duke Ernst Bogusław von Croy, which has been attributed to Andreas Schlüter. In the 18th century the church and castle were badly damaged (the nave was even used for a time as a brewery), but in 1900 the church was restored to its original state.

From Słupsk it is worth making an excursion southwards into the heart of the Pojezierze Kaszubskie (Kashubian Lakeland) to the town of **Bytów (Bütow)**, which is in fact already in Pomerelia (Western Pomerania). Its imposing *Zamek Kryżacki (Castle of the Teutonic Order)* (plate 27), an extensive, rectangular building with massive brick walls and four corner towers, was built around 1400, when the town came into the possession of the Order. It was designed for defence, with a courtyard surrounded by massive walls with defensive passageways running along them, and a three-storeyed residential building attached to the inside of the northeast wall. Originally the castle precinct was also protected outside by tall earthworks. The round corner towers are among the first in Europe to have been designed specifically for the use of artillery.

Northeast of Słupsk, at the mouth of the River Łeba (Leba) between Lake Łebsko and Lake Sarbsko, is the small coastal town of **Łeba (Leba)**, a picturesque fishing port and a busy bathing resort in the summer months. The partly-wooded dune landscape of the *Słowiński National Park* extends westwards from here as far as Lake Gardno. This sandy stretch of land with its great shifting dunes is aptly called Polska Sahara. Over 250 species of migrating birds come here, and storks can be seen nesting in villages throughout the area. The original town of Łeba was an old Kashubian fishing settlement, which stood on the west bank of the river as early as the 13th century and received its town charter in 1357, under the suzerainty of the Teutonic Order. Sand storms and sand drifts caused such damage that in the 1560's the inhabitants moved across the river to the safer west bank. The ruins of the old parish church can still be seen in the forest. The present town has a plain Baroque church (1683), whose tower was replaced with a half-timbered structure in the 18th century following a fire; there are also some romantic 19th-century fishermen's houses. Łeba only became fashionable as a holiday resort after 1899, when it was linked to the railway network, and it has managed to retain its original character, now carefully tended, to the present day.

Lębork – Wejherowo – Kartuzy – Żukowo

The road inland from the coast runs through **Lębork (Lauenburg)**, 30 km south of Łeba. The origins of the town are Slavic. A massive castle and encircling walls with 33 bastions were built in the 14th century, when it was in the territory of the Teutonic Order. During the Swedish Wars in the 17th century, and again in 1945, much of the town was destroyed, but extensive fragments of the town walls have survived, including the *Baszta Bluszczowa (Ivy Tower)*. The present appearance of the *Castle* and the Gothic *Kościół św. Jakuba (Church of St James)* is the result of restoration in the 19th and early 20th centuries. The largely reconstructed ensembles of *houses and shops* in the market place and adjoining streets are worth seeing, however. These were built in the 19th century in a playful mixture of historical styles with much use of polychromatic brickwork. Lębork is in the middle of the region still inhabited by Kashubians (see page 346), and there are many relics of old Kashubian folklore to be seen nearby – especially now that the region has been developed as a popular holiday and leisure area.

Most of the towns in this region, which in fact forms part of the historic Duchy of Pomerelia, are medieval in origin, being 14th-century foundations that developed out of earlier Slavic settlements. One exception, however, is **Wejherowo (Weihersfrei)**, formerly also called Nowe Miasto (Neustadt), about 37 km east of Lębork. It is named after Jacob Weiher, a local magnate from an old family, originally from Franconia, who founded the town in 1643 as a centre of religious tolerance, where anyone could freely practise any religion. Very soon, however, the town became a focus of post-Tridentine Catholicism, and as early as 1657 Protestants were denied the right to build their own church here. Wejherowo is therefore a centre of High Baroque architecture, of the sort that could only flourish under aristocratic Catholic patronage. Jakob Weiher founded a monastery for the Reformed Franciscans, and to the south of the town, against the backdrop of the forest, he laid out a Way of the Cross (the *Kalwaria Wejherowska*) consisting of 26 chapels of various designs. His model – and the model for the design of some of the chapels – was the Kalwaria Zebrzydowska near Kraków (see page 502). The architect of this picturesque and interesting ensemble is unknown.

Some of the chapels have been left in their original form, their noble Baroque decoration contrasting with the natural landscape around them. Others had half-timbered shells built

Lębork, view of the Prison Tower (destroyed in the Second World War), from an old postcard

around them in the 19th century, creating the bizarre and surprising effect of elegant little temples and baldachins concealed in apparently humble huts. Others were replaced, also in the 19th century, with Romantic, neo-Romanesque or Gothic structures. While these alterations detract from the historical consistency of the ensemble, they do add considerably to the charm of a stroll around the Stations of the Cross.

From Wejherowo it is only a short distance via Gdynia and Sopot to Gdańsk. However, it is worth making a detour through the fascinating countryside of the Pobrzeże Kaszubskie (Kashubian Coastland).

About 45 km south of Wejherowo, on Lake Klasztorne, is **Kartuzy (Karthaus)**, a relatively new town which has grown up since the 19th century around a Carthusian monastery once called Marien-Paradies. The first monks were brought from Prague in the 1380's, and for centuries the monastery stood in austere Carthusian isolation in the countryside. Only after the closing of the monastery in 1826 did a settlement begin to develop. In 1920 it was given the status of a town. Today it is an important economic centre and a cultural focus for the Kashubian region. The *Muzeum Etnograficzne (Ethnographical Museum)* at ul. Kościerska 1 has a display of Kashubian artefacts, ranging from historical agricultural implements, through crafts and applied arts, to musical instruments.

The main attraction of Kartuzy is the fine Gothic *Kościół Klasztorny (Monastery Church)* with its unusual Baroque hipped roof (1731–3) looking like a gigantic coffin lid. The church was built at the end of the 14th century, and the star vault was added in the 16th century. Its rich furnishings, well preserved and painstakingly restored, date mostly from the 17th century (the high altar and some of the side altars, the choir stalls and some Baroque monuments). The most precious item is a carved and gilded altarpiece of 1444, probably made by a Gdańsk workshop.

More monastic architecture is to be seen in the village of **Żukowo (Zuckau)** just outside the gates of Gdańsk, in the valley of the River Radunia (Radaune). The church of the former convent of Premonstratensian nuns, since 1834 the *Kościół Farny (Parish Church)*, has unusually rich Gothic furnishings. The abbey was founded in 1209, and the church and conventual buildings were erected in the course of the 14th century. In the 17th century there were major alterations, especially in the interior. The choir was remodelled and the vault was renewed. The tower was given a Baroque helm and a ridge turret was set on top of the steep roof. Many of the church furnishings, including the finely carved choir stalls, also date from this time. The altar paintings, sculptures and embroidered vestments of the 15th and 16th centuries remain, however, the church's most valuable treasures. Foremost amongst these is the magnificent Antwerp Triptych, imported from Flanders in the early 16th century. The story of the Life and Passion of Christ is told in the scenes of the central panel, which are carved in high relief, and in the dramatic and vivid paintings on the wings.

Dorota Leszczyńska and Michaela Marek

Pomorze Wschodnie (Eastern Pomerania) and Gdańsk – Kujawy

The lower course of the Vistula, for centuries Poland's main commercial artery, flows through the austere countryside of the historic territories of Kujawy and the Ziemia Chełminska (Kulmer Land), to the Baltic. East of the river valley begin the great expanses of Mazurian lakeland, while to the west lie the Bory Tucholskie (Tuchola Woods), a region of dense forest rich in wildlife. The Żuławy Wiślane (Vistula Marshes) at the river delta, where the Vistula enters the Zatoka Gdańska (Bay of Gdańsk), are fertile agricultural land, much of it below sea level. To the north of the great conurbation of Gdańsk, the bay is protected by a long sandbank, the Mierzeja Helska (Hel Peninsula), now an important holiday centre, while to the east of the bay another sandbank, the Mierzeja Wiślana creates the Zalew Wiślany (Vistula Lagoon). On its western side the bay is bounded by the Pobrzeże Kaszubskie (Kashubian Coastland also known as Kashubian Switzerland), an extensive moraine landscape of lakes and forests, with tall, steep hills separated by glacial valleys.

The earliest settlement was a fortified town, Truso, which stood in the 9th century on a long inlet in an area cut off from the other Polish regions by wilderness. The pattern of settlement developed from Kujawy and spread over the lakeland plains of Golub Dobrzyń and Chełmno. The colonization from Greater Poland moved northwards down the lower course of the Vistula, where it collided with the colonization being undertaken by the Pomorani, with outposts at Gniew and Tczew, and by the Pruzzi from east of the Vistula. Bolesław I Chrobry supported the mission of Bishop Wojciech (Adalbert) in 997 to Christianize the latter and thus extend Polish influence beyond the Vistula. This enterprise met with little success, however, since the bishop was soon murdered by his intended converts.

Konrad Mazowiecki summoned the knights of the Order of 'the Blessed Virgin Mary of the Teutonic House in Jerusalem' (commonly called the Teutonic Order) to defend the territory adjoining the land of the Pruzzi. In return the knights were given the Ziemia Chełmińska (the Chełmno region) to hold as a fief. The evangelizing of the Pruzzi began again, this time in a more drastic manner. In fifty years it ended with their eradication and the Germanizing of the territories.

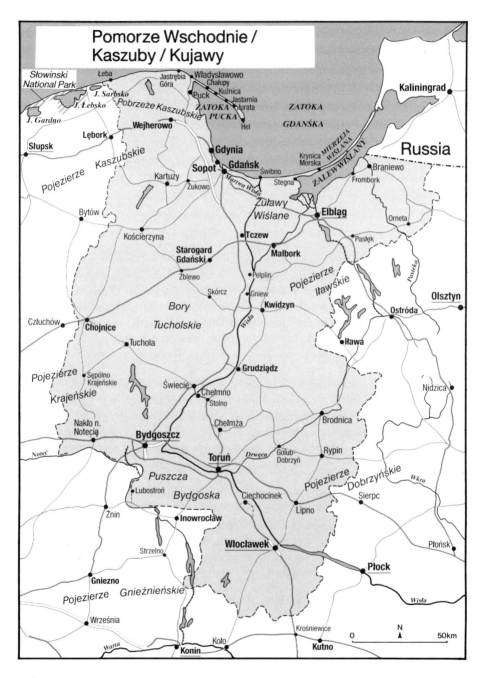

Pomorze Wschodnie / Kaszuby / Kujawy

Słowinski National Park
Leba
Jastrębia Góra
Władysławowo
Chałupy
Kaliningrad
J. Sarbsko
Puck
Kuźnica
J. Łebsko
Pobrzeże Kaszubskie
ZATOKA PUCKA
Jastarnia
Jurata
ZATOKA GDAŃSKA
J. Gardno
Wejherowo
Hel
Słupsk
Lębork
Kaszubskie
Gdynia
Russia
Pojezierze
Sopot
Gdańsk
Krynica Morska
MIERZEJA WIŚLANA
Braniewo
Kartuzy
Żukowo
Świbno
Martwa Wisła
Stegna
ZALEW WIŚLANY
Frombork
Bytów
Żuławy Wiślane
Elbląg
Orneta
Kościerzyna
Tczew
Pasłęk
Pauska
Starogard Gdański
Malbork
Zblewo
Pelplin
Pojezierze Iławskie
Olsztyn
Skórcz
Gniew
Kwidzyn
Ostróda
Bory
Człuchów
Chojnice
Tucholskie
Wisła
Iława
Tuchola
Pojezierze
Sępólno Krajeńskie
Grudziądz
Krajeńskie
Świecie
Chełmno
Nidzica
Stolno
Nakło n. Notecią
Chełmża
Brodnica
Noteć
Bydgoszcz
Toruń
Drwęca
Golub-Dobrzyń
Rypin
Puszcza
Pojezierze Dobrzyńskie
Wkra
Lubostroń
Bydgoska
Ciechocinek
Sierpc
Żnin
Inowrocław
Lipno
Strzelno
Włocławek
Płońsk
Płock
Gniezno
Gnieźnieńskie
Pojezierze
Wisła
Września
Krośniewice
N
0   50km
Warta
Koło
Kutno
Konin

344

In 1308 the Order occupied Gdańsk, in 1309 the surrounding region of Eastern Pomerania (also known as Pommerellen or Pomerelia), and in 1332 Kujawy. The Teutonic Order's 'Drang nach Osten' ('eastward drive') at first posed a great threat to Lithuania, but it was eventually halted by the Polish-Lithuanian victory at the Battle of Grunwald (Tannenberg) in 1410.

The Peace of Toruń in 1466 ended the Thirteen Years War and gave Poland Pomorze Gdańskie, Ziemia Chełmińska and part of the Prussian territories with Malbork (Marienburg) and Warmia (Ermeland), which from that time was known as Prusy Królewskie (Royal Prussia). The remaining part of the Teutonic State was placed under Polish feudal overlordship and eventually, in 1525, converted into the secular Duchy of Prussia (Ducal Prussia, or Prusy Książęce), with the last Grand Master, Albrecht von Hohenzollern-Ansbach, as its hereditary ruler. In 1657 the Duchy of Prussia freed itself from Polish suzerainty, and in 1701 Brandenburg and Prussia were joined to form the Kingdom of Prussia, which after the First and Second Partitions of Poland was also to include Royal Prussia and Gdańsk. Between 1815 and 1914 customs posts between Włocławek and Toruń marked the border between the regions under Russian and Prussian rule.

At the Versailles Conference the former Royal Prussia (which had been renamed West Prussia) passed to Poland, but without Elbląg and Gdańsk. This created the Polish Corridor separating East Prussia from the rest of the German Reich, a major factor in the increasing tension between Poland and Germany. For Poland the narrow strip of land was welcomed as the basis for the development of maritime trade through the new port of Gdynia. After the Second World War this region, which for hundreds of years had been shaped by Polish, German and Kashubian languages and cultures, and had witnessed many military confrontations, as well as much peaceful coexistence, was incorporated into the new Republic of Poland. The German population had to leave, and displaced Poles, particularly from the Wilno region, came to make their home here.

The most important conurbation for administration, culture and science is the Trójmiasto, the 'Triune City' of Gdańsk, Gdynia and Sopot. Other smaller, but important centres, of which the university and industrial city of Toruń is the most important, are situated along the Vistula.

Gdańsk

The 'Triune City' (Trójmiasto), consisting of the great Hanseatic city of Gdańsk, the port of Gdynia and the resort of Sopot, with a total population of about 700,000, extends along the Zatoka Gdańska (Bay of Gdańsk), which is bordered to the east by thickly wooded hills. The area around the Triune City, together with the Kashubian Hills (also called Szwajcaria Kaszubska, 'Kashubian Switzerland'), the Gdańsk Plain and the sand-bar on the coast, forms one of the most important holiday regions in Poland. There is indeed a Swiss beauty about the moraine hills, some 200 metres high, and the larger and smaller lakes surrounded by extensive forests.

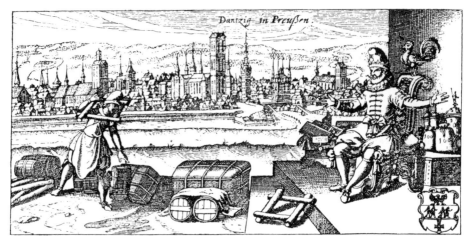

The Old Town of Gdańsk, engraving by R. J. Helmer, 1700

The Kashubian people, from whom the region takes its name, today number approximately 200,000. They now live only in a few villages near Gdańsk and Słupsk, and in some small enclaves between Lakes Łebsko and Gardno. As the descendants of the Pomorani, the Gdańsk Kashubians are the indigenous population group of Western Pomerania; they have preserved their distinctive Slavic dialect and vestiges of their fascinating folklore.

The first mention in the records of 'urbs Gyddanzc' is in the Life of St Wojciech (Adalbert) around 999. The Czech missionary bishop, who had been a pupil at the cathedral school of Magdeburg and was the confidant of the German Emperor Otto III, spent several days in Gdańsk, accompanied by two monks and soldiers of Bolesław I Chrobry, in the course of his missionary journey to the pagan Pruzzi in 997, and according to tradition he baptized a number of pagans here. The bishop martyr is venerated as a national saint at his shrine in Gniezno Cathedral (see p. 278f.).

Amber was discovered at the mouth of the Vistula as early as the Neolithic period, and the precious material found its way in the form of jewellery or implements into eastern, central and southern Europe. Because of its convenient location on the old Amber Road, Gdańsk had already developed by the year 1000 into a fortified trading and fishing settlement. In the first years of the 11th century the settlement had a population of around 2,000. It is assumed that the origins of the castle can be attributed to the activity of the first ruler of Poland, Mieszko I (ruled 960–92), in Western Pomerania and at the mouth of the Vistula.

In the 12th century Gdańsk was ruled by an independent ducal dynasty, under whose protection the town and port developed rapidly. The earliest known representative of this Gdańsk dynasty, Duke Subisław (end of the 12th century), was probably the founder of the monastery at Oliva; his son Sambor later took the title of *Princeps Pomoranorum*. In this period a merchant settlement grew up around a market place (now Pl. Dominikański). Duke Sambor probably founded the Church of St Nicholas in 1190.

Between 1220 and 1266 Gdańsk was ruled by Świętopełk (Swantopolk von Pommerellen), who granted the town its charter with German laws, founded a Dominican monastery and summoned German merchants to encourage maritime trade.

Świętopełk's son, Mściwój II, transferred Gdańsk and the whole of the duchy to Duke Przemysław II of Wielkopolska, who was crowned King of Poland in 1296. In 1308 the Teutonic Order gained possession of Gdańsk. The Knights soon converted the castle of the Dukes of Pommerellen into a residence for a Komtur (Commander) and began to enlarge the city. In 1312 the order granted special rights to the settlement of Osiek (Hakelwerk), to which fishermen and craftsmen had fled from the original town (now known as the Old Town). In 1343 the Prawe (later Główne) Miasto (Rechtstadt or Main Town), the central part of the historic town centre, was given its charter, and the following years saw a rapid development of this part of the city, which had its own town council and was surrounded by a wall. In an attempt to prevent the further expansion of the flourishing Rechtstadt the Teutonic Knights founded another town to the north of the Old Town. This was known as the Jungstadt (Young Town) and was granted municipal rights with the laws of Kulm. However, the new town was not destined to play an important part in Gdańsk's history, since in 1454 it was destroyed by the citizens of the Old Town, jealous of their privileges. Meanwhile another district, the Stare Przedmieście (Alte Vorstadt, Old Suburb), grew up to the south of the Rechtstadt. In 1440 Gdańsk became a member of the Prussian League, formed to counter Teutonic dominance. In 1454 the burghers of Gdańsk refused to obey the Teutonic Order and formed a federation with the aim of returning the region to Poland. A special privilege granted by King Kazimierz IV Jagiellończyk annexed the city and the whole of West Prussia to Poland. Over the following centuries it developed into one of the greatest ports in Europe, received privileges and donations, and grew to become a great independent commercial and cultural centre. In the 17th century Gdańsk was enlarged by the addition of another district, the Dolne Miasto (Niederstadt, Lower Town).

This was the heyday of Gdańsk as an artistic and cultural centre. The city was famous throughout Europe for its goldsmith work, as well as for furniture and clock-making. It was also a place of lively intellectual activity: the Gymnasium Academicum and the Collegium Medicum (founded in 1558) had a wide reputation. The patricians were great art collectors and created libraries. Printing houses and publishers were established. Many 16th-century scholars, such as the astronomer Johannes Hevelius (1611–87), and writers such as Martin Opitz and Jan Dantyszek (Johannes Dantiscus) were working in Gdańsk at that time, and in this cosmopolitan environment works were written in German and Polish as well as Latin. This cultural eminence continued in the following centuries: Gdańsk was the birthplace of Daniel Gabriel Fahrenheit (1686–1736), whose thermometry is still used in Anglo-Saxon countries, and of the great philosopher Arthur Schopenhauer (1788–1860).

In the Swedish Wars Gdańsk remained true to Poland, despite being Protestant. In 1734 it gave protection to the Polish elected king, Stanisław Leszczyński, and consequently suffered a long siege by the Russian and Saxon armies. After the Second Partition (1793), however, there was no resistance from the population when Gdańsk came under Prussian rule.

During the Napoleonic era Gdańsk was given the status of a free city and republic, but lost it after Napoleon's defeat. Until the end of the First World War, the maritime city, first under the rule of Prussia, then of the German Empire, experienced considerable economic development, particularly in the 'Gründerjahre' after 1870, which saw a rapid expansion of the shipyards and port.

The Treaty of Versailles of 28 July 1919 declared Gdańsk a Free City – the territory also included the famous resort of Sopot – under the control of the League of Nations. The rights of Poland were represented by the General Commissioner of the Republic of Poland in Gdańsk. Power in the city was exercised by a Senate, and the population was represented by the People's Council (Volksrat); one Danziger and one Polish representative sat on the Council of the Ports and Waterways. The rights of the city were clearly formulated; they included a common customs zone, independent representation abroad of Gdańsk interests, a military company of 182 men in the port district (with an ammunition store at Westerplatte – a strip of land to the northwest which Poland received on permanent lease). Difficulties arose, however, when it came to the exercise of these rights, since the German Reich and the German nationalist circles in Gdańsk constantly questioned the privileges granted to the Poles. When Hitler seized power in 1933 the National Socialists began to undermine the political order in the Free City.

Already in the 1920's the lack of suitable access to the sea had made it necessary for the

Gdańsk   1 Brama Wyżynna (Upland Gate)   2 Przedbramie (Outer Gate)   3 Złota Brama (Golden ▷ Gate)   4 Dwór Bractwa św. Jerzego (House of the Fraternity of St George)   5 Kamienica Uphagena (Uphagen House)   6 Dom Ferberów (Ferber House)   7 Lwi Zamek (Lion Castle)   8 Ratusz Głównego Miasta (Town Hall of the Main Town)   9 Fontanna Neptuna (Neptune Fountain)   10 Złota Kamienica (Golden House)   11 Dwór Artusa (Arthur Court)   12 Zielona Brama (Green Gate)   13 Brama Chlebnicka (Bakers' Gate)   14 Dom Angielski (English House)   15 Kościół Mariacki (St Mary's Church)   16 Kaplica Królewska (Royal Chapel)   17 Brama Mariacka (St Mary's Gate)   18 Dom Przyrodników (House of the Scientists)   19 Brama św. Ducha (Holy Ghost Gate)   20 Żuraw (Crane Gate)   21 Brama Świętojańska (St John's Gate)   22 Kościół św. Jana (Church of St John)   23 Kościół św. Mikołaja (Church of St Nicholas)   24 Baszta Jacek (Tower of St Hyacinth)   25 Baszta Na Podmurzu (Tower at the Wall)   26 Baszta Bramy Szerokiej (Tower of the Wide Gate)   27 Baszta Latarniana (Lantern Tower)   28 Wielka Zbrojownia (Great Arsenal)   29 Pomnik Jana III Sobieskiego (Jan III Sobieski Monument)   30 Dom Opatów Pelplińskich (House of the Abbots of Pelplin)   31 Szpital i Kościół św. Elżbiety (Hospital and Church of St Elizabeth)   32 Kościół św. Józefa (Church of St Joseph)   33 Ratusz Staromiejski (Town Hall of the Old Town)   34 Wielki Młyn (Great Mill)   35 Kościół św. Katarzyny (Church of St Catherine)   36 Kościół św. Brygidy (Church of St Bridget)   37 Poczta Polska (Polish Post Office)   38 Dwór Miejski (City Manor)   39 Baszta Narożna (Corner Tower)   40 Baszta Schultza (Schultz Tower)   41 Baszta Browarna (Brewery Tower)   42 Kościół św. Trójcy (Trinity Church)   43 Klasztor Franciszkanów (Franciscan Monastery)   44 Baszta Biała (White Tower)   45 Mała Zbrojownia (Little Arsenal)   46 Brama Nizinna (Lowland Gate)   47 Baszta Pod Zrębem (Loft Tower)   48 Kościół śś. Piotra i Pawła (Church of Sts Peter and Paul)   49 Dawne Gimnazjum (Town Grammar School)

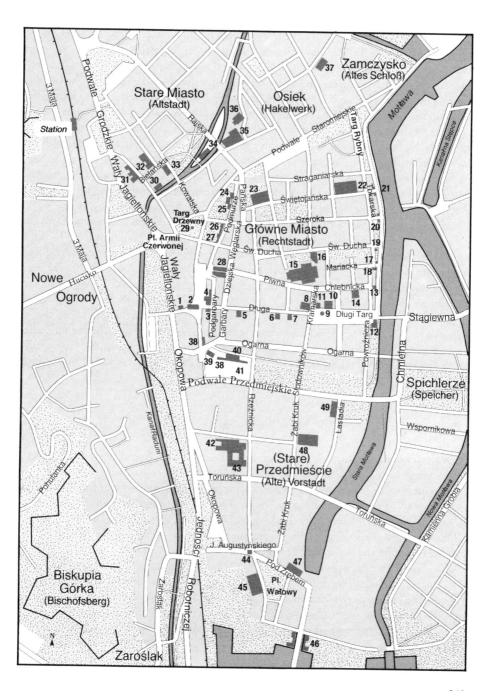

Poles to create their own port nearby. In 1924 work began on its construction at the village of Gdynia 20 km to the north of Gdańsk. Construction progressed rapidly; it was hoped that 2.5 million tonnes of goods would be passing through the port by 1930. The development of Gdynia was one of the greatest achievements of the young Polish state. The successful realization of the project owed much to two ministers between the wars, Władysław Grabski and Eugeniusz Kwiatkowski, and to the head of planning, Tadeusz Wenda.

The first shots of the Second World War were fired on 1 September 1939 by the battle cruiser 'Schleswig-Holstein' on the Polish ammunition depot at Westerplatte. Many Poles were killed in these first engagements, and many more were tortured in the Victoria School, or deported to the Stutthof concentration camp (at Sztutowo). The desperate defence of the city by German army units in 1945 and the unparalleled vengeance wrought by the Red Army on anything that looked German, left 90 per cent of historic Gdańsk in ruins.

Günter Grass has painted a memorable picture of the wartime city in his novel 'The Tin Drum' (1959), a film version of which was made by Volker Schlöndorff in 1978. Like central Warsaw, the historic centre of Gdańsk is now largely a reconstruction. The merchants' houses have not always been reproduced exactly as they were before the war, but the spirit of Gdańsk's old architecture has been carefully preserved. Today Gdańsk is the capital of a voivodship, and a cultural and scientific centre with five institutions of higher education (including a Technical University founded in 1904 and a University founded in 1970), many scientific institutions and societies, as well as archives, museums, three theatres, an opera house and a philharmonic orchestra. The St Dominic Fair, which dates back to the 13th century, is held for three weeks each August as part of the Gdańsk Days festival. In September there is a festival of Polish films.

Główne Miasto (Rechtstadt, Main Town)

As we have seen, the historic centre of Gdańsk consists of several towns which were autonomous in medieval times. The Główne Miasto, founded in 1343 and known as Rechtstadt because it had its own laws, contains historic Renaissance and Baroque buildings erected by prosperous patricians. They line most of the Royal Way running from the **Brama Wyżynna (Upland Gate)** (1) along ul. Długa (Langgasse) to the Town Hall of the Główne Miasto at the end of Długi Targ (Langer Markt) as far as the River Motława (Mottlau) and then on to the Werder Gate.

The massive Brama Wyżynna was built in 1574–76 by Johann Kramer and Willem van den Blocke following North Italian models. It was decorated in 1586–8, and altered in 1878–9. The lower storey of the building, with a large opening for vehicles and two smaller ones for pedestrians, is articulated with Tuscan pilasters. Above the entablature runs a tall frieze with two angels supporting the arms of the Polish Republic, a pair of lions supporting those of Gdańsk, and unicorns supporting those of Royal Prussia. Latin inscriptions praise justice, peace, liberty and unity as the qualities of a flourishing community.

The nearby ensemble of buildings at the **Przedbramie (Outer Gate)** (2) are a remnant of the old Gothic town fortifications. They consist of the Katownia (Torture Chamber) and, linked to it, the Wieża Więzienna (Stockturm, Prison Tower). The latter was built around 1410 to give additional protection to the Brama Długouliczna (Langgasser Tor), which stood where the Golden Gate now stands. In the early 16th century four storeys were added to the tower, and in the 1580's it was converted into the town prison.

At the beginning of the 17th century, when the medieval town fortifications seemed out of date, the Brama Długouliczna was replaced by a new building to mark the beginning of the Royal Way along ul. Długa and Długi Targ (pl. 33).

This new building, the **Złota Brama (Golden Gate)** (3) – so called because of its gilded sculptural decoration – was built in 1612–14 by Abraham van den Blocke in a Mannerist style. The two-storeyed building, articulated with columns, alludes to the structure of Roman triumphal arches. The inscriptions on the friezes of the lower storey invoke the prosperity of a community based on concord. In 1648–9 the gate was surmounted with allegorical figures which supplement the message of the inscriptions: Peace, Freedom, Wealth, Glory, Wisdom, Piety, Justice, as well as Concord herself (by Jeremias Falck and Peter Ringering). After severe damage in the war the restoration of the gate, with its decoration, was completed in 1967, but since the 1970's further measures have had to be taken, as with all the historic architecture of Gdańsk, to counter the new damage caused by industrial air pollution.

Next to the Golden Gate is the Late Gothic **Dwór Bractwa św. Jerzego (Georgshalle, House of the Fraternity of St George)** (4) built in 1487–94 by Hans Glotau. The Fraternity was a shooting club for patricians. It is a two-storey brick building with a rectangular ground plan. The shooting equipment and ammunition was kept in the hall on the ground floor, while the room upstairs was the setting for social functions. Today the house is used as the gallery of the Union of Polish Architects. Our route from here follows the Droga Królewska (Royal Way).

Ul. Długa has several interesting patrician houses with façades from the Mannerist and Baroque periods. One of the most beautiful is the **Kamienica Uphagena (Uphagen House)** (5), at No. 12. Its origins go back to the 14th century, but it was given its Late Baroque form by Johann Benjamin Dreyer in 1775–6. Its interior arrangement is typical of Danzig burghers' houses of this period: there is an office on the ground floor, and the grand hallway has a 'suspended room', a gallery-like mezzanine floor where business callers were received. In 1909 the heirs of the architect Johann Uphagen donated the house to the city, and it became a museum. In 1945 the building was completely destroyed, but the moveable furnishings had been taken to safety and it was possible to re-install the museum after the rebuilding.

A few yards further on is the **Dom Ferberów (Ferber House)** (6), at No. 28, which was remodelled in the Mannerist taste in 1560 with rich façade decoration. The attic bears the arms of Poland, Royal Prussia and Gdańsk.

No. 35, the **Lwi Zamek (Löwenschloss, Lion Castle)** (7) is an outstanding example of

Mannerist architecture. Built in 1569, probably after a design by Johann Kramer of Dresden, it is remarkable for its noble, regular proportions and the simple rhythm of its pilasters, which become more decorative with each storey. The rich decoration of the frieze and gable, in the style of Dutch Mannerism, are thought to be by Friderik Vroom of Haarlem. The interior arrangement of rooms has been retained; the hallway has a panelled ceiling, which once had four reliefs symbolizing Grammar, Arithmetic, Rhetoric and Geometry. The house has been rebuilt since 1945, but the reliefs are still missing.

At the entrance of ul. Długa into Długi Targ stands the **Ratusz Głównego Miasta (Town Hall of the Main Town)** (8). This imposing Gothic brick building (colour plate 24), was built over a period of more than 100 years, between 1379 and 1492, replacing a small half-timbered building of the mid-13th century. The names of its architects are known: the first, in the 14th century, was Heinrich Ungeradin, who was followed in the 15th century by Johann Kretschmer and Heinrich Hetzel. There were originally two storeys; the entrance in ul. Długa was marked by a tower, and the east front in ul. Kramarska had a splendid gable. In the cellars there was a prison, on the ground floor the town scales and the town chest, on the upper floor the council chamber and law court. The tower contained the council chapel and the archives.

In 1539–61 alterations were made after a fire, and the opportunity was taken to transform the town hall into a grandiose building in the Dutch style, worthy of the town's status. Another storey was added; the east front was given tall pointed blind arcading

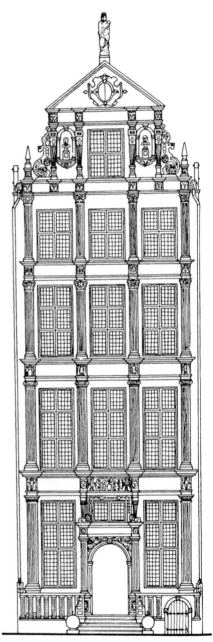

Elevation of the Lwi Zamek

and an attic bearing the arms of Poland, Prussia and Gdańsk. At the southeast corner Anton Glaser added a sundial in 1588–9, which can still be seen today. The tower too was altered, and a gilded statue of King Zygmunt II August was set on top of it.

Further changes were made in the years around 1600. The interiors were given splendid furnishings, which survived until the Second World War, and which since then have been partially reconstructed. The double stairway in front of the entrance and the Baroque doorway guarded by two stone lions with the arms of the town, were added in 1766–8 by the sculptor Daniel Eggert.

In the Second World War the town hall suffered heavy damage. Restoration began as early as 1946, and work continued on the interior until 1970. Today the town hall houses the *Muzeum Historii Miasta Gdańska (Historical Museum of the City of Gdańsk)*. It includes the reconstructed interiors of the town hall from the alterations around 1600 and a collection of Gdańsk art.

We go up the grand entrance stairs, past the Gothic mural paintings of the former Kaplica 'Mały Krzysztof' ('Little Christopher' Chapel) – the room where the archives were kept was called the 'Great Christopher' after a statue of the saint – and first enter a large hallway on the first floor decorated with Delft tiles and luxuriant woodcarving around the door frames and on the spiral staircase to the second floor. The ceiling used to have an allegorical painting showing the figure of Concord surrounded by the arms of the leading patrician families; it now has a picture of the entry of the King of Poland into the city.

The most splendid room is the *Sala Czerwona (Red Hall)*, the Great Council Chamber. Above the benches for the councillors the walls are covered with the red damask from which the room takes its name.

The ceiling has a complicated pattern of panels of various sizes with lavishly carved and gilded frames. The paintings set into it show biblical and classical scenes representing examples of private and public virtues, accompanied by appropriate emblems. The programme continues in the broad frieze running round the wall below the ceiling. Here too are large history paintings representing virtues and explained by Latin inscriptions; personifications of the virtues appear between them.

This complex iconographic programme, presumably devised by one of the city's many humanist scholars, was executed by the greatest artists of the day then working in the city: the overall arrangement of the decoration and the carvings on the ceiling were the work of Anthonis van Opbergen from the Netherlands; the paintings are by Hans Vredemann de Vries and Isaac van den Blocke, the coloured intarsia work in the frieze by Simon Hoerle, and the monumental stove, decorated with the town's coat of arms, by the sculptor Willem van der Meer. The impressive ensemble is the most prominent example of the great contribution which Dutch artists made to Danzig Mannerism.

Besides the Red Hall other rooms of interest are the *Mała Sala Rady (Small Council Chamber)* and the *Council Archive*, both of which have retained at least some of their old furnishings, supplemented by works of modern artists (Józefa Wnukowa, Hanna and Jacek Żuławski). Also impressive is the reconstructed *Kamlarnia (Treasury)*.

Next door is the Late Gothic **Dwór Artusa (Artushof, Arthur Court)** (11), which stands on Długi Targ. It was built by the town in 1476–81, after the first court was burned down around 1350. The façade was modernized in a Mannerist style in 1616–17 by Abraham van den Blocke, and it too was given an allegorical programme. Two roundels flanking the door contain busts of King Zygmunt III Waza and his son Władysław IV. The

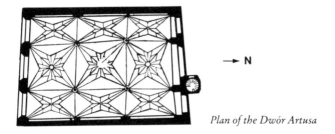

→ N

Plan of the Dwór Artusa

four statues on consoles in the upper part of the façade represent heroes of antiquity, Scipio Africanus, Themistocles, Camillus and Judas Maccabaeus, as embodiments of virtues which contribute to the wellbeing of the community. In the niches of the attic and on the roof-ridge stand allegories of the virtues. The Dwór Artusa was a gathering place for the patricians of Danzig, where ceremonies, business and day-to-day meetings all took place. Behind the great windows, therefore the interior consists of a single hall, which was gradually – especially between 1531 and 1626 – decorated by leading artists, Anton Moeller, Hans Vredemann de Vries, Martin Schoninck and Georg Stelzener. The star vaulting is supported by four slender granite columns, probably taken from the Teutonic castle in Gdańsk. Today the Dwór Artusa is preserved as a historical monument and is part of the Historical Museum of the City of Gdańsk. More than 70 per cent of its valuable furnishings were saved during the war. Many of the paintings are now in the Gdańsk National Museum. The hall is the setting for a strange story ('The Artushof') by E. T. A. Hoffmann.

The **Fontanna Neptuna (Neptune Fountain)** (9) erected around 1633 in front of the Dwór Artusa celebrates Gdańsk's greatness as a maritime trading power (plate 34). The design was by Abraham van den Blocke and the bronze statue of the sea god was modelled by Peter Husen and cast in Gdańsk by Gert Bonning.

Długi Targ (Lange Markt, Long Market), which begins at this point, was not only the market place, but also the scene for festivities of all kinds. Among its Renaissance and Baroque houses the **Złota Kamienica (Golden House)** (10), at No. 41, is particularly striking. It was built in 1609–18 by Abraham van den Blocke and Johann Voigt for the burgomaster Johann Speimann; during Prussian rule the family of Steffens lived here, and the house is sometimes called after them. It is known as the Złota Kamienica because of the gilding which covers the façade. The articulation and decoration show the influence of Netherlandish Mannerism: contemporary houses in Antwerp are very similar in composition. The wall surface has a framework of columns and windows extending over all four storeys. Sculptured allegories flow over all the architectural members. Above the doorway stands the figure of Caritas (Charity), accompanied by Spes (Hope) and Fides (Faith) in the spandrels. The three theological virtues are joined on the attic by their cardinal counterparts: Prudence, Temperance, Fortitude and Justice. In the friezes are historical scenes with explanatory inscriptions.

The beautiful ensemble of gabled houses in Długi Targ is one of the finest achievements of postwar architectural restoration in Poland.

At the east end of the square, spanning the gap between the burghers' houses, stands the **Zielona Brama (Green Gate)** (12) which leads directly to the bank of the Motława. It was built in 1564–8 by the architects Johann Kramer and Regnier of Amsterdam. The great hall on the first floor was originally intended as accommodation for the kings when they visited Gdańsk. Instead it was used for a time as an arsenal, but also for public ceremonies and theatrical performances. In the Second World War the Green Gate was completely destroyed, and since its reconstruction in 1949–51 it has been used by the city's office of architectural conservation.

The Neptune Fountain, drawing by I. Bentchev, 1987

Following the bank of the Motława northwards we come to the Late Gothic **Brama Chlebnicka (Bakers' Gate)** (13), the oldest watergate in Gdańsk (1454). In ul. Chlebnicka the **Dom Angielski (English House)** (14), at No. 16, is worth a close look. It was built around 1570 for Dirck Lylge, a Westphalian merchant who had arrived in the city shortly before, and the architect was Johann Kramer. The façade, severely articulated with columns and overspread with rich relief decoration, is characteristic of the grand burgher's houses of northern Mannerism. The name – which may in fact be Dom Anielski (Angel House) – seems to be that of the inn established in the house in the 19th century; there is no connection with the English merchants who were prominent in Gdańsk's commercial life. No. 14, one of the grandest of the city's Late Gothic burghers' houses (*c.*1520), was taken down and its façade carried off to Potsdam, where it was re-erected in 1824 in the unlikely Romantic landscape setting of Peacock Island; it can still be seen there today.

A little further on rises the majestic **Kościół Mariacki (Marienkirche, St Mary's Church)** (15), 105 metres in length and over 140,000 cubic metres in volume, the third largest church in the world (plate 36). Built in stages between 1343 and 1502 as a hall church with chapels between the exterior buttresses, a three-aisled choir and a monumental west tower, the great Gothic building dominates the whole of the Main Town. It has room for 25,000 people. It was badly damaged in the war, and rebuilt in 1947–55, an impressive feat of engineering in view of the collapse of many vaults.

Although the exterior is severe and plain, indeed almost fortress-like, the interior with its fine star vaults is luminous and impressive. The church used to be famous for its rich furnishings and decorations; but many were destroyed in the Second World War, and several were taken to the National Museum in Warsaw (see page 215). Fortunately, some of the most important pieces have returned to the church. There are numerous sculpted and painted epitaphs, especially from the 16th and 17th centuries. In the Chapel of St Reinhold next to the porch, on the ground floor of the tower, is a copy of Memling's *Last Judgement* (see page 364). St Anne's chapel, third in the north aisle, contains Gdańsk's most famous Gothic sculpture, the life-size 'Beautiful Madonna' made around 1410, probably in the city itself. The magnificent tomb of Simon and Judith Bahr at the end of the north transept was made by Abraham van den Blocke in 1620. Nearby, the 15th-century St Dorothy Altarpiece incorporates English alabaster sculpture. The Late Gothic winged altarpiece in the Holy Cross Chapel was imported from Antwerp in 1510. On the north-west crossing piers hangs an unusual painting of 1480/85 illustrating the Ten Commandments with figures in contemporary dress. Other important furnishings include the famous astronomical clock made by Hans Düring in 1464-70, the organ of 1629 and the bronze font at the west end of the nave.

The decoration of the choir gives the most vivid impression of the original appearance of the interior. High on a cross beam in the choir arch stands a crucifixion group by Master

Plan of St Mary's Church

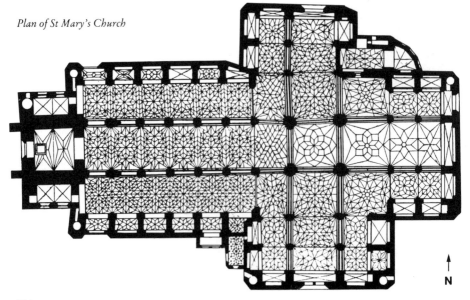

N

The Żuraw (Crane Gate), the symbol of Gdańsk, engraving, 1735

Paul, set up here in 1517. Of the same period (1511–17) is the high altar with a relief carving of the Coronation of the Virgin in the main panel and paintings on the wings. It is the work of Master Michael, who was probably from Augsburg. In the Chapel of the Eleven Thousand Virgins, on the right of the choir, stands a Crucifixion group made in Gdańsk around 1430, which is one of the most extraordinary works of that era. Its penetrating naturalism bursts the bounds of the idealizing Schöner Stil (Beautiful Style or International Gothic). The first chapel (from the transept) in the south aisle commemorates the 2,779 Polish priests who were murdered during the Second World War. There is a memorial plaque and a modern sculpture of the Man of Sorrows recalling this sacrifice, and inviting prayer.

Adjoining the Mariacki on its northeastern side is the **Kaplica Królewska (Royal Chapel)** (16), an isolated example of High Baroque in Gdańsk. It is a domed, centrally planned building with a grand façade, built in 1678–81 and founded by King Jan III Sobieski to encourage Catholics in the free practice of their religion, since St Mary's was used by the Lutherans (and remained a Lutheran Church until 1945). The architect was Tylman van Gameren, the master mason Bartolomäus Ranisch, and the sculptural decoration is by Andreas Schlüter.

357

In ul. Mariacka (Frauengasse), which leads from here to the Motława, the houses still have a characteristic feature of old Gdańsk, 'Beischläge' (or in Polish, *przedproża*), the platforms raised on flights of steps in front of the houses. At the east end of ul. Mariacka stands the Late Gothic **Brama Mariacka (Frauentor, St Mary's Gate)** (17), which was built in the second half of the 15th century and preserves fine armorial decoration from that period (on the exterior the arms of Poland, Royal Prussia and Gdańsk).

To the right of this is the **Dom Przyrodników (House of the Scientists)** (18), No. 26, which takes its name from a scientific society founded there in 1743 and now contains the Muzeum Archeologiczne (Archaeological Museum). It is one of the tallest Renaissance houses in the city, and was built in 1598 possibly by Anthonis van Opbergen, who was then the town architect. The Museum is a centre of research into early cultures in the region of Eastern Pomerania.

Further north we first pass the ruins of the **Brama św. Ducha (Holy Ghost Gate)** (19) dating from the second half of the 15th century, before reaching the **Żuraw (Krantor, Crane Gate)** (20), one of the city's most important landmarks (frontispiece and plate 35). The undecorated gatehouse, flanked on either side by a massive semicircular tower, was built at the beginning of the 1440's. Soon afterwards the new wooden crane, the biggest goods lift of the 15th century, was erected. The Żuraw was completely destroyed by fire in 1945. Since its reconstruction (1959–62) it has housed the Centralne Muzeum Morskie (Central Maritime Museum).

Running the length of the embankment, Długie Pobrzeże, is the old harbour of Gdańsk, now used for passenger traffic (colour plates 22, 23).

From here we return to the town centre; past the ruins of the **Brama Świętojańska (St John's Gate)** (21), we reach the **Kościół św. Jana (Church of St John)** (22). This Gothic brick hall church (*c.*1371–1415) was extended in the mid-15th century, given a tower and vaulting. It is now used as a lapidarium for sculpture saved from old Gdańsk. Restoration work is still continuing.

Further west, in ul. Świętojańska, near the old limits of the Main Town, stands the **Kościół św. Mikołaja (Church of St Nicholas)** (23), the only inner-city church to have come through the Second World War without serious damage.

Its history goes back to the 12th century; the little wooden church which stood here then was given in 1227 by Duke Świętopełk to the Dominicans, who had been brought from Kraków. In the second half of the 14th century they began the construction of the present church, which continued until the end of the 15th century. At the same time extensive conventual buildings were erected on the site of the present-day Pl. Dominikański. In 1813, during the Napoleonic Wars, the complex was burnt down, and the ruins were razed in 1839–40. After an interval of nearly a hundred years, during which St Nicholas's was a parish church, the Dominicans returned after the war. For their friary they use the parish house built in the 19th century in front of the west façade of the church.

The three-aisled hall church with its long choir is a brick building largely without decoration. The richest articulation is found on the southeast section, approached by ul.

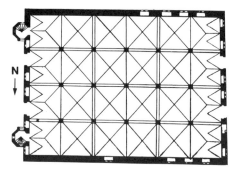

Plan of the Wielka Zbrojownia (Great Arsenal)

Świętojańska. From here the choir forms a striking ensemble with its steep gables decorated with blind arcading and a large pointed window, the octagonal tower and the low battlemented sacristy extension. The west façade, articulated only by its buttresses, is decorated by the three staggered false gables in front of the roofs of the nave and aisles.

The interior, plain except for its star vaults resting on octagonal piers, contains a rich collection of furnishings dating from the 15th to the 18th centuries. Particularly worthy of attention are the monumental retable of the high altar (1647) and the choir stalls of the mid-16th century, which have Baroque panelling with New Testament scenes. The rood, larger than life-size, was made in 1520–25 in the workshop of Master Paul, who a little earlier had made the similar Crucifixion group at St Mary's. On the left in the first bay of the nave is a Gothic Pietà (*c.*1430), characteristic of the period that followed the Schöner Stil. A walk round St Nicholas's with its wealth of monuments gives an excellent survey of the history of art in Gdańsk.

The Dominican church is attached to the 14th-century town fortifications, of which there are remains on the west side. These include the polygonal **Baszta Jacek (Tower of St Jacek)** (24), once known as 'Kiek in de Köken', which is reached along ul. Pańska. It was built in the late 14th century to serve both as a defensive tower and a watchtower. At its foot the annual Dominic Fair is held, named after the nearby monastery.

Continuing southwards we pass fragments of the town walls along ul. Podmurze and ul. Latarniana, with three more Gothic towers: **Baszta Na Podmurzu (Tower at the Wall)** (25), **Baszta Bramy Szerokiej (Tower of the Wide Gate)** (no longer standing) (26), and **Baszta Laterniana (Lantern Tower)** (27).

At the next corner (ul. Teatralna and Targ Węglowy) we find the **Wielka Zbrojownia (Great Arsenal)** (28), a long brick Mannerist building, erected in 1602–9 by Anthonis van Opbergen (plate 37). The façade has four curved gables richly adorned with strapwork; statues of soldiers and trophies indicate the building's original function, but today the upper floor is used by the college of art, and a shopping arcade occupies the ground floor.

Stare Miasto (Altstadt, Old Town)

To the north of the Main Town, beyond the town walls and a strip of land which marks the course of the moat that was once here, lies the Stare Miasto (Old Town), which was given its charter in 1375.

Our visit begins at Targ Drzewny (Holzmarkt) with the **Pomnik Jana III Sobieskiego**

(Jan III Sobieski Monument) (29) which was brought here from Lwów after 1945. Ul. Elżbietańska 3, by the Kanał Raduni (Radunia Canal), is the Dom Opatów Pelplińskich (House of the Abbots of Pelplin) (30), one of the finest Mannerist burghers' houses in Gdańsk. It was probably built as a private commission by Abraham van den Blocke in 1612, and was bought in 1648 by the wojewoda, Władysław Łoś, who donated it to the Cistercians of Pelplin.

A little further on are the Szpital and Kościół św. Elżbiety (Hospital and Church of St Elizabeth) (31), which probably go back to a private foundation in the second half of the 14th century. The small aisleless church was built around 1400. The present appearance of the hospital buildings is the result of rebuilding in 1752–3, after they had been completely destroyed by fire. The doorway was made by Krzysztof Strzycki.

The neighbouring Kościół św. Józefa (Church of St Joseph) (32) was begun in 1467 as the monastic church of the Carmelites. Because of lack of funds as well as the religious unrest in the 16th century the church and monastery remained unfinished. Precisely because of this incompleteness the fragmentary church reveals much about building methods in the middle ages. When work stopped the choir had been completed and the foundations of the nave laid. At the end of the 16th century the friars finally gave up hope of completing the work and closed off the west end of the choir with a gable, and around 1620 a lower, makeshift interior was set up, so that the choir was available for worship before the rest of the church was ready in 1623. After the disturbances in the 17th and 18th centuries, including an occasion in 1678 when the monastery was looted by a mob while the friars were on a pilgrimage procession to Oliwa, the conventual buildings were rebuilt. In the Second World War the whole complex was completely destroyed except for the outer walls. Reconstruction lasted from 1947 until the 1970's; the furnishings are modern.

Diagonally opposite St Joseph's, at the corner of ul. Bielańska and ul. Korzenna, stands the Ratusz Staromiejski (Town Hall of the Old Town) (33). This elegant square building was erected in 1587–95 by the Flemish architect Anthonis van Opbergen. The exterior is articulated only by the large windows and a string course; the walls were originally plastered in dark red. Above the attic with its row of blind arches and four slender corner pinnacles, there are two parallel hipped roofs. Only the main façade on ul. Korzenna is treated with any lavishness. The portal and string course have sculptural decoration, a dormer window with three allegorical statues gives emphasis to the middle axis (the sculptures are probably by Willem van der Meer), and a bell-tower rises above the roof-ridge.

After the abolition of the Old Town Council in 1793 (after the Second Partition) the building was adapted for other uses. In 1914 some of the fittings from a number of burghers' houses were collected here, where they still remain, forming a sort of museum of interiors within the Wojewódzki Ośrodek Kultury (Voivodship Cultural Centre).

At its southern end ul. Korzenna reaches the Kanał Raduni (Radunia Canal), built in the second quarter of the 14th century for the Teutonic Order. It was the source of energy for the many workshops which were established on its banks. The only survival of this

Targ Drzewny (The Wood Market), from an old postcard

industrial quarter of medieval Gdańsk is the **Wielki Młyn (Great Mill)** (34) of the mid-14th century, the largest building of its kind in Europe. It stands on an island between the two branches of the canal, the water of which drove 18 giant millwheels each with a diameter of 6 metres. A little later a bakery was set up in the mill; its chimney can be seen on the east gabled front. Until its destruction in 1945 the mill remained in uninterrupted operation. In 1880 the millwheels were replaced by water turbines, but apart from some conservation work the building itself remained unaltered. It was reconstructed in 1962–7.

Close by stands the great **Kościół św. Katarzyny (Church of St Catherine)** (35), the oldest parish church in the city. The original building was erected in the mid-13th century and was certainly ready by 1266, when the body of Duke Świętopełk lay in state here. In the second half of the 14th century the citizens of the recently founded town commissioned a new building, the three-aisled hall church which is still there today. A century later the bell-tower was added; it was given its Baroque helm in 1634. The tower was famous for its clock and carillon installed in 1738. The unusually low interior, which received its net-vaulting around 1500, has fragments of the original 15th-century painted decoration (in the eastern parts of the side-aisles). Over the centuries the church acquired a rich collection of furnishings, but few of these survived wartime destruction. The 16th-century carved winged altarpiece in the nave, with the Coronation of the Virgin, is of interest, as is the partly reconstructed high altar with a 17th-century painting by Anton

361

Moeller, depicting the Crucifixion in front of a panorama of the city of Gdańsk. The church contains the graves of several members of the Hoewelke family (latinized to Hevelius); in the choir is the tomb of the famous astronomer Johannes Hevelius (1611–87), the father of lunar topography. His monument was set up in the 18th century by a descendant.

The rebuilding of this venerable church was begun in 1953 and is now almost complete. The present carillon was installed thanks to the efforts of a former citizen of Danzig who founded an association to collect money from West German politicians and others, to have 37 new bells cast as replacements for the set that had been taken down during the war and destroyed.

Just behind St Catherine's is another Gothic church, the **Kościół św. Brygidy (Church of St Bridget)** (36), formerly a monastic church, which became famous in the 1980's as a centre of the Solidarity movement. This was the church that Lech Wałęsa attended.

From here the way takes us – via ul. Brygidki, Mniszki, Refektarska, Browarna, Osiek and Sieroca – to a monument of Gdańsk's tragic 20th-century history, the **Poczta Polska (Polish Post Office)** (37), where one of the first battles of the Second World War broke out. On 1 September 1939, while the battlecruiser 'Schleswig-Holstein' bombarded Westerplatte, SS units attacked the post office. Almost half the fifty post office staff who defended the building met their deaths here. The event, graphically portrayed by Günter Grass in *The Tin Drum*, is commemorated by monuments to the fallen (1957, by Maria and Zygfryd Korplalski) and a memorial by Wincenty Kućma and Krystyna Hejde-Kućma. There is also a memorial inside the building.

Panorama of the Old Town of Gdańsk, engraving, 1573

Stare Przedmieście (Alte Vorstadt, Old Suburb)

The Stare Przedmieście or Old Suburb to the south of the Main Town developed from the second half of the 14th century to become a separately organized entity. From the beginning there were many craftsmen's workshops, especially shipyards, established here in the present-day ul. Lastadia, whose wall is as old as the district itself. In the second half of the 15th century the Stare Przedmieście was given its own defensive walls, of which only fragments can be seen today.

The starting point for our tour is the southeast corner of the Main Town, where more remnants of its fortifications have survived, as well as the **Dwór Miejski (Stadthof, City Manor)** (38) at the corner of ul. Wojciecha Bogusława and ul. Ogarna. This complex consists of two long buildings erected in 1616–19 by the municipal architect Jan Strakowski along the town walls. The south building incorporated three defensive towers: the **Baszta Narożna (Corner Tower)** (39), the **Baszta Schultza (Schultz Tower)** (40), named after the 19th-century engraver Johann Karl Schultz, who loved the old architecture of Gdańsk, and the **Baszta Browarna (Brewery Tower)** (41). Originally the City Manor housed commercial institutions and the city mint. In the course of the 17th century a timber theatre was added. The synagogue established here in 1885–7 was destroyed in 1939. Today the much-altered south wing is the headquarters of the Gdańsk Scout Association.

Two blocks to the south stands the **Kościół św. Trójcy (Holy Trinity Church)** (42) with the former **Klasztor Franciszkanów (Franciscan Monastery)** (43). In 1422 the friars began to build a modest, aisleless church. At the end of the 15th century work was resumed after a long interruption, and work also continued on the building of the monastery. In the meantime the church had become too small, and so was extended into a three-aisled hall church with beautiful net vaults. Not long afterwards, in 1555, the monastery was closed down in the Reformation; the church became Lutheran (and remained so until 1945), while the monastic buildings became the property of the town and were used by the Gymnasium Academicum, Danzig's famous school. During the Napoleonic Wars the monastic complex became a military hospital and storehouse, and it was not until 1821 that the church was used for worship again.

The exterior of the church is typical of the local brick Gothic tradition with plain walls pierced by great pointed windows. The gables on the choir and entrance façades are masterpieces of this style. The interior has largely retained its lavish furnishings. The fine Late Gothic stalls (1507–11), which were in the presbytery, have now been moved into the body of the church. The brilliantly decorated high altar erected in 1632, with paintings of the Last Supper and the Ascension, probably the work of Isaac van den Blocke, was destroyed in the war. The church contains the only Gothic pulpit in Gdańsk, which, like the font, dates from the 16th century. Of particular interest amongst the rich furnishings however, are two altarpieces dated 1515 from the same Augsburg workshop: the Collect Altar, a Late Gothic winged altarpiece, with figures of saints beneath ornamental arches, and the St Francis Altar, with a carved centre panel and painted wings, repeating the same motifs in richer form. The Late Baroque pew of the Frantzius family (1781) stands in the north aisle: a magnificent wooden structure articulated with pilasters and surmounted by the majestic figure of Chronos, the god of time, who in this religious context is a reminder of the transience of earthly life. The walls have relief panels with representations of the lament for the dead, the general resurrection of the dead, and the blessed in Paradise.

In 1872 the *Muzeum Narodowe (National Museum)* was established in the old monastic buildings. It has good collections of Gothic painting and sculpture, part of the outstanding collection of European and Oriental textiles from St Mary's, as well as a gallery of Polish and French paintings and drawings. The most prominent painting in the Netherlandish section is an early masterpiece by Hans Memling, his *Last Judgement*. Painted in Bruges in 1467–73 for Angelo Tani, the Medici representative there, it was intended for a church in Florence. However, it never reached its destination, since the ship carrying the painting to London was captured by a cruiser from Gdańsk (the Hanseatic League was then at war with England). The captain presented the painting to the city and it was hung in St Mary's Church. It was removed to Paris by Napoleon in 1807 and to Berlin by the Prussians in 1815–17. As the bombing of Gdańsk intensified towards the end of the Second World War, it was taken to the safety of a mine in Saxony, but after a brief stay in Leningrad it returned to Gdańsk in 1956.

South of the museum, at the end of ul. Rzeźnicka we come across the **Baszta Biała (White Tower)** (44), one of the few surviving towers of the medieval fortifications, which were destroyed as early as the 16th and 17th centuries, when a new, wider ring of defences was built. The White Tower was erected in 1460–61 to protect a town gate which stood here at that time. In the 17th century it was adapted for the storage of gunpowder, and at the same time Pl. Wałowy (Wallplatz) was laid out as an exercise ground and on its western side the **Mała Zbrojownia (Little Arsenal)** (45) was built (1643–5, Jan Strakowski). The tower was restored in 1983–4, when it was made the headquarters of a mountaineering club, while the Little Arsenal, after alterations in the 19th century and rebuilding in 1957–60, now houses the Gdańsk taxi headquarters.

Adjoining this to the south is the site of the new ring of fortifications, surrounded by a moat specially formed from a branch of the Motława (Dopływ Motławy). The architect Cornelis van der Bosch based his designs on Italian Renaissance fortifications, which in this period were being imitated all over Europe. Here also one of the town gates has survived, the **Brama Nizinna (Lowland Gate)** (46). Built by Jan Strakowski in 1626, it is a triumphal arch of unusual design: the building is flanked by high embankments, which make the passages seem like tunnels. On the top of the gate is a little sentry post.

Returning to the centre of the Stare Przedmieście we pass at the corner of ul. Pod Zrębem and ul. Żabi Kruk, where the **Baszta Pod Zrębem (Loft Tower)** (47), another remnant of the medieval walls, collapsed in 1982.

Further north stands the **Kościół śś. Piotra i Pawła (Church of Sts Peter and Paul)** (48). There was already a church here in 1400, but it was destroyed by fire in 1424. The present building, a three-aisled hall church with a massive west tower, was built between 1425 and 1514. The exterior has a gable with blind arcading, exterior buttresses and moulded window reveals. The interior has suffered serious damage many times in its history. In the second half of the 16th century, when the church belonged to the Calvinist community, all the furnishings were removed. The church was damaged twice during the wars between 1734 and 1807, and a third time in the Second World War. Rebuilding did not start until 1975, and is still continuing. Only the south aisle is in use as a provisional parish church.

Ul. Lastadia takes us from here to the Targ Maślany (Butter Market), the west side of which is occupied by the brick building of the former **Gimnazjum (Town Grammar School)** (49), built by Karl Friedrich Schinkel in 1834–7. At the request of his friend and patron the Prussian Crown Prince Friedrich Wilhelm, it was designed not in the Neo-classical Greek style as originally intended, but in the 'deutscher Stil', i.e. brick Gothic.

We can now return to Długi Targ along ul. Kotwiczników (Anchor-smiths' Street) and ul. Powroźnicka (Rope Street), passing the Smiths' tower, the *Baszta Kotwiczników* which dates from the 14th century, and was converted into a prison in the 16th century. Since its rebuilding (1968–9) the tower has been used by the offices of the Department of Architectural Conservation.

The Port

Since the 19th century the port of Gdańsk has occupied the area along the Martwa Wisła (Dead Vistula). The regular tours by boat (departures from Zielona Brama) also pass the world-famous **Gdańsk Shipyards**. Gdańsk has been a shipbuilding city since the 14th century, but it was in the 19th century that the shipyards underwent a great expansion to serve the maritime and naval needs of Prussia. During the later period of the inter-war Free City, much of the shipbuilding activity here was concerned with illegally equipping the German navy.

It was at the Gdańsk Shipyards, renamed the Lenin Shipyards after the war, and at Szczecin and Gdynia, that unrest over price rises broke out in December 1970. This was followed by the bloody deployment of the militia against the workers' demonstrations, and the crisis brought about the downfall of the Gomułka regime.

Ten years later, in August 1980 strikes broke out again at the yards over the legalization of the independent trade union, Solidarity, led by the electrician Lech Wałęsa, later to become the Nobel Peace Prize winner in 1983 and the first democratically elected postwar President of Poland in 1990. After a two-week occupation of the shipyards, the founding of a strike committee and finally a crippling wave of strikes across the whole country, during which the shipyard workers refused to be bribed into splitting off from the rest of the country, the Gdańsk Agreement was reached between Solidarity and the Polish government. After this agreement, and on the initiative of Solidarity, a monument was erected at the shipyard to those who had died in 1970. Steel plates from the shipyard were used in its construction to form three giant crosses with anchors. Below is inscribed a poem by Czesław Miłosz: 'Który skrzywdziłeś' ('You who wronged a simple man ...').

In the 1980 agreement most of the strikers' demands were met, including the legalization of the union. Gdańsk remained closely linked with Solidarity, even after its suspension in December 1981, and above all with its president Lech Wałęsa (who carried on working as an electrician at the shipyards until 1 May 1989).

Monument at the Gdańsk shipyards commemorating those who died in the shipbuilders' uprising of 1970

In May 1988 the Lenin Shipyards were threatened with closure because of unprofitability. Several thousand workers with Lech Wałęsa in their midst, went on strike for a week demanding that Solidarity be legalized again. This time the subsequent wave of unrest was to lead to the collapse of the whole Communist system.

Wisłoujście – Westerplatte – Wrzeszcz – Oliwa

A few hundred yards from the mouth of the Dead Vistula, on the Bay of Gdańsk stands **Wisłoujście (Weichselmünde)**, a fortress built in the 14th century to protect the city from sea-borne attack. In 1482 a defensive and lookout tower was built, which also served as a lighthouse. Around 1600 Anthonis van Opbergen remodelled the inside of the fortress in the form we see today. The east rampart of five Dutch bastions was built in 1624–6 under the direction of Peter Janssen de Weert and was later extended.

Westerplatte, a peninsula projecting into the bay at the mouth of the Dead Vistula, is where the Second World War broke out at 4.45 a.m. on 1 September 1939, when the battle-cruiser 'Schleswig-Holstein' opened fire on the Polish garrison of 210 men here. The body of the garrison commander, Henryk Sucharski, was brought here from Italy in 1971 and buried on the site of the battle, and the event is commemorated by the *Monument to the Heroes of Westerplatte* by Franciszek Duszeńko, and by the surviving Guardroom No. 1.

On the way from Gdańsk to Oliwa and on to Sopot and Gdynia (Gdańsk's sister towns), we pass through the district of **Wrzeszcz (Langfuhr)**, the largest and most modern part of the Triune City, where most of its business and cultural life is now concentrated. The University of Gdańsk, the Medical School and Polytechnic are located here, as well as the Opera and Philharmonia Hall.

Following the Al. Grunwaldzka northwest from Wrzeszcz, we reach the district of **Oliwa (Oliva)**, whose history goes back to 1186, when Duke Sambor established a Cistercian monastery here with monks from Kołbacz Abbey. In the middle of all the modern building a few islands of old Oliwa have survived. The romantically sited abbey in Park Oliwski is famous. The monks built a small oratory here in about 1200. This was

Oliwa, west front of the cathedral, photograph taken in 1920

soon destroyed by the warlike Pruzzi, but was rebuilt in the course of the 13th century, when the transept and nave were added. Since 1925 the church has been a *Cathedral* (originally for the territory of the inter-war Free City of Danzig). After a fire in 1350 the church was enlarged, and at the same time an extensive monastic complex was built. In the following centuries the building preserved the appearance of a monumental Romanesque-Gothic church; the only major alteration was the remodelling of the west front in the Baroque manner in 1688.

Since the cloister cuts into the south aisle, the interior has an asymmetric nave, with a transept and ambulatory choir. It is dominated by splendid Late Gothic star vaults inserted in the late 16th century following a fire in 1577, which also destroyed all the medieval furnishings. The present furnishings date from the 17th and 18th centuries and show all stages in the development of Baroque, from the last stages of Mannerism to the Rococo. The famous organ above the entrance porch, with its moving whirligigs and trumpeting angels, is used for recitals in the summer. It was built in 1763–88 by two monks of the abbey. The beautiful illusionistic effect of the high altar, erected in 1688, is best appreciated from here. A whirl of clouds with angels singing the Virgin's praises bursts theatrically from above the columns around the apse. Along the sides of the choir a gallery was built in the late 16th century for the Dukes of Pomerelia and the Kings of Poland, who supported the monastery with donations or privileges. The Gothic monastic buildings can be visited on request including the Refectory with frescoes of the life of St Bernard.

The south wing of the former *Pałac Opacki (Abbot's Palace)*, a Rococo building of 1754–6, now contains the ethnographic department of the Gdańsk National Museum, with Kashubian folk art and a gallery of modern sculpture. In 1660 the Peace of Oliwa, bringing to an end the Swedish Wars, was signed in the abbey. Behind the monastic complex are the Abbey or Castle Gardens, which have belonged to the monastery since time immemorial. The gardens contain a fine stock of trees and a monument to Adam Mickiewicz. They were laid out in their present form in the 18th century for the abbot, Count Karl von Hohenzollern-Hechingen. There is a Palm House, Botanical Garden, and even (since 1929) an 'Alpinum'.

It is worth taking a walk from here along ul. Polanki, which is lined with fine houses and villas of the 17th and 18th centuries. Oliwa Zoo, which lies to the west of the cathedral and is approached by way of ul. Spacerowa and ul. Kawieńska, is also of interest. It was established in 1954 on the initiative of the people of Dolina Leśnego Młyna in the middle of the Las Oliwski (Oliwa Woods).

Sopot – Gdynia

Situated on the coast 10 km to the north of Gdańsk, **Sopot (Zoppot)** has been one of the most popular holiday places of the region since the mid-16th century.

It is first mentioned in the sources in 1283, when Duke Mściwój II endowed the

Cistercians of Oliwa with some villages, one of which was Sopot. At that time the trade road to Gdynia and Puck, known as the *via regia*, ran through the village. Sopot's picturesque situation inspired the patricians of Danzig to build their country houses and summer retreats here, but it was not until 1823, when Johann Georg Haffner, who had served as a medical officer in Napoleon's army, built a bathing pool here that the village of 23 houses became a bathing resort. Today it is still one of Poland's most fashionable seaside resorts, and the pier, which extends for 516 metres into the sea, is still a favourite place for a stroll.

Along the sea-front promenade stand the stately buildings of the Grand Hotel, as well as cafés, a pavilion for art exhibitions and a hydrotherapy centre (today the foully polluted water of the Bay of Gdańsk does not make for healthy bathing). To the north the main features are the more recent bathing facilities, the *Łazienki Północne (North Baths)* and a magnificent coastland park with tennis courts. Hidden among the wooded hills is the *Opera Leśna (Forest Opera)*, which was built in 1909 and modernized in 1960–61, an open-air theatre with 5,000 seats and a folding roof. The Sopot Song Festival is held here every July.

Only a few kilometres along the coast to the north we come to **Gdynia (Gdingen)**. The valley of the little River Chylońska was a suitable site for settlement and the earliest traces of habitation, dating back to the Neolithic period, have been found at Oksywie, the

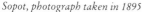

Sopot, photograph taken in 1895

northern part of Gdynia. In the early middle ages the Slavs turned the settlement into a port. The first documentary reference to Oksywie is in 1209, in a charter of Mściwój I endowing a convent of Premonstratensian nuns. From 1316 the settlement belonged to the Cistercians of Oliwa, and in 1362 Gdynia was granted 'location privilege' according to the law of Kulm, enabling it to be established as a town. In 1381 it passed into the possession of the Carthusians of Kartuzy (see page 341). In the middle of the 17th century a large brickworks was built here, and in 1683 an inn was established for travellers. Towards the end of the 18th century a post road was made to pass through Gdynia, and a paved road was laid in the early 19th century. Later there was also a railway link with Gdańsk. New opportunities for development occurred when Poland was given access to the sea by the Treaty of Versailles. The new Polish Republic had no major maritime port, since Gdańsk lay outside its borders, and so in 1922 it was decided to build a port at Gdynia. Two years later construction work began. Gdynia, which in 1875 had been a village with 1,170 inhabitants, now grew at breathtaking speed to become a major industrial centre, one of the showpieces of newly independent Poland and a rival to its older neighbour to the south. By 1931 the population had risen to 38,600, and by 1938 it had more than trebled to 120,000. The port was almost completely destroyed in the Second World War; its reconstruction and the building of the large shipyards continued into the 1960's. Today Gdynia is one of the most important ports and industrial cities in Poland.

The town centre is completely imbued with Gdynia's maritime character. Its heart is Skwer Kościuszki (Kościuszko Square). Along the pier at the Nabrzeże Prezydenta (President's Quay), between the buildings of the State Naval Academy, are an *Aquarium* and the *Oceanographic Museum*. Not far to the south of here, on Bulwar Szwedzki, stands the *Muzeum Marynarki Wojennej (Naval Museum)*, which documents the maritime history of the region from the early middle ages to the Second World War. The hill to the west, *Kamienna Góra (Steinberg)*, gives a magnificent view over the whole town and harbour.

Puck – Wiadysławowo – Jastrzębia Góra – Chałupy – Kuźnica – Jastarnia – Jurata – Hel

An excursion northwards from Gdynia takes us to the Mierzeja Helska (Hel Peninsula or Sand-bar).

The ancient trading settlement of **Puck (Putzig)** was given its town charter in the mid-14th century, and in the 16th century became the base for Zygmunt II August's war fleet. After a long period of decline Puck flourished again at the end of the 19th century. In 1920 the first Polish naval base was founded here, but it was soon superseded by Gdynia. Since the Second World War Puck has survived mainly as a fishing port.

The Gothic *Parish Church* built in the 13th and 14th centuries is worth a visit, mainly for some fine Early Baroque altarpieces from the first half of the 17th century. A few picturesque houses from around 1800 can still be seen in the market square.

Divers for amber about to set sail, wood engraving c.1890

At the point where the Hel Peninsula joins the mainland, 11 km further north, lies the resort and fishing town of **Władysławowo**, with beaches facing both the Zatoka Pucka (Bay of Puck) and the open sea. Excavations here have uncovered traces of a settlement from the period 650–400 BC. About 10 km from Władysławowo we reach the northern-most point of Poland, *Rozewie (Rizhöft)*. There was already a lighthouse here in the 15th century, which survived as one of the oldest on the Baltic coast until the building of the present *lighthouse* in 1771. It bears the name of the writer Stefan Żeromski, who liked to withdraw here to work. Today it houses the Muzeum Latarnictwa (Historic Lighthouse Museum).

Near the cape is **Jastrzębia Góra (Habichtsberg)**, one of the most beautiful seaside resorts in Poland. The village is situated at the top of cliffs 33 metres high, with a superb beach below.

The Hel Peninsula, 34 km long and only 200–500 metres wide for much of this length, which separates the Bay of Puck from the Baltic, was already inhabited two thousand years ago. Some of the little villages that line the road along it have been in existence as fishing villages since the middle ages. At **Chałupy** King Władysław IV Waza built a fort around 1635 to guard Puck harbour. The narrowest point in the sandbank is at the fishing village of **Kuźnica (Kussfeld)**, where it is barely 200 metres wide.

The village of **Jastarnia (Heisternest)** is where the earliest traces of human settlement have been discovered. The fishing port established by the Kashubian population is mentioned in documentary sources from the 14th century. Today Jastarnia is a popular centre for sailing and a bathing resort, like the neighbouring village of **Jurata** which has a fine beach fringed by woods. At its tip the peninsula widens to about 3 km. Here on its southernmost point lies the little town of **Hel (Hela)**, which has been a fishing settlement for 600 years. In the 14th century it was a flourishing town, but from the 15th century, first under Gdańsk and then under Prussia, it went into decline, and it was not until the 20th century that it again developed into a busy fishing port and a popular holiday resort. The predominantly German population of Hel was moved out by the Polish Government in 1937, when Hel was made part of the national defences. It was the last part of the coastal defence to fall, capitulating on 2 October 1939. The *Pomnik Obrońców Helu (Monument to the Defenders of Hel)* was set up in 1979. The 15th-century Gothic *Church* now houses a Museum of Fishing. The main street, ul. Świerczewskiego, still has a few picturesque old half-timbered houses with gables. In early 1945 the Peninsula was the refuge of tens of thousands of Germans fleeing the Russian advance. Many also tried to escape the Baltic towns by ship: the sinking just off Gdynia of the *Wilhelm Gustoff* and the *Goya* with some 15,000 victims was the largest maritime disaster in history.

Sobieszewo – Stegna – Sztutowo – Kąty Rybackie – Krynica Morska – Frombork – Elbląg

Bursztynowe Wybrzeże (Amber Coast) has long been the name given to the narrow strip of coastline which extends eastwards from Gdańsk to the Mierzeja Wiślana (Frische Nehrung, Vistula Sand Bar). The Baltic throws up large quantities of amber (fossilized resin) onto the beach here; great lumps of it are sometimes left by the tide and can only be retrieved from the sand with the help of special pumps. The whole coastland region, with its high dunes covered with pine woods, is very picturesque.

We reach the coastal road east of Gdańsk by way of the Żuławy Wiślane (Vistula Marshes) and continue eastwards for 12 km to the resort of **Sobieszewo (Bohnsack)**, which marks the beginning of the Amber Coast. There is a ferry across the Vistula at Świbno (Schievenhorst), which takes us to **Stegna (Steegen)** with its pretty little 17th-century half-timbered *church*.

The village of **Sztutowo**, an ancient Slavic settlement, was the site of the *Stutthof Concentration Camp*, established here within days of the German invasion. Within the first month of the war Jews were already being killed here. Between 60,000 and 70,000 people of many nationalities died a horrific death at Stutthof, which continued to function until the end of April 1945. The site has been made a museum, and the major buildings, such as the commandant's office, gas chambers and some huts have been left. There is a memorial to the victims.

Not far beyond Sztutowo, at the village of **Kąty Rybackie (Bodenwinkel)**, the Amber Coast becomes the Vistula Sand Bar, and about 15 km further on we reach the popular resort of **Krynica Morska** with its wide beach and a lighthouse surrounded by wooded dunes. There was a fortified settlement here in the early middle ages on the old Amber Road (see page 317).

From these fishing and ferry ports we can cross over to the town of **Frombork (Frauenburg)** situated in Warmia on the Zalew Wiślany (Frisches Haff, Vistula Lagoon). The town has been made famous by its connection with Nicolaus Copernicus (called Mikołaj Kopernik in Polish), who spent most of his life here as a canon. His greatest work 'De revolutionibus orbium coelestium libri VI' was written here and he was buried in the cathedral in 1543 a few days after its publication.

The town has a history going back to the early middle ages, and is still dominated by its fortified *Cathedral* (plate 38). In the 1220's the Teutonic Order subjugated the pagan Pruzzi who were settled here and in 1274 the hill on which Frombork stands became the seat of the diocese created in 1236. The construction of the cathedral, an imposing brick hall church, began in 1329 with the choir. The west front, richly decorated with blind arcading, and the west portal with carved archivolts peopled with saints, was completed in 1388. From the end of the 14th century the cathedral was surrounded with a defensive wall with several towers, and in the 16th century these defences were modernized. At the foot of the fortifications a fishing settlement developed, which later grew into a town. Within

Frombork, the house of Nicolaus Copernicus, 19th-century wood engraving

the walls the houses of the canons were built as well as the *Pałac Biskupów Warmińskich (Palace of the Bishops of Warmia)* (c.1530; remodelled in 1727 and rebuilt after destruction in 1945), which now contains the *Muzeum Mikołaja Kopernika (Nicolaus Copernicus Museum)*.

The cathedral has rich furnishings from the Gothic to the Late Baroque, including a large collection of tombs, slabs and funerary monuments (Copernicus's grave has not been identified). Of particular interest are the Late Gothic winged altarpiece (1504) in the north aisle with expressive scenes of the Passion, and a fine sculpture of the Virgin. The high altar and imposing choir stalls in the presbytery date from the first half of the 18th century, as does the lavishly decorated *Kaplica Stanisława Szembeka (Szembek Chapel)* built to house a collection of relics. The paintings are by Matthias Meyer and the superb wrought iron grille is by the Schwarz brothers of Reszel. The fortifications are well preserved. In the northeast corner stands the *Wieża Kopernika (Copernicus Tower)*, where the astronomer is supposed to have set up his observatory (his room with reconstructed furnishings can be visited). The octagonal *Wieża Radziejowskiego (Radziejowski Tower)*, which was raised in height by order of the bishop in 1685, gives an impressive view over the town. The main gate on the south side with its two semicircular bastions dates from around 1530.

In 1945 the town itself was almost completely destroyed, and the rebuilding in 1967–73 was mostly modern.

A similar tragic fate was suffered by the town of **Elbląg (Elbing)**, about 30 km southwest of here, on the southern tip of the Vistula Sand-Bar. There was a settlement in the 9th century and the convergence here of natural waterways has always favoured trade. In 1246 Elbląg received its charter – under the suzerainty of the Teutonic Order – and was fortified. Soon afterwards a harbour was built, and still in the 13th century Elbląg became a member of the Hanseatic League. Trading ties with England were to be particularly important; from 1579 to 1628 the Eastland Company had its headquarters in Elbląg, a third of the town's trade was with England and many English merchants set up offices here. Commercial success led to a notable cultural flowering: in the 16th century the town was a centre for humanist studies, and in the following century the leading humanist and educationalist Jan Amos Komenský (Comenius) taught in the grammar school, which had been founded in 1535. Rivalry with the commercial power of Gdańsk spurred on Elbląg's architects and artists to produce works of the highest quality. Until the devastating destruction of 1945, when 90 per cent of the town's fabric was lost, Elbląg was a major architectural showpiece. The most important buildings which have been rebuilt in the midst of the modern industrial town, give a hint of its former beauty.

The Dominican *Kościół N.P. Marii (Church of St Mary)* is a fine hall church built in the 13th and 14th centuries, which has been converted since the war into a gallery of modern art (Galeria EL). Before the war this was the Lutheran church and contained a number of 1/th-century monuments to English merchants, some of which survive. The *Kościół św. Mikołaja (Church of St Nicholas)* in ul. Rybacka also dates from the 13th and 14th centuries. Its Late Gothic bronze font with Marian and Christological scenes, is dated 1387 and

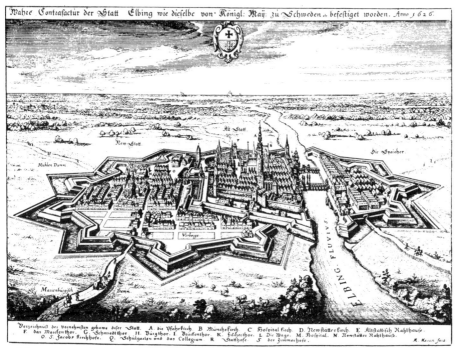

Elbląg, engraving by M. Merian, 1626

signed by Master Bernhauser. The church is also graced by the Maltsters' Altar (*c.*1520), with carved figures of the Virgin, flanked by St Barbara and St Catherine, and paintings after Dürer's engravings on the outer panels.

The many interesting old burghers' houses of all periods from Late Gothic to Neoclassicism fell victim to wartime destruction. For many years the centre of Elbląg was a wasteland, but in the last ten years the rebuilding of the old town has been undertaken. Very few of the old merchants' houses have been reconstructed in their pre-war form (ul. Garbary 16 and ul. Mostowa 17 and 18). In most cases the scale of the façades has been preserved but the gables and other features have been handled in a modern idiom. A few fragments are all that now remains of the old town fortifications. The *Brama Targowa (Market Gate)*, built in the early 14th century and raised in height during the 15th century, was the only town gate to survive bombardment in 1945. The old grammar school building (ul. Wigilijna 12) now houses the *Muzeum Elbląskie (Elbląg Museum)*.

It was near Elbląg in February 1943 that Solzhenitsyn, an officer in the Red Army, was arrested: the first step on his *via dolorosa* through the Gulag Archipelago.

Tczew – Malbork – Pelplin – Gniew – Kwidzyn – Grudziądz – Sartowice – Chełmno – Chełmża

On the lower Vistula, about 35 km south of Gdańsk, we come to the town of **Tczew** (Dirschau), formerly one of the many bases of the Teutonic Order in this fertile territory around the Vistula and the Nogat. The town has preserved two important monuments from its long history: the *Kościół Farny św. Kryża (Parish Church of the Holy Cross)* and the *Kościół Dominikanów (Dominican Church)*. Both are brick hall churches of the 14th century, though the parish church was later much altered. Its treasury contains some important 15th-century church plate.

Crossing an 890-metre-long bridge over the Vistula, (built by August Stüler of Berlin and the longest bridge in Europe when it was opened in 1857) we head for **Malbork** (Marienburg). Now an industrial town with a population of almost 40,000, it was founded in the 13th century as a castle of the Teutonic Order. In 1276 it was raised to the status of town with the laws of Kulm, and in 1309 became the seat of the Grand Master. The administrative centre of the order thus moved from Venice to Malbork. A century and a half later (1457–66) the order had to surrender its castles to the Polish Crown and the Grand Master moved to Königsberg. Over the following century the buildings fell into decay and they suffered damage during the Swedish Wars. From 1457 to 1772 Malbork, besides being the seat of a starosta, was one of the residences of the Kings of Poland. After its acquisition by Prussia in the First Partition, it was converted to barracks.

Around 1274 the Teutonic Knights had begun to build a strongly fortified castle close to the bank of the Nogat (plate 41). It was named 'Marienburg' after the Virgin Mary, the patroness of the Order, and was to become the largest brick-built castle and one of the most important Gothic secular buildings in Europe. The internal arrangement of the castle was determined at the earliest stage in the planning, and construction continued in stages until its surrender in 1457. In the centre is the square building of the Zamek Wysoki (Hoch-schloss, High Castle) with its adjoining Przedzamcze (Vorburg, Outer Bailey). On the other side of the castle the residential settlement is symmetrically grouped around a wide main street, which also served as the market place. The stronghold was protected by a highly complex system of defensive walls and towers. The most impressive view of the immense extent of the castle is from the opposite bank of the river.

Its chivalric history and impressive appearance gave the castle an important role in German Romanticism. In particular, Friedrich Gilly's atmospheric drawings of Malbork in 1799 revived interest in brick Gothic and inspired the Gothic Revival and the conservation of medieval architecture in Germany. In the course of the 19th century, as part of this enthusiasm for Gothic buildings, the buildings underwent constant alterations and restorations by Schinkel and, more elaborately, by Conrad Steinbrecht. The Hohenzollerns exploited the romantic nationalist prestige of Malbork, and Wilhelm II himself visited the castle for a Teutonic pageant. The Second World War left the town completely destroyed

Malbork, the Grand Master's Palace, drawing by D. Quaglio, 1834

and the castle badly damaged. In 1961–78 the castle buildings and fortifications were reconstructed, while the residential settlement was rebuilt in modern form, though unlike Elbląg the original street plan was adhered to, so that it is easy to imagine the town's former appearance. The castle now contains the *Muzeum Zamkowe (Castle Museum)*, with a fine collection of medieval sculpture, amber objects, old coins and medals.

The *Zamek Wysoki (Hochschloss, High Castle)* (1) is the oldest part of the complex. Construction began around 1274 with the north range, which at first contained the most important rooms: the chapel, dormitory, chapter house, prison and archives. In the years up to about 1300 the High Castle was extended to form a courtyard enclosed by four ranges. During the 14th century the whole castle precinct was an enormous building site. The building of the *Zamek Średni (Mittelschloss, Middle Castle)* (2) lasted from 1310 to c.1330. It included one of the most splendid rooms in the whole complex, the *Wielki Refektarz (Grosser Remter, Great Refectory)*, also known as the Sala Rycerska (Rittersaal, Knights' Hall) which now houses Jan Matejko's massive canvas of the Polish-Lithuanian victory over the Teutonic Knights at the Battle of Grunwald. Also in the Middle Castle are the residence of the Grosskomtur (Grand Commander), guest rooms, a hospital and a number of offices; the roof storey served as an arsenal. After the completion of the Middle Castle, it was then possible to undertake the alterations that had become necessary in the High Castle. Loggias were built around the courtyard, and the chapel in the southeast corner was extended to form the *Kościół Zamkowy N.P. Marii (Castle Church of St Mary)* (3) with the *Kaplica św. Anny (Crypt Chapel of St Anne)* below. Both of these were richly decorated with sculpture, of which only the carvings of the doorway, with scenes from the New Testament, the Legend of the Finding of the True Cross and the Last Judgment, have survived. The chancel projected far beyond the line of the wall. The niche on the exterior of the east side of the polygonal apse was filled with an enormous figure of the Virgin and Child, 8 metres high, executed in relief and covered with mosaic, which dominated the countryside around. It was destroyed almost without trace in 1945, but there are plans to reconstruct it from old colour photographs. Parallel with the work on the chapel, fortifications were built around the whole complex and extensive office buildings were erected in the outer bailey. These works continued well into the 15th century.

The 1380's and 1390's saw the construction of the most impressive building in the castle precincts, the *Pałac Wielkich Mistrzów (Hochmeisterpalast, Palace of the Grand Masters)* (4) with a grand façade projecting from the walls of the Middle Castle to the bank of the Nogat. Its architect was probably Nikolaus Fellenstein, the master mason of the Teutonic Order at that time. This magnificent building is as enigmatic as it is famous. At first sight it seems a defensive structure with its thick walls, watchtowers at the corners and battlements. On closer inspection, however, these features are revealed to be for display only, as attributes of power: the walls were articulated with large windows, originally filled with stained glass, the colonettes are merely decorative, and the crenellation is picked out in

Malbork, plan of the Marienburg   1 Zamek Wysoki (High Castle)   2 Zamek Średni (Middle Castle)   3 Kościół Zamkowy N.P. Marii i Kaplica św. Anny (Castle Church of St Mary and St Anne's Chapel)   4 Pałac Wielkich Mistrzów (Grand Master's Palace)   5 Ratusz (Town Hall)   6 Kościół św. Jana (Church of St John)

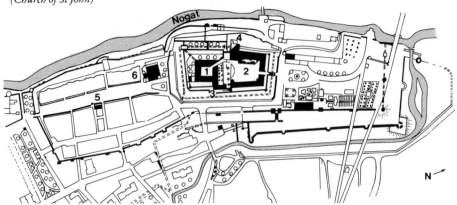

Malbork, the Summer Refectory of the Grand Master's Palace, aquatint by F. Frick, 1799

delicate relief. The interiors have equally luxurious decoration, especially the two refectories, the *Refektarz Zimowy (Winterremter, Winter Refectory)* and the *Refektarz Letni (Sommerremter, Summer Refectory)*. The star vaults in these two rooms – in each case supported on a single granite column – mark the culmination of development in vaulting technique which can be traced through all the important rooms of the castle.

Between the modern houses on the site of the old settlement below the castle, the Late Gothic *Ratusz (Town Hall)* (5), built in 1365–80 and remodelled in 1457–60, and the *Kościół św. Jana (Parish Church of St John)* (6), rebuilt between 1468 and 1523 as a Late Gothic hall church, have survived, as well as fragments of the fortifications.

The most important architectural monument in **Pelplin** is the *Cistercian Abbey* founded in 1274, with its magnificent Gothic *Church*, which came through the Second World War largely unscathed (colour plate 20). Since 1824 it has been the seat of a bishopric, which was transferred here from Chełmno. The church, one of the most important examples of brick Gothic in the former Teutonic State, is a basilica built between 1280 and 1320 on a rectangular plan intersected in the middle by the transept. The exterior is rhythmically articulated by buttresses and large windows which appear simply to have been cut into the brickwork. The only external decoration is the filigree-work of the gables, and only the doorway in the north transept, set deep in the wall with moulded jambs and archivolts, has figural sculpture, with half figures of apostles and saints at the

Pelplin, cloister in the north range of the Cistercian Abbey, photograph taken in 1950

imposts, and angels in the archivolts (the sculpture in the tympanum is modern). The severity of the architecture, in keeping with the spirit of the Cistercian Order, continues in the interior. Two rows of unornamented octagonal piers run along the whole length of the church. The transept creates no spatial effect; all that counts is the long, tall nave which continues into the choir almost without a transition. The only accent is the Early Baroque high altar built in 1623–5, which rises to a height of 26 metres, the tallest in Poland. The altarpiece (1623–4) depicting the Coronation of the Virgin, was painted by Hermann Hahn.

The differences between the various parts of the church only become apparent as one walks around it. The first four bays of the nave have lavish star vaults of the 15th century, while the star vaults in the eastern bays are simpler. The vaults in the aisles, especially the north choir aisle with a continuous ridge rib, are remarkably similar to English tierceron vaults developed in the 13th century. The marvellous net vaulting in the transept, supported by a single column, was built in 1557 by Anton Schultes.

In the monks' choir and the north transept are mid-15th-century carved Gothic stalls with wonderful tracery. The altar paintings are by leading Baroque artists of the 17th century: Hermann Hahn, Bartholomäus Strobel the Younger and Andreas Stech. The pulpit and organ also date from this period. The construction of the monastic buildings had begun in 1274 with the east range and th star-vaulted chapter house; the cloister and the other ranges were built in the first half of the 14th century, and were given an extra storey in 1859–68 for the seminary which was established here in 1828. Gothic wall paintings (early 15th century) have survived in the cloister. The library (now the seminary library) has a rich collection of medieval manuscripts and incunables, including a Gutenberg Bible. In the *Park* surrounding the monastery stands the Neoclassical Bishop's Palace, built in 1837.

About 12 km south of Pelplin on a hill by the banks of the Vistula stands the little town of **Gniew (Mewe)**, which was already in existence in the 11th century as a settlement on the trade route that ran along the river. Its heyday began after the founding of the castle of the Teutonic Order in 1283, and it has retained the form it was given in that period. The *Zamek Kryżacki (Castle)* was completed at the end of the 14th century as a square fort with corner towers. In 1922 it was gutted by fire, and although the bare masonry was secured around 1970 and new roofs were erected, there was no attempt to reconstruct the interior.

In the course of the 14th century, during construction of the castle, the town itself was laid out on a chequerboard plan around a square market place. This was originally surrounded by low Gothic burghers' houses, which were altered and given arcades, and since the 17th century have all been given Baroque or Neoclassical remodellings. The Gothic town hall that stood in the centre of the market place was replaced by a new building in the 19th century. Restoration work has revealed remains of the Gothic masonry.

The *Kościół św. Mikołaja (Parish Church of St Nicholas)* stands in its own square adjoining the market place to the southwest. It is a brick hall church built in the second half of the 14th century on the site of an earlier wooden church, and has suffered much damage and alteration in the course of its history. A thorough restoration took place in the 19th century, which included the rebuilding of the vaults, and the replacement of all the furnishings except for two Baroque altars.

At the northwest and southwest corners of the town centre there are still fragments of the 14th-century town walls.

Kwidzyn (Marienwerder), another foundation of the Teutonic Order (1233), lies about 27 km further south, on the other bank of the Vistula. The old town centre was almost completely destroyed in 1945 and 1946, when the stone – even the pavements – was carried off for the rebuilding of Warsaw; Kwidzyn was rebuilt in the 1960's as an entirely modern town except for the imposing *Zamek Kapituły (Capitular Castle)* and the former Cathedral, now the *Kościół Farny N.P. Marii (Parish Church of St Mary)*. In 1254 the town was made the seat of the Prince Bishop of the newly founded diocese of Pomesania. The chapter was established in 1285, and was drawn entirely from the ranks of the priests of the Teutonic Order. In the 1330's work began on the building of the choir of the cathedral, the first stage in the creation of the castle complex, which was to become one of the most outstanding examples of Gothic military architecture in Europe. The church is a pseudo-basilica with a two-aisled crypt below the polygonal choir and a tall and massive belltower. After many alterations, mainly in the 16th and 18th centuries, the interior was re-gothicized in the 19th century, and most of the furnishings were replaced, including the high altar. Nevertheless interesting remnants of the medieval decoration survive. The most famous are the 14th-century wall paintings in the aisles, which show scenes from the Life of Christ and the Virgin and the legends of saints; they were repainted in the 19th century and partly restored in the 1930's. (Contemporary with these paintings is an important mosaic on the outside of the south porch.)

Attached to the north aisle is the funerary chapel built in 1705 for the lavish tomb of the starosta of Kwidzyn, Friedrich von der Groeben (died 1728). He was the founder of the first Brandenburg colony in Africa, on the Gold Coast, in 1683. The figures of the starosta and his three wives on the outer wall of the chapel have given rise to many picturesque legends.

Below the windows in the choir there are more wall paintings executed c.1510. They show the Virgin and St John the Evangelist, three Grand Masters of the Teutonic Order and seventeen bishops.

The castle had been erected in an unusually short time between the 1320's and 1340's. After the 16th century, when the bishopric of Pomesania went over to Protestantism, it was used for a variety of purposes and its architecture was altered. The south and east ranges of the original quadrangle were demolished in 1798. Restoration work in the second half of the 19th century gave the castle its present appearance. After 1945 a museum was installed within its walls with works of art from the region and archaeological and ethnographical collections.

Little has remained of the original 14th-century fabric apart from the articulation of the external walls with their tall, pointed blind arcading, and some of the vaulting in the lower storey. The most spectacular feature is the 'dansker' (latrine) tower, which is connected to the west range by a covered passageway on tall brick arches.

Grudziądz (Graudenz), one of the oldest towns in Ziemia Chełmińska (Kulmer Land), is dramatically situated on the old Amber Road along the Vistula. In about 1218 the settlement was put under the control of the missionary diocese which had been founded for the conversion of the pagan Pruzzi. In 1228 it passed to the Teutonic Order. In the 15th century there was a rebellion against the Order by the burghers, who had joined the Prussian League in 1440. After bitter disputes Grudziądz was given to the Polish Crown in the Second Peace of Toruń in 1466, and in 1772 it passed to Prussia in the First Partition of Poland. The fortress built in 1772–86 was bravely defended against the Napoleonic army by Guillaume Courbière, the Prussian commander of Huguenot descent. (The interesting cast iron monument to Courbière (1815), probably by Schinkel, is no longer extant.) The Versailles Treaty of 1919 made Grudziądz part of the Polish Corridor.

The Old Town by the bank of the Vistula still largely preserves its medieval appearance, despite heavy damage in the war. Its centre is the large rectangular market place, in the middle of which the town hall stood until the 19th century. The *houses* have been rebuilt in historical styles since the war. On the north side stands the oldest surviving house, the *Apteka pod Łabędziem (Swan Pharmacy)* (No. 20) dating from the 16th century. At the northeast corner of the market place we turn into ul. Kościelna, where the *Kościół św. Mikołaja (Parish Church of St Nicholas)* was built as a pseudo-basilica in the second half of the 14th century. The traces of several remodellings – particularly of Baroque redecoration in the 18th century – were swept away by a restoration in 1896, and further damage was caused by a fire in 1945. However, the remains of Gothic wall paintings can still be seen on the piers, and there is an impressive Late Romanesque font in the sacristy dating from the second quarter of the 13th century, with carvings of dragons between foliage ornament.

Nearby, in ul. Ratuszowa, stands the former *Klasztor Jezuitów (Jesuit Monastery)*, founded in 1622, with the *Kościół św. Franciszka Ksawerego (Seminary Church of St Francis Xavier)* and the *Jesuit College*. The aisleless Baroque church with its tall façade articulated with pilasters and niches containing the figures of saints was built between 1648 and 1715. The lavish decoration of the interior has remained intact. The College building, restored in 1945–7 after severe damage, adjoins the church on the west side. Its middle range is dominated by a high tower emphasizing the entrance, with a double flight of steps leading up to it.

The castle built by the Teutonic Knights in the 14th century used to stand on the *Góra Zamkowa (Castle Hill)* at the northwestern end of the Old Town. During the wars of the 18th century most of it was destroyed and the ruins were removed in 1801 on the orders of King Friedrich Wilhelm III. Since then the hill has become a popular place for Sunday walks with a fine view over the town and countryside. The obelisk was erected in 1965. (The Grudziądz Polyptych, a masterpiece of late 14th-century painting, once in the castle chapel, is now in the National Museum in Warsaw.)

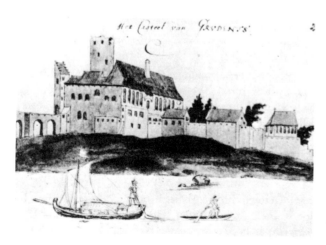

Grudziądz, view of the Castle, watercolour by A. Boot, 17th century

The right-hand side of ul. Spichrzowa is lined with a row of picturesque granaries built in the 16th century, most of which were remodelled in the 18th century and then rebuilt after the war in 1949–54. They had a double function: as storehouses and as a defensive wall along the bank, which falls steeply down to the Vistula. There is a good view of the river frontage from ul. Królowej Jadwigi. At the end of ul. Spichrzowa we come to the *Brama Wodna (Water Gate)*, the only gate to survive from the 14th-century town fortifications. It was converted into a dwelling in the 18th century and since its rebuilding in 1955–7 it has been used by an angling club.

On its east side the gate is adjoined by the complex of the former *Opactwo Benedyktynek (Benedictine Nunnery)*. The monastery was originally built as a medieval hospital foundation. After being used for a time by the Protestant community, it was given to the Benedictine nuns in 1624. The alterations they made were destroyed in the Swedish Wars, and the present Baroque buildings date from 1728–31. They were remodelled several times, before suffering destruction once again in 1945. Rebuilt in 1949–56, they now house the *Muzeum Państwowe (State Museum)*, which was founded by the Towarzystwo Miłośników Starożytności (Society of Lovers of Antiquity), with a variety of collections very much in the spirit of the 19th century. They include sections devoted to archaeological finds from the region, documentation of the political and economic development of Ziemia Chełmińska, ethnography and natural history, arms and armour, and Oriental porcelain of the 17th–19th centuries. In 1961 a gallery of contemporary painting was opened.

Continuing along ul. Wodna past these monastic buildings, we come to the convent church, the *Kościół św. Ducha (Holy Ghost Church)* and the *Pałac Opatek (Palace of the Abbesses)*, which now houses the municipal music school. The small, aisleless church was built in the 14th century as the chapel of the hospital, and with the rest of the complex has had a chequered history of destruction and remodellings. It was rebuilt after the Second World War in its Baroque form, but parts of the Gothic masonry can be seen in the façade. The interior decoration is modern.

The Palace of the Abbesses, probably built in 1750–52, has retained little of its old character, though the façade was rebuilt in its original form in 1949–50, with pilasters and wooden statues of Benedictine saints in the niches.

Sections of the old town fortifications can be seen along ul. Szkolna, with the double line of walls and a moat (Kanał Trynki), which from 1552 also served to link the Vistula to the River Osa, which flows past the town on its northeast side. For centuries the Vistula was the essential artery of Polish trade. The grain which was the basis of all the great fortunes in the land was rafted down to Gdańsk, often by the (smaller) landowners themselves. One of the important stops was the little *Chapel* of the patron saint of rafters, St Barbara, at **Sartawice**, 10 km south of Grudziądz on the other side of the river.

One of the loveliest and best preserved towns on the Amber Road is **Chełmno (Kulm)**. In 1226 it came into the possession of the Teutonic Order, and in the course of the 13th century was laid out on a regular plan. Its heyday was in the 14th century, when it was a

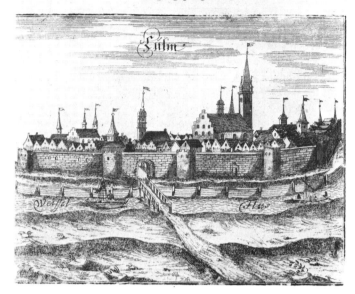

Culm /
Eine alte Stadt / an der Pohlnischen Gränße / dem
Könige gehörig.

Chełmno, view of the town, engraving by J. J. Vogel, 1684

prosperous trading town and a member of the Hanseatic League. In the middle of the 15th century disputes between the Prussian League and the Order led to an economic decline from which it never really recovered. Because of this, and because the town came through the Second World War largely unscathed, Chełmno has kept its medieval character.

The chequerboard plan of the town centre is still surrounded by the walls built in the 14th and 15th centuries with seventeen towers, but only one of the town gates has remained unaltered, the *Brama Grudziądzka (Grudziądz Gate)* on the east side of the town. (The other gates were all remodelled in 1609.) A chapel was built on the outside of the gate and the Pietà which was then placed in the niche over the entrance is still there today.

Ul. Grudziądzka takes us to the large square market place. Here the Gothic buildings were remodelled in the 19th and 20th centuries, and although they have retained their basic shape, they now sport Neoclassical or modern façades.

The *Ratusz (Town Hall)*, which stands in the centre of the square, is an architectural gem created in 1567–72 by altering the existing Gothic building. It is a rare example of Mannerist architecture in the region, comparable to the town hall at Poznań (see page 273), and it is still used by the municipal administration. The medieval origins of the building can be seen from the irregular disposition of some doors and windows on the façades.

385

There is a delightful quirkiness in the use of Italianate architectural elements and the square building is surmounted by a tall, lavishly articulated attic topped by a cresting of small decorative gables, an allusion to medieval crenellation. The tall tower was built in 1589–95.

In the south corner of the square, between ul. Toruńska and ul. Szkolna, stands the monumental *Kościół N.P. Marii (Church of St Mary)*, which is set diagonally on its square plot of land in order to preserve the exact eastward orientation of the chancel. The arrangement of the roofs of this three-aisled Early Gothic hall church is unusual for this part of the country: the nave and choir have a single saddleback roof, while the aisles each have five smaller transverse saddleback roofs with gables decorated with blind arcading. The pinnacled buttresses projecting between the bays add plasticity to the side elevations. The façade was planned with two towers, but the south tower was never completed. The parapet and spire on the north tower date from the 19th century. The interior is a rather austere conception with cross-rib vaults supported on octagonal piers, but it has rich furnishings, which have been added to over the centuries. Particularly interesting are the Late Gothic wall paintings made around 1400, which were rediscovered in 1925 under a layer of plaster. St Christopher is in the north aisle; a Crucifixion, Christ in Majesty and the Martyrdom of St Apollonia are on the north wall of the chancel; and opposite are fragments of scenes from the life of the Prophet Daniel. Also dating from the 14th century are seven of a set of figures of the Apostles made of artificial stone. In the south porch is an octagonal Romanesque font of the mid-12th century, probably imported from Gotland. The elk head suspended from the nave ceiling is an unusual feature.

In the western part of the old town centre two Gothic monasteries stand close together. The *Kościół św. Jakuba (Church of St James)* in ul. Franciszkańska was built from about 1290 for the Franciscans who had settled here thirty years earlier. The severe, three-aisled hall church has hardly changed since it was completed in the 15th century. As was usual with churches of the mendicant orders, its only decoration is its richly ornamented gables at the west and east ends, and the star vaults which were added in the 15th century. When the monastery was closed in the 19th century all the old furnishings were removed from the church.

A few steps away to the northwest, in ul. Dominikańska close to the town walls, stands a former convent founded in 1261, which originally belonged to Cistercian nuns and later passed to Benedictine nuns. The laying of the foundation stone of the *Kościół śś. Jana Chrzciciela i Jana Ewangelisty (Church of Sts John the Baptist and John the Evangelist)* is recorded in 1266, but most of the church was built in the first half of the 14th century and it was enlarged and altered several times over the centuries that followed. It was originally an aisleless building with a three-sided apse and a gallery, a type unusual in the church architecture of this region. The furnishings date from the 16th and 17th centuries and include choir stalls with lavish intarsia work, a fine pulpit (1597), organ (1619), in the chancel, and altars. On the way up to the gallery (on the north side of the chancel) is an Early Gothic tomb slab made in 1275 for Arnold Lieshorn, a burgher of the town, the earliest such work surviving in this region. Incised on the limestone slab is a portrait of the deceased, his hands clasped by a sainted abbess as intercessor.

Halfway between Chełmno and Toruń, on the shores of Jezioro Chełmżyńskie (Kulmsee), is another old town which was once important in the region, **Chełmża (Kulmsee)**. In 1251 the episcopal see of Chełmno, which had been founded only eight years previously, was transferred here. The village, then called Łoza, was therefore given a town charter and a new name. In the same year work began on the construction of the cathedral (now a parish church), which is the only important medieval building remaining in Chełmża. It was originally planned as a three-aisled basilica with four towers (very much in the spirit of Romanesque cathedrals), but as it was built it became a Gothic hall church, with only the choir and transept having a Romanesque core. Of the four only the northwest tower reached its full height and was given a bulbous Baroque cap in 1692. The choir façade is distinguished by a richly decorated Late Gothic stepped gable.

Most of the decoration dates from the 16th and 17th centuries; fragments of late 14th-century Gothic paintings survive in the aisle vaults only. The carved Baroque choir arch incorporating a Late Gothic Crucifixion from around 1500 is of interest. But the finest work in the church is the Renaissance wall tomb of Bishop Peter Kostka (died 1595), with an impressive recumbent figure by one of the Italian sculptors then working in Kraków.

Toruń

The town of **Toruń (Thorn)** set in the austere landscape of the Vistula valley has kept much of its medieval charm. The early medieval settlement was granted its town charter in 1233, two years after it had come into the possession of the Teutonic Order together with the Ziemia Chełmińska (Kulmer Land). Thanks to its situation at the intersection of important roads and its membership of the Hanseatic League (c.1280) the town soon developed into a flourishing trading centre and port, as can be seen from the intense building activity – public, ecclesiastical and private – in the 14th and 15th centuries. As they grew more prosperous the burghers of Toruń sought with increasing insistence to throw off the rule of the Teutonic Order. In 1454 Toruń played the key role in the uprising of the Prussian League against the Order. After 1466, when the Teutonic State ceded West Prussia to the Polish Crown, the town received further privileges, including the right to mint coins, which contributed to its continued commercial and cultural flowering.

Toruń's most famous son, the great astronomer and discoverer of the heliocentric universe Nicolaus Copernicus, was born on 19 February 1473. He lived here until 1491, when he went to study at Kraków.

Toruń remained prosperous until the 17th century when the Swedish occupation (1655–8) brought about a decline, from which the town was unable to recover in the short intervals between wars. Toruń was still famous, however, for its religious tolerance, but the 'Tumult of Thorn' in 1724 briefly put the town at the centre of European politics.

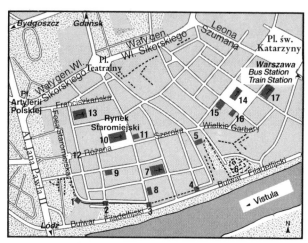

Toruń (Thorn)
1 Krzywa Wieża
  (Leaning Tower)
2 Brama Klasztorna
  (Nuns' Gate)
3 Brama Żeglarska
  (Sailors' Gate)
4 Brama Mostowa
  (Bridge Gate)
5 Wieża Monstrancji
  (Monstrance Tower)
6 Zamek Krzyżacki (Castle
  of the Teutonic Knights)
7 Kościół śś. Janów (Church
  (of the two Sts John)
8 Pałac Biskupów Kujawskich
  (Palace of the Bishops of
  Kujawy)

9 Dom Kopernika (Copernicus House)   10 Ratusz (Town Hall)   11 Dom pod Gwiazdą (Star House)
12 Kościół św. Ducha (Church of the Holy Ghost)   13 Kościół Najświętszej Panny Marii (Church of
St Mary)   14 Zbór św. Trójcy (Protestant Church of the Holy Trinity)   15 Apteka pod Lwem (Lion
Pharmacy)   16 Gospoda pod Modrym Fartuchem (Blue Apron Inn)   17 Kościół św. Jakuba (Church
of St James)

When, following ugly fighting between Jesuit students and Lutheran burghers, the Polish
court in Warsaw condemned the Lutheran burgomaster and other burghers to death for
countenancing sedition, the Protestant powers of Europe were outraged. The executions
provided the Protestant cause with martyrs (only a few of the condemned saved their skins
by repenting and turning to Catholicism) and helped Brandenburg-Prussia to extend its
influence as the defender of the Protestants in Poland. In 1793, following the Second
Partition of Poland, Toruń became part of the Kingdom of Prussia and was converted into
a border fortress and garrison. Except for the period from 1807 to 1815, when it belonged
to Napoleon's short-lived Duchy of Warsaw, it remained part of Prussian territory until
1920.

Today this voivodship capital, famous for its elaborate gingerbread, still retains much of
the atmosphere of Copernicus's time. It has hardly suffered any war damage since the 17th
century and economic stagnation has prevented any major changes to the town's medieval
fabric, much of which has survived and preserves its organic integrity.

The historic centre of Toruń consists of three parts, which were originally independent
but later grew together: the Stare Miasto (Old Town), the Nowe Miasto (New Town) and
the now largely ruined Zamek Krzyżacki (Castle of the Teutonic Order). The town's plan
is almost unchanged since the middle ages. Parts of the town walls can still be seen, as well
as many burghers' houses and granaries from the middle ages and later.

The Old Town extends along the Vistula, on whose bank, in ul. Bankowa, the southern
part of the town fortifications is preserved with four town gates. The town walls were laid

out in the 13th and 14th centuries, and strengthened in 1420–59 when additional towers were added. These include the **Krzywa Wieża (Leaning Tower)** (1) at the southeast corner of the Old Town (converted into a house in the 19th century and now the headquarters of the civic society, the 'Towarzystwo Miłośników Torunia'), and the next two gates, the **Brama Klasztorna (Nuns' Gate)** (2) at the end of ul. św. Ducha, and **Brama Żeglarska (Sailors' Gate)** (3) which leads into ul. Żeglarska. **Brama Mostowa (Bridge Gate)** (4) was added in 1432 as part of the extension of the fortifications by Master Hans Gotland, and was altered in the 19th century. The octagonal **Wieża Monstrancji (Monstrance Tower)** (5) on the east side of the Old Town in ul. Podmurna also dates from the 15th century. The New Town had its own fortifications, though nothing now remains of these.

Like all the medieval buildings of Toruń the fortifications were built of brick, the usual material in this area since stone is very scarce.

At the end of ul. Przedzamcze we come to the former **Zamek Krzyżacki (Castle of the Teutonic Order)** (6), which was first built in the middle of the 13th century, originally of wood, on the site of an early medieval settlement (10th–12th centuries), itself on the remains of a Bronze Age settlement (Lusatian Culture, 10th–4th century BC; the excavation can be seen in the reconstructed cellars). Already in the 1260's work had begun on the construction of a new brick building, one of the first such castles built by the Teutonic Order. Not long after it was completed at the end of the 14th century, the castle fell in the uprising of 1454, and was abandoned. It was not until the age of Romantic medievalism in the 19th century that the castle was restored, and it now stands as a picturesque ruin in the middle of a park; the 13th-century latrine tower, remains of an octagonal keep and the ground-floor walls of the convent buildings with their cloister have survived.

Several large churches were erected at the same time as the castle; the Parish Church of St John, the Franciscan Church of St Mary in the Old Town, and the Dominican Church of St James and its monastery in the New Town.

On the way from the castle to St John's we pass along ul. Ciasna (Tight Street), one of the characteristic alleyways in which commerce was concentrated. Here there are a number of granaries, including a Gothic one (No. 7, 14th century), and others from the 17th and 18th centuries. Nos. 4–8 now contain a branch of the *Archeologiczne Muzeum Okręgowe (Regional Archaeological Museum)* in which are displayed archaeological finds from the prehistory and early history of Ziemia Chełmińska, systematically excavated since the 19th century.

Like the other churches of Toruń the monumental building of the **Kościół śś. Janów (Parish Church of the two Sts John)** (7) has not suffered from later alterations. The oldest part, dating from the second half of the 13th century, is the chancel with one of the earliest known star vaults. The hall-church nave, also begun in the first phase of construction, was raised in the second half of the 15th century and was given a fine star vault and three parallel saddleback roofs of the same height covering the nave and aisles. The massive west tower would have become the town's principal landmark if it had reached the height of 65 metres originally planned. The architect of the Bridge Tower, Hans Gotland, was in charge

389

of its construction, but work on the church was abandoned after 26 years (1407–33).

The interior furnishings including a great array of statuary, are also largely intact, although the most important altarpieces have been taken to the National Museum in Warsaw. In the choir are Early Gothic wall paintings from the 1330's in which the figures of John the Baptist and John the Evangelist, the church's patrons, appear. One of the church's greatest treasures, a masterpiece of the Schöner Stil, was a statue of the Virgin at the end of the north aisle, which has been missing since the War. The genius of its maker, the 'Master of the Beautiful Madonnas', can still be seen in the remaining console, carved with a bust of Moses and the Burning Bush, one of the Old Testament symbols of the Virgin (c.1400). The Late Gothic carved altarpiece of St Wolfgang (1506) and the Crucifix of the second half of the 14th century placed above it, were both made for this church. The magnificent brass of the burgomaster Johann of Soest and his wife was made c.1360 in a Bruges workshop.

Nicolaus Copernicus was baptized in the westernmost chapel of the south aisle; above the bronze Gothic font which still stands there a memorial painting was set up in 1589, and a Late Baroque portrait bust was added in 1766.

Just by the west front of the church, at ul. Żeglarska 8, the Baroque façade of the Pałac Biskupów Kujawskich (Palace of the Bishops of Kujawy) (8) built for Bishop Stanisław Dąbski in 1693, has typically luxuriant decoration, rustication on the ground floor and plaster swags. The richly ornamented doorway and pediment were destroyed in alterations in the 19th century.

Copernicus was born in what is now ul. Kopernika, although the house itself is no longer standing – in the 1480's it was replaced by a new building (No. 17). After many disfiguring alterations this house, together with its 14th-century neighbour (No. 15), was reconstructed in 1972-73. The **Dom Kopernika (Copernicus House)** (9) is now a *Museum*. Among the most precious of the two thousand or so exhibits is a collection of old editions of his writings, including his magnum opus 'De revolutionibus orbium coelestium libri VI' (1543), copies of old astronomical instruments, portraits, and examples of his less well known works as a classical scholar, a physician and an ecclesiastical politician. No. 15 has been furnished as a medieval patrician house.

The Rynek Staromiejski (Old Town Market Place) is dominated by the **Town Hall** (10), a symbol of bourgeois self-confidence, which – unlike the churches – was continually added to, altered and made to suit the prevailing artistic fashion (plate 40). It is the largest and most imposing medieval town hall in Poland, and was intended from the beginning as a centre both of municipal administration and of commerce. Its history began around 1250 with the building of the tower and the market and cloth halls nearby, with the administrative and judicial offices housed on the first floor. In 1385 the tower was raised in height and slender blind arcading, projecting corner turrets and a tall pointed spire were added – signs of the growing self-assertiveness of the burghers towards the Teutonic Order. A few years later, in 1393, a spacious courtyard was created with four ranges incorporating the earlier building into a unified complex articulated by giant blind arcading. At the beginning of the

Nicolaus Copernicus (1474–1543), detail of the memorial in the Church of the two Sts John

17th century Anthonis van Opbergen, a Fleming who enjoyed a high reputation in Pomerania as an exponent of modern bourgeois architecture, was entrusted with the remodelling of the building. He added an extra storey, placed gables on the four façades and gave the main front a grand doorway (re-Gothicized in the 19th century). In 1703 the town hall was gutted by fire, and the present interiors date from the rebuilding that followed. Particularly impressive are the rich portals with intarsia-decorated doors, and the painted wooden ceilings.

Today the town hall contains the *Muzeum Okręgowe (Regional Museum)*, in which there are displays of medieval art from Toruń, applied art (goldsmith's work and coins), a portrait gallery of important figures in Toruń's history (including an authentic, 16th-century, portrait of Copernicus, as well as Polish painting from the 18th century to the present). On the ground floor the old decoration of the law court has been reconstructed together with the Crucifix and paintings intended to admonish the judges.

The *Copernicus Monument* in front of the southeast corner of the town hall was erected in 1853 to a design by the Berlin sculptor Christian Friedrich Tieck. Copernicus is shown in a scholar's gown, his right hand raised in a rhetorical gesture, while he holds in his left a model of the heliocentric cosmos. The Latin inscription on the base praises him as 'Nicolaus Copernicus of Toruń, who set the earth in motion and brought the sun to a halt'.

The buildings around the market square are burghers' houses representing a wide spectrum of architectural styles. Many of them are basically Gothic but were remodelled at various periods in a manner in keeping with their prestigious location. The **Dom pod Gwiazdą (Star House)** at No. 35 (11), now a branch of the Muzeum Okręgowe with a collection of Far Eastern art, was given its rich façade decoration in 1697. It is typical of Toruń Baroque, with plaster cartouches in high relief and garlands of fruit and flowers.

To the south, opposite the town hall, the Dwór Artusa (Artushof, Arthur Court) (14th century) stood until 1802 as one of the most lavish buildings in the town, whose façade since the 17th century was decorated with an allegorical political programme comprising the portraits of Polish kings, coats of arms, personifications of the virtues and exemplary figures from antiquity. The neo-Renaissance building which has stood on its site since 1890 contains the *Collegium Maximum* of the Uniwersytet Mikołaja Kopernika (the headquarters of the Nicolaus Copernicus University).

On the corner of ul. Różana stands the former Protestant **Kościół św. Ducha (Holy Ghost Church)** (12), which since 1945 has been used by the Jesuits. It was designed by the Dresden architect Andreas Adam Bähr in 1741 and built in 1753–6. The façade is by the Baroque architect Ephraim Schroeger, his only work in his native town. (The disfiguring tower was added to the façade in 1897–9.) The door to the sacristy has magnificent intarsia work.

On the way from the market square to St Mary's Church along ul. Panny Marii it is worth turning off into ul. Piekary, which like ul. Ciasna has preserved several Gothic and Baroque granaries. Because of their outstanding quality these have been restored to their original form. The house at No. 37 has a fine Baroque façade with stucco decoration, somewhat similar to the 'Dom pod Gwiazdą' in the Rynek Staromiejski. (The ground floor was only opened up during the First World War.)

The chancel of the **Kościół Najświętszej Panny Mary (Church of St Mary)** (13) extends as far as the corner of the Old Town Market Square, which is unusual for Franciscan churches, since the mendicant orders usually had to establish themselves on the edge of towns. This peculiarity may be explained by the fact that the arrival of the Order occurred not long after the town itself was founded.

By about 1250 the friars had a small, temporary, wooden church in Toruń, and this was rebuilt as a two-aisled masonry church in the second half of the 13th century. The present grand hall church with its long rectangular chancel was built between 1343 and 1400. Contrary to usual practice, the rebuilding began with the nave, because as a preaching order the Franciscans needed as much room as possible for the congregation. The model was the recently completed St John's Church, and here too the nave and aisles originally each had their own roofs. It was not until about 1800 that these were replaced by a single saddleback roof, which gives a false impression of the structure of the building. In accordance with the rules of their Order, the Franciscans did without a tower (which they regarded as a symbol of worldly power) and restricted the decorative elements to a minimum. The chancel is marked only by a false gable composed of three octagonal bell-turrets with blind arcading.

The interior was originally as bare as the exterior but over the centuries it accumulated a rich collection of furnishings. Its most precious item, a Gothic polyptych with scenes from the Life of Christ (1380–90) has been kept since the Second World War in the National Museum in Pelplin. Its place has been taken in the church by an altar with a crown-shaped baldachin made in 1731, the same year that the chancel arch with a Crucifixion group was erected. The Gothic choir stalls (first half of the 15th century) with their intricate tracery carving are some of the most famous in Poland. Among the tombs in the choir is the mausoleum of Anna Waza (see page 399), the sister of King Zygmunt III Waza, built in 1636 as a small chapel attached to the north wall of the presbytery. Its Baroque doors are decorated with allegorical figures and the arms of the Wazas, Sweden and Gotland.

Toruń, view of the town, engraving by M. Merian, 1652

Near the entrance to the sacristy stands the original rood (first half of the 15th century), which combines the gracefulness of the Schöner Stil with anatomical realism.

In the gallery above the north aisle, created by incorporating a range of the cloister into the church, can be seen the richly carved Mannerist organ front (1609; the organ itself is more recent). In the south aisle Gothic painting of the 1370's has survived on the inward-facing buttresses, with New Testament scenes and figures of saints in niches. These are the work of Bohemian painters, and introduced the new achievements in spatial representation of architecture developed in Italian painting. In the two eastern bays of the south aisle are two late 16th-century monuments (of the Stroband family and Martin Mochinger), which are good examples of the artistic taste and pretensions of the wealthy patrician families of Toruń. The Stroband tomb may be the work of Willem van den Blocke, the Dutch architect and sculptor who was active in Gdańsk.

On the way to Rynek Nowomiejski it is worth stopping to look at the Renaissance doorway of *Dom Eskenów (Esken House)* at ul. Łazienna 16. It was created around 1590 as part of the remodelling of what was originally a Late Gothic burgher's house, which was converted into a Neoclassical granary in about 1800. The door itself, which has a relief carving of the Prodigal Son, is now in the Muzeum Okręgowe.

Ul. Szeroka and ul. Królowej Jadwigi take us to *Rynek Nowomiejski (New Town Market Place)*, the centre of the New Town, which until 1454 was an independent entity. Unlike the Old Town, which was inhabited mainly by merchants, the New Town was mostly occupied by craftsmen. Consequently its architectural appearance was generally more modest than that of its neighbour. Moreover it has suffered more from fires, destruction in wars and architectural development in the 19th and 20th centuries.

The Ratusz Nowomiejski (Town Hall of the New Town) which used to stand in the middle of the square, was converted into a Lutheran church in the 17th century and demolished in 1818. It was replaced by the **Zbór św. Trójcy (Protestant Church of the Holy Trinity)** (14) (now a storehouse), a *Rundbogenstil* building in whose design Karl Friedrich Schinkel had a part.

Among the houses facing the square, No. 13, the **Apteka pod Lwem (Lion Pharmacy)** (15) on the corner of ul. Królowej Jadwigi, is a Gothic building, which was given a Neoclassical remodelling at the beginning of the 19th century. An inn is supposed to have been established on the site of No. 8 on the next corner (ul. Ślusarska) as early as 1489. The present **Gospoda pod Modrym Fartuchem (Blue Apron Inn)** (16), now a café, dates from the 18th century; the evocative interior was restored in the 1950's.

The southeast corner of the square is dominated by the massive west front of the **Kościół św. Jakuba (Church of St James)** (17), which served as a convent church for various orders of nuns. It was built between 1309 and about 1340 and the west tower was added in the course of the following century, together with the only other alteration to the original fabric, two rows of chapels along the aisles. The church therefore still looks much the same as when it was built, and it is possible to appreciate what an alien effect it must have produced. This basilican type of structure with exterior buttresses (now partly concealed by the 15th-century chapels) and rich decoration (friezes and blind arcading composed of coloured glazed bricks) is an import from western Europe occasionally to be found in this region. Inside, the architecture of the star vaulting of the nave and choir gives way to a curious fan-shaped vault at the rectangular east end, creating the suggestion of a polygonal apse, another unusual feature.

Many Gothic paintings on walls and vaults have survived from the original decoration (scenes from the lives of saints, ornament; restored in the 19th century), as have several statues. A figure of the Virgin (late 14th century) stands in front of the southeastern pier in the nave, and another (late 15th century) in the first chapel in the south aisle. Also in the south aisle are two Gothic Crucifixes from the former Dominican monastery, a mystic cross, surrounded by prophets holding inscribed scrolls (late 14th century, incorporated into a Baroque altarpiece) and the Czarny Krucyfiks ('Black Crucifix', mid-15th century). The Dominican monastery, a parallel foundation to the Franciscan house in the Old Town, stood on the northwest edge of the New Town, between ul. Dominikańska and ul. Most Pauliński. After destruction in the Napoleonic Wars the ruins were demolished. The fine late 15th-century panel painting in the choir is modelled on the work of Netherlandish masters and consists of many interconnecting scenes of the Passion, shown in a contemporary landscape and acted out by figures in modern dress.

Bydgoszcz – Lubostroń

West of Toruń, in Kujawy, lies **Bydgoszcz (Bromberg)**, the voivodship capital, which has suffered ever since its foundation in the 13th century from its situation in the border region between various opposing powers. In the 14th century it was fought over by the Teutonic Order and the Kingdom of Poland, and then for the next two centuries experienced its longest flowering as a busy commercial town. It was severely damaged during the Swedish Wars, and further destruction was wrought by the Russian, Prussian and French armies in the 18th and early 19th centuries. During the 19th century, when Bydgoszcz was Prussian (from 1772), and, from 1814 to 1919, the capital of the Province of Posen, the tensions between the Polish and German inhabitants increased. The town profited from this national rivalry which stimulated the activity of the many cultural circles and associations, encouraging among other things the building of schools. During this period a new economic boom changed the face of the town. In the Second World War Bydgoszcz was the scene of bloody fighting, and by 1945 it had lost more than a quarter of its population.

The Stare Miasto (Old Town), on a curve in the River Brda (Brahe), has retained at least the rough outlines of its historic appearance. In 1349, when it received its charter from King Kazimierz III Wielki, it was laid out on a regular chequerboard plan with a rectangular market place in the centre. The most important buildings – the Town Hall, five churches, the castle ruins and the medieval fortifications – were all demolished in the course of modernization during the 19th century.

The market place, in the centre of which the Town Hall stood until 1834, and which until well into the 19th century was the busy commercial and administrative centre of the town, now has a predominantly 20th-century appearance. With the exception of a few 18th-century buildings it was all rebuilt around 1900 and restored in 1973–5. At the southeast corner stands the Late Baroque building of the *Biblioteka Publiczna (Public Library)*, built in 1774–8 (No. 24). Diagonally opposite, at the corner of ul. T. Magdzińska, a Gothic house (No. 27) survives under a Neoclassical remodelling of 1775. On the west side of the square stood the Jesuit Church, which was demolished with the whole terrace in 1940. The bronze *Pomnik Walki i Męczeństwa Ziemi Bydgoskiej (Memorial of the War and the Martyrdom of the Bydgoszcz Region)* was erected in 1968 to commemorate the public executions which took place here in 1939.

At the back of the block of houses is the Baroque building of the *Kolegium Jezuickie (Jesuit College)*, which since 1879 has been used as the seat of municipal government.

The adjacent *Kościół św. Marcina i św. Mikołaja (Church of St Martin and St Nicholas)* in ul. Farna is the oldest surviving church in Bydgoszcz. It was originally built around 1400, but destroyed shortly afterwards in 1409 during the battles with the Teutonic Order. The present church was built between 1460 and 1502 as a hall church with an almost square ground-plan and a long choir with a three-sided apse. The west front is decorated with a Late Gothic stepped gable; the porch was added around 1600. The interior has fine star vaults built around 1500. Most of the furnishings date from the Baroque period. The new stained glass in the choir was inserted in 1952–4 and is based on the glass in the Sainte Chapelle in Paris.

The route along ul. Przyrzece to Wełniany Rynek (Wool Market) follows a branch of the River Brda, which washes around the Wyspa Młyńska (Mill Island). Sadly, many of the early 19th-century houses in this picturesque corner of the Old Town, known as *Wenecja Bydgoska ('Bydgoszcz Venice')*, are very dilapidated.

We now go along ul. Wierzbickiego and across Nowy Rynek (New Market Place), laid out in 1835, to the Wały Jagiellońskie, the site of the old town fortifications. These were destroyed in the Swedish Wars and their ruins were later incorporated into new houses. A *tower* dating from 1484 has survived in the courtyard of No. 3. A few remains of the walls can still be seen along Wały Jagiellońskie.

The street ends at Zbożowy Rynek (Cornmarket), which originally lay outside the walls of the town in the old Przedmieście Toruńskie (Toruń Suburb). At its northeast corner stands the former *Kościół Bernardynów N.P. Marii (Bernardine Church of St Mary)*, later the garrison church. The Bernardines were invited to Bydgoszcz in 1480 and first built a wooden church on the site. This was replaced in 1545–57 by a Late Gothic aisleless church with a long choir. The present appearance of the church is the result of a purist restoration out carried out in 1864–6, which included a remodelling of the façade. The land to the east of the church was the monastery garden from the 17th century; some of the old trees still remain.

A few paces further along ul. Bernardyńska take us to Pl. Kościeleckich which contains the neo-Gothic *Kościół św. Andrzeja Boboli (Church of St Andrzej Bobola)*, a former Lutheran church built in 1900–03.

Views of Bydgoszcz, wood engraving, 1888

We continue along ul. Przy Zamczysko and ul. Grodzka to Rybi Rynek (Fish Market), which from the middle ages until 1952 was the centre of the fish trade. On its south side (ul. Grodzka Nos. 7, 11, 12) are half-timbered *Spichlerzy (granaries)* dating from the 18th and 19th centuries. They now house the historical, archaeological and numismatic collections of the *Muzeum Okręgowe (Regional Museum)*.

On the other side of the river stood the medieval Przedmieście Gdańskie (Gdańsk Suburb), today's Śródmieście (town centre), which until the industrial expansion of the town in the 19th century was limited to the vicinity of the Most Staromiejski (Old Town Bridge).

In Pl. Zjednoczenia, on the corner of ul. Jagiellońska, rises the *Kościół Wniebowzięcia N. P. Marii (Church of the Assumption)* built around 1600 on the site of an earlier hospital church founded in 1448. In 1615 the Poor Clares took it over and had the nave rebuilt.

In 1835 the church was secularized and until 1920 was used as a storehouse. During this period the church and its furnishings were badly damaged. The appearance of the church today is the result of two restorations, one in the 1920's, the other in the 1950's. It is worth going inside to see the 17th-century ceiling paintings and high altar.

Nearby is the former convent, built in 1615–18 and altered several times since, which is now the *Muzeum Okręgowe (Regional Museum)* with a large collection of works by the Romantic Bydgoszcz painter Leon Wyczółkowski.

In Al. 1. Maja stands an interesting Art Nouveau hotel '*Pod Orłem*' *(The Eagle)* (No. 14), opposite which is the Jedynak department store, an early reinforced concrete structure erected in 1911.

Three blocks to the north, near the Park im. Kochanowskiego, is the cultural centre of the town. On the south side of ul. Słowackiego stands the imposing neo-Baroque *Wyższa Szkoła Muzyczna (School of Music)* built in 1905–6. The *Filharmonia Pomorska im. Ignacego Paderewskiego (Ignacy Paderewski Pomeranian Philharmonic Hall)* built in 1954–8 is regularly used for music festivals, such as the annual 'Musica Antiqua Europae Orientalis'.

The *Pomnik Henryka Sienkiewicza (Henryk Sienkiewicz Memorial)* by Stanisław Horno-Popławski was set up in the park in 1968.

The *Teatr Polski (Polish Theatre)*, founded in 1945, occupies a building erected in 1947–9 at the northwest corner of the square, on the corner of Al. Adama Mickiewicza and ul. 24. Stycznia 1945.

At **Lubostroń** about 30 km south of Bydgoszcz the Skórzewski family, who owned the area from 1764 to 1939, built a beautiful little Neoclassical *Palace* between 1795 and 1800; the English landscape garden covering 28 hectares was laid out at the beginning of the 19th century.

The palace, designed by one of the greatest Polish Neoclassical architects, Stanisław Zawadzki, is in the Palladian villa tradition, as revived in England in the 18th century.

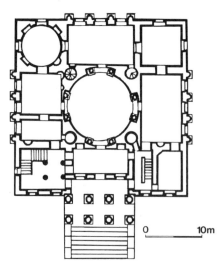

Lubostroń, plan of the Palace

0 ____ 10m

Its square ground plan and central dome are related to Palladio's Villa Rotonda and Campbell's Mereworth, but here the dome is surmounted by a statue of Atlas balancing the world on one hand. The severe symmetry of the articulation of the façades, each with a pedimented centrepiece with engaged columns, is broken only on the entrance front where a broad flight of steps leads up to a portico. The interiors too are arranged around a central rotunda which rises to the full height of the building. The rotunda was designed to incorporate the columns that were to have been used in a Temple of Providence in Warsaw planned to celebrate Polish independence, a project that was cancelled at the time of the Partitions. The decoration follows classical models: under the ring of the dome is a frieze showing a sacrificial procession, below which are bas-reliefs of scenes from the medieval history of Poland. In the rotunda the rich parquet floor inlaid with oak, beech and rosewood has also survived. The pattern is composed of motifs from the arms of Poland and Lithuania. The adjoining rooms have decorative painting by Antoni and Franciszek Smuglewicz.

Golub Dobrzyń

It is worth making a day trip to the little town of **Golub Dobrzyń (Gollub)**, picturesquely situated on a hill above the River Drwęca (Drewenz), about 40 km from Toruń, to visit its imposing and well preserved castle (plate 15).

In 1239 the Teutonic Order conquered the settlement, which belonged to the Dukes of Mazovia, and built the castle and town walls. By 1454 when Golub Dobrzyń joined the Prussian League, it had become a thriving commercial town. In the Second Peace of Toruń (1466) it passed with the rest of Warmia to the Polish Crown. Golub Dobrzyń experienced a second flowering after 1611, when it was inherited by Anna Waza, the sister of King Zygmunt III Waza. The princess instigated among other things the cultivation of vines and tobacco, which were to bring the town considerable profits. At that time Golub was a serious commercial rival to Toruń. But before the end of the 17th century the castle was destroyed in the Swedish Wars, which brought the development of the town to an end.

The district of Dobrzyń on the opposite bank of the river developed originally as a suburb of Golub. In the Prussian period (from 1772) it was raised to the status of an independent town, but after the Second World War the two towns were made into a single administrative unit.

The *Zamek Krzyżacki (Castle of the Teutonic Order)* was built by the Knights in 1302–6 as four ranges forming an almost perfect square around a courtyard. Then at the beginning of the 15th century the west front was given two round corner towers, one of which has survived, and the interior was opened to the courtyard with a two-storeyed cloister.

At the beginning of the 17th century Anna Waza converted the castle into a grand Late Renaissance palace. The elegant attic surmounting the building and the four decorative corner towers are part of her alterations. The Gothic Kaplica św. Krzyża (Chapel of the Holy Cross) on the upper storey of the south range still survives, and has a fine (re-constructed) star vault; the (14th century) tracery and the painted window frames have also been restored. The reconstructed rooms are now used by the *Muzeum Okręgowe (Regional Museum)*.

The town, which lies below the castle on a bend of the river, suffered serious damage during the two-year occupation by the Swedes and again in a fire in 1893. Parts of the fortifications have survived along the river bank, as has the *Kościół św. Katarzyny (Parish Church of St Catherine)* nearby. The church was built in the first half of the 14th century and destroyed and rebuilt several times in the course of the following centuries. However, the interior still retains important parts of the original decoration such as the Gothic door (*c.*1400) to the sacristy, with its ironwork, and the Late Gothic wall paintings on the south wall which date from the end of the 15th century and show scenes from the Passion of Christ. The Mannerist high altar (*c.*1640) incorporates a Gothic Pietà. The pulpit and rood (with four Evangelists) date from around 1730.

A visit to Golub should also include the market place, where many of the houses were remodelled in the Neoclassical manner in the 19th century.

Ciechocinek – Włocławek

Across the plain of Kujawy lies the spa town of **Ciechocinek**, about 25 km southeast of Toruń. Saline springs were discovered here as early as the 12th century. The town grew gradually from the 17th century, but its present importance is due to its development in the early 19th century by its patron Stanisław Staszic, who turned it into a spa and in 1823 established the first saltworks. Surviving from this early period are the extraordinary *Tężnie (Graduation Works)* (1827–8), perhaps the most famous early industrial architecture in Poland. They consist of enormously long (up to a kilometre) oak frames filled with brushwood, through which the brine trickles and evaporates. Between the three graduation works stands a Neoclassical pavilion, also of wood, built in 1836 over the spring. In 1908 the *Park Tężniowy (Park of the Graduation Works)* was laid out. Among its interesting and exotic trees a monument to Stanisław Staszic was erected in 1961. The extraordinary character of the flora found around Ciechocinek is due to the high salt content of the soil. The conditions are ideal for very rare salt-loving plants, and various nature parks have been established in an attempt to preserve them. The atmosphere is said to be good for a number of ailments.

Following the Vistula we come to **Włocławek**, one of the oldest towns in Poland. It is already mentioned towards the end of the 12th century as the seat of the bishop of Kujawy, transferred here from Kruszwica in 1159, whose diocese extended as far as the Baltic. It was granted its charter in 1259. Today the townscape of Włocławek, although grim, still bears witness to its turbulent history.

In the middle ages the town frequently suffered because of its situation on the disputed border of the Teutonic State, but after the Peace of Toruń in 1466 it built up a flourishing trade with the northern regions of Poland, particularly with Gdańsk. Its main source of income was agricultural produce from the fertile plain of Kujawy. This economic revival was followed by a cultural flowering, as the town developed into an important centre of humanism. The learned bishop and humanist Piotr z Bnina (Peter of Bnin) and the astronomer-astrologer Mikołaj Wódka both worked here. The period of prosperity lasted for about 150 years. In 1620 the town was devastated by fire, followed three years later by a cholera epidemic. Then came the Swedish invasion in the 1650's, and it was not until the 19th century that Włocławek experienced a revival of fortunes, becoming the major centre of cellulose processing and paper manufacture in Poland. These are still the town's most important industries.

There are few reminders of the medieval past; Włocławek today is largely a creation of the 19th century. The street plan was redrawn and the style of the buildings is predominantly Neoclassical. Only in Stary Rynek (Old Market Place) and the adjacent streets near the bank of the Vistula have a few old burghers' houses and granaries survived. The rows of houses on the east side of the market place, Gothic in origin but given Baroque remodellings in the 18th century, were converted in 1968–9 to be used by the *Muzeum Historii Miasta (Museum of Town History)*. Also in the market place is one of Włocławek's old churches, the *Kościół św. Jana (Church of St John)* dating from the 1530's. The aisleless Late Gothic building shows little of its original form. The Renaissance tower was erected in 1580 and later given a Baroque helm. The semicircular apse was built in 1622 to replace the earlier chancel. The two adjoining chapels are also later additions, being family foundations of the 17th and 18th centuries. The church was refitted with Late Baroque furnishings in the 18th century.

A short distance along ul. Tumska, which opens off the south side of the market place, we come to Pl. Mikołaja Kopernika where the *Cathedral* stands (plate 39). It was built in 1340–65 to replace a Romanesque cathedral, and has been frequently altered over the centuries to suit changing tastes of the times. The last such remodelling was a neo-Gothic restoration in the late 19th century. The bell-towers were built in the mid-19th century. However, the interior still largely retains a rich variety of furnishings from various periods. In keeping with its importance, the cathedral has particularly lavish chapels, altarpieces and, above all, tombs and monuments to bishops from the 15th to the 19th centuries. Some of the choir windows date from the period of the building's construction *c.*1360, and others are by the leading Polish Art Nouveau painter Józef Mehoffer of Kraków. Among the cathedral's greatest treasures are the Late Renaissance gilt cross (1610–15), and the Late Baroque silver altar (1744) brought here from the monastery at Łódź. In the Kaplica św. Marcina (St Martin's Chapel) some 13th-century Romanesque sculptures from the earlier cathedral are displayed. The Kaplica św. Józefa (Chapel of St Joseph) contains the tomb of Bishop Piotr z Bnina. The orange-brown Hungarian marble tomb slab of 1493, carved in high relief with a full-length portrait of the deceased, 'sad, plump and beardless' (B. Knox), is a work by Veit Stoss (see page 458).

Near the cathedral stands the small Gothic *Kościół św. Witalisa (Church of St Vitalis)* built around 1300 and given its fine star vault in the 16th century. Since the 19th century it has belonged to a seminary occupying the neighbouring neo-Gothic building of 1843.

Dorota Leszczyńska and Michaela Marek

Warmia, Mazuria, Suwałki, Białystok

Poland's north-eastern borderlands are one of the most fascinating parts of the country. Besides beautiful landscape, unspoilt lakeland and primeval forest, there is also great cultural diversity. German influence can still be seen in the area which was once East Prussia, while further east and south the presence of Lithuanians and Tatars, as well as Orthodox Christians and even Old Believers, make this one of the more exotic regions of the country.

The northern border of the voivodship of Warmia-Mazury follows the line established in the Potsdam Agreement of 1945 dividing the German province of East Prussia into a Soviet northern part and a Polish southern part. East Prussia, the successor to Ducal Prussia and the Teutonic State, was thus partitioned out of existence. Its capital Königsberg, home of Immanuel Kant, was renamed Kaliningrad and became a Russian city. The southern border follows the old inter-war frontier between East Prussia and Poland, while the eastern border of the voivodship of Podlasie, now the state boundary with Lithuania and Byelorussia, as defined in the Polish-Soviet border treaty of 1945, is essentially the 'Curzon Line' as proposed in 1920 by the British Prime Minister Lloyd George in the name of his Foreign Secretary, Lord Curzon.

Warmia is the triangular wedge of land between the towns of Frombork, Olsztynek and Reszel, and once formed a Catholic enclave in the middle of Protestant Mazuria. The name Warmia, or Ermeland, is derived from the old Prussian name for the region. In the last phase of the Teutonic State Warmia went its own way, and during the Thirteen Years' War between the rebellious towns (with Toruń at their head) and the Teutonic Order, Warmia placed itself under the protection of the Polish King. Not until 1772 did it again become part of Prussia.

Unlike Warmia, Mazuria was never a political entity. There was no Mazurian dukedom or principality, and until very recently no administrative district of that name. Mazuria was a geographical expression: the territory between Gołdap in the north and Nidzica in the south. The city of Olsztyn, which is nowadays regarded as the capital of Mazuria, used to be not in Mazuria but in Warmia.

The old territory of East Prussia experienced more than its share of suffering and destruction in the centuries up to 1945. The reason for this lay not in a supposed age-old antagonism between the Germans and Poles, but in its position at the strategic crossroads between East and West: the Teutonic Knights and the Poles both sought access to the Baltic here, the Swedes marched through on their way to Poland, Hitler's army passed through on its way to Russia, and the Red Army on its way to Germany.

The Teutonic Knights, summoned by the Polish Duke Konrad Mazowiecki, arrived here in 1226. The region was then populated by the pagan Pruzzi, after whom the land was later to be called Prussia. Their territory extended westwards as far as the lower Vistula, northwards as far as Memelland in Lithuania, eastwards to Grodno and southwards to Pułtusk and Białystok. They had been settled here without interruption from the Neolithic period onwards, and hundreds of prehistoric burial mounds, mostly from the Bronze Age and early Iron Age, have survived.

The Teutonic Knights, clad in their distinctive white mantles marked with a black cross, set about their task of pacification with gusto: some of the Pruzzi were exterminated, others driven out, and the rest of the indigenous population forced to adopt the Catholic faith. At the same time the order built monasteries and churches, castles and towns. Gradually Polish settlers were introduced, mostly farmers from the province of Mazovia, who, together with the German settlers and the remaining Pruzzi, were to form the population of Mazuria.

The decline of the Teutonic Order was caused by two factors: on one hand the continual conflicts with the Poles, which culminated in the Battle of Grunwald (known to the Germans as Tannenberg) in 1410, when the army of the Order suffered devastating defeat at the hands of the Polish-Lithuanian troops and their Mazovian allies; and on the other the intensified resistance against the power of the Order among its own subjects. In 1454, in alliance with Poland, the Prussian towns rose against Teutonic rule. The Polish King Zygmunt I Stary finally agreed to the secularization of the Teutonic State and its transformation in 1525 into the hereditary Duchy of Prussia under Polish feudal overlordship. Soon afterwards the duchy adopted the Lutheran faith. In 1618, the year which saw the outbreak of the Thirty Years War, the duchy passed by inheritance to the Hohenzollerns of Brandenburg and the Elector of Brandenburg became Duke of Prussia too. After the confusion of the Swedish Wars, the Peace of Oliwa on 3 May 1660 gave international recognition to Prussian sovereignty.

Wars continued to limit the economic development of East Prussia. In 1656–7 Tatars invaded, in 1806 Napoleon's army marched through on its way to Russia, in 1914 Russian troops devastated large parts of Mazuria. The region was the scene of fierce fighting in 1914, when Hindenburg's victory over the Russians at the Mazurian Lakes was presented by German propaganda as revenge for the defeat at nearby Grunwald five centuries before. Nor did the region suffer only the disasters of war: in 1709–12 nearly 250,000 people (a third of the population of East Prussia) died of the plague.

When the Prussian state took notice of its distant province, it was usually concerned with the northern part, particularly the city of Königsberg. In this region great estates

Gdańsk

Frombork*

Elbląg

Lidzbark Warmiński

Orneta

JEZ. TALTY

Łyna

Bartoszyce

JEZ. MAMRY

Bisztynek

Gierłoż

Kętrzyn

Reszel

Święta Lipka

W a r   m   i   a

Kan. Elbląski

Morąg

Dobre Miasto

Ryn

JEZ. RYŃSKIE

M

Mikołajki

Kwidzyń

Barczewo

Olsztyn

m   a   z   u   r   y   e

Ostróda

P o j e z i

Ruciane-Nida

JEZ. JEZIORAK

Olsztynek

Iława

JEZ. PLUSZNE

JEZ. ŁAŃSKIE

JEZ. NIDZKIE

Pus

Szczytno

Grudziądz

Stębark
Grunwald

Nidzica

Brodnica

Działdowo

Mława

 Os

Ciechanów

Wisła

Włocławek

Wyszków

Płock

WARSZAWA

Wisła

0   N   50 km

Łowicz

404

Warmia, Mazuria, Suwałki, Białystok

Gołdap

Pojezierze
Puńsk
Cz. Hańcza

Puszcza
Borecka
Suwałki
Suwalskie

Olecko
Sejny

skie

JEZ. WIGRY
Puszcza

Augustów
Augustowska

Ełk
Kopijki

NIARDWY
Prostki
Biebrza
Augustowski

Grodno

Niemen

Sokółka

Knyszyn

Puszcza
Knyszyńska
Supraśl
Kruszyniany
Wolkowysk

Tykocin
Bobrowniki

Białystok

Byelorussia

Zambrów

Narew

Puszcza

Podlaska

stów Maz.

Białowieski National Park
Bielsk Podlaski
Białowieża
Brańsk
Białowieska

Bug

Siemiatycze
Grabarka

Drohiczyn

Kobrin

Siedlce

Brest

The Battle of Grunwald (1410), woodcut, 1597

developed, while in Mazuria small farmers, fishermen and foresters predominated. The 19th century saw much emigration from Mazuria, especially towards the Ruhr, where people were attracted by the higher wages they could earn in the collieries.

East Prussia's greatest suffering came in 1945. The Nazi authorities left evacuation far too late, and tens of thousands of men, women and children lost their lives as they fled before the advancing Soviet troops. They died of hunger and cold, drowned in the march across the frozen Frisches Haff, or fell victim to dive-bombing attacks or the ferocity of Soviet soldiers. Of the 2.6 million East Prussians about 500,000 were listed as dead, of whom 200,000 were members of the Wehrmacht. The number of Germans who wished to remain in former East Prussia after 1945 was estimated at 500,000, but with the support of the Allies the Polish Communist authorities began expelling them soon after the end of the war. The only ones allowed to remain were those who were regarded as 'autochthonous': that is, 'long-established' Mazurians who had been 'Germanized' in the past and now needed to be 'Polonized' again. This process was often undertaken by force and its unpopularity resulted in more emigration.

The German province of East Prussia is now part of history. Today there can be no doubt that Mazuria is part of Poland, and between Ostróda in the southwest and Gołdap in the northeast a third generation of the new inhabitants is already growing up. Their grandparents were moved here from all regions of prewar Poland, their parents felt that they belonged here, and the children have no doubt that they are 'Mazurians'. Nor is there any reason to doubt, as some Germans still do, the historic rights of the present-day Polish state to Mazuria; it is a border region which always had a mixed population of Poles and Germans.

The appearance of the Mazurian countryside has altered little since before the war (plate 43). It is still in the words of the famous old 'Ostpreussenlied' the 'Land of the dark forests and crystal lakes', a rural region with little industry. Consequently it is one of the most popular holiday destinations for Poles and Germans. It is hard to say whether Mazuria is a lakeland plain in the midst of forests, or an extensive forest region set between lakes. Nature-lovers, ramblers, anglers and lovers of water sports, will find everything they could wish for. Many nature reserves have been created, particularly in the areas of primeval forest, to protect plants and animals. They cover a total area of 13,000 hectares, where rare species such as beavers, wild swans, herons, cranes and even elks can be found. The Pojezierze Mazurskie (Mazurian Lakeland) is divided into four areas: the Great Mazurian Lakes with Lake Śniardwy (114 sq km) near Mikołajki and Lake Mamry (105 sq km) near Giżycko – these are known as the 'Mazurian Seas' and are Poland's largest lakes; the East Mazurian Lakes with Lake Hańcza (Poland's deepest lake at 108 metres) north of the town of Suwałki; the Central and Southern Mazurian Lakes around Olsztyn; and the West Mazurian lakes north of Iława.

The beauties of this landscape are described by Marion, Countess Dönhoff in her memoir of an East Prussian childhood *Before the Storm*. Great landowning families like the Dönhoffs had an immense influence on the political, economic and cultural development of East Prussia, and the countess's analysis of the genesis of her class makes interesting reading. She also gives a harrowing account of the exodus in 1945, which for many meant the loss of their homeland. The novelist Siegfried Lenz, another East Prussian, has also tried to come to terms with this loss in some of his writings, notably *Heimatmuseum* (translated into English as *Heritage*).

East Prussians, including Agnes Miegel, the anti-Nazi writer Ernst Wiechert and Fritz Skowronnek, as well as the artists Käthe Kollwitz and Lovis Corinth, all drew inspiration for their work from the particular qualities of the East Prussian landscape and its people.

In the 18th century East Prussia was one of the great intellectual centres of Europe. Its capital, Königsberg, was the home of the three 'sages of East Prussia': Immanuel Kant (1724–1804), perhaps the greatest German philosopher, whose thought has left a lasting mark on European culture; Johann Gottfried Herder (1744–1803), whose ideas have had an enduring influence on literature, philosophy and historiography (the importance he attached to folk songs, which he collected, and folk culture generally, played a major part in the beginnings of the 19th-century nationalism); and Johann Georg Hamann (1730–88), who emphasized the importance of individual revelation in opposition to the rationalism of the Enlightenment, and who stressed the religious aspect of philosophy, creating the term 'practical Christianity'.

In the same period a leading Polish literary representative of the Enlightenment was Ignacy Krasicki (1735–1801), the last Prince-Bishop of Warmia, a favourite of King Stanisław Poniatowski and after Prussia's annexation of Warmia, of Frederick the Great. His philosophy looked back to Erasmus of Rotterdam and his poetry was influenced by poets of the Polish 'Golden Age', especially Jan Kochanowski (see page 100).

Olsztyn – Ostróda – Morąg – Olsztynek – Grunwald – Nidzica – Działdowo – Barczewo – Dobre Miasto – Orneta – Lidzbark Warmiński – Bisztynek – Reszel – Święta Lipka – Kętrzyn

Olsztyn (**Allenstein**) is situated in the midst of beautiful undulating countryside. The town is a good base for exploring the extensive forest region to the south of the town between the lakes Plusznie, Łańskie and Kośno, or indeed the whole Mazurian lake district. With a population of 145,000, almost three times that of 1945, it is now the second largest town (after Białystok) in Poland's furthermost northeastern region. Besides being the administrative centre of a voivodship and the home of several large industrial concerns (including the largest Polish tyre factory), it also has several institutions of higher education founded since the Second World War, including two agricultural colleges and a teacher training college. Its pantomime theatre has a nationwide reputation.

The town dates back to the 14th century. In 1346 the cathedral chapter of Warmia was granted the Prussian districts of Bertingen and Gudikus, and the canons built a castle in one of the bends in the River Łyna (Alle), which was to form the centre of the later settlement. The first mention of the 'New Town' is in 1348. After the Peace of Toruń in 1466 Olsztyn, together with the rest of Warmia, passed to the Polish Crown. In 1516–19 and 1520–21 Nicolaus Copernicus was working in Olsztyn as administrator of the cathedral chapter. It was during this period that he started work on his magnum opus 'De revolutionibus'. In the First Partition Olsztyn was given to Brandenburg-Prussia. It was occupied by the French army in 1807 and by Russian troops in 1914, but remained Prussian until 1945.

About half the town was destroyed in the Second World War, but it has since been rebuilt in almost the same form. The burghers' houses and old town hall in the market place have regained their original appearance. Not far from the market place stand the 19th-century, neo-Gothic Lutheran parish church (which survived the war unscathed and is still used by a few remaining Lutherans), the Catholic parish church of St James (now the cathedral of the diocese of Warmia), and the High Gate, the only surviving part of the 14th-century town walls.

The *Brama Wysoka (High Gate)*, which was used as a prison from 1850 until 1898, is a brick Gothic building with an almost square ground-plan. On the town side it is decorated with a beautiful diamond pattern of coloured headers, while the outward-facing front is articulated with pointed and segmental blind arcading; the gable and stair-tower date from 1858.

Among the *gabled arcaded houses* in the market place mention should be made of two connected Gothic houses, Nos. 10 and 11, built around 1380 and revealed in 1936 following a fire. No. 11 is one of the oldest arcaded houses in former East Prussia. Of the *Stary Ratusz (Old Town Hall)*, built in 1623–4 and thoroughly restored in 1766, only the outer walls survive; the ridge-turret (1851) and gable (1881) are later additions.

The *Kościół Farny św. Jakuba (Parish Church of St James)* (since 1945 a cathedral) is one of the greatest examples of the brick architecture characteristic of the Teutonic State. It was probably begun in 1370–80 in connection with the building of the Teutonic Order's castle, and is first mentioned in 1445. The architect followed the typical Warmian model of the three-aisled, choirless hall church with a massive tower included within its rectangular ground-plan. The 16th-century nave vaults are a complex web of brick ribs, while the aisles have diamond vaulting with a variety of patterns. The church underwent restorations in 1715–21, 1819–20 and 1859, but the most thorough restoration took place in 1866–8, when it was given its present neo-Gothic appearance. The painted decoration dates from 1925. On the tower the interruption of the building work can be clearly seen above the

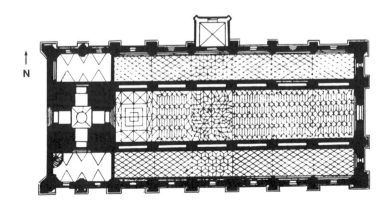

N

Olsztyn, plan of the Church of St James

third storey; on the ground floor is a richly articulated pointed doorway, above which is blind arcading, with patterns composed of glazed bricks set in the horizontal plaster friezes and around the pointed arches. The Baroque furnishings were nearly all replaced with neo-Gothic ones in 1866–71.

The former *Castle* of the cathedral chapter of Warmia survived the Second World War almost intact and is still in good condition. It now houses the *Muzeum Warmii i Mazur* with a good collection of Gothic sculpture, as well as archaeological, ethnological and scientific collections and exhibits illustrating the history of the Polish national movement in Warmia and Mazuria. The construction of the castle began in 1348, which means that it was more or less contemporary with the castles of Reszel and Lidzbark Warmiński. The most important survival from this first phase is the main building in the northeast range, which included the former residence of the land provost, a refectory and St Anne's Chapel. Some of the diamond vaulting is unusually beautiful. On the side of this range, facing the courtyard, is a two-storey arcade ornamented with a horizontal plaster frieze and pointed arches in the upper storey. The main tower rises at the west corner of the building, its square lower part decorated with a diamond

*Olsztyn, view of the Castle,
drawing by F. von Quast, 1852*

pattern in coloured headers. In the southwest range the break in the masonry halfway up and the former loopholes give an indication of the original appearance of this part of the castle. Nicholas Copernicus lived and worked here in the 16th century, when he is supposed to have designed the sundial in the arcade. The museum has various exhibits recalling the great astronomer, including his desk. In the courtyard are three Pruzzi granite statues.

The ruins of the *Zamek Kryżacki (Castle of the Teutonic Order)* at **Ostróda (Osterode)**, about 40 km west of Olsztyn, needed considerable restoration to return the building to its original appearance. A number of fires and damage in the Second World War had meant that of the old fabric of the castle (1347–70) only the cellar, the outer walls (to the height of the main storey), parts of the ground floor rooms, the main gate, and the door and windows had survived. Today Ostróda is mainly a holiday centre for the neighbouring Iława lakeland. The town stands on the east bank of Jezioro Drwęckie, which is linked by a number of rivers and canals to other lakes nearby, so that there are many delightful waterways throughout the area. In the summer months boats run daily along the Kanał Elbląski (Oberländer Kanal), with some interesting boat lifts, as far as Elbląg and Iława. Iława, or Deutsch-Eylau, was the site of the bloody but indecisive Battle of Eylau, fought in a snow storm in February 1807 between Napoleon's army and the combined Russians and Prussians. Napoleon was only able to claim victory because his troops were slower to abandon the field than the enemy. 'Le pays est couvert de morts et de blessés,' he wrote to Josephine. 'Ce n'est pas la belle partie de la guerre. On souffre, et l'âme est oppressée de voir tant de victimes.' Some 45,000 soldiers lay dead in the snow: the highest toll of any battle hitherto recorded.

Johann Gottfried Herder, humanist and poet

Morąg (Mohrungen) to the north of Ostróda is the birthplace of the great philosopher and writer Johann Gottfried Herder (see page 408). The house where he was born on 25 August 1744 did not survive the Second World War, but its site is marked by a commemorative plaque, and the street which was first named ul. Kościelna after the war was later renamed ul. Herdera. There are some Herder memorabilia and early editions in a museum in the Baroque *Palace* of the Dohna family, one of the great families of the Prussian aristocracy. It was built in 1717–19 by the local architect Johann Caspar Hindersin and has been rebuilt since its destruction in 1945. At present restoration work is under way on the interior of the attractive brick Gothic *Town Hall* (1360–80), which has rich mouldings round its doorways. The only notable buildings to survive from old Morąg are a much altered wing of the former *Castle* of the Teutonic Order and the fine *Kościół Farny (Parish Church)*. The oldest parts of the church date from the first quarter of the 14th century; furnishings and monuments survived the war. There are Late Gothic wall paintings in the chancel.

At **Olsztynek (Hohenstein)** to the south of Olsztyn little remains of the Teutonic Order castle (first mentioned in 1351); foundations, outer walls and two granite corbels on the west gable are incorporated in a 19th-century building, which is now used as a school. On the way out of the town, on the Olsztyn road, is the interesting *Muzeum Budownictwa Ludowego (Museum of Vernacular Architecture)*, whose examples of timber peasant buildings, originals as well as reconstructions, give a good insight into old building methods.

Almost 20 km to the southwest of Olsztynek, between the villages of **Grunwald (Grünfelde)**, Stębark (Tannenberg) and Łodwigowo (Ludwigsdorf) is the site of one of the greatest battles of the middle ages. On 15 July 1410 the army of the Teutonic Order,

411

led by the Grand Master Ulrich von Jungingen, suffered a crushing defeat at the hands of the combined Polish-Lithuanian forces. The Grand Master and half of his 27,000-strong army were killed; Poland-Lithuania emerged as the undisputed master of the region, and the Jagiellonians as a dynasty of European importance. The event is commemorated by a *monument* erected in 1960. According to Poland's first major historian, Jan Długosz, whose father fought there, the Polish and Lithuanian soldiers sang the 'Bogurodzica' ('Mother of God Song', see page 129) before the battle. The song is one of the earliest recorded texts in the Polish language, and already in the 15th century it was regarded as a sort of national anthem.

The battle, called Tannenberg by the Germans and Grunwald by the Poles, is at the centre of Henryk Sienkiewicz's historical novel 'Krzyżacy' (see page 103). An English translation of this stirring nationalist work, under the title 'The Teutonic Knights', was published in 1943 as part of the war effort. A film was made in 1960 by Aleksander Ford.

A little over five hundred years later, in August 1914, the German Eighth Army under the command of Hindenburg defeated the Russian Narev army in this same region. Fighting began near Stębark on 27 August 1914 and ended some 20 km further east two days later. Although the field was now some 30 km away from the medieval battlefield, Ludendorff, Hindenburg's Chief of Staff, insisted on naming it the Battle of Tannenberg (sometimes conflated with the Battle of the Mazurian Lakes). A few fragments of masonry on an unremarkable hill southwest of Olsztynek are all that remains of the huge 'Reich-sehrenmal Tannenberg' (Tannenberg Monument), erected in 1927 and blown up in 1945 by the retreating Germans. The 1914 bloodbath is remembered as one of the great First World War battles of encirclement.

Nidzica, engraving by Hartknoch, 1684

In the far south of the voivodship of Olsztyn is the town of **Nidzica (Neidenburg)** with its old *Zamek Kryżacki (Castle of the Teutonic Order)*, a massive rectangular building dominating the town. It is still in good condition and today contains a museum, library and restaurant. Started around 1370 and essentially complete by the time the town was founded in 1381, it served as a border castle facing Poland and was clearly conceived as a defensive building in the old manner, with high walls, towers and houses. The chapel contains interesting wall paintings from around 1400: the Martyrdom of the Eleven Thousand Virgins, an Adoration, figures of the four Evangelists and ornamental scroll-work. Nidzica was the birthplace in 1821 of the great 19th-century poet and historian of medieval Rome, Ferdinand Gregorovius.

Since 1980 restoration work has been continuing at another Teutonic border *Zamek (Castle)*, built in 1340–50 at **Działdowo (Soldau)**, about 25 km southwest of Nidzica and already in the voivodship of Ciechanów.

The former *Klasztor Franciszkanów (Franciscan Monastery)* at **Barczewo (Wartenburg)** northeast of Olsztyn, contains the splendid Late Renaissance black and white marble tomb of Cardinal Andrzej Batory (the brother of King Stefan Batory), who kneels in prayer above, and his nephew Baltazar, who reclines below. It was erected in 1598 to designs by the Dutch architect Willem van den Blocke, who introduced kneeling figures into funerary sculpture in Eastern Europe.

The *Kościół Farny (Parish Church)* of **Dobre Miasto (Guttstadt)** (colour plate 26) on the old road to Königsberg, is the biggest parish church in Warmia. It was built in the third quarter of the 14th century as a three-aisled brick hall church with no choir – the box form typical of the region – and still retains some of its medieval decoration. The tower is late 15th century, but the present gables were added in 1895. Adjoining the church on the south side is its priests' college, built in the 14th century. It is now used as a seminary and has kept its first-floor cloister and some restored frescoes. The public library is in the neo-Romanesque former Protestant church (1830–3) by Karl Friedrich Schinkel.

Orneta (Wormditt) suffered little damage in the war, and has a fine brick Gothic *Town Hall* (1373) with a stepped gable on its west front, and an interesting church, the *Kościół św. Jana (Church of St John)*, a 14th-century building enlarged and remodelled in 1422–94. Crowned by a host of pinnacled gables, with lavish use of blind arcading, it is 'one of the showpieces of medieval brick architecture' (Knox). The moulded brick friezes decorated with human figures and foliage on the exterior of the aisles are an unusual feature. Inside there is some fine lierne vaulting, and good Baroque altars and other fittings, including a superb font-enclosure (after 1738). Some old burghers' houses survive in the market square.

Like the rest of Warmia **Lidzbark Warmiński (Heilsberg)** was under the feudal over-lordship of Poland from 1466 to 1772. The Bishops of Warmia resided here from 1315 to 1321, again from 1350 to 1795 and intermittently until 1836, when they moved to Frombork. Lidzbark developed into an important intellectual and artistic centre, especially

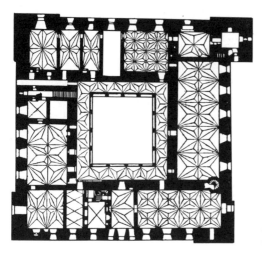

Lidzbark Warmiński, plan of the Bishops' Castle

during the Renaissance. It was here that Nicolaus Copernicus made his astronomical observations after 1506, and probably wrote the first draft of the 'Commentariolus' giving his conception of a heliocentric system. Here too Ignacy Krasicki, the last Prince-Bishop of Warmia (1765–95), wrote his satirical comic epic 'Monomachia or the Monks' War', making fun of the drunkenness and stupidity of monks, and the idleness of the monastic life.

The town lies in a curve of the River Łyna. In 1308 it received its charter with the laws of Kulm, and it still retains its medieval street plan around a rectangular market place. In the market square (Nos. 15 and 18) and ul. Długa (No. 29) a number of the fine old 18th-century gabled houses remain. A part of the old town fortifications completed in 1357 also survives: the *Wysoka Brama (High Gate)* with its two round turrets. It resembles the Crane Gate in Gdańsk, and is the only example of a Dutch type of gate in former East Prussia.

From the market place it is a short distance to the bank of the Łyna, from which there is a good view of the *Zamek Biskupów (Bishops' Castle)* now part of the local museum. The castle is a square fort with plain outer walls, loopholes below the eaves, steep roofs, flanked by two corner turrets and a massive keep – a combination of a princely residence and a stronghold. Next to Malbork (Marienburg, see page 376), which influenced its layout and form, it is probably the most important and best preserved example of the secular architecture of the Teutonic Order. It was built around 1350 and well restored in 1925, when some parts of the once splendid painted decoration were uncovered in the Summer Refectory (first decade of the 14th century), in the Chapel, in the Great Refectory (1370–80) and in the northeast corner tower (c.1500). The courtyard is surrounded by a fine two-storey arcade.

The Catholic *Kościół Farny śś. Piotra i Pawła (Parish Church of Sts Peter and Paul)* was built around 1350 (at the same time as the castle and the town fortifications) as a basilica without a tower. After a fire in 1497 it was converted to a hall church, and the present twelve-part star vaults were built on narrow corbels and arcades. The furnishings include a fine sculpture of the Agony in the Garden (*c.*1420), a granite font (14th century) and a copper-gilt bust reliquary of St Ida (*c.*1420). The old wooden *Lutheran Church* (now Orthodox), built in the Rundbogenstil with a two-tower front, is probably by Karl Friedrich Schinkel (1821–3).

Bisztynek (Bischofstein) owes its German name and coat of arms (a crozier standing on a rock) to the massive granite block known as 'Kamień wielki' ('Great Stone'), which can still be seen, and the memory of the founder of the town, Bishop Heinrich III Sorbom.

In the late middle ages **Reszel (Rössel)** was a strategically important place on the old trade route from the Zalew Wiślany (Frisches Haff) to Poland. The name comes from the old Pruzzi settlement of Resel a few miles to the north. The *Castle* of the Bishops of Warmia completed in 1371, with its great round keep, is mostly intact. Since 1980 restoration work on the interior has intensified. A gallery for contemporary art has been installed and a museum and library are due to be opened soon.

Not far from Reszel, in a valley on the road to Kętrzyn, about 70 km northeast of Olsztyn, stands a surprising and exotic-looking building. At first sight its extravagant Baroque architecture seems out of place, as if it had been brought from Bohemia. It is certainly very unlike the familiar plain brick Gothic of Warmia. This is the pilgrimage church of **Święta Lipka (Heiligelinde)** (plate 44) and its adjoining Klasztor Jezuitów (Jesuit Monastery).

The first mention of the pilgrimage chapel of the holy lime-tree *(capella in linda)* occurs in 1482. In 1617 Stefan Sadorski, secretary to King Zygmunt III Waza of Poland, acquired the Linde estate and had a new chapel built on the foundations of the old one, which had been destroyed in 1524. Later he donated the property to the Warmia Cathedral Chapter. The foundation stone of the present complex was laid in 1687, construction was placed under the direction of the master mason Georg Ertly from Wilno (now Vilnius) and the building was virtually complete by 1730. The Jesuits, who had been put in charge of the pilgrimage site in 1636, later set up a music school and open-air theatre (for religious drama) in 1722. The pilgrimage church is the most important work of Italianate Baroque in Catholic Warmia. Some fine gates by the brothers Johann and Christoph Schwarz lead to an arcaded courtyard with domed corner chapels. The church is a basilica with a high nave and narrow chancel, and the eye-catching façade is flanked by two towers with a balcony. A wide flight of steps leads up to the entrance. The central doorway is set in a deep niche, and between the two windows is a relief of the sacred lime-tree with the apparition of the Virgin Mary (1730, by the sculptor Matthias Poertzel of Königsberg). This cult is in fact a Christianization of pagan tree worship. The rich decoration of the church has remained largely unaltered, and includes an extensive programme of wall painting: on the nave vault is the Glorification of the Virgin in illusionist perspective (1722–7, by Matthias Johann Meyer), on the side walls the Passion of Christ. The large high altar (1712–14), which reaches up to the ceiling, echoes the severe columnar architecture of 17th-century Roman Baroque; it is matched by a magnificent organ. A well-stocked treasury includes 17th-century chalices, 18th-century vestments, as well as some interesting early printed books. One of its greatest treasures, a magnificent monstrance of 1720, was stolen in 1980.

Kętrzyn (Rastenburg) is an attractive little town in the middle of delightful countryside. Its location at a road and rail junction has brought about the establishment of several small industries, but it remains primarily a market town for the produce of the farmers in the region. However, the *Kościół Farny św. Jerzego (Parish Church of St George)* has some of the best diamond vaulting (16th century) in East Prussia. There is nothing here to indicate that only a few kilometres further to the east, just off the road to Giżycko, near the village of **Gierłoz (Görlitz)**, was one of Hitler's main command centres in the Second World War – the *'Wolfsschanze'* ('Wolf's Lair', Polish: Wilczy Szaniec).

Today the 'Wolf's Lair' is a pile of rubble, a riven landscape of concrete slabs and bricks, surrounded by forests, lakes and marshes. The cordon of mines surrounding Hitler's

The Holy Lime-Tree at Święta Lipka, engraving, 15th century

The bunker of the 'Wolf's Lair', one of Hitler's command centres in the Second World War

command centre was 180 metres wide and 10 km long; the concrete roof to the Führer-bunker was 10 metres thick. In this secret town there were 80 buildings including air-raid shelters, offices, hotels, officers' messes and barracks. It was from the Wolf's Lair that Hitler gave the order for Operation Barbarossa, and here too that on 20 July 1944 Colonel Claus Schenk von Stauffen-berg planted the bomb intended to kill Hitler and overthrow the Nazi regime. The Führer survived and Stauffenberg, his fellow conspirators and many sympathizers were brutally executed. 'The list of names of the conspirators sounds like a doomsday roll call from the Almanach de Gotha ... The twentieth of July 1944 marks not only the failure of a political plot, but the end of the Prussian tradition and of Prussia herself as a political force in Europe' (J. P. Stern). Hitler did not abandon the Wolfsschanze until four months later, on 20 November 1944, as the Red Army approached, and on 24 January 1945 German sappers blew it up. Around 250,000 visitors a year come to the memorial at Gierłoż which documents in photographs and film the Nazi crimes in Poland during the Second World War.

Puszcza Piska – Ruciane-Nida – Pisz – Mikołajki – Ryn – Giżycko – Węgorzewo – Ełk – Augustów – Suwałki – Sejny – Wigry

The **Puszcza Piska (Johannisburger Heide)** in the south of the voivodships of Olsztyn and Suwałki is one of the most beautiful areas in Mazuria, almost a thousand square kilometres of forests and lakes, which still retain their primeval character. It is bisected by the great curve of the Jezioro Nidzkie (Niedersee), which, like the Jezioro Bełdany (Beldahnsee) and the Jezioro Mokre (Muckersee) has a spectacular wealth of bird life, with swans, grebes, herons and even eagles. The changing colours of deciduous forests and the endless pine forests, with wild mushrooms, bilberries and red whortleberries, make this a paradise for ramblers and lovers of water sports.

The town of **Ruciane-Nida (Rudschanny)** in the middle of the region has become a popular holiday centre. Many boat trips, paddle-boat and sailing boat tours, and footpaths start here, making it the best place from which to explore the area.

Pisz (**Johannisburg**), on the eastern edge of the Puszcza Piska is another mecca for water sports. To the north we can cross the Jezioro Roś (Roschsee) and the Jegliński Canal to the Jezioro Seksty (Sextersee) and the great Jezioro Śniardwy (Spirdingsee). Those bold and fit enough can paddle southwards all the way to Warsaw along the rivers Pisa (Galinde) and Narew. Pisz has a population of 15,000 and is a centre of the timber industry. The castle of the Teutonic Order, built in 1345–70 and dedicated to the Baptist, from which the town gained its German name, fell into ruin in the 18th century and was gradually dismantled. Despite damage in the Second World War the old *Town Hall* and some *burghers' houses* in the market square survive.

Mazuria has 1,600 lakes larger than a hectare, as well as at least 3,000 smaller lakes, known to the Germans as 'Äuglein' or 'little eyes'. Some lakes are narrow and meander endlessly, linking together rivers, streams and canals and filling the deep furrows created by the meltwater from the glaciers in the last Ice Age. The glaciers were also responsible for the two great lakes, Jezioro Śniardwy and Jezioro Mamry, called the 'Mazurian seas'. Lake Śniardwy covers an area of 110 sq. km. Those who live on the shores know how the character of these 'seas' can change: in calm weather they are as smooth as glass, but storms can stir up the waters and capsize boats. At the southern tip of the Jezioro Śniardwy is *Czarny Ostrów* ('Black Island'), which used to be known as Teufelsinsel, in honour of Perkunos, Potrimpos and Pikullos, the trinity of old Pruzzi gods, who had their dwelling here. Beneath the lime-tree of Romowe, the gods are said to have been worshipped with human sacrifices.

The 250-year-old town of **Mikołajki (Nikolaiken)** has also retained the peculiar charm of small Mazurian towns. It has been called – with some exaggeration – 'Mazurska Wenecja' ('Mazurian Venice'). From Mikołajki boats leave for excursions across the great lakes. The 'Stinthengst', a giant stone fish with a crown on its mossy head, still swims beneath the town bridge across the Jezioro Mikołajskie (Nikolaiker See). According to legend he was the greatest enemy of the fishermen of Mikołajki, ripping their nets and releasing the trapped perch and whitefish, sometimes even sinking boats and drowning the fishermen. When he was finally caught the fishermen decided that he should not be killed but should instead be chained to a pier of the bridge as a warning to other fish who might think of causing trouble. Mikołajki gained some importance after the building of the canal between Lakes Śniardwy and Mamry in 1764–6, which was intended to bring timber from the wooded Puszcza Piska to this timberless region.

Unlike Pisz or Mikołajki, the town of **Ryn (Rhein)** further north has remained a quiet spot, away from the busy holiday region and off the main roads. At its centre is a *Zamek Kryżacki (Castle of the Teutonic Order)* built in 1377–80 on the strategically important strip of land between Jezioro Ryńskie (Rheinsee) and another lake. But of the original building only the three-storey main range at the south corner has survived relatively unchanged. Each fall of the later plaster has revealed parts of the brickwork with diamond patterns. The cellar and ground floor each have a long hall with groin vaults and central piers. The regional conservation authorities are planning to restore the building.

On the strip of land between Jezioro Mamry and Jezioro Niegocin (Löwentinsee) lies the town of **Giżycko (Lötzen)**, the most important holiday centre in the whole Mazurian Lakeland. From here it is a short distance to *Piekna Góra*, the 'beautiful mountain' from which there is a wonderful view over the surrounding lakes, to Wysoki Ostrów (Hohe Insel), where there is a reserve for cormorants, and to the heathland of Puszcza Borecka (Rothebucher Forst), where bison are bred. The Teutonic Order's stronghold of '*Leczenburg*', first mentioned in 1337, stood at the narrowest point in the strip of land, about 3 km west of Giżycko. In 1390 it was transferred to the present site and rebuilt in stone. This architecturally important building is in a poor state of repair, but an idea of its former beauty is given by the Renaissance gables on the narrow sides (1560, by Christoph Römer). Also worth seeing is the former Lutheran church, built in 1827 to a design by the school of Schinkel with Tuscan columns in the galleried interior.

The two most interesting buildings at **Węgorzewo (Angerburg)** are the ruined *castle* of the Teutonic Order and the former Lutheran parish church. The castle was at the north-eastern end of the chain of fortifications intended to protect the lake district between Węgorzewo and Pisz. It was first built in 1335 and rebuilt in 1398 after being

Lakes and landscape near Suwałki

419

destroyed by the Lithuanian princes. The Parish Church is a Late Gothic brick building built in 1598–1618, one of the last churches in former East Prussia to have a massive ribbed vault.

Today Węgorzewo, whose name means 'Eel Town', is a centre for fishing and fish processing. The town owes its charm to its situation on the upper stretch of the River Węgorapa, not far from the north bank of Jezioro Mamry. From here it is 20 km to the border with the Russian part of former East Prussia.

The town of Ełk (Lyck), now in the middle of the voivodship of Suwałki, was until the Second World War a border town at the southeastern tip of East Prussia. The old German-Polish border ran about 15 km south of the town. Near the villages of Prostki and Kopijki an old border marker, set up in 1545, still stands. Ełk is the birthplace of the German novelist Siegfried Lenz (born 1926), some of whose work is a literary memorial to the vanished people and traditions, history and landscape of old Mazuria. Outside the town, on an island in Jezioro Ełckie, there are still some remains of the Castle of the Teutonic Knights, built here between 1398 and 1408. In the 16th century Ełk was something of an intellectual centre: the provincial school here had the task of preparing pupils for Königsberg University.

The eastern voivodship of Podlasie, beyond the line running from Gołdap in the north and Ełk in the south, was part of Poland before 1945. Earlier the frontier between the two parts of the Jagiellonian empire, Poland and Lithuania, ran across this region. From 1795 to 1807 parts of it were under Prussian rule, before becoming part of the Duchy of Warsaw. At the Congress of Vienna in 1815 Suwałki and Augustów in the north were made part of the Kingdom of Poland, while Białystok in the south became part of Russia. In 1918 the whole region was incorporated into the new Republic of Poland, but in July 1920, under pressure from the Red Army, Białystok was briefly a Republic of Soviets, and Julian Marchlewski and Feliks Dzierżyński set up a 'Provisional Revolutionary Committee' there. In September 1939 Suwałki was occupied by German forces and incorporated into East Prussia, while Białystok was taken by Soviet troops. In 1941, when Germany turned against Russia, Białystok became a German administrative district. The borders after the Second World War kept both towns in Poland, but some of their old hinterland, including the town of Grodno, passed to the Soviet Union (and are now in the independent republics of Lithuania and Byelorussia, or Belarus).

The ethnic composition of the regions reflects something of this turbulent history. There are Lithuanians living round Puńsk and Sejny, while to the south, along the border and in Białystok, there are Byelorussians, who have their own language. Polonized Tatars, still holding to Islam, are to be found in two villages east of Białystok, near the Byelorussian border, where their forebears were granted land by King Jan III Sobieski in gratitude for their loyal military service. Finally, a few villages round Suwałki and Augustów are home to some Old Believers (Polish: *Starowiercy*) of Russian origin, whose ancestors fled their homeland in 1654.

The town of **Augustów**, now with a population of about 25,000, was founded by King Zygmunt II August in 1561. Its 19th-century development was due above all to the building of the Augustowski Canal in 1824–39, connecting the rivers Biebrza (which joins the Narew and Vistula), Czarna Hańcza and Niemen. Today Augustów is mainly used as a base for visiting the nearby lakeland and the Puszcza Augustowska, which covers an area of more than 1,000 sq km and is therefore Poland's largest uninterrupted area of forest. Polish insurrectionaries had their hideouts in the Puszcza Augustowska during the fighting in 1831 and 1863, and during the Second World War Polish partisans used it as a base for attacks on the German occupiers. This is a landscape of striking beauty: dense coniferous forests, to which access is sometimes difficult, and primitive heathland, bogs and beautiful lakes, linked by rivers and canals. Because of the crowds of holidaymakers who visit the Puszcza Augustowska, the regional authorities are concerned to protect the rich variety of flora and fauna which flourish in this region, and access to some areas has been restricted. The *Wigry National Park* has deer, boar, moose, bison, black storks, white-tailed eagles, swans and cranes; it is also famous for its fish and its forest fungi. Around the River Biebrza itself beavers, wolves and reindeer can be seen, and thousands of waterfowl.

The historic centre of **Suwałki** is characterized by Late Neoclassical architecture typical of the 19th-century Kingdom of Poland, including the Catholic *Kościół Farny (Parish Church)* (1820–45, Aigner and E. Marconi), the *Ratusz (Town Hall)* (first half of 19th century), the *Gimnazjum (Grammar School)* (1833, Corazzi), and a number of *burghers' houses*. No. 31 in ul. Kościuszki is an old Polish *country house*, where the poet and pioneer feminist, Maria Konopnicka (1842–1910), was born. Every Pole is familiar with the Polish national song *Rota* ('The Oath'), for which she wrote the words. Also worth seeing are the *Muzeum Etnograficzne (Ethnographical Museum)* at ul. Kościuszki 81, and the Old Believers' church.

Just 10 km from the Lithuanian border is the old pilgrimage centre of **Sejny**. The church of the *Klasztor Dominikanów (Dominican Monastery)* is a Late Renaissance building erected in 1610-19, and remodelled around 1760 as a Late Baroque hall church with a two-towered façade; the furnishings are Rococo. The village also has an old Synagogue, now a museum. The annual fair which has been held for centuries in Sejny is famous throughout the region.

About 10 km to the east of Suwałki, by the shores of Jezioro Wigry, stands the great Baroque church (1704–45, by Pietro Putini) of the former Camaldolensian monastery of **Wigry**, founded here by King Władysław IV Waza in the 17th century. The monastic buildings have been converted into an hotel.

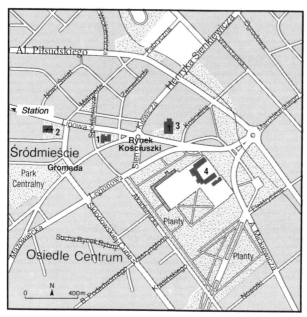

Białystok
1 Ratusz (Town Hall)
2 Cerkiew św. Mikołaja
(Orthodox Church of
St Nicholas)
3 Kościół Wniebowzięcia NMP
(Church of the Assumption)
4 Pałac Branickich (Branicki
Palace)

Białystok – Tykocin – Supraśl – Kruszyniany – Bohoniki – Puszcza Białowieska – Grabarka – Drohiczyn

The voivodship of Białystok on the Byelorussian border is a gently undulating landscape of woods and field, little lakes and moors, with a sparse population and hardly any industry. **Białystok**, the voivodship capital, with a population of 240,000 the largest town in north-eastern Poland, does have some industrial development, particularly in the fields of textiles, metal, timber and food production.

Białystok was a town of no great importance until the 18th century, when the Hetman Jan Klemens Branicki made it his residence. Industry followed in the next century: the first textile mill was set up here in 1824. By 1879 there were 47 mills in operation, and the town began to rival Łódź as a textile centre. The great strikes of 1905–6 were led by the textile workers. Białystok was one of the great centres of East European Jewry. In 1906 Russian right-wing extremists, with the connivance of the tsarist authorities, unloosed a terrible pogrom against the Jewish inhabitants. Thirty-five years later the Nazis set up one of the notorious ghettoes, in which the Jews were penned in inhuman conditions. Like Mordche Gebirtig in Kraków and Hirsh Glik in Wilno, Pejsach Kaplan described in songs and poems the sufferings of the Jews of Białystok. The Nazi policy of extermination not only claimed thousands of innocent human victims, it also destroyed irreplaceable works of Jewish culture: the houses typical of eastern Jewry have gone, together with all the wooden synagogues, many of which were remarkably original works of architecture with wonderful painted decoration. Following the Warsaw Ghetto Uprising, the Jews of Białystok took arms against their tormentors – although there was no hope of victory. By the end of the war over half the population of the town had been killed.

The historic town centre is the Rynek Kościuszki, a triangular market square laid out in the 18th century, where the Late Baroque *Town Hall* (1) built in 1745–61, stands. This now houses the *Muzeum Regionalne (Regional Museum)*, which contains archaeological and ethnological collections as well as a small collection of Polish painting; its most important treasures are the 16th-century frescoes from the monastery at Supraśl (see page 441). In ul. Lipowa stands the massive Orthodox *Cerkiew św. Mikołaja (Church of St Nicholas)* (2), a Neoclassical building of 1846; the rich polychromy of its interior (1910) is a copy of the frescoes in the Orthodox Cathedral of St Sophia in Kiev. To the east of the market place stands the *Kościół Wniebowzięcia NMP (Church of the Assumption)* (3), built in 1617–21, which contains the tomb of the Hetman Jan Klemens Branicki. A plaque on No. 26 in ul. Zamenhofa commemorates the site of the birthplace of the oculist Ludwig Zamenhof (died 1917), who created Esperanto, the universal language that he hoped would foster universal brotherhood.

Białystok's most important building is the Baroque *Pałac Branickich (Branicki Palace)* (4) (plate 42). Because of its grandiose architecture and fine gardens it was known as 'Wersal Podlaski' ('Podlasian Versailles') – though for this title it had to vie with the palace

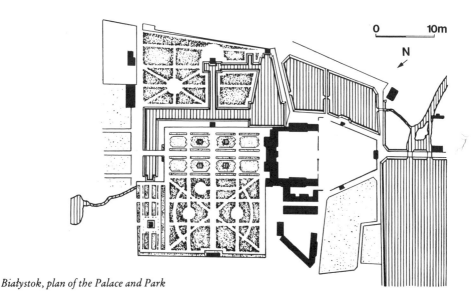

Białystok, plan of the Palace and Park

of Radzyń Podlaski (see page 255). The palace was originally built in the late 15th or early 16th century as a small Gothic palace with two round towers at the ends, on the site of an earlier castle. The building was remodelled in the second half of the 17th century and four single-storey corner pavilions were added. Towards the end of the century there was a further extensive remodelling by Tylman van Gameren, who rotated the axis of the house around 180 degrees, raised the corner buildings on the sides facing the courtyard and the garden, and added a single-storey arcaded hall between the corner buildings. The third phase of remodelling was for the Hetman Jan Klemens Branicki in 1728–58 under the direction of Johann Sigismund Deibel, who raised the whole building of the *corps de logis* to three storeys, gave the entrance front a symmetrical alignment, and created two narrow courtyards surrounded by single-storey buildings. The only surviving interior is a Rococo staircase supported by sculptures of slaves. Branicki had a 400-seat theatre with Polish and French actors and a corps de ballet 'but the only attention Hetman Branicki paid to this impressive establishment was to have the younger ballerinas read fairy-tales to him in his dotage. The stables contained 200 horses, the library 170 books' (A. Zamoyski). The palace has not had a happy history in the 20th century. It was looted by Russian troops in 1915. Dzierżyński proclaimed the Polish Soviet Republic from the principal balcony in 1920. The palace was damaged during the German occupation, but has been reconstructed since 1945. The interior is not open to the public, since it now houses a medical school; part of the gardens are used for botanical experiments by the Institute of Experimental Biology.

A few 19th-century *synagogues* and a single *Jewish cemetery* (of six) remain.

About 30 km west of Białystok, a little beyond the main Warsaw road, lies the historic town of **Tykocin**. In 1548 the town, which had been granted its charter and the municipal laws of Kulm in 1425, was acquired by King Zygmunt II August, who had a great fortress built here, with an arsenal, treasury and library. Soon the town was also playing an important part as a trading centre between east and west. During the Swedish Wars it was the scene of fierce fighting, and much damage was caused by fires and sieges. Of the mighty castle only the foundations now remain, but some of the later buildings are still standing. The impressive Early Baroque *Synagogue* (1642) is now a Jewish museum. The former Missionaries' College was founded by Hetman Jan Klemens Branicki, and its church, now the *Kościół Farny Trójcy Świętej (Parish Church of the Holy Trinity)*, was built in 1742–9, with a façade linked by curving wings to two flanking towers (inside are paintings by Szymon Czechowicz). In 1763 Branicki erected the statue of his grandfather, the military commander Stefan Czarniecki (1599–1665), who had been given a hereditary grant of land here in gratitude for his defeat of the Swedes. Nearby are the restored buildings of the *Alumnat*, a hospice for old soldiers founded in 1633. In the side-streets around the market square many wooden, single-storey houses survive.

63 HREBENNE Church of St Nicholas ▷

65 Uchanie Parish church, tomb of Paweł Uchański and his wife Anna

66 Leżajsk Church of the Annunciation, Baroque organ

◁ 64 Baranów Sandomierski Leszczyński Palace

68 Zamość Plasterwork vault decoration in a patrician house in the Main Square

67 Opatów 'Lament of Opatów' (detail)

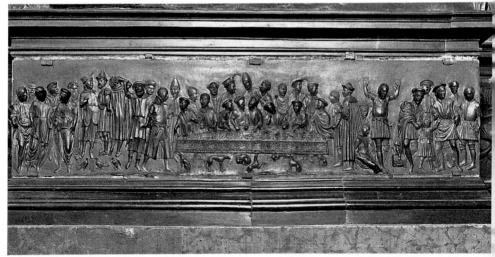

70 Wrocław St John Nepomuk Monument
69 Wrocław Town Hall

71 WROCŁAW
Cathedral, door to
the sacristy

72 WROCŁAW
Church of St Mary
Magdalene, Roman-
esque doorway

73, 74, 75   TRZEBNICA   Convent church, tympanum reliefs on the north door

76   LUBIĄŻ   Cistercian abbey, ceiling painting in the Princes' Hall

78 BĘDZIN Piast castle
77 OPOLE Terrace of houses on the market place in the old town
79 HENRYKÓW Cistercian abbey

81 Góra Świętej Anny Monument to the Third Polish Uprising in Upper Silesia in 1921

80 Paczków Church of the Virgin

83 Płakowice Renaissance palace ▷

82 Katowice The Sports and Entertainment Hall in the city centre

The town of **Supraśl**, northeast of Białystok, was once a great textile centre; manufacturers from Łódź and many German workers settled here after 1830. The Gothic Renaissance church (1503-11) of the Orthodox *Klasztor Zwiastowania NMP (Monastery of the Annunciation)*, razed to its foundations by the Germans in 1944, has been meticulously rebuilt since 1984. Fragments of the original wall-paintings are displayed in the 17th-century Archimandrite's Palace, which has interesting plasterwork. Other buildings in the extensive monastic complex have also been restored or are being reconstructed, and the monastery is enjoying a revival. The famous Supraśl Codex, an 11th-century lectionary once in the library here, is one of the earliest surviving texts in Old Church Slavonic. It is now divided between St Petersburg, Ljubljana and Warsaw.

It is a good 50 km from Supraśl to the Byelorussian border and the villages of **Kruszyniany** and **Bohoniki** – the Tatar settlements still lived in by the descendants of the Tatar soldiers of Jan III Sobieski, who were granted land here in the late 17th century. Picturesque Kruszyniany, an enclosed settlement with about fifty houses, most of them wooden, is proud of its 200-year-old *Meczet* (Mosque), which is a timber building with two towers and an unobtrusive minaret. The building is well maintained and the faithful still meet regularly for worship; the imam based in Warsaw is occasionally present. On a hill not far away is the Muslim cemetery, where the tomb of the last imam of Kruszyniany is the most prominent of the bilingual Arabic-Polish gravestones with their Polonized Muslim names, which rise above the tall grass. Despite the financial support for the mosque from the Middle East, it seems that the days of these settlements of Polish Tatars are numbered: only the elderly carry on living here and they are periodically overwhelmed by curious tourists and noisy school parties. The younger ones have already moved to Białystok or Warsaw, where they have running water instead of having to use an old outdoor hand-pump.

Once the hunting ground of Polish, Lithuanian and Russian royalty, the **Puszcza Białowieska (Białowieża Forest)** southeast of Białystok is the largest area of primeval forest left in Central Europe. Part of it, on the border with Byelorussia, is now the Białowieski National Park. It is most famous for its bison, some of which can be seen in a special enclosure, and its wild horses (tarpans or Biłgoraj ponies, the basis of the stock used by the Greeks and all the other chariot-driving peoples of the Eastern Mediterranean, which are being bred back to their original type), lynxes, beavers, racoons, polecats and wolves, as well as red deer, reindeer and wild boar. The national park also contains a vast range of rare flora and 13 kinds of bats. Scientists from Poland and all over the world stay at the village of Białowieża, where some buildings from a vast 19th-century Tsars' hunting lodge survive, to work on zoological and botanical projects. Public access is limited to specific areas, which can be visited with a guide, using horse-drawn carts or bicycles. There is a good museum at Białowieża, which has a room devoted to the history of bee-keeping.

Grabarka, about 15 km east of Siematycze, is the most important religious centre for the Orthodox Christian community in Poland, which numbers several hundred thousand. They hold a festival here every August in the old Gothic timber church (recently damaged by arsonists).

The little town of **Drohiczyn** lies west of Siemiatycze, on the River Bug. Here time seems to have stood still; many of the houses are of wood, the ferry across the river is still pulled by hand. From the high river bank the view extends as far as the Byelorussian border. Among the town's impressive Baroque churches, the *Kościół Benedyktynek (Benedictine Nunnery Church)*, built in 1744, has an unusually powerful façade. There is also an *Orthodox church*.

Reinhold Vetter

Małopolska (Lesser Poland)

The first Polish state had been centred on Wielkopolska (Greater Poland) in the west with its cities of Poznań and Gniezno, but when Poland re-emerged as a political entity in the 14th century after years of fragmentation, the centre of power was shifted to the southeast, to the region known as Małopolska, with Kraków as its capital. The region had originally been settled by the Vistulanians (Wiślanie), who took their name from Poland's greatest river, the Vistula (Polish: Wisła).

The historic region of Małopolska encompasses the whole area between the present state frontier with Slovakia along the Carpathians to the south; the rivers Soła, Przemsza and Pilica to the north and northwest; the Vistula and Wieprz to the north; and the state border with the Ukraine along the Bug to the east. The part of Małopolska which lay east of the Bug, with the former capital of East Galicia, Lwów (Lemberg), became part of the Soviet Union. Lwów, known by its Ukrainian name Lviv, is now the second city of the Republic of the Ukraine.

For the purposes of this guide we have divided Małopolska into four sections based on present-day voivodships: the historic city of Kraków; the region around Kraków (Ziemia Krakowska) extending to the Carpathian mountains (Tatry and Beskidy) to the south; the rich Małopolska Plain (Wyżyna Małopolska) to the northwest around Częstochowa, Radom and Kielce; and the eastern region between the Vistula and Bug and the Carpathians (Bieszczady) to the east with the Lublin Plain (Wyżyna Lubelska) and Sandomierz Basin (Kotlina Sandomierska).

Kraków

Cracovia totius Poloniae urbs celerrima atque amplissima regia atque academia insignis (Cracow, the most famous and glorious town in all of Poland, distinguished by virtue of its royal residence and the Academy – M. Merian).

A visit to Kraków (Latin: *Cracovia*, hence the English form Cracow), Poland's old capital, is a journey into Poland's past. It was here that the kings of Poland were crowned and were buried; and even after they transferred their residence to Warsaw in the 16th century the old metropolis, where most of the Royal Elections and Diets had been held, still remained 'the noblest and most famous city of Sarmatia'. The whole city of Kraków is a monument to the cultural achievement of Poland, and works by foreign artists (Veit

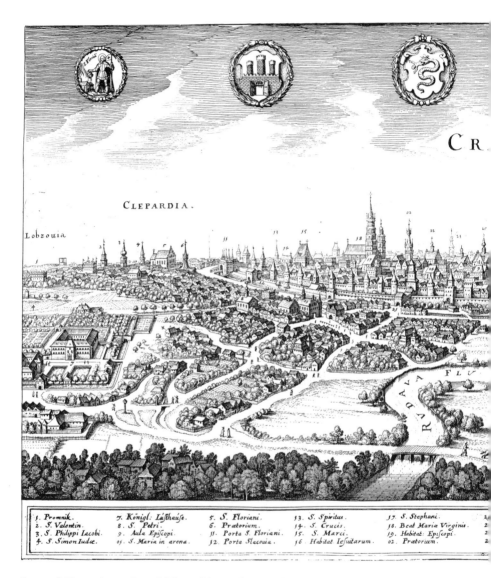

1. *Promnik*.	7. *Königl: Lusthause*.	5. *S. Floriani*.	13. *S. Spiritus*.	17. *S. Stephani*.
2. *S. Valentin*.	8. *S. Petri*.	6. *Prætorium*.	14. *S. Crucis*.	18. *Beat Mariæ Virginis*.
3. *S. Philippi Iacobi*.	9. *Aula Episcopi*.	11. *Porta S. Floriani*.	15. *S. Marci*.	19. *Habitat: Episcopi*.
4. *S. Simon Iudæ*.	01. *S. Maria in arena*.	12. *Porta Slacouia*.	16. *Habitat Iesuitarum*.	02. *Prætorium*.

Stoss of Nuremberg, Bertel Thorvaldsen of Copenhagen, Peter von Nobile of Vienna) are evidence of the economic and cultural links with other European centres over the centuries.

There are traces of human habitation near Kraków as early as the Late Palaeolithic period (2–3 mill.–10,000 BC). On the Wawel, the flat-topped hill above the Vistula,

25. S. Francisci. 29. Curia Pontificis. 33. Templ. Bernhardinorū. 37. Oppid. Iudeorū. 41. S. Catharina. 46. Porta:
26. Templum Iesuitarum. 30. Palatia Regis. 34. S. Heduigis. 38. S. Laurentij. 42 S. Leonardi. Scardinia.
27. S. Andreæ. 31. S. Stanislai. 35. S. Agneta. 39. T. Corp. Christi. 43. Rupell S. Stanislai.
28. S. Martinus. 32. S. Michaelis. 36. Porta Vistulæ. 40. Prætorium. 44. S. Iacobi. 45. S. Benedicti.

considerable archaeological evidence of settlements from the Neolithic period (from 10,000 BC), the Lusatian Culture (*c.*1200–*c.*800 BC) and the Iron Age (from 1000 BC) has been found. Two artificial hills *(Kurhany)* date from prehistoric times: the *Krakus Mound* to the north and the *Wanda Mound* to the south. (This hill-building activity was resumed in the 19th century with the *Kościuszko Mound* to the west and in the 20th century with

445

the *Piłsudski Mound*, which commemorate the two outstanding figures in modern Polish history.)

The Krakus Mound is supposedly the tomb of the legendary Krak, a military leader and king, who built a castle on the Wawel rock opposite. (The Wanda Mound commemorates Krak's daughter Wanda, who is said to have drowned herself in the Vistula rather than marry a German prince.) In the 8th and 9th centuries the Slavic Vistulanians settled here. For a time they were independent, but they soon came under the rule of the Czech Přemyslids. The first written mention of the town is in the account by Ibrahim Ibn Ja'qūb, a Jewish merchant from Cordoba, who visited Kraków in 965, around the time that Mieszko I (ruled c.960–992), the ruler of the Polanians, made it part of the Piast state.

Because of its location on five important trade routes, Kraków was then already an important centre, visited by merchants who made their way along the Amber Road from the Baltic to southern Europe, and from the West to the lands of the Rus and Byzantium. In 963 a wooden fort was built on the Wawel with a massive palace chapel, replaced only 55 years later, under the Piasts of Wielkopolska, by the first cathedral. The Wawel was then an island in the Vistula, the 'Queen of Polish rivers'; on the riverbanks below an important fortified town was already developing. In 1038 Kazimierz I Odnowiciel ('the Restorer') made Kraków the capital of the country, and Bolesław III Krzywousty confirmed this in 1138. Kraków remained the political centre and seat of princely rule as the country fragmented into lesser princedoms (1138–1306); in 1257 the town was granted the laws of Magdeburg by Bolesław V Wstydliwy ('the Chaste'), Prince of Sandomierz and Kraków, and in 1259 its first stone walls and towers were built.

Meanwhile the Tatar invasions (1241–2, 1259 and 1287) had been disastrous for the town. During the civil wars and confusion after the death in 1288 of its ruler Leszek Czarny ('the Black'), Kraków changed hands many times, and suffered a year-long siege as a result of a revolt led by the German community, after which only those who could correctly pronounce certain difficult Polish words were pardoned.

Leszek's brother, Władysław I Łokietek, slowly reconquered Poland, and he was finally crowned King in the ruins of the Wawel Cathedral in 1320. The church he subsequently built here was the coronation church of the Polish kings until the end of the monarchy, although Kraków remained the capital and royal residence only until 1596. The most important examples of medieval architecture in the town below the Wawel are the Church of St Mary (since 1222 the parish church) and the Sukiennice (Cloth Hall), which developed in the late 14th century from a bazaar street in the market place.

King Kazimierz III Wielki (ruled 1333–70) turned Kraków into a brilliant metropolis. In 1349 he founded the University, the first on Polish soil; his vice-chancellor Janko of Czarnków was the assiduous chronicler of the period between 1370 and 1384, which ushered in the 'Golden Age' of Poland under the Jagiellonians (1386–1572), the most important period in the town's history. The University, refounded in 1400 by Władysław II Jagiełło with a legacy from his consort Jadwiga, attracted between 8000 and 10,000 foreign students in the 15th century alone. In 1405 a burgher of Kraków called Stobner

The refounding of Kraków University by Władysław II Jagiełło (left, holding the captured banners of the Teutonic Order and being baptised) and his late wife Jadwiga (right, supported by the University's original founder, Kazimierz III Wielki); St Jan Kanty prays in his cell below

endowed a chair in Mathematics and Astronomy, the only one in Europe at that time. Among the many leading theologians working at the university was Mateusz of Kraków (1345–1410), who later became Rector of Heidelberg University. In the mid-15th century Jan Długosz (1415–80) wrote the first history of Poland here. Nicolaus Copernicus studied at the university from 1491 to 1494. Filippo Buonaccorsi from San Gimignano (known as Callimachus, 1437–96), one of the greatest humanists in Europe, was a confidant of the Archbishop of Lwów, Grzegorz of Sanok (1406–77), who gathered a host of artists and intellectuals about him. The German geographer Hartmann Schedel described the city in his World Chronicle in 1493: 'In Kraków there is a famous university, which is rich in many outstanding and very learned men, where many liberal arts are taught ... Here people live more lavishly than elsewhere in Poland. You can find here everything that human nature requires.'

The burghers, who were gaining in self-confidence and wealth, were, after the royal court, the second greatest promoters of this cultural development. It has left its mark on the city to this day. By 1430 Kraków had become a member of the Hanseatic League and had many German merchants and craftsmen among its inhabitants, as well as active communities of Ukrainians, Czechs, Rumanians, Italians and Jews. The contacts with the cultural elite of Germany and Bohemia were particularly strong. The outstanding example of this is the Nuremberg artist Veit Stoss, who lived in Kraków for 19 years and between 1477 and 1489 created for its German burghers the greatest late medieval carved altarpiece in Europe (colour plate 7). In 1473 Kraków had 17 towers and gates, in 1575 there were 33, and in the 17th century 47; each one was assigned to one of the craftsmen's guilds for upkeep and defence.

Kraków enjoyed its greatest flowering in the 16th century under the tolerant and cultured Jagiellonian kings, Zygmunt I Stary and Zygmunt II August. Italian architects and artists not only remodelled the royal residence on Wawel Hill in the Renaissance manner, they also left evidence of their work on almost all the town buildings. This Florentine Renaissance manner survived in Kraków as a coherent and consistent style well into the following century. The first Italian to work in Kraków was Francesco Fiorentino (Franciszek Florentczyk), who first appeared in 1501–2 and was responsible for the tomb niche of King Jan I Olbracht in Wawel Cathedral and the first stage of the remodelling of the royal castle. After Fiorentino's death in 1516 his successor was Bartolommeo Berrecci, another Florentine, who created the Sigismund Chapel. Perhaps the most spectacular reminders of the splendours of the royal court are the 136 surviving Brussels tapestries (of 356), some of them worked with gold thread, which decorated the rooms of the castle and the cathedral on the Wawel.

Closely connected with the court in the 16th century were a number of famous humanist scholars, including several Bishops of Kraków (Piotr Tomicki, Samuel Macie-jowski and Filip Paniewski). They were served by a vigorous publishing industry, which produced, amongst others, the first book printed in Cyrillic and the first in Hungarian and Romanian.

An important school of painting was created by Tommaso Dolabella of Venice, who lived in Kraków from 1598 until his death in 1650. The most important architects of the first half of the 17th century were Giovanni Trevano of Lugano (Church of Sts Peter and Paul), Andrea Spezza, and Andrea and Antonio Castelli; the leading sculptors were Giovanni Battista Falconi, Giovanni Francesco Rossi and, outstanding among them, Baldassare Fontana (St Anne's Church).

The many surviving works of art and architecture from the Renaissance and Mannerist periods (16th–17th centuries) give a vivid picture of the life of the burghers of the town.

After Warsaw was made the capital, when King Zygmunt III Waza transferred the royal residence there between 1596 and 1611, Kraków lost some of its importance. During its occupation by the Swedes in 1655–7 and again in 1702, Kraków suffered heavy damage and looting. The 18th century brought a deep political and economic crisis, and by the time of the Partitions (1772–95) the population had sunk from 40,000 to 9,000. Some 150 monasteries in Kraków and the vicinity were closed. Despite this decay, the town was the starting

The Great Fire of 1850, lithograph by S. Sandmann

point for the Kościuszko Uprising in 1794. Of more lasting influence were the university reforms of its Rector, Hugo Kołłątaj, which ensured that Kraków would remain a beacon of Polish culture in the centuries to come.

In the Third Partition (1795) Kraków passed to Austria and became part of the Kingdom of Galicia and Lodomeria. On 15 July 1809 the city became part of the Duchy of Warsaw, but the Congress of Vienna in 1815 made it a free city (the 'Republic of Kraków') under the supervision of the three partitioning powers. There followed thirty years of independence, during which the population rose to about 80,000. Much refurbishment of the city centre was carried out. Kraków became a centre of resistance against foreign rule in Poland, and after the failed Revolution of 1846 it was again annexed by Austria.

In 1850 a great fire swept through a large area of the old city; part of the market place, ul. Grodzka and many churches, including those of the Dominicans and the Franciscans, were severely damaged. Consequently, the later 19th century was able to see the creation of some major new buildings or new interiors in what remained essentially a Late Medieval and Early Renaissance city.

In the last quarter of the century, during the tolerant period of the reign of Emperor Franz Joseph (to whom some Cracovians still look back with nostalgia), Kraków developed as a centre of intellectual and cultural life in Poland and a base for the revival of national culture. After 1866, the use of Polish was permitted at the Jagiellonian University,

449

Polish dramatists worked at the National Theatre and great Polish actors and actresses appeared there, including the immortal Helena Modrzejewska. The Academy of Art, founded in 1873, enjoyed a high reputation throughout Central Europe.

In the lively café society (of which traces survive, notably the Jama Michalika café itself, see page 455) decadent art and socialist adventurers flourished alike (both Piłsudski and Lenin were active here). More mainstream art and nationalist aspiration crystallized around the personality of Poland's leading history painter, Jan Matejko (1838–93), who spent his whole life in Kraków. His works are as much a part of Polish consciousness as the novels of Sienkiewicz. Matejko's best pupils, Józef Mehoffer (1869–1946) and Stanisław Wyspiański (1869–1907), both members of the Vienna Secession and leading lights in the local Młoda Polska movement, made Kraków the undisputed centre of the visual arts in Poland and home to an individual strain of Art Nouveau decoration.

The investment programme of the Austrian Monarchy up to the First World War resulted in an increase in population from 50,000 (1870) to 150,000 (1915) and made Kraków one of the largest towns in Austria-Hungary. The vigorous building activity – with many new monasteries and churches, some of which were for religious orders that had been driven out of Russian-occupied Poland – resembled that of late 19th-century Vienna. The University was expanded in 1883–7, and the Collegium Novum and Academy of Fine Arts were built. Museums and galleries were also erected, as well as the new town theatre (1891–3). The restoration of Wawel Cathedral, the Cloth Hall, the Franciscan

Kraków 1 Brama Floriańska (St Florian Gate) 2 Arsenał Miejski (Town Arsenal) 3 Sukiennice ▷
(Cloth Hall) 4 Wieża Ratuszowa (Town Hall Tower) 5 Kościół św. Wojciecha (Church of
St Adalbert) 6 Kościół Mariacki (Church of the Assumption of the Virgin) 7 Kościół św. Barbary
(Church of St Barbara) 8 Kamienica Szara (Grey House) 9 Kamienica Montelupich (Montelupi
House) 10 Kamienica Pod Jaszczurami (House of the Lizards) 11 Kamienica Hetmańska (Hetman's
House) 12 Pałac Potockich (Potocki Palace) 13 Pałac Pod Baranami (Palace of the Rams) 14 Pałac
Pod Krzysztofory (Christopher Palace) 15 Kamienica Pod Murzynkiem (House of the Moor)
16 Kamienica Pod Matką Boską (House of the Mother of God) 17 Dom Jana Matejki (Jan Matejko
House) 18 Jama Michalika 19 Barbakan (Barbican) 20 Pomnik Grunwaldzki (Battle of Grun-
wald Monument) 21 Kościół św. Krzyża (Church of the Holy Cross) 22 Teatr im. Juliusza
Słowackiego (Juliusz Słowacki Theatre) 23 Dom Pod Krzyżem (House of the Cross) 24 Pałac
Czartoryskich (Czartoryski Palace) 25 Kościół Pijarów Przemienienia Pańskiego (Piarist Church of
the Transfiguration) 26 Pałac Lubomirskich (Lubomirski Palace) 27 Pałac Wodzickich (Wodzicki
Palace) 28 Pałac Popielów (Popiel Palace) 29 Muzeum Historyczne (Historical Museum)
30 Collegium Maius 31 Collegium Physicum (Kołłątaj Collegium) 32 Collegium Nowodworskie
33 Kościół św. Anny (Collegiate Church of St Anne) 34 Collegium Novum 35 Teatr Stary
(Old Theatre) 36 Pałac Sztuki (Palace of Art) 37 Kamienica Szołayskich (Szołayski Museum)
38 Kamienica Morsztyna 'Pod Gruszką' (Morsztyn House) 39 Kościół św. Marka (Church of
St Mark) 40 Pałac Wielopolskich (Wielopolski Palace) 41 Kościół św. Franciszka (Franciscan
Church) 42 Więzienie św. Michała (St Michael's Prison) 43 Kościół Dominikanów św. Trójcy
(Dominican Church of the Holy Trinity) 44 Collegium Juridicum 45 Kościół ś.ś. Piotra i Pawła
(Church of Sts Peter and Paul) 46 Kościół św. Andrzeja (Church of St Andrew) 47 Kościół
św. Idziego (Church of St Giles) 48 Wawel 49 Smocza Jama (Dragon's Cave) 50 Klasztor
Bernardynów (Bernardine Monastery) 51 Kościół Misjonarzy (Church of the Missionaries)

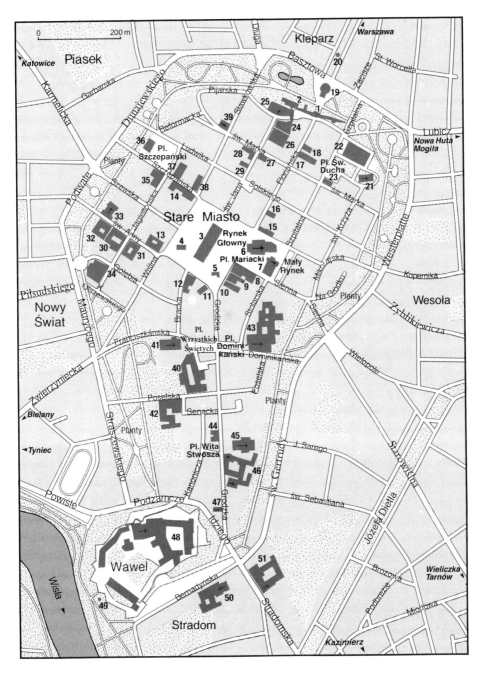

Katowice
Piasek
Kleparz
Warszawa
Basztowa
Długa
Pijarska
Karmelicka
Garbarska
Dunajewskiego
Sławkowska
Reformacka
20
19
25
2
1
Zacisze
St. Worcella
Szpitalna
24
Lubicz
Nowa Huta
Mogiła
36
Pl.
Szczepański
Ludwika
Planty
św. Marka
26
18
22
28
37
Szczepańska
27
17
Floriańska
Pl. Św.
Ducha
35
29
23
Szewska
Portwale
38
14
Sołskiego
św. Marka
św. Anny
21
św. Jana
Stare Miasto
16
33
15
Szpitalna
32
13
3
Rynek
Główny
Mikołajska
31
4
6
30
Pl. Mariacki
Mały
Rynek
Westerplatte
34
Gołębia
Wiślna
5
7
Sienna
Kopernika
Wesoła
12
10
8
Na Gródku
Planty
11
9
Bracka
Grodzka
Sławkowska
Stolarska
Zyblikiewicza
Piłsudskiego
Olszewskiego
Nowy
Świat
Maurycego
Pl.
Wszystkich
Świętych
Pl.
Domini-
kański
43
Dominikańska
Franciszkańska
41
40
Poselska
Wielopole
Starowiślna
Zwierzyniecka
Straszewskiego
42
Senacka
Planty
Poselska
Bielany
Planty
44
45
J. Sarego
Tyniec
Pl. Wita
Stwosza
św. Gertrud
Powiśle
Podzamcze
46
św. Sebastiana
Kanonicza
Grodzka
47
Jozefa Dietla
Wawel
48
51
Wieliczka
Tarnów
Brozowa
Wisła
Bernardyńska
50
Stradomska
Podbrzezie
Miodowa
49
Stradom
Kazimierz

451

church and other monuments laid the foundation for the tradition of Polish architectural conservation (which now has a worldwide reputation), and encouraged the growth of a sense of national identity, which had the eager support of the imperial authorities in Vienna. It was with Austrian support that in 1914 Józef Piłsudski marched out of Kraków with his soldiers to fight the Russians. But the destruction in Galicia during the war was as severe as that in Belgium.

When Poland regained its independence in 1918 a number of monumental buildings were erected at a suitable distance from the old city centre, including the School of Mines (1922–39) and the rebuilt Jagiellonian Library (1931-9). Some of these are magnificent structures, drawing on the lessons of the Secession in a grander idiom. There were particularly close cultural and scientific ties with the city of Lwów not very far away, which had several important scientific institutions and a lively art world.

Kraków's brief rise in the years after 1918 came to an abrupt end with the outbreak of the Second World War in September 1939. The Nazi Generalgouverneur Hans Frank set up his headquarters in the restored Wawel Castle. The nature of Nazi rule soon became clear. In the 'Sonderaktion Krakau' in November 1939 the academic staff of the university were summoned, supposedly to hear a talk about the effect of the new order on higher education; they found themselves forced into covered wagons and transported to Sachsenhausen concentration camp. Hitler's stated aim was to liquidate the Polish intelligentsia. In ul. Montelupich the Gestapo set up a prison in which about 15,000 prisoners were tortured before being shot or taken to a concentration camp. The labour camps in Luboń and Płaszów were notorious. Near the Kazimierz district, which had been founded in the 14th century by King Kazimierz III Wielki as an independent town and had gradually become the home of the Kraków Jews, the Nazis established one of the biggest ghettoes in Poland; very few of its inmates survived.

The city itself, which the Germans had been preparing to blow up, survived owing to speedy manoeuvres by the troops of the Soviet Marshal Koniev, and was captured on 18 January 1945 with negligible damage. After the war Kraków played an important part in the revival of cultural life in Poland. Many scientists and artists, mostly from Lwów (which was now part of the Soviet Republic of the Ukraine) came to live and work here. The art treasures which had been removed by the Nazis, including the Marian Altarpiece by Veit Stoss and the paintings of the Czartoryski Museum returned; the world famous tapestries, which had been smuggled out to Canada in 1940, eventually came back too.

The increasing number of students and the new work force, predominantly from the agricultural regions of Poland, meant that by 1985 the population had increased to 745,000, making it the third largest city in Poland. Part of this increase was due to the Communist plan to drown the spirit of this Catholic, conservative and intellectual city in an industrial proletarian flood, by building Nowa Huta, a massive steel works and housing project on the edge of Kraków. However, the mainly peasant population that gravitated to Nowa Huta remained immovably Catholic and allied itself with the Catholic intelligentsia. Kraków's proudest moment was the election in 1978 of Pope John Paul II, who was born

Karol Wojtyła in Wadowice, 55 km to the southwest, and who had been the city's archbishop for ten years.

The many disasters in the city's history have done relatively little damage to the fabric of Kraków. In 1978 it became the first European city to be included in the UNESCO list of world cultural heritage sites. There are almost 1,000 old burghers' houses, 100 churches and 48 chapels, dozens of palaces and hundreds of thousands of works of art in 26 museums. Despite economic difficulties and administrative delays, work on the conservation and restoration of this heritage has continued. The greatest danger to the monuments (and indeed to the population) is posed, however, by the appalling air pollution for which the Nowa Huta steelworks are in great part responsible.

The traditions and customs of the citizens of Kraków recall the turbulent past. A watchman on the taller of the two towers of St Mary's still blows a warning trumpet signal every hour, the *Hejnał Mariacki*, which breaks off abruptly at the point where his predecessor 700 years ago was struck down by a Tatar arrow. The more successful resistance to the Tatars made by the inhabitants of the Zwierzyniec district is commemorated every year at the 'Green Carnival' held eight days after Corpus Christi, when a merry procession with the Tatar Khan and his entourage makes its way from the Norbertine convent to the Kraków market place. The Khan, or *Lajkonik* ('the man on the little horse'), is dressed in a brightly coloured costume designed by Stanisław Wyspiański. Other ceremonies include *Juvenalia* which begin on a day in the second half of June, when the Rector of the University relinquishes the exercise of his office for a few days to the students, who then go in procession through the town centre in historical and imaginative costumes. On Midsummer's Eve (St John's Eve, 23 June) a colourful ceremony is held on the Vistula at the foot of the Wawel, when wreaths *(wianki)* with lighted candles are floated on the river. In the weeks before Christmas home-made cribs create a colourful spectacle in the market place, and an actor disguised with an animal mask (*Turoń*) plays merry pranks.

Stare Miasto (Old Town)

Within the ring of medieval fortifications, most of them demolished and turned into the public gardens known as the *Planty*, the medieval layout of the town (after 1257) has been preserved intact. At the centre of the rectangular grid of streets is the enormous *Rynek Główny (Main Market Place)* (plate 49); at 200 metres by 200 metres, it is the biggest square in Europe. The main streets run from here to the site of the old fortifications; a few years ago the whole of the Old Town within the Planty was made a pedestrian zone. (Plan: page 451.)

Kraków is bisected by the Royal Way, the route followed by the coronation procession of the kings of Poland. It began just outside the town, at the church of St Florian, Kraków's patron saint, and led to the Cathedral on Wawel Hill and then on to the Paulite

Church Na Skalce ('on the Rock') where the kings performed a ritual purification. The visitor can conveniently follow the Royal Way, and it is the spine of the following description of the town. It starts, moreover, near the train and bus stations.

The *Kościół Kolegiacki św. Floriana (Collegiate Church of St Florian)* stands at the northern end of Pl. Matejki, the centre of the *Kleparz* district of Kraków. The history of this church, whose present appearance is the result of a Baroque rebuilding after the Swedish Wars, goes back to 1185, when the relics of St Florian were transferred to Kraków from Rome, in order to give the growing town some relics of its own. The ashes became so miraculously heavy just before reaching Kraków that the procession had to stop, and it was at this auspicious spot that the church was built. Since then the Roman martyr has been one of Kraków's patron saints. The rich furnishings of the royal church date from the 17th and 18th centuries. The most important paintings are St Florian by Jan Tricius, and parts of a 16th-century triptych by Hans Süss von Kulmbach, the Nuremberg painter who worked in Kraków.

Pl. Matejki – from which there is a fine view of the Barbican and the towers of St Mary's Church – is dominated by the imposing **Pomnik Grunwaldzki (Battle of Grunwald Monument)** (20), dedicated in 1910 by Ignacy Paderewski, the pianist, patriot and President of Poland, to mark the 500th anniversary of the battle. The equestrian figure is King Władysław II Jagiełło. It was erected in Kraków because the Austrian Empire was more lenient towards such expressions of Polish nationalism than were the authorities in Wilhelmine Germany. The monument was destroyed by the Nazis during the Second World War, but reconstructed in 1976. The sculptures are by Marian Konieczny (who was also responsible for the *Monument to Stanisław Wyspiański* outside the Museum of Modern Art, and the now demolished *Lenin Monument* in Nowa Huta). Below the Grunwald monument is a much simpler Monument to the Unknown Soldier, with an Eternal Flame. The building on the right is the Academy of Art, built in 1880 (see page 422).

Ahead is the **Barbakane (Barbican)** (19). By the end of the 17th century the fortifications of Kraków consisted of 47 towers, set in three kilometres of double walls and a moat of between 3 and 24 metres wide. A good impression of how the fortifications looked is given by the panorama on pages 444–5. Demolition, mooted by the Austrians, was eventually carried out by the Republic of Kraków between 1822 and 1847 as a display of municipal modernization. Even at this early date, however, a conservationist backlash, headed by Professor Feliks Radwański of the Jagiellonian University, ensured that a representative section of the walls and three towers were preserved, together with the Barbican. This famous building is a cylindrical brick structure (a 'rondel') with an inner courtyard and charming turrets. It was built in 1489–99 (as part of preparations accompanying the unsuccessful expedition to Moldavia) and is the most spectacular fortification of this type in Central Europe. The unusual design is based on Arab models; it allows defenders to train fire on the flanks of any attacker. The Barbican was set in a moat 20 metres wide at this point, and joined by a bridge to the **Brama Floriańska (St Florian**

Gate) (1) behind. This gate was built in stone before 1307; its height was raised in brick in the late 15th century and it was given its Baroque roof in 1657 and a fine stone relief of St Florian facing the town along the street named after him (plate 45). The walls at St Florian's Gate date back to the 13th-14th centuries and were reconstructed after 1900, and again in 1949–50, together with the covered wooden defensive walkway. On the east side of the gate stands the fine late 15th-century Baszta Pasamoników (Haberdashers' Tower, named after the guild responsible for its upkeep), to the west is the Baszta Stolarska (Joiners' Tower), which is beyond the octagonal Baszta Ciesielska (Carpenters' Tower), built in the early 14th century. Between these two bastions the **Arsenał Miejski (Town Arsenal)** (2) was built in 1565 (remodelled in the 19th century). A covered passageway across ul. Pijarska connects this building with the Czartoryski Palace (see page 423).

Leading from the St Florian Gate to the Market Square is Kraków's most fashionable street, ul. Floriańska. Mainly occupied by shops and cafés, the houses are in fact some of the oldest buildings in Kraków. The first building of note is, however, a monument of Kraków's more recent past. No. 45 is **Jama Michalika** (18) a café, cabaret, and major literary landmark. The house originally belonged to the Belza family, then to the Order of the Holy Ghost. In the 18th century it was known as the Kamienica Pod Jelonkiem (House of the Fawn). In 1895, Jan Michalik opened his confectioner's and the Lwowska Café, and they soon became a favourite meeting place of Bohemian circles. In 1905 Jan August Kiesilewski started a legendary cabaret here, the Zielony Balonik ('Green Balloon'). Jama Michalika is one of the great surviving Art Nouveau interiors; furniture, fittings, stained glass (by Henryk Uziembło), paintings have hardly changed since the last days of the Austro-Hungarian Empire. The decoration was overseen by Franciszek Mączyński and the set designer Karol Frycz. Continuing down ul. Floriańska, No. 41 is the **Dom Jana Matejki (Jan Matejko House)** (17), the famous history painter's 16th-century house. Seven years after his death (1893) a *Museum* was set up in the building. The Baroque-style façade, with the implements of the painter's craft, is the work of

Reconstruction of the Barbican and St Florian Gate, after Essenwein

Tomasz Pryliński and Matejko himself. No. 17 has chains outside, rare survivals of an ancient, city-wide system of crowd control. At No. 14, on the other side of the street, is the Hotel Pod Różą ('The Rose'), where many of Kraków's most famous visitors have stayed including Fausto Sozzini, the Sienese religious reformer, who came to Poland in 1579 and spread Antitrinitarianism ('Socinianism') among the Polish nobility, Tsar Alexander I, Franz Liszt, but (despite what the commemorative plaque says) not Balzac, who stayed at the now vanished 'White Rose' in ul. Stradomska. The inscription on the handsome Renaissance doorway reads 'May this house stand until the ant drinks the ocean and the tortoise circles the earth'. Some older houses on the eastern side include No. 13, the residence of the Kmita family, with fine Renaissance windows; No. 7, the **Kamienica Pod Matką Boską (House of the Mother of God)** (16), 15th century with a niche containing a stone figure of the Virgin and Child; and, at the corner of the Market Place, the **Kamienica Pod Murzynkiem (House of the Moor)** (15), No. 1, with coloured plaster reliefs of American Indians, not Moors, on its façade.

Ul. Floriańska opens onto the superb perspectives of the **Rynek Główny (Main Market Place)**, dominated by the great Cloth Hall at its centre, the Town Hall Tower behind, the huge Mariacki church set at an angle to its northeast corner, and the incongruously tiny Church of St Adalbert towards the southern corner. The Market Place was laid out after the town was granted its charter by Duke Bolesław V Wstydliwy. As well as being the commercial hub of Kraków, it was the scene of many state occasions. Homage to the Kings was sworn in the square (including the famous Prussian Homage when the Teutonic Knights accepted the Polish Kings as overlords); and executions took place here on a scaffold. Kościuszko raised the standard of revolt here in 1794. The solemn oath of freedom that Kościuszko swore here was re-intoned by Lech Wałęsa on 3 May 1981.

The **Sukiennice (Cloth Hall)** (3), originally a Gothic building, started before 1344 and finished by 1392, was given a Renaissance remodelling in 1556–60 by Gian Maria Padovano, after a fire. This is the period of the barrel vault and the attic, with its series of masks on high pedestals, probably made after designs by Santi Gucci. This is the earliest example of the 'Polish attic' or 'Polish parapet', which later became widespread. The hall's present appearance (colour plate 6) is the result of a reconstruction in 1875–9, by Tomasz Pryliński with the participation of the famous painter and Cracovian Jan Matejko. The characteristic neo-Gothic arcades and oriels along the sides and the projecting attics at the transverse axis date from this thorough reshaping. The ground floor, largely Gothicized, still houses small shops selling hand-made leather goods, textiles, jewellery, and other articles aimed at the tourist trade, as well as two cafés, of which Lenin was once a patron. The *Galeria Malarstwa Polskiego (Gallery of Polish Painting)* on the first floor, founded in 1879, contains important works by Polish painters of the 19th and 20th centuries: Matejko, Michałowski, Gierymski, Chełmoński, Podkowiński, Siemiradzki, Kossak, and others. In the eastern part of the market place, between St Mary's Church and the Cloth Hall, stands the famous *Pomnik Adama Mickiewicza (Monument to Adam Mickiewicz)*, a statue of the greatest poet of Polish Romanticism (1798–1855). It is the work of Teodor Rygier and was erected in 1898, dismantled by the Nazis in 1940 and not re-erected until 1956. The banning by the authorities of one of Mickiewicz's patriotic plays 'Dziady', in 1968 led to massive demonstrations at the statue, and it remained a focus of dissident interest throughout the remaining years of the Communist régime. It is also the site of the annual Christmas Crib competition. The figures at its base represent Poland, Poetry, Science and Courage.

Southwest of the Cloth Hall we reach the **Wieża Ratuszowa (Town Hall Tower)** (4), all that remains of the old town hall, another victim of the Republic of Kraków's modernizations, demolished in 1820. The tower dates from around 1383, was raised in height in the 16th and 18th centuries and given its Baroque helm in the 17th century. The last restoration took place in 1965. The cellars of the tower, with their massive medieval vaults, are now used as a café and a theatre *(Maszkaron)*. In front of the tower a fenced-in plaque on the ground marks the place where on 24 March 1794 Kościuszko swore to free Poland from foreign rule (the 'Act of Insurrection of the Citizens and Inhabitants of the Palatinate of Kraków'). Here in 1918 most of the Austrian eagles in the town were piled up as a symbol of Polish independence. At the southeast corner of the square stands the little **Kościół św. Wojciecha (Church of St Adalbert)** (5), which dates from the 11th–12th centuries. This Romanesque building was altered in the 18th century when a Baroque dome and lantern were added. In the crypt beneath the church is a permanent exhibition of the *Archaeological Museum* about the history of Kraków Market Square.

But the most important building in the Market Square is the Gothic **Kościół Mariacki (St Mary's, or Church of the Assumption of the Virgin)** (6), which, like so many churches in Kraków, goes back to a foundation of Bishop Iwo Odrowąż in 1222. The original building was almost completely destroyed by a Tatar raid in 1241. The present three-aisled basilica was built in 1355–1408; the side chapels were added in the second half of the 15th century and the early 16th century. Two imposing towers form the west front: the tall one (81 metres), built at the end of the 14th century, has a helm ringed by eight turrets (1478, by Maciej Heringk) and a spire with a gilded crown (1666). This is the tower from which the hourly *Hejnał Mariacki* (see page 453) is sounded (it is broadcast at midday on Polish radio). From the top of the tower (entrance at the west corner) there is a magnificent view over the city. Entrance to the church is through an elaborate Baroque vestibule (1750–53, by Francesco Placidi), incongruous against the blank Gothic walls. The nave, which is typical of the great Kraków basilicas of the reign of Kazimierz III Wielki (compare St Catherine's and Corpus Christi in Kazimierz), was built in 1392–7 under the direction of Niklas Wernher of Prague and has the same width and height as the chancel built in 1355–65. Both nave and chancel are decorated with paintings designed by Jan Matejko. The very beautiful angels in the chancel are praising Our Lady with words from the Litany; elsewhere the walls show the symbols of the Kraków guilds and of the various Polish lands. The decoration was executed in 1889–92 by Stanisław Wyspiański, Józef Mehoffer and Włodzimierz Tetmajer among others, and makes an interesting contrast with their work in the Franciscan church (see page 462). Three stained glass windows of the chancel apse date from the middle ages (*c*.1370): the 120 panels tell the story of the Old and New Testaments in the manner of the Biblia Pauperum. The star vaulting dates from 1442; in the chapels it is decorated with fine Art Nouveau painting.

The long chancel, though crowded with altars, pews and paintings, is dominated by what is probably the most famous work of art in Kraków, the Marian Altarpiece by Veit Stoss (Wit Stwosz in Polish) of Nuremberg.

The city had been collecting funds for the altarpiece since 1473; Stoss arrived in 1477 and had more or less completed the carving by 1486 when he returned to Nuremberg; painting, gilding and assembly were undertaken by other craftsmen. The altar was finished by July 1489; it had cost 2,808 florins, which was roughly the equivalent of the municipal budget for a whole year. This huge sum was contributed by private donations from the German community, for whom the Mariacki was a source of civic pride, and the altarpiece has been understood by some writers as an aggressive statement of German burgher culture increasingly under threat from the Jagiellonian kings. 'The altarpiece still registers this kind of aggressiveness in a quite disturbing way: it is the largest of all the surviving retables and is distinguished by a stridently opulent polychromy' (Baxandall). Nevertheless, Stoss went on to create the greatest of the Jagiellonian tombs in Wawel Cathedral in 1492 (see page 474).

The altarpiece measures about 11 by 13 metres when open, and has about 200 figures carved from limewood, painted and gilded. The most impressive effect is created by the central scene with its over-life-size figures representing the Death of the Virgin, above which is her Assumption into heaven. In the predella is the Tree of Jesse; the (restored) superstructure has the Coronation of the Virgin. The 18 panels on the wings have reliefs showing scenes from the Lives of Christ and the Virgin. The paintwork and gilding were uncovered after the war, when the altarpiece returned in 1946 from Nuremberg, where it had been taken by the Nazis. Another piece by Stoss is a stone crucifix of 1491, commissioned by Heinrich Slacker, which hangs in a Baroque altarpiece in the south aisle. Also sometimes attributed to him is the huge crucifix on the rood beam (1490). The three side chapels are patrician foundations dating from 1423–46. The Kaplica Kaufmannów (Kaufmann Chapel) on the upper floor of the south tower has fine balustrades executed in 1520 by the workshop of Bartolommeo Berrecci; the Kaplica św. Łazarza (St Lazarus Chapel) has a tracery balustrade of 1510–20. The Baroque entrances to the chapels are of inlaid marble.

The church contains a wealth of other interesting furnishings. Most of the altars date from the Baroque period, including 26 made of black marble from Dieczyn (18th century), and some with paintings by the great Venetian Giovanni Battista Pittoni. Gian Maria Padovano made the marble tabernacle (*c*.1533–6) decorated with angels, at the arch between nave and chancel, and an alabaster ciborium in the nave (1551–2). The St Stanislas Triptych in the chapel above the south porch (*c*.1504) is attributed to Stanislaus Stoss, the brother of Veit. The lower part of the choir stalls dates back to 1586, and the reliefs on the backs are by Fabian Möller (1635). The lavishly decorated stalls include the Councillors'

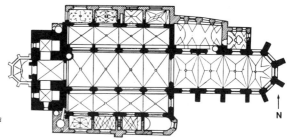

Plan of the Church of the Assumption of the Virgin (Mariacki, St Mary's)

N

pew (1516–21), the Mayor's (Syndicus) pew by the south pier (1602–9), the Fogelweder pew by the north pier with its Late Renaissance intarsia work, and the Judges' pew of 1634 in the north aisle.

The church has a plethora of funerary monuments, including some very splendid ones. The Mannerist Montelupi tomb (early 17th century), the Cellari tomb (before 1616) (in the chancel), are both made of sandstone, marble and alabaster with many expressive busts of members of the families in an architectural framework, richly decorated in the manner of the Pińczów workshop (see page 525). The tomb of the castellan Marcin Leśniowski is in the Kaplica św. Walentego (St Valentine's Chapel), with a recumbent figure of the deceased on a sarcophagus (sandstone and marble, late 16th century). Hundreds of funerary memorials and tablets can be found on the interior walls and they are particularly numerous on the outside walls. Some have figures in relief, such as those for the members of the Salomon family made in the early 16th century by the workshop of Peter Vischer the Elder of Nuremberg (who also made the bronze tomb slab of Peter Salomon, died 1516, in the chancel). In the Kaplica św. Jana Chrzciciela (Chapel of St John the Baptist) is the tomb slab (1532–8, workshop of Hans Vischer) of Seweryn Boner, castellan of Kraków, the nephew and successor of Jan Boner, the Alsatian banker who became burgrave and trusted adviser to King Zygmunt I Stary, and his wife Zofia. The Treasury, created around 1600, a Late Renaissance extension to the sacristy on the north side of the chancel, contains a rich collection of liturgical metalwork (including a very fine early 15th-century chalice) and vestments.

Just behind the Mariacki to the south is the **Kościół św. Barbary (Church of St Barbara)** (7), a two-aisled building built in 1394–1402, which once served as a cemetery chapel. It was handed over to the Jesuits in 1583 and in the following years was remodelled as a Baroque church. For a time it housed a famous Jesuit college. Under Austrian rule, when services in the Mariacki were conducted in German, this tiny building was the principal Polish language church for Kraków. The ceiling paintings are by Peter Franz Molitor (1765). The stone figure of Christ on the Mount of Olives in the little chapel at the entrance to the church is a copy after the original attributed to the circle of Veit Stoss.

Most of the old burghers' houses and palaces around the Main Market Place have been remodelled more than once. As well as their interesting façades with attics, they also have

459

charming courtyards, which sometimes connect streets. No. 6, the **Kamienica Szara (Grey House)** (8), the oldest burgher's house in the town, was built in the 13th and 14th centuries. Gothic vaults and Renaissance ceilings survive inside, but the west façade to the market square was considerably reshaped in the 17th century. The massive Baroque doorway created by sculptors of the Castelli family dates from the same period. The house belonged to the noble family of Zborowski and later to the Zebrzydowskis. It was here in 1574 that Henryk Walezy (Henri de Valois – later Henri III of France) was received on his arrival in Poland as the first elected king; the Zborowskis were his greatest supporters. In 1794 the house was used by Tadeusz Kościuszko as his headquarters, and it later became the seat of the short-lived provisional government during the Kraków Uprising of 1846.

No. 7 is the **Kamienica Montelupich (Montelupi House)** (9), a Gothic building given a Renaissance remodelling in 1554. Its owners were the Montelupi, a Florentine family who organized Poland's first postal service in the 16th century (commemorative plaque).

No. 8, the **Kamienica Pod Jaszczurami (House of the Lizards)** (10) is named after the coat of arms on its façade. (The original relief is now in the National Museum.) Built in the 15th century, the building now houses the best known student club in Kraków (the 'Jaszczury').

No. 9, the *Kamienica Bonerów (Boner House)* (also called Kamienica Firlejów, or Firlej House), another Gothic building altered in the 16th century and given a decorative Renaissance attic, was the scene in 1605 of the proxy marriage of the Russian pretender, the first False Dmitri, to Maryna Mniszech, the daughter of the wojewoda of Sandomierz. This was the culmination of years of intrigue, but failed to provide a firm foothold in Moscow for Polish adventures.

No. 11 was the house of the Venetian envoy, No. 12 was lived in by the great stucco artist Baldassare Fontana (see St Anne's, page 469), and No. 13 has been an apothecary's shop for centuries. Over the way, No. 15 is the oldest restaurant in Kraków, called *Wierzynek* after its 14th-century owner, who is supposed to have started the restaurant's tradition by holding a lavish feast here for the royal guests of King Kazimierz III Wielki, after a great meeting of monarchs in 1364. The food here still has a high reputation and the dining rooms have fine Renaissance ceilings. It was Nicholas Wierzynek who paid for the chancel of the Mariacki.

The **Kamienica Hetmańska (Hetman's House)** (11), or 'Old Mint', at No. 17 dates from the 14th century. After being used as the mint, the house became the Kraków residence of the Field Hetman. The ground floor has some magnificent rooms with Gothic rib-vaults. The bosses of these vaults are carved with the arms of the provinces of the Kingdom of Poland and two heads, one of which has been identified as Elżbieta, the daughter of Władysław II Łokietek and sister of Kazimierz III Wielki.

No. 20, on the corner of ul. Bracka, is the **Pałac Potockich (Potocki Palace)** (12), which is also known as the Wodzicki, Zbaraski or Jabłonowski Palace, after other owners. The palace has a fine Neoclassical façade added in 1773, with allegorical figures. The 17th-century arcaded courtyard seems to be intended as a copy of the courtyard of Wawel Castle.

The **Pałac Pod Baranami (Palace of the Rams)** (13) at No. 27 was created around 1600 by remodelling earlier burghers' houses. It belonged at different times to some of the greatest magnate families: the Ostrogskis, Radziwiłłs, Wielopolskis, Wodzickis and Potockis. It was given its present Neoclassical façade as late as 1860. The courtyard contains the remains of arcades, and the ground floor and basement is used by Poland's most famous cabaret the 'Piwnica pod Baranami'.

The *Pałac Spiski (Spiski Palace)* at No. 34, further along the south side of the square, is also the result of the remodelling of a Gothic house in the 18th and 19th centuries. The same is true of the house next door, the **Pałac Pod Krzysztofory (Christopher Palace)** (14) at No. 35, on the corner of ul. Szczepańska. This was the residence in the 17th century of Crown Marshal Adam Kazanowski. Later owners, members of the Wodzicki family, built a beautiful Baroque well next to the colonnaded loggia. This palace was then considered the most magnificent residence in Kraków, after the Wawel itself. The main doorway dates from a second Baroque remodelling, by Jacopo Solari, which took place in 1682–4. The plasterwork on the first floor was created in about 1700 by Baldassare Fontana with classical scenes and rich garlands. Further alterations to the building were made in 1916. In 1848 the palace was the seat of the revolutionary government; it now houses a gallery of the 'Grupa Krakowska' artists' association showing contemporary art. The first floor is occupied by a permanent exhibition of the *Muzeum Historyczne Miasta Krakowa (Historical Museum of the City of Kraków)*.

Goethe stayed for a short time in 1790 at No. 36, on the north side of the square (commemorative plaque). Two blocks along on the same side, to the left of St Mary's (Pl. Mariacki 3) stands the *Kamienica Hipolita (Hippolytus House)*. Its courtyard has a 17th-century wooden gallery, and a room on the first floor is decorated with plasterwork by Baldassare Fontana. The house next door, No. 4, with a Baroque rusticated façade and an attic (17th century) by Jan Zatorczyk is the residence of the archpriest of the Mariacki and is known as the *Prałatówka (Prelate's House)*. Its Baroque doorway leads into an entrance hall with 17th-century plasterwork, hung with paintings by Hans Süss von Kulmbach, which were commissioned by the patrician Jan Boner for the church; the house has other important furniture and paintings too. The street leads to the *Mały Rynek (Small Town Square)*. This was originally the meat market, and some of the ancient butcher's booths can still be seen.

Returning now to the Market Place, the street that leads from its southern corner is ul. Grodzka, the oldest street in Kraków. This forms part of the Royal Way and runs to the Wawel. A little way down it we come to Pl. Wszystkich Świętych, a long square dominated at its eastern end by the Dominican church, with its grand doorway, and at the western by the Franciscan church with its bright Wyspiański murals. On the other side of the square, ul. Grodzka picks up with an Art Nouveau shop whose attic imitates that of the Cloth Hall – a typical piece of Cracovian self-reference. To the right, behind a little stretch of green,

Mały Rynek (Little Market Place), 19th-century watercolour

stands the 17th-century **Pałac Wielopolskich (Wielopolski Palace)** (40), now used by the city administration. The statues above the main doorway are 19th-century, and there is a handsome Art Nouveau extension at right angles to the main block. In the square is a forbidding statue (1937–9, by Xawery Dunikowski) of a City President, Józef Dietl. In the corner house, No. 6, known as the Larisch Palace, the Society of the Friends of Fine Arts opened its headquarters in 1854.

To the right of the Pałac Wielopolski stands the **Kościół św. Franciszka (Franciscan Church)** (41) with its monastery (13th–15th centuries). This was founded by the wojewoda Teodor and first completed in 1269. Shortly afterwards Władysław Łokietek made a dramatic escape from the monastery in a basket lowered over the city walls. A more far-reaching event in Polish history was the baptism here in 1386 of Władysław II Jagiełło, the pagan Lithuanian chosen by the Poles as their king. Prince Bolesław V Wstydliwy ('the Chaste') is buried in the church, as are his sister, the Blessed Salomea, and Jan Piotr Kochanowski (1532–84), the translator of Ariosto and Tasso. The monastery was the home of Father (now Saint) Maksymilian Kolbe before his deportation to Auschwitz.

The church is a tall, plain brick building with some fine vaulting. It is remarkable now for its magnificent – and magnificently restored – Art Nouveau murals and glass, commissioned from the visionary painter-playwright Stanisław Wyspiański after the church had been burned out in the disastrous city fire of 1850. Roses, lilies, pansies and countless other flowers form a hymn to the great creating nature of St Francis' vision. The glass shows God the Creator in the west window, and St Francis and the Blessed Salomea behind the altar. The nave frescoes are by Wyspiański's pupil, Tadeusz Popiel. In the North Chapel the Stations of the Cross are by another famous Polish Art Nouveau painter, Józef Mehoffer, who studied in Paris and was strongly influenced by Van Gogh. In the South Chapel is a superb 15th-century Madonna of Mercy, a popular image known in Kraków as the Melancholy Benefactress. The cloisters, on the south side of the church, are famous for their medieval frescoes (from various periods but mostly in a poor state) and for their collection of 15th to 20th century portraits of bishops. The altar at the southeast corner is an appealing mixture, with an Art Nouveau Madonna against a 15th-century wall and under a 17th-century vault.

The complex of buildings across the street from the church (on the corner of ul. Franciszkańska and ul. Bracka) is the Archbishop's Curia with the residence of the Cardinal Archbishop Franciszek Macharski, the successor of Karol Wojtyła since his elevation to the papacy. Following the Planty southwards towards the Wawel, past the Franciscan monastery, the next street we come to is ul. Poselska. The group of buildings which stretch from here to the Planty is the former **Więzienie św. Michała (St Michael's Prison)** (42). After the war this became the *Archaeological Museum* of the City of Kraków. Until the 17th century it was the residence of the Tęczyński family and the court of the Abbots of Tyniec (see page 491); it was later converted into a monastery by the Carmelites and dedicated to St Michael. The Austrians expelled the friars in the 19th century and transformed the buildings into a prison and courthouse. Nearby, at ul. Poselska 7, is the *Kamienica Hebdowska (Jan Hebda House)*, which dates from the early 14th century. It is named after its first owner, an archdeacon of Gniezno and canon of Kraków. Later it belonged to the Benedictines of Tyniec and after 1612 became the residence of their abbots. The fine Art Nouveau building opposite is the back of the Town Hall; on the left is a plaque marking the site of Joseph Conrad's childhood home. His father Apollo Korzeniowski, a patriotic poet and political agitator, had moved to Kraków after his release from exile in Russia.

Returning to Pl. Wszystkich Świętych, we follow it eastwards as it becomes Pl. Dominikański with the **Kościół Dominikanów św. Trójcy (Dominican Church of the Holy Trinity)** (43) and the Dominican Monastery. The Dominican friars were given the site in 1222 by Bishop Iwo Odrowąż of Kraków at the instigation of his kinsman St Jacek (latinized to Hyacinth), as their first base in Poland. The three-aisled basilica was built in the 13th century, but has undergone several alterations. The imposing stepped gable of the east front was added in 1462; the height of the choir was raised in the second half of the 14th century, when the five-bay nave was built, and the net vaulting dates from before 1438. Inside the protective neo-Gothic vestibule is a beautiful late 14th-century stone portal with its exceptional foliate and animate carving. The original interior of the church was devastated by the same great fire in 1850 that gutted the Franciscan church at the other end of the square. In a fascinating contrast, the Dominicans decided to redecorate in an elaborate but light neo-Gothic. The delicate vault painting – ironically less medieval in effect than Wyspiański's overwhelming Art Nouveau murals – and the spire-encrusted confessionals, stalls and high altar are of a very high quality. In the chancel three of the original monuments survive: on the right the Baroque memorial to Bishop Iwo Odrowąż, the indefatigable establisher of this and many other religious houses in Małopolska, and on the left the simple tomb slab of Leszek Czarny ('the Black'), Prince of Kraków (whose death in 1288 led to thirty years of confusion before his younger brother, Władysław Łokietek, managed to have himself crowned King at the Wawel), next to a major monument of Renaissance sculpture: the bronze tomb slab of the great Italian humanist scholar Filippo Buonaccorsi (Callimachus), designed by Veit Stoss and cast at Nuremberg by Peter Vischer the Elder around 1496–1500. Buonaccorsi is shown in his study sitting at a richly carved desk, and Vischer has carefully shown the textures of the wood, the velvet hangings and the hat. Of the several richly decorated Baroque chapels, the finest is the *Kaplica Myszkowskich* (1603–14) (fifth chapel in the south aisle), which makes striking use of contrasting black and white marbles. The busts of the Myszkowski family can be seen in the dome – a mingling perhaps of the motif of the Hall 'Under the Heads' in the Wawel with the form of the Renaissance Sigismund Chapel, the model here as so often in Kraków for the structure. The next chapel contains a miraculous image of Our Lady of the Rosary. On the north side, the *Kaplica Zbraskich* (1627–33, by Constantino Tencalla and the brothers Castelli) (1627–33) to the right of the west door is an oval variation on the Sigismund Chapel. The large flight of steps in the north aisle leads up to the *Kaplica św. Jacka* (Chapel of St Hyacinth), which has a free-standing altar by Baldassare Fontana with the figure of the saint standing on a sarcophagus supported by gilded angels. The chapel's interior architecture, whose recent restoration reveals a very delicate use of colour, is by Andrzej Jastrząbek (1614–18) with a cycle of paintings showing the life of the saint and figures of angels by Tommaso Dolabella (1619–25). The plasterwork is also by Fontana, and the ceiling painting by Karl Dankwart. Below the great flight of steps a fine Renaissance door leads to the cloisters, with medieval frescoes and monuments and a Romanesque refectory. During the years of communist rule, an influential anti-communist youth club flourished here, and the church is still a favourite with the students of Kraków. The church treasury is one of the most splendid in Kraków and has some magnificent medieval vestments.

Returning to ul. Grodzka, the visitor continues towards the Wawel, past many houses with carved house signs, often of exotic animals (the earliest dates from the 14th century). No. 46 has attractive Rococo plasterwork, and the **Collegium Juridicum** (44) at No. 53 should be mentioned for its beautiful doorway and arcaded Renaissance courtyard.

Opposite is Kraków's oldest Baroque church, the **Kościół ś.ś. Piotra i Pawła (Church of Sts Peter and Paul)** (45) which was built on the site of a Gothic church. The building was begun in 1595 by the Jesuit Giuseppe Brizio for his order (which had just been summoned to Poland), and follows Roman models, in particular the Gesù and S. Andrea

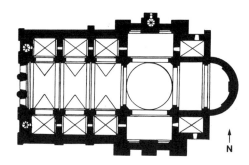

Plan of the Church of Sts Peter and Paul

N

della Valle. After some construction difficulties, it was completed in 1605–19 by the Lombard Giovanni Battista Trevano, court architect to Zygmunt III Waza. Although disconcertingly austere, the interior has the finest Baroque plasterwork in Kraków, by Falconi (1619–33), mainly in the enfilade of chapels either side of the nave. The furnishings are equally sparse and grandiose: organ (by Baldassare Fontana), altar and the (earlier) pulpit. A few fine monuments include a curious assemblage of sculptural and painted elements in the south transept. The row of Apostles in front of the church are ugly new copies of the Baroque originals by David Heel, which were destroyed by pollution.

Nearby a contrast is provided by the **Kościół św. Andrzeja (Church of St Andrew)** (46), a rare monument of the Romanesque in Małopolska, built around 1079–98 and altered *c*.1100. The west front, built of white limestone, is dominated by the two Romanesque towers with square bases, octagonal upper storeys and Baroque caps (1639). The very severe elevation is alleviated only by the triple window between the towers, which lights a gallery inside. The interior decoration is a jewel-like Baroque, with plasterwork by Baldassare Fontana (the Four Virtues in the cupola) and an elaborate boat pulpit. The frescoes are by Karl Dankwart. The church was transferred from the Bernardines to the Poor Clares in 1318, and has a richly stocked treasury with several of the oldest Christmas crib figures in Europe (14th century) and a mosaic icon of the Virgin made in Constantinople in the first half of the 13th century. This image was credited with saving the lives of the Cracovians who sought refuge here during the Tatar invasion of 1241.

On the other side of the little square opposite, Pl. św. Marii Magdaleny, we come to perhaps the most picturesque street in Kraków, ul. Kanoniczna, which has well-preserved rows of houses from the 15th and 16th centuries. Above almost all the fine entrance doorways are coats of arms, which formerly took the place of house numbers. For some years the houses have been undergoing careful restoration, and it is worth taking a look at their interesting courtyards. No. 5 was the headquarters of Tadeusz Kantor's Cricot 2 theatre, and No. 9 is the *Wyspiański Museum*, and was once the home of the 18th-century patriot and reformer of the university, Hugo Kołłątaj. At the end of the street are two particularly impressive houses, the *Dom Dziekański (Deanery)*, No. 21, a 16th-century Renaissance palace with sgraffito decoration on the façade (designed by Santi Gucci) and

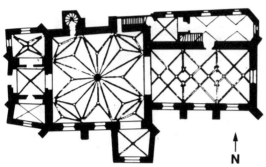

N *Plan of the Church of the Holy Cross*

the *Dom Długosza (Długosz House)*, No. 25, which in the 15th century was a royal bath-house and residential building, and was later given to the great Polish historian Jan Długosz, tutor to the sons of Kazimierz IV Jagiellończyk. A bronze plaque commemorates the fact that here Stanisław Wyspiański's father Franciszek had his sculpture workshop.

Back in ul. Grodzka, the church next door to the Poor Clares' convent (which is attached to St Andrew's) is the *Kościół św. Marcina (Church of St Martin)* built by Giovanni Battista Trevano in the 17th century and used since 1816 for Lutheran worship. The altar painting is 'Christ Stilling the Storm' by Henryk Siemiradzki. At the end of ul. Grodzka, as it reaches the foot of the Wawel hill, stands the small, early 14th-century Gothic *Kościół św. Idziego (Church of St Giles)* in which the stalls and door-frames are made up of fragments of the old shrine of St Jacek (1581–3), removed from the Dominican church in the 17th century (see page 463). Here ul. Grodzka reaches the imposing mass of Wawel Hill, the goal of the Royal Way (see page 471).

Of the streets that run parallel to ul. Floriańska, the easternmost is ul. Szpitalna. Jammed against the walls of this north-eastern corner of medieval Kraków, the burghers established the town hospital. All that now survives in Pl. św. Ducha (Holy Ghost Square) is the **Kościół św. Krzyza (Church of the Holy Cross)** (21). The chancel (14th century) is attached to a dramatic nave (15th century) whose Late Gothic vaulting is supported by a single pier, resembling a palm-tree and reminiscent of some English chapter houses. The furnishings are mostly Baroque but there are Late Gothic sculptures and paintings, early 15th-century murals, and a fine bronze font dating from 1423, which is decorated with the figures of Adam and Eve and other scenes. There is a monument to the world-famous Polish actress Helena Modrzejewska.

The square is now overshadowed by the **Teatr im. Juliusza Słowackiego (Juliusz Słowacki Theatre)** (22), whose eclectic style clearly owes much to Garnier's Opéra in Paris. It was erected in 1891–3 to the designs of Jan Zawiejski, who had studied with Ferstel at the Technische Hochschule in Vienna and had been involved in the building of Vienna University. The theatre is the most important of the many buildings he created in Kraków during his term as its municipal architect between 1900 and 1922. Like the Great

Theatre in Warsaw, this was a building intended to express and encourage national feeling; and as in Warsaw it involved the demolition – not without considerable conservationist protest – of a group of historical buildings, in this case all the main structures of the medieval hospital.

In front of the Słowacki Theatre is a *Monument* to Aleksander Fredro (1798–1878) with a bust of the dramatist by Cyprian Godebski. The foyer is hung with portraits of famous theatrical figures. The painting on the stage curtain is by Henryk Siemiradzki.

The **Dom Pod Krzyżem (Cross House)** (23) at Pl. św. Ducha 5, which was built around 1470 as a hostel for poor scholars, and the house next door now contain a gallery of the History of the Kraków Theatre. Ul. Szpitalna continues down to the Mały Rynek.

The street west of ul. Floriańska is ul. św Jana. The church which closes it off at its northern end is the **Kosciol Pijarów Przemienieria Pańskiego (Piarist Church of the Transfiguration)** (25), built in 1718–27, probably to the plans of Kasper Bażanka. The façade was added by Francesco Placidi in 1759–61, while the balustrade with the double flight of steps leading up to the entrance above the large crypt was not built until 1893 (Tadeusz Błotnicki). All the vaults inside have paintings (1727–31) by Franz Eckstein of Brno. The sculptures were made by Chrystian Bola between 1718 and 1733. The altar paintings date from the 18th century (Szymon Czechowicz – a pupil of Carlo Maratta – and Andrzej Radwański).

Part of the monastery buildings are connected by a covered bridge to the neo-Gothic **Pałac Czartoryskich (Czartoryski Palace)** (24), which houses the *Czartoryski Museum*, Poland's most important family art collection. Founded by the great patroness and collector Princess Izabella Czartoryska (née Flemming) (see page 542) in the family palace at Puławy, the collection went to Paris after the Uprising of 1830, but was offered to the city of Kraków in the 1870's by Prince Władysław Czartoryski. A suitable home was created by converting the Old Arsenal, the former Piarist monastery and some adjoining burgher's houses (1879–84, by Maurice Ouradon). Besides objects connected with Polish national heroes, a large collection of antiquities, and a fine armoury, the museum also has an extremely good collection of European paintings. Particular strengths are Sienese primitives and Dutch 17th-century paintings (including Rembrandt's brooding 'Stormy Landscape with the Good Samaritan'), but the museum is famous above all for Leonardo da Vinci's 'Lady with an Ermine'. The animal in fact identifies her as Cecilia Gallerani, the mistress of Leonardo's patron, Ludovico il Moro, since Leonardo is punning on the Greek word for a weasel, *gale*, and Ludovico's own nickname, Ermelino.

If we now follow ul. św. Jana south, past a number of fine old houses, we come to the **Pałac Lubomirskich (Lubomirski Palace)** (26), No. 15, whose Neoclassical façade of 1873–4 conceals what were originally three burghers' houses. The fine entrance hall has decorative plasterwork. At the next corner stands the **Pałac Wodzickich (Wodzicki Palace)**, (27), No. 11, surmounted by a balustraded attic with sculptures. The Austrian Hofkommissar, Count Deym, was living here in 1848 when he was forced by Prince Adam Potocki and a deputation of citizens of Kraków to release Polish prisoners being held for their liberal and democratic views. The house opposite, No. 20, is known as either the **Pałac Popielów (Popiel Palace)** (28) or the Dom Kołłątajowski (Kołłątaj House). It was formed in 1774 by putting two burghers' houses under a single roof. In 1812 it belonged to Kościuszko's friend Konstanty Popiel, and later to his son Paweł, who took part in the 1830 Uprising. At that time the palace was the centre of social life in Kraków. The Late Baroque façade was probably designed by Francesco Placidi. The doorway, flanked by atlantes, is of a type popular in Prague and Silesia.

The **Muzeum Historyczne Miasta Krakowa (Historical Museum)** (29) is at No. 12, the Kamienica Krauzowska (Krauze House), originally a Gothic building, but remodelled by Giovanni Petrini and Giovanni Battista Trevano in 1611. Here in 1913 Klemens Bąkowski founded the Towarzystwo Miłośników Historii i Zabytków Krakowa (Society of the Friends of the History and Monuments of Kraków). The main part of the museum is in the Pałac Pod Krzysztofory (see page 461). In the Krauze House the exhibits illustrate the history of Kraków's municipality, and of the city's many guilds and associations (foremost amongst them the Gun Cock Fraternity, which still exists, and whose silver cockerel prize, given by the king in 1565, is the star exhibit).

At the next corner is the eponymous *Kościół św. Jana (Church of St John)*, a little Baroque church (1621–3) set at an angle on earlier foundations.

The last of the streets parallel with ul. Floriańska, ul. Sławkowska, is lined with handsome old buildings. (Before taking it down to the Rynek Glowny, however, it is worth looking briefly over the Planty to see the magnificent Industrialists' Club, now a bank, on the other side, with its globe-capped tower and decorated attic.) One block down ul. Sławkowska is the brick Gothic **Kościół św. Marka (Church of St Mark)** (39), a foundation of Bolesław V Wstydliwy. The nave and tower date from the 15th century. A famous monumental carved Crucifixion (*c.*1500) on the outer wall of the chancel (on ul. Sławkowska) has been removed for restoration. The rich interior furnishings include a high altar made in 1618 by the workshop of Baltazar Kuncz. The Crucifix (added later) is Late Gothic. (The side street leads to Pl. Szczepański (see page 470) past the *Kościół Reformatów (Church of the Reformed Franciscans)*, with 18th-century Stations of the Cross in the garden opposite.) On the street corner opposite St Mark's (ul. Sławkowska 13) is the *Pałac Tarnowskich (Tarnowski Palace)*, formed in the 17th century out of two burghers' houses. The hollowed-out stones on either side of the main entrance were for extinguishing torches. Inside is an impressive entrance hall with Baroque doorways. The *Kamienica Gotycka (Gothic House)* (No. 4) dates from the 15th century and was given a Baroque remodelling in the 17th century.

Southwest of the market place, between the site of the old ramparts and ul. św. Anny and ul. Jagiellońska is the complex of buildings forming the centre of Kraków University (entrance in ul. św. Anny). Originally called the Kraków Academy, it is now known as the Jagiellonian University, a nationalistic name invented by the Republic of Kraków. The university was in fact founded by King Kazimierz III Wielki in 1364 (following the example of the Emperor Charles IV in Prague), but had to be refounded by Władysław II

Jagiełło, using a legacy of jewels from his wife Jadwiga, great-niece of Kazimierz. In 1400 the King acquired a house belonging to the Pęcherz family for the university. This building with its prominent stone buttress is now the corner of the **Collegium Maius** (30) built in 1492–7 by the Saxon Master Johann, and is one of the best preserved medieval university buildings in Europe. This was a vigorous centre of Renaissance culture, Copernicus and Callimachus being amongst the luminaries. The beautiful courtyard has a cloister with star vaulting and carved columns, and in the centre is a Baroque well-head decorated with the arms of Poland, the City of Kraków, Queen Jadwiga and King Władysław Jagiełło. On the ground floor is the Alchemy room, with appropriate paraphernalia. A staircase leads to the first floor balcony and the main rooms. The *Aula (Hall)* was completed in the early 16th century; it is richly panelled and furnished and includes a portal and a door from the old town hall (see page 457) dating from around 1600 (the inscription is the motto, *Plus ratio quam vis*, 'With reason rather than with force'). The *Stuba Communis (Common Room)* has a three-sided oriel overlooking the street and a fine star vault, as well as a 'Danzig' (spiral) staircase' (*c*.1700) from a house in ul. św. Ducha in Gdańsk. It was installed here in 1949 during the restoration work by Karol Estreicher jun., completed in 1964 for the 600th anniversary of the university's foundation. Restoration involved the removal of 19th-century accretions made when the building housed the Jagiellonian Library (later transferred to a new building in Al. Mickiewicza). Since the Second World War, when the university was brutally closed and its buildings occupied by the Nazi Institut für Deutsche Ostarbeit (Institute for the Study of the Eastern Territories), the Collegium Maius has been used as a *Museum* of the history of the university and its fascinating collections. Sadly, some items were lost when the contents were carried off by the Nazis, but many important historic objects can still be seen, including four university maces of the 14th–15th centuries, seals, old globes (among them the Jagiellonian Globe, a clock dating from shortly after 1510, with the first known representation of America), prints, furniture and paintings (portraits of kings and professors).

Opposite the Collegium Maius stands the large Neoclassical building of the **Collegium Physicum** (or Kołłątaj Collegium, after the great 18th-century reformer of the University) (31), designed in 1790 by Feliks Radwański. On its façade is a plaque commemorating Karol Olszewski and Walery Wróblewski, the two scientists who in 1882 were the first to liquefy oxygen, hydrogen and nitrogen. The last quarter of the 19th century was perhaps the greatest period in the university's history, since it then became a major force for national integration, attracting students from all three zones of the Partition.

The **Collegium Nowodworskie** (32), at ul. św. Anny 12, was built as a school by Jan Leitner in 1639–43. The fine arcaded courtyard and the staircase date from this period. The school's famous alumni include the military leaders Jan Sobieski and Józef Bem, and the artists Jan Matejko and Stanisław Wyspiański. Today the building is used by the university's medical school.

On the other side of the street is the impressive, richly articulated façade of the **Kościół św. Anny (Collegiate Church of St Anne)** (33), one of Poland's most beautiful Baroque

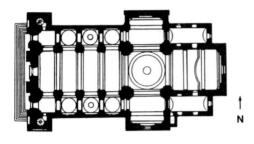

Plan of the Collegiate Church of St Anne

↑
N

churches. The medieval University church was replaced by the present building when it became too small for the cult of St Jan Kanty (1390–1473, beatified 1680 and canonized 1767, a University professor whose frugal cell can be seen in the Collegium Maius). St Anne's was built by the royal architect Tylman van Gameren in 1689–1703, and it follows the model of S. Andrea della Valle in Rome in having a four-bay nave flanked by chapels, a dome over the crossing and a three-bay chancel. The magnificent plasterwork (with figures) and the altars (1695–1704) are the most important work of Baldassare Fontana; the illusionistic frescoes and paintings are by Carlo and Innocenzo Monti and Karl Dankwart. The fine furnishings include the shrine of St Jan Kanty, near some Turkish standards presented by King Jan III Sobieski, a co-founder of the new church, and a Neoclassical monument to Copernicus, installed under the nationalist Republic of Kraków by the rector, despite the fact that Copernicus' works were still on the Index.

We now follow the Planty southwards to the *Nicolaus Copernicus Monument*, which stands in front of the brick building of the **Collegium Novum** (34), built in a neo-Gothic style in 1883–7 by Feliks Księżarski on the site of old university buildings. In the large *Aula* hang paintings illustrating the history of the university, as well as portraits of professors. A plaque commemorates the professors arrested here in 1939, many of whom later died in concentration camps (see page 452). Hitler, like Stalin, was determined to liquidate the Polish intelligentsia and leave nothing but a semi-literate and enslaved proletariat.

The house at the next corner (ul. Gołębia 11) is the *Collegium Minus*, which in the 15th century housed the Faculty of Liberal Arts, and was altered in the 17th and 18th centuries. In the 19th century this was the Faculty of Fine Arts. It was here that Jan Matejko studied painting under Kornel Stattler, a friend of Thorvaldsen, the Nazarenes and Mickiewicz.

Ul. Jagiellońska leads to *Pl. Szczepański*, a slightly dilapidated square with Kraków's finest Art Nouveau architecture. On the corner with ul. Jagiellońska stands the **Teatr Stary (Old Theatre)** (35). The original theatre, built in 1843, was transformed in 1904–6 by Tadensz Stryjeński and Franciszek Mączyński into the most representative example of the Art Nouveau in Małopolska. The façade decoration by Józef Gardecki includes a frieze with a sinuous Art Nouveau relief below the overhanging eaves, while the attic above is in the old Cracovian manner.

On the same side of the square is a fine apartment block dated 1909 (No. 2) with a stained glass overdoor and staircase lights. The west side of the square is taken up by the **Pałac Sztuki (Palace of Art)** (36) a transitional Art Nouveau building begun in 1901 by Franciszek Mączyński. Around the building runs a frieze based on drawings by Jacek Malczewski, and the niches hold busts of famous Cracovian artists: Matejko, Wyspiański, Kossak, Księżarski and Szujski. The Towarzystwo Przyjaciół Sztuk Pięknych (Society of the Friends of the Fine Arts) has its headquarters in the building, which is used for temporary art exhibitions. Other exhibitions, including the famous Graphics Triennial, are held in a Brutalist concrete building opposite the Pałac Sztuki, on the Planty. This controversial but impressive structure incorporates a Baroque house, and was built on the site of a celebrated Futurist café.

The rest of Pl. Szczepański has some other interesting Art Nouveau buildings, and a Functionalist concrete block that houses the offices of Solidarity. At No. 9 on the east side is the **Kamienica Szołayskich (Szołayski Museum)** (37), which contains the most important collection of Gothic art in Małopolska. Its star piece is the wooden figure of a 'Beautiful Madonna' (*c*.1410) discovered in Krużlowa by Stanisław Wyspiański.

Continuing east up ul. Szczepańska to return to the Main Market Place, the visitor passes some fine Baroque houses, of which the most distinguished is the **Kamienica Morsztyna (Morsztyn House)** (38), also known as Pod Gruszką (Pear House) at ul. Szczepańska 1, on the corner. This originally dates from the 14th century, but has been remodelled several times since. On the first floor is a room with Late Gothic vaulting, which was decorated around 1700 by Baldassare Fontana with rich plasterwork depicting, among other things, Allegories of the Arts. The lower parts of the walls are covered with Dutch tiles from the second half of the 17th century.

Wawel: Castle and Cathedral

The **Wawel** (48) – the religious, spiritual and patriotic heart of Poland – is the most splendid of Poland's castles. Surrounded by defensive walls, the Gothic cathedral (plate 48) and the royal residence, at once a fortress and a palace, stand on a hill 25 metres above the Vistula. A long carriage road leads up the north flank of the hill, facing the city. In the wall are plaques commemorating the gifts made by many Poles for the restoration of the Wawel between the wars. On a 16th-century bastion above is a proud equestrian *Monument to Tadeusz Kościuszko* (1921, by Leonard Marconi, statue by X. Rygier). It was destroyed by the Nazis in 1940, but re-erected in 1960 as a gift of the city of Dresden. Behind it are two towers. The lower is called Zygmuntowska (see below); originally defensive in purpose, it now houses the famous Zygmunt Bell. The taller, or Clock Tower, with its magnificent helm (*c*.1715, by Kasper Bażanka) has the four great Slav saints at the corners: Casimir, Wenceslas, Stanislas and Adalbert (Wojciech).

Entering the castle precincts by the Vasa Gateway (with ghostly worn tombstones) the visitor finds the Cathedral to the left, the Cathedral Museum to the right, and ahead a large courtyard, cleared of its minor buildings by the Austrians to make a parade ground (and now arranged to show the foundations of an earlier church). The open space allows a superb view of the Cathedral's southern façade – an extravagant collection of styles, focused on the superb gilt dome of the Sigismund Chapel. (This is surmounted by a crown-bearing angel and the chapel is inscribed *'Domine dilexisti decorem domus tue non nobis domine non nobis sed nomine tue MDXX'* – not unto us but to thy name alone, O Lord.) The dragon spouts are worth noting. The little 20th-century pavilion at the southwest corner is the entrance to Piłsudski's tomb (1936–38, by A. S. Bohusz).

The *Kościół Katedralny śś. Wacława i Stanisława Biskupa (Cathedral of St Wenceslas and St Stanislas)* (g) is the centre of the Polish nation, the scene of royal coronations and victorious thanksgivings, and the mausoleum of kings and heroes. Though surprisingly small, its every detail is important to the Polish soul. 'This basilica has so many ties with the history of the Polish nation, with eras of prosperity and various other conditions of this monarchy, that if it were that no other history of the Polish nations had ever been written, the walls and marble of this sanctuary would for the most part tell it.' (Bishop Józef Olechowski to King Stanisław August Poniatowski on his visit in 1787, quoted by Michał Rożek).

The present building is the successor of the Romanesque church of St Gereon (1018 to after 1038) and the church of Prince Władysław I Herman (1075–1145), destroyed in the great fire of 1305. It was in the burnt-out shell that Władysław Łokietek became the first

*The Wawel 1 Castle 2 Sigismund Chapel
3 Potocki Chapel*

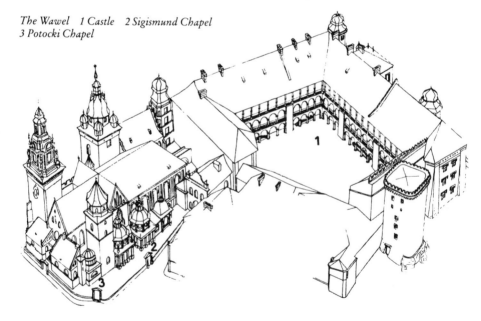

king to be crowned in Kraków in 1320; almost immediately afterwards he began the choir of the present church, which now stands as a three-aisled basilica with a transept and ambulatory, surrounded by 18 Gothic and Baroque chapels – a plan that proved very influential for Polish architecture. The choir dates from 1320–46, and the aisles were built around 1350. On the north side rises the *Wieza Zygmuntowska (Sigismund Tower)* (14th century) in which hangs the biggest bell in Poland, 'Zygmunt': cast in 1520 by Hans Belam from the metal of 40 captured cannons, it is 2.4 metres in diameter, weighs 8 tonnes, and is only rung on national occasions and great feast days; 11 men are needed to ring it. From the window of the bell-chamber there is a fine view over the town and the Vistula. The northwest tower is the *Clock Tower*, and the southwest is the *Wieza Wikaryjska (Tower of the Silver Bells)*, the lower half of which survives from the Romanesque cathedral, and in which the oldest bell dates from the 13th century. The restoration of the cathedral took place in 1895–1910 under the direction of Sławomir Odrzywolski and Zygmunt Hendel.

Like the rest of the cathedral's exterior, the entrance is picturesque rather than grandiose or coherent: a flight of steps between two lean-to brick chapels. The ashlar gable is carved with the Piast eagle, and there is a small figure of St Stanisław, to whom the church is dedicated. The massive prehistoric bones suspended by chains just to the left of the door have been there since the early middle ages; supposedly the bones of Krak's dragon (see page 482), they are in fact the shin of a mammoth, the skull of a rhinoceros and the rib of a whale. When they fall, according to legend, the end of the world will be at hand. A Baroque portal (1636–9) holds the famous doors (third quarter of the 14th century) strengthened with iron mounts in the form of the letter 'K', the cypher of King Kazimierz III Wielki, in whose enlightened reign the cathedral was consecrated (1364). Inside, the first object to meet the eye is the great shrine of St Stanisław (Stanislas) beneath the crossing. Bishop Stanisław is said to have been murdered (at the Skałce in Kazimierz, see page 484) in 1079 by King Bolesław II, because he had condemned the king's injustices. His cult grew, though unlike Thomas à Becket it was nearly 200 years before he was canonized, in 1253. The powerful myth of the martyr killed for standing up to the excesses of the secular power finds an echo not only literally in the murder of Father Jerzy Popiełuszko in 1984, but also in the notion of Poland the martyr-nation. The saint's remains were placed here in 1254, and the spot became the spiritual focus of the cathedral. It was here that the standards captured at Grunwald were brought in 1410. The present Baroque shrine is of black marble and gilded bronze and was designed by Giovanni Battista Trevano as a square baldacchino with arches, surmounted by a dome with the figures of the patron saints of Poland at the corners (by Antonio Lagastini). Above the altar is the silver sarcophagus of the saint, a superb work by the silversmith Peter van der Rennen of Gdańsk, made in 1669–71; the four kneeling angels supporting the sarcophagus, and the plaques with scenes from the life of the bishop were made in silver at Augsburg. The ensemble is completed by four marble tombs on the crossing piers: to Marcin Szyszkowski, who commissioned the Stanisław shrine (1630, by Trevano) and to his successor bishops, Gembicki (died 1657) who commissioned the high altar (1634, bust and beautiful skull and crossbone capitals by Giovanni Rossi), Małachowski (died 1699) and Łubieński (died 1719) (both by Kasper Bażanka). The nave is hung with Brussels tapestries (c.1650, by Jacob van Zenner) which tell the story of Jacob. Below them, on the right, is the tomb of Władysław Jagiełło (died 1434), one of the glories of Polish art. It was carved in the first half of the 15th century, of red Hungarian marble. (Colour harmonies – particularly black, gold, white, red – are a striking feature of the cathedral's interior.) Around the tomb are weepers carrying the coats of arms of the King's lands; below are hounds and falcons, alluding to the King's love of the chase. The Renaissance canopy, designed by Berrecci and executed by Giovanni Cini was commissioned in 1525 by the King's grandson, Zygmunt I Stary, while he was building his own funerary chapel.

Opposite Jagiełło's tomb is the matching tomb of his son Władysław III Warneńczyk (died 1444) by Antoni Madeyski (1906). (It is in fact empty, since his body was never recovered after the battle of Warna.) The organ loft is by Francesco Placidi (1756–9). In the chancel the Baroque high altar was made in the mid-17th century after a design by Giovanni Battista Ghisleni. The stalls were made in 1620 and the backs added in 1901 (Sławomir Odrzywolski). Of particular interest is the tomb of Cardinal Fryderyk Jagiellończyk set into the platform in front of the high altar; it was cast in bronze by Peter Vischer the Elder at Nuremberg in 1510.

Walking around the cathedral from the southwest corner, the first chapel, to the right of the entrance, is the *Kaplica Świętokrzyska (Holy Cross Chapel)* (I), whose walls and three-bay star vault were decorated in 1470 with paintings in a Russian-Byzantine manner by painters from Pskov. (This is one of four surviving sets of murals of this style in Poland, see pages 141–2; 'a fine and rare example of the mutual permeation of western and eastern cultures in the vast territories of the Jagiellonian monarchy' – Michał Rożek.) Of particular iconographic interest are the choirs of angels and the scene of the Lamentation. The Holy Cross Chapel is also the funerary chapel of Kazimierz IV Jagiellończyk and his wife, the Habsburg princess Elizabeth. The king's tomb, made in 1492 of mottled red marble from Salzburg, is an outstanding work by Veit Stoss. The energetic, twisted shield-bearers contrast with the earlier ones on the tomb of Władysław Jagiełło in the nave. The sensual canopy was carved by Jörg Huber of Passau. The monumental Neoclassical tomb of Bishop Kajetan Sołtyk on the south wall was made in 1789 to a design by Chrystian Piotr Aigner. The bishop was exiled for his Polish patriotism, and his departure is shown on the sarcophagus. Above, the Polish eagle is resurgent, while Fame holds open the tomb that Time tries to close. The Trinity triptych (1467, School of Kraków) and the Adoration (end of the 15th century) are of interest, and the windows are by Mehoffer.

The adjoining *Kaplica Potockich (Potocki Chapel)* (II) was erected by Jan Michałowicz (the 'Polish Praxiteles'), who was also responsible for the alabaster tomb of Bishop Filip Padniewski (1572–5). The busts of Count Artur Potocki and his mother were designed by Bertel Thorvaldsen and carved by R. Monti in 1833–4, when the chapel was being remodelled in a Neoclassical style for the Potockis by the Viennese architect Peter von Nobile. The figure of Christ Blessing is also by Thorvaldsen. On the aisle wall here is the bronze

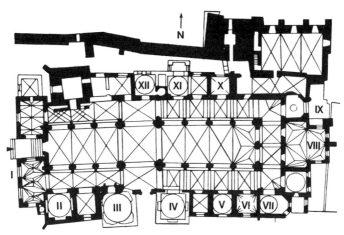

Plan of Wawel Cathedral   I Kaplica Świętokrzyska (Holy Cross Chapel)   II Kaplica Potockich (Potocki Chapel)   III Kaplica Wazów (Vasa Chapel)   IV Kaplica Zygmuntowska (Sigismund Chapel)   V Kaplica Zadzika (Chapel of Bishop Zadzik)   VI Kaplica Olbrachta (Chapel of King Jan Olbracht)   VII Kaplica Tomickiego (Chapel of Bishop Tomicki)   VIII Kaplica Mariacka (Lady Chapel)   IX Kaplica Gamrata (Chapel of Bishop Gamrat)   X Kaplica Zebrzydowskiego (Chapel of Bishop Zebrzydowski)   XI Kaplica Lipskich (Lipski Chapel)   XII Kaplica Maciejowskiego (Chapel of Bishop Maciejowski)

memorial by Peter Vischer of Nuremberg to Piotr Kmita the Elder, a magnificent gentleman and wojewoda of Kraków (died 1505). Next comes the *Kaplica Wazów (Vasa Chapel)* (III) designed by Giovanni Battista Ghisleni. The exterior is closely based on the Sigismund Chapel (see below), but the interior is Baroque, decorated with plasterwork and mural paintings. The solemn black and white decoration is redolent of Counter-Reformation gloom, as are the intricate bronze doors (1673, by Michael Weinhold of Gdańsk) which show the arms of the Vasas and of the lands they ruled, together with skeletons trampling on vanities in the lower register.

The *Kaplica Zygmuntowska (Sigismund Chapel)* (IV), recognizable from the outside by its gilded dome, is the finest and most famous of all the chapels, and is universally described as a gem of Renaissance architecture. It was commissioned as a family mausoleum by King Zygmunt I Stary, heartbroken by the death of his first wife Barbara Zapolya in 1515. The design was submitted in 1517 by Bartolommeo Berrecci; work began in 1519 on the site of Kazimierz III Wielki's chapel, and continued until 1533, led by Berrecci and a team of Tuscan masons. The architect, who is not known in his native Florence, left his signature, a prominent inscription 'BARTHOLO FLORENTINO OPIFICE' which can be read in the lantern of the dome. The building is the finest example of Tuscan Renaissance architecture north of the Alps. The sandstone interior with its richly articulated coffered dome forms a contrast to the red marble of the sculptures by Berrecci and his pupils. These represent the patron saints of King Zygmunt I and his burgrave (administrator) Seweryn Boner; the Evangelists; and Kings Solomon and David (portraits of Zygmunt I and Boner) in roundels on the south wall; but the most exuberant sculpture is in the lunettes above, where tritons and nereids disport themselves. (The compositions are full of classical allusions, the expression in the visual arts of the flourishing humanist culture of the late Jagiellonian court.) Set into the west wall are the magnificent recumbent effigies of King Zygmunt I Stary (died 1548) by Berrecci (above), and King Zygmunt II August (died 1572) (below). The latter was added by the last Jagiellon, his sister, Queen Anna Jagiellonka (wife of King Stefan Batory) who had the double tomb created in 1574–5 by Santi Gucci using the earlier sculpture of their father's tomb. The queen had her own tomb (1583) placed opposite the chapel entrance, where it stands in front of Zygmunt's royal stall, over which the crown is still held aloft by angels. Her final alteration was to have the dome's exterior gilded; this now has to be redone every two or three years, such are the effects of pollution. Unlike the rest of the chapel, the altarpiece is not of Italian workmanship; it is a pentaptych made in 1531–8 by a Nuremberg workshop, with chased silver reliefs showing the life of the Virgin (by Melchior Baier and Pankraz Labenwolf after designs by Peter Flötner), and paintings of the Passion (by Georg

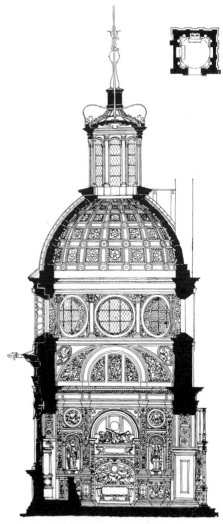

Section through the Sigismund Chapel showing the double tomb of the Zygmunt I Stary and Zygmunt II August

Pencz, a pupil of Dürer). Of the two grilles, the grander is c.1530 and made in the Vischer workshop.

Opposite the chapel is the sarcophagus of Queen Jadwiga, the much revered queen of Poland who sacrificed her own love to marry Władysław Jagiełło, the pagan ruler of Lithuania. This tomb by Antoni Madeyski (1902) is a focus of Polish nationalism. It is based on the Ilaria tomb by Jacopo della Quercia in Lucca, but is as unmistakably Art Nouveau as the marble decoration of the stalls. Jadwiga's remains are now housed around the corner, at the foot of her favourite crucifix. Her grave goods – a wooden sceptre and orb (whose humble materials have also given rise to legends of her self-sacrifice) – are in a case nearby.

After the Chapel of Bishop Jan Konarski, with its sheep's head capitals, comes the *Kaplica Zadzika (Chapel of Bishop Zadzik)* (V), a Baroque structure of 1645–50. Above the entrance hangs a portrait of Queen Anna Jagiellonka, presumably painted before 1587 by Marcin Kober. The bronze bust of the bishop is probably by Sebastiano Sala, who designed this chapel, once used as the king's robing room at the coronation. Next comes the *Kaplica Olbrachta (Chapel of King Jan Olbracht)* (VI) built in 1501. The chapel is Gothic but the king's tomb (1502–5, by Francesco Fiorentino) is the earliest Renaissance work in Poland, together with the west range of Wawel Castle; the tomb slab with the relief figure of the king is attributed to Jörg Huber.

Opposite is the very fine tomb of Kazimierz III Wielki, the Great (died 1370), the last Piast king of Poland, in whose reign this cathedral was consecrated. Commissioned by the king's nephew and successor, Ludwik Węgierski (the Hungarian), the tomb is carved from Hungarian marble, only the sandstone of the canopy being Polish. The king's other great foundation, the University, is perhaps commemorated by the figures below, who seem to be shown in disputation. Kazimierz's remains were removed for reburial in the 19th century, occasioning widespread nationalist demonstrations.

The next chapel was made into a dramatic Late Baroque ensemble when it was re-modelled in the 18th century for Bishop Załuski by F. Placidi, who also made the splendid door frame. Inside is the swinging Rococo statue of the 14th-century Bishop Grot. The altar painting is by Salvatore Monsilio, and the Renaissance tomb is of a Castellan of Kraków, Walenty Dembiński.

The *Kaplica Tomickiego (Chapel of Bishop Tomicki)* (VII) at the east end of the church was built by Bartolommeo Berrecci in 1530–35; Berrecci (or perhaps Padovano) was also responsible for the bishop's tomb, in the form of a sarcophagus with a marble figure. The larger chapel directly behind the high altar is the *Kaplica Mariacka (Lady Chapel)* (VIII), also known as the Kaplica Batorego (Chapel of Stefan Batory). This Gothic chapel (1380–92) with its tripartite vaulting was remodelled in 1594–5 by Gucci to house the tomb of King Stefan Batory. The choir stalls and the royal tomb of marble and alabaster are also Gucci's work; the contorted effigy of the king, surrounded by emblems of his military prowess, is the last in this superb series of royal funerary portraits. The ceiling painting is by Kasper Kurcz. The Baroque ciborium dates from *c.*1647, at about which time the gallery was also built; it connects the chapel to the castle by a passageway. The *Kaplica Gamrata (Chapel of Bishop Gamrat)* (IX), with a fine Renaissance grille, was remodelled in the mid-16th century by Gian Maria Padovano, who also made the tomb. The choir ambulatory contains the richly decorated Baroque tombs of King Michał Korybut Wiśniowiecki (died 1673, of a surfeit of gherkins) and King Jan III Sobieski (died 1696), created in 1753–60 of black marble, plaster and alabaster after a design by Francesco

Placidi; Turkish and Tatar captives hold up the sarcophagi, and the reliefs show the battle at Chocim (1673) and the victory at Vienna (1683). At the end of the ambulatory is the harrowing *Crucifix of Queen Jadwiga* (figure 14th century, frame and silver altarpiece 1743), much venerated since, according to tradition, Queen Jadwiga used to pray before it. Her relics were personally transferred here by Pope John Paul II in 1987. Behind stands the *Sacristy*, with early Gothic bas-reliefs; it leads to the Treasury (see below) and the Zygmunt Tower. Opposite, next to the fine bronze plaque to Stanisław Borek, a canon of Kraków (1558) is the sandstone tomb of Władysław I Łokietek who began the present cathedral (1333, restored 1838; the canopy is modern).

The *Kaplica Zebrzydowskiego (Chapel of Bishop Zebrzydowski)* (X) was remodelled for the bishop and his tomb is by Jan Michałowicz of Urzędow, 1562–3; the *Kaplica Skotnickich (Skotnicki Chapel)* has a Neoclassical monument to the painter Michał Skotnicki, by Stefano Ricci, a pupil of Canova, copied from his tomb in Santa Croce in Florence. The *Kaplica Lipskich (Lipski Chapel)* (XI) was redesigned by Francesco Placidi with dramatic hidden lighting effects; tombs of Bishop Andrzej (1634) and Cardinal Jan Aleksander (1743). Steps here lead to the crypt of Mickiewicz and Słowacki. The *Kaplica Maciejowskiego (Chapel of Bishop Maciejowski)* (XII), with a monument by the Padovano workshop (1552) contains a small Romanesque sculpture in its vestry.

The *Vestibule* is a Rococo staircase (1773–5, by Dominik Puck) which leads to the chapter house, cutting through the 15th-century chapel of Hincza of Rogów and its frescoes. Next to it is a wall plaque to Bishop Andrzej Trzebicki (died 1673), who as executor of the will of the last Vasa supervised the completion of the Vasa Chapel (and whose very fine portrait by Daniel Schultz survives in the Franciscan cloister; see page 462); by this is a Neoclassical monument to Stanisław Ankwicz (1840, by Francesco Pozzi of Florence), whose broken Neoclassical column is charmingly set against one of the Cathedral's own Gothic columns. The last two chapels are 19th-century foundations: the *Kaplica Czartoryskich (Czartoryski Chapel)* which contains a triptych attributed to Stanislaus Stoss, and the *Chapel of the Holy Trinity*, rebuilt by Francesco Maria Lanci for Anna Wąsowicz (her curious Neoclassical-Gothic Revival tomb is by Adamo Tadolini and Luigi Pampaloni). On the right is a monument by Bertel Thorvaldsen to Włodzimierz Potocki, a soldier in Napoleon's armies; the nationalist murals and the glass are by Włodzimierz Tetmajer (1902–4).

The *Treasury* at the northeast corner of the cathedral contains reliquaries, liturgical objects, royal regalia and manuscripts from the 8th to 17th centuries. Among the most outstanding pieces are: the 'Cross of Kazimierz IV Jagiellończyk', fashioned in the 13th century out of two crowns; the head reliquaries of St Florian and St Stanisław (Kraków, 1504); the reliquary of St Sigismund (Nuremberg, 1533); the 'Glass of St Jadwiga' (11th–12th centuries, and 15th century); paintings attributed to Quentin Massys and Hans Dürer; and the fine chasuble of Piotr Kmita with extraordinary stump-work scenes of the martyrdom of St Stanisław (early 16th century). The treasury also has the spearhead of the Lance of St Maurice, given to Bolesław I Chrobry by the Emperor Otto III at their meeting at Gniezno in AD 1000 (see page 15). The Chapter Library has a good collection, including some outstanding illuminated manuscripts: *Predicationes* (North Italy, *c.*800), the St Emmeram Gospels (Regensburg, *c.*1100), and the Olbracht Gradual (Kraków, early 16th century).

Beneath the cathedral the labyrinthine *Crypt* – including the surviving parts of the Krypta św. Leonarda (Crypt of St Leonard) *c.*1100 (entrance from the interior of the cathedral at the west end) – is full of the sarcophagi of Polish kings and their relatives, as well as famous Poles such as the poets Adam Mickiewicz and Juliusz Słowacki, and the national heroes Tadeusz Kościuszko, Józef Poniatowski and Józef Piłsudski. Kościuszko's grand marble sarcophagus was carved by Paolo Filippi to a design by Francesco Lanci; the simpler Poniatowski sarcophagus is by the local Ferdynand Kuhn. The pewter sarcophagi of the kings are richly decorated, some with figures in relief. The finest, made in Gdańsk, are those of Zygmunt II August (1572), Stefan Batory (1587), Anna Jagiellonka (late 16th century) and Zygmunt III Waza (1632). The sarcophagi of Władysław IV Waza and his first wife, Cecilia Renata of Austria, were made in Toruń by Christian Bierpfaff (*c.*1644–7). The altar is by Viollet-le-Duc.

From the parade square, the passage through a gateway by the Cathedral's flank leads to the *Castle* proper. Between the 9th and 13th centuries a prince's seat stood on this site, and by the 11th century it had become a royal castle. The foundations of the *Kaplica Mariacka (Chapel of St Mary)* also called the Kaplica śś. Feliksa i Adaukta (Rotunda of Sts Felix and Adauctus) (a), quatrefoil in plan with a round extension, have survived from around the year 1000, as well as the *Pozostałości Katedry* (b) (the remains of the first and

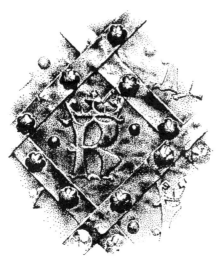

The cypher of Kazimierz III Wielki on the doors of Wawel Cathedral, drawing by I. Bentchev, 1987

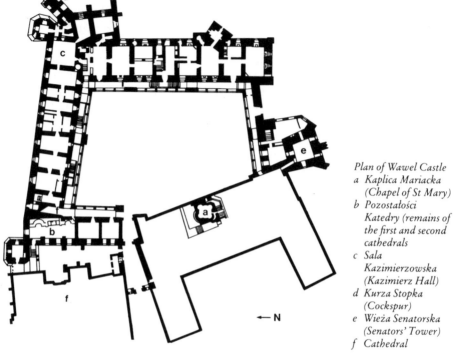

Plan of Wawel Castle
a Kaplica Mariacka
(Chapel of St Mary)
b Pozostałości
Katedry (remains of
the first and second
cathedrals
c Sala
Kazimierzowska
(Kazimierz Hall)
d Kurza Stopka
(Cockspur)
e Wieża Senatorska
(Senators' Tower)
f Cathedral

← N

second cathedrals) and the Gothic curtain walls of the 13th-14th centuries. Like the present cathedral (the third), the royal castle dates from the 14th century and was built during the reign of Kazimierz III Wielki; and it too has been much altered. Surviving from the time of Kazimierz are the *Sala Kazimierzowska (Kazimierz Hall)* (c) in the Łokietek Tower and the residential pavilion built at the end of the 14th century known as the *Kurza Stopka ('Cockspur')* because of its absurd position. In the late 14th and early 15th centuries the castle's defences were strengthened by curtain walls and towers, including the *Wieża Senatorska (Senators' Tower)* (e), the *Wieża Złodziejska (Thieves' Tower)* and *Wieża Sandomierska (Sandomierz Tower)*. Much was destroyed in a fire in 1499, and it was not until the reign of King Aleksander and especially his son Zygmunt I Stary, while Duke of Głogów, that the castle grew into the magnificent Renaissance palace that we see today. Artists were brought from Italy and all over Europe, and for fifty years from 1503 work proceeded continuously, interrupted only by fires. The next major campaign, also carried out mainly by Italian architects, began after another fire in 1595. A long decline began in 1655-7, with heavy plundering by the Swedes, compounded when they accidentally set fire to the castle on their return in 1702. There was yet more destruction when the Austrians turned the Wawel into a barracks. Intermittent restoration from the 17th to the

19th centuries achieved little, and it was not until the 20th century that, fuelled by patriotic enthusiasm and contributions, a proper and extended programme of restoration began, which was to continue into the 1960's. The castle was last used as a seat of government by Hans Frank, the Generalgouverneur of the Nazi Generalgouvernement, and his deputy, the Austrian quisling Seyss-Inquart. (Curzio Malaparte wrote an extraordinary account of a visit to Frank's court on the Wawel in his book *Kaputt*). Nazi occupation resulted in some damage, but luckily the speedy Soviet advance in 1944 (under Marshal Koniev) prevented the planned destruction of all the buildings on Wawel Hill. Since the war, the castle has been a museum.

The passageway from the parade ground to the castle opens up suddenly into the great courtyard (plate 47); how much more impressive this must have been when the rest of Wawel Hill was crowded with buildings. The magnificent space was designed by Francesco Fiorentino (1507–36), Master Benedykt of Sandomierz (1524–9) and Bartolommeo Berrecci (1530–36). It is surrounded by galleries with arcades (partly reconstructed) with columns on the lower two storeys and tall shafts supporting the overhanging eaves, beneath which are fragments of the original painted decoration, roundels with busts of the Roman Emperors by Dionizy Stuba (1537). This decoration originally continued round the entire courtyard, which was altogether more colourful than it is today, the roofs being covered with multi-coloured tiles, and the ground made up with crushed brick – an ideal surface for the tournaments that were staged here. The contrast between the classical columns with their varied capitals, and the complex Late Gothic mouldings around the doors and windows underlines the transitional character of the building. Among the state rooms the former Sala Tronowa (Throne Room and Hall of Deputies), known as *'Pod Głowami' ('Under the Heads')* (1529–35) is outstanding. It is famous for its wooden ceiling, with carved heads in the coffers (1531–5) and the painted frieze by Hans Dürer (brother of Albrecht), who was working in Kraków from 1529 to 1534, and by Anton of Breslau (1532–5) (colour plate 5). In this hall hang some of the Flemish tapestries which King Zygmunt II August bought between 1553 and 1571 from the Brussels workshops. With the other tapestries in the castle and cathedral they now form the most important collection of this sort in the world. There are three series of biblical stories (Adam and Eve, Noah, and the Building of the Tower of Babel – after cartoons by Michiel Coxcie), a series of landscapes and animals, and a series of grotesques, landscapes and coats of arms. The castle also contains a number of interesting portraits of Polish kings, and paintings of battles and ceremonies.

The north range was remodelled in 1596–1620 by Giovanni Trevano for Zygmunt III Waza. Trevano's work included the *Schody Senatorskie (Senators' Stairs)* (f) and the Baroque decoration of the rooms, such as the great overmantel of various coloured marbles in the *Sala Pod Ptakami ('Under the Birds')*. The walls are covered with Cordovan leather from Schloss Moritzburg in Dresden. Several stoves with decorative tiles, dating from the second half of the 18th century have survived the destruction that took place at the time of the Partitions of Poland (and a collection of tiles from vanished stoves of the

15th to the 18th centuries can be seen in the museum). The most important room on the second floor is the *Sala Senatorska (Senators' Hall)*, used for formal sessions of the Senate and – as its 16th-century balcony suggests – for balls and theatrical performances. The small vestibule that is passed on leaving this room has superb early Baroque door frames.

The *State Art Collections* in Wawel Castle include the former art treasures of the Polish kings. The Crown Treasury has liturgical objects dating back to the 11th century, as well as royal regalia, most notably the *Szczerbiec* ('jagged'). This sword was made around 1200, as an imitation of the sword that Bolesław Chrobry dented on the Golden Gate of Kiev when he conquered Red Ruthenia in 1018, and the copy was used from at least 1320 as the coronation sword of the Kings of Poland. (Most of the other Polish Crown Jewels were removed and destroyed by the Prussians after the Third Partition.) Like other valuable objects in the collection the sword was taken to Canada for safety during the Second World War. Apart from the tapestries already mentioned, there are also old paintings, furniture, and a remarkable collection of Ottoman art with Turkish and Persian tents of the 17th and 18th centuries, and arms, armour, flags, carpets and ceramics. Most of the objects were captured by King Jan III Sobieski outside Vienna in 1683. Seven rooms on the ground floor and in the basement contain the large *Armoury* numbering about 1,000 items (16th–18th centuries).

After a visit to the castle and cathedral a stroll down to the bank of the Vistula is recommended, past the **Smocza Jama (Dragon's Lair)** (49), a limestone cave. The fire-breathing (gas flame) statue of a dragon by Bronisław Chromy (1963) outside, represents the beast which, according to legend, was vanquished by the bold cobbler Skuba, who fed it a sheep stuffed with sulphur so that it rushed to drink in the river and exploded – not unlike the dragon of Brno. The cave, anciently a pub and brothel, was walled up by Zygmunt II August in 1565, but became a pub again in the 17th and 18th centuries, and was only cleaned up in the 19th century, when Emperor Franz Joseph went to have a look at it.

Szczerbiec – the coronation sword of the Kings of Poland

View of Kraków with Kazimierz (left), woodcut, 1493

Stradom and Kazimierz

The continuation of ul. Grodzka, ul. Stradomska (which becomes ul. Krakowska) runs southwards from the Old Town to the district of Kazimierz. The street first passes through *Stradom*, the district below the castle. In Pl. Bernardyński at the foot of the Wawel stands the **Klasztor Bernardynów (Bernardine Monastery)** (50), built on the site of a Gothic church destroyed by Swedish troops in 1655. The Baroque basilica was designed by Krzysztof Mieroszewski in 1670–80; it is a provincial variation on the Gesù in Rome. The interior furnishings, however, are more interesting and include several 17th- and 18th-century altars, some of which have paintings by Franciszek Lekszycki done after engravings of works by Rubens and Van Dyck. The sculpture of St Anne with the Virgin and Child in the Chapel of St Anne is by the workshop of Veit Stoss. In the aisle hangs a celebrated painting of the 'Dance of Death' (17th century) a typical example of a theme popular in Poland in the Baroque period. A more recent example of popular art is the vast diorama of the Deposition set up in one of the chapels during Passion Week.

Continuing down ul. Stradomska the visitor comes to the **Kościół Misjonarzy (Church of the Missionaries)** (51), one of the finest, if unfinished, examples of Late Baroque architecture in Kraków, built in 1719–28 to the designs of Kasper Bażanka. The centre-piece of the façade is based on that of Bernini's S. Andrea al Quirinale in Rome. The monumental painting on the high altar is by Tadeusz Kuntz, an 18th-century artist who, like Bażanka, was close to Roman Baroque. There were other important paintings in the monastic buildings, including a portrait of Stefan Batory by Marcin Kober, now removed.

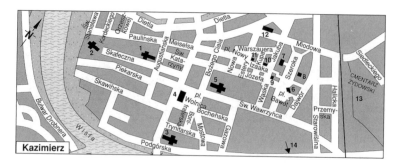

Stradom is separated from *Kazimierz* by the broad ul. Dietla, which was laid out in 1873 on the site of a filled-in branch of the Vistula. The original appearance of the two towns is shown in the early woodcut on page 483 and the panorama on pages 444–5. Ul. Dietla is lined with rich houses, many of which were the homes of well-to-do Jews; Kazimierz, founded as an independent town by Kazimierz III Wielki in 1335, was the focus of Jewish life in Małopolska after the Jews were expelled from Kraków in 1495, and became one of the great centres of European Jewry. Eventually Kazimierz was divided into a Jewish quarter to the east, and a Christian one to the west, separated by a wall.

The visitor turns right towards the first of the great brick churches founded by King Kazimierz, the **Kościół św. Katarzyny (Church of St Catherine)** (1) (14th–15th centuries) which belongs to the Augustinian Canons. Unlike most of the churches in Kraków, and particularly its sister foundation in Kazimierz, the church of Corpus Christi, the church is bare and flooded with clear light, as a consequence of a series of disasters, including floods, two earthquakes, and use by the Austrians as a storehouse. A slender chancel (1345–78) was completed by a more earthbound basilica (*c*.1400). The vigorous Baroque altar dates from 1634, and the large tomb is that of the Castellan Spytek Jordan (1603), known to Vasari as 'il grandissimo signore in Polonia' for his wide patronage of the arts (but who was also a typically obstreperous member of the szlachta). The cloisters have remains of 15th- and 16th-century frescoes, and the sacristy is an interesting room supported by a single pillar; the ceiling bosses spell out the name of the founder Kazimierz. The little wooden building at the corner is a 15th-century belfry.

We continue down ul. Skałeczna, past the southern vestibule of St Catherine's (*c*.1400). This has some of the most delicate carving in Kraków, and is typically Cracovian in its contrast of curved and straight lines playing over large plane surfaces. A covered bridge spans the street from church to monastery. At the end of the street is an attractive Baroque gateway with fine ironwork, which leads to the Paulite Monastery and the Baroque **Kościół Michała Archanioła i św. Stanisława Biskupa 'Na Skałce' (Church of St Michael the Archangel and St Stanislas 'on the Rock')** (2), built in 1734–8 to a design by Anton Gerhardt Müntzer on the site of an earlier church. The second dedication recalls that it is supposed to have been in the Romanesque predecessor of the present church that Bishop Stanisław was murdered at the hands of King Bolesław Śmiały in 1079. Legend has it that St Stanisław's hacked-off finger fell into a pool nearby, whose waters thus acquired miraculous healing powers. This pool is the tank to be seen on the right, with gateway, walls, obelisks and a statue of the saint in the middle (all *c.1723*). After Stanisław's canonization, the rock became a place of pilgrimage, and each king performed a solemn rite of penitence and expiation here. The interior of the church has some fine altars by Antonio Solari, who completed the building. The plasterwork is by Johann Georg Lehnert. In 1880 the crypt was turned into a mausoleum for Poles who had made a contribution to the arts. Those interred here include the historian Jan Długosz (died 1480), the composer Karol Szymanowski (died 1937), and the painters Henryk Siemiradzki (died 1902) and Stanisław Wyspiański (died 1907).

If we continue down ul. Krakowska towards the Vistula, the church on the left at No. 48 is the recently restored **Kościół św. Trójcy (Trinity Church)** (3), also known as the Kościół Bonifratrów (Church of the Merciful Brethren). By Francesco Placidi (1741–58), this is one of the few truly Rococo buildings in Kraków. The small interior has illusionist frescoes by the Moravian painter Joseph Pilz (1757–8).

At the centre of Kazimierz, in Pl. Wolnica, stands the **Town Hall** (4), built in the 14th century and remodelled in the 16th. Further expansion was carried out at the end of the 19th century, and since 1947 the building has housed the Ethnological Museum (founded

The Town Hall of Kazimierz in an early 19th-century watercolour

1905), despite Nazi destruction one of the richest in Poland (Christmas cribs, costumes, paintings). To the north of Pl. Wolnica rises the Gothic **Kościół Bożego Ciała (Church of Corpus Christi)** (5), the other great church in Kazimierz to survive from the time of Kazimierz III Wielki. It was founded by the king in 1340 as a parish church. The long chancel was built in 1369–87, and the nave completed in 1405, by Hans and Nikolaus Czipser, respectively; in the same year the church was handed over to the Canons Regular brought from Kłodzko in Silesia. The gable of the west front was erected in the late 15th century, the tower in 1556–82, and the cap was added in the 17th century. A cemetery and conventual buildings, including a fine cloister with columned arcades and a small Gethsemane, surround the church. Inside, the predominant colours are a rich blend of black and gold. The furnishings are particularly good: a high altar of 1634–7 and extravagantly carved choir stalls (1624–32, workshop of Baltazar Kuncz with paintings by the circle of Tommaso Dolabella), besides many altarpieces, a little early 15th-century stained glass (in the choir), and an impressive figure of St Barbara (early 16th century). The decoration culminates in the mid-18th century pulpit, shaped like a boat and complete with rigging and supporting sirens. Bartolomeo Berrecci, whose Sigismund Chapel on the Wawel spawned countless imitations all over Kraków and Małopolska, including chapels in this church, was buried here after his assassination (slab in left aisle wall, surrounded by naïve 17th-century paintings). The church was used by King Charles X Gustavus as his headquarters during the Swedish siege of Kraków.

The eastern part of Kazimierz was the crowded, bustling home of the Jews of Kraków from 1495 until 1941, when the Nazis moved them to the ghetto at Podgórze, across the river (see below). Today eastern Kazimierz is a relatively run-down area. Of the 68,400 Jews who lived here in 1939, only 2,000 survived the war, and most of these emigrated, leaving a tiny, elderly community.

The most notable building here is the **Old Synagogue** (6) (ul. Szeroka 24), the second oldest synagogue to survive in Europe (after Prague). It was built in the 15th-16th centuries and remodelled or restored several times: in 1557–70 (after a fire) by Matteo Gucci (the attic dates from this period); in 1904–13 by Zygmunt Hendel; and in 1957–9 after the devastation of the war. The interior has two naves and two slender columns holding up sexpartite vaults. From the (reconstructed) *bimah* Kościuszko made an impassioned appeal to the Jews in 1794, to which they responded patriotically, as they did again in the Uprisings of 1830 and 1863. The Torah shrine in the wall is original. The synagogue now houses the *Jewish Museum*. In the courtyard in front a monument marks the spot where 30 Poles were shot by the Nazis.

The Old Synagogue is the southern end of ul. Szeroka, which is effectively a large square and was the teeming centre of Jewish Kazimierz before the war. Further up the square is the **R'emuh Synagogue and Cemetery** (7). The synagogue, still in use by Kraków's 600-strong Jewish community, was founded in 1553 by the royal banker Israel Isserles and named after his son, the great sage and rabbi Moses Isserles R'emuh (1525–75). The cemetery has been in existence since 1551, but its present form is a post-war reconstruction, using tombstones from the whole Kraków region, including many which had been buried during the Swedish wars to avoid desecration. The wall is built of tombstone fragments. On R'emuh's tomb, which is fenced off, the inscription reads: 'From Moses [Maimonides] to Moses [Isserles] there was no greater Moses'. Pilgrims still come here to pay their respects at the grave of this great teacher and to see the spot where he sat in the synagogue. Other (unused) synagogues are at ul. Szeroka 16, the **Bociana Synagogue** (8) (also called the *Wolf Popper* or the *Storch Synagogue*) (1620); ul. Józefa 38, the **Wysoka (High) Synagogue** (9) (1556–63); ul. Kupa 16, **Isaak's Synagogue** (10) (1638, some painting survives); ul. Warszauera 8, the **Kupa Synagogue** (11) (first half of 17th century, some surviving paintings); and ul. Miodowa 24, the **Temple (or Reformed) Synagogue** (12) (1860–62, interiors intact, and occasionally used). There was a bath house *(mikvah)* at ul. Szeroka 6; and the **New Cemetery** (13), which is still in use, is at ul. Miodowa 55, beyond the main road and the railway line. This road leads over the river to Podgórze, where the Jews of Kazimierz were interned in a ghetto by the Nazis before being deported to Auschwitz and other death camps.

Podgórze, Płaszów, Wesoła and Nowa Huta

Podgórze on the right bank of the Vistula was not developed until 1784, when the Austrians raised an insignificant village to the status of a free town, named Josephstadt after the reigning emperor. As the border of the Free Republic of Kraków was the Vistula, Podgórze between 1815 and 1848 was the Austrian border town. According to legend, the conical '*Kopiec Kraka*' *(Krakus Mound)* is supposed to be the burial mound of the founder of Kraków. Archaeological investigations have so far revealed only wooden supporting posts. The huge neo-Gothic church at the top of the Rynek Podgórski is the *Kościoł św. Józefa (Church of St Joseph)* (1905–9, by J. Sas-Zubrzycki).

Eastern Podgórze was the site of the Nazi Ghetto, where the Jews of Kraków were crammed in March 1941 for two years before their complete destruction. They were rounded up for deportation to the death camps in what is now **Pl. Bohaterów Getta (Square of the Ghetto Heroes)** (14). At No. 18 there is a museum in the building of the Apteka Pod Orłem, the Ghetto pharmacy, which was run by Dr Tadeusz Pankiewicz, the only non-Jew permitted to live in the Ghetto. The seat of the Jewish Fighters' Organization (ŻOB) was at No. 6 in the square. There are some other Jewish buildings nearby; and in ul. Lwowska a small section of the Ghetto wall survives. Anyone caught crossing it was summarily shot.

At **Płaszów**, to the east of Podgórze, the Nazis built a labour camp in 1942, on the site of two Jewish cemeteries, many of whose stones were used as foundation material. There are two memorials to the 80,000 people who lost their lives there, nearly all of them Jews. Nearby was the factory of Oskar Schindler, who smuggled hundreds of Jews to safety under the cover of using them as slave labour.

On the eastern edge of the Old Town of Kraków is the district of **Wesoła**, where (at ul. Kopernika 44) the Late Baroque *Kościół św. Teresy (Church of St Theresa)* (or Kościół Karmelitanek, Church of Carmelite Nuns), probably designed by Kasper Bażanka, was built in 1719–33. The centrepiece of the Late Baroque interior is the marble high altar (1725); there is also an elegant Gothic statue of the Virgin and Child (*c.*1380). The convent has a large collection of 18th-century wax figures.

Running eastwards through Wesoła in the direction of Mogiła is ul. Kopernika, one of Kraków's most beautiful streets. It contains the monumental buildings of the University Hospital (second half of the 19th century) and a number of churches of the 17th and 18th centuries, as well as the *Kościół Jezuitów na Wesołej (Jesuit Church in Wesoła)*, built in 1909–21 and designed by Franciszek Mączyński, which contains some good examples of modern church art: monumental architectural sculpture by Xawery Dunikowski, altars by Karol Hukan, wall paintings by Jan Bukowski. At the end of ul. Kopernika stands, appropriately enough, the *Obserwatorium Astronomiczne (Astronomical Observatory)* founded by Feliks Radwański, now unusable because of air pollution, and a *Botanical Garden*, first established in 1788 by the enlightened Rector of the University, Hugo Kołłątaj, which contains examples of almost every type of flora in Poland.

Ul. Lubicz leads to the industrial suburb of **Nowa Huta ('New Works')** situated about 10 km east of the city centre. Work began on the construction of the steel mills – then called the Lenin Steelworks – in the former village of Mogiła in 1949. The decision to place an industrial conurbation here was a political one (see page 452); there were no raw materials for steel production nearby, nor a large population needing work. Although the plan to create an atheist and communist proletariat at the heart of historic Poland failed, Kraków was inevitably marked by its transformation into a large industrial city – not least of course by the terrible pollution.

The modern buildings of Nowa Huta give a good idea of the development of postwar architecture in Poland, beginning with the Soviet-inspired eclecticism of the 1950's. Churches were not part of the original plan but after a long struggle, permission was eventually granted to build one: the *Kościół Matki Boskiej Królowej Polski (Church of the Mother of God, Queen of Poland)* (also known as the 'Ark Church'), a bold design which gives interest to the otherwise monotonous district of Bieczyce. Built in 1967–77 to the designs of Wojciech Pietrzyk, its boat-like shape is made up of abstract forms derived from Le Corbusier's Ronchamp, but with homely Polish touches: wooden shingles on the eaves and ceiling, and mountain pebbles set into the concrete exterior. The extraordinary bronze crucifix inside (by Bronisław Chromy) is eight metres high.

Mogiła, Kleparz and Zwierzyniec

In 1222 Bishop Iwo Odrowąż of Kraków founded a Cistercian monastery at Kacice. Three years later the monks moved to **Mogiła**. In 1266 Odrowąz consecrated the *Kościół*

Najświętszej Panny i św. Wacława (Church of St Mary and St Wenceslas). The *Opactwo Cystersów (Cistercian Abbey)* is one of the most important works of Early Gothic architecture in Małopolska. The church follows the usual Cistercian plan: a three-aisled basilica with pairs of chapels in the transepts. In the 18th century the nave and nave vault were remodelled. The Late Baroque west front (1779–80) was designed by Franz Moser. The most notable feature of the interior are the wall paintings by Stanisław Samostrzelnik, the great Renaissance miniaturist (see pages 290–1), who was a monk here. They were made at the same time as the monumental depiction of the Crucifixion in the cloister (1537–8). The abbey has a good collection of paintings and an interesting library.

Opposite the abbey church stands the *Kościół św. Bartlomieja (Church of St Bartholomew)*, one of the oldest wooden churches in Poland. The richly carved doorway (by Maciej Mączka) bears the date 1466; the Baroque belfry (which doubles as a gate tower) was built in 1752.

The centre of the **Kleparz** district, north of the Barbican, is Pl. Matejki with the Pomnik Grunwaldzki (see page 454). Outside the church of St Florian ul. Warszawska and ul. 29 Listopada run northwards to the large *Cmentarz Rakowicki (Rakowicki Cemetery)*, which was laid out in 1803. Here, as in all cemeteries in Poland, dozens of candles are lit on the graves each year on All Saints' Day. Many of the tombs are of high artistic quality.

One of Kraków's strangest monuments stands in the western part of the **Zwierzyniec** district, to the west of the Old Town (approached via ul. Zwierzyniecka or ul. Marszałka Józefa Piłsudskiego). This is the *Kopiec Kościuszki (Kościuszko Mound)*, inspired by the prehistoric Wanda and Krak hills nearby, but created in 1820–23 in honour of the national hero Tadeusz Kościuszko and built with earth from the battlefields on which he fought (including those in America). There is a good view over the city from the top. The most important building in Zwierzyniec is the large *Klasztor Norbertanek (Norbertine or Premonstratensian Nunnery)*, founded in 1162, with its *Kościół św. Augustyna (Church of St Augustine)*. The church dates from the 13th century (a Late Romanesque doorway survives on the south side), but its present appearance is due to remodelling in 1596 and 1626. It was given a new Neoclassical interior in 1777 by Sebastian Sierakowski. The *Kościół Salwatora (Church of the Saviour)* on Bronisław Hill is one of the oldest churches in Kraków. Three previous Early Romanesque churches on the site (the earliest *c.* 1000) have been uncovered by archaeological excavations. The present church was rebuilt in the 12th century and remodelled in the early 17th century when the Late Gothic nave and tower were built. The chancel has been returned to its original Romanesque state. There are many local traditions associated with Zwierzyniec. Every year, eight days after Corpus Christi, the procession of *Lajkonik* (see page 453) forms outside the Norbertine Church, before making its way through the streets of Kraków to the market square, and on Easter Monday a fair is held here called 'Emaus'. *Szopki Krakowskie*, the colourful, fantastic structures inspired by the old architecture of Kraków, and often barely recognizable as Christmas cribs (see page 453), are a tradition started by the masons of Zwierzyniec.

Ivan Bentchev

Ziemia Krakowska (Kraków Land)

The beautiful rolling countryside around Kraków is rich in artistic treasures, though the boundaries of the area under Kraków's direct cultural influence in the southwestern part of Małopolska (Lesser Poland) cannot be established with precision. The region corresponds roughly, however, to the present voivodships of Kraków, Tarnów (with part of the voivodship of Krosno), Nowy Sącz, the eastern part of Bielsko-Biała and Katowice, as well as the southern part of Kielce. To the west is the historic frontier between Małopolska and Silesia, while to the south the Western Carpathians and the High Tatras form the natural frontier of the Polish state.

Bielany – Tyniec – Rudno – Krzeszowice – Racławice – Oświęcim-Brzezinka (Auschwitz-Birkenau) – Wilamowice

The great forest park of *Las Wolski* begins a few kilometres west of Kraków city centre (by way of ul. Tadeusza Kościuszki and ul. Księcia Józefa). In the southern part of the park, on Srebrna Góra ('Silver Mountain'), high above the Vistula, rises the monumental façade of the Camaldulensian church of **Bielany**. The *Kościół Wniebowzięcia Najświętszej Marii Panny (Church of the Assumption)* was founded by Mikołaj Wolski, Crown Marshal of Poland, and built in 1605–42. At the Polish court Wolski, a much-travelled diplomat and collector, was a leading patron of Counter-Reformation art. The extensive complex of buildings was built to Roman designs for the community of monks he summoned from Monte Corona near Perugia. First to be built were the monks' hermitages (1605–09), a feature of the ascetic Camaldulensian Order. In 1617, just as the church was nearing completion, the main façade collapsed. The rebuilding to a design by Andrea Spezza, Wallenstein's architect, was not completed until around 1630. Spezza's façade was to become influential in Polish architecture: it consists of a massive centrepiece accentuated by a pediment and flanked by square corner towers. Inside the church, the spacious barrel-vaulted nave has three richly decorated chapels on either side. The Early Baroque decoration creates an impressive ensemble with its mural paintings, plasterwork and wood-carving, and details in black marble. The two easternmost chapels, the *Kaplica św. Benedykta (Chapel of St Benedict)* (1632–6), and the *Kaplica św. Romualda (Chapel of St Romuald)* opposite are particularly lavish. Each contains a cycle of paintings (1633–43) by Tommaso Dolabella showing the lives of St Ladislas (King of Hungary and patron saint of King Władysław IV, who founded the Chapel of St Benedict) and St Romuald, the founder of the Order.

The whole complex is an excellent example of the axiality which was an essential part of the Baroque concept of space: the church façade not only dominates the grandiose forecourt, it also holds together visually the symmetrically arranged monastic building to the north and south, as well as the group of monks' hermitages to the east. The grandeur and coherence of the design reflects the confident spirit of the Counter-Reformation. The monastery complex is closed to women, except for the main church on occasional feast days only.

Southwest from Bielany and on the other side of the river is **Tyniec**, where the *Opactwo Benedyktynów (Benedictine Abbey)* stands on a limestone cliff above the Vistula. (It can also be reached by boat from central Kraków.) The abbey was founded in 1076–9 by Bolesław II Śmiały, and grew to become the most magnificent Benedictine house in Poland in the 11th century. The complex has undergone considerable alterations in the course of its history. Excavations have shown that the original building of the *Kościół śś. Piotra i Pawła (Church of Sts Peter and Paul)* was a three-aisled Romanesque basilica with three apses at its east end. A cloister with rich sculptural decoration was built on the south side of the church. After destruction by the Tatars in the 13th century the church was rebuilt between the 15th and 17th centuries with a fine west portal. Its interior dates from the mid-18th century and is probably the work of Francesco Placidi. Particularly impressive are the life-size statues that adorn the high altar of black marble. The monastic buildings, on the north side of the church, fell into ruin in the 19th century but have been gradually rebuilt since 1947. The lapidarium has a collection of fragments of medieval architectural sculpture going back to the monastery's origins in the Romanesque period, including double capitals from the cloister (1100). The well in the monastery forecourt goes down to the level of the Vistula lapping at the foot of the cliff below. Post-war excavations have revealed not only the foundations of the Romanesque church, but also tombs containing precious grave goods (now in Wawel Castle in Kraków).

Returning to Liszki we take the main road westwards via Zagórze and Poręba-Żegoty, to the village of **Rudno**. Here, on a wooded hill, stand the impressive ruins of the *Zamek Tenczynek (Tenczyn Castle)*, until 1638 the property of the powerful Tęczyński family. The remains of an older 14th-century castle served as the foundations for the splendid Late Renaissance magnate's residence erected in 1579. The castle was rebuilt after a devastating fire in 1656, but abandoned in the mid-18th century. The defensive walls and fortifications still retain some Late Gothic features of the 15th century, such as the round bastion to the southeast of the complex. The ruins were restored in the late 1940's and can now be visited.

Ogrodzieniec • ▲ **Góra Janowskiego**
(504 m)

Wolbrom

Książ Wielki

Miechów

Pustynia

Bytom

Dąbrowa
Górnicza

Chorzów

Gliwice

Zabrze

Katowice

Sosnowiec

Błędowska

Olkusz

Imbramowice

Pieskowa
Skała

Wysocice

Skała
Ojców

Nationalpark
Ojcowski

Wieçławice
Michałowice

Modlnica

Chrzanów

Igołomia

Chełmek

Poręba-Żegoty

Kraków

Wisła

Zagórze

Brzezinka

Tyniec

Niepoło

Podłęże

Wieliczka

Wadowice

Kalwaria
Zebrzydowska

Lanckorona

Kobiernice

Bielsko-Biała

Myślenice

Muc

Wisła

Żywiec

Sucha
Beskidzka

Babiogórski
National Park

Rabka

Gorczański
National
Park

Zab

BESKID ŻYWIECKI

BESKIDY

Nowy Targ

Sromowce Niżr

Chochołów

Zakopane

T A T R Y

Tatra National Park

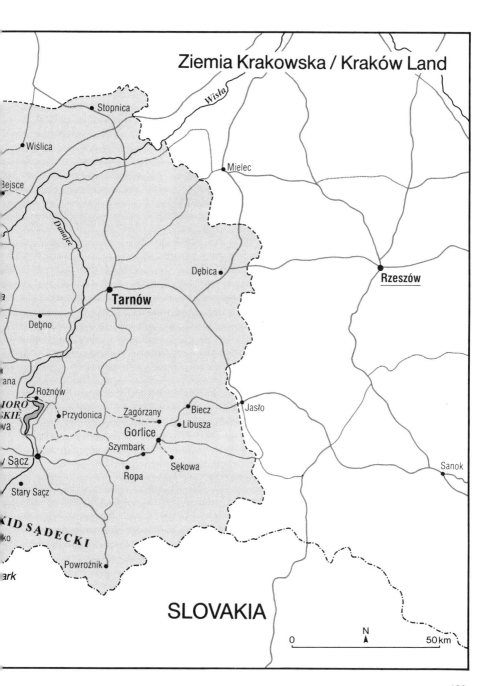

Ziemia Krakowska / Kraków Land

Wisła

Stopnica

Wiślica

Bejsce

Mielec

Dunajec

Dębica

Rzeszów

Tarnów

Dębno

ana

Rożnów

JORO
KIE
va

Przydonica

Zagórzany

Biecz

Jasło

Libusza

Gorlice

Szymbark

Sęcz

Sękowa

Sanok

Ropa

Stary Sącz

KID SĄDECKI

ko

Powroźnik

ark

SLOVAKIA

0   N   50 km

Oświęcim, view of the Castle,
engraving, 1878

A few kilometres north of here in the town of **Krzeszowice** the *Parish Church* (1823–44) designed by Karl Friedrich Schinkel for Count Arthur Potocki, younger son of the extraordinary Count Jan Potocki, is a good example of the architect's neo-Gothic style and still has some original furnishings. The façade is decorated with statues of the Evangelists and the arms of the Potocki and Branicki families. Schinkel also provided designs for the nearby Potocki Palace, which in fact was built by Francesco Maria Lanci (1850-58). The palace was a residence of Generalgouverneur Hans Frank during the Nazi occupation.

The road north from here to Przeginia passes through the village of **Racławice**, which has an interesting Late Gothic timber church. It is best known as the site of the famous victory of Tadeusz Kościuszko and his peasant scythe-men over the Russian army on 4 April 1794.

The town of **Oświęcim** is about 8 km south of Chelmek, in the voivodship of Małapolska. In the middle ages, from 1317 to 1564, it was the seat of an independent duchy. The ruins of the *Gothic Castle* and its tower stand on a hill beyond the town. Since the Second World War this unexceptional earlier history has been eclipsed by the horror associated with **Auschwitz**, the German name of Oświęcim. The walls, watchtowers and barbed-wire fences, loading ramps, execution walls and crematoria of the Nazi machinery of genocide are still standing. Between 1.1 and 1.4 million people from 28 countries, most of them Jews, met their deaths at *Oświęcim-Brzezinka (Auschwitz-Birkenau)*, the biggest and most horrific of the Nazi concentration camps. In May 1940 the main camp Auschwitz I was created out of old Austrian barracks. It was used as a model camp for showing to visiting foreign delegations. 'Arbeit macht frei' ('work makes you free') reads the inscription over the round-arched main entrance. From spring 1942, when experiments with Cyclon-B poison gas were being carried out, this main camp was linked by a railway line to a new extermination camp (Auschwitz II) at Birkenau, two kilometres away, where most of the systematic killing took place. At the external camp at Monowice (Monowitz)

The railway entrance to Birkenau

(Auschwitz III), and at 39 subsidiary camps in the vicinity, prisoners worked as slave labour in various industries, including I. G. Farben's chemical works at nearby Dwory and the German armaments industry. Before the Soviet Army liberated Auschwitz, the Nazis destroyed crematoria and gas chambers in an attempt to remove all traces of their crime. It is worth remembering that Auschwitz is famous not only because of its size, but also because, unlike other death camps, there were enough survivors to tell the tale. Sobibór, Treblinka, Bełżec and others had finished their work and been ploughed underground before the war's end.

On the site of the main camp and in Birkenau, museums and memorials have been established since the war (open every day). From 1967 the great *Monument to the Victims of Auschwitz* was erected in Birkenau to the design of Polish and Italian sculptors and paid for by the International Auschwitz Committee. In 1984 a *Klasztor Karmelitek (Carmelite Convent)* was established in a former hall in Auschwitz I and led to a bitter dispute between the Polish Church and the world Jewish community. In 1987 Pope John Paul II canonized the Franciscan priest Maksymilian Kolbe, and controversy was caused in 2000 by the canonization of the Carmelite nun Edith Stein murdered because she was Jewish.

A few kilometres beyond Oświęcim, the village of *Wilamowice* is a rare survival of medieval German colonization, where the original Frisian dialect and costumes have been preserved to this day.

Modinica – Ojców – Grodzisko – Pieskowa Skała

To the northwest of Krakow begins the Wyżyna Krakowsko-Częstochowska (Kraków-Częstochowa Plain) – also called the Jura Krakowska. This limestone plateau, 300-400 metres above sea level, has a remarkably varied landscape, including approximately 500 caves created by subterranean watercourses.

In the village of **Modlnica** is a fine example of a simple *country house* of 1783–7. The little Late Gothic timber *church*, built in 1553, is also worth a visit.

About 22 km northwest of Kraków is the small town of **Ojców**, from which the *Ojcowski National Park* takes its name. The park includes the picturesque Dolina Prądnika (the valley of the Prądnik, a tributary of the Vistula), a 200-metre-deep gorge cut into the Jura limestone cliffs. The formation has created a microclimate, and there is a rich variety of trees including a birch found nowhere else. There are many birds, bats in the caves, and beautiful swallowtail butterflies. A clearly marked footpath leads over hills and chasms with bizarre rock formations to Ojców, the starting point for the 'Szlak Orlich Gniazd' ('Way of the Eagles' Nests'), which in the 11th and 12th centuries was an important trade route linking Kraków with Wielkopolska. Many castles and watchtowers were built to guard it. One of these was the *Zamek Kazimierzowski (Kazimierz Castle)* on the cliff at Ojców, which was built by Kazimierz III Wielki as a base for a strong guard detachment. The castle passed into the possession of the starosta Mikołaj Koryński, who set about an extensive remodelling in 1620–30 to turn the castle into a magnificent residence. After the Partitions of Poland the castle sank into decline and in 1829 was almost completely demolished. All that is left is two towers and the remains of the walls of the castle chapel. From here there is a superb view over the Prądnik Valley.

The way continues to **Grodzisko**, where the *Pustelnia błg. Salomei (Hermitage of the Blessed Salomea)* is situated on a cliff-top high above the river. Salomea was the sister of Bolesław V Wstydliwy ('the Chaste'), and married Duke Koloman of Halicz. On the foundations of the medieval *Klasztor Klarysek (Convent of Poor Clares)* Jan Sebastian Piskowski, a canon of Kraków, the confidant of and adviser to the Poor Clares of Kraków, built an unusual architectural ensemble to his own designs in 1677–90, starting with the baroquization of the small church at its centre (by Piskowski). A doorway in the outer wall leads to the rectangular forecourt dominated by a large *statue* of St Clare. On the wall stand the figures of saints and rulers who have a connection with the region and with the Blessed Salomea: St Jadwiga (Hedwig) and the Blessed Kinga (Cunegunda), and their respective husbands Duke Henryk Brodaty and Duke Bolesław V Wstydliwy, as well as Salomea's own husband Duke Koloman. Behind the church, set a little deeper into the cliffs, is a small courtyard which has a 17th-century chapel with three artificial grottoes at its end. These are (from left to right): the Grottoes of St Mary Magdalene, of the Death of the Virgin, and of St John the Baptist. An obelisk on the back of a stone elephant, made in 1698 on the model of Bernini's statue in the Piazza Minerva in Rome, stands in the centre of the courtyard. Finally, by way of the 50 'Rosary Steps' behind the grotto chapels, we reach the *Hermitage of the Blessed Salomea* (also called the Hermitage of St Mary Magdalene), which seems to teeter on the edge of the abyss.

An attractive footpath runs from Grodzisko to **Pieskowa Skała**. A kilometre north of Grodzisko, on the right-hand side of the road, rise the Skały Wdowie (Widow Rocks), behind which begins the long Dolina Kamieniec (Kamieniec Valley). After about 7 km the castle comes into sight on a hill beyond the lone standing rock formation known as Maczuga Herkulesa (Hercules' Club). *Zamek Pieskowa Skała (Pieskowa Skała Castle)* was spared the fate of most of the eagles' nests and has been preserved almost intact. It was granted to Piotr Szafraniec by the Crown in 1377. Extensive alterations in several stages in the 16th century transformed the medieval castle into a grand magnatial residence for the Szafraniec family. The haphazard cluster of medieval buildings was linked together to form an integrated complex with three-storey open arcades around an inner courtyard, decorated with ferocious moustachioed masks. The castle interiors were decorated on the model of the Wawel Castle. The later owners of Pieskowa Skała, the Wielopolski family, were responsible for some other minor alterations. The castle was damaged by fire in 1718. Around 1780 Jan Hieronim Wielopolski restored the property and much of its Renaissance character was lost. After a troubled history the building had reached such a state of decline and its owners had fallen so deeply in debt that it had to be sold by public auction. Thanks to the initiative of the writer Adolf Dygasiński the castle was saved in 1903 and converted into a convalescent home. Lengthy restoration work (1948–70) returned the building to its Renaissance appearance: the arcades around the courtyard were uncovered, as well as the wallpaintings on the exterior and interior walls and the famous open loggia with its view over the Prądnik Valley.

The castle is entered across a draw-bridge through a gateway in its impressive outer defences. An open courtyard leads to the inner, arcaded court. The rooms of the two residential floors are arranged in a long enfilade and retain their Renaissance fireplaces and doorways. In the northwest corner of the courtyard stands the Baroque castle chapel, which is decorated with fine plasterwork. Above the crypt, which contains four sarcophagi of the former lords of the castle, we come to the oldest part of the building, where until the 1870's the Dorotka Tower stood. Legend relates how the wife of one of the Szafraniec family spent many years imprisoned in the cellars of the tower as a punishment for marital infidelity. The castle is now a branch of the State Art Collections of the Wawel in Kraków. It houses an excellent and well displayed collection of Polish and European art from the middle ages to the 19th century, with some fine furniture and sculpture.

Wysocice – Imbramowice

The towns of Wysocice and Imbramowice are situated at the northern tip of the voivodship of Małopolska, and are reached by way of the picturesque and narrow road which follows the River Dłubnia which it crosses just after the village of Iwanowice. At **Wysocice** the *Kościół św. Mikołaja (Church of St Nicholas)* is a particularly well preserved example of a Romanesque stone church from the first quarter of the 13th century. The small aisleless nave opens at the east end into a rectangular chancel with a semicircular apse, and at the west end has a characteristic open gallery in the tower. The south doorway has a tympanum sculpture showing Christ enthroned between the figures of two saints, and the Nativity. A diamond-shaped niche in the east gable, above the apse, contains a sculptured figure of an enthroned Virgin and Child.

Continuing northwest for a few kilometres, we arrive at the *Klasztor Norbertanek (Convent of Premonstratensian Nuns)* at **Imbramowice**, founded by Bishop Iwo Odrawąż of Kraków in 1223. A fire caused such damage to the *Kościół śś. Piotra i Pawła (Church of Sts Peter and Paul)* that it was almost entirely rebuilt in 1711–20. Kasper Bażanka's severe exterior belies the lavishly decorated interior conceived on the model of the Baroque churches of Rome, with a sophisticated arrangement of marble altars. The fine sculptural decoration is by Antoni Frąckiewicz, and the illusionistic painting by Wilhelm Wioch. The convent has an interesting collection of works of art from the Romanesque to the Late Baroque. The prize piece is a painting by Jan Breugel the Elder, the 'Madonna in the Garland of Flowers'.

Olkusz –Sławków – Ogrodzieniec

Olkusz is one of Poland's oldest mining towns; lead and silver ore have been extracted here since the 13th century. The town enjoyed a high reputation and received many privileges from the Polish kings. The parish church, the *Kościół św. Andrzeja (Church of St Andrew)*, was founded by King Kazimierz III Wielki. It is a brick-built three-aisled hall church with a long chancel, but though erected around the middle of the 14th century, it gradually lost its Gothic character in the course of numerous fires and restorations. During extensive restoration work in 1960–68 several layers of wall paintings were uncovered, dating from the 14th, 15th and 16th centuries. (These inspired the restorer Józef Dutkiewicz to cover the vaults with distinctive painted decoration.) The most outstanding work of art in the church, however, is the 'Olkusz Polyptych' in the high altar, an important work of the Kraków School. The four wings of this altarpiece, painted in 1485 by Jan Wielki and Stanisław Stary, are filled with 16 panels of scenes of the Life of the Virgin and the Passion. The central panel contains a 15th-century carving of the enthroned Virgin and Child. Outstanding among the Baroque furnishings are the organ, made around 1612 by Johann Hummel of Nuremberg, and the richly decorated pulpit of 1639. The church treasury contains a silver cross 1.5 metres high and weighing 7 kg, which was given by the miners of Olkusz in the 17th century.

Twelve kilometres west of Olkusz, at **Sławków** is 'the finest example of an old Polish inn, one of the few that still survive in our small towns' (J. Z. Łoziński), a timber building dating from 1771.

From Dąbrowa Górnicza we take the road northeast for about 26 km to catch sight of the highest point of the Kraków Jura, Góra Janowskiego (504 metres). The bizarre rock formations look like human figures and animals.

Few castles in Poland have such a mysterious setting as the nearby ruins of **Zamek Ogrodzieniec**. Jan Boner, the banker and burgrave of Kraków, took over the castle in 1523 and bequeathed it to his nephew Seweryn, who in 1530–45 erected a massive palace on the foundations of the medieval fortifications. Following its destruction by the Swedes in 1655–7 it was partly rebuilt, though it never regained its original splendour. Until 1810 the central part was still lived in, but when this too became dilapidated the palace was used as a quarry. After the war the ruins were saved from further collapse and opened to the public.

Before returning by a direct route to Olkusz, we pass through an unexpected landscape, the sandy desert known as the *Pustynia Błędowska*. Covering an area of 32 square kilometres, this little Sahara has sand banks and dunes up to 10 metres high; mirages can be seen on hot days in high summer and the green banks of the River Przesza can look like an oasis. It was here that Field Marshal Rommel trained his 'Afrika-Korps' during the German occupation.

Więcławice – Niedźwiedź

To the north of Kraków lies the little village of **Więcławice** (near Michałowice), where the wooden *Kościół św. Jakuba Młodszego (Church of St James the Less)* (1748) is worth visiting mainly for its Late Gothic winged altarpiece of 1477, which was brought here from the Wawel Cathedral in Kraków. In the centre is St Nicholas, enthroned with St Stephen and St Lawrence.

A few kilometres further north, off the road to the right, is the Late Gothic parish church of **Niedźwiedź**, the *Kościół św. Wojciecha (Church of St Adalbert)*, a stone building of 1486–93, which contains several outstanding works of Late Gothic church art: a superbly carved wooden figure of the Virgin rather precariously holding the Christ Child (*c.*1420), one of the family of 'Schöner Stil' Madonnas; and two altar panels (*c.*1530) painted on both sides with scenes from the Life of Christ.

Wieliczka – Staniątki – Niepołomice – Igołomia – Kościelec

Wieliczka, Poland's ancient salt town, situated 15 km to the southeast of Kraków, has always been high on the list of the country's tourist attractions. Goethe and Balzac were among the many famous visitors to its salt mine, the oldest in Europe. The entrance to the *Kopalnia Soli (Salt Mine)* is only a few yards from the market place. About a third of the wealth of the Polish kings came from the 'white gold' of Wieliczka and Bochnia, and it was thus the crucial economic factor behind the treasures of Kraków. Later the mine was the raison d'être of Austria Hungary's first railway line. The mine was in commercial use as early as 1044, and is first mentioned in a document as *Magnum Sal* in 1119. Medieval miners suffered an annual mortality rate of 10 per cent, but were given good pay and free

Salt production in the Wieliczka salt mine, engraving by J. Nilson, 1719 (detail)

funerals. A tour takes two hours, goes down to a depth of 135 metres and covers about 3 km of the galleries and passages, where salt was mined from the 16th to the 19th centuries. Of the eight existing levels three are open to visitors. Some of the subterranean chambers have been converted into a *museum* displaying objects found during mining (petrified fauna and flora), old mining equipment and tools. At a depth of 101 metres is the mine's showpiece, the magnificent *Kaplica św. Kingi (Chapel of St Kinga)*, a vast chamber hewn between 1896 and 1963 with its altars and sculptures all carved in salt by miners. There are two other, older chapels: the *Kaplica św. Antoniego (Chapel of St Anthony)* (1675) and the more architecturally ambitious 17th-century *Kaplica św. Krzyża (Chapel of the Holy Cross)* with carved columns and arches. The mine also has some beautiful subterranean lakes. The microclimate in the mine is beneficial to those with respiratory problems; the therapeutic department of an asthma sanatorium was established here in 1964. Also worth seeing is the crystal grotto discovered in 1860, which is under strict protection.

On the way from Wieliczka to Niepołomice (8 km) we turn off to the right at Podłęże to visit the *Klasztor Benedyktynek (Convent of Benedictine Nuns)* at **Staniątki**. The monas-tery was founded in 1228, and the *Kościół Najświętszej Marii Panny i św. Wojciecha (Church of St Mary and St Adalbert)* was built in the second half of the 13th century. It is one of the earliest three-aisled hall churches in Poland. After destruction and fires the church underwent thorough renovation in the 17th and 18th centuries. In 1760 the interior was given Rococo painted decoration by Andrzej Radwański. The convent has some good Gothic woodcarvings, including a figure of Christ (c.1510).

The village of **Niepołomice** is situated at the extreme western end of the Puszcza Niepołomicka, a region where one can still get an impression of what Małopolska's old primeval forests were like. For centuries this was a royal hunting ground, and in 1550–71 a Renaissance hunting lodge with a large arcaded courtyard was built here for the last Jagiellonian king, Zygmunt II August. The *Kościół Najświętszej Marii Panny i 1000 Męczenników (Church of St Mary and the 1000 Martyrs)* belongs to the group of double-edged churches founded by King Kazimierz III Wielki between 1350 and 1358. The last of the Piast kings had not had an easy relationship with the Church. He was known for his hot temper, and his turbulent private life often gave the clergy cause for criticism. Kazimierz had one such critic, Marcin Baryczka, drowned after a fierce argument, and he was promptly excommunicated by Pope Clement VI. The rift was healed in 1350, and the King agreed to build these churches in expiation for his sins.

Other examples in this group of 'expiatory churches' are at Wiślica (see page 504) and Stopnica (see page 505). They all share a grandeur of spatial conception, with vaults springing from two or three piers, which unusually are arranged along the middle axis. This practically does away with the classic articulation of a medieval church interior with clearly defined nave and aisles. Unfortunately at Niepołomice this treatment of the interior space has been obscured by later alterations, but it does retain fragments of exquisite wall paintings of female martyrs (c.1360–70) in a Tuscan-Emilian style and painted by an Italian workshop. Later additions include two remarkable chapels: the Mannerist *Kaplica Branickich (Branicki Chapel)* with the richly decorated tomb of Katarzyna and Grzegorz Branicki, made in 1595–9 by the Kraków-based workshop of Santi Gucci, and the *Kaplica św. Karola Boromeusza (Chapel of St Charles Borromeo)*, founded in 1640 by the Lubomirskis, which has Early Baroque decoration. The plasterwork and illusionistic paintings in the dome are by Giovanni Battista Falconi.

At **Igołomia**, north of Niepołomice, stands the early 19th-century *Pałac Wodzickich (Wodzicki Palace)* in the middle of an extensive landscaped park. It is one of the best examples in Poland of a Neoclassical palace and was probably designed by Chrystian Piotr Aigner; the excellent plasterwork of the round salon, which rises through two storeys, is attributed to Friedrich Baumann.

The parish church of **Kościelec**, the *Kościół św. Wojciecha (Church of St Adalbert)* was founded by Bishop Wiesław of Kraków between 1230 and 1240. It was devastated by the Arian Protestants in the mid-16th century. For a long time the church was left abandoned, and it was not rebuilt until 1628–34. Some features survive from the Romanesque period: the triforia with paired columns and foliate capitals, and a doorway in the west front set with slender colonnettes decorated with vine motifs.

Lanckorona – Kalwaria Zebrzydowska

The little town of **Lanckorona** has a picturesque location on the southern slope of the Góra Lanckorońska to the southwest of Kraków. It forms a unified architectural ensemble arranged around two focal points: the spire of the church and the ruins of the castle on the edge of the forest. Lanckorona's importance lies in the fact that it has preserved unchanged the original spatial planning of a typical small Polish town, and has kept most of its 19th-century timber houses. The town was the scene of high drama in 1756 when orthodox Jews discovered scenes of carnality, concupiscence and illegal union amongst novices at a Frankist prayer meeting.

A few kilometres further on, just over the border to the voivodship of Bielsko-Biała, is the famous pilgrimage centre of **Kalwaria Zebrzydowska**. This was the first such Calvary (or Way of the Cross) to be created in Poland and was the model for a series of similar complexes elsewhere (for example, Kalwaria Wejherowska in Pomerania, see page 340). They have an important place in the history of Counter-Reformation religious architecture and the urban spatial planning associated with it, and pilgrimages to such places still play an important part in popular Polish Catholicism. The ensembles recreated the Stations of the Cross as a loose grouping of chapels and courts based on the topography of old Jerusalem. The architectural complex at Kalwaria Zebrzydowska includes the Church dedicated to the Virgin Mary, a Bernardine monastery, and Mount Calvary itself, with no fewer than 42 chapels scattered over the surrounding hills. The construction of this ensemble was made possible by generous donations from the wojewoda of Kraków, Mikołaj Zebrzydowski (1600–20), and later from Jan Zebrzydowski (1620–41). The earliest part of the monastery was built in 1603–9 under the direction of the Italian Jesuit architect Gian Maria

N →

Kalwaria Zebrzydowska, plan of the Church of the Mother of God of the Angels and the Bernardine Monastery

Bernardoni and Paulus Baudarth from Flanders, and there were many alterations and additions in the 17th and 19th centuries. The addition of a four-bay nave with two towers flanking the façade was completed in 1702. Inside the church, the Mannerist retrochoir stalls with 26 scenes from the Life of the Virgin, the richly carved pulpit (mid-17th century), and the open-work Baroque high altar all merit close attention, though the modern ceiling paintings may disappoint. The church has recently been elevated to the dignity of a basilica by Pope John Paul II, a regular pilgrim all his life to the monastery and to the famous Stations of the Cross.

A Via Dolorosa was created here in 1604, inspired by the description of Jerusalem by Christian Adrian Cruys (1584). In 1632 the complex was extended in an impressive manner with the addition of the 'Marian Stations'. Buildings such as the 'House of Mary (1612–14), the 'House of Caiaphas' (1609) and the 'Palace of Herod' (1609), together with other chapels and courts have imaginative ground-plans (elliptical, hexagonal with semi-circular apses) and furnishings. In the *Kościół Grobu Matki Boskiej (Church of the Tomb of the Mother of God)*, built in 1611–30 on a rectangular ground-plan, is a version of the Virgin's tomb made by Paulus Baudarth in the form of a monumental domed sarcophagus. The oldest building in the complex is the *Kościół Ukrzyżowania (Church of the Crucifixion)* of 1600-01, which contains four paintings by Franciszek Lekszycki of scenes from Christ's Passion. During Passion Week and on the festival of the Assumption the Calvary is the setting for re-enactments of the Bible story, attended by vast crowds.

Miechów – Książ Wielki – Skałbmierz – Wiślica – Stopnica – Bejsce – Książnice Wielkie

The southern tip of the present voivodship of Święty Krzyż and the northern part of the Małopolska voivodship belong historically to the Ziemia Krakowska.

Heading northwards from Kraków, past the towns of Wieclawice and Niedźwiedź, after 39 km we come to the town of **Miechów**. Already in the middle ages the monastic complex of the *Kościół św. Grobu i św. Jakuba Młodszego (Church of the Holy Sepulchre and St James the Less)* and the former *Klasztor Bożogrobców (Monastery of Canons Regular of the Holy Sepulchre)* made the town an important pilgrimage centre. The monastery was founded after 1169. Some masonry from that period and from the period after 1233 survives in the walls of the present church, built in 1394–1410. In 1749–71 the interior was baroquized and later decorated with rich sculptural Rococo decoration by Wojciech Rojowski: statues of Apostles and Saints on the piers; altars, pulpit, stalls and organ. The *Kaplica Grobu Chrystusa (Chapel of the Tomb of Christ)* (c. 1553) is Poland's earliest extant 'copy' of the Holy Sepulchre in Jerusalem. Also worth a visit is the Treasury, which contains a magnificent Late Gothic chalice (c. 1500) and a large collection of chasubles.

A few kilometres to the north in **Książ Wielki** the majestic *Pałac Mirów (Mirów Palace)* has withstood the vicissitudes of history almost unaltered. It was built in 1585–95 by Santi

Gucci for Piotr Myszkowski, Bishop of Kraków, and is a good example of a Mannerist residence designed on a strictly symmetrical, axial plan. The rectangular site is skirted by retaining walls with a decorative bastion. On the eastern part of this platform stands the palace itself, a compact building fitted crossways into the site, with a narrow forecourt and two pavilions containing the chapel and library. Behind the palace is a geometrical garden.

Beyond Miechów the route continues southeast for 31 km to **Skalbmierz**, where the chief interest is the *Kościół św. Jana Chrzciciela (Church of St John the Baptist)*, formerly a collegiate church (now the parish church). Most of the present church is a Late Gothic building erected in the first half of the 15th century to replace a Romanesque basilica. The nave opens into a long choir, which is flanked on the north and south by square Romanesque towers of ashlar, which were retained from the previous building. The most striking feature of the rich Baroque decoration of the interior is the monumental frame built round the chancel arch and containing a Crucifixion group of the last quarter of the 17th century. The church also has a painting of the Adoration of the Magi probably by Jacob Jordaens or his workshop.

We now take the southeast road out of Skalbmierz for 10 km before turning off to the northeast towards Kazimierza Wielka. After about 20 km we reach the Collegiate Church of **Wiślica**. The *Kościół Narodzenia Najświętszej Marii Panny (Church of the Nativity of the Virgin Mary)* (plate 54) is the grandest of King Kazimierz III Wielki's expiatory churches, all built shortly after 1350 (see page 501). The very individual effect of their

Wiślica, fragment of the Romanesque plaster floor in the Church of the Nativity of the Virgin Mary

interiors is best preserved at Wiślica. Most characteristic are the piers along the middle axis (in this case three), which support the vaults and divide the space into two naves, to which the three-bayed chancel is attached. The two-nave plan was used in the middle ages for monastic refectories and other large rooms, but it is unusual to find it used for churches. It was, however, adopted for some medieval synagogues such as the 14th-century Old-New Synagogue in Prague and the Old Synagogue in Kraków (see page 486). The vaulting bosses at Wiślica are carved with the coats of arms of the provinces of Poland, the symbols of the Evangelists and the head of Christ. The walls of the chancel are covered with Byzantine-Ruthenian paintings (1397–1400) similar to those found in the Holy Cross Chapel in Wawel Cathedral and the Castle Chapel at Lublin. Above the south doorway is a Late Gothic relief of 1464 showing King Kazimierz III Wielki kneeling as he presents his church to the Virgin and Child. In the crypt are remains of the two earlier Romanesque churches (mid-12th century and second quarter of the 13th century), including a unique survival: a Romanesque plaster floor (4 by 2.5 metres) incised with foliage scroll borders and two groups of figures (perhaps the founder and his family) in attitudes of prayer. Among the many precious furnishings are a stone Madonna (c.1300), and three other Late Gothic statues of saints, as well as a Late Gothic crucifix of the first half of the 16th century.

The other interesting building in the town is the *Wikariat w Wiślicy (vicarage of Wiślica)*, a Late Gothic house built in 1460 for Jan Długosz, a canon of Kraków and Poland's first great historian, who was vicar here.

To visit the third of the expiatory churches, we must make a detour via the spa town of Busko-Zdrój to **Stopnica** 17 km away. The *Kościół śś. Piotra i Pawła (Church of Sts Peter and Paul)* was the third of King Kazimierz's foundations and was built in stone between 1362 and 1370. Most of the present church is in fact an accurate replica built in 1954–60 after 80 per cent of the building had been destroyed in the war. The stone antependium carved with coats of arms is original, however, as are the heraldic bosses in the vault.

At **Bejsce** the Gothic *Kościół św. Mikołaja (Church of St Nicholas)* was built in brick around 1400. The church's main claim to fame is the Renaissance funerary chapel of the Firlej family. Mikołaj Firlej, the wojewoda of Kraków, had the chapel built in 1593–1600 by masters from the celebrated Pińczów Workshop nearby (see page 525). It was constructed on a square plan and lavishly decorated with marble and sandstone: 'Nowhere does the zoomorphic trend of the vernacular reach such buoyant density and fantastic dynamism …' (J. Białostocki). The whole of the west wall is taken up with the monumental tomb of Mikołaj Firlej and his first wife Elżbieta. The couple were originally to have been shown lying down, but at a late stage more up-to-date kneeling figures were chosen, following the model of the Branicki Chapel at Niepołomice (see page 501).

To the southwest of Bejsce lies the village of **Książnice Wielkie**, whose parish church, the *Kościół Wniebowzięcia Najświętszej Marii Panny (Church of the Assumption)* has been altered several times and owes its present appearance to restoration in the 19th century. It is famous for its winged altarpiece, almost as big as Veit Stoss's masterpiece in the

Mariacki in Kraków, of which it is a weak imitation, carved by one of his assistants, Master Michał of Kraków, in 1491, only two years after the original. The centre panel contains the scene of the Death of the Virgin, with her Assumption into Heaven above, and her Coronation as Queen of Heaven in the baldacchino-like super-structure.

Western Carpathians: Kobiernice – Żywiec – Sucha Beskidzka – Zakopane – Chocołów – Dębno Podhalańskie – Stary Sącz

The southern part of the Ziemia Krakowska is made up of the Carpathian Mountains (Polish: Karpaty): to the west the Beskid Żywiecki range with the town of Żywiec as its centre, to the east the Beskid Sadecki centred on Nowy Sącz, to the south the Tatry (High Tatras) with the winter sports resort of Zakopane, and lastly the Pieniny Mountains. The latter are famous for the picturesque Dunajec Valley with rocky precipices rising 300 metres. A popular form of excursion is a trip on a raft steered through the rapids by the mountain folk,

Bejsce, section through the Firlej Chapel in the Church of St Nicholas

the *górale*, wearing their traditional costume (just visible in plate 50). The inhabitants of all this region have held doggedly to their old language and music, their folk costumes, traditional timber architecture, as well as their traditions of glass painting and woodcarving.

The górale national costume is very picturesque: the women wear kerchiefs and skirts with floral patterns, white blouses and red coral necklaces; the men wear white felt trousers decorated with embroidery, an elaborately embroidered fur doublet, with woven leather shoes, round felt hats and a garment called the *cucha*, a cloth jacket thrown over the shoulders. A famous górale folk festival is held at Zakopane every September.

The High Tatras (colour plate 10) are a high mountain range with deep lakes, of which the most famous, Morskie Oko, has long been a favourite subject for many painters and writers. Valleys such as Dolina Chochołowska and Dolina Kościeliska have many caves, some of which can be visited.

The folk costumes of the inhabitants of the Beskids are particularly colourful; the women of Żywiec wear clothes decorated with lace and embroidery. In the *Skansen (Open-air Museum)* at Żywiec examples of houses of traditional rural construction can be visited. There is an interesting farm museum at Orawka.

All over this mountainous region there are historic buildings: palaces, villas and peasants' houses, little wooden churches – Roman Catholic and Greek Catholic (Uniate). Roadside chapels and figures of saints are a common sight.

The Pieniny, Tatra and Babia Góra National Parks have great natural beauty. All three have fine alpine scenery, and fauna such as chamois, marmot, lynx, bear and golden eagle. The Pieniny Gorge is unique, however, for its flora. Never scoured by glaciers, and with a complex geology and singular microclimate, it still shelters plants from the ice age – including pines, junipers and orchids otherwise completely unknown in this region, and vestiges of tropical jungle plants. Over 160 species of birds and 1,800 species of butterflies live here, including the Apollo. Pieniny was the first ever international park (1932). According to legend, the richness of the flora is due to the saintly Princess Kinga who walked over the mountains scattering seed. Mt. Zamkowa is still called the 'Gardens of Kinga'.

Taking the road via Kalwaria Zebrzydowska and the small village of Wadowice, which has recently attained fame as the birthplace of Pope John Paul II, we come to **Kobiernice** with a typical Neoclassical nobleman's *country house*, built in the first half of the 19th century. Twenty-eight kilometres further south we reach a reservoir by which stands the town of Żywiec, famous for its excellent beer. The Komorowski family had a *Palace* built here in 1569–71, with an elegant Renaissance courtyard surrounded by columned arcades on the ground floor and first floor. The south range was built in 1708–23 for later owners, the Wielopolski family. The complex was thoroughly restored for the Habsburgs in the last third of the 19th century, when the palace was given its neo-Gothic exterior.

There is another Late Renaissance *Palace* of the Komorowski family, also thoroughly rebuilt, in the town of **Sucha Beskidzka**, to the east of Żywiec.

Further south the road via Rabka and Nowy Targ first passes through a narrow gorge before arriving at Poland's leading winter sports centre, **Zakopane** (plate 51). Thanks to its ideal position on the north slopes of the High Tatras, with the natural protection afforded by the surrounding mountain peaks, Zakopane has developed into one of the most popular Polish resorts. In the second half of the last century it was still a small, inaccessible górale village. Zakopane's rapid expansion began around the turn of the century, when the village became popular in artistic circles. Since then generations of Polish writers, scientists and artists have been inspired by the folklore of the górale and the beauty of the High Tatras. In the 1880's the painter and theoretician Stanisław Witkiewicz created his 'Zakopane Style' of architecture here; it is still in use today. His son, Stanisław Ignacy Witkiewicz, a leading figure in avant-garde art and literature between the wars, also lived at Zakopane. The composer Karol Szymanowski found a refuge for creative work at the Villa Atma (now a museum) and used motifs from the music of the górale, particularly in his ballet score 'Harnasie' (1926). Other important figures in the arts also lived and worked here: the

Zakopane: at the foot of the High Tatras, photograph taken in 1930

composers Mieczysław Karłowicz and Artur Malawski, the 'Young Poland' writers Jan Kasprowicz and Kazimierz Przerwa-Tetmajer, and after the war the sculptors Antoni Kenar and Władysław Hasior.

In spite of the rapid rate of the resort's modernization and expansion, the centre of the town has largely retained its original character. Among the villas, perhaps the most interesting is the *Willa Pod Jedłami (The Firs)* (plate 52) a typical example of Witkiewicz's 'Zakopane Style', which took the vernacular wooden architecture of Podhale and the High Tatras as its model. The villa, built in 1897, is a timber construction on a tall masonry base, with magnificent terraces and balconies and dormer windows in the high, shingle covered hipped roof. Woodcarvings with stylized górale motifs show Jugendstil influence. The 'Zakopane Style' can be found applied to ecclesiastical architecture in the picturesque wooden chapel designed by Witkiewicz for the village of Jaszczurówka, a few kilometres to the east of Zakopane and easily reached by beautiful woodland paths (colour plate 12).

Before making an excursion into the High Tatras it is worth climbing Gubałówka Hill to admire the view of the mountains, and to visit the *Muzeum Tatr (Tatra Museum)*, which has a large local ethnographic collection, models of górale houses and mountain huts, interiors with old equipment, costumes and glass paintings, as well as natural history collections from the High Tatras and Podhale. The Botanical Garden attached to the museum contains examples of the exceptional flora of the region.

Dębno, 13th-century wood panel, drawing by I. Bentchev, 1987

The best example of the village timber architecture of the Podhale region is at **Chochołów**, 19 km northwest of Zakopane. The peasants' houses and farm buildings are those of a traditional working village; the three oldest date from 1818, 1825 and 1826. Following the Biały Dunajec river northeast for about 30 km, via Nowy Targ and Łopuszna, we come to **Dębno Podhalańskie**. The Gothic *Kościół św. Michała Archanioła (Church of St Michael the Archangel)*, dating from the second half of the 15th century, is one of the finest surviving examples of timber church architecture of the 15th-16th centuries (plate 53). Prestige buildings were usually stone–built in this period, but there were also many churches and chapels for which wood was used, often with great skill. Of the large number of timber churches in Ziemia Krakowska, none from before 1450 has survived, though of the 529 churches mentioned by the historian Jan Długosz, writing in 1470 in his 'Liber beneficiorum', 419 were built of wood. The oldest surviving wooden churches all date from the second half of the 15th century: besides Dębno Podhalańskie, there are other early examples at Lipnica Murowana (see page 512) and Haczów (see page 561).

Dębno church has the aisleless nave with a rectangular chancel characteristic of the timber churches of rural Małopolska. The tall steep roof and galleries surrounding the exterior of the chancel, and the bell tower, which was added later, are all shingled. The church is famous for its superb decorative carpentry and its interior painted decoration, which has survived complete. The ceiling, walls, chancel arch, west gallery balustrade, pulpit and founder's pew are covered with a carpet-like profusion of patterns with more than seventy motifs. Other Late Gothic timber churches of this type can be seen not far away at Przydonica, Sękowa and Libusza (see pages 510–11).

Heading northeast from Dębno Podhalańskie, via Krościenko and Zabrzeż, we reach the picturesque old town of **Stary Sącz**. Here, on the crest of a hill sloping down to the Dunajec, stands the *Kościół św. Trojcy (Church of the Holy Trinity)* with its nunnery of Poor Clares. The convent was founded in 1280 by the Blessed Kinga (Cunegunda), the daughter of King Béla IV of Hungary, after the death of her husband Duke Bolesław V Wstydliwy (literally 'the Bashful' – so called because his marriage with the pious Kinga was never consummated). It was here that Kinga spent the last twelve years of her life. The Gothic church, completed in 1332, was altered in the 15th and especially in the 17th centuries. The rich Baroque and Rococo decoration includes three plasterwork altarpieces in the choir (1696–9, by the workshop of Baldassare Fontana) and the spectacular pulpit (probably 1671) with a carved Tree of Jesse growing from beneath the preacher's box to the top of the elaborate, spiky canopy. The conventual buildings were erected in 1601–4 under the direction of Giovanni de Simoni. The greatest of the convent's many treasures are a Late Gothic painting (c.1470–80) of Christ as the Man of Sorrows with the Virgin, and a reliquary dating from the second half of the 13th century, which tradition connects with St Kinga herself. Also dating from the time of the convent's foundation are two late 13th-century illuminated graduals. The whole precinct is enclosed by a wall, which was given loopholes and sgraffito work in the early 17th century; the façade of the chaplain's house, built in 1605, has similar decoration.

Central Carpathians: Nowy Sącz – Rożnów – Przydonica – Ropa – Sękowa – Zagórzany – Libusza – Biecz – Powroinik

The town of **Nowy Sącz**, beautifully situated on the River Dunajec south of the large reservoir of Jezioro Rożnowskie, is the economic and cultural centre of the southern part of the Ziemia Krakowska. Remnants of the old town walls have survived, as have parts of the former *Klasztor Franciskanów (Franciscan Monastery)* (late 13th century) with its church (Gothic and Baroque). The *Muzeum Miejskie (Town Museum)* has an interesting collection of Orthodox icons, which like other such collections in the region come from deserted Uniate and Orthodox churches. But the museum's most important paintings are 300 or so works by the famous naïve painter Nikifor of Krynica (1895–1968), who was also from the Orthodox tradition.

Visitors wishing to explore the nearby Pieniny Mountains, a compact limestone massif (plate 50), should choose Nowy Sącz as their base. The village of Sromowce Niżne, a starting point for raft trips on the Dunajec (see page 506), is within easy reach. These rafts are nearly all that is left of what was once the basic means of transport in Poland, essential to the economy and celebrated in poetry.

North of Nowy Sącz, in the village of **Rożnów**, which also lies on the Dunajec, is an early 19th-century *manor house*, typical of the Małopolska region with its grandiose single-storey façade and colonnaded porch at the back. The house has been restored since the war, and contains Neoclassical wall paintings, doors and fireplaces. Nearby are the remains of a fortress built before 1568 for the Hetman Jan Tarnowski, the earliest example in Poland of modern fortification of the Italian type.

Before skirting the reservoir southwards from Roznów to return to Nowy Sącz, it is worth making a detour to **Przydonica**, to visit the Late Gothic *Kościół Matki Boskiej*

Różańcowej (Church of Our Lady of the Rosary) (1527). It belongs to the same architectural type as the church at Dębno Podhalańskie (see page 509), and it too has a richly decorated interior. The chancel has Late Renaissance wall paintings of 1596 showing scenes from the life of St Stanislas, the Passion of Christ, and saints.

Ropa, about 30 km east of Nowy Sącz, has a magnificent manor house, a Baroque and Neoclassical house with outbuildings, which was created in 1803 for the Siemeński family by enlarging a small 16th century building. Not far away, at **Szymbark** another manor house, also restored after the war, can be visited. Picturesquely situated on the bank high above the River Ropa, it is an impressive example of a 16th-century fortified house; the façades, doorways and windows are decorated with beautifully carved stonework and the walls are surmounted by an elaborate parapet.

On the way to Zagórzany we turn off to the south at Gorlice to visit the third of the Late Gothic timber churches mentioned above – the *Kościół śś. Filipa i Jakuba Apostoła (Church of Sts Philip and James)* at **Sękowa,** built in 1520. The effect of the building is created by its shingled roofs: the main roof is unusually tall and steep and surrounded by a lower roof over an open exterior ambulatory. The rectangular tower on the principal facade was added later, probably in the 17th century.

Surrounded by a beautiful landscape park, the romantic *Palace* at **Zagórzany** was built in 1834–9 by Francesco Maria Lanci, in a style inspired by neo-Gothic English castles. It was restored in the 1950's and 1960's and is now used as a youth centre.

A few kilometres east of Zagórzany we come to **Libusza,** where the fourth of these timber churches stands. The interior of the *Kościół Narodzenia Najświętszej Marii Panny (Church of the Nativity of the Virgin),* built in 1513, has well-preserved and very beautiful Late Gothic murals (1523), considered to be the finest in Małopolska. They show scenes from the Life of the Virgin, the Passion of Christ and figures of saints, framed by luxuriant garlands of flowers and foliage.

Biecz is one of Małopolska's grandest little medieval towns. It is known as 'Little Kraków' and indeed its history has been closely linked to that of the old capital. In the middle ages it was a major centre of the wine trade with Hungary. It is first mentioned, with its castellan, in the 13th century, and in 1303 was granted its town charter, which was confirmed by Kazimierz III Wielki in 1363. Biecz was once a fortified town, surrounded by a massive wall with 16 towers and a castle, but only remnants of the walls and town gates survive. However, the most important buildings of the old town are still extant: the *Town Hall* (15th-16th centuries) a massive tower dominating the market place, and the *Kościół Bożego Ciała (Corpus Christi Church).* The latter, built of brick with stone dressings and completed in 1521, is one of the finest Late Gothic churches in Małopolska. Its superb interior is dominated by the glorious high altar (before 1604) with a painting of the Deposition (North Italian, mid-16th century). The furnishings include ten Baroque side altars, richly decorated choir stalls, a remarkable music-stand of 1633 with relief carvings of saints and musicians, painted epitaphs (c.1600) and the Renaissance tomb of Mikołaj Ligęza (1575). The town once boasted a school for executioners.

At **Powroźnik** close to the Slovak border is one of the finest churches built by the Uniate Christians of the Carpathian region: the *Kościół św. Jakuba Młodszego (Church of St James the Less)*, which is now used by the Western Rite Catholics, was built in 1611–43. The interior is divided into three spaces: the vestibule with the tower, a square nave and a long chancel. This arrangement shows the influence of the treatment of space in Late Gothic rural timber architecture, but it has been adapted to suit the liturgical requirements of the Eastern Rite. The iconostasis (1738–43), some surviving icons and fragments of 17th-century wall painting give an idea of the former character of this interior. The chief external features of the building are three onion domes of diminishing size on tower, nave, and chancel.

Lipnica Murowana – Wiśnicz Nowy – Bochnia – Dębno – Tarnów

The northwest road from Nowy Sącz, via Muchówka, leads to **Lipnica Murowana**, which is already in the voivodship of Tarnów. The town has retained its medieval street plan with a square market place. The ground plan of the old timber cemetery church, the *Kościół św. Leonarda (Church of St Leonard)* (second half of the 15th century), is the same as that of the church at Haczów (see page 561), and the church is encircled by an external open gallery. The exterior walls are mostly covered with wooden shingles, as are the roofs of most timber churches in Poland today, although traditionally thatch was also used. The ceiling is decorated with stencilled plant motifs, dating from around 1500 and later. The walls are covered with Baroque paintings of the life of Christ and saints.

Wiśnicz Nowy, view of the Castle and Monastery, painting by J. Łosik, 1905

On a hill on the eastern side of the town of **Wiśnicz Nowy**, to the northwest of Lipnica Nowa, stands the town's imposing *Castle*, originally built of stone towards the end of the 15th century for the Kmita family. Between 1615 and 1630 it was transformed into an Early Baroque residence for the Lubomirski family, probably by the architect Maciej Trapola, and surrounded by a pentagonal fortification with bastions. The entrance gate on the east side also dates from this period, as do many of the handsome doorways throughout the castle. The vault of the two-storey gallery and the tower room on the third floor have the remains of plasterwork by Giovanni Battista Falconi. In the chapel some elements of an illusionistic painting have survived. Trapola was probably also the architect of the *parish church*, and of the Monastery of the Discalced Carmelites, prominent in the illustration opposite, but razed by the Nazis (1942–4).

Bochnia, halfway between Kraków and Tarnów, was granted a town charter as early as 1253 because of the boom in salt mining. Legend links the discovery of salt at Bochnia and Wieliczka with a miracle. When Duke Bolesław V of Kraków asked for the hand of the Hungarian princess Kinga, she begged her father, King Béla IV, to give something as a dowry which would be equally useful to all subjects in her future domain. The king took her to a salt mine in Maramureş and advised her to take salt with her to Poland, since it was a treasure which everyone could use. The princess threw her ring into the deep shaft and made a wish that the salt would travel with her to Poland. . . Not long after her marriage she was travelling through her new possessions and rested at Bochnia. There she remembered her ring and commanded her people to start digging at a particular spot. Soon they found a large salt crystal which was then broken to reveal the very same gold ring that Kinga had thrown down the mine in Hungary. The parish church of the charming little town is the Late Gothic *Kościół św. Mikołaja (Church of St Nicholas)*, which has a Baroque interior (after a fire in 1655) and a bell tower (1609) of larchwood. The *Muzeum Regionalne (Regional Museum)* is housed in the former Dominican monastery on the market place. There is a *Jewish cemetery* on Krzeczków hill.

The *Castle* at **Dębno** is the best example in Małopolska of a Late Gothic residence built on a regular plan (plate 55). Originally built around 1470 for Chancellor Jakub Dębiński, probably by the workshop of the architect Marcin Proszko of Kraków, the castle was remodelled in 1596 and in the 17th and 18th centuries. Particularly interesting are the 15th-century oriel windows (which open to the inside through extraordinary arches with cusps and stepped mouldings), the main gate, and the sgraffito decoration around the windows.

The historic town of **Tarnów** is one of the few in Poland where the whole of the old centre has been made a protected conservation area. The town has kept its medieval street plan and many medieval buildings. The first mention of Tarnów in documentary sources is in 1105, and it received its town charter in 1330. Its rapid development, like that of Biecz (see page 511), was due above all to its location on the trade route to Hungary. In the 16th century members of the ruling Tarnowski family were great patrons of the arts in the town. Tarnów became a leading cultural centre with important Renaissance buildings and for a time a section of Kraków University was even located here. During the First

Tarnów, view of the medieval town, engraving by Z. Vogel, 1800

World War Tarnów and its environs were the scene of bitter fighting between the Russian and Austrian forces and there are large military cemeteries here.

Around the rectangular market place are a few 16th-century *burghers' houses* (Nos. 19–21) with fine doorways, arcades and attractive façades. Parts of the interior painted decoration have also survived.

Like these burghers' houses, the *Town Hall* is now a museum, with an excellent collection of paintings and drawings, applied arts, and ethnological items. It is a Late Gothic brick building (15th century), which was given its present Renaissance form when it was remodelled in the late 16th century. The broad frieze with blind arches surmounted by a 'Polish attic' with volutes and masks is closely related to the style of the Sukiennice in Kraków (see page 456).

The *Kościół Narodzenia Najświętszej Marii Panny (Church of the Nativity of the Virgin),* since 1785 the Cathedral, was built as a collegiate church around 1400 and considerably altered in the 19th century. The most beautiful remaining feature of its Late Gothic decoration is the south doorway of 1505 with sculptures on the theme of Christ's Passion, the design of which is based on a Dürer woodcut made in the same year. Two sections of the original canons' stalls have also survived, but the most important and impressive feature of the interior is a magnificent group of 16th-century tombs. That of Barbara von Rocnow (1517) with its excited drapery, fluttering scroll and proto-Renaissance niche, is a striking contrast with the sobriety of Barbara Tarnowska's tomb, started only ten years later. Here the figure of the young wife of the Hetman Jan

Tarnowski, who died in 1527 at the age of thirty, is probably by Bartolommeo Berrecci (1527–30) and is certainly one of the most beautiful female figures in Renaissance sculpture in Europe. Its frame was made later (it was finished after 1536) by Giovanni Maria Padovano, who was also responsible for the large double tomb of the Hetman himself and his son Jan Krzysztof erected in 1561–70. Three more Jan Tarnowskis, two recumbent figures side by side on the wall and an infant above, are represented on another wall tomb, probably by Bartolommeo Berrecci (c.1530–35). Another remarkable tomb is that of the Ostrogskis, probably made by Willem van den Blocke and Johann Pfister in 1612–20, with statues showing the two deceased kneeling at the foot of the cross. The treasury contains an outstanding collection of Late Gothic goldsmiths' work from Tyniec Abbey, including two splendid 15th-century chalices made in Kraków and a richly decorated cross reliquary. From the church tower (72 metres high) there is a good panoramic view of the whole town.

The Jewish cemetery (between ul. Słoneczna, ul. Szpitalna and ul. Starodąbrowska) is very old (1583) and has some finely carved stones. There are the remains of a synagogue on ul. Żydowska.

Ivan Bentchev

Częstochowa, Kielce, Radom

Częstochowa – Olsztyn Castle – Szczekociny – Koniecpol

Częstochowa is famous above all for a miraculous image of the Virgin Mary, which is one of Poland's most potent symbols. The town itself (population 245,000), an important industrial centre, forms a strong contrast to the surrounding country. Enormous steel works and textile mills loom over the town and cast a shadow over the living conditions of its inhabitants, but only a few kilometres away is some of the most delightful countryside in Poland. This is the limestone Wyżyna Krakowska-Częstochowska (or Kraków-Częstochowa Jura), a popular area for excursions. Nowhere else in Poland are there so many caves with such bizarre and fantastic rock and dripstone formations.

Located at the intersection of major trade routes, Częstochowa was granted its town charter, with the laws of Magdeburg, around 1375. There is documentary evidence that the extraction of ore was begun at the same time and iron smelting works were also erected near the town. At the behest of King Ludwik Węgierski, Duke Władysław of Opole founded a monastery in 1382 for the monks of the Paulite Order (which had been founded in the King's capital, Buda, in 1215). The *Klasztor Paulinów (Paulite Monastery)* was built on a limestone outcrop called *Jasna Góra ('Bright Hill')* about three kilometres from the town centre.

For 600 years the history of the town has been inextricably linked with the destiny of the monastery on Jasna Góra. From the writings of the Kraków historian Jan Długosz we know that already by the 14th century there were hundreds of pilgrims from Poland, Prussia, Hungary and Silesia to the 'Czarna Madonna' ('Black Madonna'). The Paulite monastery is a unique example in the troubled history of Poland of a treasure house which has survived unscathed, with its excellent collections documenting the most important events in the political and cultural history of Poland.

Two crucial events in the 17th and 18th centuries were to make the fortified monastery a symbol of Polish freedom. The first was in 1655, when, under the leadership of Prior Augustyn Kordecki, monks, soldiers and a group of nobles withstood a siege by vastly superior Swedish forces led by King Charles X Gustavus. This successful defence of Jasna

Góra marked the beginning of the liberation of Poland from Swedish occupation. The second event came more than a century later, in the late autumn of 1770, when an army of the anti-Russian Confederation of Bar commanded by Kazimierz Puławski defended itself here against the forces of the Empress Catherine II.

The extensive complex comprising the *Kościół Wniebowzięcia i Znalezenia św. Krzyża (Church of the Assumption and of the Finding of the Holy Cross)* (1) and the monastic buildings is surrounded by a rectangular fortress with towers. It is approached via a series of gates: the *Brama Lubomirskich (Lubomirski Gate)* (13), a triumphal arch by Johann Baptist Limberger (1723), the *Brama Stanisław August (Stanisław August Gate)* (14), 1767 and rebuilt 1957, and lastly the *Brama Jagiellońska (Jagiellonian Gate)* (15) built in the first half of the 17th century. The tall, slender tower of the church dominates the silhouette of the town and is visible from a great distance. The church (plate 59) is basically a Late Gothic building, erected before 1463, but it was remodelled as a basilica after a fire in 1690. Between 1690 and 1730 Silesian artists created the rich Baroque interior: all the vaults have lavish plasterwork and panels with paintings executed in 1690–93 by Karl Dankwart. The Late Gothic cross-rib vaulting which survived in the aisles was given the same baroquizing treatment. The plaster decoration on the entablature frieze was made by Johann Franz

The Swedish siege of the Paulite Monastery on Jasna Góra in 1655, engraving of 1659

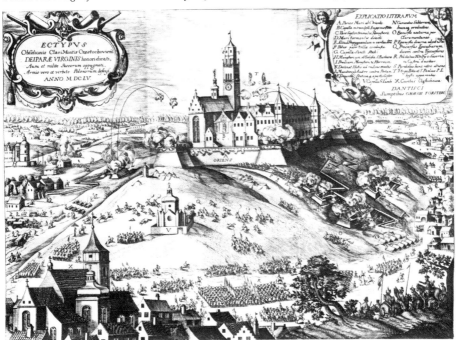

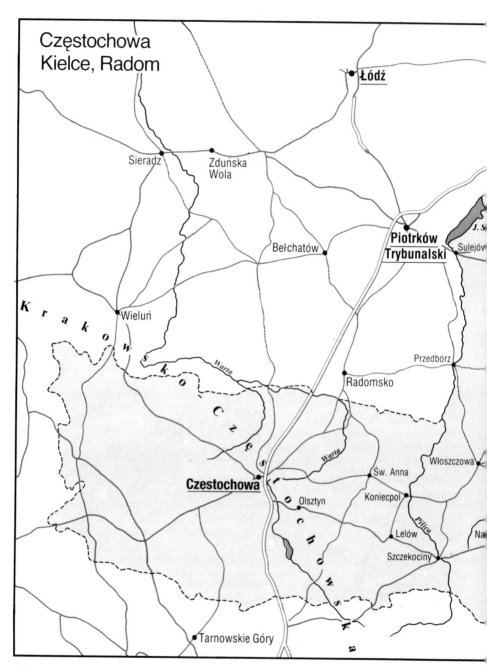

Częstochowa
Kielce, Radom

Łódź

Sieradz

Zduńska
Wola

Bełchatów

Piotrków
Trybunalski

J. S

Sulejóv

K r a k o w s k o

Wieluń

Warta

Przedbórz

Radomsko

C z ę

Warta

Św. Anna

Włoszczowa

Częstochowa

s t o c h o w s k a

Olsztyn

Koniecpol

Pilica

Lelów

Na

Szczekociny

Tarnowskie Góry

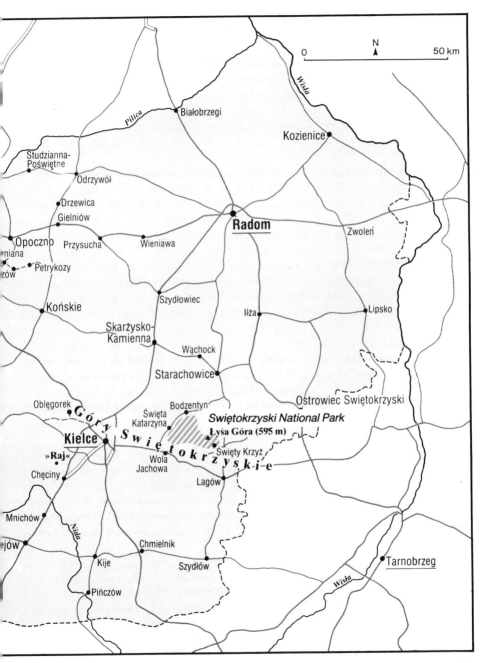

Krembs (1728). The walls were given a coloured marble effect in 1760–62; the bases of the piers are of black marble. The altars are also mostly made of marble with gilding and white plaster statues.

On the south side of the church three domed, centrally planned extensions were added: the *porch* (1620–30) (2) with a Late Renaissance doorway; the *Kaplica św. Pawła (Chapel of St Paul)* (3), Early Baroque, completed in 1671, with mural paintings showing scenes from the life of the Apostle; and at the fourth bay, the *Kaplica śś. Relikwii (Chapel of the Holy Relics)* (1641–8) (4) in the lower part, with the *Kaplica Jabłonowskich (Jabłonowski Chapel)* containing the black marble tomb of the Wojewoda Stanisław Jabłonowski (1751–4) above.

Within the high altar in the *Kaplica Narodzenia Najświętszej Marii Panny (Chapel of the Nativity of Virgin)* (7), a separate building on the north side of the monastery church, is the object which has made Jasna Góra famous: the miraculous image of the Virgin and Child known as the 'Czarna Madonna'. This icon, which shows a Virgin of the type known in Byzantine art as the 'Hodegetria', was probably brought to Częstochowa from Red Ruthenia (now part of Ukraine) by Władysław of Opole in 1384. During a Hussite attack in Holy Week of 1430 the miraculous image was torn from the altar before the eyes of the monks and then taken out to the forecourt of the church, where it was attacked with swords and finally pierced with a dagger. In the following years King Władysław II Jagiełło commissioned three different workshops one after another to repair the painting, which was broken into three pieces. Eventually they managed to fix the wooden panels together, surround them with a rigid frame and stretch over them an accurate copy in tempera on canvas of the original painting. In memory of the 1430 attack two deep wounds were scratched in the left cheek of the painting of the Virgin. The news of the almost miraculous restoration of the image, and King Władysław II Jagiełło's extraordinary commitment to it, attracted thousands of pilgrims and transformed the Paulite monastery into one of the most popular pilgrimage shrines in Europe. In 1650 the Grand Hetman Jan Ossoliński donated a new high altar, in which the Black Madonna is still kept today. The wooden panel is concealed by a splendid ebony cover and decorated with superb silver ornaments. Since 1673 the image has been protected by a silver screen which is removed to the accompaniment of fanfares. There are also many precious votive 'garments' for the Black Madonna: coverings made of velvet and silver plate and studded with precious stones, with spaces left for the face and hands. Ever since the proclamation of the Virgin Mary as 'Queen of the Crown of Poland' in 1717, the Black Madonna has been venerated under this title.

Of the original late Gothic furnishings of the chapel all that could be saved from the fire was the monumental crucifix on the side altar to the right. Recent researches have suggested that it is a late 15th-century work from the circle of Veit Stoss.

The ceiling of the nave of the chapel has intricate plasterwork. Above the chancel arch are two paintings, one showing the Virgin vanquishing heresy (1656) – she sits on a cloud with the Church Fathers as a dragon entangles various book-wielding Protestants below –

Częstochowa, plan of
the Monastery on
Jasna Góra
1 Kościół (Church)
2 Kruchta (Porch)
3 Kaplica św. Pawła
(Chapel of St Paul)
4 Kaplica śś. Relikwii
i Kaplica Jabłonowskich
(Chapel of the
Holy Relics and
Jabłonowski
Chapel)
5 Dzwonnica
(Bell-tower)
6 Wieczernik
(Cloister Chapel)
7 Kaplica
Narodzenia NMP
(Chapel of the
Navity of the
Blessed Virgin)
8 Stary Świat
(Old World)
9 Refektarz
(Refectory)
10 Pokoje Królewskie (Royal Rooms)
11 Studnia Klasztorna (Monastery Well)
12 Arsenał (Arsenal)
13 Brama Lubomirskich (Lubomirski Gate)
14 Brama Stanisława Augusta (Stanisław August Gate)
15 Brama Jagiellońska (Jagiellonian Gate)

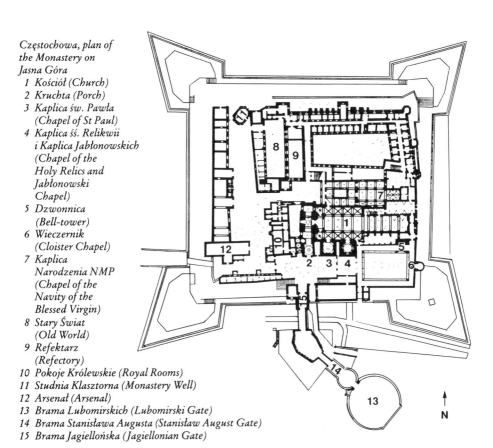

and the other depicting the 1655 siege of Jasna Góra by the Swedes, painted soon after the event in 1656–7.

The sacristy, treasury, magazine and arsenal contain one of the richest collections of applied art in Poland. For more than six centuries kings and magnates had made valuable donations to the Paulites and had sent artists in their service to Jasna Góra. Pilgrims had made votive offerings as an expression of their veneration for the Black Madonna. The collection of several thousand pieces of goldsmith's work includes the Baroque, jewel-encrusted monstrance of Prior Augustyn Kordecki, made in 1672 by the Warsaw goldsmith Wacław Grottko; a Late Gothic cross reliquary donated by King Zygmunt I Stary, made in Nuremberg in 1510; and a large number of votive plaques made of sheet silver.

There are also more than a hundred liturgical vestments, the oldest of them dating from the 15th century. They include a purple chasuble given by the Archpriest of St Mary's in

Kraków, embroidered with a remarkable stump-work Crucifixion with the Virgin fainting at the foot of the Cross, as well as the lavishly bejewelled 'Pearl Chasuble' made in 1720 for Prior K. Moszyński.

The finest room in the monastic buildings, to the north and west of the Chapel of the Nativity of the Virgin, is the *Refectory* (9) on the ground floor of the west range, with a vault painted by Karl Dankwart (after 1693). The Library above has decoration by the monastery's cabinet maker, Grzegorz Woźniakowic, ornamented with intarsia work (1733–9). Among the illuminated manuscripts in the monastery's extensive archives are an Italian breviary of 1480, and a missal donated by King Jan I Olbracht and painted by miniaturists at Wawel Castle in Kraków in 1506–7.

The other rooms of the monastery contain more than 150 paintings, mainly works by monks of Jasna Góra, some showing the influence of the Venetian artist Tommaso Dolabella, who worked at the royal court at Kraków in the 17th century, where his narrative skill had been greatly appreciated.

A few miles to the southeast of Częstochowa, in the midst of the picturesque limestone cliffs of the Wyżyna Krakowska-Częstochowska, are the ruins of **Olsztyn Castle**. This Gothic fortress was built for Kazimierz III Wielki around the middle of the 14th century on the border of Małopolska and Silesia and was extended several times over the following centuries. Like many other buildings it fell victim to the devastations of the Swedish army in 1655.

At **Szczekociny** further along the road to Jędrzejów, is the very elegant *Palace* built for Urszula Dembińska, the wife of the starosta, in 1770–80 probably by Franz Ferdinand Nax. The main block is linked by curving arcaded galleries to the two pavilions flanking the forecourt. Behind the palace is a large French garden, with an adjoining landscaped park.

We turn north at Szczekociny to reach **Koniecpol**. The *Kościół św. Trójcy (Church of the Holy Trinity)*, founded by the Hetman Stanisław Koniecpolski, is an Early Baroque building erected in 1633–40 on a rectangular plan with a plain façade with pilasters and volutes. The church is symmetrically placed on an axis with the courtyard, which has interesting towers and a rusticated doorway. The Late Baroque turret was added between 1758 and 1778. Many of the furnishings (choir stalls, confessionals) date from the same period, and the church also contains a Mannerist painting of the Crucifixion from the second half of the 16th century.

Kielce – Oblęgorek

Kielce, situated about 120 km to the northeast of Kraków, was formerly the centre of Poland's old industrial region, and is still an important industrial town and voivodship capital, with a population of approximately 200,000. It is not far from some of Małopolska's important historic and artistic sites, such as Jędrzejów, Pińczów, Święty Krzyż, Bodzentyn and Wąchock. Kielce is also a convenient starting point for visits to the woods of the rolling Góry Świętokrzyskie (Holy Cross Mountains), the oldest mountain range in Poland, whose paleozoic rock thrusts through the chalk foothills and cliffs around the town.

In 1394 Kielce was granted its charter with the municipal laws of Magdeburg. A few years earlier the Bishops of Kraków had established their summer residence here. The town had a great economic boom in the 16th century, when it began to exploit the reserves of lead, copper and iron ore in the vicinity. In 1815 Poland's first school of mines was established at Kielce. The town achieved a sad notoriety in July 1946, when a Polish mob, inflamed by rumours of Jews abducting Christian children, attacked the surviving Jews in Kielce. Forty-two Jews were murdered. This pogrom, and other anti-Jewish attacks, convinced most Polish survivors of the Holocaust that there was no future for them in postwar Poland.

Over the centuries the Bishops of Kraków at Kielce were not only great princes of the church, pastors and the final authority on theological questions, but some of them were also magnanimous patrons of the arts. Bishop Kajetan Sołtyk, for instance, supported the famous theatre at Kielce during its 18th-century Enlightenment flowering. In the 20th century Kielce again became an important theatrical centre, when in 1955–6 the Żeromski Theatre under the direction of Irena and Tadeusz Byrski prepared the way for the thaw in Polish theatre after the Stalinist period.

The two most important architectural monuments, the Cathedral and the Palace of the Bishops of Kraków (now the National Museum), are to be found south of the town centre (Pl. Partyzantów).

The *Katedra Wniebowzięcia Najświętszej Marii Panny (Cathedral of the Assumption)*, an Early Baroque basilica, was until 1815 a collegiate church. It was erected in 1632–5 and altered several times since, most notably in 1869–72, when the neo-Baroque façade was

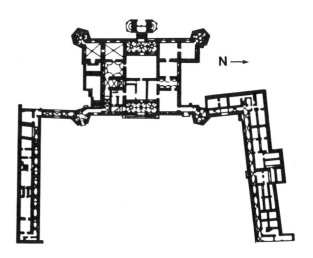

N→

Kielce, plan of the Palace of the Bishops of Kraków

523

built. The most remarkable features of the Late Baroque interior are works by the outstanding woodcarver Antoni Frączkiewicz of Kraków (1726–30): several altars with figures of the Patriarch Joseph, King David and St George; the large painting of the Assumption by Szymon Czechowicz (1730); the Renaissance tomb of Elżbieta Zebrzydowska (died 1553) with a red marble effigy, attributed to Giovanni Maria Padovano. The church treasury contains various gifts from Kazimierz III Wielki, including a Gothic chalice made in Kraków in 1362 and a bust reliquary of St Mary Magdalene of around 1370.

The Early Baroque *Pałac Biskupów Krakowskich (Palace of the Bishops of Kraków)* (plate 56) is a fine example of palace architecture in the 'Waza Style'. The closed, axial scheme of a North Italian villa is supplemented by the northern European features of polygonal corner towers and a hipped roof. The residence was built for Bishop Jan Zadzik in 1637–41, by Tommaso Poncino, probably following designs by Giovanni Battista Trevano. Particularly impressive is the former dining hall, now called the Hall of Portraits, which has a wooden ceiling with painted decoration. Around the top of the walls runs a frieze with portraits of the Bishops of Kraków. The ceilings of the adjoining rooms have scenes painted on canvas by Tommaso Dolabella (1641) showing events from contemporary church history, such as the Condemnation of the Arians.

The old grammar school of Kielce houses the *Muzeum Żeromskiego (Żeromski Museum)*, commemorating its most celebrated pupil, the writer Stefan Żeromski (1864–1925), whose greatest work was *Ashes*, a massive treatment of the Napoleonic Wars (see page 103). A few kilometres to the northwest of Kielce, at **Oblęgorek** is a reminder of another great Polish man of letters: the manor house presented to Henryk Sienkiewicz (1846–1916), the author of *Quo Vadis?* and winner of the Nobel Prize for Literature, as a 'gift from the public' in 1900 to celebrate 25 years of literary activity. In 1958 it was opened as the *Muzeum życia i twórczości H. Sienkiewicza (Museum of Sienkiewicz's Life and Work)*. Southwest of here, on the way to Chęciny (see below), is perhaps the most beautiful dripstone cave in Poland, known as *Raj* ('Paradise').

Chęciny – Mnichów – Jędrzejów – Pińczów – Młodzawy – Szydłów

The ruined *castle* at **Chęciny** is one of the more imposing architectural monuments in the uplands of Małopolska. The castle was begun at the end of the 13th century for Bishop Jan Muskata of Kraków, the representative of King Václav II (Wenceslas II) of Bohemia, and completed after 1311 for King Władysław I Łokietek; it was remodelled around 1630. The long polygonal plan of the surrounding wall has survived, with two cylindrical towers and remains of the treasury, a residential building and a gate. Chęciny itself (population 4,000) was granted its town charter in the early 13th century and has kept its medieval street plan: the town centre is a rectangular market place, with streets running from its corners. The famous Polish organ-builder Szymon Sadkowski was born here, and the organ in the

Kościół św. Józefa (Church of St Joseph) is one of the finest in Poland. It was made after 1675 and today remains in its original state with nine stops, mechanical action, slider wind chest and manual. Chęciny also has a reconstructed 17th-century *synagogue* (c.1638, now a cultural centre) with some 19th-century frescoes. There is a picturesque Jewish *cemetery* near the town.

A few kilometres to the south, at **Mnichów**, the timber *Kościół św. Stefana (Church of St Stephen)*, built in 1765–7, is one of the most beautiful examples of a transposing of the language of masonry architecture into the idiom of timber construction. The church uses the basic formal elements of the Late Baroque: the nave has a two-towered façade at its west end, and a dome on a drum rises above the crossing (colour plate 11). The original Rococo interior has largely been preserved. The two altars in the transept, the pulpit, font and confessionals are carved from lime and larch.

At **Jędrzejów** the *Kościół Najświętszej Marii Panny i św. Wojciecha (Church of St Mary and St Adalbert)* (plate 60) was founded in 1140 by the future Archbishop of Gniezno, Janik Gryfit, as the church for the first Cistercian monastery in Poland, a daughter house of Morimont in Burgundy. The arrival of the monks in 1149 marked the end of the first wave of Cistercian foundations in Poland. A second wave (also from Morimont) followed in 1170–80 and led to the founding of the abbeys of Koprzywnica (see page 549), Sulejów (see page 531) and Wąchock (see page 528).

The abbey church at Jędrzejów, consecrated in 1201, was a typically Cistercian, Late Romanesque basilica, with arcades resting on piers, and a transept with two chapels on the east side of each arm. The whole church was vaulted with cross-rib vaults – the greatest Cistercian innovation in architecture. The building was remodelled several times. The Gothic nave arcades were built in the 15th century, but the most important changes came in 1728–54, when the choir was lengthened, the whole interior was given Late Baroque vaulting, two symmetrical domed chapels were built flanking the north and an impressive two-towered façade with a blocked door and windows was built at the east end. The interior has Late Baroque paintings by Andrzej Radwański on the walls and vaults (1734–9), and the high altar and the richly carved choir stalls dating from 1730–50 are probably from the workshop of Antoni Frączkiewicz. Of the monastic buildings only the west and south ranges of the cloister survive.

Jędrzejów's other great attraction is the *Muzeum Zegarów Słonecznych (Gnomoniczne) (Sundial [Gnomonical] Museum)* at Rynek 7/8, which has one of the most extensive collections of sundials in Europe, as well as a library of rare astronomical books. The collection was presented to the state in 1962 by the scholar and collector Tadeusz Przypkowski.

Fifteen kilometres west of Jędrzejów lies the village of Nagłowice, the birthplace of the 'father of Polish literature', Mikołaj Rej (1505–69). Rej, a Protestant and polemical humanist, promoted the use of the Polish vernacular in place of Latin (see page 98).

To the southeast of Jędrzejów, beyond Kije, we come to the valley of the Nida with the little town of **Pińczów**. In the second half of the 16th century Pińczów became the centre of the Reformation in Poland and was known as the 'Sarmatian Athens'. Protestant theologians from abroad taught at the Calvinist school established here in 1551, and it was here that Petrus Statorius wrote the first Polish grammar, 'Polonicae grammatices institutio', published in 1568, and that Daniel of Łęczyca printed the writings of the great humanist Andrzej Frycz Modrzewski (1503–72) (see page 99).

In 1943–4 the Home Army was so successful in eliminating German troops from the hills around the town that the area was known as the 'Republic of Pińczów'.

The former Paulite church, *Kościół św. Jana Ewangelisty (Church of St John the Evangelist)*, was completed in 1642 but was founded by Cardinal Zbigniew Oleśnicki of Kraków in 1436. The interior was given a rich Baroque decoration: the high altar, nine side-altars and choir stalls with carvings showing scenes from the lives of hermit saints and free-standing figures of apostles and saints. Adjoining the church to the southeast is the former *Klasztor Paulinów (Paulite Monastery)* with its cloister.

On a hill above the town stands the *Kaplica św. Anny (Chapel of St Anne)* built in 1600. Its founder, Zygmunt Myszkowski, very probably entrusted the design to Santi Gucci. The little chapel at Pińczów is one of the few free-standing Renaissance chapels in Poland and is a striking and elegant architectural concept of two domed cubes, one large, the other small. The exquisitely executed architectural sculpture is an important example of work by what is known as the 'Pińczów Workshop', a group of stonemasons in the late 16th and early 17th century who produced sculptured door and window frames for many churches and magnates' residences.

Southwest of Pińczów, in the little village of **Młodzawy**, is the *Kościół Ducha św. i Matki Boskiej Bolesnej (Church of the Holy Ghost and the Mater Dolorosa)*, which was

View of Szydłów, engraving, 1869

built between 1716 and 1740, probably to a design by Kasper Bażanka. Particularly impressive is the magnificent stone façade with its severe pilaster articulation, massive volutes and gesticulating figures of saints perched atop the pediment.

Northeast of Pińczów lie *Chmielnik*, where there was a wholesale massacre of the nobility of Małopolska by the Golden Horde, and *Raków*, where the Polish Brethren at the turn of the 16th century preached an early form of Unitarianism and practised a primitive communism. Between them is **Szydłów** where the most striking feature is a set of fortifications built by King Kazimierz III Wielki in the mid-14th century. With their battlemented walls and the remains of towers, the most striking of which is the *Brama Krakowska (Kraków Tower)*, they give a good impression of the medieval appearance of the town.

Świętokrzyski – Nowa Słupia – Święta Katarzyna – Bodzentyn – Wąchock

The centre of the uplands of Małopolska, the Góry Świętokrzyskie (Holy Cross Mountains) to the east of Kielce, are well worth a visit, with their weathered mountain peaks and magnificent forests of fir and larch, including the rare Polish larch as well as natural curiosities such as the bare quartzite fields of Łysa Góra ('bald mountain'), and a plethora of rare species of flora and fauna. This wildlife is protected in the **Świętokrzyski National Park**. The area was the centre of much iron working in the first millenium, and there is a *Museum of Ancient Metallurgy* at **Nowa Słupia**. The wooded ridges of the mountains have been used as a hide-out by Polish resistance fighters on several occasions. In 1863 Marian Langiewicz, a commander of the insurrectionaries, set up his headquarters here; and in the Second World War the partisans used the mountain as a base from which to conduct their guerrilla campaign against the German occupiers.

Święta Katarzyna, a small town 20 km from Kielce, is mainly used as a starting point for walks through the Góry Świętokrzyskie. On Łysa Góra at the eastern edge of the national park, reached after a drive of about 36 km, stands the *Kościół św. Krzyża (Holy Cross Church)*, which was part of a Benedictine abbey until 1818, became a notorious prison in Tsarist times and is now an oblate monastery with a museum and hostel run by the PTTK. The original abbey was founded by King Bolesław III Krzywousty in the first third of the 12th century. Already in the 8th and 9th centuries there had been a pagan cult centre on the site, and parts of a stone rampart from this structure survive.

The present church was built in 1781–9. Its main points of interest are its Late Baroque west front and Neoclassical interior, which includes altar paintings (c.1800) by Franciszek Smuglewicz.

Of the Late Gothic *monastery* built for King Kazimierz IV Jagiellończyk and Cardinal Zbigniew Oleśnicki in the mid-15th century, only the cloister is extant: the cross-rib vaults have heraldic bosses. The east range contains the 17th-century domed chapel of the Oleśnickis, later decorated with Rococo paintings by Matthias Reichan (1782); the double tomb of the wojewoda Mikołaj Oleśnicki and his wife is made of coloured marbles (1611–20). Ten kilometres north of Święta Katarzyna, on the edge of the Świętokrzyski National Park, is the town of **Bodzentyn**, where the *Kościół Wniebowzięcia Najświętszej Marii Panny (Church of the Assumption)*, built in 1440–52, has the great high altar made for Wawel Cathedral at the time of its Renaissance remodelling. Carved in 1545–6 by Italian artists involved in the building of the Zygmunt Chapel, it was transferred to the collegiate church of Kielce only a year later, and finally in 1728 to Bodzentyn. The carved figures (among them St Stanislas and St Wenceslas) are by Giovanni Cini and the Crucifixion was painted by Petrus Venetus in 1547. The church also has the central panel of a Late Gothic winged altarpiece showing the Death of the Virgin with angelic choirs and the kneeling figure of the donor, Bishop Jan Konarski. This masterpiece of early-16th-century Polish painting is attributed to Marcin Czarny of Kraków. The church itself, built in 1440–52 on the model of the great Cracovian basilicas, stands next to the imposing ruins of a castle which was once the residence of the Bishops of Kraków.

The *Opactwo Cystersów (Cistercian Abbey)* of **Wąchock**, to the northeast of Kielce, and close to the towns of Starachowice and Skarżysko-Kamienna, is one of the group of Cistercian monasteries in Małopolska (see page 525). The monastery and the *Kościół Najświętszej Marii Panny i św. Floriana (Church of St Mary and St Florian)* were founded in 1179 by Bishop Gedko of Kraków for monks from Morimond Abbey in Burgundy. The monastic buildings were erected in 1218–39, probably by members of an Italian masons' workshop under the direction of Master Simon, whose name is carved on the church's façade. The church is a basilica with piers and the cross-rib vaulting characteristic of the Cistercians. Its exterior walls are given effective articulation by alternate courses of yellow and reddish-brown sandstone ashlar. The interior furnishings include several Baroque and Rococo altars and a richly decorated pulpit and choir stalls (*c.*1750).

The best preserved part of the original monastic buildings (plate 57) is the east range of the cloister, which contains a particularly fine chapter house. The room has cross-rib vaulting divided into nine compartments, and the transverse arches rest on four columns whose capitals – like the corbels on the walls – are decorated with beautifully carved foliage ornament. The refectory in the south range also has cross-rib vaulting with corbels and bosses with

o   1 m

Wąchock, a Romanesque window in the Church of St Mary and St Florian plant decoration. From the early 16th-century cloister a portal (part Gothic, part Renaissance) leads into the church. The monastery has a number of beautifully carved tomb slabs, ranging from a Romanesque example (first half of the 13th century) with an abbot's crozier and interlace and volute decoration, to a Late Gothic slab (after 1521) with the incised figure of Abbot Rafał Zaborowita.

Szydłowiec – Radom – Wieniawa – Drzewica – Studzianna – Poświętne

The *Castle* at **Szydłowiec**, built for Mikołaj Szydłowiecki in 1510–26, consists of a quadrangular courtyard surrounded by ranges on the west, north and east sides. The interior retains two Renaissance doorways, window surrounds, coffered ceilings and wall paintings (attributed to Stanisław Samostrzelnik) in their original state.

The *Town Hall*, erected in 1602–5, with its tall attic and frieze of blind arcading, clearly shows its derivation from the Sukiennice in Kraków. It stands in the centre of the market place and has four little round towers at the corners and a large rectangular tower with an octagonal superstructure on the main front. The façades were restored in 1989.

The Late Gothic *Kościół św. Zygmunta (Church of St Sigismund)* was built in 1493–1509. An aisleless church with a long chancel, it has good star vaulting. The interior furnishings are of interest, above all the Late Gothic polyptych, with a central panel showing the Assumption of the Virgin (before 1509, by a Kraków workshop). The Apostles are shown gathered around the empty tomb, while the Virgin is welcomed by Christ in Heaven, and the small figures of the donor, Jan Szydłowiecki, with his wife and three daughters, kneel below. Also to be seen in the church are the lavishly carved Mannerist high altar (1618–27), and a Late Gothic carving of the Coronation of the Virgin (before 1531). Two tombs deserve attention: the marble slab with the figure of the Grand Treasurer Mikołaj Szydłowiecki, made by Bartolommeo Berrecci after 1532, and the Neoclassical tomb of the Radziwiłł family (1807) with a female figure by Giacopo Monaldi (1795). There is a very large *Jewish cemetery* (ul. Wschodnie) with some fine carving.

Radom, with a population of 200,000 and a number of big factories, is one of Poland's most important industrial towns. The town hit the headlines in the Western press in 1976, when the workers protested against price rises with strikes and demonstrations.

The former *Gmach Komisji Wojewódzkiej (Building of the Voivodship Committee)* in ul. Żeromskiego (No. 30) is a good example of the Late Neoclassicism that characterized the architecture in Congress Poland after 1815. The building was erected in 1825–7 to a design by Antonio Corazzi and has an impressive 15-bay façade with a central pediment and projecting ends.

The *Town Hall* in the market place is by the leading Warsaw architect Enrico Marconi (1847–8), who took the Italian palaces of the quattrocento as his model for the rusticated façade and round-arched windows.

In ul. Żeromskiego stands the *Kościoł św. Katarzyny (Church of St Catherine)* with the adjoining Bernardine monastery founded in 1468. The compact, brick-built ensemble has been altered several times in its history. The excellent Late Gothic crucifix in the church is worth close attention.

Wieniawa lies to the west of Radom, on the road to Piotrków Trybunalski. Its main point of interest is the 16th-century *Kościół św. Katarzyny (Church of St Catherine)*, in which the Kaplica św. Stanisława (Chapel of St Stanislas) contains a very fine Renaissance polyptych (1544) with woodcarvings showing scenes from the life of St Stanisław. The central panel is filled with a dramatic representation of the saint's murder by King Bolesław II, a popular theme in late medieval Polish art.

Radom, view of the old market place, drawing, 1808

About 35 km northwest of here, after passing through Przysucha (the home town of the 'Holy Jew' and site of his grave) and Gielniów, we come to **Drzewica** with its ruined *Castle*. This was built between 1527 and 1535 and combines Late Gothic with Renaissance elements. Particularly striking is the contrast between the massive defensive walls and the tall, decorated gables of the main building and the chapel, which rise above the level of the battlements.

Beyond Odrzywół we come to **Studzianna-Poświętne**. Here the *Kościół śś. Filipa Nereusza i Jana Chrzciciela (Church of St Philip Neri and St John the Baptist)* dates from the first half of the 18th century and follows the Baroque spatial scheme of the Collegiate Church of St Anne in Kraków (see page 470). The monumental façade has pilaster articulation, with a two-storey pedimented centrepiece and domes on octagonal drums rising above the projecting ends. The main entrance is flanked by columns, and on either side above and below are pedimented niches filled with statues of saints. The Baroque furnishings include a number of magnificent altars, as well as two silver candlesticks decorated with the arms of King Zygmunt III Waza, made at Augsburg in 1620. Adjoining the church to the east is a long range of the Oratorian monastery.

Białaczów – Petrykozy – Sulejów

The *palace* at **Białaczów** was built in 1797–1800 by the Marshal (Speaker) of the Sejm, Stanisław Małachowski, who had played a prominent part in the creation of the Constitution of 3 May 1791. The designer was the famous Warsaw architect Jakub Kubicki. The palace follows a Palladian plan (English Palladianism was popular with the late-18th-century Polish reformers) with the main block linked to the secondary buildings by means of curved arcades, which together with two pavilions surround a large cour d'honneur. The English landscape park contains romantic garden architecture designed by Francesco Maria Lanci (1825–30), including mock-medieval ruins and an orangery.

Ten kilometres east of here, at **Petrykozy**, stands the *Kościół św. Doroty (Church of St Dorothy)* founded by Stanisław Małachowski in 1791. The aisleless Neoclassical building was designed by Johann Christian Kamsetzer. The articulation of its compact east front is an exercise in geometry: the pedimented projecting centre is surmounted by a tower-like superstructure with a large semicircular window.

Returning now to Białaczów and on through Miedzna–Drewniana we come to Żarnów where we take the Piotrków road to **Sulejów**, which has one of the best preserved medieval Cistercian churches in Poland. The monastery was founded in 1177 by Kazimierz II Sprawiedliwy, and like the other Cistercian houses of Małopolska was settled by monks from Morimont in Burgundy. The Late Romanesque *Kościół Najświętszej Marii Panny i św. Tomasza (Church of St Mary and St Thomas)* was consecrated in 1232 and is very similar to Wąchock and Koprzywnica: a basilica (with piers) built of ashlar, presumably by the Italian masons' workshop of Master Simon (see page 528), it has the characteristic division of space and cross-rib vaulting. Much of the architectural sculpture survives. The fine west door has slender columns with ornamented capitals in its jambs, and an inner archivolt carved with interlace decoration. The rose window above still contains part of its original tracery (plate 58). (Doorway and window are at present undergoing restoration.) A Romanesque tympanum set into the façade above the entrance to the north aisle (12th/13th centuries) is carved with a symbolic representation of the Passion of Christ (the Cross flanked by the sun and moon, and a crowing cock). The austere monumentality of the church's interior contrasts with its Baroque furnishings: an imposing ensemble of altars made of black marble and alabaster, a richly decorated pulpit, choir stalls and organ gallery.

Many of the monastic buildings were destroyed in the 19th century, but fortunately the square *chapter house* (second quarter 13th century) on the east side of the cloister has survived. Its vaults are supported on a pillar in the middle of the room. The foliage ornament on its intricately carved capital matches that of the corbels on the walls; one of the four vaulting bosses is carved with four men's heads. The other monastic buildings are in ruins.

Large sections of the Late Gothic fortifications (15th-16th centuries) survive, though various other buildings were added to them between the 15th and the 19th centuries. One gate-tower is extant, the *Brama Krakowska (Kraków Gate)*, as well as the Abbot's Tower and a tower to the southeast, which had a Renaissance attic added in the 16th century. Some of the buildings attached to the fortifications have been converted into a passable PTTK Hotel.

Reinhold Vetter

Between Vistula, Bug and Carpathians

Lublin – Majdanek

Lublin is the largest Polish city east of the Vistula, and the most important economic, cultural and educational centre in southeastern Poland. The Catholic University, founded in 1919, is the only such institution in Central Europe. Karol Wojtyła taught here when he was Bishop of Kraków. Many lecturers at this university were among the first victims of the Nazis in their suppression of intellectuals during the German occupation, but the survivors helped to make Lublin a centre of the underground press against the Nazi occupiers. A second, state university, founded in the closing stages of the Second World War in 1944, was given the name of the great Polish scientist, Marie Curie-Skłodowska.

Like Tarnów, Przemyśl and other towns in southeastern Poland, Lublin was a very important centre of Polish Jewry before the Second World War. In 1939 there were 45,000 Jews out of a total population of 115,000. Lublin had been the seat of the Council of the Four Lands (see page 91) between 1581 and 1764, and it was famed for its scholars. The Talmudic library was the largest in the world. Alfred Döblin wrote a vivid description of his visit here in 1924 on his journey through Poland to study the living conditions of the Jews. The world Döblin saw, a world also described by Isaac Bashevis Singer in his *Magician of Lublin*, has vanished. There are two major Jewish cemeteries.

The urban character of Lublin was shaped by the Renaissance and humanism. The most important stages in its development occurred in the 16th and 17th centuries. Under the influence of Kraków, then Poland's political and cultural centre, the first Renaissance buildings were erected at the beginning of the 16th century. But the greatest artistic achievements in the Lublin region came after 1600 with the development here of a local form of Mannerism. Churches of the 'Lublin Renaissance' have naves combining the proportions of Late Gothic architecture with rich plaster vaulting of distinctive design.

During the Reformation Lublin was the scene of fierce religious disputes. The Hussite Biernat of Lublin (*c*.1465–after 1529) was the first writer to write exclusively in Polish instead of Latin. The poet Sebastian Klonowic (*c*.1545–1602) was also mayor of the city, and Jan Kochanowski (1530–84), the greatest poet of the Polish Renaissance (see page 98), died here.

Between the Vistula,
the Bug and the
Carpathians

Radom

Czarnolas
Janowiec

Czemierniki
Gołąb
Puławy
Kazimierz
Dolny
Nałęczów
Opole Lubelskie

Lubartów
Lublin
Majdanek
Puchaczów

Chełm

Uchanie
Hrubieszów

Tarłów
Kraśnik

Opatów

Ujazd
Koprzywnica
Staszów
Rytwiany
Baranów
Sandomierski

Sandomierz

Stalowa Wola

Zamość

*Roztoczański
National Park*

Biłgoraj

Tomaszów
Lubelski

Tarnobrzeg

Mielec

Leżajsk

Hrebenne

Łańcut

Tarnów

Rzeszów

Przeworsk
Jarosław

UKRAINE

Lvov

Przemyśl

Stara Wieś

Krasiczyn

Krosno
Haczów

Dukla
Sanok

J. SOLIŃSKIE

K A R P A T Y

B I E S Z C Z A D Y

SLOVAKIA

*Bieszczady
National Park*

N

0   50 km

534

Lublin's history can be traced back to the 7th century, when the first settlement began on the site of the present town. In 1317 King Władysław I Łokietek granted the town its charter with the laws of Magdeburg, and in the period that followed Lublin developed into an important centre on the trade routes between Małopolska and Lithuania, and between Wielkopolska and the Ukraine. In 1569 the Sejm met in the town and instituted the Union of Lublin, which united Poland and Lithuania to make a single political entity, the Rzeczypospolita ('Republic' or 'Commonwealth'). In 1578 Lublin became the seat of the crown tribunal for South and East Poland.

It was not until centuries later, towards the end of the Second World War, that Lublin again played a major part in Polish history: on 25 July 1944 the 'Polish Committee of National Liberation', which had been founded at Chełm a few days earlier to serve as the first Polish administration after the liberation of the country from Nazi rule, began its work. Lublin functioned as the capital of Poland until 1 February 1945. The first postwar publishing house, Czytelnik ('Reader') was founded here, as was the first literary magazine of the new Poland, Odrodzenie ('Rebirth').

From Pl. Łokietka, named after the king who gave Lublin its charter, we enter the historic Old Town through the **Brama Krakowska (Kraków Gate)** (1). With its massive Gothic brick tower, the gate forms part of the fortifications built after the Tatar invasion in 1341. Its basic form is still preserved although it has undergone several alterations and additions over the years. In the first half of the 16th century a lower foregate was added, decorated with projecting turrets and battlements; in 1574–84 the octagonal upper storey was added to the tower; and finally in 1782 it was given a Baroque cap. Since 1965 the Brama Krakowska has housed the historical section of the Lublin regional museum. From the top storey of the gate the view takes in the **Nowy Ratusz (New Town Hall)** (2), an early 19th-century Neoclassical building, and the roofs and towers of the Old Town. The market place is dominated by the solid building of the **Stary Ratusz (Old Town Hall)** (3). This was originally a Gothic building erected in 1389. After rebuilding in 1579 it was used for meetings of the Crown Tribunal, and in 1781 was given a thorough Neoclassical remodelling by Domenico Merlini. Not far away in one of the old burghers' houses is the 'Pod Czarcią Łapą' ('The Devil's Claw') café. Legend tells how a poor widow, about to be deprived of her last belongings by the court, appealed to the Devil for help. The following night demon judges dressed in black appeared in the rooms of the tribunal and found in favour of the poor woman, signing their verdict with a claw mark on the table (which can still be seen in the castle museum; see page 538). The poet Jan Kochanowski, who lived near Lublin on his Czarnolas estate, died suddenly in the town hall in 1584.

Three of the burghers' houses facing the market place are of particular interest. The **Kamienica Klonowica (Klonowic House)** at No. 2 (4), where the family of the poet and town councillor Sebastian Klonowic lived around 1600, was given its present Neoclassical appearance at the end of the 18th century; the sgraffito roundels representing Klonowic with his fellow poets Jan Kochanowski, Wincenty Pol and Biernat of Lublin, were not added until 1939. The **Kamienica Lubomelskich (House of the Lubomelski family)** (5)

View of Lublin, 1719

at No. 8 was erected around 1540 and remodelled in 1782 (Neoclassical façade and balustrade) and in 1874; the vaulted interior, with a corner fireplace, is used as a wine bar. The cellar is decorated with Renaissance wall paintings from the period *c.*1570: between floral scrollwork there are panels with allegorical scenes and inscriptions from classical authors. The **Kamienica Konopnicòw (House of the Konopnica family)** (6) at No. 12, was built around 1600 and given a fine Renaissance façade with attic. The groups of two and three windows on the first and second floors are set in exuberant surrounds carved by the Pińczów workshops (herm-pilasters as jambs and supports, with portrait roundels, dragons and cartouches).

A little street, ul. Gruella, leads from the market place to the **Wieża Trynitarska (Trinitarian Tower)** (7), built in 1693–9 and given a neo-Gothic remodelling in 1819–21, probably by Antonio Corazzi, as the bell-tower of the cathedral. Next we come to the **Katedra śś. Jana Chrzciciela i Jana Ewangelisty (Cathedral of Sts John the Baptist and John the Evangelist)** (8). Until the suppression of the Order in 1773 this was the Jesuit church; since 1818 it has been a cathedral. The designer of this Late Renaissance building was the Jesuit architect Gian Maria Bernardoni, but its erection was entrusted to local builders in 1592–1604. It has a three-bay nave with pier arcades and aisles flanked by chapels. After a fire in 1752 the upper storeys of the towers were built together with their helms, and in 1820 the Neoclassical column portico designed by Antonio Corazzi was added. The cathedral was one of the first churches in Poland where the interior space was treated in a genuinely Baroque manner, though this too was altered by a major remodelling after the fire of 1752. Joseph Mayer completed the Late Baroque illusionistic painted decoration of the whole interior in 1757 (Apocalypse, patron Saints of the church and of the Jesuits, and, in the celebrated acoustic Sacristy, scenes of the Expulsion of Heliodorus from the Temple and others).

From the Wieża Trinitarska next to the cathedral, ul. Trybunalska and ul. Klonowicza lead past the Państwowy Teatr Lalki (State Marionette Theatre) to what is perhaps the most beautiful church in the Old Town, the **Kościół Dominikanów (Dominican Church)** (9). The present church with nave and aisles is probably the result of a reshaping of an aisleless Gothic church founded in the 14th century. It was completed in 1668, and dating from the same period are the rows of chapels on either side, the façade articulated with pilasters, string courses and volutes, with a tall, Late Renaissance gable, and the two rectangular flanking towers. The domed chapels built in the first half of the 17th century have rich architectural decoration. One of these is the Firlej Chapel, a fine piece of Late Renaissance architecture, whose dome was covered on the interior with a network of ornamented plaster strips enclosing plasterwork motifs. The other is the Holy Cross Chapel (colour plate 4) with an octagonal interior decorated in 1655–8, probably by Giovanni Battista Falconi with plasterwork decoration (figures of the prophets) and a painting of the Last Judgement by Tomasz Muszyński in an elliptical dome. The sculptural decoration in the church includes a number of Rococo altars made around 1760 in the workshops at Puławy. The finest piece of goldsmith's work in the cathedral treasury is an Early Baroque monstrance dating from the second quarter of the 17th century.

Lublin   1 Brama Krakowska (Kraków Gate)   2 Nowy Ratusz (New Town Hall)   3 Stary Ratusz (Old Town Hall)   4 Kamienica Klonowica (Klonowic House)   5 Kamienica Lubomelskich (House of the Lubomelski family)   6 Kamienica Konopniców (House of the Konopnica family)   7 Wieża Trynitarska (Trinitarian Tower)   8 Katedra (Cathedral)   9 Kościół Dominikanów (Dominican Church)   10 Brama Grodzka (Castle Gate)   11 Zamek (Castle)   12 Cerkiew (Orthodox Church)   13 Kościół Nawrócenia św. Pawła (Church of the Conversion of St Paul)   14 Kościół NMP (Church of St Mary)   15 Kościół św. Ducha (Church of the Holy Ghost)   16 Kościół Karmelitów (Carmelite Church)

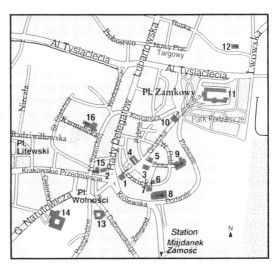

*Lublin, the old market place,
lithograph by A. Lerue, 1857*

The **Brama Grodzka (Castle Gate)** (10), which marks the northeastern end of the Old Town, was created in 1785 to designs by Domenico Merlini. The gable is decorated with the cypher of the last Polish king, Stanisław August Poniatowski.

The only remaining part of the original **Zamek (Castle)** (11), built around the middle of the 14th century, is a single massive round tower, which was incorporated into the state prison built on the castle site by Ignacy Stompf in a bizarre neo-Gothic style. In the 19th century it was used by the Tsarist occupying power, and later by the Gestapo. Today, however, the once feared building houses the *Lublin Museum of Polish Painting, Folk Art and Archaeology*.

The most important and interesting of Lublin's historical monuments is the medieval *Kaplica św. Trójcy (Chapel of the Holy Trinity)* at the east end of the longer range of the castle. It has the form of a hall church with a long choir with a crypt below, and was built around 1395 at the behest of Władysław II Jagiełło. The whole of the interior is covered with wall paintings in the style favoured by the Orthodox Church, the best preserved of the four surviving ensembles of such wall paintings in Poland (see pages 141–2) by the painter Andrei and his assistants, who probably came from the Ukraine. Jagiełło had become a convert to the Roman Catholic Church when he was made King of Poland, but he was familiar with the art of the Orthodox Church in his Lithuanian territories and regarded the introduction of Eastern Christian art in Roman Catholic churches as a means of reinforcing his claims to these eastern regions. The paintings are arranged in registers: the

Glorification of the Holy Trinity in the vault, Old Testament scenes in the wall arches, the Christological cycle in the upper part of the walls, figures of saints on the octagonal central pillar, as well as secular subject matter including a portrait of Jagiełło himself. The paintings were discovered beneath the plaster towards the end of the 19th century; they were restored in 1954–6.

To the west below the castle hill lies the oval *Pl. Zebrań Ludowych* (*'Square of the People's Assemblies'*), which was created on the site of what until 1943 was the centre of the Jewish ghetto in Lublin. To the northeast of the castle, in the Kalinowszczyzna quarter, old tombstones with Hebrew inscriptions can still be found on the site of the old *Jewish cemetery*.

Also not far from the castle, in ul. Ruska, stands Lublin's only surviving **Cerkiew (Orthodox Church)** (12), originally a Late Renaissance edifice erected in 1607–33 and rebuilt around 1875.

Between ul. Dąbrowskiego and Podgrodzie, a few minutes' walk from the Brama Krakowska, stands the Late Renaissance **Kościół Nawrócenia św. Pawła (Church of the Conversion of St Paul)** (13), which was created in 1602–7 by remodelling a Late Gothic church. The decoration of the interior is the earliest example of Lublin Mannerist plasterwork.

The **Kościół Najświętszej Marii Panny (Church of St Mary)** (14) in ul. Narutowicza was erected in 1412–26 to commemorate the victory of Władysław II Jagiełło over the Teutonic Knights at Grunwald (1410). Nearby in the former Brigittine convent is a museum dedicated to the works of the poet Józef Czechowicz (1903–39) and other Lublin writers. Czechowicz, an early translator of Joyce and Eliot, and himself 'a writer with a distinctive, untranslatable voice, full of foreboding' (Miłosz) was killed in a bombing raid on his home town.

Somewhat in the shadow of the massive *New Town Hall* in Krakowskie Przedmieście is the **Kościół św. Ducha (Church of the Holy Ghost)** (15), originally a 15th-century Late Gothic church but rebuilt in 1602–8 in the characteristic style of Lublin Mannerism, and re-erected after a fire as a Baroque building in the mid-18th century. It was founded in 1419 by the burghers of Lublin as part of a hospital.

The **Kościół Karmelitów (Carmelite Church)** (16) in ul. Hanki Sawickiej has an impressive Renaissance façade incorporating plaster figures.

Krakowskie Przedmieście leads to *Pl. Litewski* (*'Lithuanian Square'*), once a place of assembly for the Polish nobles. An obelisk erected by Stanisław Staszic in 1826 commemorates the Union of Poland and Lithuania. Just next to it is a monument to the Soviet Army and a plaque commemorating the Constitution of 3 May 1791. The square is surrounded by several Neoclassical buildings: the former town palace of the Czartoryskis, now the seat of the Lublin Scientific Society; the Collegium Juridicum next door, formerly a palace of the Lubomirski family; and finally the former palace of the Radziwiłłs, now the rectorate of the Marie Curie-Skłodowska University. The Yeshivah (1930, Agenor Senduchowski) was built by Rabbi Meir Shapiro with money contributed from all over the world. Once a great centre of Talmudic studies, it is now the Medical Academy.

At **Majdanek**, 3 km from Lublin on the road to Zamość, the Nazis established a concentration and extermination camp. Here between 1941 and 1944 according to (incomplete) records around 360,000 people – the great majority of them Jews, though there were also Poles and Russians – were murdered. In the summer of 1944, the advancing Soviet army used the camp to imprison Poles from the Home Army. The barracks and gas chambers, watch towers and trenches for mass shootings remain. In 1969 a great roughhewn monument designed by Maria Albin Boniecki was erected, and there is also a museum documenting the atrocities.

Nałęczów – Kazimierz Dolny – Janowiec – Puławy – Gołąb

To the west of Lublin are three important towns: the old spa town of Nałęczów, the little Renaissance town of Kazimierz Dolny, and Puławy, which became a centre of patriotic artistic and cultural life in the years following the Third Partition of Poland in 1795.

Although the ferrous springs at **Nałęczów** were discovered before 1800, the town only became famous as a health resort and spa in the 19th century, when a house at Nałęczów, or an occasional stay there, was essential to members of Poland's cultural elite. Bolesław Prus, then the leading Polish novelist and a major figure in the Positivist movement stayed here (there is a *Prus Museum* in the Baroque Małachowski Palace of 1727), as did Stefan Żeromski, a leading figure in Młoda Polska (Young Poland). Henryk Sienkiewicz, the patriotic historical novelist and author of *Quo Vadis* was also a guest here. The spa buildings and pensions of Nałęczów were built in historicist and Art Nouveau styles, and are still redolent of the Belle Epoque.

Kazimierz Dolny, one of Poland's most magically beautiful towns, owes some of its charm to its curious topographical location. On its southern side is the gorge of the Vistula, which divides the southeastern Polish uplands from the Lublin plateau. The town is laid out in terraces on the right bank, which rises about 100 metres above the river and is fissured by ravines caused by erosion. Kazimierz Dolny takes its name from the Piast prince Kazimierz II Sprawiedliwy ('the Just'), who granted the village to the Premonstratensian Order in the 12th century. Later a royal starosta was installed here. In the mid-14th century Kazimierz Dolny was granted a charter according to the municipal laws of Magdeburg. In its heyday in the 16th and 17th centuries the town developed into one of the most important centres of the huge Polish grain trade, which was mainly in the hands of Jewish merchants working for a few patrician families (such as the Przybyło and the Celej), who used their wealth to engage in architectural rivalry with the nearby town of Zamość. It was in this period that the most interesting buildings in Kazimierz were erected.

On a hill not far from the market place rises the *Kościół św. Jana Chrzciciela i św. Bartłomieja (Church of St John the Baptist and St Bartholomew)*, one of the finest examples of Lublin Mannerism, built in two campaigns, in 1586–9 and 1610–13, under the

Monument on the site of Majdanek concentration camp

direction of the Lublin architect Jakub Balin. The interior is characterized by pilasters and arcades with Mannerist plasterwork in the vaults (panels, rosettes, ornamental surrounds). Two of the funerary chapels flanking the nave are particularly worthy of attention: the Chapel of the Assumption, a Baroque building with an elliptical dome, coupled columns in the corners and a doorway surmounted by plaster figures; and the Górski Chapel with its rich plasterwork decoration. The magnificent organ built in 1607–20 – one of the builders may have been Szymon Lilius – is the earliest complete organ to have survived in Poland. Leading organists from Poland and abroad come regularly to give recitals on this splendid instrument.

Above the church and visible from a great distance, are the ruins of the *Castle* with its tall watchtower. It was built in the 14th century for Kazimierz III Wielki, the last of the Piast kings. Nos. 1 and 2 on the south side of the market place are the *Kamienice Przybyłów (Houses of the Przybyło Brothers)*, two adjoining patrician houses completed in 1615, consisting of a single storey above a three-arch loggia, with tall attics, and highly decorative ædicules and gables. The Mannerist façades display a plethora of carved motifs: figures, plants and animals, with inscriptions, strapwork and scrollwork. Between the windows are the figures of the patron saints of the two brothers: St Nicholas on the left, the house of Mikołaj Przybyło, and a larger figure of St Christopher on Krzysztof's house on the right. (Notice the crayfish in St Christopher's river.) Each window is flanked by female or male herms. Another patrician house stands at ul. Senatorska 11, the *Kamienica Celejowska (House of Bartłomiej Celej)* built in 1635. It is of a similar type to the houses on the market place, with a single storey and lavish decoration, but it lacks a loggia. The lightly rusticated façade sets off the elaborate windows and doors decorated with plant motifs. Above the cornice is a massive attic, almost the same height as the house below, with a frieze of niches and pilasters, and cresting composed of fantastic figures and turrets and segments of pilasters and niches. Niches contain the figures of the Virgin and Christ, as well as St Bartholomew and John the Baptist.

The Baroque *Klasztor Reformatów (Monastery of the Reformed Franciscans)* in ul. Klasztorna on a hill in the upper town, fits harmoniously into the urban townscape, as does the former *Synagogue* in ul. Lubelska. Built in the 17th century, this reminder of the town's once thriving Jewish community was reconstructed after the war and is now used as a cinema.

On the other side of the river, above the little town of **Janowiec** an extensive complex of ruins is all that remains of the castle of the Firlejs, once one of the greatest families in Poland. It was built in several stages, the earliest parts dating from before 1537. One gatehouse has survived, as well as a curved bastion and part of the Late Gothic and Renaissance curtain walls, embrasures, window surrounds; some Baroque sgraffito decoration remains in the rooms of the first floor. The *parish church* contains the Late Renaissance tomb of Andrzej and Barbara Firlej by Santi Gucci, erected in 1586–7.

North of Kazimierz Dolny, on the road and rail routes from Warsaw to Lublin, lies **Puławy**, now an industrial town with a population of 50,000. Its most prominent buildings are the factories producing nitrogen and artificial fertilizers, but Puławy has much more to offer than these; its name has passed into Polish national history as a symbol of Polish political and cultural sovereignty. Around 1800 Izabela Czartoryska, the wife of the enlightened Prince Adam Czartoryski, turned Puławy into a great patriotic cultural centre, a meeting place for the best scholars, writers and artists. She founded a museum for 'National Remembrance', the first Polish museum and the nucleus of the later Czartoryski Museum in Kraków. The court theatre of the Czartoryskis was one of the best and most famous in Poland. The centre of the complex is the *Pałac Czartoryskich (Czartoryski Palace)*, built on the model of an Italian villa to a design by Tylman van Gameren in 1676–9. It was later modified several times: in 1722–36 by Johann Sigismund Deibel and Karl Meyer, and in 1788–1801 by Chrystian Piotr Aigner. Its present Late Neoclassical appearance is due to two further remodellings, in 1840–44 by Józef Górecki and in 1858 by Julian Ankiewicz, who transformed the palace into a three-storey building with corner pavilions and an arcaded gallery at the front. The rooms inside were treated in the Neoclassical or Gothic Revival manner. After 1790 the *Pałac Marynki (Marynka Palace)*, a rectangular, single-storey building, was erected under the direction of Aigner in the southeastern part of the park. Its façade is articulated by pilasters, with a four-column portico and a salon with a semicircular projection on the garden front.

Izabela Czartoryska was responsible for laying out the *Park Krajobrazowy (Landscape*

*Puławy, Temple of the
Sibyl, 19th-century
lithograph*

Garden) in which many Romantic buildings were erected, mainly by Aigner, between 1788 and 1810. Particularly noteworthy are the Neoclassical *Świątynia Sybilli (Temple of the Sibyl)* (1798–1801), built in the form of a rotunda with Corinthian columns after the model of the Temple of the Sybil at Tivoli, and the *Dom Gotycki (Gothic House)* of 1809, square, two storeys, with a gallery of pointed arches and a colonnade portico.

To the north of Puławy, the village of **Gołąb** is worth visiting for its *Kościół Farny śś. Floriana i Katarzyny (Parish Church of St Florian and St Catherine)*, a Late Renaissance building erected in 1628–36. It is notable chiefly for its exterior, which is characterized by

543

the contrast between the brick walls articulated by pilasters and arcades, and the stone or stucco elements, ornamental window surrounds, and gables decorated with obelisks and volutes. Between the towers on the west front is a doorway whose fantastic surround is linked to the windows above. In the cemetery beside the church is the *Kaplica Loretańska (Loreto Chapel)*, a distant imitation of the Casa Santa at Loreto, created in 1634–8 by the future Chancellor Jerzy Ossoliński. Ossoliński was a devout, Jesuit-educated opponent of the religious toleration that had been characteristic of Poland in the previous century; the Loreto Chapel, typical of such Counter-Reformation shrines, is an expression of his desire to revive the power of Catholicism in Poland.

Not far from Gołąb, on the other side of the Vistula is the town of *Czarnolas*, the beloved home of Jan Kochanowski. It now has a museum commemorating the great poet of the Polish Renaissance. In the other direction, the town of **Kock** was famous as a centre of Hasidism, and was the seat of the Morgenstern dynasty of tzaddiks. Their house is still standing, and the grave of tzaddik Menachel Mendel Morgenstern in the cemetery still draws many pilgrims. The town also has a monument to Bereł Joselewicz, a Jewish colonel in Kościuszko's army.

Opole Lubelskie – Lubartów – Czemierniki – Puchaczów – Kraśnik

The voivodship of Lublin has a number of churches of considerable art-historical interest. At **Opole Lubelskie**, southwest of Lublin, the *Kościół Wniebowzięcia Najświętszej Marii Panny (Church of the Assumption)* was built in 1650–75. Its walls and vaults are decorated with Late Baroque paintings: the Assumption in the chancel, Christ in Majesty in the nave, and the Legend of the Cross in the north chapel, painted by Antoni Dębicki. Among the paintings the portrait of the wojewoda Jan Tarło (1744) is noteworthy.

At **Lubartów**, to the north of Lublin, the *Kościół św. Anny (Church of St Anne)* is (with Włodowa and Chełm) one an unusual group of Late Baroque centrally planned churches dating from the second third of the 18th century, inspired by Austrian architecture and designed by Paolo Antonio Fontana. In all these churches the central element of the sophisticated architectural composition is an octagonal nave, approximately elliptical in shape. The west front is flanked by two widely separated towers. The interior (*c.* 1738) has Rococo decoration.

Just west of Lubartów, the Zamoyski palace at *Kozłówka* is a magnificent Baroque structure begun in 1735 by Paolo Antonio Fontana and extended by Jan Heurich in 1899-1904. Its furnishings and paintings are still in situ. It also houses an extraordinary museum of Socialist Realist art.

The *Kościół św. Stanisława (Church of St Stanislas)* at **Czemierniki**, also situated to north of Lublin, was built in 1603–17 and is notable for the Late Renaissance decorative plasterwork by Jan Wolff (1614) on the vaults of the nave and chapels.

At **Puchaczów** to the east of Lublin, the Late Baroque *Kościół Wniebowzięcia Najświętszej Marii Panny (Church of the Assumption)* has an unusual, highly curved façade with a projecting tower in the middle.

The Late Gothic *church*, also dedicated to the Assumption, at **Kraśnik**, on the road to Sandomierz, south of Lublin, has three large paintings from the workshop of Tommaso Dolabella (*c.*1627) commemorating the victory over the Turks at Lepanto. The musician Jan of Lublin was a canon at Kraśnik; his famous 'Tabulatura', which fills 260 pages, is one of the most important sources of 16th-century organ music.

Sandomierz – Opatów – Tarłów – Ujazd – Koprzywnica – Staszów – Rytwiany – Baranów Sandomierski

On the edge of the Małopolska Plateau, a few kilometres south of the confluence of the San and the Vistula, lies **Sandomierz**, a town where the harmony of landscape, architecture and art is almost as beautiful as Kazimierz Dolny.

The settlement at Sandomierz was granted the municipal laws of Magdeburg by the Piast prince Leszek Czarny around 1244. The memory of two catastrophes in the town's history is still kept alive by the inhabitants: the repeated attacks of the Tatars in the 13th century, and the devastation wrought in the 17th century by the army of King Charles X Gustavus of Sweden. The heyday of Sandomierz was the period of the Jagiellonians and the Polish-Lithuanian Union. The trade in grain and timber on the Vistula was thriving, and a number of major secular and ecclesiastical buildings were erected, which made Sandomierz the most beautiful town in Małopolska after Kraków.

At the heart of the town are the market square and the historic town hall, while to the south of the town centre stands the *Kościół Katedralny Narodzenia Najświętszej Marii Panny (Cathedral of the Nativity of the Virgin)*, built in 1360–82 on the initiative of Kazimierz III Wielki on the site of an earlier Romanesque church of 1191. The Baroque façade was added in 1670. The interior has Gothic cross-rib vaults with beautiful sculptural decorations on the piers and bosses, including the coats of arms of the provinces of the Kingdom of Poland. The walls of the choir are covered with Ruthenian painting (*c.*1430, see pages 141–2), showing scenes from the cycles of the Life of the Virgin and the Life of Christ, figures of Evangelists and saints. The rich furnishings include the Late Baroque marble high altar (1755–6), allegorical figures on the piers (1770–76, by Maciej Polejowski of Lwów), a Baroque organ gallery and the organ itself (1684–97, by Andrzej Nitrowski), Early Baroque choir stalls, Renaissance tomb slabs and Baroque funerary monuments. The early 18th-century paintings in the side aisles show the massacre of the inhabitants of Sandomierz by the Tatars in 1259, and the blowing up of the castle by the Swedes in 1656. The restored *castle* can in fact be seen from the cathedral, as can the *Dom Długosza (Długosz House)* (1476–8), once the home of Poland's first great historian Jan Długosz (1415–80) (see page 87) and now the Diocesan Museum, and finally the former *Kolegium Jezuitów (Jesuit College)*, also called the Collegium Gostomianum after the wojewoda Hieronym Gostomski, who founded it in 1602; one range survives from 1605–15.

On a little hill to the southwest of the cathedral stands another of the town's architect-

VISTUL

*The destruction of Sandomierz by troops of King Charles X Gustavus of Sweden,
engraving, 1656 (detail)*

ural gems, the *Kościół Dominikański św. Jakuba (Dominican Church of St James)*. The
Late Romanesque church is the earliest brick-built basilica in Poland and the most
important example in Central Europe of the architecture of the mendicant orders, who
settled in the Polish towns in the second and third quarters of the 13th century. The most
impressive feature of its exterior is the famous Late Romanesque doorway in the centre of
the west front. This entrance with trefoil arches and decoration composed of shaped bricks
was reconstructed in 1907–8. Attached to the south side of the choir is the surviving east
range of the former monastery. Also attached to the choir is the Late Renaissance chapel
commemorating the 49 Dominicans killed by the Tatars in 1260; the interior has Early
Baroque plasterwork dating from 1642.

Further west in the town we come to the Gothic *Kościół Farny św. Pawła (Parish
Church of St Paul)* which was altered in the mid-17th century and again in 1706–9. The
simple exterior contrasts with the rich architectural decoration and carvings of the interior;
broad pilasters with stylized capitals support a vault covered with typical Lublin plasterwork. The church bells, in a freestanding bell tower at the gate to the graveyard, are among
the oldest in Poland (1314 and 1389).

The market place, which slopes gently down to the east, is rich in beautiful architecture,
and is dominated by the sturdy Renaissance brick *Town Hall* built around the middle of
the 16th century and incorporating an almost square tower of the 14th century. It is
surmounted by a splendid attic with a broad frieze of arcading. Above this are round

openings alternating with small consoles, and then a cresting consisting of vertical elements, volutes and stone masks. The tower on the west side, which begins with a square plan and then becomes octagonal, dates from the second quarter of the 17th century; the helm was only added in 1873. Of the houses in the market square the most interesting is No. 10, the *Kamienica Oleśnickich (Oleśnicki House)*, erected in 1770–80 on old foundations and given a Late Baroque façade. Underground passages link the building with the town hall.

To the north the historic Old Town ends at the *Brama Opatowska (Opatów Gate)*, a Gothic brick building of the 14th century, square with five storeys, and surmounted by a 16th-century Renaissance attic.

Opatów Gate also leads to the *Kościół św. Michała (Church of St Michael)*, which until 1903 belonged to Benedictine nuns. The most important of the carved Baroque furnishings (1686–92) is the pulpit (1694–5), which is made in the form of a genealogical tree of the Benedictine Order, based on the Tree of Jesse iconography, with various Church Fathers and Benedictine saints standing on the branches of a tree-trunk growing out of St Benedict. On the west side of the church stands the former convent, which since 1903 has housed a seminary. Some of the Holy Cross Sermons discovered at St Petersburg in 1890 once belonged to this Benedictine nunnery. They are based on a 13th century original and are some of the earliest documented literature in Polish; their archaic language is a valuable source for the study of Old Polish. Sandomierz and its art treasures are threatened by geological faults; in 1967 a serious landslide carried away a part of the Vistula embankment; the safety measures that were then brought into force have so far prevented more serious calamities.

One of the most beautiful Romanesque churches in southeast Poland is at **Opatów**, a little town west of Sandomierz, which however has been known since 1282 as *Magna Civitas Opatów* ('the great city of Opatów). The *Kościół Farny św. Marcina (Parish Church of St Martin)*, originally a collegiate church, was built around the middle of the 12th century, in the greatest period of the Romanesque in Poland. This was when the splintering of the state into princedoms strengthened the position of the feudal and ecclesiastical hierarchy. Dukes and church dignitaries expressed their power by the establishment of richly endowed foundations. The cathedrals and monastic churches, as well as the colleges of canons, all took on more magnificent, even monumental forms. This three-aisled basilica is typically grand, with a four-bay nave, a west front with two towers, an eastern transept with two smaller side apses, and a square chancel which originally also had an eastern apse. Several parts of the Romanesque decoration remain: the main doorway, double windows in the south tower, a frieze on the façade and some damaged imposts of the arcade piers.

A thorough remodelling took place in the first half of the 16th century. It included the creation of a Late Gothic net vault in the nave, the erection of the stepped gables of the chancel and transept, and the building of new doorways. The Baroque helms of the towers and the ridge-turret date from 1734. Of the furnishings inside, the most interesting are a group of Renaissance tombs of the Szydłowiecki family, made in 1533–40. Chancellor Krzysztof Szydłowiecki was the most important political figure after the king, and was also a major patron of the arts, supporting among others the Cistercian monk Stanisław Samosztrelnik, the leading painter of the period. The tomb of Szydłowiecki on the north wall of the north transept (1532–4), was cast in bronze by Bernard Zanobi de Gianotis and Giovanni Cini, who were among the Italian artists brought to the court on the Wawel in Kraków by Zygmunt I Stary. For the Szydłowiecki tomb they adapted the design of the tomb of Kazimierz IV Jagiellończyk at Kraków, without its architectural frame, but with a strong emphasis on the attributes of the status and power of the deceased: his sword and lance with pennant. The remarkable feature of the tomb is the *Lament Opatowski (Lament of Opatów)* (plate 67), a bronze bas-relief on the side of the tomb chest, showing the town mourning the death of the Chancellor. In the upper part of the tomb is a monument to Szydłowiecki's son Zygmunt, who died in childhood. On the west wall elements from various different tombs have been assembled, including the effigy of Anna Szydłowiecka, the daughter of the Chancellor, the tomb of her infant brother Ludwik Mikołaj (possibly by Bartolommeo Berrecci), and a plaque with an inscription from the tomb of Krzysztof Szydłowiecki.

On the opposite bank of the Opatówka stands the *Klasztor Bernardynów (Bernardine Monastery)* with its *Kościół Wniebowzięcia Najświętszej Marii Panny (Church of the Assumption)*, a building dating from 1751–65 with an harmonious Rococo interior; particularly impressive is the high altar by Maciej Polejowski. He was one of a group of sculptors from Lwów, whose work is also found in other Polish towns such as Chełm, Przemyśl, Leżajsk and Dukla.

The *Kościół Farny św. Trójcy (Parish Church of the Holy Trinity)* at **Tarłow** is interesting mainly for the rich plasterwork decoration of its chancel vault and the two domed chapels at the east end. The south chapel (the funerary chapel of the Oleśnickis) contains realistic plaster reliefs (mid-17th century) in the Sarmatian manner, showing Death appearing to representatives of various social stations and trades, and different generations.

At **Ujazd**, to the west of Sandomierz, stand the mighty ruins of the Mannerist *Zamek Krzyżtopór (Krzyżtopór Castle)*, built for the wojewoda of Sandomierz, Krysztof Ossolinski, by his architect Lorenzo Muretto (known in Polish as Wawrzyniec Senes after his birthplace, Sent in the Grisons). It was sacked only a few years later in 1655–7 by soldiers of the Swedish army, but although it is now roofless, most of the outer walls are still standing. On either side of the entrance giant bas-reliefs make a punning reference to the name of the castle: a big cross (Polish: *krzyż*, a symbol of the Counter-Reformation) and an axe (Polish: *topór*) form the cross-axe in the Ossoliński coat of arms. The symmetry and complicated ground-plan of the building are striking. The castle is surrounded by pentagonal fortifications corresponding to its own plan; the large inner courtyard is trapeze-shaped, and within the palace itself is another, smaller courtyard in the shape of an ellipse. Enough of the wall decoration survives to show the grandiose mingling of Roman and Venetian motifs. The articulation of the walls is based on a double row of triumphal arches, with quatrefoils that originally contained paintings glorifying the Ossoliński family.

The former *Opactwo Cystersów (Cistercian Abbey)* at **Koprzywnica** is one of the unified group of four Cistercian monasteries in Małopolska (the others being Jędrzejów, see page 525; Wąchock, see page 528, and Sulejów, see page 531). The church, a Late Romanesque basilica of ashlar, with a nave of four bays and a transept, was built together with the monastery in 1218–38, probably by an Italian workshop led by Master Simon. The interior has Romanesque round-arched arcades and an Early Gothic cross-rib vault on pointed transverse arches. The façade with its projecting frontispiece, and the tower over the crossing with its helm, are both Late Baroque (1770–90, by the architect and priest Józef Karśnicki).

Inside, the Gothic wallpaintings are impressive, and there is a painting in the north aisle of St Wenceslas and various bishops. The rich furnishings include ten side altars and the splendid high altar with a painting of the Assumption (1645) by Bartolomäus Strobel the Younger, an artist in royal service.

In the parish church of **Staszów** west of Sandomierz, the *Kaplica Tęczyńskich (Tęczyński Chapel)* is – like the Myszkowski Chapel in the Dominican Church in Kraków (see page 464) – a product of the famous workshops of Pińczów near Kielce (see page 526) dating from 1610–18. It is a square building with slightly sloping marble-clad walls with all-over rustication and a dome resting on an octagonal drum and surmounted by a decorated stone lantern with carved stonework.

At **Rytwiany**, not far from Staszów, stands the *Kościół Zwiastowania Najświętszej Marii Panny (Parish Church of the Annunciation)*. Until 1819 the church was part of a

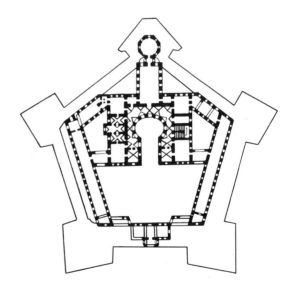

Ujazd, plan of Krzyżtopór Castle

Camaldulensian Monastery, a Counter-Reformation foundation of the Tęczyński family. Three ranges of the former monastic buildings are still standing. The Early Baroque church was begun in 1624 and both its interior decoration and façade were completed by 1655. The church is noteworthy for the logical simplicity of its ground-plan, which is characteristic of Italian architecture of the Camaldulensian Order, and the richness of the plaster decoration of the interior. It is a rectangular, closed building with a nave and side-chambers (sacristy and chapter house) suggesting a basilican arrangement. All the façades are symmetrically designed with doorways in the middle and two rows of windows in two storeys. The gilded plasterwork on the walls of the nave and choir is articulated by herm pilasters with an unbroken entablature.

Heading southwards from Sandomierz on the road to Tarnów and Rzeszów, we reach **Baranów Sandomierski** with the magnificent Late Renaissance *Pałac Leszczyńskich (Leszczyński Palace)* (plate 64). Construction of this residence for the magnate Rafał Leszczyński was begun in 1569, probably to a design by Santi Gucci, and completed in 1606.

The palace quadrangle is surrounded on three sides by ranges, while on the fourth is a wall with a central tower, which serves as the entrance with steps leading to the courtyard; at the corners of the palace are four cylindrical towers. The exterior façades are unarticulated; the wall is surmounted by a decorated attic, which acts as a transition to the gables of the side-ranges. The wall and the side ranges have two-storey open arcaded passages with columns, and at the back of the tower is a double flight of steps, also with arches on columns. The most important part of Tylman van Gameren's modernization of the interiors after 1683 was the creation of the plasterwork and painted decoration of the apartments. After a fire in 1849 the palace was rebuilt; the most recent restoration work was completed in 1965. Today the palace contains among other things a *Museum of the Sulphur Industry* installed by the sulphur-processing firm at Tarnobrzeg, who were generous donors for the restoration and maintenance of the building.

Chełm – Włodawa – Uchanie – Zamość – Roztoczański – Bełżec

Chełm is only an hour by car from Lublin. It is the administrative capital of the least populous voivodship in Poland and is just 23 km from the Ukrainian border on the River Bug.

There has been a town here for nearly a thousand years. From 1387 it belonged to the Polish crown, and in 1392 Władysław II Jagiełło granted it a town charter with the municipal laws of Magdeburg. Today there are few visible signs that Chełm, like many other eastern Polish towns, was until 1939 a home (Chełm means 'home') of eastern Jewry. The Jews of Chełm were the traditional butt of Jewish humour. Like the men of Gotham they were proverbially stupid. 'The sages of Chełm began to argue about what was more important to the world: the sun or the moon. The reigning wise man then ruled: 'The moon *must* be more important than the sun, because without the light of the moon our nights would be so dark we could not see anything. The sun, however, shines only by day – which is when we don't need it.' Nearly all the Jewish citizens were murdered at the *Sobibór* death camp on the Bug about 45 km to the north of the town. The camp was set up in April 1942, the third, after Chełmno nad Nerem and Bełżec, to be specially designed for systematic murder. In October 1943 Sobibór was the scene of revolt by the Jewish prisoners of Camp I; three hundred were killed but three hundred managed to escape and many joined the partisan Units. A monument marks the site of the camp, which was razed to the ground by the retreating SS. About 250,000 Jews were killed here.

Until their removal and dispersal after the Second World War, another important group in Chełm were the Łemkowie, a Ukrainian people who lived in this region (see page 562).

On 21 July 1944 the 'Polish Committee of National Liberation' was established here before moving to Lublin, where it became the first post-war Communist government.

The *Kościół Farny (Parish Church)*, which until 1864 belonged to the Piarist Order, is a prominent landmark. Designed by Paolo Antonio Fontana and built in 1753–63, it is the most impressive of his group of Late Baroque centrally planned churches in the Lublin area (see page 544). The towers are attached at the sides of the nave, which has the form of an elliptical octagon; the articulation of the west front is characterized by the surrounds of the windows and niches, the pilasters and broken entablature. Inside the four chapels are linked by archways to form an ambulatory. The walls and vaults have illusionistic painting by Joseph Mayer (*c.* 1758): in the nave are scenes from the Life of the Virgin, in the choir scenes from the Acts of the Apostles, and in the chapels episodes from the Life of St Joseph Calasanz, the founder of the Piarists. The Rococo furnishings (1774–81) are mostly the work of the woodcarver Michał Filewicz. The 18th-century Greek Catholic Cathedral (now a Roman Catholic church), also perhaps by Fontana, has a fine façade and is attached to a Basilian monastery. The former chalk mines, tunnelled under Chełm over the centuries, can still be visited.

About 50 km north of Chełm lies **Włodawa**, a peaceful border town where time has stood still. Here timber houses still predominate. Here too is another of Fontana's Late Baroque churches with elliptical naves (see above and page 544), *Kościół Farny św. Ludwika (Parish Church of St Louis)*, whose façade is even more richly articulated than that of the church at Chełm; the middle part is surmounted by a gable with pilasters, and the niches, windows and doorways have a variety of surrounds. The church was built by Fontana in 1739–52, and the Rococo painted decoration inside is by Gabriel Sławiński and Antoni Dobrzeniewski.

On the other side of the large market place stands the Neoclassical *Cerkiew (Orthodox Church)*. With its spacious *Synagogue* (1767), together with a rabbinical school, the town is the biggest surviving Jewish intellectual centre outside Kraków.

At **Uchanie**, halfway between Chełm and Zamość, the *Kościół Farny Wniebowzięcia Najświętszej Marii Panny (Parish Church of the Assumption)* contains two double-decker Mannerist tombs, that of Arnulf and Stanisław Uchański by the workshop of Santi Gucci (c.1590), and another, dating from the early 17th century and more ornate, with alabaster effigies of Paweł and Anna Uchański (plate 65), by the master responsible for the Firlej Chapel at Bejsce (see page 505). The church's façade has rich plaster decoration with bands of interlace, plant and animal motifs in the window surrounds, in the spandrels above the arcades and in the frieze of the entablature. The same decoration continues inside, especially in the vaults with a network of ornamented mouldings surrounding large panels (rosettes, armorial cartouches). Together with the Firlej Chapel in the Dominican church at Lublin (see page 537), this is one of the best works of Jan Wolff.

Zamość, about 80 km southeast of Lublin, is a pattern-book example of European town-planning in the Late Renaissance period. Zamość was the first town of this type in Poland and one of the earliest in Europe to be planned and built as a complete work of art. It was a new town, laid out and constructed from the ground up, and developed into the ideal form of community life as envisaged by some Italian Renaissance theorists.

Its founder and patron, Jan Zamoyski (1542–1605), the Chancellor and Poland's leading statesman in the reign of Stefan Batory (1576–86), intended that the town should fulfill all the urban functions which he regarded as important: it was to be a commercial centre, a stronghold, a religious centre and a cultural focus – a magnate's residence town par excellence. Zamoyski entrusted this commission to the architect Bernardo Morando of Padua, who planned and directed the building work until his death in 1610. He presented his plans in 1579, the surveys were carried out in 1581–3, and by 1587 the fortifications were completed. Then work continued until the beginning of the 17th century on Zamoyski's palace, the collegiate church, academy, arsenal, town hall, non-Catholic churches and the first stone houses. In the years that followed the town was soon flourishing. Besides

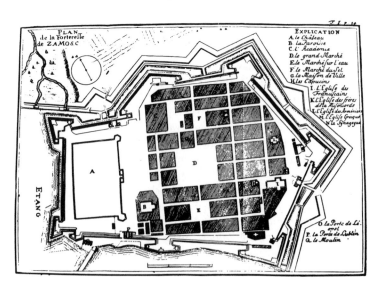

Zamość, plan of
the town,
engraving, 1704

native Poles, Armenians, Greeks, Jews, Germans and Italians also moved to Zamość. Trade, learning, poetry and the theatre flourished, but after the 17th century Zamość never again achieved the same importance.

Later Zamoyskis left their mark too. Jan's heir, Tomasz (1594–1638) made the town a centre of oriental studies, and encouraged the manufacture here of Persian carpets. Andrzej (1716–92), like the others Chancellor of Poland, was the first nobleman to enfranchise his serfs. Another member of the family has recently been made Mayor.

The massive fortress withstood the Swedish attack in 1655, and was also an important defensive point in the Napoleonic Wars (1812–13). As part of Congress Poland the town expanded, and in 1821 became the property of the state. The demolition of the fortress in 1866 meant that Zamość was able to expand.

In the Second World War Zamość of course did not escape Nazi atrocities. During the German occupation three prisoner-of-war camps were established here, in which around 20,000 people died, many of them executed in the arsenal, called the Rotunda (see below). As part of the Nazis' Germanization policy for the region many Polish families were deported from Zamość (which was to be renamed Himmlerstadt) and the surrounding villages, and German families were moved in.

The early 17th-century houses around the *Rynek Wielki (Great Market Place)*, a square with sides 100 metres long, and on the Rynek Solny (Salt Market), ul. Staszica and ul. Ormiańska are impressive, with arcaded passages, decorated window surrounds and doorways, and with splendid plasterwork in the vaults and ceilings (plate 68). The finest and best preserved building is one of the Armenian houses on the north side of the market place: the *Kamienica Pod Aniołem (Angel House)*, No. 26 (1). It was originally built with a

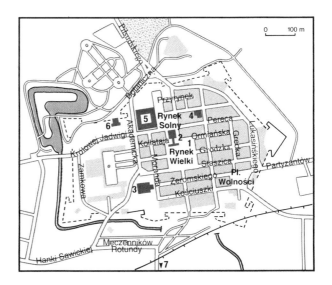

Zamość
1 *Kamienica Pod Aniołem
  (Angel House, No. 26)*
2 *Ratusz (Town Hall)*
3 *Kościół Kolegiacki
  (Collegiate Church)*
4 *Synagoga (Synagogue)*
5 *Akademia (Academy)*
6 *Brama Lubelska (Lublin
  Gate)*
7 *Rotunda*

553

Zamość, Collegiate Church, original elevation of the west front

single storey above an arcade, with an attic. This was replaced by a second storey in the 18th century and the building lavishly decorated with rich plasterwork decoration consisting of orientalizing plant and animal motifs and a figure of the Angel Gabriel. In the interior the pairs of windows are framed by stone reliefs, and there are admirable doorways, wooden ceilings and friezes. Sadly some of the other houses, for example in ul. Kołłątaja, are showing signs of decay, since shortage of money has put a halt to renovation work.

At *Rynek Wielki 37*, on 25 December 1870, Rosa Luxemburg, the future co-founder of the German Communist Party, was born in the family of a well-to-do Jewish businessman. The Luxemburgs moved three years later to Warsaw.

The *Town Hall* (2), erected on the north side of the market place in 1639–51 under the direction of Jan Jaroszewicz and Jan Wolff on the foundations of a smaller building (1591–1600) by Morando, has a tall, slender tower, octagonal at the top, with a Baroque helm added in 1770, which dominates the town. The main front has a monumental double stairway resting on arches, which dates from 1767–8 and was originally built with a small guardhouse attached. The attic was reconstructed in 1937–8.

The *Kościół Kolegiacki Zmartwychwstania i św. Tomasza (Collegiate Church of the Resurrection and St Thomas)* (3) is considered by Polish art historians to be the finest Late Renaissance church in the country. It was built in 1587–98 and its façade was given a Neoclassical remodelling at the beginning of the 19th century. The three-aisled interior contains important Mannerist sculptures and plasterwork, and the coffering and stucco work of the barrel vault are based on designs by Bernardo Morando. The Zamoyski Chapel in the south aisle contains the black marble and bronze tomb slab of Jan Zamoyski, the town's founder.

The former *Synagogue* (4) in ul. Bazyliańska, used as a library since its restoration after the war, is a Late Renaissance building dating from 1610–20. The tops of the vaults, lunettes and niches in the great hall have lavish Lublin-style plasterwork. The stone torah-shrine dates from before 1650.

One of Zamoyski's most interesting initiatives was the founding of a humanist *Academy* (5) in 1595. It was intended to educate a civic elite – not a university, but a sort of continuing secondary school. The Academy's building, which now houses the grammar school, stands in ul. Akademicka. A plaque on the façade mentions the man to whom Zamoyski entrusted his new foundation: the Renaissance poet Szymon Szymonowic (1558–1629), whose place in the history of Polish literature rests on his *Sielanki* ('Idylls') published in 1614, bucolic verse which is rendered with a sharp ear for the real voices of peasant life.

Opposite the Academy stands the old *Brama Lubelska (Lublin Gate)* (6).

The *Rotunda* (7), a 19th-century gunpowder magazine in the park on ul. Wyspiańskiego, is now a museum commemorating the terrible events here during the war. In the Rotunda between 1939 and 1944 almost 8,000 people were killed in the Nazi terror.

The **Roztoczański National Park** can easily be reached from Zamość and is of great natural beauty. The extensive forests of fir, beech and spruce were already protected areas before the Second World War; rare fauna and flora are still to be found here.

The large death camp at **Bełżec** (42 km from Zamość on the road to Lwów), where 600,000 people were killed, was entirely destroyed by the Germans in the spring of 1943. There is a monument (1963).

Timber churches of Tomaszów Lubelski, Hrebenne and Radruż

For many centuries timber was the Polish building material par excellence. Wood was not used only by the peasantry however: many members of the szlachta built their grander houses in wood too. Małopolska was the region of Poland where the most architecturally important wooden buildings, especially churches, have survived. Until the late 17th century the builders of these timber churches kept to the Late Gothic forms, with narrow roofs, though these were enriched with Baroque caps. Later, in the 18th century, they imitated stone architecture and adopted double-tower façades and crossing-domes. The timber Greek-Catholic (Uniate) churches along the eastern border of Małopolska remained largely unaffected by subsequent artistic trends.

The *Kościół Farny (Parish Church)* at **Tomaszów Lubelski**, to the south of Zamość, is one such Baroque wooden church; it dates from 1727. It has the characteristic façade with two towers and is surmounted by a broad cornice with curved coping, which runs round the church and separates off the upper part of the towers with their onion-domes. Inside are slender piers linked by arches dividing the nave from the aisles, into which trapezoidal wall projections are built. The furnishings are Late Baroque.

At **Hrebenne**, between Zamość and Lwów, a border post between Poland and the Ukraine was opened some years ago. Here the *Kościół św. Mikołaja (Church of St Nicholas)* (plate 63), formerly used by a Uniate congregation but now of the Latin Rite, is worth a visit. It consists of three square parts, the larger one being the nave and the smaller ones the sanctuary and vestibule, each surmounted by octagonal drums and domes. The walls and roofs are articulated by three sets of eaves: one runs round the whole church halfway up the wall, a second one is formed by the roofs of the three parts of the building, and a third is at the lower rim of the domes. Sadly, the original shingled eaves and domes have now been replaced by metal, and the shingles on parts of the outside walls by plain boarding, depriving the exterior of some of its charm.

Another former Greek Catholic church, the *Kościół św. Paraskewy (Church of St Paraskeva)* at **Radruż** just on the Ukrainian border, and already in the voivodship of Przemyśl, is a fine example of the timber architecture of the Uniate Christians. It too consists of three square parts: nave, sanctuary and vestibule. Roofed passageways, open at the side, run round the church. The sanctuary and vestibule have pitched roofs, while over the nave is a pyramidal roof with a little round turret.

Rzeszów – Łańcut – Leżajsk – Przeworsk – Jarosław – Przemyśl

Rzeszów, situated on the east-west route from Kraków via Przemyśl and Lwów to the Black Sea, is, after Kraków, the largest town in southern Poland. After the First Partition in 1772 this formed part of Galicia, a land of the Habsburg Crown. The traditional appearance of the town has been much changed by wartime destruction and the development of large industrial complexes. Two former synagogues, the ruined *Small Synagogue* dating from the early 17th century, and the *Great Synagogue* built in 1705–10, together with a monument, recall the city's vanished Jewish population and the big ghetto in which they had to live. Rzeszów is a more modern town than Tarnów or Przemyśl and has less of artistic interest.

The former Bernardine church (1624–9), the *Kościół Wniebowzięcia Najświętszej Marii Panny (Church of the Assumption)* was founded by the castellan Mikołaj Spytek Ligęza, the then owner of the town. In the niches of the side walls of the high altar are alabaster figures representing members of the Ligęza family by Johann Pfister. The Gothic *Kościół Farny (Parish Church)* is notable above all for the Renaissance tombs in the chancel. The Baroque buildings of the former *Klasztor Pijarów (Piarist Monastery)* now house the Rzeszów regional museum. To the south of the town, on the edge of the Wisłok valley, stands a *castle* of the Lubomirski family, which dates from the 17th century and has fortifications (bastions, moats) laid out on the Italian model.

A few kilometres to the east of Rzeszów, in the midst of an English park, stands the palace of **Łańcut**, the most important architectural monument in this region. It was built in 1629–41 to designs by Maciej Trapola for Stanisław Lubomirski, who had acquired the estate from the heirs of the notorious noble bandit, Stanisław Stadnicki ('the Devil of Łancut'). The Lubomirskis were eventually succeeded by the Potockis. Built on a rectangular plan with four corner towers, the palace as it appears today is the result of several remodellings in the 18th and 19th centuries. The first alterations in 1771–86 for Princess Izabela Lubomirska (see Wilanów, page 219 ff) involved the erection of the second storey, and in 1795–1807 the addition of wings north and south of the façade, the north wing containing the library. At the end of the 18th century Izabela Lubomirska's son-in-law, the writer Jan Potocki, a great traveller, anthropologist, political thinker and pioneer of Slavonic studies, best known as the author of the fantastic novel *The Saragossa Manuscript*, lived here for a short time, and after the French Revolution Łańcut was briefly the home of Louis XVIII. A second major remodelling took place in 1889–1912, when the present neo-Baroque façades were created by the French architects Armand Beauqué and Albert Pio. The palace and its collections survived the First World War intact and remained the property of the Potockis until 1944, when Count Alfred Potocki packed its most valuable contents into fourteen freight cars and took them off to Vienna. Before he left, the Count also set up signs that read 'National Museum', and as a result the palace escaped damage and looting. It has since been very well restored. Of the many richly decorated interiors some merit particular attention: the Ballroom which rises through two storeys, the Sculpture Gallery (late 18th century) with illusionistic paintings of a vine-covered trellis, the Cabinet of Mirrors (mid-18th century) with its Rococo panelling, the Chinese Apartments (c.1800), the Pompeian Room (c.1780), the apartments of Izabela Lubomirska, and the Theatre built in 1792 (with a stage modernized in 1911 by the Viennese architects Ferdinand Fellner and Hermann Helmer). The palace contains a rich collection of paintings, sculpture (an important Canova), porcelain, glass and furniture (much of it assembled since the departure of the Potockis), as well as the *Carriage Museum* in the old riding arena, with carriages, hunting brakes and coaches (many of them once the property of the Potockis), the most extensive collection of this kind in Europe. The stables nearby now house a museum of icons.

On the southeast side of the palace is a large *Orangery* built in 1799–1802 by Chrystian Piotr Aigner, who also designed the romantic neo-Gothic *Castle* in the park. Of the 16th-century fortifications, laid out like a five-pointed star, two bastions remain on the western side. The town of Łańcut has a fine *synagogue* built in 1761, of a type that was current in this region in the 17th and 18th centuries: the barrel vaults are supported by four sturdy columns set close together, which also mark the corners of the tabernacle over the bimah. At Łańcut this tabernacle has retained its plasterwork decoration, showing deer flanking the crown of the Torah. Pilgrims still visit the tomb of a famous tzaddik, Reb Hururtz, in the old Jewish cemetery.

At **Leżajsk**, northeast of Łańcut, the *Kościół Zwiastowania Najświętszej Marii Panny (Church of the Annunciation)* is famous for its *organ*, which is probably the finest in Poland and is one of the largest and most ambitious Baroque organs in Europe (plate 66). This mammoth instrument (1678–93, by Jan Głowiński of Kraków) with its 78 stops and nearly 6,000 pipes fills the west wall of the nave and the two aisles. The organ loft and the black-and-gold front of the organ case (completed 1729, by Stanisław Studziński and Jan Głowinski) are covered with an unusually rich ornamental and figural decoration, including a representation of Sobieski's victory over the Turks at Vienna in 1683.

The other furnishings of the church include much woodcarving (there are 13 Rococo altars with fine statues by Antoni Osiński). The choir stalls, with their gnarled shellwork

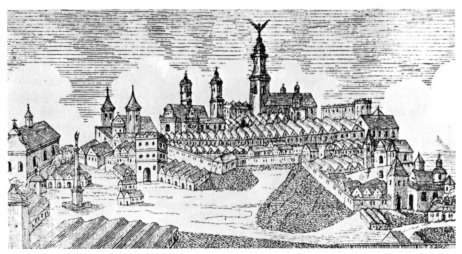

Jarosław in the 17th century, engraving, 1846

decoration, figures and intarsia work, are particularly impressive. The wall and ceiling paintings are by Stanisław Stroiński, and the altarpiece is by Franciczek Lekszycki.

At **Przeworsk** the *Kościół Bernardynów św. Barbary (Bernardine Church of St Barbara)*, a Late Gothic brick building of the late 14th century with an early 17th-century Mannerist gable at the east end, provides another good example of the richness of Baroque church furnishing in the mid-17th century. The cloister in the adjoining monastic buildings contains early 16th-century wall paintings. In the 17th and 18th centuries Przeworsk was famous for its weaving mills and its annual fairs. The Gothic *Kościół Farny (Parish Church)* (1430–33) in ul. Krakowska has fortified walls intended as protection against Tatar raids. In its tower hangs the famous 'Sylvester' bell cast in 1627 and weighing almost three tonnes.

The townscape of **Jarosław** on the River San is dominated by three hills, each surmounted by a monastery. The town is first mentioned in 1152, but was probably founded by Jarosłav, Prince of Kiev (978–1054). It was granted its charter in 1375. In the late middle ages and in the early modern period Jarosław was well-known for its fair, second only to Leipzig, and attracting up to 300,000 people. The *Kościół Na Polu (Church in the Fields)*, built for the Jesuits in 1629–35, but since 1777 a Dominican church, is impressive above all for its Late Baroque east façade on the side fronting the town. Two projecting towers with bevelled corners and concave walls, each crowned by a Baroque helm, flank the centrepiece and are linked by a balustrade. This double-tower façade was doubtless built under the influence of Silesian architects.

The regular trade fairs at Jarosław attracted Italian, Greek and Armenian merchants to the town. Among these was the banking family of Orsetti, whose magnificent patrician residence, *Kamienica Orsettich* in the market place, can be visited. Built after 1581, it has a tripartite loggia and a tall Late Renaissance attic decorated with pilasters, blind arcading, aedicules and volutes.

Przemyśl, which is located just by the present Ukrainian border, also used to be an important trading centre. There was a settlement here in prehistoric times, and after the Second World War the remains of buildings of the early Piast period (a protective rampart, rotunda and ducal residence, *c.*1000) were excavated, as well as the foundations of a 12th-century Romanesque cathedral. In the Habsburg period Przemyśl was a Babel, with twelve languages in regular use, and newspapers published in four of them. Jewish intellectuals in the town who had survived the Nazi terror, played a leading part in the Zionist movement. Przemyśl is also the seat of a bishop and before 1945 of a Uniate bishop, and today is an important cultural centre; a large number of learned and cultural organizations do notable work here, including the Fredreum, Poland's oldest (1869) and most enterprising amateur theatre. It also became a heavily fortified town in 1873, when the Austrians built a massive fortress and extensive defences around Przemyśl to guard against the Russian threat. These were destroyed in the Russian siege of 1914–15 and the fierce fighting that ensued, but fortunately the historic town centre, where the oldest house dates back to the 16th century, survived.

Just off the market place stands the *Kościół Franciszkanów św. Marii Magdaleny (Franciscan Church of St Mary Magdalene)* (1754–78) (colour plate 8), which has an impressive façade with a double stairway with stone figures of the Virgin, St Giles and St Antony on the balustrade of the raised platform. The centrepiece is flanked by groups of three columns, surmounted by a curved gable and flanked by towers with pilasters and simple helms. The painted polychromy with marbling on the exterior has recently been restored. The lavishly furnished interior is also articulated with a projecting cornice and pilasters. On the walls and vaults are illusionistic Rococo paintings by Stanisław Stroiński and others with an elaborate iconographic programme. Woodcarvers from Lwów were responsible for the unified Rococo sculptured programme and furnishings: the high altar built into the apse, the pulpit, organ and wooden capitals of the pilasters.

Further to the west stands the *Kościół Katedralny św. Jana Chrzciciela (Cathedral Church of St John the Baptist)*, originally a Late Gothic hall church with a choir ending in a three-sided apse, built on the site of a 13th-century rotunda between 1470 and 1571. In 1724–44 the church underwent a Baroque remodelling in the course of which the four-bay nave was turned into a pseudo-hall with semi-circular arcades and articulated with pairs of pilasters. Between 1883 and 1913 the choir was re-gothicized. On the vaults of the choir foliage-scroll painted decoration dating from 1549 was discovered in 1972 and restored. Attached to the sides of the eastern bay of the nave are two domed chapels: on the south the Fredro Chapel (1724), Late Baroque, elliptical and decorated with red and black marble; on the north the octagonal Drohojowski Chapel, originally built in 1568, but rebuilt in 1720 with illusionistic Rococo painting probably by Stanisław Stroiński. The furnishings of the cathedral mostly date from between 1883 and 1913, but earlier features

Krasiczyn Castle in the valley of the San

include the alabaster Pietà (known as the 'Jacków Madonna', late 15th century, probably from northern France or the Low Countries) on the Renaissance altarpiece to the right of the choir arch, and the Mannerist tomb of the Fredro family (1589, completed after 1622). Beneath the choir the foundations of the Late Romanesque stone rotunda with a horse-shoe. shaped apse was discovered in 1961.

A few kilometres west of Przemyśl, also in the San valley, stands one of Poland's most beautiful Late Renaissance castles, *Zamek Krasiczyn (Krasiczyn Castle)*, built in 1592–1618 by Galeazzo Appiano and others for the magnatial family of the Krasickis (colour plate 9, plate 62). It was erected on a square ground-plan with an arcaded courtyard and massive round bastions at the corners, with its walls surmounted by decorative attics. Each of the bastions has a name: Szlachecka (Nobility), Królewska (King), Papieska (Pope), Boska (God). The façade is ornamented with sgraffito work depicting Polish kings, and scenes from the history of Ancient Rome and from the Old and New Testaments. Inside the domed God Bastion is the chapel, which has elaborate plasterwork decoration. Badly dam-aged in the Second World War, the castle has been under restoration since the 1950's, but parts of interior can be visited on a guided tour. The castle stands in an extensive and beau-tiful parkland with ancient and unusual trees.

The town of **Krosno**, in the far southeast of Poland, stands on a hill high above the valley of the Wisłok. The town received its charter with the municipal laws of Magdeburg in 1342. Krosno is famous for its glass, which is exported throughout Europe. The *Museum* in the former Bishop's Palace, however, is devoted to an industry which one would hardly expect to find here, but which thrived in this region a hundred years ago. Ignacy Łukasiewicz, the inventor of the paraffin lamp, sank the first oil well in 1854 at Bóbrka near Krosno, and the region to the southwest of Lwów was once the centre of oil extraction in Galicia.

The market place has some fine old 16th- and 17th-century houses with arcaded loggias, including the *Kamienica Wójtowska (Sheriff's House)* with a Renaissance doorway (1550). The pillory in the market has also survived.

The Late Gothic *Kościół św. Trójcy (Church of the Holy Trinity)*, built in 1473–1512, contains many paintings; particularly interesting are the Coronation of the Virgin painted in 1480, and a series of 17th-century paintings on the theme of death from the circle of Tommaso Dolabella.

The Early Baroque funerary chapel of the Oświęcim family in the north aisle of the *Kościół Franciszkanów (Franciscan Church)* is richly decorated with plasterwork (by Giovanni Battista Falconi). In the niches of the chapel are full-length portraits of members of the family including the portraits of Stanisław and Anna Oświęcim (1647–8) by a painter from the circle of Peter Danekerts de Rij. The altar (1650) shows St Stanislas Raising Piotrowin from the Dead. There are some fine Renaissance and Mannerist tombs, the most impressive of which, commemorating Jan Kamieniecki, is by Gian Maria Padovano (1560–73).

The Baroque *Kościół Farny* at **Dukla** near the Slovak border is impressive for its unified Rococo decoration. The illusionistic ceiling paintings from the period around 1775 were probably executed by Antoni Stroiński. Two chapels are divided from the nave by fine Neoclassical grilles with the arms of the family of Crown Marshal Jerzy August Mniszech. In the south chapel stands the tomb of his wife Amalia Mniszech, the white marble effigy lying on a black marble sarcophagus with bronze mounts (1773). The *Dukla Pass* south of the town leads through the picturesque Beskid mountains to Slovakia and beyond. It was the scene of bloody engagements in the First World War, and a ferocious battle in the Second, in which over 60,000 Soviet soldiers fell.

Haczów, south of Krosno, has the largest extant Gothic timber church in Poland, the magnificent *Kościół Wniebowzięcia Najświętszej Marii Panny (Church of the Assumption)*. The square nave and the chancel with its narrower three-sided apse were erected after 1450. Around 1624 the front with a quadrangular tower with sloping walls and surmounted by a bell-chamber, as well as the covered galleries that run all round the church at ground level, were added. On the outside the walls and roofs are covered with shingles, while below the eaves are corbels with decorative carvings, some of them in the form of human masks. The walls inside have paintings of 1494, (a large cycle of scenes of the Passion and the Life of the Virgin and depictions of the saints, in the style of panel painting in Małopolska), arranged in several registers.

The *Kościół Farny (Parish Church)* of **Stara Wieś**, like the church 'Na Polu' at Jarosław, shows the influence of Silesian architects. It was built in 1728–60 as a Paulite church and the Rococo decoration of the interior (c.1760) is probably by the Silesian sculptor Franz Joseph Mangold, whose most famous work is at the university at Wrocław (see page 575). Among the outstanding features are the plaster altarpieces, the pulpit with its rich sculptural decoration, and the furnishings and painted decoration of the sacristy.

In **Sanok** the oldest buildings are the *castle* (12th century) and the *Klasztor Franciszkanów (Franciscan Monastery)*, where the betrothal of King Władysław II Jagiełło took place in 1412. The *Castle Museum* has the largest collection of icons in Poland. Ranging in date from the 14th to the 19th century, most of them come from the Uniate churches of the villages in the vicinity, whose inhabitants were forcibly resettled by the Polish government in 'Operation Vistula' after the suppression of the Ukrainian Resistance in 1947. The *Skansen (Open-Air Museum)* has examples of timber architecture: 19th-century peasants' cottages, farm buildings and beehives characteristic of the two principal ethnic groups in this region: the Bojkowie (Boyks) and Łemkowie (Lemks).

Sanok is also the starting point for walks in the beautiful mountain region of the *Bieszczady* at the junction of three countries: Poland, Slovakia and the Ukraine. The area around the *Solińskie Reservoir* has retained its primeval character with a wide variety of fauna and flora. Some of the most unusual landscape in Europe is to be found in the **Bieszczadzki National Park** which contains bison (also known as wisent), raccoons, wolves, bears, lynxes, Aesculapius vipers, eagles and other rare species. The park is best visited by the 140 km long panoramic route, Pętla Bieszczadzka.

The *Synagogue* at **Lesko** is one of the most interesting in Poland. Built c.1700, and restored in 1980, it has a unique, decorated façade and rich interior wall decorations. The *Jewish Cemetery* opposite is especially evocative.

Reinhold Vetter

Śląsk (Silesia)

Although Silesia remains today a recognizable historical, cultural and geographical region, it is no longer a single political entity. The borders of the old Prussian province of Silesia, which had survived as internal Polish boundaries since the war, were swept away in 1975 as part of a reform of local government. They were partly reinstated with the introduction the new voivodship boundaries in 1999, when most of the historical region of Silesia was divided into the three voivodships of Dolny Śląsk, Opole and Śląsk. (When Poles talk about 'Śląsk', they generally mean Górny Śląsk, or Upper Silesia; the rest of the region is usually referred to by its full name, Dolny Śląsk, or Lower Silesia.) However, some parts of historic Silesia, such as Żagań and Zielona Góra, lie outside these voivodships and are included in our section on Wielkopolska, while other regions formerly belonging to Silesia are now in Germany (part of Oberlausitz, or Upper Lusatia) and the Czech Republic (Hlučinsko and the Olsa region).

Geographically the territory of Silesia is centred on the collection area of the upper and middle Oder and its tributaries. The Oder forms the axis of the region, while the mountains to the south and southwest form a natural frontier. At its southeastern corner Silesia adjoins the Western Beskids (Beskid Śląski), and along its southwestern border the Sudety range, which runs parallel to the Oder and consists mainly of granite and slate. At the foot of the bleak mountainous region is a hilly landscape with fertile stretches of land covered with loess, extending from the Ruda in Upper Silesia to Upper Lusatia.

Even in prehistoric times Silesia's geographical position made it a land through which much traffic passed. Communications with the neighbouring regions were mainly by road, for until the 18th century the Oder was of no great importance as a waterway. In the middle ages a major role was played by the 'High Road', an east-west link, which ran from the Lower Rhine to the Black Sea and passed through the Silesian foothills. At the same time all the roads from the north (Gdańsk, Toruń, Poznań, Szczecin) met at Wrocław, where they crossed the 'High Road' and then entered the passes into Bohemia and Moravia. Already in Roman times the Amber Road ran from the Baltic through Silesia to the south.

Throughout its long history Silesia was frequently a bone of contention between various European powers, or was drawn into their struggle for mastery in other European regions.

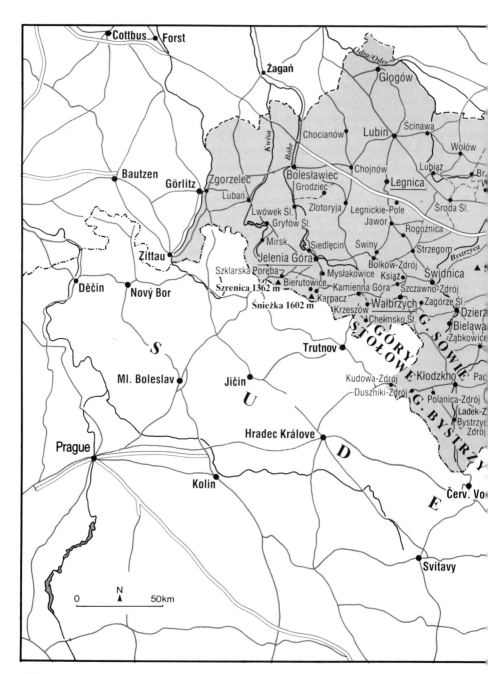

Cottbus • Forst

Żagań

Głogów

Odra/Oder

Chocianów

Lubin

Ścinawa

Wołów

Bautzen

Görlitz

Zgorzelec

Chojnów

Lubiąż

Legnica

Br
W

Luban

Bolesławiec

Grodziec

Lwówek Śl.

Złotoryja

Legnickie-Pole

Środa Śl.

Gryfów Śl.

Jawor

Rogoźnica

Mirsk

Siedlęcin

Świny

Strzegom

Bystrzyca

Zittau

Jelenia Góra

Bolków-Zdrój

Świdnica

Szklarska Poręba

Mysłakowice

Książ

Děčin

Nový Bor

Szrenica 1362 m

Bierutowice

Kamienna Góra

Szczawno-Zdrój

Karpacz

Wałbrzych

Zagórze Śl.

Śnieżka 1602 m

Krzeszów

Chełmsko Śl.

G. SOWIE

Dzierż

Bielawa

Ząbkowice

GÓRY STOŁOWE

Trutnov

Ml. Boleslav

Jičin

Kudowa-Zdrój

Kłodzko

Pac

Duszniki-Zdrój

Polanica-Zdrój

G. BYSTRZY

Ladek-Z
Bystrzyc
Zdrój

Prague

Hradec Králove

D

E

Kolin

Červ. Vo

Svitavy

N

0   50km

S

U

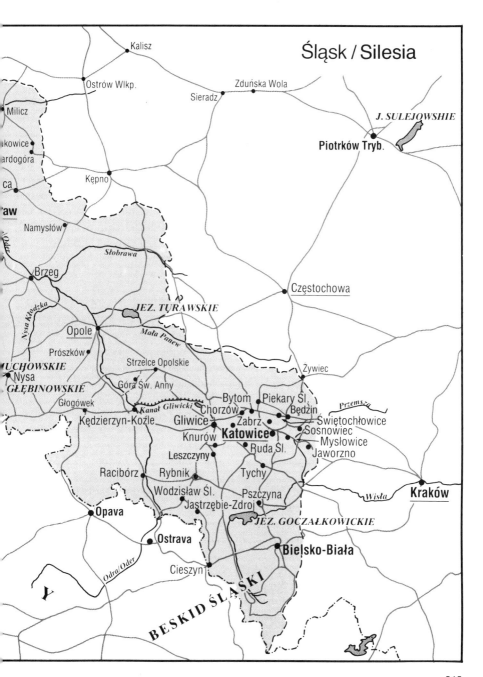

Śląsk / Silesia

Military conflicts, such as the Thirty Years War in the 17th century and the Seven Years War in the 18th had devastating consequences for the land and its people.

Archaeological finds in the Silesian region go back to the Palaeolithic period. Around the middle of the last millennium before Christ Celtic tribes migrating from Bohemia and Moravia settled here. In the 2nd century AD they were driven out by a Germanic group, who are called 'Lugieri' in the classical sources and are now known as the 'Oder-Warthe Group'. From the 6th century Slavic peoples began to settle the land; the peoples listed by the 9th-century writer known as the Bavarian Geographer include the Dedosize, Slensane, Opolane and Golensize; later the Boborane and Trebowane are mentioned in a document of the Emperor Henry IV in 1086. The leading role of the Slensane (or Ślężanie) was eventually reflected in the name given to the whole region: in Latin (and English) Silesia, in Polish Śląsk, and in German Schlesien. By 990 at the latest Slavic Silesia was incorporated into the Polish state which had been established in 966. The bishopric of Wrocław was founded at the time of the creation of an autonomous Polish church province in 1000. Władysław II Wygnaniec (the Exile) (ruled 1138–46) founded an independent Silesian Piast dynasty. Like the rest of Poland Silesia broke up into a number of principalities under various lines of Piast dukes (the Piasts of Cieszyn, of Głogów-Żagań, of Legnica-Brzeg, of Opole, of Wrocław, and others).

Despite the integration of Silesia into the Polish seniorate (see page 16), the Silesian Piast dukes were obliged by Emperor Frederick Barbarossa in 1163 to pay tribute to the Holy Roman Empire. In the subsequent period they became increasingly dependent on Bohemia, and hence on the Holy Roman Empire. In 1336, under pressure from the Emperor Charles IV, King Kazimierz III Wielki finally renounced any Polish claim to Silesia.

It was the Piast dukes themselves who summoned German farmers, merchants, craftsmen, miners and clergy to the country to bring prosperity to Silesia, which was rich in resources but sparsely populated. The first German inroads had already been made in the early 13th century when Duke Henryk Brodaty (the Bearded) and his wife St Jadwiga (Hedwig) encouraged the establishment of Cistercian monasteries from Germany. The new settlers brought with them the German language and German culture. In 1526 Silesia became part of the Habsburg monarchy. The political consequence of this was to limit the power of the princes and to strengthen that of the nobility and the great burghers in the towns; economically Silesia became more dependent on the crown, and at the same time mining, ironworking, glass-blowing and linen weaving experienced a great boom. (Silesian linen, or Sleazie, was noted for its fine, even insubstantial texture – hence, possibly, the English word sleazy.)

Habsburg rule in Silesia also prepared the way for the Counter-Reformation. In the mid-18th century much of Silesia came under Prussian rule as a result of Frederick the Great's success in the various Silesian Wars. The Preliminary Peace of Breslau in 1742 forced the Empress Maria Theresa to give the whole of Silesia to Prussia (except for 'Austrian Silesia', which is now part of the Czech Republic), and the Treaty at Schloss Hubertusburg in 1763 put a final seal on Prussian rule.

The capture of Wrocław by Frederick II in 1757, by an unknown painter

As part of Prussia Silesia was subjected to the rigid administration of an absolutist state, but on the other hand the Stein-Hardenberg reforms at the beginning of the 19th century were to sweep away much Habsburg backwardness.

Silesia experienced the breakneck modernization of the 19th-century German Reich: the building up of major industries, the formation of modern social classes, a population explosion, urbanization, and development of the modern spectrum of political parties. After the First World War Silesia once again became a contentious issue, with the newly revived nations of Poland and Czechoslovakia staking a claim, in particular for the important industrial region of Upper Silesia. In addition three Polish uprisings between 1919 and 1921, the last led by Wojciech Korfanty (1873–1939), had fought for a partition of Upper Silesia. This happened in 1921 when a controversial decision by the League of Nations confirmed a clause in the Treaty of Versailles that forced Germany to cede a considerable part of Upper Silesia to Poland. Hitler seized Upper Silesia in the early days of the Second World War, but this re-Germanization was short-lived. The post-war settlement gave almost all of Silesia (except for the small region in the south which remained part of Czechoslovakia) to Poland. With the removal of the Germans the population is overwhelmingly Polish, though the small remaining ethnic German community causes the Polish authorities some anxiety.

Today the voivodships of what used to be Silesia form a key region in Poland: the Upper Silesian Industrial Region is the backbone of the Polish economy, and Lower Silesa (Wałbrzych, Lubin, Głogów) makes an important contribution to industry and agriculture. The capital, Wrocław, is a major centre of culture and learning, while the Sudeten and Beskid mountains are popular holiday areas.

The region's many monuments, most of them carefully restored or reconstructed, give a vivid impression of Silesia's turbulent history. The remains of cult buildings on Ślęża (Zobten), Silesia's holy mountain, are evidence of the pagan and early Christian past. Romanesque buildings such as the monastic church at Trzebnica or the magnificent doorway of the Church of St Mary Magdalene in Wrocław, recall the Silesia of the Polish Piasts. Gothic Cistercian monasteries (the oldest is Lubiąż, see page 585) point to the German influences in the 13th and 14th centuries. Silesian art in the 14th century also came under Bohemian influence, apparent in a series of churches (including the parish church of Świdnica) and in Gothic funerary sculpture in the tradition of the Přemyslid tombs in Prague. Bohemian influence continued in the 18th century with a major church by K. I. Dientzenhofer at Legnickie Pole, while Silesian Baroque produced some architectural works of European importance, such as the University at Wrocław. These would not have been possible without the conditions created by Habsburg rule. The Counter-Reformation spurred the Catholic Church to a remarkable burst of building activity in a region which was split almost equally between Catholics and Lutherans. At the same time, an increasingly powerful nobility built new castles, and made good the war damage in their towns. Sculpture and painting profited from the building boom in the 17th and 18th centuries, when the greatest Silesian painter, Michael Willmann, produced his masterpieces. Later, the enlightened absolutism of Prussia with its more favourable attitude towards Protestantism, together with the character of austerity that emanated from the centre, Berlin, were to form the basis for Neoclassicism in Silesia. At the beginning of the present century Silesia, in particular Wrocław under its city architect Hans Poeltzig, was the scene of important architectural innovation, of which the most impressive example is Max Berg's Jahrhunderthalle (see page 581).

Wrocław

The beginnings of **Wrocław (Breslau)** were on Ostrów Tumski (Cathedral Island), where archaeologists have uncovered the remains of a castle protected by earthworks and wooden defences, and a settlement, all dating from the 10th century.

By the year AD 1000 this was already a celebrated fortified trading centre, and in the 12th century it developed into the metropolis of Silesia. The magnate Peter Wlast (Piotr Włosławiec) built a series of lavish churches, of which only the little Romanesque church of St Giles next to the Cathedral has survived complete.

The medieval layout of the centre of Wrocław, still recognizable today, is the result of rebuilding after the Tatar invasion of 1241. It consists of a system of streets intersecting at right angles with the market place in the middle. In 1335 Wrocław was the first Silesian hereditary principality to come under the control of Bohemia. It was a favourite city of the Emperor Charles IV, and its economy flourished until around 1420, when the Hussite Wars spread from Bohemia and Moravia into Silesia. In 1475 the first printed work in Polish appeared here, but Germanization was also underway. Among the most impressive Gothic brick buildings of the 14th and 15th centuries are the Town Hall and a number of churches (the Cathedral of St John the Baptist on Ostrów Tumski, St Mary on the Sand, St Elizabeth).

By the time the Habsburgs assumed power in Silesia the majority of the population of Wrocław had already turned Lutheran. The Counter-Reformation went on the offensive here, but it did not result in the sort of militant confrontation that took place elsewhere – indeed later visitors were surprised at how untroubled the coexistence of Lutherans and Catholics was in Wrocław. Trade and commerce were firmly based in local crafts, among which linen-weaving had been important since the 16th century. The Austrian period was marked by much new building, and the Baroque architecture of the time is prominent in the city: the University (originally built as a Jesuit college), and various institutional buildings and burghers' houses. The important school of Silesian Baroque German poetry was closely connected with Wrocław. Its three greatest figures were the 'father of German poetry' Martin Opitz (1597–1639), who among other things had the stamina to translate Sir Philip Sidney's *Arcadia*, the religious poet Johann Scheffler known as Angelus Silesius (1624–77), the author of *Der cherubinische Wandersmann*, a book of religious epigrams, and the poet and dramatist Andreas Gryphius (1616–64).

Ferdinand Lassalle (1825–64), founder of the General German Workers' Association, engraving, 1863

Prussian rule, which began in 1741, encouraged manufacturers, and in the 19th century there was a massive development of industry. The university, especially after the Congress of Vienna in 1815, became an outstanding scientific, cultural and political centre. Although predominantly German, in 1848 it was one of the intellectual centres of the Polish national movement in Prussia.

Ferdinand Lassalle, the German revolutionary and founder of the Allgemeiner Deutscher Arbeiterverein (the first pan-German Socialist party), was born in Wrocław on 13 April 1825. He was killed in a duel in Geneva in 1864 but his grave can be found in the Jewish Cemetery of Wrocław, with an inscription provided by the Polish Socialist Party in 1947. Prussian Neoclassicism can be seen at the former Hatzfeld Palace, the Bishop's Residence on Ostrów Tumski and the old Bourse.

Wrocław (population 630,000) is now the fourth largest city in Poland. The people who found a new home here after the Second World War came from all parts of Poland. Many were from the city of Lwów and elsewhere in the regions beyond the River Bug which Poland had lost to the Soviet Union, while others came from the destroyed cities and villages of central Poland, and others from the poorer parts of southern Poland. They had to rebuild a city whose centre had been up to 90 per cent destroyed, the result of the Nazis' decision to make 'Festung Breslau' a fortress to be defended at any cost against the Soviet advance. It had finally capitulated on 6 May, after Berlin and a day before the German surrender.

Today's Wrocław is thus a curious hybrid. Its historic buildings have been restored and it retains much of its Silesian heritage, but many of its older inhabitants have roots not in Prussian Silesia but in Austrian Galicia. The distinctive Lwów accent can still be heard here, and there are many reminders of close links with the former Galician capital.

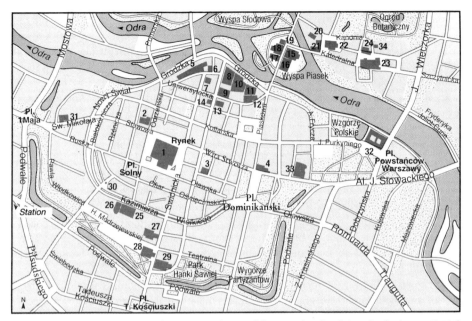

Wrocław 1 Ratusz (Town Hall) 2 Kościół św. Elżbiety (Church of St Elizabeth) 3 Kościół św. Marii Magdaleny (Church of St Mary Magdalene) 4 Kościół św. Wojciecha (Church of St Adalbert) 5 Uniwersytet (University) 6 Kościół Uniwersytecki (University Church) 7 Instytut Antropologii (Anthropological Institute) 8 Biblioteka im. Ossolińskich (Ossoliński National Library) 9 Kościół św. Macieja (Church of St Matthias) 10 Mauzoleum Piastów Wrocławskich (Mausoleum of the Wrocław Piasts) 11 Instytut Filologii (Philological Institute) 12 Kościół św. Wincentego (Church of St Vincent) 13 Kamienica Piastów Opolskich (House of the Opole Piasts) 14 Kamienica Piastów Legnicko-Brzeskich (House of the Legnica-Brzeg Piasts) 15 Kościół N. Marii Panny Na Piasku (Church of St Mary on the Sand) 16 Biblioteka Uniwersytecka (University Library) 17 Kościół św. Anny (Church of St Anne) 18 Klasztor Augustianek (Convent of Augustinian Nuns) 19 Szpital św. Anny (Hospital of St Anne) 20 Kościół św. Marcina (Church of St Martin) 21 Kościół śś. Piotra i Pawła (Church of Sts Peter and Paul) 22 Kościół św. Krzyża (Church of the Holy Cross and St Bartholomew) 23 Katedra św. Jana Chrzciciela (Cathedral of St John the Baptist) 24 Kościół św. Idziego (Church of St Giles) 25 Muzeum Archeologiczne i Muzeum Etnograficzne (Archaeological and Ethnographical Museums) 26 Kościół Opatrzności Bożej (Church of God's Providence) 27 Kościół św. Doroty i św. Stanisława (Church of St Dorothy and St Stanislas) 28 Opera 29 Kościół Bożego Ciała (Corpus Christi Church) 30 Plac Bohaterów Getta (Square of the Ghetto Heroes) 31 Kościół św. Barbary (Church of St Barbara) 32 Muzeum Narodowe (National Museum) 33 Muzeum Architektury (Museum of Architecture) 34 Muzeum Archidiecezjalne (Archidiocesan Museum) 35 Panorama Racławicka (Panorama of the Battle of Racławice)

Almost 100,000 people work in two dozen large industrial concerns, including the railway carriage works Pafawag, the generator works Dolmel and the bus factory Jelcz. The ten academic institutions in the city have about 40,000 students in all. At the university two departments have a worldwide reputation: mathematics and German studies. The experimental theatre of Jerzy Grotowski which used to perform here, and the fantastic creations of the pantomime theatre of Henryk Tomaszewski are well known. Music-lovers travel to festivals such as 'Wratislavia Cantans' in September, for choral music, and 'Jazz on the Oder' in May. Wrocław is a city of libraries, chief amongst them being the Ossoliński National Library, which was transferred here from Lwów after the war, and the old University Library with its mainly German collection. There are also extensive public gardens, the largest zoo in Poland and a botanical garden.

The intersection of ul. Świdnicka and ul. Oławska at the heart of the city gives the best view of Wrocław's Gothic **Ratusz (Town Hall)** (1) which remains the city's unmistakable landmark (plate 69). The building of a town hall began when the Rynek (Main Square) was laid out in 1242, and in 1261 there is mention of a town hall tower; the Cloth Hall, Town Hall Cellar and Council Chamber were all under construction from 1299 on. The present town hall was built between 1343 and 1357, though remodellings continued until the second half of the 16th century. Restoration work was undertaken in 1884–91 and 1933–8, and extensive rebuilding was necessary after the Second World War (1949–62).

The town hall tower, 66 metres high and visible for miles around, is surmounted by a Renaissance helm, and the east and south façades in particular have rich Gothic architectural and sculptural decoration. The middle gable of the east façade, with its pointed tower and elaborate tracery made around 1500, is a piece of medieval bravura. Below it is a large rectangular panel containing an astronomical clock made in 1580. The oriel window of the chapel is supported by two female figures, and everywhere in the corners of the windows lurk stone figures of animals and humans. The decoration of the southeast oriel was the work of the sculptor Briccius Gausske of Görlitz. The corbels are carved with the heads of John the Baptist and the Virgin. The oriel of the Bailiff's Room and the central oriel dominate the south façade, which has rich carvings from the second half of the 15th century. The hollows in the string courses contain small sculptures which form a sort of town chronicle in stone.

The entrance to the town hall is on the west side. The porch contains the remains of Renaissance mural paintings which came to light in the course of restoration after the war. The adjoining *Burghers' Hall*, which is divided in two by an arcade of pointed arches, is one of the oldest sections of the building. The Bailiff's Room, built in 1299, has two notable Renaissance doorways, which lead to the Green Room and the Mayor's Room. The walls of the *Council Room* are covered with Renaissance panelling with rich intarsia work, above which hang paintings by the 17th-century Silesian painter Michael Willmann. A Gothic stone doorway of 1428 takes us to the office of the town clerk, which has a Late Gothic vault with painted bosses.

The three-aisled *Refectory* on the upper floor is the largest and most beautiful room in the town hall. The magnificent bosses of the cross-rib vault have Christian motifs, plant and animal shapes, portraits of well-known burghers, and coats of arms: the Polish eagle of

House fronts on Plac Solny

the Piasts, the eagle of Silesia and the lion of Bohemia. Another striking feature of the room is the central oriel, with a richly carved interior.

The east wall of the *Council Elders' Room* has ashwood panelling decorated with oak intarsia. The elaborate star vault of the *Treasury* has bosses with the arms of the King Władysław II Jagiełło. The *Princes' Hall* has an equally complex cross-rib vault supported on a central column, whose capital is carved with figures and plant motifs. Since 1956 a statue of the comedy-writer Aleksander Fredro (1798–1876), brought from Lwów, has stood in front of the west façade of the town hall, replacing a statue of Frederick the Great. It was here in March 1945 that Mayor Spielhagen of Breslau was summarily shot for opposing the Nazis' exhortations to the city to stand firm in the face of inevitable defeat.

Thanks to the efforts of Polish architectural conservators, the main square and *Plac Solny (Salzmarkt, Salt Market)*, which adjoins it to the southwest, have regained the appearance they had around 1800 – before the alterations of the 19th and 20th centuries. Burghers' houses, Gothic and Renaissance, Baroque and Neoclassical, predominate (colour plate 3). On the west side these include 'Pod Gryfami' (Griffin House), No. 2, with a gable dated 1587 built by Friedrich Gross, the city architect; the House of the Blue Sun, No. 7, and 'Pod Złotym Słońcem' (House of the Golden Sun), No. 6, where the Bohemian and Habsburg rulers stayed when they visited the city; and 'Pod Siedmioma Elektorami' (House of the Seven Electors), No. 8, now the offices of the Polish publishers Ossolineum. On the south side, opposite the Fredro Memorial, Nos. 20 and 21, now carefully restored, were for a long time the headquarters in Breslau of the Fugger banking family. Plac Solny is dominated by the interesting Neoclassical building of the *Old Bourse*, built in 1822–4 by Carl Ferdinand Langhans.

From the main square it is only a short distance to three important Gothic churches: St Elizabeth in ul. św. Mikołaja, St Mary Magdalene in ul. Szewska, and St Adalbert in ul. św. Katarzyny.

The **Kościół św. Elżbiety (Church of St Elizabeth)** (2) was begun around 1330; the chancel was completed in 1361, and the nave and chapels around 1380. Work continued into the 16th century on the tower at the side. The nave of the tall, six-bay basilica is completely surrounded by chapels. The chancel beyond the transept has three aisles and three apses. Brian Knox described St Elizabeth's in 1971: 'In the war the church was little damaged and inside it is now a lovely cool white space, still full of furniture and of monuments too numerous to describe.' That was before the fires of September 1975 and June 1976. Large parts of the furnishings were destroyed including the magnificent Baroque organ of 1750–51 by the famous Silesian organ-builder Michael Engler, the Late Gothic tabernacle (1453–5) by Jodocus Tauchen, the early 16th-century choir stalls, and the elaborate pulpit of dark Italian marble. The altarpiece of the Virgin, made in 1470–80 by a German master influenced by Veit Stoss and one of the greatest Late Gothic carved altarpieces, was not destroyed, but is now in the National Museum in Warsaw, as is a painted wooden sculpture of the Annunciation. Some important Gothic sculptures do remain in the Chapel of St Elizabeth: a Crucifixion donated around 1400 by Dytwin Dumlose, a member of the town council, and a figure of St Barbara, as well as the funerary monuments for the Imperial Councillor Heinrich von Rybisch (1544) and the town councillor Nicolaus Jenckwicz. After lengthy restoration work, undertaken with financial assistance from Germany, St Elizabeth's is now open again.

The **Kościół św. Marii Magdaleny (Church of St Mary Magdalene)** (3) was completed, except for the towers and chapels, in 1362; the west doorway was built around the end of the 14th century. The six-bay basilica has a chancel with a flat east end across all three aisles. At the west end stands a massive double tower. The church's south façade has Wrocław's most important Romanesque monument, the portal from the church of the Premonstratensian monastery of St Vincent at Ołbin (Elbing) to the northwest of the Ostrów Tumski. Originally made between 1193 and 1200 when the monastery was founded by a Danish magnate, Peter Wlast, it was rebuilt here in 1546, after the monastery church was demolished. One archivolt is decorated with scenes from the Infancy of Christ (plate 72). The tympanum carved with the Death of the Virgin and the Deposition from the Cross has been removed for safekeeping to the Muzeum Narodowe (see page 581).

Outside the church are many well-preserved gravestones and epitaphs, the finest of which are those of Margarethe Irmisch (1518) and Oswaldus Winchler (1571), the cantor of Breslau. Inside, the pulpit (Jakob Gross, 1581), font (Johannes Laubesser, 1576) and a fine Pietà of c.1380 are of interest.

Construction of the **Kościół św. Wojciecha (Church of St Adalbert)** (4) began after the Tatar invasion of 1241, but it was not consecrated until 1330. An aisleless nave with a transept adjoins a three-aisled basilican chancel. The west gable, with pinnacles running through and white-plastered blind arcading, was added to the nave in 1492. The church has a splendid Baroque funerary chapel, built in 1715 by the architect Benedikt Müller. The marble and alabaster sarcophagus made in 1725 is the work of the sculptor Leonhard Weber of Świdnica; the sarcophagus lid is supported by allegorical figures of the cardinal virtues, Fortitude, Justice, Temperance and Prudence.

Between the churches of St Mary Magdalene and St Wojciech, at ul. Wita Stwoswa No.

31, stands the former *Pałac Hatzfeldów (Hatzfeld Palace)*, built in 1765–76 under the direction of the Silesian architect Carl Gotthard Langhans, who later designed the Brandenburg Gate in Berlin. The columned portico and entrance hall were restored or replaced after severe war damage, and the foyer and staircase give an idea of the palace's former splendour. The building now houses a gallery of contemporary art.

The starting point for further exploration of the city is the Pl. Uniwersytecki on the northern edge of the Old Town, near the bank of the Oder. The imposing Baroque building of the **Uniwersytet (University)** (5), an institution which traces its origins to a foundation of the Emperor Leopold I in 1702, was built – probably to the designs of Italian architects – in 1728–40. A centre of Catholic education, it was under the control of the Jesuits until their suppression in 1774, and in 1811 was merged with the Friedrich Wilhelm University, which moved to Wrocław from Frankfurt an der Oder. An asymmetrical astronomical tower dominates the long frontage facing the river. Four allegorical statues, made by Franz Joseph Mangold, represent the four faculties of the old Jesuit College: Canon Law, Theology, Astronomy and Medicine. The south front, which faces the town, has a magnificent Baroque doorway. On the parapet above the portal are four sandstone statues by Johann Albrecht Siegwitz representing the cardinal virtues. The university is famous for the splendour of the grandest of its public rooms, the *Aula Leopoldina* (colour plate 2), created in 1731–2 by the Moravian painter Johann Christoph Handtke and the sculptor Franz Joseph Mangold. The interior is dominated by three main themes. The statues of emperors were intended to honour the ruling house of Habsburg. Between the windows are paintings of the protectors of learning (including Frederick II of Prussia, who was shortly to seize Silesia). The ceiling painting shows a Christian interpretation of the origin of all sciences, with pictures of famous scholars decorating the window embrasures. The bust is of the provincial governor of Silesia, Count Johann Anton Schaffgotsch.

Directly next door to the University buildings stands the former Jesuit church, the Kościół Imienia Jezus (Church of the Name of Jesus), now the **Kościół Uniwersytecki (University Church)** (6), built in 1689–98 on the pattern of the Gesù in Rome. The enormous ceiling painting – like the rest of the church's decoration its theme is the Glorification of the Name of Jesus – was created in 1704–6 by Johann Michael Rottmayr, one of the greatest Central European fresco-painters of the Late Baroque.

Also in the Pl. Uniwersytecki is the former Jesuit Seminary of St Joseph, later called the Dom Steffensa (Steffens House) and now the home of the **Instytut Antropologii (Anthropological Institute)** (7). It was here on 8 February 1813 that Professor Henrik Steffens, a Norwegian professor of physics, made his famous speech to the students and citizens of Breslau urging them to take up the struggle against Napoleon – a key event in the awakening of Germany. It was also at Wrocław a few weeks later that King Friedrich Wilhelm of Prussia issued his proclamation 'An mein Volk' summoning the Prussian people to war against the French, and here too that he instituted the Iron Cross.

The **Biblioteka im. Ossolińskich (Ossoliński National Library** or **Ossolineum)** (8) is

575

now one of Wrocław's greatest cultural institutions. It was founded in 1827 in Lwów by Józef Maksymilian Ossoliński as a repository of Polish culture (rather like the Raczyński Library in Poznań, which was established around the same time). The library arrived at Wrocław from Lwów on a special train on 21 July 1946 and is now housed in the former St Matthias Hospital (ul. Szewska No. 37). This Baroque building, erected between 1675 and 1715 by the French Baroque master Jean-Baptiste Mathey for the Prague-based Order of Knights of the Cross with a Red Star, active in the Silesian Counter-Reformation, who had founded a hospital here in 1254. It later housed a Jesuit-run Catholic school attached to the University. Above the rusticated ground floor rise two ranges with pediments facing the river, linked by a lower centre range with a dome and lantern. Amongst its collections the Ossolineum has many manuscripts by the two greatest writers of Polish Romanticism, Juliusz Słowacki and Adam Mickiewicz, including the manuscript of the latter's 'Pan Tadeusz'.

Up the street from the library, as we go into the city along ul. Szewska, stands the 13th-century Gothic **Kościół św. Macieja (Church of St Matthias)** (9), in which Angelus Silesius is buried. In its forecourt is one of the two *Posągi św. Jana Nepomucena (St John Nepomuk Columns)* by Johann Georg Urbański (1723) – the presence of this medieval Bohemian saint (a favourite with the Counter-Reformation Jesuits) is another reminder of Habsburg rule in Silesia. Turning back to the river and walking along the front, the next two buildings after the Ossolineum are both former religious houses. The former *Kościół św. Klary (Church of St Clare)* attached to the *Ursuline* (originally Poor Clares) *Convent* (1699–1701, Johann Georg Knoll) contains the **Mauzoleum Piastów Wrocławskich (Mausoleum of the Wrocław Piasts)** (10), created in 1693–9 around the 14th-century tomb of Duke Henryk VI Dobry and his predecessors. The former Premonstratensian monastery next door (Franciscan until 1530, and originally Gothic, but remodelled in the 17th century) houses the **Instytut Filologii (Philological Institute)** (11) of the university. The three-storey conventual buildings adjoin the north side of the **Kościół św. Wincentego (Church of St Vincent)**, originally a Late Romanesque basilica, remodelled as a Gothic hall church in the 14th century by its Franciscan owners, and in 1530 given to the Premonstratensian canons when their monastery at Ołbin was demolished. It was then re-dedicated to St Vincent (the original dedication had been to St James). Opposite St Matthias's, at the intersection of ul. Szewska and ul. Uniwersytecka, stand two former town palaces: the **Kamienica Piastów Opolskich (House of the Opole Piasts)** (13) of 1532, and the **Kamienica Piastów Legnicko-Brzeskich (House of the Legnica-Brzeg Piasts)** (14) (1336–1675), which has a fine Renaissance façade.

The **Kościół N. Marii Panny Na Piasku (Church of St Mary on the Sand)** (15), known to the German population as the 'Sandkirche' ('Sand Church'), is reached across the Most Piaskowski (Sand Bridge). The church was built between 1334 and 1390; it was consecrated in 1369. Parts of an earlier Romanesque church are incorporated in the Gothic building: around 1150 the house of Augustinian Canons on Mount Ślęża (Zobten) about 30 km southwest of Wrocław (see page 584) moved here to Wyspa Piaskowa (Sand Island).

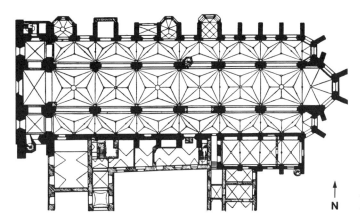

Plan of the Church of
N St Mary on the Sand

The three-aisled church of six bays marks an important development of the hall church in Silesia. The piers with oblong cross-section, the shape of the star vaults in the nave, the Piast vaulting (see page 578) in the aisles, the lack of a break between nave and choir and the way the side apses are tucked in at the side of the main apse, all create a strongly dominant east-west axis. The church was badly damaged in the war, but has been well restored (1960–65): 'This is the most majestic interior of all German brick church architecture' (B. Knox). Above the entrance to the sacristy is a Romanesque tympanum from the earlier building, carved with the Virgin and Child flanked by the kneeling figures of the founder of the church, Maria, the widow of Peter Wlast, holding a model of the earliest church on the site, and her son Świętosław. The interior has a number of very fine Gothic winged altarpieces, and a font decorated with scenes from the Life of Christ.

The buildings of the Augustinian Canons were built in 1709–15, perhaps by the local architect Johann Georg Kalkbrenner. Since 1810 they have housed the **Biblioteka Uniwersytecka (University Library)** (16) which has one of the largest collections of books in German outside German-speaking countries; there are 225,000 volumes dating from before 1800. Opposite the 'Na Piasku' church stand the Baroque **Kościół św. Anny (Church of St Anne)** (17), now used by a Uniate congregation, the former **Klasztor Augustianek (Convent of Augustinian Nuns)** (18), and lastly the former **Szpital św. Anny (Hospital of St Anne)** (19) with an original Gothic double doorway and the tomb of the founder of St Mary's Church, Abbot John of Prague (died 1386).

Most Tumski (Cathedral Bridge) leads to Ostrów Tumski (Dominsel, Cathedral Island), where the first settlement of Wrocław began. The little 13th-century Romanesque **Kościół św. Marcina (Church of St Martin)** (20) is thought to have been the chapel of the first Piast castle. Nearby is a monument to Pope John XXIII erected in 1968. On the bridge stands the Gothic **Kościół śś. Piotra i Pawła (Church of Sts Peter and Paul)** (21), with a fine vault supported on a central column. In front of the church is the *Orphantropheum (Orphanage)*, an impressive Baroque building erected in 1702–15 by Johann Blasius Peitner.

Next we come to the tall **Kościół św. Krzyża i św. Bartłomieja (Church of the Holy Cross and St Bartholomew)** (22), Wrocław's oldest hall church (1288–1350) and the starting point for the Silesian school of Gothic architecture. In the relatively short nave we find for the first time the distinctive flat Silesian nave piers for the arcade, and – another Silesian speciality – the characteristic 'jumping vaults' (also called 'Piast vaults') in the aisles. This curious tripartite structure allows a regular transition between two wall bays and a single interior bay, and creates an interesting effect of movement. The arrangement of the transept and chancel with three polygonal apses is also very original, as is the existence of a Lower Church (St Bartholomew's), a three-aisled, five-bay hall church. The church was founded by Duke Henryk IV Probus of Wrocław (ruled 1270–90), whose impressive tomb (now in the Muzeum Narodowe) stood in the choir until 1944. He can be seen, however, together with his wife Mechthild, in an Early Gothic tympanum (c.1350) in the north wall. In front of the Holy Cross Church stands the second *Posąg św. Jana Nepomucena (Nepomuk Column)* (plate 70). This one was made by Johann Georg Urbański and completed in 1732 by Johann Albrecht Siegwitz.

Past the Neoclassical *Archbishop's Palace* of 1795 (a late work by Carl Gotthard Langhans), ul. Katedralna leads to the **Katedra św. Jana Chrzciciela (Cathedral of St John the Baptist)** (23), a Gothic replacement of an earlier Romanesque church, built between 1244 and 1419. Almost completely destroyed in 1945, but now reconstructed in its essentials, the cathedral is an Early Gothic three-aisled basilica with two towers and a long choir with an ambulatory. On the exterior wall of the north aisle stands a copy of a sandstone figure of St John the Baptist, recreated from fragments and photographs of the original made in 1160–70 and severely damaged in 1945, which is now in the Muzeum Archidiecezjalne (Archdiocesan Museum, see page 579). Also now in the museum are the side panels of the altarpiece of the high altar (originally with five wings) by Bartholomäus Fichtenberger. The centre panel and the wings are all decorated with chased silver by the Breslau goldsmith Paul Nitsch (1573–1609); the other parts of the altar are missing. The doorway leading to the sacristy from the south choir aisle dates from 1517 and is one of the earliest works of the Renaissance in Silesia (plate 71). Flanking the entrance, the pilasters raised on high plinths support a richly carved entablature above which is a round-arched tympanum with a sculpture of Salome receiving the head of John the Baptist from a fashionably clad executioner, while the donor, Bishop Jan Turzon, kneels to one side. In the north aisle the entrance leads to the Chapel of St John the Baptist, in which a fragment of the tomb of Bishop Turzon has survived (a slab with the white marble effigy of the bishop). Turzon, a humanist and patron of the arts who came from Kraków, died in 1520; his Renaissance tomb and its chapel were completed in 1537. Three other interesting chapels adjoin the choir. On the left is the Elector's Chapel, a superb Borromini-inspired Baroque interior built for Franz Ludwig, Elector of Mainz and Prince-Bishop of Breslau, by Johann Bernhard Fischer von Erlach in 1716–24, with illusionistic frescoes by the prolific Lombard painter Carlo Innocenzo Carloni, plasterwork by Santino Bussi, and sculptures by the Bohemian master Ferdinand Maximilian Brokoff. The Gothic Lady

Chapel in the middle (*c*.1350) contains the marble tomb of Bishop Przecław of Pogorzela (Preczlaus von Pogarell) (died 1376). On the right is the Chapel of St Elizabeth built for Franz Ludwig's predecessor, Cardinal Friedrich of Hesse-Darmstadt, by Giacomo Scianzi in 1680–86, with a marble altar (1700) and the Cardinal's tomb (which has a large kneeling figure by Domenico Guidi). The cathedral organ, once the organ of the Jahrhunderthalle (see page 583), is the biggest in Poland.

Next door to the cathedral stands the Late Romanesque **Kościół św. Idziego (Church of St Giles)** (24) (first half of the 13th century) which survived the Tatar raids and is the oldest remaining church in Wrocław.

The **Muzeum Archidiecezjalne (Archdiocesan Museum)** (34) at ul. Kanonia No. 12 has religious art and artefacts from the Romanesque period to the present. Its fine collection includes the much-damaged figure of St John the Baptist (*c*.1160–70) from the cathedral. Among the museum's greatest treasures are some Romanesque illuminated manuscripts, including the Trzebnica Psalter and the Lubiąż Gradual.

On the opposite side of the Old Town in ul. Kazimierza Wielkiego, the boulevard which follows the course of the 13th-century city walls, the former *Pałac Spaetgenów (Spätgen Palace)* was begun *c*.1720, was added to later by Jan Baumann (1750–63), and used to be the Royal Palace of Frederick the Great and his successors. The Neoclassical façade is by Carl Gotthard Langhans (1796–7), and the long south wing is by Friedrich August Stüler (1846). It now houses the **Muzeum Archeologiczne** and **Muzeum Etnograficzne (Archaeological and Ethnographical Museums)** (25). In the same street stands the **Kościół Opatrzności Bożej (Church of Divine Providence)** (26) a Baroque church built in 1750 as a Calvinist place of worship by Jan Baumann, which was the model for many Lutheran churches in Silesia. To the east of the palace is another of Wrocław's great Gothic churches, the **Kościół śś. Doroty i Stanisława (Church of St Dorothy and St Stanislas)** (27) founded in 1351 for Augustinian Hermits by the Emperor Charles IV to commemorate his meeting here with King Kazimierz III Wielki of Poland. The church was consecrated in 1381 and the tall nave and aisles were built after 1400, with the characteristic Silesian combination of star vaults in the nave and Piast vaults in the aisles. It contains a number of good Baroque altarpieces and an impressive Late Baroque monument to Heinrich Gottfried von Spätgen (1753, Franz Joseph Mangold). In 1524 a discussion held in the church brought about a peaceful settlement of the religious conflicts in Wrocław: the church itself remained Catholic and was taken over by the Franciscans, but several of the other great churches of the city became Lutheran and remained so until 1945. The Neoclassical **Opera** (28) further down ul. Świdnicka is by Carl Ferdinand Langhans; it opened (as the Stadttheater) in 1841 with a performance of Goethe's *Egmont* and re-opened after the war on 8 September 1945 with the most Polish of operas, Moniuszko's *Halka*. Opposite the opera-house is the **Kościół Bożego Ciała (Corpus Christi Church)** (29) of the Knights Hospitaller of St John, with an elegant brick gable facing the street and elaborate vaulting within.

Before the war Breslau had one of the largest Jewish populations in Germany. The centre of Jewish life before 1933 was the Karlsplatz, now the **Pl. Bohaterów Getta (Square of the Ghetto Heroes)** (30), where there is now a monument to the Warsaw Ghetto Uprising. The large but derelict synagogue nearby is the Orthodox *Storch Synagogue*, built in 1829 by Carl Ferdinand Langhans. Not far from here was the house where the pioneer socialist Ferdinand Lassalle was born, the son of a Jewish businessman. The *Jewish Cemetery* where he is buried has recently been restored. It had been founded in 1856 and is the graveyard of a predominantly assimilated and Germanized community; it is closer in feel to Christian cemeteries of the same period than to the Jewish cemeteries of traditional Eastern European communities.

The **Kościół św. Barbary (Church of St Barbara)** (31) in ul. św. Mikołaja on the west side of the Old Town was built towards the end of the 14th century and used to contain the great double-winged St Barbara Altarpiece of 1447, now in the National Museum in Warsaw. The church is used by the Russian Orthodox community.

The building which now houses the **Muzeum Narodowe (National Museum)** (32) at Pl. Powstańców Warszawy No. 5 was built as government offices by the Prussians. It contains an important collection of medieval sculpture and painting, and as well as pieces from Silesia it includes works brought here from Lwów after the war. The collection includes two major works of early medieval sculpture from Wrocław churches: a tympanum from the monastery at Ołbin from the end of the 12th century (the rest of the portal is at the Church of St Mary Magdalene, see page 574), and the 13th-century tomb of Duke Henryk IV Probus from the Holy Cross Church (see page 578), a monument which, with its carved mourners, was to set the pattern for funerary sculpture in the region. Its other treasures include the Skarbimierz Madonna (*c.*1360), and some large Polish paintings brought from Lwów, including Matejko's 'Konrad Wallenrod' and Bellotto's 'Entry of Jerzy Ossoliński into Rome'. There are also many works by recent Silesian artists and by foreign artists.

Returning towards the town centre along ul. Purkyniego, we pass on the left a round modern building which contains another legacy from Lwów, the **Panorama Racławicka (Panorama of the Battle of Racławice)** (35), a potent symbol of Polish nationalism, which has become one of Poland's leading tourist attractions since it was finally opened to the public in its new setting in 1985. The cylindrical painting by Jan Styka and Wojciech Kossak is 15 metres high and 114 metres in circumference, and shows the famous battle fought on 4 April 1794 north of Kraków (see page 494), when Tadeusz Kościuszko and his Polish scythemen defeated the Russians at the start of the insurrection. The painting was commissioned by the patriotic Polish citizens of Lwów in 1894 to celebrate the centenary of the battle, a nationalist gesture possible in the tolerant atmosphere of Austrian Galicia. The painting was damaged by bombs in 1944 but was brought to Wrocław together with the Ossolineum Library in 1945. A political liability in communist Poland, the painting lay neglected in storage for decades until it was eventually restored in the changed climate of 1980.

A turning on the left brings us to the **Muzeum Architektury (Museum of**

The Jaxa Tympanum (Museum of Architecture Wrocław)

Architecture) (33) at ul. Bernardyńska No. 5, which occupies the former Bernardine monastery. The history of the city is told from the middle ages to the present day, with much material showing it before its wartime destruction. Among the fragments of architectural sculpture on display is the Jaxa Tympanum dating from 1162, which was found among the ruins of the monastery at Ołbin and is the earliest surviving work of this kind in Poland.

In the early years of the 20th century Breslau was an important centre of innovation in architecture. The most remarkable building to survive from this period is the **Hala Ludowa (People's Hall)** in the Park Szczytnicki to the east of the city. It was built in 1912–13 by the municipal architect Max Berg as the Jahrhunderthalle, commemorating the Prussian king's call to arms against Napoleon in 1813 (an event as crucial in the German nationalist story as the Battle of Racławice is in the Polish). The vast circular hall, 130 metres in diameter, is spanned by a single dome with tiers of windows supported by thirty-three concrete ribs, and was one of the most daring pieces of engineering yet attempted in that material. Its great organ is now in Wrocław Cathedral. The park in which the Hall is set has a number of delightful buildings, including the unexpected Modernist Kindergarten.

Trzebnica – Piotrkowice – Milicz – Goszcz – Oleśnica – Ślęża – Wojnowice – Środa Śląska – Lubiąż

Święta Jadwiga (St Hedwig of Andechs-Meran) is deeply venerated in Poland, and especially in Silesia. The daughter of a Bavarian count, she was born in 1174 and married at the age of twelve to the future duke of Silesia Henryk I Brodaty ('the Bearded'). Like her royal kinswomen St Elizabeth of Hungary and St Agnes of Bohemia she was famous for her piety. The *Cistercian Convent* at **Trzebnica (Trebnitz)** 25 km north of Wrocław was founded in 1202 by Duke Henryk at her request and settled with nuns from Bamberg. It was the first nunnery to be established in Silesia. After her husband's death in 1238 she retired here until her own death in 1243; her canonization followed soon after, in 1267. The town of Trzebnica (population 10,000) remains a much-visited pilgrimage centre.

Trzebnica is one of the most important places in Silesian history. The *Kościół Klasztorny (Convent Church)*, a Romanesque brick basilica, the earliest of its kind in Silesia, was built between 1203 and 1240, and has beautifully carved stone details. The choir beyond the transept has an apsidal east end. The most important early feature is the fine Early Gothic sculpture of the two *tympana* (plates 73, 74 and 75). The north portal (*c.*1230) at the west end (originally one of three) shows King David playing his lute to Bathsheba and her handmaid; the second, in the north wall of the transept shows the Coronation of the Virgin (after 1270). After Jadwiga's canonization an elegant Gothic chapel to house her shrine was added to the south transept, the earliest example of High Gothic in Silesia. 'After the heavy approaches ... this confection is as refreshing as water ice.' (B. Knox).

In the second half of the 17th century the interior of the church underwent a thorough baroquization, for which the sculptor Franz Joseph Mangold and the painter Christian

The building of the Cistercian monastery at Trzebnica; miniature from the Hedwig Codex, c.1353 by the court workshop of Duke Ludwik of Legnica-Brzeg (now in Malibu, California)

Oleśnica, view of the town in the 18th century, engraving by F. B. Werner

Philipp Benthum were principally responsible. In front of the high altar stands the Baroque marble sarcophagus (1680) of Duke Henryk I, who is buried here with his comrade-in-arms, the Grand Master of the Teutonic Knights, Konrad von Feuchtwangen. In the Chapel of St Jadwiga are the rather grander marble tomb of the saint also dating from 1680, but incorporating her original 13th-century Gothic tomb slab, and the tomb of her great-great-grandson, Duke Konrad II of Oleśnica (died 1403). At the end of the saint's sarcophagus is an oval medallion commemorating the last Piast princess, Katarina of Holstein-Emenhorst (died 1707). The shrine of St Jadwiga is always decorated with fresh flowers, mostly in the Polish national colours of white and red – although in her own day Jadwiga's religious foundations did much to increase the influence of German culture in Silesia. The massive Late Baroque *abbey buildings* (1697–1726) are to the south of the church.

To the northwest of Trzebnica lies **Piotrkowice (Gross Peterwitz)** where the Baroque *Palace* merits a visit. It was commissioned by Count Colonna, who had married the heiress to the estate, and was completed in 1693, probably by Italian architects and craftsmen, whose work is evident in the richly modelled façade.

Milicz (Militsch), to the northeast of Trzebnica, has an important reminder of Protestantism in Silesia. This is one of the six *'Grace Churches' ('Gnadenkirchen')*, which the Habsburg Emperor Joseph I was forced by King Charles VII of Sweden in the Peace of Altranstädt in 1707 to allow the Lutherans in Silesia. A half-timbered building like the earlier 'Peace Churches' (see page 589), it was built, together with a group of parish buildings, on the edge of the Old Town in 1709–14. The most striking feature of these Silesian Protestant churches are their galleried interiors, designed to fit the maximum congregation into a limited space. The pulpit has Rococo carvings and the font is also of interest. Like many other Lutheran churches in the region it is now used for Catholic worship.

The *Palace* at **Goszcz (Goschütz)**, near the town of Twardogóra, was built in 1730–40 for Count Heinrich I Leopold von Reichenbach. It was burned out in 1947, but the outer walls remain largely undamaged. The centrepiece and some stone sculptures give an idea of the former beauty of the building, which represented a transition between the Austrian Baroque of Silesia's Habsburg period and Prussian Rococo. The office buildings are in decay, and now house a farming cooperative; the orangery has been demolished.

Oleśnica (Oels), 30 km east of Wrocław, was for a long time the residence of the Silesian dukes and before Germanization was a stronghold of Polish Protestantism from 1538, when Duke Jan introduced the Reformation here. He was also responsible for alterations to the *Castle* (remodelling the Gothic parts of the old castle before 1548, and building a new four-storey addition between 1559 and 1562). In the fine arcaded courtyard the difference between the Early Renaissance and Late Renaissance parts can clearly be seen. The adjoining Gothic *Parish Church* contains the Renaissance tombs of the Dukes of Oleśnica. On the edge of the historic town centre extensive fragments of the medieval fortifications (including the 14th-century Wrocław Gate) have survived.

Halfway between Wrocław and Wałbrzych (Waldenburg) to the southwest rises **Ślęża (Zobten)** (718 metres), Silesia's holy hill and the highest point in the Central Silesian range. The hill takes its name from the Slavic tribe of the Slenzane. Its exposed situation and historic importance have made it the symbol of Silesia. Archaeological excavations have revealed many finds. In the Bronze Age and early Iron Age there was a cult centre on

Lubiąż, view of the Cistercian Abbey, 18th-century engraving

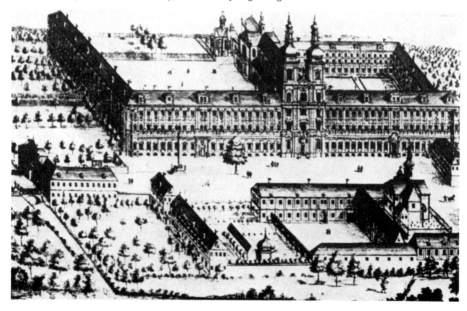

the summit; the visible form of the sanctuary is, however, attributed to the Celts, who migrated here around 500 BC. It consists of stone cult circles which mark out the sacred area, and which are still extant in three places, a smaller encircling earthwork on Kościuszki hill (Mittelberg) 3 km away, and enigmatic stone figures ('Bear F' and 'Woman with a Fish'). The Germanic Vandals (c. 100 BC–AD 400) and the Slavs (from the 6th century) also used the place as a religious site. In 1121–38 the Wrocław magnate Peter Wlast summoned Flemish Augustinian Canons to Silesia, but scholars are not agreed about the exact site of their monastery on the hill. In 1150 it was transferred to Wyspa Piaskowa in Wrocław (see page 576). Surviving architectural fragments and carved lions of Lombard type from the doorways indicate the existence of a stone monastery church. A castle was built on the hill in the 14th century, and destroyed in 1428. A 19th-century neo-Gothic chapel, replacing an 18th-century predecessor struck by lightning, now stands on the summit, and there is a magnificent view over much of Silesia.

West of Wrocław, at **Wojnowice (Wohnwitz)**, stands an impressive Renaissance Palace, built after 1513 for Nikolaus Schebitz, later governor of the principality of Wrocław. The high pitched roofs have stepped gables; the doors and windows, the loggia in the well courtyards, and the arcaded hall in the main wing are richly decorated.

The Parish Church of **Środa Śląska (Neumarkt)**, a 'new town' laid out in 1214 on the road to Lubin (Lüben), is an early 13th-century Late Romanesque basilica with a Gothic chancel (1378–88). The 14th-century bell-tower started the tradition of such free-standing towers in Silesia.

Still further west is **Lubiąż (Leubus)**, the earliest Cistercian monastery in Silesia and a masterpiece of Silesian Baroque. Its two towers rising above the extensive monastic buildings can be seen from afar (colour plate I). In 1175, after its foundation by Duke Boleslaw I, German monks came here from the Cistercian abbey of Pforta an der Saale in Saxony. The monastery has had an extremely troubled history. It was burned down in 1432 during the Hussite Wars; in the Thirty Years' War the monastic buildings were again badly damaged, but in the second half of the 18th century, after a magnificent rebuilding, the monastery enjoyed an economic boom. With secularization in 1810 the archives, library and art treasures were taken to the museums in Wrocław. After 1830 the monastic buildings were used as a lunatic asylum, and in 1945–8 they became a military hospital for Soviet soldiers. The ground floor has been converted into exhibition rooms, and practically nothing now remains of the once splendid decoration. Some of the paintings by Michael Willmann, the Baroque painter (known in his time as the 'Silesian Raphael') who retired to Lubiąż and was responsible for much of its painted decoration, have been transferred to various churches in Warsaw (see page 165). Remains of the choir stalls and altars are in the National Museum in Wrocław.

The *Abbey Church* is first mentioned in 1208; all that survives is a Romanesque piscina. The present six-bay basilica with transept and three-bay Cistercian choir was built in 1307–40. The 14th-century Piast Chapel with its Baroque decoration contains early 14th-century Flemish brasses, which mark the burial place of three Silesian princes, Bolesław

Wysoki ('the Tall'), died 1204, Przemko of Ścinawa, died 1289 and Konrad of Żagań, died 1304. (Parts of these are now in the Archaeological Museum in Warsaw.) The richly sculptured choir stalls, of which only fragments remain, are attributed to the Austrian Joseph Steindl. In 1729 the church was enclosed by new Baroque monastic buildings and a porch was added, surmounted by two towers. In the abbot's range is the Princes' Hall which rises through two storeys and has an illusionistic ceiling painting by Christian Philipp Benthum (plate 76). The Summer Refectory in the monastery range also has a large ceiling painting by Felix Anton Scheffler. Apart from the exhibition rooms the whole monastery is in a dilapidated state, though the German government has recently agreed to provide a billion złotys towards the restoration of the Princes' Hall.

Legnica – Legnickie Pole – Jawor – Złotoryja – Grodziec – Lubin – Głogów

With a population of 100,000, **Legnica (Liegnitz)** is the third biggest city in Lower Silesia (after Wrocław and Wałbrzych), as well as being the administrative centre of a voivodship and the centre of some important industries (copper works, electrical engineering). The River Kaczawa (Katzbach) divides a region of fertile fields and great forests.

Within the area of the present town in the 10th century there probably stood the chief fortified town of the Trebowane, one of the tribes which had then settled in Silesia. After the Tatar invasion in 1241 the town had to be almost completely rebuilt. From 1248 Legnica was the residence of the Piast Dukes of Legnica-Brzeg (Liegnitz-Brieg), who were the very last of the Piast lines, dying out in 1675. The town was given the laws of Magdeburg in 1293 and developed into a powerful centre of industry and trade. It was here in 1526 that the first Lutheran university in Europe was established by Duke Fryderyk II (though it only lasted until 1539). In 1813, during the Wars of Liberation, the Silesian army of the Prussian and Russian allies under Blücher defeated Napoleon's army under Macdonald, by the Katzbach about 10 km to the south of Legnica (not far from the old battlefield of Legnickie Pole, see page 588).

The historic town centre has kept its medieval layout. In the market place stands the Late Baroque *Town Hall* (1) (1737–41) by the Legnica town architect Franz Michael Scheerhofer. With its grand pilaster order this municipal building resembles a Baroque town palace; the entrance tower and double stairway with lamps add grandeur. The *Fontanna Neptuna (Neptune Fountain)* next to the Town Hall was erected in 1731. To the south the market place is dominated by the *Kościół śś. Piotra i Pawła (Church of Sts Peter and Paul)* (2), built in 1328–78 as a Gothic hall church, and much altered in 1894. In its north and west façades two 14th-century portals with tympanum carvings (Adoration of the Magi, Virgin and Child) are preserved. Inside is a Late Gothic polyptych (1498), the tomb of Duke Wacław of Legnica (died 1364) and his wife (died 1367), and in the chancel a bronze 13th-century font decorated with reliefs of trefoil arches and scenes from the Life of Christ. The only other old buildings of interest which survive in the market place are the

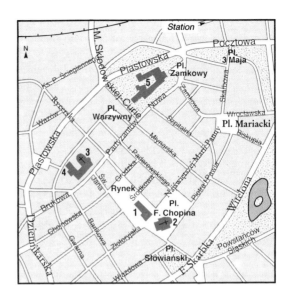

Legnica (Liegnitz) 1 Ratusz (Town Hall) 2 Kościół ś.ś. Piotra i Pawła (Church of Sts Peter and Paul) 3 Kościół św. Jana (Church of St John) 4 Mauzoleum Piastów Legnickich (Mausoleum of the Legnica Piasts) 5 Zamek Piastów (Piast Castle)

Budy Rybne (Herring Shops), a group of houses with Renaissance sgraffito decoration (c.1570) and Baroque and Neoclassical gables; restoration work since the Second World War has opened up the old arcades on their ground floor.

Taking ul. Partyzanów from the Rynek we pass the *Palace of the Abbots of Lubiąż*, a Late Baroque building with a grand pilastered façade (1734–45, probably by Martin Frantz), now the regional museum. Nearby is the *Akademia Rycerska (Military Academy)*, a foundation going back to 1648, but made a school for the Silesian nobility in 1708 under imperial and later Prussian patronage. John Quincy Adams, then American Minister at Berlin, was impressed when he visited Legnica in 1800: 'Besides the mathematics, fortification, and all the properly military studies, they are taught the Latin and French languages, and natural philosophy; as also the use of many instruments invented for the purpose of agriculture and the arts. Of these instruments they have a collection of models in miniature, by which the professors teach the students their use and construction.' The school is a large plain rectangular building around a quadrangle and was designed by Johann Christian Hertel (1726–35).

The *Kościół św. Jana (Church of St John)* (3), north of the market, built for the Jesuits in 1714–27 to replace an earlier Franciscan church, is one of the most important Baroque churches in Silesia. The elegantly curving two-tower façade which rises steeply in the narrow street, shows the influence of the Dientzenhofers of Bohemia. The theme of the frescoes inside is the apotheosis of the Piast dynasty. Adjoining the church is the choir of the earlier St John's church, retained because in the 1670's it was made the *Mauzoleum*

587

Piastów Legnickich (Mausoleum of the Legnica Piasts) (4), founded to commemorate the Piast dynasty, which came to an end with the death of the fifteen-year-old Duke Georg Wilhelm in 1675. The chapel was designed by Carlo Rossi as an oval octagon lined with niches containing the splendidly decorated ducal sarcophagi. Paintings above depict great events in Piast history explained in Latin inscriptions by the Silesian Baroque dramatist Daniel Casper von Lohenstein. Set against the piers are statues (by the Viennese sculptor Matthias Rauchmüller) of the young duke, his mother Ludovika (the foundress of the chapel), his father Duke Christian, and his sister, Karolina of Holstein-Helmenhorst. The inscriptions on the plinths are in the form of a succinct but expressive conversation. The mother exclaims 'Heu mihi soli' ('Alas I am alone'), her late husband reminds her: 'Nescia gnati' ('You forget our son'), the young duke responds: 'At sequor ipse' ('But I am following you'), and his sister is in despair: 'Spes ubi nostrae' ('Where are our hopes?'). Next to the church is the Baroque Jesuit College.

To the north of the market place we reach the former *Zamek Piastów (Piast Castle)* (5). A massive fortress was first built on this site between 1201 and 1238 – the lower storeys of the octagonal Peter Tower and the round Jadwiga Tower date from this period. In the mid-16th century the castle was converted into a Renaissance palace. The most important Renaissance survival is the east gateway, built in 1532 by Georg von Amberg with lavish, elaborately carved Italianate decoration. Following a fire in 1835 the castle was rebuilt in a neo-Gothic style under the direction of Karl Friedrich Schinkel. In 1824 the same architect had rebuilt the *Kościół Mariacki (Church of St Mary)* (in Pl. Mariacki southwest of the castle) in a similarly austere neo-Gothic. Unlike most of the Protestant churches in Silesia, St Mary's has not been taken over by the Catholics, and it is still used for worship by the town's small Lutheran community.

A few kilometres south of Legnica on the road between Świdnica and Wałbrzych is **Legnickie Pole (Wahlstatt)**. Here on 9 April 1241 Duke Henryk II with his Polish knights met the Tatar army in battle. The Tatars routed the Poles and dismembered the Duke, but decided to advance no further and withdrew to Moravia.

The *Church* in the market place was founded by St Jadwiga, Henryk II's mother. According to legend the original church was on the site of the battle, but the building which survives today dates only from the 14th century. In 1961 it was turned into the Museum of the Battle of Legnica.

The Baroque *Kościół św. Jadwigi (Church of St Jadwiga)*, a masterpiece by the greatest of the Dientzenhofer dynasty of architects, Kilian Ignaz Dientzenhofer, was erected in 1727–31 as part of a convent of Benedictine nuns. Built on an oval plan, it has an imposing twin-tower façade with boldly curving helms surmounted by crowns. The hexagonal interior is a fine example of Dientzenhofer's mastery of the plastic handling of space. Covering the oval dome is the magnificent ceiling painting (The Finding of the True Cross) by the Bavarian artist Cosmas Damian Asam (1733). The altarpiece on the high altar is by Franz de Backer (before 1731), and four of the side altars have paintings by Wenzel Lorenz Reiner of Prague (also before 1731). The church was commissioned by Abbot Othmar

Tatars bearing the head of Duke Henry II outside Legnickie Pole; miniature from the Hedwig Codex, c.1353

Zinke of Broumov (now just over the Czech border), one of Dientzenhofer's most prolific patrons.

At **Jawor (Jauer)**, also on the road to Świdnica, is one of the three *'Peace Churches'* *('Kościoły Pokoju' 'Friedenskirchen')* which were conceded to the Silesian Protestants as part of the Peace of Westphalia in 1648 on condition that the churches were built outside the town walls, that there were no belltowers, and that no stone or brick was used in their construction: only timber and clay were permitted. The half-timbered church, designed by Albrecht von Säbisch, an architect of fortifications from Wrocław, and built by Andreas Kemper in 1654–5, has room for a congregation of 6,000. The impressive interior with its four tiers of galleries has colourful painted decoration in a rustic style.

Złotoryja (Goldberg), southwest of Legnica, derives its name from the fact that in the 13th and 14th centuries gold was mined here, though by the 16th century copper was more important. The *Kościół Mariacki (Church of St Mary)* is of interest for its Late Romanesque south transept portal and chancel which were extended to make a Gothic hall church in the 14th century.

To the northwest of Złotoryja is the town of **Grodziec (Gröditzberg)**. There was already a castle on the hill of the same name (390 metres high) in the 10th century, which probably served to guard the western border of Silesia. Around 1500, under the direction of the architect Wendelin Rosskopf of Gierłoż a large Late Gothic *Castle* was built on a hexagonal ground-plan. Extensive restorations in the 19th and early 20th centuries saved the buildings from ruin but also brought many disfigurements. The most important features of the complex are the keep, the gatehouse and the hall; in the pilasters and vaulting Late Gothic and Renaissance forms are found side by side.

The towns of **Lubin (Lüben)** and **Głogów (Glogau)** are the centres of the Lower Silesian copper basin. The veins of copper discovered in this region in 1957 are among the largest in Europe. Industrialization has brought with it severe environmental pollution and in 1986 the Sejm added the region to the list of 'ecological disaster areas'. The walls of the *chapel* of Lubin Castle, completed in 1349, still stand, as does the tympanum of a doorway with figures of the suffering Christ with St Jadwiga and St Mary Magdalene. One of the three 'Peace Churches' once stood in Głogów, before it was destroyed by fire in 1758. Like Wrocław, Głogów was declared a 'fortress' in the last months of the Second World War and did not capitulate until 1 April 1945. The old town was totally destroyed, and rebuilding has been slow. The restored *Katedra św. Marii Panny (Cathedral of St Mary)*, a three-aisled hall church completed in 1466, retains elements of an earlier Romanesque church in the choir and crossing. The Baroque Jesuit church and college have also been restored. Głogów's most famous son was the great German Baroque poet and playwright Andreas Gryphius (1616–64) (see page 569), who was Syndikus (secretary) to the principality.

Jelenia Góra – Jagniątków – Karpacz – Szklarska Poręba – Karkonosze – Bierutowice – Mysłakowice – Siedlęcin – Lwówek Śląski – Płakowice – Bolesławiec – Bolków – Świny – Krzeszów

'Nothing can be more beautiful than the situation of Hirschberg itself; an handsomely built town, with a number of noble edifices, situated in a valley, surrounded by hills, more or less elevated, on every side; with the sublime gloom of the Giant Mountains as the background of the scene,' wrote John Quincy Adams on his visit in 1800.

Jelenia Góra (Hirschberg) at the confluence of the Bóbr (Bober) and the Kamienna (Zacken) dominates the valley between the Karkonosze (Riesengebirge, Giant Mountains) and the Góry Kaczawskie (Katzbachgebirge). With a population of almost 90,000 the town is not only an important industrial centre (with large pharmaceutical works and factories producing cellulose and artificial fibres) but also an important holiday resort. Its recorded history goes back to 1288, and its development was associated above all with the rise of cloth-making, including linen weaving, and cut glass.

The town centre has retained its medieval plan. The Market Place with burghers' houses, the Town Hall and Neptune Fountain is one of the most beautiful in Silesia. The houses of the linen merchants, some built in the 17th and 18th centuries on late medieval foundations, others restored or reconstructed, are fine examples of the various architectural periods especially the Baroque and Rococo. The *Town Hall*, completed in 1747, dominates the square.

The oldest ecclesiastical building is the *Kościół śś. Erazma i Pancracego (Church of Sts Erasmus and Pancras)*, whose tower, 70 metres high, is the town's most prominent landmark. The Baroque high altar in the Gothic chancel of the church was made in 1713–18 by the local carpenter David Hielscher. Its fourteen figures come from the workshop of the sculptor Thomas Weissfeld of Wrocław, while the painted altarpiece showing the Transfiguration is by Johann Kretschmer of Głogów. Nearby, ul. 1. Maja, is the architecturally interesting *Kościół św. Krzyża (Holy Cross Church)*, formerly Lutheran and built as one of the 'Grace Churches' permitted in 1707 (see page 583). It is a stone building erected on a Latin cross plan in 1709–18 by Martin Frantz, an architect from Reval (now Tallinn) on the Baltic who had settled at Legnica. He took as his model Jean de Vallée's Church of St Catherine in Stockholm. The magnificent ensemble of altar and organ occupies the whole of the east wall of the interior. This unusual arrangement was stipulated by the church's patron, Christoph Menzel, a merchant of Jelenia Góra, who wanted the organ to face the congregation behind or above the altar. The galleried interior has painted decoration by Franz Hoffmann (a pupil of Willmann) and Felix Anton Scheffler. Around the churchyard are the elaborate Baroque family vaults (now decayed) of the town's linen merchants.

The spa town of *Cieplice Śląskie-Zdrój (Bad Warmbrunn)* is now joined to Jelenia Góra. A spa was already in existence here in the 13th century; it was looked after first by the Hospitallers (1281–1381) and later by the Cistercians of Krzeszów (1404–1810), to whom it was entrusted by the Counts Schaffgotsch who acquired the town in 1381. The Late Baroque *Schaffgotsch Palace* (1784–9, Johann Georg Rudolf) dominates the town centre. In the 19th century its gardens became the Kurpark with spa buildings by Karl Gottfried Giessler, a pupil of Langhans, and a Neoclassical theatre (1836) by Albert Tollberg, a pupil of Schinkel. Development of the spa continued in the 20th century and today it is one of the most popular health resorts in Poland.

The town of *Sobieszów (Hermsdorf)* has also been incorporated into Jelenia Góra. It is situated at the foot of *Chojnik (Kynast)*, a granite precipice 627 metres high. Little survives of the original castle on the summit of the hill, dating back to Bolko II, Duke of Świdnica and Jawor, which was much altered in the 15th, 16th and 17th centuries. The only feature of interest remaining is the oriel window of the chapel (1393), projecting at a right angle from the wall and supported by a stone console in the form of a bearded head.

Jagniątków (Agnetendorf), a few kilometres to the south, was the home of the writer and dramatist Gerhart Hauptmann (1862–1946), whose best known work, the pioneering Naturalistic play *Die Weber* ('The Weavers') of 1892 dealt with the Silesian weaver's uprising of 1844. Hauptmann was awarded the Nobel Prize for literature in 1912. The large house he built in 1900–01, *Haus Weisenstein*, with a grand hall painted in 1922 with murals by Johannes Avenarius inspired by Hauptmann's works, is now a children's home. Jagniątków is situated in the Karkonosze (Riesengebirge), whose highest peak, Śnieżka

(Czech: Sněžka; German: Schneekoppe), 1,602 metres high, is the tallest in the whole 300 kilometres of the Sudety range. The best-known holiday and winter sports resorts in this region are **Karpacz (Krummhübel)** directly at the foot of Śnieżka and **Szklarska Poręba (Schreiberhau)** not far from Mount Szrenica (1,362 metres). The **Karkonosze National Park** has a fine variety of pines, mountain ash, and the Carpathian birch. Mouflons are sometimes to be seen, and the park is unusually rich in owls. **Bierutowice (Brückenberg)**, now part of the town of Karpacz, is worth a visit for the sight of one unusual attraction, the only example of Scandinavian Romanesque architecture in Central Europe. This is the *Kaplica Wang (Wang Chapel)*, one of the Norwegian stave churches dating from the time of the St Olaf, built at Wang in Valders in the early 13th

Gerhart Hauptmann (1862–1946) in 1897

century. When threatened with demolition it was bought at auction in 1841 by the painter Johan Christian Clausen Dahl, a Norwegian who had settled in Dresden. Dahl then sold it to the young Prussian King Friedrich Wilhelm IV, an obsessive Romantic who had it dismantled and transported to Germany where he at first intended to re-erect it on Pfaueninsel near Berlin. However, he was persuaded by Count Reden of Bukowiec (Buchwald) to have it reassembled in an idealized form in the mountains close to his estate at Mysłakowice. The stone tower was added by August Stüler. The church is used for Lutheran worship on Sundays, and is generally open for parties of visitors in the holiday season.

The estate at **Mysłakowice (Zillerthal-Erdmannsdorf)** was acquired in 1832 by Friedrich Wilhelm III, and over the following years the *Schloss* was much altered, first by Schinkel (1832–7) and then by his pupil August Stüler (1841–3) in a neo-Gothic style inspired by English picturesque Gothic of the early 19th century. In 1837 the king had set aside a large part of the estate as a settlement for several hundred Protestant refugees from the Zillerthal in the Tyrol, and some suitably Tyrolean-style houses were erected for them. The former Protestant *Church* is, however, in an Italian round-arched style. Built in 1837–40, it is based on designs by Schinkel and has a tall slender campanile. In the interior the exposed roof timbers are richly decorated.

To the northwest of Jelenia Góra at **Siedlęcin (Boberröhrsdorf)** stands one of Silesia's most important architectural monuments, the residential tower of a *Castle* dating from the

13th century but partly destroyed in 1443. The knights' hall on the third floor, with deep window embrasures and a ceiling with massive beams, retains some fine mural paintings with a large figure of St Christopher, a *memento mori* scene of the Quick and the Dead, and scenes from an unidentified chivalric romance (perhaps Hartmann von Aue's *Iwein*). These are the only surviving examples of secular wall painting of the early 14th century in Silesia.

Lwówek Śląski (Löwenberg), on the road from Jelenia Góra to Boleslawiec, has almost the finest *Town Hall* in Silesia. It was built in the late 15th and early 16th centuries, probably under the direction of Wendelin Rosskopf. The Burghers' Hall on the ground floor extends across the two adjoining parts of the building; it is divided in two by a row of piers supporting sinuous rib-vaulting reminiscent of Benedikt Ried's work in Prague, while the windows have vigorously carved classical elements and the walls and window embrasures are decorated with Renaissance paintings. Several of the tombs from the former *Kościół Franciszkanów (Franciscan Church)* have been moved to the town hall, including the beautiful tomb slab of the Piast duke of Jawor, Henryk I, and his wife Agnieszka (*c.* 1350).

The *Kościół Wniebowzięcia Najświętszej Marii Panny (Church of the Assumption)* was built in the 13th century, but altered around 1500. The westwork with the two towers and the doorway survives from the earlier building. The portal dating from 1270 has naturalistic foliage on the capitals and archivolts, with a tympanum carved with the Coronation of the Virgin. The town fortifications of Lwówek Śląski (double wall, gatetowers), dating from the 13th and 15th centuries, have survived almost intact.

Not far away at **Płakowice (Plagwitz)** stands a remarkable 16th-century nobleman's seat begun by Rampold von Talkenberg, and later owned by Caspar von Schaffgotsch. The entrance to the three-storey *Palace* is through a fine Renaissance doorway with decorative bas reliefs. The ground-floor arcaded loggia in the courtyard has columns with Ionic capitals supporting a balcony with a magnificent balustrade.

A few kilometres to the north is **Bolesławiec (Bunzlau)** (population 40,000), which has long been the most important town in Silesia for pottery. The Guild of Potters here was founded in 1543, and their work – brown earthenware or colourful stoneware – later made the town world famous. There are still many ceramic factories here, and in the town museum examples of pottery from the 17th century to the present day are displayed. The 'Grosser Topf' ('Great Pot'), a massive vessel 2.25 metres tall made in 1753, was destroyed in 1945. The town's other claim to fame is as the birthplace of Martin Opitz (1597–1639), known as the father of German poetry and the 'Swan of Bober' (the river Bóbr flows close to the town and is often mentioned in his works). The interior of the Late Gothic *Kościół Farny (Parish Church)* (1482–93) was baroquized in 1662–92 by Giulio Simonetti. A cast-iron obelisk covered with inscriptions in Russian and German stands in the market place. It was designed by Karl Friedrich Schinkel and commemorates the Russian Marshal Mikhail Kutuzov, who died here in 1813 during the Napoleonic campaign.

Bolków (Bolkenhain) halfway between Jelenia Góra and Walbrzych, lies in the shadow of a mountain ridge 400 metres high, on which stand the massive ruins of an old Piast *Castle*. Duke Bolko I had castle and town strengthened in the 13th century.

Another ruined *Castle* can be seen at Świny (Schweinhaus), with a 14th-century residential tower visible from afar. The fortress is mentioned for the first time in the Cosmas Chronicle in 1108 (as 'Zvini in Polonia'). In the middle ages it was the seat of the Schwenichen family.

South of Kamienna Góra (Landeshut), at the foot of the Karkonosze Mountains, stands the town of **Krzeszów (Grüssau)**, whose history is bound up with that of its famous monastery. This was founded in 1242 by Benedictines, but in 1292 was taken over by Cistercians from Henryków, who

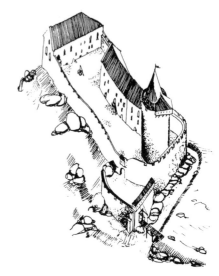

Bolków, reconstruction of the castle

stayed there for more than five hundred years, through all the troubles of the Hussite Wars and the Thirty Years War, until the monastery was secularized by the Prussians in 1810. Since the Second World War a community of Benedictine nuns from Lwów has lived here. The *Kościół Najświętszej Marii Panny Łaskawej (Church of St Mary)* (1728–35) was designed by the monastery's architect, A. J. Jentsch from Jelenia Góra. The church's impressive twin-tower façade has rich sculptural decoration by the leading Prague sculptors Ferdinand Maximilian Brokoff and Matthias Bernhard Braun. Particularly impressive is the magnificent sense of movement and expression in the figure of Moses with the Tables of the Law. Inside, the massive church has a transept and projecting galleries between piers with angled pilasters, and is vaulted in the Bohemian manner developed by the Dientzenhofers. The rich furnishings – altars, pulpit, choir stalls and organ case – were produced by the abbey's sculpture workshop under the direction of Anton Dorasil and later of Marianus Lachel. The organ, with 52 stops and 2,600 pipes, is one of the finest achievements of Silesian organ building. The painting above the high altar is by Peter Brandl of Prague (1731–2), and the ceiling painting by Georg Wilhelm Neunhertz (1733–6). The Princes' Chapel, built after 1735, containing the tombs of the founder, Duke Bolko I Waleczny (the Brave) (d.1301) of Świdnica, and his successors, is one of the finest Baroque mausolea in Silesia. The sculptures are by Dorasil and Ignazio Provisore, the murals by Neunhertz. Of the monastery buildings, which were planned on a monumental scale in the second half of the 18th century, only the three-storey south range was completed. Their size was to have expressed the influence and importance of the abbey, whose land once stretched from the Karkonosze to the Góry Wałbrzyskie (Wałbrzych Hills).

The *Kościół św. Józefa (Church of St Joseph)* at Krzeszów has a magnificent cycle of frescoes of the life of St Joseph by Michael Willmann, the 'Silesian Rembrandt', in 1692–5. The cult of St Joseph intensified during the Counter-Reformation.

An interesting feature of the town of **Chełmsko Śląskie (Schömberg)** is the timber architecture of the early 18th-century arcaded *weavers' houses*, known as the Houses of the Twelve Apostles and the Seven Brothers.

Wałbrzych – Szczawno-Zdrój – Książ Castle – Rybnica Leśna – Strzegom – Rogoźnica – Krzyżowa – Świdnica

Wałbrzych (Waldenburg) (population 120,000) is the second largest town in Lower Silesia. It is one of the centres of the Polish coal-mining industry, with three pits, several coking plants, an iron works, as well as electrical engineering and porcelain factories. The mining of seams of coal under the town has meant that the population has moved away from the centre to surrounding villages which have been incorporated into the town. Subsidence is a problem, and the serious pollution has put the town on the list of environmental disaster areas.

The town is first mentioned in 1426, but it was not until the 18th century that it became economically and politically important with the development of the linen trade. The weavers suffered greatly through the increase in exports which brought longer working hours and higher production levels. They rose several times in revolt to draw attention to their appalling working conditions and the injustices of their employers. Wałbrzych became the centre of the linen trade, especially after the advent of mechanization; but the transformation into a major industrial town only came with the development of collieries.

The Baroque *Kościół św. Marii Panny (Church of St Mary)*, built in 1714 to replace a timber building, is the town's oldest church. The neo-Gothic *Town Hall* was built in 1855–6 by Hermann Friedrich Wäsemann. Burghers' houses of the 18th century still line the market place: 'Drei Rosen' (1777), 'Tageblatt-Haus' (1793) and 'Ankerhaus' (1799). The former Lutheran church was erected in 1785–8 to the Neoclassical designs of Carl Gotthard Langhans.

Szczawno-Zdrój (Bad Salzbrunn) was famous for its mineral springs as early as the 17th century, and in the 19th century developed into a popular spa. At the entrance to the Korona Piastowska sanatorium in ul. Wojska Polskiego, once known as 'Hauptmanns Hotel zur Krone' or the 'Hotel preussichen Krone', is a plaque commemorating the birth here of the writer Gerhart Hauptmann (1862–1946) (see page 591) and his brother Carl (1858–1921), sons of the hotel proprietor. The spa theatre, where Hauptmann had his first experience of the stage, is the venue for the annual Henryk Wieniawski Music Festival (June).

Not far from Wałbrzych, in the midst of extensive old parkland, the spectacularly sited **Książ Castle (Schloss Fürstenstein)** dominates the wooded valley of the River Pełcznica. In the 13th century the castle of the Dukes of Świdnica stood here, known as *clavis ad Silesiam*, the key to Silesia. Only the keep remains (with a neo-Baroque roof added in the 19th century). The 16th-century reconstruction (for the Hochberg family) kept the original plan, with the individual buildings arranged in an oval around the keep. The residential ranges with a Baroque staircase between were added in 1722–4. The architect was Felix Anton Hammerschmied, the carved stonework was by Johann Schwibs and the ceiling painting of Mount Parnassus by Felix Anton Scheffler. The Hochbergs, grown rich from their coalmines, extended the castle on a massive scale in 1909-23, with neo-Renaissance wings designed by Scheinert and Walcher von Moltheim. The châtelaine at that time was an Englishwoman, the vivacious Princess Daisy of Pless, née Cornwallis-West, possibly a natural daughter of Edward VII. The Nazis confiscated the property and.in 1941 began work on the conversion of the castle into Hitler's headquarters. The huge bunker can still be seen, but Hitler never moved in.

The 'Old Castle' on the other side of the valley is in fact a neo-Gothic artificial ruin designed by Christian Wilhelm Tischbein and completed in 1797. At Fürstenstein in August 1800 King Friedrich Wilhelm III and Queen Luise of Prussia attended a mock-medieval tournament. It was witnessed by John Quincy Adams: 'The carousal was in a style of great magnificence ... the close adherence to the forms usual in the times when knighthood was in its glory; the pomp and solemnity of the representation; the contrast between the grandeur of the spectacle and the old ruined walls, the relics of five centuries; and between the romantic wildness of the extensive prospect around, and the crowded thousands who were present to see the show; all contributed to produce a pleasing effect.' Nearby, the castle's stud farm can also be visited.

The interesting little *Church* at **Rybnica Leśna (Reimswaldau)**, in the valley of the Rybna a few kilometres south of Wałbrzych, is one of the rare 'Schrotholzkirchen'. It was built of rough-hewn wood in 1557, as one of the places of worship erected by Protestants long before the Lutheran 'Peace Churches' or 'Grace Churches' of the 17th and 18th centuries. It has a free-standing bell-tower, which also serves as the gate tower in the surrounding wall. The interior of the church was painted in the 17th century with rustic motifs.

Szczawno-Zdrój, Gerhart Hauptmann's birthplace: 'Hauptmanns Hotel zur Krone'

The town of **Strzegom (Striegau)**, on the road to Jawor and Legnica, was founded in 1239. Together with Świdnica and Jawor it defended the mountain passes, and at the same time protected an increasingly important trade route running along the Sudety mountains. The main activity was cloth-making and linen-weaving, but prosperity was shattered by the Thirty Years War. In 1713 the town was settled by pensioners from the War of Spanish Succession. In the 19th century granite quarrying was started in the nearby cliffs. The earliest piece of architecture in Strzegom is the *Kościół śś. Piotra i Pawła (Church of Sts Peter and Paul)* with its very steep roof and two unfinished towers. It was built in the 14th century as a three-aisled basilica entirely of undressed stone with a projecting transept and a long chancel with three apses. The vaulting of the nave shows Bohemian influence; it is very similar to Parler's in St Vitus' Cathedral in Prague. The three portals of the Gothic church (second half of the 14th century) have tympana with figures. In the triangular gable above the west doorway are statues of the Virgin Mary, John the Baptist and Christ in Majesty.

Rogoźnica (Gross Rosen) is notorious for the concentration camp established in 1940, some two kilometres from the village, on the railway line from Strzegom to Jawor. In February 1944 work started on the 'Auschwitzer Lager', intended to take inmates from Auschwitz as the Soviet army advanced. There is a memorial on the site of the camp to the 200,000 people, mainly Jews, who were murdered here after being forced to work as slaves in the granite quarries of Strzegom.

By contrast, the town of **Krzyżowa (Kreisau)**, a few kilometres south of Świdnica, has since the Second World War become an important symbol of resistance to Nazi rule. The *Schloss* here was owned by the Moltke family (it had been acquired in 1867 by the great Prussian field marshal Helmuth von Moltke, who is buried nearby), and it was here that Count Helmut James von Moltke, the field marshal's great-nephew, with his friend Count Peter Yorck von Wartenburg, brought together the 'Kreisauer Kreis' ('Kreisau Circle'), a group of democratically-minded people, who discussed the future of Germany after Hitler and his dictatorship. Moltke, who was executed on 23 January 1945 at Berlin-Plötzensee, had foreseen that one of the ways in which Germany would have to pay for its crimes against other peoples, particularly against the Poles, was by territorial losses after the end of the war. At present the schloss is in a very bad state of repair and because of danger of collapse can no longer be entered. However, like the Princes' Hall at Lubiąż Abbey, it is to be restored at the expense of the German government, as agreed in the German-Polish treaty of 8 November 1990.

Świdnica (Schweidnitz), which around 1550 already had a population of 5,000, was then as big as Wrocław and in economic terms was scarcely less important. Here the trade was in livestock and grain from Poland, wood and furs from Russia, cloth from Flanders and wines from Hungary, while the famous Schweidnitz beer was exported all over Central Europe. The first settlement developed on this site around 500 BC. From 1314 Świdnica was the capital of the greatest of the Silesian Piast duchies. The last heiress, Anne of Świdnica, married the Emperor Charles IV in 1353.

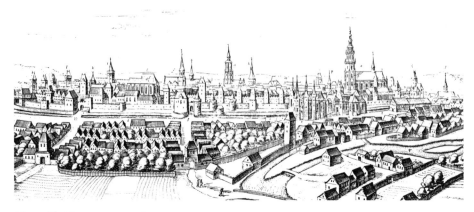

View of Świdnica, engraving by M. Merian, 17th century

The Gothic *Kościół śś. Stanisława i Wacława (Church of St Stanislas and St Wenceslas)* was begun around 1330 but not completed until the late 15th century; the church tower, which is surmounted by a Renaissance cap with three openings, is 104 metres tall, the highest in Silesia. Between 1532 and 1535 the basilica was remodelled as a hall church, and around 1700 the interior was given a Baroque redecoration by the Jesuits, including huge altarpieces, some by Willmann. Although the medieval high altarpiece gave way in 1694 to a large Baroque replacement, its Late Gothic central panel (showing the Death of the Virgin) has fortunately survived. The creator of this work was probably one of the large circle of pupils around Veit Stoss in Kraków. The doorway on the north side of the nave has carvings of Samson and Delilah, and Aristotle and Phyllis. The other interesting religious building in Świdnica is the *Kościół św. Trócjy (Trinity Church)*, the best known of the Silesian Peace Churches (see page 589). The churchyard is neglected and the tombstones with German inscriptions are overgrown, but the church itself is in a good state of repair. The cruciform building (half-timbered to meet the requirement that no stone or brick could be used), with tier upon tier of galleries and a flat ceiling, was built in 1657–8 by Albrecht von Säbisch, who was also responsible for the similar Peace Church at Jawor (see page 589). The church can hold a congregation of 3,000 seated and 4,500 standing. The interior has fine folk Baroque furnishings added in the 18th century, the work of local carpenters and sculptors. Świdnica escaped much damage in the Second World War and is one of Silesia's most attractive towns. The market square has some fine burghers' houses, mostly with Late Baroque façades, but some earlier. The early 16th-century *Town Hall* was remodelled in 1717–26, but retains a vaulted interior and a mid-16th century tower.

Kotlina Kłodzka – Kłodzko – Polanica-Zdrój – Duszniki-Zdrój –
Kudowa-Zdrój – Wambierzyce – Bystrzyca Kłodzka – Lądek-Zdrój –
Zagórze Śląskie – Ząbkowice Śląskie – Henryków – Ziębice

The **Kotlina Kłodzka (Glatzer Talkessel)**, a region which extends southwards from Wałbrzych into the Czech Republic, is hemmed in by mountain ranges: to the west are the Góry Sowie (Eulengebirge, 'Owl Mountains') and the Góry Stołowe (Heuscheuer Gebirge, 'Table' or 'Barn Mountains'), to the southwest the Góry Bystrzyskie (Habelschwerdter Gebirge), to the southeast the massif of the Masyw Śnieżnika (Glatzer Schneegebirge, 'Snow Mountains'), and finally to the east the Góry Złote (Reichensteiner Gebirge, 'Gold Mountains'), also famous for their arsenic mines. The whole region is very attractive and provides many opportunities for rambling and winter sports.

The commercial and tourist centre is **Kłodzko (Glatz)**, which in the middle ages was an important fortress town on the trading route between Poland and Bohemia. The town centre has preserved its 14th-century plan. In the market place stands the *Town Hall*, originally Gothic but altered in the late 19th century. Its Renaissance tower (1654) dominates the townscape. The interior of the Gothic *Kościół Naj Marii Panny (Church of St Mary)* (14th/15th centuries) underwent a thorough baroquization in 1660–70. In front of the church gate stands a *Nepomuk Column*, a symbol of the Bohemian-Habsburg Counter-Reformation in Silesia. The stone *bridge* (14th century) across a branch of the Nysa Kłodzka, with its Baroque statues of saints, is reminiscent of the Charles Bridge in Prague. On the hill above the town stands the *fortress* built for Frederick II in the mid-18th century to replace an earlier castle. The road west from Kłodzko follows the valley of the Góry Stołowe and Góry Bystrzyckie to the Czech border town of Náchod, passing through three popular spas and holiday resorts: **Polanica-Zdrój (Bad Altheide)**, **Duszniki-Zdrój (Bad Reinerz)** and **Kudowa-Zdrój (Bad Kudowa)**. The international Chopin Festival is held every August in the old theatre of Duszniki-Zdrój (where on 26 August 1826 the composer gave his first public concert outside Poland), while at Kudowa-Zdrój there are regular music festivals in honour of Stanisław Moniuszko. Kudowa Zdrój has 'champagne baths', thanks to the arsenic. At Duszniki-Zdrój an early 17th-century paper mill now houses a Museum of the Paper Industry. The *Kościół śś. Piotra i Pawła (Church of Sts Peter and Paul)*, baroquized in 1708–30, has an extraordinary Baroque pulpit shaped like the mouth of Jonah's whale. In the market are burghers' houses and a Marian column (1725).

Wambierzyce (Albendorf), in the Góry Stołowe 10 km northwest of Kłodzko, is Lower Silesia's most important pilgrimage centre. Its focus is a miraculous statue of the Virgin Mary. At the turn of the 18th century an elaborate *Way of the Cross* was created for the owner, Daniel Paschasius von Osterberg, who wished to turn the place into a Silesian Jerusalem. The present big Late Baroque *Church* is approached up a broad flight of steps and has a two-storey pilastered façade with projecting end bays. It was built from 1716 to 1721 on a complex centralized plan around an octagon, with a processional sequence of chapels containing tableaux of scenes from the Life of Christ and the Virgin. There are a number of large 17th-century altarpieces by Michael Willmann.

South of Kłodzko lies the town of **Bystrzyca Kłodzka (Habelschwerdt)**, where the former Protestant church now houses the *Muzeum Filumistyczne (Museum of Fire-Making)* with a fabulous collection of match boxes. The town became a centre of the match industry in the second half of the 19th century. In the market place is the *Town Hall* (16th century, altered in 1854) and some interesting *burghers' houses* with attractive Renaissance and Baroque façades. The surviving *town fortifications* date back to the early 14th century and include the Brama Wodna (Water Gate) (1568) and the Brama Kłodzka (Kłodzko Gate) with the adjoining Wieża Rycerska (Knights' Tower).

Lądek-Zdrój (Bad Landeck) in the middle of the Góry Złote is a spa town which counted Goethe and Turgenev among its visitors in the 19th century. The first bath house was established here in 1498. The town suffered badly in the Thirty Years War, but in 1678 a new bath house was built in the 'Turkish' manner. The spa was patronized by the Prussian royal family in the 18th and early 19th centuries: Frederick the Great bathed here in 1765, and in 1813 Friedrich Wilhelm III met Tsar Alexander I at Lądek to formalize the Prussian-Russian alliance against the fleeing Napoleon. The town has a delightful market place with Late Baroque house fronts (built after a devastating fire in 1739). The ruins of *Zamek Grodno (Kynsburg)* near **Zagórze Śląskie (Kynau)** on the northern edge of the Góry Sowie, is another impressive example of 14th-century Silesian fortification. Further east are two towns which were at the centre of the Weavers' Revolt in June 1844 (see page 591). The main landmark of **Ząbkowice Śląskie (Frankenstein)** is the bell-tower of the *Kościół św. Anny (Church of St Anne)*, which since subsidence at the end of the 16th

Henryków, plan of the Cistercian Church

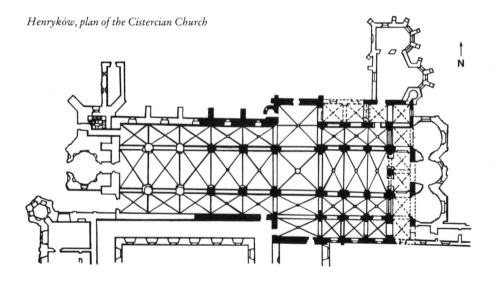

century has also been known as the Leaning Tower. The *Castle* of the Dukes of Ziębice, now a ruin in the northwest of the town, was remodelled in 1524–30 by Benedikt Ried, the architect to the Bohemian kings, for Duke Karl, who had become Burgrave of Prague. From the 15th century Ząbkowice Śląskie was one of the centres of Silesian cloth-making and linen-weaving. Not far, on a wooded hill at *Kamieniec Ząbkowicki (Kamenz)*, the neo-Gothic brick castle, now ruined, was designed by Karl Friedrich Schinkel for Princess Marianne of the Netherlands (wife of Prince Albrecht of Prussia) and built in 1838–73. This late masterpiece by the great Prussian architect shows the influence of his study of Malbork. Gutted in 1946, the castle is being restored as an hotel.

A few kilometres east of here, on the upper courses of the Oława (Ohle) stands the former abbey of **Henryków (Heinrichau)** (plate 79). Together with Lubiąż, Trzebnica and Krzeszów, this was one of the medieval monastic centres that played a decisive part in the German settlement of Silesia. In 1227 a Cistercian monastery was established here as a daughter house of Lubiąż. A year later the first church was consecrated. The abbey is also important for the early history of Polish literature: the 'Liber Fundationis claustri Sanctae Mariae Virginis', a history of the abbey written by the monks here around 1270, includes in its Latin text the earliest surviving sentence written in Polish. The Foundation Book vividly depicts daily life at the monastery.

The medieval *Kościół Klasztorny (Abbey Church)* of Henryków is the earliest surviving example of a Cistercian Gothic church in Silesia, and one of the most important. The choir dates from the 13th century, the nave from the 14th. The medieval building, a typical example of the Cistercian style, was mostly retained in the Baroque remodelling of the monastic buildings between 1682 and 1685 by Matthias Kirchberger. A Baroque gable and domed porch were added to the west front, and an openwork Baroque cap placed on the northwest tower. At the same time the interior was baroquized and furnished with magnificent altars, paintings by Michael Willmann, organ, pulpit and splendid choir stalls with statues of gesticulating saints. In the Chapel of St Mary Magdalene only the tomb slab remains of the tomb of Duke Bolko II of Ziębice (died 1341) and his wife, Jutta.

In 1810 the abbey was secularized. Through the Prussian Princess Friderike Louise Wilhelmine, who became Queen of the Netherlands, it passed to the House of Orange, but in 1863 came into the possession of the Grand Dukes of Saxe-Weimar-Eisenach. Today the former conventual buildings are used by an agricultural college. It is worth making a detailed tour of the buildings to the refectory, the Princes' Hall with its frescoes, and the series of rooms in the Abbot's lodgings.

At **Ziębice (Münsterberg)** the most interesting building is the *Kościół Farny (Parish Church of St Mary and St George)*. The nave was built in 1265–75, and in the 15th century the Romanesque chancel was replaced by a three-aisled Late Gothic chancel with three apses at the east end. Of the 16th-century Town Hall only the *Tower* survives, as do parts of the town fortifications including the Paczków Gate. The *Church of the Knights Hospitaller* was built in 1726–30. The town also has a Neoclassical Lutheran church by Carl Gotthard Langhans, one of several he built in Silesia.

Opole – Prószków – Olesno – Głogówek – Nysa – Otmuchów – Paczków – Brzeg – Góra św. Anny

Opole (Oppeln) developed at an ancient river crossing on the Oder. It is now a town with a population of more than 120,000. From 1919 until 1938 Opole was the capital of the separated German province of Upper Silesia. The limestone quarries in the vicinity provide the raw material for the town's most important industry, the making of cement. Other industries here mainly involve the processing of agricultural products.

The name of the town is derived from *opole*, an old Slavonic term for a small settlement. Archaeological excavations in the northern part of the Wyspa Pasieka (the island between the Oder and the millstream opposite the town centre) have revealed an 8th-century Slav town; the walls of houses and some objects (household tools, shoes, amulets) were found. The Bavarian Geographer (mid-9th century) mentions Opole as the capital of the Opolani, one of the six Slavic tribes then living in Silesia.

In the centre of Opole on the right bank of the Oder, is the market place with the *Town Hall*, completed in 1936 as an imitation of the Palazzo Vecchio in Florence. The Baroque and Rococo façades of the *burghers' houses* have been reconstructed since the Second World War (plate 77).

The *Kościół Najświętszej Marii Panny (Church of St Mary)*, originally 14th-century, was given its present Renaissance appearance when it was remodelled in the 16th century; it was later given a neo-Romanesque façade. The furnishings inside are mostly Baroque. Not far from the church is a Gothic building (1435) which now houses the *Muzeum Śląska Opolskiego (Museum of Opolian Silesia)*, with historical and ethnographical collections. To the north of the town centre stands the *Cathedral* (built in the first half of the 15th century as a collegiate church and raised to cathedral status since the war), which contains the tomb of the last Piast prince of Opole, Jan II (died 1532). The *Kościół Franciszkanów (Franciscan Church)* in ul. Zamkowa, which leads to Wyspa Pasieka, essentially dates from the 14th century but was altered in the 17th/18th centuries. Inside, the Gothic Kaplica św. Anny (Chapel of St Anne) (1309) contains the tombs of the Dukes of Opole with more than 20 tomb slabs in all.

The *Castle* at **Prószków (Proskau)**, south of Opole, has impressive sgraffito decoration (after 1671) on its exterior façades, with allegories, depictions of famous philosophers and scenes from various wars. Originally the castle, built after 1563 for Georg von Proskau, was a two-storey Renaissance building with an arcaded courtyard and bastion-like corner structures. After destruction in the Thirty Years' War it was rebuilt between 1677 and 1683 under the direction of an Italian architect, Giovanni Seregno. Later some parts were given a Baroque remodelling, which included the addition of two towers to the main front.

Olesno (Rosenberg), about 25 km northeast of Opole, has one of the most remarkable pieces of timber architecture in the whole of Poland. The *Kościół św. Anny (Church of St Anne)*, built in 1518, was enlarged in 1668–70 with the addition of a star-shaped ensemble of five radiating chapels by Matthias Snopek.

Głogówek (Oberglogau) near the Czech border is well worth a visit to see the *Kościół św. Bartłomieja (Church of St Bartholomew)*. The interior of this 14th-century building was made splendidly Baroque in 1775–81. The frescoes by Franz Anton Sebastini from Bohemia glorify the life and work of the church's patron saint. The numerous statues are by the sculptor Johann Schubert of Moravia.

Nysa (Neisse) is one of Silesia's oldest towns. In the 12th century it was the seat of the Piast Dukes of Nysa, but after 1198 it passed to the Bishops of Wrocław and in 1308 was granted its town charter. In the 16th and 17th centuries Nysa played an important part in the religious and cultural life of Silesia. At the Jesuit College (called the Carolinum after its founder in 1624, Archduke Karl of Austria) two future kings of Poland, Michał Korybut Wiśniowiecki (reigned 1669–73) and Jan III Sobieski (reigned 1674–96), received their education. The town also experienced a great economic boom in this period. As elsewhere in Silesia, the main trade was in linen and yarns, but Nysa was also famous for its trade in Austrian and Hungarian wines, which were stored in massive cellars. Today the main industries are metallurgy, food-processing and tanning.

The oldest architectural monument is the *Kościół św. Jakuba (Church of St James)* near the market place. Excavations have shown that this big, nine-bay hall church, built in the 14th/15th centuries, was preceded by a Romanesque basilica erected after 1198. The present church, now repaired after partial destruction in the Second World War, dates from 1392–1430. The west gable was built in the 16th century, and the vaulting of the nave was much altered in the 19th century. There are twenty chapels in all and they contain a wealth of monuments. The most famous is the tall tomb of Bishop Balthasar von Promnitz (died 1539) made of Salzburg marble, with the life-size figure of the bishop under a baldacchino. The church also has a free-standing bell-tower built of granite. Not far away is the Late Gothic *Kościół św. Barbary (Church of St Barbara)*, first mentioned in 1372 and rebuilt after destruction in 1743.

View of Nysa, engraving by M. Merian, 17th century

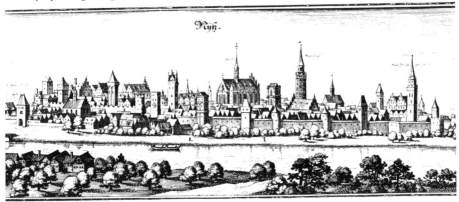

A particularly interesting Renaissance survival is the *Waga Miejska (Town Weigh-House)* completed in 1604, which stands in the market place. The arched entrance on the ground floor of the overhanging house is rusticated, while the main storey is decorated with sculptures and sgraffito work. The stepped gable is surrounded by a multiplicity of architectural and sculptural elements. The whole building was reconstructed in 1947–8.

The Baroque *Kościół śś. Piotra i Pawła (Church of Sts Peter and Paul)* to the south of the town centre was built in 1719–30 for the Canons Regular of the Holy Sepulchre by Michael Klein, an architect from Hungary who had settled in Nysa. The church with its two-towered façade is best known for a splendid ceiling painting by the brothers Felix Anton and Christoph Thomas Scheffler, showing the Adoration of the Cross by the Church Triumphant.

On the eastern side of the town centre the Baroque *Kościół Jezuitów (Jesuit Church)* built in 1688–92 clearly shows the influence of the Gesù in Rome. The interior is decorated with frescoes by Karl Dankwart, and the plasterwork is by Giovanni Battista Quadro. Next to the church stands the building of the former *Jesuit College (Carolinum)* founded in 1622–4 (college buildings 1669–73, school building 1722–5 by Christoph Tausch and Michael Klein). Parts of the medieval town walls have survived, including the *Brama Wrocławska (Wrocław Gate)* (16th century) and the *Baszta Ziębicka (Ziębice Tower)* (16th/17th centuries). The *Palace of the Bishops of Wrocław* (1608–24 and 1708–29, by Christoph Tausch, Michael Klein and Felix Anton Hammerschmied) has been rebuilt after being burned down in 1945.

A few kilometres west of Nysa, between the lakes Jezioro Nyskie and Jezioro Otmuchowskie, lies the town of **Otmuchów (Ottmachau)** which has a history going back to the 12th century, when King Bolesław III Krzywousty built a fort here. The town was not damaged in the Second World War and all its old architectural monuments survive. These include the northeast wing of the *Castle* of the Bishops of Wrocław, built in the 16th century on the hill between the River Nysa (Neisse) and the town centre, and – a little below – their *Palace*, built in 1706–7 by Michael Klein. The *Wieża Wróbla (Sparrow Tower)* to the northeast of the market place once formed part of the 14th-century town walls. In the market place itself stands the Renaissance *Town Hall* completed in 1538, with an early 17th-century tower; the square is surrounded by Baroque burghers' houses. The left bank of the Nysa runs beside the Baroque *Kościół św. Mikołaja (Church of St Nicholas)*, which was erected in 1690–93 to plans by Johann Peter Tobler. Inside, the frescoes are by Karl Dankwart (1698), and the painting on the high altar is by Michael Willmann (1696).

Paczków (Patschkau), the 'Polish Carcassonne', at the foot of the Góry Złote, is another town which has preserved its historical appearance. The 14th-century *town walls* with their towers and gates are almost completely preserved. The market place has some *burghers' houses* with Renaissance and Baroque façades. The Renaissance tower (1552), 45 metres high, dominates the town. The fine *Kościół św. Marii Panny, św. Jana Ewangelisty i św. Jana Baptysty (Church of the Virgin, St John the Evangelist and St John the*

Brzeg, gatehouse of the Piast castle

Baptist) (plate 80) is strongly fortified. It is a three-aisled hall church built in the second half of the 14th century, which in the 16th century was given Renaissance battlements concealing the roof. The most valuable of the church's furnishings is a silver crucifix, partly gilded, dating from 1516. On its front are four containers for relics around the figure of Christ attached in the centre.

The name of **Brzeg (Brieg)** halfway between Opole and Wrocław recalls the original fishing village, *Wysokibrzeg* ('high bank'), which was already in existence around 1200. It was situated at an old Oder crossing, and was later incorporated into the fortified town, together with the castle. The exact date of the founding of the town is not known, but it was probably in 1246 or 1250. Today it is an important industrial centre with a population of 37,000, but its greatest period was during the Renaissance, when the Lutheran dukes fostered the Reformation, humanism and culture, and the buildings which still dominate the townscape were built. Outside the gates of Brzeg, at the village of Małujowice (Mollwitz) 5 km west of the town, the Prussian forces gained their first victory over the Austrian army in 1741. During the siege of Brzeg, which was captured on 4 May 1741, the magnificent Piast palace was set ablaze by the Prussian cannons.

The Gothic *Kościół św. Mikołaja (Church of St Nicholas)* was built between 1370 and 1417 as a three-aisled basilica with two massive towers. It has one of the most spacious church interiors in Silesia. The narrow nave, with its steeply pitched roof, rises far above side aisles which have been extended by the addition of chapels and have flatter roofs. The *Town Hall* shows the sophistication attained in Silesian Renaissance architecture and is now the only complete Renaissance town hall to survive in the region. It was built in 1570-77 by Jacopo Pahr of Milan and his son-in-law Bernardo Niuron of Lugano, after its medieval predecessor had been destroyed by fire in 1569. The most interesting interior is the council chamber, whose Rococo remodelling dates from 1746. There are also a few burghers' houses with Renaissance façades still remaining in the town centre.

The best preserved part of the old *Piast Castle* (now the Museum of the Silesian Piasts) is its richly decorated gate. Above an archway flanked by pilasters rises an attic decorated with coats of arms and statues of Duke Georg II and his wife Barbara of Brandenburg. Above them are inscriptions which include the date of their marriage in 1553. Between the first and second floors are two rows of portrait busts, the Kings of Poland above and the Dukes of Brzeg below. Next to the gate is the castle chapel, an apsidal brick Gothic building (1369-71) containing the mausoleum of the Piast dukes (1567). The castle was started in 1544 by Georg II's father, Duke Friedrich II, but did not receive its Renaissance form until after his death in 1547, when Georg II called in the architects Pahr and Niuron. Pahr was also in charge of the building of the *grammar school* on the south side of the square in front of the castle. It was a great centre of Lutheran education in the 17th century.

About 30 km southeast of Opole lies **Góra Świętej Anny (Sankt Annaberg)**, which has become a religious and political symbol of Upper Silesia. The black basalt hill, 410 metres high, called Chełm, dominates the woods and fields for miles around. On it stands the Reformed Franciscan monastery with its Baroque *pilgrimage church,* the centre for the veneration of a plain carved wooden figure of St Anne with the Virgin and Child dating from the 15th century. Around the church, built in 1657-73 and restored in 1958, is a total of 35 chapels. On top of the hill is a monument erected in 1953 to commemorate the Third Polish Uprising in Upper Silesia in 1921 (plate 81, see page 568), when after heavy fighting the Poles were driven from the hilltop by the Germans. The present monument stands on the platform built as part of the 1936–8 German monument commemorating the same events, which includes a Nazi *Thingplatz*, an amphitheatre to be used for folk assemblies.

Katowice – Bytom – Gliwice – Będzin – Siewierz – Rybnik – Racibórz – Bielsko Biała – Cieszyn

The Katowice region is the most industrialized and most densely populated part of Poland. The huge industrial conglomeration which spreads out around the city of Katowice itself is known as GOP (Górnośląski Okręg Przemysłowy, or Upper Silesian Industrial Region) and has traditionally been the backbone of the Polish economy. It includes thirteen large towns,

Zabrze, the Old Post Office after restoration

among them Katowice (population: 362,000), Sosnowiec (252,000), Bytom (238,000), Gliwice (211,000), Zabrze (Hindenburg) (197,000), which effectively form a single industrial conurbation. There are sixty collieries operating here, including Europe's biggest, the 'Piast' pit near Tychy. There are also twenty ironworks, headed by the mighty 'Huta Katowice', and eleven coking plants. The damage done to the environment is enormous: in 1986 the Sejm designated Upper Silesia an 'ecological disaster area'.

The origins and development of industry in the GOP are based on the minerals found here, in particular metallic ores (iron, zinc and lead) and coal. The mineral riches of Upper Silesia were known in the middle ages and in the 13th century miners from Bytom were already digging for lead and silver. Upper Silesia, like the Ruhr, Prussia's other great industrial region, grew rapidly in the second half of the 19th century with the development of modern industry. The population ballooned and many working families were forced to live in terrible conditions and suffer great privations. The present appearance of Upper Silesia is characterized mainly by development in the late 1960's and early 1970's.

Although **Katowice (Kattowitz)** – briefly renamed Stalinogród in 1953 – is primarily an industrial town, it has also developed into a major centre of learning and culture since the war. The Uniwersytet Śląski (Silesian University) was founded here in 1968, and the town now has more than 20,000 students and six institutions of higher education. Films made at the studios in Katowice have dealt with the historic and social problems of Upper Silesia. A *monument* north of the town centre (1967), in the shape of three clipped wings, commemorates those who took part in the Uprisings of 1919–21. Opposite is the *Sports and Entertainment Hall* (1965–71, by Maciej Gintowt and others) (plate 82), a pioneering use of concrete.

The *Muzeum Górnośląskie* at **Bytom (Beuthen)** tells the cultural history of the region. The town also has one of the rare 18th-century 'Schrotholzkirchen' (see page 596).

Gliwice (Gleiwitz) has a long tradition of metal founding. In the late 18th century sculptures were cast here after models by famous sculptors and it was here in 1813 that the first Iron Cross was made. Between the wars Gliwice was just on the German side of the border. A plaque at the radio transmitter station on the edge of the town commemorates the alleged Polish attack (in fact staged by the Nazis) used as the pretext for the invasion of Poland in September 1939.

Będzin, to the north of Katowice, is one of the oldest towns in Upper Silesia. In the 17th century it was famous for its cloth, and in 1766 the first coal mine was started here. The Gothic *Castle* of the Piasts (13th/14th century) on a hill above the town (plate 78) can be seen for miles around. At **Siewierz** the simple, aisleless *Church of St John the Baptist* dates from the early 12th century. It has a west gallery supported on arches.

The big coal heaps, some of them up to 100 metres high, which dominate the landscape around **Rybnik**, southwest of Katowice, show that this is another major centre of Upper Silesian coal-mining. The name of the town ('fish pond') is a reminder that in the 10th century a fishing settlement existed on the site of the present town.

At an ancient river crossing, where the Oder enters Silesia, stands **Racibórz (Ratibor)**. A *castle* stood here in the 12th century guarding the trade road leading from the Moravian Gate to Kraków. According to legend the castle even withstood the Tatar invasion in 1241 and, although much altered over the centuries, it is still there. There is an elegant late Gothic chapel, founded in 1288 and dedicated to St Thomas Becket. Racibórz is one of the most attractive historic towns of Upper Silesia. Its most prominent building is the *Kościół Farny (Parish Church of St Mary)*. The chancel dates from around 1285, and the Baroque high altar (1656) and elaborate choir stalls (1653) are worth seeing. There is a modern monument to the Polish Mother, commemorating the Silesian women who kept the flame of Polish culture alive.

Bielsko-Biała (Bielitz) has been a centre of the textile industry since 1806, when the first wool-spinning machine was set up here. The town is the starting point for holiday-makers seeking relaxation in the Silesian Beskids – at Żywiec on the reservoir of the River Sola, at Wisła near the source of the Vistula, or at Szczyrk, the most important spa in the region.

Thirty kilometres west of Bielsko-Biała stands the divided town of **Cieszyn**, the former capital of an ancient duchy known in German as Teschen. The river Olza (Olsa) was chosen as the border in 1920 by the Council of Ambassadors of the victorious powers after bitter Polish-Czech disputes over the area following the defeat of the Austro-Hungarian

Empire in the First World War. In October 1938 Polish forces crossed the river to retake the Czech part (called Český Těšín), but were themselves swept away by the Germans less than a year later. The Polish and Czech governments-in-exile continued to quarrel over the town, but Stalin's solution of the dispute in 1945 was the same as that of 1920 – so the town remains split. Cieszyn stands near the centre of the Moravian Gate, the narrow corridor which is the only point between Bavaria and the Black Sea where Southern Europe can be reached without crossing an Alpine pass; this was a crucial place for traders and plundering hordes alike. The town today is full of greenery and its *Kościół św. Mikołaja (Church of St Nicholas)*, a much-restored Romanesque rotunda built in the second half of the 11th century as the chapel of the ducal castle, is one of the oldest churches in Poland. Of the castle itself only the 14th-century Piast Tower remains. Also of interest are the *Town Hall* (1800), the *burghers' houses* in the market place (18th century), the *Kościół Dominikanów (Dominican Church)*, now the parish church (originally 13th century but baroquized in the late 18th century), the *Kościół św. Trojcy (Trinity Church)* (1585), the *Palace* built in 1832 for Archduke Karl, Duke of Saxe-Teschen, by Josef Kornhäusel of Vienna, and the *Muzeum Cieszyńskie (Cieszyn Museum)* in the old palace of the Counts Larisch (1796), which tells the history of this border region. The 'Street of the Three Brothers' commemorates the legendary founding of the town in 810, when the three sons of Leszko III met at the well here and called their new town 'cieszę się' ('I am happy') because they were so pleased to see each other again.

Reinhold Vetter

Photographic Acknowledgements

Colour plates

Ifa Bilderteam, Munich 3, 22, 23
Jürgens Ost und Europa Photo, Cologne 26
Muzeum Narodowe, Kraków 5, 7
Polska Agencja Interpress, Warsaw 16
Tadeusz Suminski, Warsaw 6, 10, 14, 17, 24, 25
Krzystof Wócjik, Warsaw 1, 2, 4, 8, 9, 11, 18, 19, 20, 21

Black and white plates

Arkady, Warsaw 12, 13, 21, 55, 59, 72, 74, 75
Ifa Bilderteam, Munich 7
Edmund Kupiecki, Warsaw 18, 22, 54, 58, 68, 71, 83
Polska Agencja Interpress, Warsaw 8, 9, 17, 52, 53, 81, 82
Tadeusz Suminski, Warsaw 1, 2, 3, 4, 5, 6, 10, 11, 26, 32, 38, 41, 42, 43, 44, 45, 46, 47, 48, 49, 50, 51, 61, 64, 77
Krzystof Wójcik, Warsaw 14, 15, 16, 19, 20, 23, 24, 25, 27, 28, 29, 30, 31, 33, 35, 36, 37, 39, 40, 56, 57, 60, 62, 63, 65, 66, 67, 69, 70, 73, 76, 78, 79, 80

Text illustrations

Arkady, Warsaw 162, 214, 352, 472, 476, 506, 554, 560, 573, 594, 605
Polish Embassy 85
J. G. Herder-Institut, Marburg 229, 327, 330, 334, 339, 341, 357, 367, 369, 380, 412
Adam Kraft Verlag, Mannheim 371, 373
Ryszard Kubiczek, Kraków 455
Hanna Manczak-Wincinciuk, Warsaw 134
Isolde Ohlbaum, Munich 106
Panstwowe Wydawnictwo Naukowe, Warsaw 287, 289, 313, 528
Polska Agencja Interpress, Warsaw 13, 35, 100, 105, 111, 265, 286, 291, 482, 541, 543
Presseagentur Sven Simon, Bonn 82
Gerhard Rautenberg Verlag, Leer 361
Tadeusz Suminski, Warsaw 249, 419
Ullstein Bilderdienst, Berlin 55, 58, 63, 154, 247, 366, 417, 495, 508, 592
Urania Verlag, Leipzig 279, 285
Westpreussisches Landesmuseum, Münster-Wolbeck Frontispiece, 385, 397

All other text illustrations from authors' personal archives and those of DuMont Buchverlag.
Maps and plans by DuMont Buchverlag, Cologne.
Maps and plans on pages 17, 23, 38, 39, 42, 52 and 484 by Pallas Athene.

Glossary

altarpiece Painting and/or sculpture placed behind the altar table. Medieval altarpieces are sometimes called retables.

altarpiece, winged Altarpiece consisting of a central panel ('shrine') flanked by hinged side panels with paintings or carvings. (See also triptych, polyptych.)

antependium Altar frontal made of precious fabric, or elaborate metalwork or woodwork.

apotheosis A person being turned into a god; more generally: a glorification, transfiguration.

apse Semicircular or polygonal vaulted space often terminating a chancel or chapel.

architrave Lowest of the three parts of an entablature (qv).

archivolt Moulded frame on the face of an arch, sometimes decorated with figure sculpture in medieval portals.

ark The cabinet in which the Torah scrolls are kept in a synagogue. Also called the *aron ha-kodesh* or *hekhal*.

ashlar Blocks of stone hewn in regular rectangular shapes with flat faces and laid in horizontal courses.

atlas (pl. atlantes) Male figure supporting an entablature.

attic The area of wall above the main entablature of a building, sometimes decorated with statues, inscriptions, etc., and hiding the roof. (See also Polish parapet.)

barrel vault A vault with semi-circular (or pointed) section.

basilica (a) Church with three, five or more aisles, the central aisle (i.e. nave) being higher than those at the side, so that the nave is lighted by a clearstory (qv); (b) Title conferred by the Pope on certain privileged churches.

Bernardines Observant Order of St Francis, which claimed to observe Francis's original Rule. Named after St Bernardino of Siena.

bimah Platform in synagogue from which the Torah scrolls are read. In Ashkenazi synagogues it is situated in the centre, on the main axis of the building.

blind arcading Arcading applied to the wall surface for articulation, with no openings behind it.

Bohemian cap Form of dome with an imaginary round base, fitted into a square or rectangular plan; also called a sail vault.

boss Projection at the intersection of ribs in a vault, often decorated with carving.

Calvary Sculptural representation of the place of Christ's Crucifixion, usually as part of a sequence of Stations of the Cross. Elaborate Calvaries were built in Counter-Reformation Poland.

capital Upper part of a column, pier or pilaster with ornamental, figural or plant decoration. (See orders.)

cartouche Ornamental frame for inscriptions, emblems, coats of arms, etc.

Castellan (Polish: Kasztelan) A regional officer of state in Poland-Lithuania.

cerkiew Polish term for an Orthodox or Uniate church, distinguished from a Roman Catholic *kościół* or Protestant *zbór*.

chancel The part of a church containing

the altar, usually at the east end and raised a few steps above the nave.

Chancellor (Polish: Kanclerz) A major officer of state in Poland-Lithuania. Before the Union of Lublin there were separate chancellors for the Crown Lands and the Grand Duchy of Lithuania.

chapter house Room in a monastery (or similar foundation) where the monks or canons assemble.

chasuble Priest's vestment resembling a poncho worn for celebrating Mass.

choir Part of church where the divine office is sung, usually in the chancel (qv).

choir stalls Seating along the sides of the choir for the clergy, usually of wood and richly decorated.

ciborium (a) Vessel to contain the consecrated host; (b) Canopy over the high altar.

clearstory (or clerestory) Upper part of main walls of chancel, transepts or nave of a basilican church, pierced by windows.

coffering Flat or vaulted roof decorated with a regular pattern of square, polygonal or round fields set into the surface.

collegiate church A church served by an organized body (college) of priests not under monastic vows.

Commonwealth see Republic.

confederation see rokosz.

Congress Kingdom The Kingdom of Poland (with the Russian Tsar as King) created by the Congress of Vienna in 1815.

console Ornamental bracket projecting from wall.

cornice Upper part of an entablature, or any projecting element along the top of a building, wall, etc.

corps de logis The principal section of a Baroque palace, distinct from the less imposing side ranges.

cour d'honneur The courtyard at the entrance front of a Baroque palace facing the corps de logis and flanked by lesser buildings.

cross-rib vault see rib vault.

crossing The intersection of the nave, chancel and transepts of a church.

dansker (Polish: gdanisko) The latrine tower of castles and monasteries, particularly those of the Teutonic Order.

diamond vault (crystalline vault) A Late Gothic vault with a pattern of ridges and geometric depressions, resembling folded paper.

domical vault (cloister vault) A dome-shaped vault rising from a round or polygonal base, with segmental curved surfaces meeting at angles.

drum A cylindrical structure (round or polygonal) supporting a dome.

entablature The upper part of an order (qv).

Familia, the Family The descendants of Prince Kazimierz Czartoryski and his wife Izabela Morsztyn, who played a leading role in Polish politics in the 18th and 19th centuries. (Stanisław August Poniatowski was the son of Konstancja Czartoryska. Adam Jerzy Czartoryski was his first cousin once removed.)

flèche Slender spire set on the ridge of a roof.

frieze Horizontal strip of wall with ornament or figures.

Generalgouvernement (Polish: Generalna Gubernia) In the Second World War the area of Poland under German rule but not incorporated into the Reich. It included Warsaw but its capital was Kraków. The name is derived from the French form of the Russian 'gubernia' (province) and was first applied to German-occupied Poland in the First World War.

górale Mountain people of southern Poland.

groin vault A vault formed by the intersection of two barrel vaults of the same size, creating ridges (groins) where they meet.

hall church Church in which the aisles and nave are the same (or almost the same) height.

Hanseatic League (Hanse) A trading organization mainly of Baltic and North Sea towns, which originated in the 12th century and effectively ended in the 17th century. Its period of greatest power was the 14th century.

Hasidism Jewish revivalist movement which started in 18th-century Poland.

herm Pillar terminating in a male or female bust.

Hetman Military commander, an officer of state in Poland-Lithuania.

Hospitallers, Knights of St John of Jerusalem Military religious order founded in the 11th century in Jerusalem.

iconostasis Screen with three doors, separating the sanctuary from the nave in Eastern Orthodox (and Uniate) churches, usually covered with icons (qv).

icons Revered images of Christ or saints, usually panel paintings, which play an important part in Eastern Orthodox (and Uniate) devotion.

impost Part of a wall on which the end of an arch rests.

incunable (or incunabulum) Book printed before 1500.

intarsia Inlaid work in wood, ivory, stone, tortoiseshell, mother-of-pearl etc.

International Gothic see Schöner Stil.

Interrex The regent during the election of a Polish king; usually the Primate of Poland.

jamb The vertical side of a doorway or window.

kahal A Jewish community, the unit of social life similar to a parish.

Kashubians A Slavic people living in northwestern Poland.

keep Main tower of a castle.

latifundium Large estate of magnate family (mostly in the east of the old Polish-Lithuania).

Łemki Ukrainian-speaking people living in southeastern Poland.

Lion Madonna Statue of the Virgin and Child standing on a lion, found in West Prussia and Silesia in the late 14th century.

lisene Projecting vertical band on the exterior of a building to articulate the wall surface.

loggia Gallery open on one or more sides, usually through a pillared arcade.

lunette semicircular area of wall or opening in wall. (See also tympanum.)

Marshal of the Sejm (Polish: Marszałek Sejmu) Speaker of the Parliament.

mensa Slab forming table top of altar.

monstrance Vessel, usually elaborately decorated, used in the Roman Catholic Church for displaying the consecrated host.

mouldings Contours given to projecting elements, e.g. archivolts.

nave (a) The part of a church west of the crossing; (b) The central aisle of this part, between the side aisles.

net vault A Late Gothic rib vault with a network of ribs forming a pattern of lozenges.

Norbertines See Premonstratensian Order.

Old Believers (Polish: Starowiercy) Russian Orthodox Christians who rejected the 17th-century Church reforms in Russia. Some communities were given sanctuary in Poland, where a few still remain.

orders, classical The column with shaft, base, capital and entablature, usually made according to established forms: Doric, Tuscan, Ionic, Corinthian or Composite.

Orthodox Church The Eastern Church (Russian, Ukrainian, etc.) which rejects the authority of the Pope, looks to the Byzantine tradition and (in Eastern Europe) uses the Old Slavonic liturgy. (See also Old Believers, Uniates.)

Paulite Order The Order of Hermits of St Paul of Thebes, founded at Budapest in 1215, with several houses in Poland, most notably Częstochowa.

pendentive Concave spandrel between two walls and the base of a circular dome (see also squinch).

Piasts The descendants of Piast, the legendary founder of the Polish royal line. The last Piast ruler of Poland was Queen Jadwiga (d.1399). The last of the Piast princes, Georg Wilhelm of Brzeg-Legnica, died in 1675. The term Piast was later used for all Polish (as opposed to foreign) candidates for the Polish throne.

pilaster Shallow rectangular column projecting from a wall surface.

pinnacle Decorative spirelet placed on buttresses or parapets of Gothic buildings.

piscina Stone basin in niche near the altar with outflow, for the rinsing of eucharistic vessels.

Polish parapet A form of attic developed in Małopolska, decorated with volutes and blind arcading (e.g. on the Sukiennice, Kraków).

polyptych Painting or carving on several hinged panels. (See also triptych.)

Pommerellen (Pomerelia) The old name for Eastern Pomerania.

Poor Clares The Second Order of St Francis, founded by him and St Clare for women, with an austere contemplative rule.

portico A space with roof supported by columns forming the entrance or centrepiece of a façade.

predella Narrow band of images at the base of an altarpiece immediately above the altar.

Premonstratensian Order Order of Canons, and later Nuns, founded in 1120 by St Norbert of Xanten (hence also called Norbertines).

presbytery Part of the church, usually east of the choir, containing the altar.

Prussia (a) Land on the Baltic inhabited by a pagan race of Balts various called Pruzzi, Pruthenians, Borussians or, confusingly, Prussians; (b) This region as later governed by the Teutonic Order of Knights (qv) and later divided into Royal Prussia (west) directly under the Polish king, and Ducal Prussia (east) held as a fief of the Polish king by a branch of the Hohenzollern dynasty; (c) The territories of the Hohenzollerns, Electors of Brandenburg, after they assumed the title of Kings of Prussia in the 18th century.

Referendary A legal officer at the royal court in charge of assessing pleas and appeals.

Reformed Franciscans A breakaway group of Observant Franciscans (see Bernardines) formed in the 17th century.

Republic of Nobles The name given to the Polish-Lithuanian Commonwealth (see Republic) because of the great power held by the szlachta (qv).

Republic, Commonwealth (Polish:

Rzeczpospolita) The Polish-Lithuanian state after the Union of Lublin (1569) was so called, although it had an elected monarchy. The Polish state created after the First World War was called the 'Second Republic'.

retable Shelf above altar (see also altarpiece).

rib vault A vault composed of a framework of intersecting arched stone ribs apparently supporting the masonry cells between them. If there are only two intersecting arched ribs it is a cross-rib arch. In more complex rib vaults the secondary ribs are called liernes and the tertiary ribs tiercerons.

rokosz Confederation formed as a sort of legalized rebellion (e.g. Confederation of Bar, 1768–72).

Rundbogenstil (German for 'round arch style') A simple style of architecture based on the round arch, popular in the early 19th century.

Rus East Slavic peoples, sometimes confusingly called 'Russians'. They include the 'Great Russians', the 'Little Russians' (i.e. Ukrainians) and 'White Russians' (Byelorussians or Belorus). (See also Ruthenians.)

rustication Masonry cut to give effect of massive blocks.

Ruthenians The East Slavic Rus (qv), especially the Ukrainians and Byelorussians. The term was used for Eastern Slavs in the Austro-Hungarian Empire. (See also Łemki.)

sail vault See Bohemian cap.

Sarmatism A 17th-century peculiarly Polish aristocratic cult of the ideals of idyllic 'Old Sarmatia'. The Polish nobility saw itself as descending from the (non-Slavic) Sarmatian tribes, and therefore different from the peasantry.

Schöner Stil 'Beautiful', or International Style of the later 14th-century Gothic.

Sejm The Polish (formerly Polish-Lithuanian) Parliament. In the middle ages 'Sejm' is sometimes translated as 'Diet'.

sejmik (pl. sejmiki) Local assembly (dietine) in Poland-Lithuania, which sent a representative to the Sejm (qv).

sgraffito Incised decoration on plaster, with the top coat cut away to reveal a different coloured layer beneath.

shingles Wooden tiles used for covering roofs and spires.

Solidarity (Polish: Solidarność) The independent trade union founded in Gdańsk in 1980. Under the leadership of Lech Wałęsa it forced political reforms from the Communist government, but was banned under martial law in 1981. It re-emerged in 1989, but in the new Polish democracy it has lost its political role.

spandrel The triangular wall-surface between the curve of an arch, a horizontal drawn at its apex and a vertical drawn at its springing.

squinch Arch or sequence of arches built across the corners of a building to support a round or polygonal superstructure.

star vault (or stellar vault) A rib vault with a star-shaped pattern of ribs.

Starosta (literally: 'eldest') (a) A regional officer of state in Poland-Lithuania; (b) In the period 1919–39, a district administrative officer.

stetl (Yiddish: little town) Jewish village in Eastern Europe.

strapwork Decoration resembling cut leather or metalwork, originating in the mid-16th-century Netherlands.

string course   Projecting horizontal band on the exterior wall of a building marking the division into the storeys.

szlachta   The Polish nobility, especially the lesser nobility or gentry.

tabernacle   Ornamented recess or receptacle for the Holy Sacrament.

Tatars   Mongol nomadic people who made devastating raids into Europe in the 13th century. Some Tatar mercenaries fought for Jan III Sobieski in the 17th century and were granted land in Poland, where a few of their descendants remain.

Templars, Knights Templar   Military religious order founded in 1118 at Jerusalem. Their great power and wealth led to their suppression by the Pope in 1312.

Teutonic Order of Knights   Military religious order founded at Acre in 1197, which came to the Baltic in the early 13th century to convert pagans and colonize – 'wading in the blood of northern heathendom' as Mickiewicz put it in the first line of *Konrad Wallenrod*. From 1309 their headquarters were at Malbork and later at Königsberg. The Teutonic State was secularized in 1525, but the Order continued in the Catholic Habsburg lands and survives today as a priestly (non-chivalric) order.

Torah scrolls   The text of the Pentateuch (Torah is Hebrew for 'teaching' or written Jewish Law) written on parchment scrolls. (See also ark.)

tracery   Ornamental intersecting stone bands in a Gothic window. Blind tracery can be used to decorate wall surfaces, vaults, choir stalls, etc.

triforium   Arcaded wall passage facing the nave, above the arcade and below the clearstory.

triptych   Painting or carving on three panels, hinged so that the outer panels can fold over the centre.

tympanum   Area between the lintel and arch of a doorway. Sometimes filled with sculpture.

tzaddik (Polish: cadyk; Hebrew for 'righteous man')   Hasidic master (rebbe), the charismatic leader of a community.

Uniates (Greek Catholics)   Eastern-Rite Christians who accepted the supremacy of Rome at the Union of Breść (1596) and were allowed to keep their own liturgy and practices (e.g. married priests). In Poland most Uniates are Ukrainian speaking. (See also Orthodox Church.)

vaults   See barrel vault; groin vault; rib vault; star vault; net vault; diamond vault; domical vault.

voivodship (Polish: województwo)   Administrative district like a county. The voivodship boundaries were redrawn in 1975.

volute   Spiral scroll, found in Ionic capital, on attics, etc.

westwork   Fortress-like structure forming the west end of some Romanesque churches.

wojewoda   A voivode or palatine, the ruler of a region as the representative of the sovereign. (See voivodship.)

Young Poland (Młoda Polska)   Artistic and literary movement at the turn of the century.

Practical Information

Contents

Poland in Brief

Area: 312,677 km² (UK: 224,103 km²). Greatest length: 650 km, greatest width: 680 km. Poland borders the Baltic Sea to the northwest along a 524 km coastline. The border to the west with Germany runs for 460 km and that with the Czech and Slovak Republics to the south for 1310 km. The north and northeast Polish borders are with Ukraine, Byelorussia, Lithuania and Russia and are 1244 km long in total.

Population: 39,000,000 in 2000 (UK: 57,000,000).

Population Density: This varies greatly in different parts of the country: Upper Silesia is the most densely populated region, and the least populated is the lakeland in the northeast.

Capital: Warsaw

Economy: Farmland covers 18.7 million hectares (about 60% of the total land mass of Poland), three quarters of which is arable. Agriculture employs a third of the workforce and yet contributes only 5% to the GDP. The inefficiency of Polish farming is immediately apparent in the antiquated methods still used: strip farming, and oxen and horses as beasts of burden.

Poland is a highly industrialized country, but what Polish industry achieves in quantity it loses in quality, the result of outdated equipment and inefficient infrastructure. Further difficulties have resulted from Poland's separation from Russia, formerly its main export market, and its attempts to compete with a Western market. Restructuring has been painful for some: in the year 2000 14% of the population was unemployed. Unemployment is rising and wages and pensions have not kept pace with price rises.

A third of Poland's gross domestic product comes from heavy industries including steel, chemicals and machinery. The main industrial area is centred around Upper Silesia. This region is also the location of Poland's chief mineral resource, coal, which supplies a large portion of the domestic demand for electricity, as well as much appalling pollution.

Administrative Regions/Voivodships: Since the administration reforms of 1999 Poland has been divided into 16 voivodships (*województwa*) based on the historic regions of the country. Each *województwo* is divided into smaller administrative districts called *powiaty*.

Geography: The main agricultural area of Poland is located along a flat central belt running west to east through the country and includes Wielkopolska, Lower Silesia, Kujawy, Mazovia and Podlasie. Pomerania, Warmia and Mazuria lie to the north of this in a forested area with post glacial lakes. To the south are the uplands of Małopolska and Upper Silesia. Further south are two mountain ranges: the geologically very old Sudety Mountains (250 km long) and a relatively newer range of mountains known as the Carpathians running along the southern border with Slovakia. There are nine main rivers in Poland (the Vistula is the longest) which all flow northwards towards the Baltic Sea. The Baltic itself is very shallow and virtually tideless and so collects in pollution from the surrounding industrialized countries. It has the lowest levels of salt of any sea in the world.

Climate: Poland is under the influence of a continental climate from the east and a maritime climate from the west. Winter runs from December to March often with heavy snowfalls. The coldest months are January and February, when the temperature is usually below freezing. Spring is showery but bright with temperatures increasing towards June with the approaching Summer. July and August are usually hot (19–30°C, 62–80°F) but these months also bring rain with them (average annual rainfall is 600 mm). Autumns are, in general, mild.

Air Temperatures in °C and °F (average daytime extremes)

	January		July	
Kraków	-5.5°C/22°F	0°C/32°F	14.4°C/58°F	24.4°C/76°F
Gdynia	-2.7°C/27°F	1.6°C/35°F	14.4°C/58°F	21.1°C/70°F
Poznań	-4.4°C/24°F	0.5°C/33°F	13.8°C/57°F	24.4°C/76°F
Przemyśl	-6.6°C/20°F	0°C/32°F	13.8°C/57°F	23.8°C/75°F
Warsaw	-5.5°C/22°F	0°C/32°F	14.4°C/58°F	23.8°C/75°F

Flora and Fauna: Woodland accounts for 27% of Poland's landmass and a further 4% is peat bog with tundra vegetation. Fauna includes wolves, deer, wild boar and hares. Wild bison are to be found in the Białowieski Park, one of 13 National Parks which cover 0.6% of Poland. There are over 200 species of birds to be found. Poland also has a long tradition of Arab horse breeding; many of the studs can be visited.

Ethnic Groups: Poland's population today is overwhelmingly Polish (98%). The largest minority groups consist of Ukrainians and Byelorussians. Boyks and Lemks from the southeast of the country were settled in other parts of Poland in the late 1940's. A small German-speaking minority survives in Upper Silesia. Lithuanian-speakers are found near the Lithuanian border. There is still a tiny Tatar community (see page 441). Gypsies form an important minority group. Only 5000 to 10,000 Jews are still living in Poland.

Religion: Over 90% of the population of Poland are practising Roman Catholics, but there is a sizeable (Polish-speaking) Orthodox community particularly around Białystok, as well as Ukrainian-speaking Uniates (Greek Catholics) originating from the southeast of the country. Some Lutheran churches are still functioning in regions which were once German. Very few surviving synagogues are still used for Jewish worship (Warsaw, Kraków). The Tatar minority maintains a few mosques.

Travelling to Poland

...by Air

There are LOT (Polish Airlines) and British Airways flights daily from London to Warsaw. There are also some flights from London to Kraków, London to Gdańsk, and from Manchester to Warsaw. BA and LOT now operate their service to Poland in partnership.

LOT has flights to Poland from New York, Chicago and Toronto, but no direct flights from Ireland, or from Australia and New Zealand.

LOT offices:
UK: 313 Regent Street, London W1 (tel. 020 7580 5037).
USA: 500 Fifth Avenue, Suite 408, New York (tel. 212 869–1074).
333 North Michigan Avenue, Chicago (tel. 312 236–3388).
6420 Wilshire Boulevard, Suite 410, Los Angeles (tel. 213 658-5656).
Canada: 1000 Sherbrooke Street W., Montreal (tel. 514 844-2674).
130 Bloor Street W., Toronto (tel. 416 364 -2035).
Australia: 388 George Street, Suite 2001, Sydney (tel. 232-8430).

Warsaw's main airport (Warszawa-Okęcie) is about 8 km south of the city centre, within easy reach by taxi or bus (no. 175). The airports at Gdańsk and Kraków also have good public transport links to the city centres.

...by Car

The following are the principal border crossing points for entering or leaving Poland by car:

Germany–Poland
Ahlbeck–Świnoujście
Linken–Lubieszyn
Pomellen–Kołbaskowo
Schwedt–Krajnik Dolny
Seelow–Kostrzyn
Frankfurt an der Oder–Słubice
Frankfurt an der Oder–Świecko
Guben–Gubin
Forst–Olszyna
Bad Muskau–Łęgnica
Görlitz–Zgorzelec
Zittau–Sieniawka

Czech Republic–Poland:
Habartice–Zawidow
Harrachov–Jakuszyce
Pomezni Boudy–Przełęcz Okroj
Kralovec–Lubawka
Náchod–Kudowa Słona
Dolni Lipka–Boboszów
Mikulovice–Głuchołazy
Krnov–Pietrowice
Bohumin–Chałupki
Česky Těšín–Cieszyn

Slovakia–Poland
Trstená–Chyżne
Javorina–Łysa Polana
Mníšek nad Popradom–Piwniczna
Vyšny Komárnik–Barwinek

Ukraine–Poland
Mostiska–Medyka (from Lviv)
Raba Russkaja–Hrebenne
Liuboml–Dorohusk

Byelorussia–Poland
Damachave–Sławatycze
Brest–Terespol (from Moscow)
Grodno–Kuźnica Białostocka

Lithuania–Poland
Lazdijai–Ogrodniki
Kalvaria–Budzisko

Russia–Poland
Krasnolesie–Gołdap
Bagrationowsk–Bezledy
Mamonovo–Gronowo

...by Coach

The journey time from London to Warsaw is about 28 hours. Eurolines operate services from London to Warsaw (via Poznań) and London to Kraków (via Poznań, Wrocław, Opole and Katowice).
Eurolines, 52 Grosvenor Gardens, London SW1 (tel. 020 7730 8235).

...by Rail

International trains run daily between Poland and many western European cities. The jour-

ney time from London to Warsaw (via Berlin) is approximately 24 hours.

...by Sea

From January 2002 Finnlines have operated a weekly roll-on roll-off ferry service between Hull and Gdynia. For further information contact:

Nordic Ferry Center Oy, Lönnrotinkatu 21, FIN-00120 Helsinki, Finland
tel. +358-9-2510 200, fax. +358-9-2510 2022
info@ferrycenter.fi

Polferries, Stena Line and Unity Line run regular ferries between Scandinavia and the ports of Świnoućie, Gdynia and Gdańsk.

Polferries, ul. Chałubińskiego 8, 00-613 Warszawa, tel. 022 8300930 (information), 022 8300097 (reservations), fax 022 8300071, e-mail: booking@polferries.pl

Gdynia Stena Line, ul. Kwiatkowskiego 60, 81-156 Gdynia, tel. 058-660 92 00, fax 058-660 92 09

Unity Line, Pl. Rodla 8, 70-419 Szczecin, tel. +48 91 35 95 692,fax +48 91 35 95 673
e-mail: info@unityline.pl

Information

Outside Poland
The main state tourist information office outside Poland is Polorbis, from which free literature of a basic but wide-ranging sort can be obtained.

UK: Polorbis, 82 Mortimer Street, London WIN 7DE (tel. 020 7636 2217).

US: Polish National Tourist Office, Information Center, 333 North Michigan Avenue, Suite 228, Chicago, Illinois 60601 (tel. 236-9013).

Orbis, 342 Madison Avenue, Suite 1512, New York, NY 10173 (tel. 212 867-5011).

In Poland

Within Poland tourist information can be obtained at local travel agencies. There are also tourist information ('it') points at all border crossing points and tourist centres, in the larger railway stations and at the reception desks of larger hotels, with information material, brochures and local maps.

Warsaw: pl. Zamkowy 1/13 (tel. 022-635 18 81)

Kraków: ul. Pawia 6 (tel. 012-22 04 71 and 22 60 91)

Lublin: ul. Krakowskie Przedmieście 78 (tel. 081-244 12)

Olsztyn: Wysoka Brama (tel. 089-27 27 38)

Poznań: Stary Rynek 77 (tel. 061-52 61 56)

Wrocław: ul. Kazimierza Wielkiego 39 (tel. 071-44 31 11)

Within Poland the state travel agency and tourist service is Orbis:

Orbis, ul. Marszałkowska 142, 00-061 Warsaw (tel. 022-27 80 31).

There are also a number of other agencies of which the best known are:

Almatur, ul. Kopernika 23, Warsaw (tel. 022-826 35 12).

Gromada, ul. Cicha 7, Warsaw (tel. 022-827 49 68) organizing stays at spas and tickets for cultural events.

The PTTK (Polish Association for Tourism and the Countryside) organizes walking tours and canoe trips and provides guides to accompany walkers. It has offices in the larger towns throughout the country.

Maps and Guides

Good road maps (scale: 1:750,000) can be bought at map shops such as Stanfords, 12–14 Long Acre, London WC2, where specialist guides are also obtainable. Books about Poland, including books on art and architecture published in English in Poland, can be obtained from Orbis Bookshop, 66 Kenway Road, London SW5 0RD (tel. 020 7370 2210); from Hippocrene Books, 171 Madison Avenue, New York, NY 10016 (tel. 212-685 4371), or in Poland itself.

Detailed town plans and regional maps can usually be obtained from local Orbis offices and tourist information centres in Poland.

Visas and Travel Documents

Visas are no longer required by UK or US nationals. However, Australian and New Zealand citizens still require a visa.

Embassies and Consulates

Polish Embassies and Consulates

UK: Polish Consulate General, 73 New Cavendish Street, London WIN 4HQ (tel. 020 7580 0476).

2 Kinnear Road, Edinburgh E3H 5PE

USA: Polish Embassy, 22–24 Wyoming Avenue, NW, Washington DC 20008 (tel. 202 234-3800).
Consulate General, 233 Madison Avenue, New York, NY 10016 (tel. 212 889-8360).

Canada: 443 Daly Avenue, Ottawa, Ontario (tel. 613 789 0468).

Australia: 10 Trelawny Street, Woollahara, Sydney, NSW2025 (tel. 02-363 9816).

New Zealand: The Terrace, Wellington (tel. 712456).

Embassies and Consulates in Poland

UK: Al. Róż 1, 00-556 Warsaw (tel. 022-628 1001).

USA: Al. Ujazdowskie 29/31, 00-902 Warsaw (tel. 022-628 30 41). (Consulate) ul. Stolarska 9, Kraków (tel. 012-422 14 00).

Canada: ul. Piękna 2/8, 00-540 Warsaw (tel. 022-629 80 51).

Australia: ul. Estońska 3/4, 00-989 Warsaw (tel. 022-617 60 81).

New Zealand: ul. Migdałowa 4, Warsaw (tel. 022-645 14 07)

Irish Republic: ul. Humańska 10, Warsaw (tel. 022-849 66 55)

Seasons

The coldest months are January and February, when the temperature is usually below freezing. Snowfalls are often heavy and the winter sports resorts in the Tatras and other mountains are busy. Spring is showery but bright, and the Easter festivities are an attraction. July and August are usually hot (19°–30°C, 62°–80°F); the Baltic resorts are busy and the heat in the cities may be uncomfortable. Autumns tend to be mild and the changing colours of the woodland are very beautiful.

Customs Regulations

Import

No duty is charged on objects for personal use, and gifts up to the value of $100, 0.75 litre of wine and 0.25 litre of spirits, 250 cigarettes or 50 cigars or 25 grams of tobacco. All other articles must be declared. Weapons, ammunition, pornography and narcotics may not be imported.

Export

The following may be exported without duty: all articles declared on entering the country, gifts up to the value of $100, 250 cigarettes or 25 grams of tobacco, 0.75 litre of wine, works of art or sculpture made since 1945 to any value. Objects made before 1945 may not be exported unless they are accompanied by an export licence from the Ministry of Culture.

A–Z of Practical Information

Accommodation

Hotels and Pensions

Polish hotels are divided into five categories according to quality: 1, 2, 3 and 4 stars and luxury hotels. The highest standard is to be found in the Orbis Hotels (list obtainable from Polorbis) and the international hotel chains such as Intercontinental, Novotel, Marriott, Sheraton and Holiday Inn. These specialize in catering for foreign tourists and businessmen and will be found in Warsaw, Bydgoszcz, Gdańsk, Gdynia, Katowice, Kraków, Lublin, Łódź, Nowy Sącz, Płock, Poznań, Sopot, Sosnowiec, Szczecin, Toruń, Wrocław, Zakopane and Zielona Góra.

Orbis also runs pensions (*pensionaty*) at the holiday resorts of Zakopane, Krynica, Karpacz, Ciechocinek, Międzyzdroje and Mrągowo. Besides the Orbis hotels there is also a large number of hotels belonging to the tourist regional authorities or travel agencies, e.g. Gromada, Turysta or PTTK. Information can be obtained from Polorbis and from local Orbis representatives in Poland.

PTTK Hostels

The Polish Association for Tourism and the Countryside (PTTK) owns a large number of tourist hostels along their recommended walking routes in the mountains as well on canoe and sailing routes, and in some towns. These hostels can be spartan. The PTTK also runs large, comfortable tourist hotels with restaurants and cafes are found in Kraków, Poznań, Płock, Sandomierz, Sanok, Sopot, Szczecin, Szczyrk, Warsaw and Zakopane.

Information can be obtained from all PTTK offices in larger towns.

Student Hotels

International student hotels, run by the travel and tourist agency Almatur, offer cheap accommodation in student halls of residence between July and October. There are reductions for holders of International Student Cards (ISIC). The names of the hotels can be obtained from Orbis representatives or from Almatur, ul. Kopernika 23, Warsaw, (tel. 022-826 35 12).

Information and reservations are usually obtainable through Polorbis.

Youth Hostels

The Polish Youth Hostel Association (PTMS) provides accommodation in many school buildings in the summer holidays. The PTMS is a member of the International Youth Hostel Federation (IYHF). A list of 200 recommended official youth hostels (*Schroniska Młodzieżowe*) is included in the International Youth Hostel Handbook (obtainable in bookshops), though many of these are open only in the summer holiday period. A discount of 25 per cent is given on production of an IYHF membership card, which can be obtained from Warszawa, ul. Chocimska 28, 0 022 49 83 54, though it is best to obtain one before you go from the Youth Hostel Association, 14 Southampton Street, London WC2, (tel. 020 7836 8542) or American Youth Hostel Association, National Administrative Office, 733 15th Street NW, Suite 840, Washington DC 20005 (tel. 202–783 6161).

Inns
Along the main tourist routes good food and overnight accommodation can be found at rural inns (*zajazdy*).

Private Rooms
Accommodation offices (*Biura Zakwaterowania*) can be found in all large towns.

Tourist information offices provide information about private rooms, and many houses display signs advertising rooms (*pokoje*) or overnight lodging (*noclegi*). There has been enormous growth in this sector and prices are very low.

Camping
There are about 240 camp sites in Poland run by the Polish Camping Federation (PFC) and the International Camping and Caravanning Federation. The sites in categories I, II and III all have running water, toilet facilities and electricity; category II sites also have washrooms, and category III sites have washrooms with hot and cold water and restaurants. The camping season is from 1 May to 30 September. Polorbis can supply a list of camp sites in categories I and II. It is not possible to book places on sites in advance.

Electrical Current

220 volt alternating current.

Health

Drinking Water
Officially the tap water is safe, but it is best to drink mineral waters.

Inoculations
None required for UK or US citizens.

Other nationals should make enquiries at the nearest Polish embassy.

Medical Treatment
Poland has a bilateral health agreement with the United Kingdom. Visitors taking a NHS card will still be charged for doctors' visits and 30 per cent of the cost of medicines. No such agreement exists for US citizens. All travellers are recommended to take out health insurance.

Treatment from a doctor must generally be paid for in złotys, but sometimes partly in foreign currency (receipts must be kept).

Pharmacies
Pharmacies (*apteki*) are open from 8 am to 8 pm; medicines must be paid for in złotys (receipts should be kept). Supplies of contraceptives are erratic.

The number of AIDS cases in Poland is growing. Precautions are advisable.

Language

Polish is a West Slavonic language, like the languages of the Czechs, Slovaks and Lusadan Sorbs. Like them it is written using the Latin alphabet, though the orthography with its accumulations of consonants may seem daunting. Once the rules have been understood, however, it is relatively easy for West Europeans to master the pronunciation of Polish names and phrases, since words are pronounced as they are spelt, and the stress falls regularly on the penultimate syllable.

Characteristic Polish sounds are nasal vowels (ą, ę) similar to the sound in French, and the 'softened' consonants, which sound rather like a consonant followed by a slight 'y'. (Compare the hard t in 'too' and the soft t in 'tube'.)

Polish orthography differentiates soft and hard sybillants (ś and sz, ć and cz and, ź and ż or rz).

Nasal vowels are indicated by a tail [̨] (called ogonek) (ą, ę).

Softened consonants are indicated by an acute accent [́] (ń, ć) or by being followed by the letter 'i' (which is often not pronounced).

Unlike English, but like other Slavonic languages (and like Latin), Polish is a strongly inflected language: nouns and verbs change their endings depending on their function in a sentence. Thus the Polish for 'Poland' is Polska, but 'to Poland' is do Polski and 'in Poland' is w Polsce.

The prospect of grappling with conjugations and declensions (in three genders) – not to mention the perfective and imperfective aspects of verbs – will probably be enough to put most visitors off attempting to gain any deeper knowledge of the language. For those who do want to make the effort the most easily available beginner's book is B. W. Mazur, Colloquial Polish, London (Routledge) 1983. Some knowledge of Polish is very useful, particularly in places away from the main tourist areas, and any efforts at speaking the language will be warmly appreciated.

Pronunciation Guide
Vowels

a	as in pack
e	as in peg
i	as in peace (i is not pronounced when it is there simply to soften a consonant, so ciastko [cake] and jesień [autumn] each have just two syllables)
o	as in pot
ó	as in put
u	as in put
y	as in pin
ą	as in pawn (but more nasal)
ę	as in penguin (but more nasal)

Consonants

b	approximately as in English
c	as in pets
d	approximately as in English
f	approximately as in English
g	always a hard g, as in gun
h	approximately as in English
j	like y in yet
k	approximately as in English
l	approximately as in English
ł	like w, as in peewit
m	approximately as in English
n	approximately as in English
ń	softened, as in onion
p	approximately as in English

r	rolled behind front teeth	castle, château	zamek
s	always unvoiced as in *sin*	palace	pałac
t	approximately as in English	theatre	teatr
w	*v* as in *v*ole	museum	muzeum
z	approximately as in English	house	dom
ch	as in the Scottish lo*ch*	bridge	most
ć (or ci)	a soft *ch* as in *ch*in	gate	brama
cz	a hard *ch* as in *ch*urch	park	park
dz	approximately as in English	garden	ogród
dź	like the English *j* in *j*eans	hotel	hotel
dż	like the English *j* in *j*ungle	restaurant	restauracja
ś (or si)	a soft *sh* as in *sh*in	self-service bar	bar samoobsługowy
sz	hard *sh*, as in *sh*ort	toilet	toaleta
szcz	as in pu*shch*air	gents	dla panów; męski (▼)
ź (or zi)	soft, like the French *g* in *G*igi	ladies	dla pań; damski (●)
ż and rz	hard, like the French *j* in *j*ournal	cashier	kasa
		pharmacy	apteka
please	proszę	doctor	lekarz
thank you	dziękuję	entrance	wejście
(very much)	(bardzo)	exit	wyście
you're welcome	proszę	menu	jadłospis
(response to	(bardzo)	coffee	kawa
'thank you')		tea	herbata
good day	dzień dobry	water	woda
good evening	dobry wieczór	mineral water	woda mineralna
good night	dobranoc	drink	napój
goodbye	do widzenia	beer	piwo
greetings	witam	wine	wino
hello, bye (familiar)	cześć!		
yes	tak	1	jeden
no	nie	2	dwa
sorry	przepraszam	3	trzy
excuse me	proszę	4	cztery
(sir/madam)	Pan/Pani	5	pięc
where is ...?	gdzie...?	6	sześć
can I help you?	słucham?	7	siedem
I didn't hear	słucham?	8	osiem
street	ulica	9	dziewięć
square	plac	10	dziesięć
church	kościół	11	jedenaście
town hall	ratusz	12	dwanaście

627

13	trzynaście	Sunday	niedziela
14	czternaście		
15	piętnaście	January	styczeń
16	szesnaście	February	luty
17	siedemnaście	March	marzec
18	osiemnaście	April	kwiecień
19	dziewiętnaście	May	maj
20	dwadzieścia	June	czerwiec
30	trzydzieści	July	lipiec
40	czterdzieści	August	sierpień
50	pięćdziesiąt	September	wrzesień
		October	październik
60	sześćdziesiąt	November	listopad
70	siedemdziesiąt	December	grudzień
80	osiemdziesiąt		
90	dziewięćdziesiąt	spring	wiosna
100	sto	summer	lato
200	dwieście	autumn	jesień
300	trzysta	winter	zima
400	czterysta		
500	pięćset		
600	sześćset		
700	siedemset		
800	osiemset		
900	dziewięćset		
1000	tysiąc		
2000	dwa tysiące		
1,000,000	milion		

53	pięćdziesiąt trzy
469	czterysta sześćdziesiąt dziewięć
1785	tysiąc siedemset osiemdziesiąt pięć

Monday	poniedziałek
Tuesday	wtorek
Wednesday	środa
Thursday	czwartek
Friday	piątek
Saturday	sobota

Money and Exchange

Currency: 1 złoty (zł) = 100 groszy (gr).
Bank notes come in denominations of 10, 20, 50, 100 and 200 zł, and there are coins of 1, 2, 5, 10 and 50 gr, and 1, 2 and 5 zł.

Foreign currency may be brought into Poland in any quantity or form (cash, travellers' cheques, Eurocheques, credit cards); the foreign currency taken out may exceed that taken in, but a bank certificate of the currency exchange is required. Undeclared currency will be confiscated on leaving the country, since import and export of złotys is prohibited.

Foreign currency can be exchanged at frontier posts, banks, hotel exchange offices, travel agencies, PZM frontier offices as well as numerous private exchange bureaux (identified as *kantor wymiany walut*) which have sprung up in all towns and cities and accept cash only. Diners Club, Eurocard, Mastercard, JCB and Visa can be used to obtain złotys at Orbis hotels. Keep all conversion slips.

Credit cards are accepted by big hotels and the best known restaurants, but their acceptance cannot be taken for granted and travellers should be prepared.

Museums and Galleries

Most museums are open daily from 10 am to 6 pm, closed on Mondays and holidays. On one day of the week (usually Thursday) entrance is free.

Biskupin
Muzeum (branch of the Warsaw State Archaeological Museum), 88-410 Gąsowa
Częstochowa
Jasna Góra Monastery (Treasury, Armoury and Knights' Hall), ul. ks. Kordeckiego 2
Gdańsk
Muzeum Narodowe w Gdańsku (National Museum) ul. Toruńska 1
Centralne Muzeum Morskie (Central Maritime Museum) ul. Szeroka 67/68
Muzeum Historii Miasta Gdańska (Museum of the History of Gdańsk) ul. Długa 46 (Town Hall of Main Town)
Gniezno
Muzeum Początków Państwa Polskiego (Museum of the Beginnings of the Polish State) ul. Kostrzewskiego
Jędrzejów
Państwowe Muzeum im. Przypkowskich: Muzeum Zegarów Słonecznych (Przypkowski State Museum: Sundial Museum)

Rynek 7/8
Kórnik (near Poznań)
Castle library and collections
Kozłówka (near Lublin)
Muzeum Zamoyskich (Zamoyski Museum), with Museum of Socialist Realism, 21-132 Kamionka
Kraków
Zamek Królewski na Wawelu (Royal Castle on Wawel) Wawel 5 (State Art Collections: Royal Apartments, Treasury, Armoury and Oriental collection)
Muzeum Katedralne (Cathedral Museum) Wawel 3
Muzeum Narodowe: Galeria Szuki Polskiej XIX wieku w Sukiennicach (National Museum: Cloth Hall), Rynek Głowny (19th-century Polish art)
Muzeum Narodowe: Nowy Gmach (New Building), Al. 3. Maja 1. (20th-century Polish art; Applied arts)
Kamienica Szolayskich (Szolayski House) Plac Szczepańskich 9 (medieval collections: currently closed for repairs)
Muzeum Książąt Czartoryskich (Czartoryski Museum) ul. św. Jana 19
Muzeum Stanisława Wyspiańskiego (Stanisław Wyspiański Museum) ul. Kanonicza 9
Dom Jana Matejki (Jan Matejko's House) ul. Floriańska 41
Muzeum Uniwersytetu Jagiellońskiego (Museum of the Jagiellonian University) ul. Jagiellońska 15
Muzeum Historyczne Miasta Krakowa (Historical Museum of the City of Kraków) Rynek Głowny 35, Pałac Krysztofory
Stara Synagoga (Old Synagogue), ul. Szeroka 24 (Judaica)
Muzeum Archeologiczne (Archaeological Museum), ul Senacka 3

Muzeum Archidiecezjalne (Archdiocesan Museum), ul. Kanonicza 19–20

Centrum Sztuki i Techniki Japońskiej 'Manggha' (Manggha Centre of Japanese Art and Technology), ul. Konopnickiej 26

Łańcut

Muzeum Zamek (Castle Museum). The Potocki collections

Muzeum Gorzelnictwa (Museum of Distilling) Vodka museum attached to one of Poland's oldest distilleries

Łódź

Muzeum Sztuki (Art Museum) ul. Więckowskiego 36 (20th-century art)

Rezydencja 'Księży Młyn' ('Prince's Mill' Residence), ul. Przedzalniana 72. The palace of the Herbst family

Muzeum Historii Przemyslu Tkackiego (Museum of the History of the Textile Industry) ul. Piotrkowska 282

Łowicz

Muzeum Ziemi Łowickiej (Łowicz Regional Museum) Stary Rynek 5-7. Local folklore

Lublin

Muzeum Zamkowe (Castle Museum) ul. Zamkowa 1

Malbork

Muzeum Zamkowe (Castle Museum) ul. Hibnera 1

Nieborów

Pałac Radziwiłłów (Radziwiłł Palace. Branch of the National Museum in Warsaw

Olsztyn

Muzeum Mazur i Warmii (Museum of Mazuria and Warmia) ul. Zamkowa 2

Olsztynek

Muzeum Budownictwa Ludowego (Open-air Museum of Vernacular Architecture) ul. Sportowa 5

Opole

Muzeum Śląsku Opolskiego (Museum of Opole Silesia) ul. św. Wojciecha 13

Pieskowa Skała

Zamek (Castle) (Branch of Wawel Castle Collections in Kraków)

Płock

Muzeum Diecezjalne (Diocesan Museum), ul Tumska 3a

Poznań

Muzeum Narodowe w Poznaniu (National Museum) Al. Marcinkowskiego 9

Muzeum Historii Miasta Poznania (Museum of the History of Poznań) Stary Rynek 1

Muzeum Arcybiskupstwa (Archiepiscopal Museum) ul. Lubraziskiego 1

Muzeum Instrumentów Muzycznych (Museum of Musical Instruments) Stary Rynek 45

Szczecin

Muzeum Narodowe w Szczecinie (National Museum) ul. Staromłyńska 27. Sculpture and painting

Muzeum Morskie (Maritime Museum), Waly Chrobrego 3

Muzeum Miasta Szczecina (Szczecin Museum) Stary Ratusz, Pl. Rzepichy 1

Szydłowiec

Muzeum Ludowych Instrumentów Muzycznych (Folk Musical Instrument Museum), Zamek Szydłowiecki

Toruń

Muzeum Okręgowe (Regional Museum) Rynek Staromiejski 35. Oriental collections

Muzeum Mikolaja Kopernika (Nicholas Copernicus Museum) ul. Kopernika 17

Warsaw

Muzeum Narodowe (National Museum) Al. Jerozolimskie 3

Muzeum Etnograficzne (Ethnographical

Museum) ul. Kredytowa 1

Muzeum Historyczne Miasta Warszawy (Historical Museum of the City of Warsaw) Rynek Starego Miasta 28

Zamek Królewski (Royal Castle) pl. Zamkowy 4

*Łazienki Królewskie (*Łazienki Royal Palace and Gardens) ul. Agrykola 1 (Palace on the Water, Myślewicki Palace and Old Orangery)

Wilanów: Muzeum-Pałac (Wilanów Palace Museum), ul. S.K. Potockiego 10/16

Muzeum Xawerego Dunikowskiego (Xawery Dunikowski Museum) Palac Królikarnia, ul. Puławska 113

Państwowe Muzeum Archeologiczne (State Archaeological Museum) ul. Długa 52

Muzeum w X Pawilonie Warszawskiej Cytadeli (Museum in Block X of the Warsaw Citadel) ul. Skazańców 25

Muzeum Więzienia Pawiak (Museum of the Pawiak Prison) ul. Dzielna 24/24

Państwowa Galeria Sztuki Zachęta ('Zachęta' State Art Gallery) pl. Malachowskiego 3 (Polish and foreign artists)

Galeria Foksal (old-established avantgarde gallery), ul. Foksal

Kolekcja im. Jana Pawla II (John Paul II Collection), pl. Bankowy (collection of paintings founded by the Porczyńskis in 1987)

Muzeum Plakatu (Poster Museum), ul. Wiertnicza 1

Wieliczka (near Kraków)

Kopalnia Soli (Salt mine)

Wrocław

Muzeum Narodowe w Wrocławie (National Museum) Pl. Powstańców Warszawy 5

Oddział Numizmatyczny Biblioteki Naro-dowego Instytutu Ossolińskich (Numismatic Department of the Library of the National Ossoliński Institute) ul. Szewska 37

Muzeum Poczty i Telekomunikacji (Post and Telecommunications Museum) ul. Krasińskiego 1

Muzeum Arcybiskupstwa (Archiepiscopal Museum) ul. Kanonia 12

Panorama Racławicka (Racławice Panorama) ul. Purkyniego 11

Zakopane

Muzeum Tatrzańskie (Tatra Museum) ul. Krupówki 10

Muzeum Karola Szymonowskiego, Willa Atma (Szymonowski Museum, Villa Atma), ul. Kaprusie 19 (Branch of the National Museum in Kraków)

Concentration Camp Museums

Państwowe Muzeum Oświęcim-Brzezinka (State Museum of Auschwitz-Birkenau), ul. Więźniów Oświęcimia 20

Majdanek, 3 km southeast of Lublin

Music, Theatre and Film

Musical life is rich in Poland, with many concerts at museums, palaces, churches, and in summer in the open air as well as at concert halls (*filharmonie*). There are opera houses, some of them very beautiful, at Bytom, Poznań, Bydgoszcz, Gdynia (Teatr Muzyczny), Gdańsk (Opera Bałtycka), Sopot (Opera Leśna, open-air: summer only), Łódź, Kraków, Wrocław and Warsaw.

Every voivodship capital has a theatre, as do many of the smaller towns. The Teatr Witkacego in Zakopane, for instance, which is named after the playwright Witkacy, is 'a beautiful old building, dating back to

Witkacy's time; marvellous interior; there are always actors at the entrance to welcome you. In the large drawing room the tea is waiting – you feel you have been invited to an artistic salon and that everything that will happen will be part of your life.'

There are highly theatrical Passiontide processions at Góra Kalwaria, Kalwaria Zebrzydowska and other pilgrimage centres, and a famous *misterium*, or passion-play, at Gardzienice.

Film is extremely popular in Poland, and there are cinemas everywhere. Films in English are often shown.

National Parks

Poland has 23 National Parks (*Parki Narodowe*). The oldest is Białowieski, which was established in 1947 and is now on the UNESCO list of world heritage sites, while the most recent is Uscie Warty established in 2001. Three new parks are planned in the east of the country: Jurajski, Mazurski and Turnicki.

The National Parks include virtually all types of European landscape, often in an almost unspoilt state, with a wealth of rare plants and animals such as beavers, brown bears, lynx, wolves and (especially in Białowieski) bison.

Most of the National Parks charge an entrance fee.

The following is a list of National Parks with the addresses of administrative offices.
- Babiogórski PN (3392 ha) in the High Tatras: Zawoja 1403, 34-223 Zawoja, tel. (33) 877 5110 fax (33) 877 55-54
- Białowieski PN (10,502 ha) primeval forest on the Byelorussian border: Park Pałacowy 5, 17-230 Białowieża
- Biebrzański PN (59,223 ha) Osowiec-Twierdza 8: 19-110 Godiadz, tel. (86) 272 0620
- Bieszczadzki PN (29,202 ha) in the south-east, on the Ukrainian border: 38-714 Ustrzyke Górne 19
- Bory Tucholskie PN (4798 ha): ul. Długa 23, 89-606 Carzykowy, tel. (52) 398 83-97
- Drawieński PN (11,342 ha): ul. Leśników 2a, 73-220 Drawno, tel. (95) 768-2051, fax (95) 768 2510
- Gorczański PN (7030 ha) near Nowy Targ: Poręba Wielka 590, 34 735 Niedźwiedź
- Gór Stołowych PN (6340 ha) sandstone outcrops in the south-west: ul. Słoneczna , 57-250 Kudowa-Zdrój
- Kampinoski PN (38,544 ha) west of Warsaw: Krasińskiego 49, 38-232 Izabelin
- Karkonoski PN (5575 ha) in the Sudety mountains: Chałubińskiego 23, 58-750 Jelenia Góra
- Magurski PN (19,962 ha): Krempna 59, 38-232 Krempna, tel. (13) 441 40-99/22
- Narwiański PN (7350 ha): Kurowo 59, 18204 Kobylin Borzyny
- Ojcowski PN (2146 ha) limestone landscape north of Kraków, 32-047 Ojców
- Pieniński PN (2346 ha) near Nowy Sącz: ul. Jagiellońska 107, 34-450 Krościenko
- Poleski PN (9762 ha): ul Chełmska 7, 22-234 Urszulin
- Roztoczański PN (8482 ha) between Kraków and Lublin: ul. Plażowa 2, 22-470 Zwierzyniec
- Słowiński PN (18, 619 ha) on the Baltic coast: ul. Bohaterów Warszawy 1, 76-214 Smołdzino
- Świętokrzyski PN (7632 ha) near Kielce: ul. Suchedniowska 4, 26-010

Bodzentyn

- Tatrzański PN (21,164) near Zakopane, High Tatras: ul. Chałubińskiego 42a, 34-500 Zakopane
- Uście Warty PN (7956 ha) wetlands at confluence of Warta and Odra rivers: Chyrzno 1, 69-113 Górczyca, tel. (95) 752 40-26/27
- Wielkopolski PN (7584 ha) south of Poznań: Jeziory, 62-050 Mosina, tel. (61) 813 22-06, fax (61) 813 62-99
- Wigierski PN (15,085 ha): Krzywe 82, 16-400 Suwałki
- Woliński PN (10,937 ha) on Wolin Island: ul Niepodległości 3, 72 Międzyzdroje

News

British and American newspapers can be bought in larger bookshops and newsagents. *The Warsaw Voice* is the leading English-language weekly.

Hourly radio news in English can be heard on RMF in Kraków and Radio Z in Warsaw.

Between 23 June and 30 September Radio Warszawa (1200 metres LW) broadcasts a daily *Lato z radiem* ('Summer by Radio') programme which gives weather forecasts, tourist information and messages for motorists in Polish and several languages. (0 022 45 92 77).

BBC World Service programmes can be received on shortwave 9.41 MHz (31.88).

Opening Times

Pharmacies: Mon–Sat 8 am–8 pm
Banks: Mon–Fri 9 am–5pm

Food Shops: Mon–Fri 7 am–8 pm (but nowadays many shops stay open later.
Shops: Other than food shops, most shops are open Mon–Sat 10 am–6 pm.
Orbis: Mon–Sat 11 am–4 pm (in large towns Mon–Sat 8 am–6 pm)
Post Offices: Mon–Fri 8 am–7 pm
Museums: Tue-Sun 10 am–4pm
Restaurants: Lunch from 1 pm; Dinner from 6.30 pm

Photography

Kodak and Fuji film is widely obtainable. Mini-labs for processing films found in all cities and tourist centres.

Post

Post offices (*poczty*) are open Mon–Fri 8 am to 7 pm (main post offices in the larger towns are open day and night); the telecommunications offices in towns are open until midnight.
Postage stamps can be obtained in most hotels and often at stalls selling postcards. A postcard usually takes up to 5 days to arrive in western Europe.

Public Holidays

New Year	1 January
Easter (Sun. and Mon.)	March/April
May Day	1 May
Constitution Day	3 May
Corpus Christi	May/June
Assumption	15 August
All Saints	1 November

Independence Day	11 November
Christmas Eve	24 December
Christmas Day	25 December
Boxing Day	26 December

On Easter Monday (*Lany Poniedziałek*, 'Pouring Monday') it is traditional to sur-prise the unwary with a bucketful of cold water.

Corpus Christi (*Bożego Ciała*) is marked with church processions though the streets of Polish towns (the procession in Łowicz is particularly impressive).

There are fairs all over Poland on the feast of the Assumption (*Wniebowzięcia*).

On All Saints' Day (*Wszystkich Świętych*) Poles visit cemeteries, which are ablaze with candle-light after dark.

Christmas Eve (*Wigilia*) is when families gather for their traditional Christmas meal.

Shopping and Souvenirs

Cepelia shops sell original craft items (woodcarving, textiles etc.), some of which are of good quality. Desa shops sell graph-ics, paintings, sculpture and orna-ments, while jewellery (including amber) can be bought from Jubiler shops.

The range of goods available in ordinary Polish shops has increased enormously in the last decade; prices vary wildly. Street trading plays an important part in the cities, with people pouring over the borders of eastern Europe to sell their wares.

Spas

There are over forty health spas in Poland. Among those recommended are: Krynica-Zdrój, Ciechocinek, Busko-Zdrój, Wieliczka, Kołobrzeg, Kudowa-Zdrój, Szczawno-Zdrój, Nałęczów, Polanica-Zdrój. They specialize in treatment of diseases of the respiratory tract, motor organs, urinary tract, metabolism, diges-tive organs and skin. Further information can be obtained from Polorbis, or from the Spas department of the Ministry of Health ul. Miodowa 15, Warsaw (tel. 022-31 34 41 ext. 589 455).

Telephones

Codes for some Polish cities:

Częstochowa	034	Poznań	061
Gdańsk	058	Szczecin	091
Katowice	032	Toruń	056
Kraków	012	Wrocław	071
Łódź	042	Warsaw	022
Lublin	081		

Emergency Telephone Numbers:

Police	997
Fire Brigade	998
Accident Rescue Service	999

Tipping

Service is included in the bill (10 per cent for restaurants, taxis, etc.). However, it is usual to round up the total when paying.

Travelling within Poland

...by Car

Poland is covered by a dense network of roads. The surface of most of these is good, except for minor roads, which are often potholed. Compared with western Europe the roads are relatively empty, but there are many cyclists, horse-drawn vehicles and agricultural vehicles, which usually have inadequate lights. Polish motorists can be excitable and unpredictable.

Accidents
Accidents should always be reported to the police (*policja*). In the case of serious accidents the Polish authorities may impound the vehicle documents, passport and even the vehicle until the cause of the accident has been established. For insurance purposes it is necessary to keep a record of the details of the other party involved in the accident, a document from the police and details of the legal authorities.

Breakdowns
The AA and the RAC strongly recommend taking out 5-star Cover (AA) or Eurocover Motoring Assistance (RAC) if you are intending to drive in Poland.

Car Hire
Cars can be hired in Warsaw, Gdańsk, Kraków, Katowice, Łódź, Poznań, Szczecin and Wrocław (from Orbis and elsewhere). The driver must be over 21, have a valid passport and national driving licence. Credit cards from Avis, Hertz and Europcar are accepted. The hire charges are similar to those in the West.

Documents for Vehicles
Motorists need a national driving licence and a vehicle registration document, as well as a green insurance card. The carrying of a warning triangle, a fire extinguisher, sets of replacement bulb for headlights and indicator lights, and a first aid kit is also compulsory. Headlight deflectors are highly recommended.

Garages
It is a good idea to take a list of garages for your make of car. Owners of obsolete vehicles are advised to carry a basic collection of spare parts. Garages are listed in telephone directories (at all post offices) under the make of car or under *Reparacje Samochodów* or *Usługi Motoryzacyjne*.

Petrol
Petrol (*benzyna*) is cheaper than in the UK. Unleaded petrol (*benzyna bezołowiowa*) is available.

Telephone Numbers

Police	997
Ambulance	999
Roadside Assistance (PzMot)	9637

Traffic regulations
The speed limit in residential areas is 20 kph (12 mph), in other built-up areas 60 kph (37 mph), outside built-up areas 90 kph (56 mph), on motorways (*autostrady*) 110 kph (68 mph) and on trunk roads (*magistrale*) 100 kph (61 mph), for cars with trailers outside built-up areas usually 70 kph (43 mph). Overtaking is forbidden near road junctions. Trains have priority at road junctions where the roads are of equal status.

Cars may not stop within 100 metres of a level crossing. Outside built-up areas motorcyclists must ride with dipped head-lights even in daytime. From November to March the use of dipped headlights in daytime is compulsory. Parking is only permitted with sidelights.

Drink-drive laws are strict: virtually no alcohol may be consumed before driving. The wearing of seatbelts is compulsory. There are on-the-spot fines for parking and minor offences.

Motoring clubs provide information about the use of caravans. You may not allow your own car to be driven in Poland by a Polish resident.

Trunk roads

E–77	Warsaw – Radom – Kielce – Kraków – Zakopane
E–33	Frankfurt an der Oder – Poznań – Konin – Warsaw – Siedlce – Biała Podlaska
E–67	Wałbrzych – Wrocław – Sieradz – Łódź – Warsaw – Białystok
E–65	Świnoujście – Szczecin – Gorzów Wlkp. – Zielona Góra – Jelenia Góra
E–75	Gdańsk – Grudziądz – Toruń – Łódź – Piotrków Trybunalski
E–40	Legnica – Wrocław – Opole – Chorzów – Kraków – Rzeszów – Przemyśl
E–77	Gdańsk – Ostróda – Warsaw

...by Coach

A network of coach services is run by the national bus company (PKS) and can be useful for visiting rural and mountainous areas.

Tickets can usually be bought in advance at the coach terminals.

...by Cycle

It is possible to hire bicycles in Poland, but it is probably advisable to bring your own (complete with spare parts), since demand often outstrips supply.

...by Rail

Within Poland there is an extensive rail network, and fares are remarkably low by Western European standards. Trains are clean and punctual, but often overcrowded. It is advisable to book in advance and essential to reserve seats, especially during the main holiday periods July and August, Easter and Christmas. This can be done at Orbis offices. A 'Polrailpass', obtainable at Polish tourist agencies, allows the visitor to travel on all local, fast and express trains listed in the timetables of Polish State Railways (PKP) for eight days, fifteen days, twenty-one days or a month. This helps you avoid queuing, but it probably works out more expensive than buying tickets for each journey.

Information about timetables, fares and conditions of carriage can be obtained from Polorbis or from PKP offices.

Urban Transport

Taxis

Taxis can usually be found at centrally situated taxi ranks. Fares are usually higher at night and on Sundays and holidays.

There are also radio taxis, listed in telephone directories.

Buses and trains

Tickets are bought in advance at a kiosk; tickets must be cancelled in a machine on boarding the vehicle.

Food in Poland

The Polish king Stanislaw Leszczyński kept an excellent table whilst in exile at his court in Nancy and one day had the immortal idea of sprinkling his cake with rum and setting it alight, rather like a Christmas pudding. The rum babas are thus a Polish invention, and babas of all kinds have been baked in Poland for centuries, always in special, tall moulds, and were often so light and delicate that they had to be cooled on pillows. They were made on a grand scale: Old Polish baba recipes frequently began with the instruction 'take three score eggs ...'. Today babas are still very popular in Poland, and no Easter table is complete without them. They can be bought like many excellent cakes and pastries, from patisseries (look for *ciastkarnia*, *cukiernia* or simply *ciastka*) in every town. Polish doughnuts (*pączki*) are also recommended. They are rather different from their English or American cousins and are sometimes filled with rosepetal jam. The most famous ones come from A. Blikle, the patisserie which has been established in Warsaw's Nowy Świat for over a hundred years. Polish bread is also excellent – even the smallest village bakers generally have several varieties. Cakes and desserts can best be enjoyed in the many cafés (*kawiarnie*). Social life in Polish towns centres round them, and few Poles pass a day without popping into one.

Poles love eating meat. Climate and history have combined to create a solid, filling, meat-based cuisine. Polish sausages are world-famous and the collapse of the communist system has meant that the charcuteries are once again full of the many kinds of sausage (*kiełbasa*). Liver sausage (*pasztetówka*) and black pudding (*kaszanka*) are markedly different from their Western counterparts, and are certainly worth trying. Dried and smoked sausages are also highly recommended, *krakowska*, *myśliwska* and authentic *kabanos*, in particular. *Bigos*, a hunter's stew, has become Poland's national dish, praised by Adam Mickiewicz in the great Polish epic, *Pan Tadeusz*:

W kociołkach bigos grzano; w słowach wydać trudno
Bigosu smak przedziwny, kolor i woń cudną

The bigos is cooking in the pot, it is difficult in words
To express its marvellous flavour, colour and
              wonderful aroma ...

It is based on a mixture of fresh cabbage and sauerkraut, with many kinds of meat and sausage. Home-made is best, of course, but a good restaurant is unlikely to disappoint you. Pork chops are traditionally served rather like *Wiener Schnitzel*, coated with egg and breadcrumbs, and fried; ask for *kotlet schabowy*. *Zrazy wołowe* – the Polish version of beef olives – are also very good.

Shooting game has been a traditional Polish sport for centuries. In season you will often find game on the menu in restaurants. Hare in cream (*zając w śmietanie*) is highly recommended, as are wild duck (*dzika kaczka*) and pâté of wild boar (*pasztet z dzika*). In spring and summer, poussins, roasted 'Polish style' with excellent stuffing (*kurczak nadziewany po polsku*) are worth looking out for, and are usually served with a salad of cucumbers in soured cream (*mizeria*) and new potatoes (*młode kartofle*). Dill (*koper*) could be called the Polish national herb, and you will generally find it sprinkled over both *mizeria* and *kartofle*. It is also widely used in pickles, particularly in salted cucumbers, which are not preserved in vinegar, but fermented with salt in wooden barrels. In summer so-called *ogórki małosolne* (literally 'little salted'), which have been pickled for only a few days, have a unique flavour and are worth seeking out in the shops and street markets.

Polish home-made *konfitura* contains whole fruit and is runnier than jam. *Konfitura z poziomek* (made from wild strawberries) is deliciously aromatic. You can pick wild strawberries and bilberries in most Polish woods in July, and in autumn a wide variety of wild mushrooms. Mushroom-picking is a popular Polish pastime, but one has to be careful as many are poisonous. It may be safer to leave it to the experts. since in Poland wild mushrooms are not newly fashionable, they do not carry a designer price tag and do not come in tiny chichi punnets. In the autumn, particularly in a good mushrooming year, they can be seen everywhere, sold from huge rustic baskets or a newspaper spread on the ground, in open-air markets, greengrocers and simply in the streets. If you recall the price of fresh wild mushrooms back home, you will be pleasantly surprised at how little you will have to pay for copious quantities of them. The number of varieties, their subtle beauty – all understated velvets and suedes – and the gorgeous smell are also a joy. At other times of the year you can buy a string of dried mushrooms (*grzyby suszone*) or a jar of pickled mushrooms (*grzyby marynowane*) as a souvenir. Honey also makes an excellent gift –

heather (*miód wrzosowy*) and buckwheat (*miód hreczany*) honey are especially good. It is also worth looking our for *powidła śliwkowe* – a healthy low-sugar plum spread, not unlike English fruit cheeses, which is traditionally baked in stone pots.

It is difficult to find a clear dividing line between Polish and Jewish cuisine, since they have influenced each other for centuries. Both share a love of fish – and this means mostly freshwater fish, except of course for herring. Try a variety of marinated herring (*śledzie*) – in oil (*w oleju*), vinegar (*w occie*), or cream (*w śmietanie*), stuffed pike or carp Jewish style (*ryba po żydowsku*), and carp in aspic (*karp w galarecie*). All of these appear on the table at the most important occasion in the Polish calendar – Christmas Eve.

Poland has a great variety of excellent soups. If you want a slightly more adventurous version of the ubiquitous borsch (*barszcz czerwony*), try the substantial Ukrainian variety (known as *barszcz ukraiński* or *barszcz małorosyjski*) made with savoy cabbage, haricot beans and meat. Its summertime counterpart is *chłodnik*, a classic cold soup, which contains young beetroot, cucumber, dill, soured cream and sometimes diced veal. Occasionally freshwater crayfish (*szyjki rakowe*) may also be added. Crayfish are likely to reappear as the polluted rivers and lakes are beginning to be cleaned. They are called *raki* and are usually served cold, with dill, Scandinavian fashion, or in a soup: *zupa rakowa*. Other soups include *krupnik* (pearl barley and winter vegetable soup), *kapuśniak* (with sauerkraut), *żur z kiełbasą* (a delicious sour soup based on fermented flour, served with sliced sausage), *zupa grzybowa* (wild mushroom soup). There are also many summer fruit soups: *jabłkowa* (apple), *wiśniowa* (cherry), *jagodowa* (bilberry) and so on. Halfway between a soup and a main course are the famous *flaki po warszawsku* (tripe *à la varsovienne*).

Poland is also a land of pasta eaters. There are several varieties of *pierogi* – pasta envelopes filled with cream cheese, potatoes and fried onions (*pierogi ruskie*), sauerkraut and wild mushrooms (*pierogi z kapustą i grzybami*), meat (*pierogi z mięsem*), or fruit – try bilberries in season (*pierogi z jagodami*). (A word of warning though: Poles are slow to adapt to modern dietary ways. Unless you ask them not to, they will tend to pour ladles of melted butter or margarine over your plate of pasta.) The sophisticated version of pierogi is called *kołduny*. These come from Lithuania, are small, filled with chopped lean meat and always served in clear broth (*rosół*). Other kinds of pasta are *knedle* (not unlike Austrian *knödel* or English dumplings) – pasta rounds with different stuffings, and potato-based *pyzy* (delicious with meat or wild mushroom sauce) or kopytka. Many varieties of noodles (*kluski*) are added to soups or served with sauces.

One Polish speciality not to be missed is cheap, homely and widely available: a large heart-shaped soft white cheese (*biały ser*), somewhat similar to curd cheese. With rye bread and radishes it makes an excellent snack. Avoid *chudy*, made with skimmed milk, and go for *pełnotłusty*, which is sinfully full fat but has a much nicer taste. Among the other cheeses worth seeking out are *bryndza* and *oscypek*. Both are prepared from ewes' milk in the mountain regions of southern Poland but are usually available everywhere. *Bryndza* is somewhat reminiscent of feta cheese, while *oscypek* is smoked and thus develops an appetising dark skin over its creamy interior. It is also highly decorative, being made in carved wooden moulds, and keeps for ages.

Lastly, it would be unthinkable to visit Poland and not try its famous beers and vodkas. Both have been made in Poland for centuries. Particularly well-known brands of beer (*piwo*) include Żywiec and Okocim.

Apart from clear vodka, called *czysta* (the most popular brand is *Polonez*, but *Wyborowa* and rye-based *Żytnia* are good, while *Królewska* and *Chopin* have bravely flamboyant bottles), there is an endless choice of flavoured vodkas. The delicately aromatic *żubrówka* is coloured pale green from the blade of bison grass in each bottle; *jarzębiak* is made with rowan berries; *pieprzówka* is spiced with black pepper; *cytrynówka* – with lemon; *goldwasser* or *złotówka* has floating flecks of real gold; Jewish *pejsachówka* is a dry spirit based on plums, and *wiśniówka* is a sweet vodka or cherry brandy. My favourite is *Soplica*. In character similar to brandy, it is dry, aromatic and quite splendid. Its name is derived from the family portrayed in *Pan Tadeusz*. *Siwucha* used to be the home-spun moniker for vodka in ancient Poland. The brand available nowadays panders to the somewhat dubious nostalgia for communist times and the cheapest vodka sold then; it was popularly referred to as *strażacka*, fireman's vodka, because of its red label, now replaced by red wax on the cork.

To enjoy vodkas at their best, serve clear ones straight from the freezer, dry flavoured vodkas chilled, and sweet vodkas at room temperature.

Many Poles have their own recipes for home-flavoured vodka (*nalewka*), often passed down for generations. One of the most famous (or infamous) is *żmijówka* – with a poisonous snake coiled at the bottom of the bottle!

Natalia von Svolkien

Further Reading

* very readable   ▲ good illustrations   ■ useful for reference

General History

*Ascherson, Neal: *The Struggles for Poland*, London (Pan) 1989
Braun, Jerzy (ed.): *Poland in Christian Civilization*, London (Veritas Foundation) 1985
*Davies, Norman: *The Heart of Europe: A Short History of Poland*, Oxford (OUP) 1986
*Davies, Norman: *God's Playground: A History of Poland (2 vols)*, Oxford (OUP) 1982
Kłoczowski, Jerzy: *A History of Polish Christianity*, Cambridge (CUP) 2000
*Lukowski, Jerzy, and Hubert Zawadzki: *A Concise History of Poland*, Cambridge (CUP) 2001
Suchodolski, Bogdan: *A History of Polish Culture*, Warsaw 1986
*Zamoyski, Adam: *The Polish Way*, London (John Murray) 1988

Pre-20th Century History

Bogucka, M.: *The Lost World of the 'Sarmatians'*, Warsaw (PAN, Institute of History) 1996
Butterwick, Richard: *Poland's Last King and English Culture: Stanisław Poniatowski 1732–1798*, Oxford (OUP) 1998
Christiansen, Eric: *The Northern Crusades. The Baltic and the Catholic Frontier 1100–1525*, London (Macmillan) 1980
Długosz, Jan: *The Annals of Jan Długosz* (an English abridgement by H. Michael), Chichester (IM Publications) 1997
Federowicz, J. K. et al. (eds.): *A Republic of Nobles. Studies in Polish History to 1864*, Cambridge (CUP) 1982
Fiszman, S. (ed.): *The Polish Renaissance in its European Context*, Bloomington (Indiana UP) 1988
Jedlicki, J.: *A Suburb of Europe: Nineteenth-Century Polish Approaches to Western Civilization*, Budapest (Central European UP) 1999
Leslie, R.F.: *Polish Politics and the Revolution of November 1830*, London (Athlone Press) 1956
Lukowski, Jerzy: *Liberty's Folly: the Polish-Lithuanian Commonwealth in the Eighteenth Century*, London (Routledge) 1991
Porter, B. : *When Nationalism Began to Hate: Imagining Modern Politics in Nineteenth-Century Poland*, New York (OUP) 2000
Segel, Harold B.: *Renaissance Culture in Poland: the Rise of Humanism*, Ithaca (Cornell UP) 1989
Tazbir, Jan: *A State Without Stakes: Polish Religious Toleration in the Sixteenth and Seventeenth Centuries*, New York (Kościuszko Foundation) 1973
Walicki, Andrzej: *Philosophy and Romantic Nationalism: the Case of Poland*, Oxford (OUP) 1982

20th Century History

Ascherson, Neal: *The Polish August: The Self-limiting Revolution*, London (Allen Lane) 1981
Bethell, Nicholas: *Gomułka: his Poland and his Communism*, London (Longman) 1969
Ciechanowski, J. M.: *The Warsaw Rising of 1944*, Cambridge (CUP) 1974
Davies, Norman: *White Eagle, Red Star: the Polish-Soviet War 1919–1920*, London (Orbis) 1983
*Garton Ash, Timothy: *The Polish Revolution: Solidarity*, London (Penguin) 1999
Leslie, R. F. (ed.): *The History of Poland Since 1863*, Cambridge (CUP) 1980
Lipski, Jan Józef: *A History of KOR: the Committee for Workers' Self Defence*, Berkeley (University of California Press) 1985
Polonsky, Anthony: *Politics in Independent Poland 1921–1939. The Crisis of Constitutional Government*, Oxford (OUP) 1972
Torońska, Teresa: *Oni* ['Them']: *Stalin's Polish Puppets*, London (Harvill) 1987

Art and Architecture

For those with some knowledge of Polish, most of the country has now been covered by the Polish equivalent of Pevsner's *Buildings of England*, the well-illustrated series ▲ ■ *Katalog zabytków sztuki w Polsce* [Catalogue of Monuments of Art in Poland] edited by Jerzy Z. Loziński and published by the Institut Sztuki Polskiej Akademii Nauk in Warsaw.

A more concise illustrated survey of art and architecture in Poland, ▲ ■ *Pomniki sztuki w Polsce*, also edited by Loziński, is in the course of publication. One and a half volumes have so far appeared:
Volume I: *Małopolska,* Warsaw (Arkady) 1984 (also available in German translation)
Volume II (part 1): *Pomorze*, Warsaw (Arkady) 1992

A useful one-volume gazetteer to Poland's historic architecture, also in Polish, with colour illustrations has recently been published:
▲ ■ Faryna-Paskiewicz, H., M. Omilanowska and Robert Pasieczny: *Atlas Zabytków Architektury w Polsce*, Warsaw (PWN) 2001

Several volumes of a well-illustrated *History of Polish Art*, published in Poland, are available in English translation:
▲ Świechowski, Zygmunt: *Romanesque Art in Poland*, Warsaw (Arkady) 1983
▲ Labuda, A.: *Gotyk w Polsce*, Warsaw (Arkady)
▲ Kozakiewicz, Helena and Stefan: *Renaissance in Poland*, Warsaw (Arkady) 1976
▲ Karpowicz, M.: *Baroque in Poland*, Warsaw (Arkady) 1991
▲ Karpowicz, S.: *Rokoko w Polsce*, Warsaw (Arkady)
▲ Lorentz, Stanislaw and Andrzej Rottermund: *Neoclassicism in Poland*, Warsaw (Arkady) 1986

▲ Białostocki, Jan: *The Art of the Renaissance in Eastern Europe*, Oxford (Phaidon) 1976
▲ Bujak, Adam (photos), Michal Rożek (text): *Nekropolie Królów i Książąt Polskich*, Warsaw (SiT) 1991

▲ Buxton, David: *The Wooden Churches of Eastern Europe: an introductory survey*, Cambridge (CUP) 1981

■ Chrcisciski, J. A. and A. Rottermund: *Atlas of Warsaw's Architecture*, Warsaw (Arkady) 1978

Crossley, Paul: *Gothic Architecture in the Reign of Kasimir the Great 1320–1380*: *Church Architecture* (Biblioteka Wawelska 7), Cracow 1986

■ Dehio, Georg and Ernst Gall (revised Michael Antoni): *West- und Ostpreussen (Handbuch der deutschen Kunstdenkmäler)*, Munich (Deutscher Kunstverlag) 1993

Dmochowski, Zbigniew: *The Architecture of Poland*, London (Polish Research Centre) 1956

Fryś-Pietraszkowa, Ewa et al.: *Sztuka Ludowa w Polsce*, Warsaw (Arkady) 1988

▲ Iwanusiw, Oleh Wolodymyr: *Church in Ruins*, St Catharines, Ontario (St Sophia) 1987

Jaroszewski, Tadeusz Stefan: *The Book of Warsaw Palaces*, Warsaw (Interpress) 1985

▲ * Knox, Brian: *The Architecture of Poland*, London (Barrie and Jenkins) 1971

▲ Krzysztofowicz-Kozakowska, Stefania: *Polish Art Nouveau*, Kraków (Wydawnictwo Kluczynski) 1999

■ Lewicka, Maria: *The Old Town in Warsaw, Atlas of Architecture*, Warsaw (Arkady) 1992

Lileyko, J.: *The Royal Castle in Warsaw*, Warsaw (Interpress) 1981

Morawińska, A.: *Polish Painting, 15th–20th Centuries*, Warsaw (Auriga) 1984

Olszewski, Andrzej K.: *An Outline of Polish 20th Century Art and Architecture*, Warsaw (Interpress) 1989

▲ Ostrowski, Jan K., et al. *Land of the Winged Horsemen: Art in Poland 1572-1764* (Yale UP) 1999

▲ Szablowski, Jerzy (ed.): *Zbiory Zamku Królewskiego na Wawelu*, Warsaw (Arkady) 1990

Waldorff, Jerzy: *The Rest is Silence* [Powązki Cemetery, Warsaw], Warsaw (Interpress) 1989

▲ Zachwatowicz, Jan: *Polish Architecture*, Warsaw (Arkady) 1966

Memoirs and biography

Brandys, Kazimierz: *Warsaw Diary 1977–81*, London (Chatto) 1983

Curie, Eve: *Madame Curie*, London (Heinemann) 1938 (and later editions)

*Dönhoff, Marion Gräfin: *Before the Storm. Memories of my youth in old Prussia*, New York (Knopf) 1990

*Gombrowicz, Witold (tr. Lillian Vallee): *Diary* (3 vols), London (Quartet) 1988–94

*Hoffmann, Eva, *Lost in Translation, London (Minerva) 1990*

Jędrzejewicz, Wacław: *Piłsudski: A Life for Poland*, New York (Hippocrene) 1982

Lifton, Betty: *The King of Children* [Janusz Korczak], London (Chatto (pb Pan)) 1988

*Malaparte, Curzio (tr. Cesare Foligno): *Kaputt*, London 1948 (pb. 1964 and later)

Miłosz, Czesław: *Native Realm*, London (Penguin) 1981

Moczarski, K. (ed. Marianna Fitzpatrick): *Conversations with an Executioner*, Englewood Cliffs NJ (Prentice Hall) 1981

Pasek, Jan Chryzostom (ed. and tr. C. S. Leach): *Memoirs of the Polish Baroque*, Berkeley (University of California Press) 1976

Piłsudski, Józef: *Memoirs of a Polish Revolutionary and Soldier*, London (Faber) 1931

Potocki, Count Alfred: *Master of Lancut*, London (W. H. Allen) 1959

Sikorska, Grażyna: *Jerzy Popiełuszko, a Martyr*, London (Fount) 1985

*Wat, Alekander (tr. Richard Lourie): *My Century. The Odyssey of a Polish Intellectual*, Berkeley (University of California Press) 1988

Zamoyski, Adam: *The Last King of Poland*, London (Jonathan Cape) 1992

Polish Jewry

Abramsky, Chimen; Jachimczyk, Maciej and Polonsky, Antony (ed.): *The Jews in Poland*, Oxford (Blackwell) 1986

Adelman, Alan, and Robert Lapides: *The Lodz Ghetto – Inside a Community under Siege*, London (Viking) 1990

Bartoszewski, Władysław T.: *The Warsaw Ghetto: a Christian's testimony*, London (Lamp Press) 1989

Bauman, Janina: *Winter in the Morning*, London (Virago) 1986

Duda, Eugeniusz: *Krakowskie Judaica*, Warsaw (Wydawnictwo PTTK 'Kraj') 1991

Fink, Ida: *A Scrap of Time*, London (Penguin) 1989

*Gilbert, Martin: *The Holocaust. The Jewish Tragedy*, London (Collins) 1986

Gross, Jan T.: Neighbors, (Princeton UP) 2001

Gruber, Ruth Ellen: *Jewish Heritage Travel. A Guide to Central and Eastern Europe*, New York (John Wiley & Sons) 1992

Herling-Grudziński, Gustaw: *A World Apart*, Oxford (OUP) 1985

*Hoffmann, Eva: *Shtetl: the History of a Small Town and an Extinguished World,* London (Weidenfeld and Nicholson) 1995

Keneally, Thomas: *Schindler's Ark*, London (Hodder & Stoughton) 1982

▲ Krajewska, Monika: *The Time of the Stones*, Warsaw (Interpress) 1983

*Levi, Primo: *If this is a Man / The Truce*, London (Abacus) 1987

Polonsky, Antony and Władysław Bartoszewski (ed.): *The Jews in Warsaw*, Oxford (Blackwell) 1991

de Pomiane, Edouard (tr. Josephine Bacon): *The Jews of Poland: Recollections and Recipes*, Garden Grove, CA (Pholiota) 1985

Richmond, Theo: *Konin: A Quest* London (Cape) 1995

Singer, Isaac Bashevis: *In My Father's Court*, London (Secker and Warburg) 1967 (Penguin 1980)

Singer, Isaac Bashevis: *The Collected Stories*, London (Penguin) 1984

Singer, Isaac Bashevis: *The Magician of Lublin*, London (Secker and Warburg) 1961 (Penguin 1980)

*Szpilman, Władysław: *The Pianist* London 1998

▲ Vishniac, Roman: *A Vanished World*, London (Allen Lane) 1983

Literature

Miłosz, Czesław: *The History of Polish Literature*, Berkeley (University of California Press) 1983

Pre-20th century Polish Literature in Translation

Fredro, Aleksander (tr. Harold B. Segel): *The Major Comedies of Alexander Fredro*, Princeton (Princeton UP) 1969

Krasicki, Ignacy (tr. T. H. Hossington): *The Adventures of Mr Nicholas Wisdom*, Evanston (Northwestern UP) 1992

Potocki, Jean (tr. Ian Maclean): *The Manuscript Found in Saragossa*, London (Penguin) 1998

Prus, Bolesław (tr. David Welsh et al.): *The Doll,* London (Central European Press) 1994

Prus, Bolesław (tr. Jeremiah Curtin): *The Pharaoh and the Priest*, London 1910
Sienkiewicz, Henryk (tr. Adam Zamoyski): *Charcoal Sketches, and Other Tales*, London (Angel) 1990
Sienkiewicz, Henryk (tr. Alicija Tyszkiewicz): *The Teutonic Knights*, Edinburgh (Nelson) 1943
Sienkiewicz, Henryk (tr. C. J. Hogarth): *Quo Vadis?*, Gloucester (Alan Sutton) 1989
Sienkiewicz, Henryk (tr. W. S. Kuniszak): *Trilogy (With Fire and Sword, The Deluge, Fire in the Steppe)*, New York (Hippocrene) 1991–92

20th-century Polish Prose in Translation
Andrzejewski, Jerzy (tr. D. J. Walsh): *Ashes and Diamonds*, Harmondsworth (Penguin) 1965
Borowski, Tadeusz (tr. Barbara Venner): *This Way for the Gas, Ladies and Gentlemen*, Harmondsworth (Penguin) 1976 (first publ. 1967)
Gombrowicz, Witold (tr. Alasdair Hamilton): *Pornografia,* London (Calder and Boyars) 1966
Gombrowicz, Witold (tr. Eric Mosbacher): *Ferdydurke*, New York (Grove Press) 1968
Gombrowicz, Witold (tr. Nina Karsov and Carolyn French): *Transatlantyk*, London (Yale UP) 1998
Gombrowicz, Witold (tr. Krystyna Griffith-Jones and Catherine Robins): *Princess Ivona*, London (Calder & Boyars) 1969
Herbert, Zbigniew (tr. Michael March and Jaroslaw Anders): *Barbarian in the Garden*, Manchester (Carcanet) 1985
Hłasko, Marek (tr. Norbert Guterman and Tomasz Mirkowicz): *The Eighth Day of the Week, & Killing the Second Dog*, London (Minerva) 1992
Kapuściński, Ryszard *Imperium*, London (Granta) 1994
Konwicki, Tadeusz (tr. David Welsh): *A Dreambook for Our Time*, Harmondsworth (Penguin) 1976
Konwicki, Tadeusz (tr. Richard Lourie): *A Minor Apocalypse*, London (Faber) 1983
Konwicki, Tadeusz (tr. Richard Lourie): *The Polish Complex*, New York (Farrar, Strauss) 1982
Kott, Jan (ed.): *Four Decades of Polish Essays*, Evanston (Northwestern UP) 1990
Lec, Stanislaw Jerzy (tr. Jacek Gałązka): *Unkempt Thoughts*, New York (St Martin's Press) 1962
Lem, Stanisław (tr. Joanna Kilmartin and Steve Cox): *Solaris*, London (Faber) 1970
Mrożek, Sławomir (tr. Henry Deissel): *The Emigrants*, London (French) 1984
Mrożek, Sławomir (tr. Nicholas Bethell): *Six Plays*, London (Jonathan Cape) 1967
Przybyszewska, Stanisława (tr. D. Gerould & B. Taborski): *The Danton Case and Thermidor*, Evanston (Northwestern UP) 1992
Reymont, Władysław (tr. Michael H. Dziewicki): *The Peasants*, New York (Knopf) 1942
Schulz, Bruno (tr. Celina Wieniewska): *The Fictions of Bruno Schulz: The Street of Crocodiles and Sanatorium Under the Sign of the Hourglass*, London (Picador) 1988
Schulz, Bruno: *Letters and Drawings with Selected Prose*, ed. Jerzy Ficowski, New York (Fromm) 1988
Szczypiorski, Andrzej (tr. Klara Glowczewska): *The Beautiful Mrs Seidenman*, London (Sphere) 1990
Wat, Aleksander (tr. Lilian Vallee): *Lucifer Unemployed,* Evanston (Northwestern UP) 1990
Witkiewicz, Stanisław Ignacy (tr. Louise Iribarne): *Insatiability*, London (Quartet) 1985
Witkiewicz, Stanisław Ignacy (ed. Daniel Gerould): *The Witkiewicz Reader,* (Northwestern UP) 1992
Żeromski, Stefan (tr. Helen Stankiewicz-Zand): *Ashes*, New York (Knopf) 1928

German Literature in Translation
Bienek, Horst (tr. Ralph R. Read): *The First Polka*, London (Gollancz) 1976
Grass, Günter (tr. R. Manheim): *The Danzig Trilogy (The Tin Drum, Cat and Mouse,* and *Dog Years)*, London (Sidgwick and Jackson) 1959, 1961, 1963

Grass, Günter (tr. R. Manheim): *The Call of the Toad*, London (Sidgwick and Jackson) 1992

Hauptmann, Gerhart (tr. Frank Marcus): *The Weavers*, London (Methuen) 1980

Hauptmann, Gerhart (tr. Stanley Radcliffe): *Lineman Thiel and other tales*, London (Angel) 1990

Hoffmann, E. T. A. (tr. R. C. Hollingdale et al.): *Tales of Hoffmann*, London (Penguin) 1982

Lenz, Siegfried (tr. Krishna Winston): *Heritage*, London (Methuen) 1981

Poetry

Czerniawski, Adam (ed.): *The Burning Forest. An Anthology of Polish Poetry*, Newcastle (Bloodaxe) 1988

Herbert, Zbigniew (tr. John and Bogdana Carpenter): *Selected Poems*, Oxford (OUP) 1977

Herbert, Zbigniew (tr. John and Bogdana Carpenter): *Report from the Besieged City, and Other Poems*, Oxford (OUP) 1987

Kochanowski, Jan (tr. Seamus Heaney and Stanisław Barańczak): *Laments*, London (Faber) 1995

Mickiewicz, Adam (tr. Irene Suboczewski) *Konrad Wallenrod and Grażyna*, Lanham, London (Univ. Press of America) 1989

Mickiewicz, Adam (tr. Kenneth R. Mackenzie) *Pan Tadeusz*, London (Polish Cultural Foundation) 1986 (tr. first publ. 1964)

Mickiewicz, Adam; Zygmunt Krasiński and Juliusz Słowacki (tr. Harold B. Segel): *Polish Romantic Drama* [Mickiewicz: *Forefathers' Eve, part III*; Krasiński: *Undivine Comedy*; Słowacki: *Fantasy*], Ithaca, London (Cornell UP.) 1977

Miłosz, Czesław: *Collected Poems 1931–1987*, London (Penguin) 1988

Miłosz, Czesław (ed. and tr.): *Post-War Polish Poetry*, Berkeley (Univ. of California) 1983 (3rd ed.)

Norwid, Cyprian Kamil (tr. Adam Czerniawski) *Poezje – Poems*, Kraków 1986

Peterkiewicz, J., and Singer, B. (eds.): *Five Centuries of Polish Verse 1450–1970*, Oxford (OUP) 1970

Różewicz, Tadeusz (tr. Adam Czerniawski): *Selected Poems*, Harmondsworth (Penguin) 1976

Różewicz, Tadeusz (tr. Adam Czerniawski): *Conversations with the Prince*, London (Anvil) 1982

Staff, Leopold (tr. Adam Czerniawski): *An Empty Room*, Newcastle (Bloodaxe) 1983

Szymborska, Wisława (tr. Adam Czerniawski): *People on a Bridge*, London (Forest Books) 1990

Szymborska, Wisława (tr. Stanisław Barańczak and Clare Cavanagh): *View with a Grain of Sand, Selected Poems*, London (Faber) 1996

Wat, Aleksander (tr. Czesław Miłosz and Leonard Nathan): *Selected Poems*, London (Penguin) 1991 (first publ. NY 1969)

Performing Arts: Music, Theatre, Cinema

Drozdowski, Bohdan: *Twentieth Century Polish Theatre*, London (John Calder) 1979

Grodzicki, August (tr. Lucyna Tomaszewska): *Polish Theatre Directors*, Warsaw (Interpress) 1979

Grotowski, Jerzy (ed. Eugenio Barba): *Towards a Poor Theatre*, London (Methuen) 1969

Kantor, Tadeusz (tr. Mariusz Tchorek and G. M. Hyde): *Wielopole, Wielopole*, London (Boyars) 1990

Michałek, Bolesław (ed.): *Le Cinéma polonais*, Paris (Centre Pompidou) 1992

Michalski, Grzegorz, Ewa Obniska, Henryk Swolkień and Jerzy Waldorff: *An Outline History of Polish Music*, Warsaw (Interpress) 1979

Travel

Adams, John Quincy: *Letters on Silesia, written during a Tour through that Country in the Years 1800, 1801*, London (J. Budd) 1804

Coxe, William: *Travels in Poland, Russia, Sweden, Denmark*, Dublin 1792

Döblin, Alfred (tr. J. Neugroschel): *Journey to Poland*, London (I. B. Tauris) 1991

Fauvel, Jean-Jacques: *Pologne – Guide Bleu*, Paris (Hachette) 1967

Mason, V.: *The Land of the Rainbow*, London 1941

de Montfort, Annie and Henri: *Pologne – Guide Bleu*, Paris 1939

Wraxall, N. W.: *Memoirs of the Courts of Berlin, Dresden, Warsaw and Vienna in the Years 1777, 1778 and 1779*, London 1806 (3rd ed.)

Persons and Subjects

Figures in *italic* refer to illustrations

Places

Place name concordance

German	Polish
Agnetendorf	Jagniątków
Albendorf	Wambierzyce
Alle	Łyna (river)
Allenstein	Olsztyn
Angerburg	Węgorzewo
Auschwitz	Oświecim
Bad Altheide	Polanica-Zdrój
Bad Kudowa	Kudowa-Zdrój
Bad Landeck	Lądek-Zdrój
Bad Reinerz	Duszniki-Zdrój
Bad Salzbrunn	Szczawno-Zdrój
Bad Warmbrunn	Cieplice Śląskie-Zdrój
Beldahnsee	Jezioro Bełdany
Beuthen	Bytom
Bielitz	Bielsko-Biała
Birkenau	Brzezinka
Bischofstein	Bisztynek
Biskupiner See	Jezioro Biskupińskie
Bober	Bóbr (river)
Boberröhrsdorf	Siedlęcin
Bodenwinkel	Kąty Rybackie
Bohnsack	Sobieszewo
Bolkenhain	Bolków
Brahe	Brda (river)
Breslau	Wrocław
Brieg	Brzeg
Bromberg	Bydgoszcz
Brückenberg	Bierutowice
Bunzlau	Bolesławiec
Bütow	Bytów
Cammin	Kamień Pomorski
Camminer Bucht	Zalew Kamieński
Crossen	Krosno Odrzańskie
Danzig	Gdańsk
Deutsch-Eylau	Iława
Dirschau	Tczew
Drewenz	Drwęca (river)
Drewenz-See	Jezioro Drwęckie
Driesen	Drezdenko

German	Polish
Drossen	Ośno Lubuskie
Elbing	Elbląg
Elbing (near Wrocław)	Ołbin
Ermeland	Warmia
Eulengebirge	Góry Sowie
Eylau	Iława
Frankenstein	Ząbkowice Śląskie
Frauenburg	Frombork
Friedeberg	Strzelce Krajeńskie
Frisches Haff	Zalew Wiślany
Fürstenstein	Książ
Galinde	Pisa (river)
Gdingen	Gdynia
Glatz	Kłodzko
Glatzer Schneegebirge	Góry Śnieżki
Glatzer Talkessel	Kotlina Kłodzka
Gleiwitz	Gliwice
Glogau	Głogów
Gnesen	Gniezno
Goldberg	Złotoryja
Gollub	Golub Dobrzyń
Görlitz	Gierłoż
Goschütz	Goszcz
Graudenz	Grudziądz
Greifenberg	Gryfice
Gröditzberg	Grodziec
Gross Peterwitz	Piotrkowice
Grünberg	Zielona Góra
Grünfelde	Grunwald
Grüssau	Krzeszów
Guttstadt	Dobre Miasto
Habelschwerdter Gebirge	Góry Bystrzyckie
Habelschwert	Bystrzyca Kłodzka
Habichtsberg	Jatrzębia Góra
Heiligelinde	Święta Lipka

German	Polish
Heilsberg	Lidzbark Warmiński
Heinrichau	Henryków
Heisternest	Jastarnia
Hela	Hel
Hermsdorf	Sobieszków
Heuschener Gebirge	Góry Stołowe
Hindenburg	Zabrze
Hirschberg	Jelenia Góra
Hohensalza	Inowrocław
Hohenstein	Olsztynek
Jamunder See	Jezioro Jamno
Jauer	Jawor
Johannisburg	Pisz
Johannisburger Heide	Puszcza Piska
Kalzig	Kalsk
Kamenz	Kamieniec Ząbkowicki
Karthaus	Kartuzy
Kattowitz	Katowice
Katzbach	Kaczawa (river)
Katzbachgebirge	Góry Kaczawskie
Katzengebirge	Bełczyna
Klastawe	Chlastawa
Kolbatz	Kołbacz
Kolberg	Kołobrzeg
Königsberg	Kaliningrad
Königsberg (in Poland)	Chojna
Köslin	Koszalin
Kosten	Kościan
Kreisau	Krzyżowa
Krummhübel	Karpacz
Kruschwitz	Kruszwica
Kulm	Chełmno
Kulmer Land	Ziemia Chełmińska
Kulmsee (town)	Chełmża
Kulmsee (lake)	Jezioro Chełmżyńskie
Kussfeld	Kuźnica
Küstrin	Kostrzyn
Kynau	Zagórze Śląskie
Lagow	Łagów
Landeshut	Kamienna Góra
Landsberg an der Warthe	Gorzów Wlkp.
Langenbielau	Bielawa
Langfuhr	Wrzeszcz
Lauenburg	Lębork

German	Polish
Lausitz	Lusatia
Leba	Łeba
Lebus	Lubusz
Lemberg	Lwow (Ukrainian: Lviv)
Leubus	Lubiąż
Liegnitz	Legnica
Lissa	Leszno
Lötzen	Giżycko
Löwenberg	Lwówek Śląski
Löwentinsee	Jezioro Niegocin
Lüben	Lubin
Ludwigsdorf	Łodwigowo
Lyck	Ełk
Marienburg	Malbork
Marienwerder	Kwidzyn
Mauersee	Jezioro Mamry
Meseritz	Międzyrzecz
Mewe	Gniew
Misdroy	Międzyzdroje
Mohrungen	Morąg
Mollwitz	Małujowice
Mottlau	Motława (river)
Muckersee	Jezioro Mokre
Münsterberg	Ziębice
Neidenburg	Nidzica
Neisse	Nysa
Nemitz	Dziwna (river)
Netze	Noteć (river)
Neumarkt	Środa Śląska
Neustadt	Weihersfrei
Niederschlesien	Dolny Śląsk (Lower Silesia)
Niedersee	Jezioro Nidzkie
Nikolaiken	Mikołajki
Nikolaiker See	Jezioro Mikołajskie
Oberglogau	Głogówek
Oberländer Kanal	Kanał Elbląski
Oberschlesien	Górny Śląsk (Upper Silesia)
Oder	Odra (river)
Oels	Oleśnica
Ohle	Oława (river)
Olsa	Olza (river)
Oppeln	Opole
Osterode	Ostróda
Ottmachau	Otmuchów
Pansin	Pęzino
Paradies	Gościkowo
Patschau	Paczków

German	Polish	German	Polish
Peterswaldau	Pieszyce	Sorau	Żary
Petrikau	Piotrków	Spirdingsee	Jezioro Śniardwy
Plagwitz	Płakowice	Stargard	Stargard Szczeciński
Poberow	Pobierowo	Steegen	Stegna
Posen	Poznań	Sternberg	Torzym
Proskau	Prószków	Stettin	Szczecin
Putzig	Puck	Stettiner Haff	Zalew Szczeciński
Pyritz	Pyrzyce	Stolp	Słupsk
		Stolpe	Słupia (river)
Radaune	Radunia	Striegau	Strzegom
Rastenburg	Kętrzyn	Stutthof	Sztutowo
Ratibor	Racibórz		
Reichensteiner		Tannenberg	Stębark
Gebirge	Góry Złote	Teschen	Cieszyń
Reimswaldau	Rybnica Leśna	Teufelsinsel	Czarny Ostrów
Rhein	Ryn	Thorn	Toruń
Rheinsee	Jezioro Ryńskie	Trebnitz	Trzebnica
Rizhöft	Rozewie	Treptow	Trzebiatów
Roschsee	Jezioro Roś		
Rössel	Reszel	Usedom	Uznam, island
Rothebucher Forst	Puszcza Borecka		
Rudschanny	Ruciane-Nida	Wahlstatt	Legnickie Pole
Rügenwalde	Darłowo	Waldenburg	Wałbrzych
Rügenwaldermünde	Darłówko	Wartenburg	Barczewo
		Warthe	Warta (river)
Sagan	Żagań	Weichselmünde	Wisłoujście
Sankt Annaberg	Góra Świętej Anny	Weihersfrei	Wejherowo
Schivelbein	Świdwin	Wipper	Wieprza (river)
Schlesien	Śląsk (Silesia)	Witwenfelsen	Skały Wdowie
Schneekoppe	Śnieżka	Wohnwitz	Wojnowice
Schömberg	Chełmsko Śląskie	Wormditt	Orneta
Schreiberhau	Szkarska Poręba		
Schweidnitz	Świdnica	Zielenzig	Sulęcin
Schweinhaus	Świny	Zillerthal-	
Schwiebus	Świbodzin	Erdmannsdorf	Mysłakowice
Schwirsen	Świerzno	Zobten (mount)	Ślęża
Sextersee	Jezioro Seksty	Zobten (town)	Sobótka
Soldau	Działdowo	Zoppot	Sopot
Soldin	Myślibórz	Zuckau	Żukowo
Soldiner See	Jezioro Myśliborskie	Züllichau	Sulechów

PALLAS GUIDES

CZECH AND SLOVAK REPUBLICS
Erhard Gorys

Highly informative and quite admirable *The Art Newspaper*

Rich and rewarding *Traveller Magazine*

The Czech and Slovak Republics, at the heart of the new Europe, offer the traveller an unforgettable combination of monuments and magnificent landscapes. Prague was the jewel of the Holy Roman Empire, and is still one of the most beautiful cities in the world. Less well known is the countryside of Bohemia and Moravia, where rich plains are ringed by grandiose mountains, and a thousand castles stand guard over Baroque cities. Most recent delights include Edward VII's favourite spa, Mariánské Lázně, which still offers the perfect retreat for convalescents, *flâneurs* and hikers alike. In Slovakia, which has still been scarcely explored by tourists, unspoilt medieval towns nestle amongst some of the most dramatic Alpine scenery in Europe.

This guide is the indispensible companion for any traveller exploring the treasures of the Czech and Slovak Republics.

Erhard Gorys studied art history and jurisprudence at Göttingen and Cambridge, and his studies have taken him to North Africa, the Near East, and Eastern Europe. He has written several guide books, including the Pallas Guide to Israel, and an archaeological handbook.
Sebastian Wormell, the translator and editor, studied art history at Heidelberg, Cambridge and the Courthauld Institute, and has lectured for London University. He has also edited the Pallas Guide to *Poland*.

462 pp including 24 colour plates, 65 b/w plates, 136 illustrations, diagrams and maps, 2 fold out maps, full indexes and practical information Second revised edition
ISBN 1 873429 51 7   £15.95

PALLAS GUIDES

YEMEN
Peter Wald

An extensively researched and in-depth cultural guide
to this incredible country *Wanderlust*

An acclaimed and scholarly guide *Anderson's Travel Companion*

All in all, nothing surpasses Wald's guidebook if one wants to get to know and
understand South Arabia, or savour its fascination *Yemen Report*

An eminently readable, exhaustive historical account, fascinating in itself,
leavened with chapters on jewellery, birdlife, and the last imam's
sexual prowess and love of Heinz tinned Russian salad *TLS*

'Arabia Felix' to the Romans, 'Happy Arabia', Yemen is a land of astonishing drama, wildness and beauty, and it has a history to match. Ten thousand years of trade along its Red
Sea and Indian Ocean coasts, over its mountains and across its deserts, have made this a
meeting point of people and ideas: both monotheism and writing were born in Yemen, and
there are many fascinating archaeological remains of the sophisticated and mixed cultures
that flourished here. Contemporary Yemeni culture is perhaps most famous for its incredible mud architecture, whose forms date back for millenia but continue to develop under
influences from as far away as Java. The capital, San'a, is one of the beautiful cities of the
world and a UNESCO World Heritage Site. The Yemenis are as warm and welcoming a
people as a traveller is ever likely to meet.

Peter Wald has been exploring Yemen for over thirty-five years, and wrote this book with
the help of his wife, a well-known ethnographer in Yemen. It is one of the most complete
books on this fascinating country ever published.

384 pp including 100 colour plates, 16 duotone plates, 212 text illustrations and diagrams,
2 fold out maps, full indexes and practical information. Second revised edition
ISBN 1 873429 23 1   £17.99

PALLAS GUIDES

WEST COUNTRY
Peter Sager

An unsung genius   *Val Hennessy, Daily Mail*

Certainly the best book on the country   *New York Times*

Excellent and in-depth   *Anderson's Travel Companion*

A wonderful thing   *Jan Morris*

Peter Sager, widely acclaimed for his guidebooks to Wales and East Anglia, now turns his attention to the West Country. From the mysteries of Stonehenge, behind barbed wire, to the suboceanic tin mines of Cornwall, from Hardy's cottage to the Tintagel of Tennyson and Swinburne, from the Marquess of Bath's Kama Sutra paintings at Longleat to the light-basking work of the St Ives School, passing by sculptors, poets, furniture makers and eccentrics of all kinds, this is another comprehensive and mercurial guide by the 'unsung genius' of travelling in Britain.

Peter Sager, born in 1945, is an art critic and radio editor, and since 1975 has been a reporter for Die Zeit based in Hamburg. In 1989 he won Germany's most prestigious award for journalism, the Egon-Erwin-Kisch Award. He and his family spend all their holidays in Britain, and he has written books on Wales, Southern England, East Anglia, and Scotland.
David Henry Wilson, the translator, was born in 1937. A university lecturer in Britain and Germany, he also writes plays, children's book and novels. He lives with his family in Somerset.

276 pp including 2 fold out maps, 146 colour plates, illustrations, diagrams and maps, full indexes and practical information   ISBN 1 873429 08 8   £14.95

PALLAS GUIDES

DORDOGNE
Joy Law

An exemplary regional guide *British Book News*

She captures the region well in her book, and has drunk in
full draughts of its heady sunshine *The Old Lady*

The best sort of travel book *The Spectator*

Required reading *TLS*

Joy Law has an intimate knowledge and vast enthusiasm for the region
and has compiled a marvellous travelling companion
The Journal, Newcastle upon Tyne

Joy Law's intimate account of Dordogne is the fruit of nearly forty years of living in and exploring the province. Whether she's taking the reader to some unexpected architectural treasure or singing the praises of the fabulous gastronomy of Dordogne – the home of truffles, foie gras, walnut oil and other legendary pleasures – her enthusiasm is always infectious.

Designed to be savoured at leisure before, during or after a holiday, this guide also has some of the most comprehensive information on all aspects of Dordogne available anywhere, together with a gazetteer, specially drawn maps and full index to make it indispensable on the road.

Joy Law has had a house in Dordogne for thirty-five years. She was editorial director of a London publishing house and worked at the Royal College of Art in charge of Publications and Exhibitions. Her other books include *Fleur-de-Lys: the Kings and Queens of France*; *The Midi, Languedoc and Roussillon*; and a prize-winning history of her commune, *St Julien de Lampon*.

318 pp including 26 colour plates, 2 fold out maps, 90 illustrations, diagrams and maps, full index and practical information   ISBN 1 873429 28 2   £14.95

PALLAS ATHENE

Find out more about our books at:

WWW.PALLASATHENE.CO.UK

Pallas Guides
Pallas for Pleasure
Pallas Arts
Pallas Passions
Pallas Editions